THE SOCIOLOGY
OF
ORGANIZATIONS

THE SOCIOLOGY OF ORGANIZATIONS

Basic Studies

Second Edition

EDITED BY

Oscar Grusky

George A. Miller

THE FREE PRESS

A Division of Macmillan Publishing Co., Inc.

NEW YORK

Collier Macmillan Publishers

LONDON

THE FREE PRESS
A Division of Macmillan Publishing Co., Inc.
866 Third Avenue, New York, N.Y. 10022

Collier Macmillan Canada, Ltd.

Library of Congress Catalog Card Number: 80-1060

Printed in the United States of America

printing number

5 6 7 8 9 10

Library of Congress Cataloging in Publication Data

Grusky, Oscar   comp.
    The sociology of organizations.

    Includes bibliographies and index.
      1. Organization—Addresses, essays, lectures.
I. Miller, George Armitage   II. Title.
HM131.G3   1981   302.3′5   80-1060
ISBN 0-02-913060-3
ISBN 0-02-912930-3 pbk.

Contents

Contents

Preface
to the Second Edition

The field of organizations has experienced many changes since the first edition of this book was published. Several of these are reflected in the choices made in putting together this volume. Four themes in particular guided our decisions: maintain historical continuity by reprinting the classics; stress the variety of promising new theories; emphasize the interplay among the individual, the structure of the organization, and its environment; and draw attention to an organization's relations with other organizations as well as with other resources in its environment.

This edition consists of twenty-five selections. Thirteen of these are new and twelve appeared in the previous edition. The reader will note that all seven of the selections in Part One, on classical theory, also appeared in the first edition. This is as it should be, since a classic by definition is of acknowledged excellence and should have a timeless quality.

Five of six selections in Part Two, on current theoretical perspectives, are new. This especially rich and provocative group of studies reflects the many new directions that sociological thinking on organizations has taken in the 1970s. Our aim was to celebrate the diversity as well as the quality of ideas.

Unlike the first edition, which focused on selected substantive problems, this edition is organized by level of analysis: the person, the structure of the focal organization, and the organization's relationship to its environment. This new format allows the instructor more flexibility in assigning materials, just as it allowed us greater flexibility in picking from a huge range of potential candidates.

Because of the variety of sources and the diversity of authors, the pieces collected here show, naturally, variety and diversity of writing and editorial styles. Beyond basic typographics, no attempt has been made to impose any artificial consistency of style on this collection. Unless otherwise noted, methods of documentation, numbering systems, spelling, punctuation, and other such matters of style are here reproduced as in original sources.

Inevitably the value of this collection rests mainly on the contributions of the authors. We are indeed grateful to them. We are also grateful to our respective institutions, UCLA and the University of Utah, for their support. Grusky acknowledges the partial assistance of the National Institute of Mental Health (USPHS MH 14583), which supports his training program in mental health evaluation research. We appreciate the typing assistance of Andrea Anzalone and the editorial help of Gladys Topkis, Michael Sander, and Kitty Moore.

O. G.

G. A. M.

Preface
to the First Edition

In 1952 the Free Press published the *Reader in Bureaucracy* edited by Robert K. Merton, Ailsa P. Gray, Barbara Hockey, and Hanan C. Selvin. This important book directed interest to the problems of organizations for over two decades and remains a major contribution to this day. Since the present volume is by the same publisher, some comparisons of the non-invidious kind are in order.

First, unlike its predecessor, we sought deliberately to present a uniquely sociological orientation. That is not to say that nonsociologists were excluded from the "club," but rather that the aim was to present the student, insofar as possible, with the conceptual elements of a sociology of organizations. This field emerged from what was earlier called industrial sociology and the sociology of occupations, on the one hand, and the more general area, social organization, on the other. The object of study—the organization—has been labelled the complex, the formal, the bureaucratic, and the large-scale organization. The study of organizations has now reached a stage of development where the outlines of a sociological perspective can be identified. We do not consider it anti-interdisciplinary to believe such a condition both desirable and deserving of encouragement.

Second, we decided against dividing up the work of major theorists by selected substantive areas in favor of reprinting large, unified sections of their work in one place. The main advantage of this procedure is that it enables the reader to grasp the whole perspective. Obviously, however, reading the entire work of the author is superior to either approach. This technique sought to encourage direct theoretical comparisons among the classical theorists as well as between classical and current theoretical perspectives. We called upon the work of Talcott Parsons to serve as a bridge between the classical and current theorists.

The current theorists were also presented in one unit with the aim of emphasizing the broad interrelationships between the specialized field of organizations and the general study of social systems. In this respect as well, Parsons is a leader. We hope the instructor will encourage students to reexamine empirical studies presented later in the book in terms of contrasting theories. For this purpose, the theoretical material is lengthy and detailed and the empirical studies, whenever possible, are presented in full.

ix

Third, a broadly based selection of research techniques is provided in the early part of the book so as to emphasize the obviously close relationship between methods and theory. A comparison with the *Reader in Bureaucracy,* which dealt exclusively with field methods, is evidence of the degree of progress, increased sophistication, and self-awareness that has characterized the field since the 1950s.

Fourth, the selections on substantive problems differentiated the two collections most of all and in the case of the present volume, presented the most difficult problems. Like its predecessor, we sought to focus on universal organizational problems. Yet, not only are the problems different, but the way of approaching them, and especially the more rigorous theoretical and methodological equipment used, distinguish the studies included in this book. Moreover, a somewhat broader range of organizational types may be found including religious organizations, prisons, the military, industry, ships, unions, and so on. Sociologists may very well fault us for failing to stress such important problem areas as interorganizational relationships, organization-client relations, debureaucratization, and others. Some may also feel that too much attention is given to problems stemming from professionalization. This emphasis reflects both the great commitment of contemporary researchers to this topic and the realities of living and working in a postindustrial society.

The decisions to include and exclude studies were very difficult ones. Almost every selection has been used at some time during our combined total of twelve years of teaching an advanced undergraduate course on formal organizations at UCLA. We apologize to the many talented scholars whose work we were compelled by space limitations to omit and thank the authors and publishers who graciously permitted the use of their material. We are deeply grateful to Peter Blau for advice and suggestions, to Carl Beers of The Free Press for his interest and assistance, and to Keiko Shimabukuro for secretarial help.

O. G.

G. A. M.

PART ONE

Classical Theoretical Perspectives

Social scientists are notorious for their lack of agreement on what constitutes the basic issues or most fruitful approaches to their fields, or even as to who in the past have been the major contributors to their discipline. However, when the position of Max Weber is evaluated, organizational sociologists, almost to a person, are in agreement on his preeminence. It is therefore altogether fitting— one could say that there was almost no alternative—for the present collection to begin with the work of this man.

The excerpts selected cover three main areas: Weber's three pure types of authority, a detailed description and analysis of the characteristics and development of bureaucracy, and the process of routinization of charismatic authority. The concept of legitimacy is fundamental to Weber's treatment of organizations. By legitimacy he referred to the acceptance of influence because of its perceived justifiability. The three ideal types of authority are based on the types of legitimation applied. In the rational-legal or bureaucratic kind, members accepted a ruling as proper because it was based on abstract rules that they accepted as just. Under traditional authority legitimacy was based on the simple fact that things had normally been accomplished in that fashion in the past. Acceptance of charismatic authority was based on the member's emotional commitment to the leader or to his mission.

The longest selection describes both the fundamental features of bureaucratic organizations and their historical development. The ponderousness of the system, its emphasis on efficiency, and the political characteristics of bureaucracies, with illustrations from Greece, Rome, Weber's native Germany, and even the United States, are analyzed. Weber sought to account for organizational changes in part by an extensive analysis of the succession process. The

1

last brief selection examines the mechanisms involved when an established system seeks to maintain itself beyond the first generation of leadership.

Michels is most famous for his study of the process of goal displacement, whereby organizations subvert their original objectives and replace them with other goals, sometimes even with objectives that are alien to their original purposes. *Political Parties* is a detailed study of pre–World War I European labor unions and Socialist parties. The excerpts from this book illustrate some of the major components of Michels' theory of organizational leadership. The organizations studied, although originally seeking a socialist revolution, soon abandoned this goal in part because of the leaders' desires to maintain their relatively high status position. Organizations become conservative because, once in power, leaders refuse to engage in activities that will endanger their position. Moreover, the leaders are able to ensconce themselves in office because of the built-in advantages of their position. These advantages include control over communication to the ordinary members and superior political skills and experience. This does not mean that every organization, even those with avowedly democratic objectives, *must* become oligarchical, but instead that voluntary, political organizations and perhaps other types as well contain certain elements that can interfere with rank-and-file control. The problem is to specify the conditions and circumstances, no doubt varying for particular types of organizations, that encourage or interfere with the democratic process. Readers will be especially interested in Lipset, Trow, and Coleman's *Democracy,* which explicates and qualifies several propositions from Michels by means of a detailed study of the history and political structure of the International Typographers Union (see Part Four).

The selection from Taylor's *Scientific Management* presents the basic assumptions of this classic approach to the study of organizations. A major feature of this orientation rests in the notion that careful definition of the requirements of each worker's job can assure effectiveness, as defined by the management. Hence, in Taylor's system: "The work of every workman is fully planned out by the management . . . and each man receives in most cases written instructions, describing in detail the task he is to accomplish, as well as the means to be used in doing the work" (p. 39). In addition to rigorous planning of work tasks, scientific management encouraged close supervisory control of the worker and the application of narrow economic incentives. The administrative theory of Gulick and Urwick (editors), *Papers on the Science of Administration* (New York: Institute of Public Administration, Columbia University,

1937), which is not represented in this volume, is closely related to the scientific management approach. This orientation also emphasized the importance of breaking complex tasks down into simpler components and thereby specifying the task expectations associated with each position.

The case of Schmidt, a pig-iron handler, which is presented in the excerpt, illustrates the principles of task specification, close control, and economic incentives. The derogation of the worker and his assumed inferiority, that is, the moral components of the approach, are also apparent in the account.

The human relations approach sought to counter scientific management's focus on formal requirements and simple economic rewards as crucial motivational elements. The point of view was that *non*economic, social rewards were more important in inducing workers to behave in line with or in opposition to managerial goals. The famous studies of the Relay Assembly Test Room, the Mica Splitting Test Room, and the Bank-Wiring Observation Room served as the empirical basis for the conclusions that informal group behavior was fundamental to the operation of industrial and other organizations. However, other elements in the social structure of the plant, such as technology and formal structure, were not totally overlooked. Nevertheless, as shown in the Roethlisberger and Dickson selection from *Management and the Worker,* which summarizes the main theoretical perspective, these features are not emphasized. While only one half-page is devoted to the formal organization of the plant, seven times as much space is devoted to the plant's informal organization. The human relations approach stressed—some would say "discovered"—the key role of informal group behavior for the functioning of complex organizations. The reader may be especially interested in two other studies that are noteworthy contributions to the human relations approach: Elton Mayo, *The Human Problems of an Industrial Civilization,* (New York: MacMillan, 1933), and Burleigh Gardner, *Human Relations in Industry* (Chicago: Irwin, 1945). In addition, the reader will find it useful to examine criticisms of this perspective by Henry Landsberger (*Hawthorne Revisited* [Ithaca, N.Y.: Cornell University Press, 1958]), Morris S. Viteles (*Motivation and Morale in Industry* [London: Staples, 1954]), Alex Carey ("The Hawthorne Studies: A Radical Criticism," *American Sociological Review,* 32 [June 1967], 403–416), and Richard H. Franke and James D. Kaul ("The Hawthorne Experiment: First Statistical Interpretation," *American Sociological Review,* 43 [October 1978], 623–43).

The next classical theoretical perspective is that of Chester I. Barnard, former president of New Jersey Bell Telephone Company and a man of varied experiences in business, academic, and government organizations. Barnard's theory of cooperation stresses the joint importance of factors emanating from the system as a whole and from the individual member. The distinction underlies the use of the concepts of effectiveness and efficiency, as well as the analysis of the three requirements for organization: willingness to cooperate, common purpose, and communication. There is a much stronger focus on motivational elements than on structural features in Barnard's orientation. Hence, the brief excerpt from Barnard's theory of authority stresses personal predilection and perception as elements in the acceptance or rejection of authority. The interest in incentives as a means of inducing members of an organization to cooperate in achieving the organization's objectives served as the cornerstone of his theory and was a direct intellectual predecessor to the March and Simon theory described in Part Two.

The next selection is from the foremost sociological theorist of recent times, Talcott Parsons. Like Weber before him, Parsons has sought as his point of departure the exploration of the general relation of economics and sociology. Parsons has tried in this essay to isolate the fundamental defining features of organizations. Four main categories derived from his well-known general classification system are applied: the value system of the organization, the mechanisms of procuring resources, the means of policy making, allocating, and integrating the units of the system, and the organization's institutional connections to the larger society. The focus on goal attainment is seen as the basic characteristic of the organization. Parsons' concern with the organization's value pattern and the relationship of this value pattern to the more generalized values of the society is a forerunner of open-systems theory and a key feature of his orientation. Parsons' approach also resembles Max Weber's in its concern with the problem of power, "the generalized capacity to mobilize resources in the interest of attainment of the system goal.'" The concluding substantive section presents Parsons' typology of organizations: economic, political, integrative, and pattern-maintenance systems.

In the final selection Blau suggests that comparative analysis of a large number of organizations is essential if one seeks to establish valid relationships among organizational attributes. He describes three general approaches to the study of organization and argues that each approach is limited in the kinds of problem with which it can deal. He notes that organizations have attributes that do not pertain to the characteristics of their individual members, and that these attributes can be studied on their own without the time and effort required to survey organizational members. Blau's selection inspired our reorganization of this book. Parts Three, Four, and Five are divided so as to correspond to his three general approaches and are entitled: "The Person in the Organization"; "Organizational Structure"; and "Organizations and Their Environments."

The reader should seek to evaluate the utility of each theoretical perspective presented in enhancing his understanding of the substantive problems raised later in this volume. He or she also will find it valuable to contrast the orientations of the classical theorists with the current theorists presented in Part Two.

Bureaucracy

Max Weber

The Three Pure Types of Legitimate Authority

There are three pure types of legitimate authority. The validity of their claims to legitimacy may be based on:

1. Rational grounds—resting on a belief in the "legality" of patterns of normative rules and the right of those elevated to authority under such rules to issue commands (legal authority).
2. Traditional grounds—resting on an established belief in the sanctity of immemorial traditions and the legitimacy of the status of those exercising authority under them (traditional authority); or finally,
3. Charismatic grounds—resting on devotion to the specific and exceptional sanctity, heroism or exemplary character of an individual person, and of the normative patterns or order revealed or ordained by him (charismatic authority).

In the case of legal authority, obedience is owed to the legally established impersonal order. It extends to the persons exercising the authority of office under it only by virtue of the formal legality of their commands and only within the scope of authority of the office. In the case of traditional authority, obedience is owed to the *person* of the chief who occupies the traditionally sanctioned position of authority and who is (within its sphere) bound by tradition. But here the obligation of obedience is not based on the impersonal order, but is a matter of personal loyalty within the area of accustomed obligations. In the case of charismatic authority, it is the charismatically qualified leader as such who is obeyed by virtue of personal trust in him and his revelation, his heroism or his exemplary qualities so far as they fall within the scope of the individual's belief in his charisma.

SOURCE: *The Theory of Social and Economic Organization,* ed. and trans. by A.M. Henderson and Talcott Parsons, p. 328. Copyright © 1947, renewed 1975 by Talcott Parsons. Reprinted with permission of Macmillan Publishing Co., Inc.

1. The usefulness of the above classification can only be judged by its results in promoting systematic analysis. The concept of 'charisma' ('the gift of grace') is taken from the vocabulary of early Christianity. For the Christian religious organization Rudolf Sohm, in his *Kirchenrecht,* was the first to clarify the substance of the concept, even though he did not use the same terminology. Others (for instance, Hollin, *Enthusiasmus und Bussgewalt*) have clarified certain important consequences of it. It is thus nothing new.

• • •

Characteristics of Bureaucracy

Modern officialdom functions in the following specific manner:

I. There is the principle of fixed and official jurisdictional areas, which are generally ordered by rules, that is, by laws or administrative regulations.

1. The regular activities required for the purposes of the bureaucratically governed structure are distributed in a fixed way as official duties.

2. The authority to give commands required for the discharge of these duties is distributed in a stable way and is strictly delimited by rules concerning the coercive means, physical, sacerdotal, or otherwise, which may be placed at the disposal of officials.

3. Methodical provision is made for the regular and continuous fulfilment of these duties and for the execution of the corresponding rights; only persons who have the generally regulated qualifications to serve are employed.

In public and lawful government these three elements constitute "bureaucratic authority." In private economic domination, they constitute bureaucratic "management." Bureaucracy, thus understood, is fully developed in political and ecclesiastical communities only in the modern state, and, in the private economy, only in the most advanced institutions of capitalism. Permanent and public office authority, with fixed jurisdiction, is not the historical rule but rather the exception. This is so even in large political structures such as those of the ancient Orient, the Germanic and Mongolian empires of conquest, or of many feudal structures of state. In all these cases, the ruler executes the most important measures through personal trustees, table-companions, or court-servants. Their commissions and authority are not precisely delimited and are temporarily called into being for each case.

SOURCE: *From Max Weber: Essays in Sociology,* edited and translated by H.H. Gerth and C. Wright Mills, pp. 196–204, 214–16. Copyright © 1946 by Oxford University Press, Inc; renewed 1973 by Dr. Hans H. Gerth. Reprinted by permission.

II. The principles of office hierarchy and of levels of graded authority mean a firmly ordered system of super- and subordination in which there is a supervision of the lower offices by the higher ones. Such a system offers the governed the possibility of appealing the decision of a lower office to its higher authority, in a definitely regulated manner. With the full development of the bureaucratic type, the office hierarchy is mono-cratically organized. The principle of hierarchical office authority is found in all bureaucratic structures: in state and ecclesiastical structures as well as in large party organizations and private enterprises. It does not matter for the character of bureaucracy whether its authority is called "private" or "public."

When the principle of jurisdictional "competency" is fully carried through, hierarchical subordination—at least in public office—does not mean that the "higher" authority is simply authorized to take over the business of the "lower." Indeed, the opposite is the rule. Once established and having fulfilled its task, an office tends to continue in existence and be held by another incumbent.

III. The management of the modern office is based upon written documents ("the files"), which are preserved in their original or draught form. There is, therefore, a staff of subaltern officials and scribes of all sorts. The body of officials actively engaged in a "public" office, along with the respective apparatus of material implements and the files, make up a "bureau." In private enterprise, "the bureau" is often called "the office."

In principle, the modern organization of the civil service separates the bureau from the private domicile of the official, and, in general, bureaucracy segregates official activity as something distinct from the sphere of private life. Public monies and equipment are divorced from the private property of the official. This condition is everywhere the pro-duct of a long development. Nowadays, it is found in public as well as in private enterprises; in the latter, the principle extends even to the lead-ing entrepreneur. In principle, the executive office is separated from the household, business from private correspondence, and business assets from private fortunes. The more consistently the modern type of business management has been carried through the more are these separations the case. The beginnings of this process are to be found as early as the Middle Ages.

It is the peculiarity of the modern entrepreneur that he conducts himself as the "first official" of his enterprise, in the very same way in which the ruler of a specifically modern bureaucratic state spoke of him-self as "the first servant" of the state. The idea that the bureau activities of the state are intrinsically different in character from the management of private economic offices is a continental European notion and, by way of contrast, is totally foreign to the American way.

IV. Office management, at least all specialized office management—and such management is distinctly modern—usually presupposes thorough and expert training. This increasingly holds for the modern executive and employee of private enterprises, in the same manner as it holds for the state official.

V. When the office is fully developed, official activity demands the full working capacity of the official, irrespective of the fact that his obligatory time in the bureau may be firmly delimited. In the normal case, this is only the product of a long development, in the public as well as in the private office. Formerly, in all cases, the normal state of affairs was reversed: official business was discharged as a secondary activity.

VI. The management of the office follows general rules, which are more or less stable, more or less exhaustive, and which can be learned. Knowledge of these rules represents a special technical learning which the officials possess. It involves jurisprudence, or administrative or business management.

The reduction of modern office management to rules is deeply embedded in its very nature. The theory of modern public administration, for instance, assumes that the authority to order certain matters by decree—which has been legally granted to public authorities—does not entitle the bureau to regulate the matter by commands given for each case, but only to regulate the matter abstractly. This stands in extreme contrast to the regulation of all relationships through individual privileges and bestowals of favor, which is absolutely dominant in patrimonialism, at least in so far as such relationships are not fixed by sacred tradition.

The Position of the Official

All this results in the following for the internal and external position of the official:

I. Office holding is a "vocation." This is shown, first, in the requirement of a firmly prescribed course of training, which demands the entire capacity for work for a long period of time, and in the generally prescribed and special examinations which are prerequisites of employment. Furthermore, the position of the official is in the nature of a duty. This determines the internal structure of his relations, in the following manner: Legally and actually, office holding is not considered a source to be exploited for rents or emoluments, as was normally the case during the Middle Ages and frequently up to the threshold of recent times. Nor is office holding considered a usual exchange of services for equivalents, as is the case with free labor contracts. Entrance into an office, including one in the private economy, is considered an acceptance of a specific obligation of faithful management in return for a secure existence. It is decisive for the specific nature of modern loyalty to an office that, in the pure type, it does not establish a relationship to a *person,* like the vassal's or disciple's faith in feudal or in patrimonial relations of authority. Modern loyalty is devoted to impersonal and functional purposes. Behind the functional purposes, of course, "ideas of culture-values" usually stand. These are *ersatz* for the earthly or supramundane personal master: ideas such as "state," "church," "community," "party," or "enterprise" and thought of as being realized in a community; they provide an ideological halo for the master.

The political official—at least in the fully developed modern state—is not considered the personal servant of a ruler. Today, the bishop, the priest, and the preacher are in fact no longer, as in early Christian times, holders of purely personal charisma. The supramundane and sacred values which they offer are given to everybody who seems to be worthy of them and who asks for them. In former times, such leaders acted upon the personal command of their master; in principle, they were responsible only to him. Nowadays, in spite of the partial survival of the old theory, such religious leaders are officials in the service of a functional purpose, which in the present-day "church" has become routinized and, in turn, ideologically hallowed.

II. The personal position of the official is patterned in the following way:

1. Whether he is in a private office or a public bureau, the modern official always strives and usually enjoys a distinct *social esteem* as compared with the governed. His social position is guaranteed by the prescriptive rules of rank order and, for the political official, by special definitions of the criminal code against "insults of officials" and "contempt" of state and church authorities.

The actual social position of the official is normally highest where, as in old civilized countries, the following conditions prevail: a strong demand for administration by trained experts; a strong and stable social differentiation, where the official predominantly derives from socially and economically privileged strata because of the social distribution of power; or where the costliness of the required training and status conventions are binding upon him. The possession of educational certificates—to be discussed elsewhere—are usually linked with qualification for office. Naturally, such certificates or patents enhance the "status element" in the social position of the official. For the rest this status factor in individual cases is explicitly and impassively acknowledged; for example, in the prescription that the acceptance or rejection of an aspirant to an official career depends upon the consent ("election") of the members of the official body. This is the case in the German army with the officer corps. Similar phenomena, which promote this guildlike closure of officialdom, are typically found in patrimonial and, particularly, in prebendal officialdoms of the past. The desire to resurrect such phenomena in changed forms is by no means infrequent among modern bureaucrats. For instance, they have played a role among the demands of the quite proletarian and expert officials (the *tretyi* element) during the Russian revolution.

Usually the social esteem of the officials as such is especially low where the demand for expert administration and the dominance of status conventions are weak. This is especially the case in the United States; it is often the case in new settlements by virtue of their wide fields for profit-making and the great instability of their social stratification.

2. The pure type of bureaucratic official is *appointed* by a superior authority. An official elected by the governed is not a purely bureaucratic figure. Of course, the formal existence of an election does not by itself mean that no appointment hides behind the election—in the state, especially, appointment by party chiefs. Whether or not this is the case does not depend upon legal statutes but upon the way in which the party mechanism functions. Once firmly organized, the parties can turn a formally free election into the mere acclamation of a candidate designated by the party chief. As a rule, however, a formally free election is turned into a fight, conducted according to definite rules, for votes in favor of one or two designated candidates.

In all circumstances, the designation of officials by means of an election among the governed modifies the strictness of hierarchical subordination. In principle, an official who is so elected has an autonomous position opposite the superordinate official. The elected official does not derive his position "from above" but "from below," or at least not from a superior authority of the official hierarchy but from powerful party men ("bosses"), who also determine his further career. The career of the elected official is not, or at least not primarily, dependent upon his chief in the administration. The official who is not elected but appointed by a chief normally functions more exactly, from a technical point of view, because, all other circumstances being equal, it is more likely that purely functional points of consideration and qualities will determine his selection and career. As laymen, the governed can become acquainted with the extent to which a candidate is expertly qualified for office only in terms of experience, and hence only after his service. Moreover, in every sort of selection of officials by election, parties quite naturally give decisive weight not to expert considerations but to the services a follower renders to the party boss. This holds for all kinds of procurement for officials by elections, for the designation of formally free, elected officials by party bosses when they determine the slate of candidates, or the free appointment by a chief who has himself been elected. The contrast, however, is relative: substantially similar conditions hold where legitimate monarchs and their subordinates appoint officials, except that the influence of the followings are then less controllable.

Where the demand for administration by trained experts is considerable, and the party followings have to recognize an intellectually developed, educated, and freely moving "public opinion," the use of unqualified officials falls back upon the party in power at the next election. Naturally, this is more likely to happen when the officials are appointed by the chief. The demand for a trained administration now exists in the United States, but in the large cities, where immigrant votes are "corralled," there is, of course, no educated public opinion. Therefore, popular elections of the administrative chief and also of his subordinate officials usually endanger the expert qualification of the official as well as the precise functioning of the bureaucratic mechanism. It also weakens the dependence of the officials upon the hierarchy. This holds at least for the large administrative bodies that are difficult to supervise. The superior qualification and integrity of federal judges, appointed by the President, as over against elected judges in the United States is well known, although both types of officials have been selected primarily in terms of party considerations. The great changes in American metropolitan administrations demanded by reformers have proceeded essentially from elected mayors working with an apparatus of officials who were appointed by them. These reforms have thus come about in a "Caesarist" fashion. Viewed technically, as an organized form of authority, the efficiency of "Caesarism," which often grows out of democracy, rests in general upon the position of the "Caesar" as a free trustee of the masses (of the army or of the citizenry), who is unfettered by tradition. The "Caesar" is thus the unrestrained master of a body of highly qualified military officers and officials whom he selects freely and personally without regard to tradition or to any other considerations. This "rule of the personal genius," however, stands in contradiction to the formally "democratic" principle of a universally elected officialdom.

3. Normally, the position of the official is held for life, at least in public bureaucracies; and this is increasingly the case for all similar structures. As a factual rule, *tenure for life* is presupposed, even where the giving of notice or periodic reappointment occurs. In contrast to the worker in a private enterprise, the official normally holds tenure. Legal or actual life-tenure, however, is not recognized as the official's right to the possession of office, as was the case with many structures of authority in the past. Where legal guarantees against arbitrary dismissal or transfer are developed, they merely serve to guarantee a strictly objective discharge of specific office duties free from all personal considerations. In Germany, this is the case for all juridical and, increasingly, for all administrative officials.

Within the bureaucracy, therefore, the measure of "independence," legally guaranteed by tenure, is not always a source of increased status for the official whose position is thus secured. Indeed, often the reverse holds, especially in old cultures and communities that are highly differentiated.

In such communities, the stricter the subordination under the arbitrary rule of the master, the more it guarantees the maintenance of the conventional seigneurial style of living for the official. Because of the very absence of these legal guarantees of tenure, the conventional esteem for the official may rise in the same way as, during the Middle Ages, the esteem of the nobility of office rose at the expense of esteem for the freemen, and as the king's judge surpassed that of the people's judge. In Germany, the military officer or the administrative official can be removed from office at any time, or at least far more readily than the "independent judge," who never pays with loss of his office for even the grossest offense against the "code of honor" or against social conventions of the salon. For this very reason, if other things are equal, in the eyes of the master stratum the judge is considered less qualified for social intercourse than are officers and administrative officials, whose greater dependence on the master is a greater guarantee of their conformity with status conventions. Of course, the average official strives for a civil-service law, which would materially secure his old age and provide increased guarantees against his arbitrary removal from office. This striving, however, has its limits. A very strong development of the "right to the office" naturally makes it more difficult to staff them with regard to technical efficiency, for such a development decreases the career opportunities of ambitious candidates for office. This makes for the fact that officials, on the whole, do not feel their dependency upon those at the top. This lack of a feeling of dependency, however, rests primarily upon the inclination to depend upon one's equals rather than upon the socially inferior and governed strata. The present conservative movement among the Badenia clergy, occasioned by the anxiety of a presumably threatening separation of church and state, has been expressly determined by the desire not to be turned "from a master into a servant of the parish."

4. The official receives the regular *pecuniary* compensation of a normally fixed *salary* and the old age security provided by a pension. The salary is not measured like a wage in terms of work done, but according to "status," that is, according to the kind of function (the "rank") and, in addition, possibly, according to the length of service. The relatively great security of the official's income, as well as the rewards of social esteem, make the office a sought-after position, especially in countries which no longer provide opportunities for colonial profits. In such countries, this situation permits relatively low salaries for officials.

5. The official is set for a *"career"* within the hierarchical order of the public service. He moves from the lower, less important, and lower paid to the higher positions. The average official naturally desires a mechanical fixing of the conditions of promotion: if not of the offices, at least of the salary levels. He wants these conditions fixed in terms of "seniority," or possibly according to grades achieved in a developed system of expert

examinations. Here and there, such examinations actually form a character *indelibilis* of the official and have lifelong effects on his career. To this is joined the desire to qualify the right to office and the increasing tendency toward status group closure and economic security. All of this makes for a tendency to consider the offices as "prebends" of those who are qualified by educational certificates. The necessity of taking general personal and intellectual qualifications into consideration, irrespective of the often subaltern character of the educational certificate, has led to a condition in which the highest political offices, especially the positions of "ministers," are principally filled without reference to such certificates.

• • •

The Quantitative Development of Administrative Tasks

The proper soil for the bureaucratization of an administration has always been the specific developments of administrative tasks. We shall first discuss the quantitative extension of such tasks. In the field of politics, the great state and the mass party are the classic soil for bureaucratization.

This does not mean that every historically known and genuine formation of great states has brought about a bureaucratic administration. The permanence of a once-existing great state, or the homogeneity of a culture borne by such a state, has not always been attached to a bureaucratic structure of state. However, both of these features have held to a great extent, for instance, in the Chinese empire. The numerous great Negro empires, and similar formations, have had only an ephemeral existence primarily because they have lacked an apparatus of officials. And the unity of the Carolingian empire disintegrated when its organization of officials disintegrated. This organization, however, was predominantly patrimonial rather than bureaucratic in nature. From a purely temporal view, however, the empire of the Caliphs and its predecessors on Asiatic soil have lasted for considerable periods of time, and their organization of office was essentially patrimonial and prebendal. Also, the Holy Roman Empire lasted for a long time in spite of the almost complete absence of bureaucracy. All these realms have represented a cultural unity of at least approximately the same strength as is usually created by bureaucratic polities.

The ancient Roman Empire disintegrated internally in spite of increasing bureaucratization and even during its very execution. This was because of the way the tax burdens were distributed by the bureaucratic state, which favored the subsistence economy. Viewed with regard to the intensity of their purely *political* unities, the temporal existences of the empires of the Caliphs, Carolingian and other medieval emperors were essentially unstable, nominal, and cohesive conglomerates. On the whole, the capacity for political action steadily diminished, and the relatively great unity of *culture* flowed from ecclesiastic structures that were in part strictly unified and, in the Occidental Middle Ages, increasingly bureaucratic in character. The unity of their cultures resulted partly from the far-going homogeneity of their social structures, which in turn was the aftermath and transformation of their former political unity. Both are phenomena of the traditional stereotyping of culture, which favors an unstable equilibrium. Both of these factors proved so strong a foundation that even grandiose attempts at expansion, such as the Crusades, could be undertaken in spite of the lack of intensive political unity; they were, one might say, performed as "private undertakings." The failure of the Crusades and their often irrational political course, however, is associated with the absence of a unified and intensive state power to back them up. And there is no doubt that the nuclei of intensive "modern" states in the Middle Ages developed concomitantly with bureaucratic structures. Furthermore, in the end these quite bureaucratic political structures undoubtedly shattered the social conglomerates, which rested essentially upon unstable equilibriums.

The disintegration of the Roman Empire was partly conditioned by the very bureaucratization of its army and official apparatus. This bureaucratization could only be realized by carrying through at the same time a method of taxation which by its distribution of burdens was bound to lead to relative increase in the importance of a subsistence economy. Individual factors of this sort always enter the picture. Also the "intensity" of the external and the internal state activities play their part. Quite apart from the relation between the state influence upon culture and the degree of bureaucratization, it may be said that "normally"—though not without exception—the vigor to expand is directly related to the degree of bureaucratization. For two of the most expansive polities, the Roman Empire and the British world empire, during their most expansive periods, rested upon bureaucratic foundations only to a small extent. The Norman state in England carried through a strict organization on the basis of a feudal hierarchy. To a large extent, it received its unity and its push through the bureaucratization of the royal exchequer, which, in comparison to other political structures of the feudal period, was extremely strict. Later on, the English state did not share in the continental development towards bureaucratization, but remained an administration of notables. Just as in the republican administration of Rome, this English rule by notables was a result of the relative absence of a continental character, as well as of absolutely unique preconditions, which at the present time are disappearing. The dispensability of the large standing armies, which a continental state with equally expansive tendencies requires for its land frontiers, is among these special preconditions. In Rome, bureaucratization advanced with the transition from a coastal to a continental ring of frontiers. For the rest, in the domination structure of Rome, the strictly military character of the magistrate authorities—in the Roman manner unknown to any other people—made up for the lack of a bureaucratic apparatus with its technical efficiency, its precision and unity of administrative functions, especially outside the city limits. The continuity of administration was safeguarded by the unique position of the Senate. In Rome, as in England, one presupposition for this dispensability of bureaucracy which should not be forgotten was that the state authorities increasingly "minimized" the scope of their functions at home. They restricted their functions to what was absolutely demanded for direct "reasons of state."

At the beginning of the modern period, all the prerogatives of the continental states accumulated in the hands of those princes who most relentlessly took the course of administrative bureaucratization. It is obvious that technically the great modern state is absolutely dependent upon a bureaucratic basis. The larger the state, and the more it is or the more it becomes a greater power state, the more unconditionally is this the case.

The United States still bears the character of a polity which, at least in the technical sense, is not fully bureaucratized. But the greater the zones of friction with the outside and the more urgent the needs for administrative unity at home become, the more this character is inevitably and gradually giving way formally to the bureaucratic structure. Moreover, the partly unbureaucratic form of the state structure of the United States is materially balanced by the more strictly bureaucratic structures of those formations which, in truth, dominate politically, namely, the parties under the leadership of professionals or experts in organization and election tactics. The increasingly bureaucratic organization of all genuine mass parties offers the most striking example of the role of sheer quantity as a leverage for the bureaucratization of a social structure. In Germany, above all, the Social Democratic party, and abroad both of the "historical" American parties are bureaucratic in the greatest possible degree.

Qualitative Changes of Administrative Tasks

Bureaucratization is occasioned more by intensive and qualitative enlargement and internal deployment of the scope of administrative tasks than by their extensive and quantitative increase. But the direction bureaucratization takes and the reasons that occasion it vary widely.

In Egypt, the oldest country of bureaucratic state administration, the public and collective regulation of waterways for the whole country and from the top could not be avoided because of technical economic factors. This regulation created the mechanisms of scribes and officials. Once established, this mechanism, even in early times, found its second realm of business in the extraordinary construction activities which were organized militarily. As mentioned before, the bureaucratic tendency has chiefly been influenced by needs arising from the creation of standing armies as determined by power politics and by the development of public finance connected with the military establishment. In the modern state, the increasing demands for administration rest on the increasing complexity of civilization and push towards bureaucratization.

Very considerable expansions, especially overseas, have, of course, been managed by states ruled by notables (Rome, England, Venice), as will become evident in the appropriate context. Yet the "intensity" of the administration, that is, the transfer of as many tasks as possible to the organization of the state proper for continuous management and discharge, has been only slightly developed among the great states ruled by notables, especially Rome and England, if we compare them with bureaucratic polities.

Both in notable and bureaucratic administrations the *structure* of state power has influenced culture very strongly. But it has done so relatively slightly in the form of management and control by the state. This holds from justice down to education. The growing demands on culture, in turn, are determined, though to a varying extent, by the growing wealth of the most influential strata in the state. To this extent increasing bureaucratization is a function of the increasing possession of goods used for consumption, and of an increasingly sophisticated technique of fashioning external life—a technique which corresponds to the opportunities provided by such wealth. This reacts upon the standard of living and makes for an increasing subjective indispensability of organized, collective, interlocal, and thus bureaucratic, provision for the most varied wants, which previously were either unknown, or were satisfied locally or by a private economy.

Among purely political factors, the increasing demand of a society, accustomed to absolute pacification, for order and protection ("police") in all fields exerts an especially persevering influence in the direction of bureaucratization. A steady road leads from modifications of the blood feud, sacerdotally, or by means of arbitration, to the present position of the policeman as the "representative of God on earth." The former means placed the guarantees for the individual's rights and security squarely upon the members of his sib, who are obligated to assist him with oath and vengeance. Among other factors, primarily the manifold tasks of the so-called "policy of social welfare" operate in the direction of bureaucratization, for these tasks are, in part, saddled upon the state by interest groups and, in part, the state usurps them, either for reasons of power policy or for ideological motives. Of course, these tasks are to a large extent economically determined.

Among essentially technical factors, the specifically modern means of communication enter the picture as pacemakers of bureaucratization. Public land and water-ways, railroads, the telegraph, et cetera—they must, in part, necessarily be administered in a public and collective way; in part, such administration is technically expedient. In this respect, the contemporary means of communication frequently play a role similar to that of the canals of Mesopotamia and the regulation of the Nile in the ancient Orient. The degree to which the means of communication have been developed is a condition of decisive importance for the possibility of bureaucratic administration, although it is not the only decisive condition. Certainly in Egypt, bureaucratic centralization, on the basis of an almost pure subsistence economy, could never have reached the actual degree which it did without the natural trade route of the Nile. In order to promote bureaucratic centralization in modern Persia, the telegraph officials were officially commissioned with reporting all occurrences in the provinces to the Shah, over the heads of the local authorities. In addition, everyone received the right to remonstrate directly by telegraph. The modern Occidental state can be administered the way it actually is only because the state controls the telegraph network and has the mails and railroads at its disposal.

Railroads, in turn, are intimately connected with the development of an interlocal traffic of mass goods. This traffic is among the causal factors in the formation of the modern state. As we have already seen, this does not hold unconditionally for the past.

Technical Advantages of Bureaucratic Organization

The decisive reason for the advance of bureaucratic organization has always been its purely technical superiority over any other form of organization. The fully developed bureaucratic mechanism compares with other organizations exactly as does the machine with the non-mechanical modes of production.

Precision, speed, unambiguity, knowledge of the files, continuity, discretion, unity, strict subordination, reduction of friction and of material and personal costs—these are raised to the optimum point in the strictly bureaucratic administration, and especially in its monocratic form. As compared with all collegiate, honorific, and avocational forms of administration, trained bureaucracy is superior on all these points. And as far as complicated tasks are concerned, paid bureaucratic work is not only more precise but, in the last analysis, it is often cheaper than even formally unremunerated honorific service.

Honorific arrangements make administrative work an avocation and, for this reason alone, honorific service normally functions more slowly; being less bound to schemata and being more formless. Hence it is less precise and less unified than bureaucratic work because it is less dependent upon superiors and because the establishment and exploitation of the apparatus of subordinate officials and filing services are almost unavoidably less economical. Honorific service is less continuous than bureaucratic and frequently quite expensive. This is especially the case if one thinks not only of the money costs to the public treasury—costs which bureaucratic administration, in comparison with administration by notables, usually substantially increases—but also of the frequent economic losses of the governed caused by delays and lack of precision. The possibility of administration by notables normally and permanently exists only where official management can be satisfactorily discharged as an avocation. With the qualitative increase of tasks the administration has to face, administration by notables reaches its limits—today, even in England. Work organized by collegiate bodies causes friction and delay and requires compromises between colliding interests and views. The administration, therefore, runs less precisely and is more independent of superiors; hence, it is less unified and slower. All advances of the Prussian administrative organization have been and will in the future be advances of the bureaucratic, and especially of the monocratic, principle.

Today, it is primarily the capitalist market economy which demands that the official business of the administration be discharged precisely, unambiguously, continuously, and with as much speed as possible. Normally, the very large, modern capitalist enterprises are themselves unequalled models of strict bureaucratic organization. Business management throughout rests on increasing precision, steadiness, and, above all, the speed of operations. This, in turn, is determined by the peculiar nature of the modern means of communication, including, among other things, the news service of the press. The extraordinary increase in the speed by which public announcements, as well as economic and political facts, are transmitted exerts a steady and sharp pressure in the direction of speeding up the tempo of administrative reaction towards various situations. The optimum of such reaction time is normally attained only by a strictly bureaucratic organization.*

Bureaucratization offers above all the optimum possibility for carrying through the principle of specializing administrative functions according to purely objective considerations. Individual performances are allocated to functionaries who have specialized training and who by constant practice learn more and more. The "objective" discharge of business primarily means a discharge of business according to *calculable rules* and "without regard for persons."

"Without regard for persons" is also the watchword of the "market"

---

* Here we cannot discuss in detail how the bureaucratic apparatus may, and actually does, produce definite obstacles to the discharge of business in a manner suitable for the single case.

and, in general, of all pursuits of naked economic interests. A consistent execution of bureaucratic domination means the leveling of status "honor." Hence, if the principle of the free-market is not at the same time restricted, it means the universal domination of the "class situation." That this consequence of bureaucratic domination has not set in everywhere, parallel to the extent of bureaucratization, is due to the differences among possible principles by which polities may meet their demands.

The second element mentioned, "calculable rules," also is of paramount importance for modern bureaucracy. The peculiarity of modern culture, and specifically of its technical and economic basis, demands this very "calculability" of results. When fully developed, bureaucracy also stands, in a specific sense, under the principle of *sine ira ac studio.* Its specific nature, which is welcomed by capitalism, develops the more perfectly the more the bureaucracy is "dehumanized," the more completely it succeeds in eliminating from official business love, hatred, and all purely personal, irrational, and emotional elements which escape calculation. This is the specific nature of bureaucracy and it is appraised as its special virtue.

The more complicated and specialized modern culture becomes, the more its external supporting apparatus demands the personally detached and strictly "objective" *expert,* in lieu of the master of older social structures, who was moved by personal sympathy and favor, by grace and gratitude. Bureaucracy offers the attitudes demanded by the external apparatus of modern culture in the most favorable combination. As a rule, only bureaucracy has established the foundation for the administration of a rational law conceptually systematized on the basis of such enactments as the latter Roman imperial period first created with a high degree of technical perfection. During the Middle Ages, this law was received along with the bureaucratization of legal administration, that is to say, with the displacement of the old trial procedure which was bound to tradition or to irrational presuppositions, by the rationally trained and specialized expert.

•　•　•

The Concentration of the Means of Administration

The bureaucratic structure goes hand in hand with the concentration of the material means of management in the hands of the master. This concentration occurs, for instance, in a well-known and typical fashion, in the development of big capitalist enterprises, which find their essential characteristics in this process. A corresponding process occurs in public organizations.

CLASSICAL THEORETICAL PERSPECTIVES

The bureaucratically led army of the Pharaohs, the army during the later period of the Roman republic and the principate, and, above all, the army of the modern military state are characterized by the fact that their equipment and provisions are supplied from the magazines of the war lord. This is in contrast to the folk armies of agricultural tribes, the armed citizenry of ancient cities, the militias of early medieval cities, and all feudal armies; for these, the self-equipment and the self-provisioning of those obliged to fight was normal.

War in our time is a war of machines. And this makes magazines technically necessary, just as the dominance of the machine in industry promotes the concentration of the means of production and management. In the main, however, the bureaucratic armies of the past, equipped and provisioned by the lord, have risen when social and economic development has absolutely or relatively diminished the stratum of citizens who were economically able to equip themselves, so that their number was no longer sufficient for putting the required armies in the field. They were reduced at least relatively, that is, in relation to the range of power claimed for the polity. Only the bureaucratic army structure allowed for the development of the professional standing armies which are necessary for the constant pacification of large states of the plains, as well as for warfare against far-distant enemies, especially enemies overseas. Specifically, military discipline and technical training can be normally and fully developed, at least to its modern high level, only in the bureaucratic army.

Historically, the bureaucratization of the army has everywhere been realized along with the transfer of army service from the propertied to the propertyless. Until this transfer occurs, military service is an honorific privilege of propertied men. Such a transfer was made to the native-born unpropertied, for instance, in the armies of the generals of the late Roman republic and the empire, as well as in modern armies up to the nineteenth century. The burden of service has also been transferred to strangers, as in the mercenary armies of all ages. This process typically goes hand in hand with the general increase in material and intellectual culture. The following reason has also played its part everywhere: the increasing density of population, and therewith the intensity and strain of economic work, makes for an increasing "indispensability" of the acquisitive strata for purposes of war. Leaving aside periods of strong ideological fervor, the propertied strata of sophisticated and especially of urban culture as a rule are little fitted and also little inclined to do the coarse war work of the common soldier. Other circumstances being equal, the propertied strata of the open country are at least usually better qualified and more strongly inclined to become professional officers. This difference between the urban and the rural propertied is balanced only where the increasing possibility of mechanized warfare requires the leaders to qualify as "technicians."

The bureaucratization of organized warfare may be carried through in the form of private capitalist enterprise, just like any other business. Indeed, the procurement of armies and their administration by private capitalists has been the rule in mercenary armies, especially those of the Occident up to the turn of the eighteenth century. During the Thirty Years' War, in Brandenburg the soldier was still the predominant owner of the material implements of his business. He owned his weapons, horses, and dress, although the state, in the role, as it were, of the merchant of the "putting-out system," did supply him to some extent. Later on, in the standing army of Prussia, the chief of the company owned the material means of warfare, and only since the peace of Tilsit has the concentration of the means of warfare in the hands of the state definitely come about. Only with this concentration was the introduction of uniforms generally carried through. Before then, the introduction of uniforms had been left to a great extent to the arbitrary discretion of the regimental officer, with the exception of individual categories of troops to whom the king had "bestowed" certain uniforms, first, in 1620, to the royal bodyguard, then, under Frederick II, repeatedly.

Such terms as "regiment" and "battalion" usually had quite different meanings in the eighteenth century from the meanings they have today. Only the battalion was a tactical unit (today both are); the "regiment" was then a managerial unit of an economic organization established by the colonel's position as an "entrepreneur." "Official" maritime ventures (like the Genoese maonae) and army procurement belong to private capitalism's first giant enterprises of far-going bureaucratic character. In this respect, the "nationalization" of these enterprises by the state has its modern parallel in the nationalization of the railroads, which have been controlled by the state from their beginnings.

In the same way as with army organizations, the bureaucratization of administration goes hand in hand with the concentration of the means of organization in other spheres. The old administration by satraps and regents, as well as administration by farmers of office, purchasers of office, and, most of all, administration by feudal vassals, decentralize the material means of administration. The local demand of the province and the cost of the army and of subaltern officials are regularly paid for in advance from local income, and only the surplus reaches the central treasure. The enfeoffed official administers entirely by payment out of his own pocket. The bureaucratic state, however, puts its whole administrative expense on the budget and equips the lower authorities with the current means of expenditure, the use of which the state regulates and controls. This has the same meaning for the "economics" of the administration as for the large centralized capitalist enterprise.

In the field of scientific research and instruction, the bureaucratization of the always existing research institutes of the universities is a function of the increasing demand for material means of management. Liebig's laboratory at Giessen University was the first example of big enterprise in this field. Through the concentration of such means in the hands of the privileged head of the institute, the mass of researchers and docents are separated from their "means of production," in the same way as capitalist enterprise has separated the workers from theirs.

In spite of its indubitable technical superiority, bureaucracy has everywhere been a relatively late development. A number of obstacles have contributed to this, and only under certain social and political conditions have they definitely receded into the background.

The Leveling of Social Differences

Bureaucratic organization has usually come into power on the basis of a leveling of economic and social differences. This leveling has been at least relative, and has concerned the significance of social and economic differences for the assumption of administrative functions.

Bureaucracy inevitably accompanies modern *mass democracy* in contrast to the democratic self-government of small homogeneous units. This results from the characteristic principle of bureaucracy: the abstract regularity of the execution of authority, which is a result of the demand for "equality before the law" in the personal and functional sense—hence, of the horror of "privilege," and the principled rejection of doing business "from case to case." Such regularity also follows from the social preconditions of the origin of bureaucracies. The nonbureaucratic administration of any large social structure rests in some way upon the fact that existing social, material, or honorific perferences and ranks are connected with administrative functions and duties. This usually means that a direct or indirect economic exploitation or a "social" exploitation of position, which every sort of administrative activity gives to its bearers, is equivalent to the assumption of administrative functions.

Bureaucratization and democratization within the administration of the state therefore signify and increase the cash expenditures of the public treasury. And this is the case in spite of the fact that bureaucratic administration is usually more "economical" in character than other forms of administration. Until recent times—at least from the point of view of the treasury—the cheapest way of satisfying the need for administration was to leave almost the entire local administration and lower judicature to the landlords of Eastern Prussia. The same fact applies to the administration of sheriffs in England. Mass democracy makes a clean sweep of the feudal, patrimonial, and—at least in intent—the plutocratic privileges in administration. Unavoidably it puts paid professional labor in place of the historically inherited avocational administration by notables.

This not only applies to structures of the state. For it is no accident that in their own organizations, the democratic mass parties have completely broken with traditional notable rule based upon personal relationships and personal esteem. Yet such personal structures frequently continue among the old conservative as well as the old liberal parties. Democratic mass parties are bureaucratically organized under the leadership of party officials, professional party and trade union secretaries, et cetera. In Germany, for instance, this has happened in the Social Democratic party and in the agrarian mass movement; and in England, for the first time, in the caucus democracy of Gladstone-Chamberlain, which was originally organized in Birmingham and since the 1870's has spread. In the United States, both parties since Jackson's administration have developed bureaucratically. In France, however, attempts to organize disciplined political parties on the basis of an election system that would compel bureaucratic organization have repeatedly failed. The resistance of local circles of notables against the ultimately unavoidable bureaucratization of the parties, which would encompass the entire country and break their influence, could not be overcome. Every advance of the simple election techniques, for instance the system of proportional elections, which calculates with figures, means a strict and interlocal bureaucratic organization of the parties and therewith an increasing domination of party bureaucracy and discipline, as well as the elimination of the local circles of notables—at least this holds for great states.

The progress of bureaucratization in the state administration itself is a parallel phenomenon of democracy, as is quite obvious in France, North America, and now in England. Of course one must always remember that the term "democratization" can be misleading. The *demos* itself, in the sense of an inarticulate mass, never "governs" larger associations; rather, it is governed, and its existence only changes the way in which the executive leaders are selected and the measure of influence which the *demos,* or better, which social circles from its midst are able to exert upon the content and the direction of administrative activities by supplementing what is called "public opinion." "Democratization," in the sense here intended, does not necessarily mean an increasingly active share of the governed in the authority of the social structure. This may be a result of democratization, but it is not necessarily the case.

We must expressly recall at this point that the political concept of democracy, deduced from the "equal rights" of the governed, includes these postulates: (1) prevention of the development of a closed status group of officials in the interest of a universal accessibility of office, and (2) minimization of the authority of officialdom in the interest of expanding the sphere of influence of "public opinion" as far as practicable. Hence, wherever possible, political democracy strives to shorten the term of office by election and recall and by not binding the candidates to a special expertness. Thereby democracy inevitably comes into conflict with

25

the bureaucratic tendencies which, by its fight against notable rule, democracy has produced. The generally loose term "democratization" cannot be used here, in so far as it is understood to mean the minimization of the civil servants' ruling power in favor of the greatest possible "direct" rule of the *demos,* which in practice means the respective party leaders of the *demos.* The most decisive thing here—indeed it is rather exclusively so—is the *leveling of the governed* in opposition to the ruling and bureaucratically articulated group, which in its turn may occupy a quite autocratic position, both in fact and in form.

• • •

The Permanent Character of the Bureaucratic Machine

Once it is fully established, bureaucracy is among those social structures which are the hardest to destroy. Bureaucracy is *the* means of carrying "community action" over into rationally ordered "societal action." Therefore, as an instrument for "societalizing" relations of power, bureaucracy has been and is a power instrument of the first order—for the one who controls the bureaucratic apparatus.

Under otherwise equal conditions, a "societal action," which is methodically ordered and led, is superior to every resistance of "mass" or even of "communal action." And where the bureaucratization of administration has been completely carried through, a form of power relation is established that is practically unshatterable.

The individual bureaucrat cannot squirm out of the apparatus in which he is harnessed. In contrast to the honorific or avocational "notable," the professional bureaucrat is chained to his activity by his entire material and ideal existence. In the great majority of cases, he is only a single cog in an ever-moving mechanism which prescribes to him an essentially fixed route of march. The official is entrusted with specialized tasks and normally the mechanism cannot be put into motion or arrested by him, but only from the very top. The individual bureaucrat is thus forged to the community of all the functionaries who are integrated into the mechanism. They have a common interest in seeing that the mechanism continues its functions and that the societally exercised authority carries on.

The ruled, for their part, cannot dispense with or replace the bureaucratic apparatus of authority once it exists. For this bureaucracy rests upon expert training, a functional specialization of work, and an attitude set for habitual and virtuoso-like mastery of single yet methodically integrated functions. If the official stops working, or if his work is forcefully interrupted, chaos results, and it is difficult to improvise replacements from among the governed who are fit to master such chaos. This holds for public administration as well as for private economic management. More and more the material fate of the masses depends upon the steady and correct functioning of the increasingly bureaucratic organizations of private capitalism. The idea of eliminating these organizations becomes more and more utopian.

The discipline of officialdom refers to the attitude-set of the official for precise obedience within his *habitual* activity, in public as well as in private organizations. This discipline increasingly becomes the basis of all order, however great the practical importance of administration on the basis of the filed documents may be. The naïve idea of Bakuninism of destroying the basis of "acquired rights" and "domination" by destroying public documents overlooks the settled orientation of *man* for keeping to the habitual rules and regulations that continue to exist independently of the documents. Every reorganization of beaten or dissolved troops, as well as the restoration of administrative orders destroyed by revolt, panic, or other catastrophes, is realized by appealing to the trained orientation of obedient compliance to such orders. Such compliance has been conditioned into the officials, on the one hand, and, on the other hand, into the governed. If such an appeal is successful it brings, as it were, the disturbed mechanism into gear again.

The objective indispensability of the once-existing apparatus, with its peculiar, "impersonal" character, means that the mechanism—in contrast to feudal orders based upon personal piety—is easily made to work for anybody who knows how to gain control over it. A rationally ordered system of officials continues to function smoothly after the enemy has occupied the area; he merely needs to change the top officials. This body of officials continues to operate because it is to the vital interest of everyone concerned, including above all the enemy.

During the course of his long years in power, Bismarck brought his ministerial colleagues into unconditional bureaucratic dependence by eliminating all independent statesmen. Upon his retirement, he saw to his surprise that they continued to manage their offices unconcerned and undismayed, as if he had not been the master mind and creator of these creatures, but rather as if some single figure had been exchanged for some other figure in the bureaucratic machine. With all the changes of masters in France since the time of the First Empire, the power machine has remained essentially the same. Such a machine makes "revolution," in the sense of the forceful creation of entirely new formations of authority, technically more and more impossible, especially when the apparatus controls the modern means of communication (telegraph, et cetera) and also by virtue of its internal rationalized structure. In classic fashion, France has demonstrated how this process has substituted *coups d'état* for "revolutions": all successful transformations in France have amounted to *coups d'état*.

27

The Routinization of Charisma

In its pure form charismatic authority has a character specifically foreign to everyday routine structures. The social relationships directly involved are strictly personal, based on the validity and practice of charismatic personal qualities. If this is not to remain a purely transitory phenomenon, but to take on the character of a permanent relationship forming a stable community of disciples or a band of followers or a party organization or any sort of political or hierocratic organization, it is necessary for the character of charismatic authority to become radically changed. Indeed, in its pure form charismatic authority may be said to exist only in the process of originating. It cannot remain stable, but becomes either traditionalized or rationalized, or a combination of both.

The following are the principal motives underlying this transformation: (*a*) The ideal and also the material interests of the followers in the continuation and the continual reactivation of the community, (*b*) the still stronger ideal and also stronger material interests of the members of the administrative staff, the disciples or other followers of the charismatic leader in continuing their relationship. Not only this, but they have an interest in continuing it in such a way that both from an ideal and a material point of view, their own status is put on a stable everyday basis. This means, above all, making it possible to participate in normal family relationships or at least to enjoy a secure social position in place of the kind of discipleship which is cut off from ordinary worldly connections, notably in the family and in economic relationships.

These interests generally become conspicuously evident with the disappearance of the personal charismatic leader and with the problem of succession, which inevitably arises. The way in which this problem is met—if it is met at all and the charismatic group continues to exist—is of crucial importance for the character of the subsequent social relationships. The following are the principal possible types of solution:

(*a*) The search for a new charismatic leader on the basis of criteria of the qualities which will fit him for the position of authority. This is to be found in a relatively pure type in the process of choice of a new Dalai Lama. It consists in the search for a child with characteristics which are interpreted to mean that he is a reincarnation of the Buddha. This is very similar to the choice of the new Bull of Apis.

In this case the legitimacy of the new charismatic leader is bound to certain distinguishing characteristics; thus, to rules with respect to which a tradition arises. The result is a process of traditionalization in favour of which the purely personal character of leadership is eliminated.

SOURCE: *The Theory of Social and Economic Organization,* ed. and trans. by A. M. Henderson and Talcott Parsons, pp. 363–73. Copyright © 1947, renewed 1975 by Talcott Parsons. Reprinted with permission of Macmillan Publishing Co., Inc.

(*b*) By revelation manifested in oracles, lots, divine judgments, or other techniques of selection. In this case the legitimacy of the new leader is dependent on the legitimacy of the technique of his selection. This involves a form of legalization. It is said that at times the *Schofetim* of Israel had this character. Saul is said to have been chosen by the old war oracle.

(*c*) By the designation on the part of the original charismatic leader of his own successor and his recognition on the part of the followers. This is a very common form. Originally, the Roman magistracies were filled entirely in this way. The system survived most clearly into later times in the appointment of "dictators" and in the institution of the "interrex." In this case legitimacy is acquired through the act of designation.

(*d*) Designation of a successor by the charismatically qualified administrative staff and his recognition by the community. In its typical form this process should quite definitely not be interpreted as "election" or "nomination" or anything of the sort. It is not a matter of free selection, but of one which is strictly bound to objective duty. It is not to be determined merely by majority vote, but is a question of arriving at the correction designation, the designation of the right person who is truly endowed with charisma. It is quite possible that the minority and not the majority should be right in such a case. Unanimity is often required. It is obligatory to acknowledge a mistake and persistence in error is a serious offence. Making a wrong choice is a genuine wrong requiring expiation. Originally it was a magical offence.

Nevertheless, in such a case it is easy for legitimacy to take on the character of an acquired right which is justified by standards of the correctness of the process by which the position was acquired, for the most part, by its having been acquired in accordance with certain formalities, such as coronation. This was the original meaning of the coronation of bishops and kings in the Western World by the clergy or the nobility with the "consent" of the community. There are numerous analogous phenomena all over the world. The fact that this is the origin of the modern conception of "election" raises problems which will have to be gone into later.

(*e*) By the conception that charisma is a quality transmitted by heredity; thus that it is participated in by the kinsmen of its bearer, particularly by his closest relatives. This is the case of hereditary charisma. The order of hereditary succession in such a case need not be the same as that which is in force for appropriated rights, but may differ from it. It is also sometimes necessary to select the proper heir within the kinship group by some of the methods just spoken of; thus in certain Negro states brothers have had to fight for the succession. In China, succession had to take place in such a way that the relation of the living group to the ancestral spirits was not disturbed. The rule either of seniority or of designation by the followers has been very common in the Orient. Hence, in the house of Osman, it has been obligatory to eliminate all other possible candidates.

Only in Medieval Europe and in Japan universally, elsewhere only sporadically, has the principle of primogeniture, as governing the inheritance of authority, become clearly established. This has greatly facilitated the consolidation of political groups in that it has eliminated struggle between a plurality of candidates from the same charismatic family.

In the case of hereditary charisma, recognition is no longer paid to the charismatic qualities of the individual, but to the legitimacy of the position he has acquired by hereditary succession. This may lead in the direction either of traditionalization or of legalization. The concept of "divine right" is fundamentally altered and now comes to mean authority by virtue of a personal right which is not dependent on the recognition of those subject to authority. Personal charisma may be totally absent. Hereditary monarchy is a conspicuous illustration. In Asia there have been very numerous hereditary priesthoods; also, frequently, the hereditary charisma of kinship groups has been treated as a criterion of social rank and of eligibility for fiefs and benefices.

(*f*) The concept that charisma may be transmitted by ritual means from one bearer to another or may be created in a new person. The concept was originally magical. It involves a dissociation of charisma from a particular individual, making it an objective, transferrable entity. In particular, it may become the charisma of office. In this case the belief in legitimacy is no longer directed to the individual, but to the acquired qualities and to the effectiveness of the ritual acts. The most important example is the transmission of priestly charisma by anointing, consecration, or the laying on of hands; and of royal authority, by anointing and by coronation. The *caracter indelibilis* thus acquired means that the charismatic qualities and powers of the office are emancipated from the personal qualities of the priest. For precisely this reason, this has, from the Donatist and the Montanist heresies down to the Puritan revolution, been the subject of continual conflicts. The "hireling" of the Quakers is the preacher endowed with the charisma of office.

Concomitant with the routinization of charisma with a view to insuring adequate succession, go the interests in its routinization on the part of the administrative staff. It is only in the initial stages and so long as the charismatic leader acts in a way which is completely outside everyday social organization, that it is possible for his followers to live communistically in a community of faith and enthusiasm, on gifts, "booty," or sporadic acquisition. Only the members of the small group of enthusiastic disciples and followers are prepared to devote their lives purely idealistically to their call. The great majority of disciples and followers will in the long run "make their living" out of their "calling" in a material sense as well. Indeed, this must be the case if the movement is not to disintegrate.

Hence, the routinization of charisma also takes the form of the appropriation of powers of control and of economic advantages by the followers or disciples, and of regulation of the recruitment of these groups. This process of traditionalization or of legalization, according to whether rational legislation is involved or not, may take any one of a number of typical forms.

1. The original basis of recruitment is personal charisma. With routinization, the followers or disciples may set up norms for recruitment, in particular involving training or tests of eligibility. Charisma can only be "awakened" and "tested"; it cannot be "learned" or "taught." All types of magical asceticism, as practiced by magicians and heroes, and all novitiates, belong in this category. These are means of closing the group which constitutes the administrative staff.

Only the proved novice is allowed to exercise authority. A genuine charismatic leader is in a position to oppose this type of prerequisite for membership. His successor is not, at least if he is chosen by the administrative staff. This type is illustrated by the magical and warrior asceticism of the "men's house" with initiation ceremonies and age groups. An individual who has not successfully gone through the initiation, remains a "woman"; that is, is excluded from the charismatic group.

2. It is easy for charismatic norms to be transformed into those defining a traditional social status on a hereditary charismatic basis. If the leader is chosen on a hereditary basis, it is very easy for hereditary charisma to govern the selection of the administrative staff and even, perhaps, those followers without any position of authority. The term "familistic state" will be applied when a political body is organized strictly and completely in terms of this principle of hereditary charisma. In such a case, all appropriation of governing powers, of fiefs, benefices, and all sorts of economic advantages follow the same pattern. The result is that all powers and advantages of all sorts become traditionalized. The heads of families, who are traditional gerontocrats or patriarchs without personal charismatic legitimacy, regulate the exercise of these powers which cannot be taken away from their family. It is not the type of position he occupies which determines the rank of a man or of his family, but rather the hereditary charismatic rank of his family determines the position he will occupy. Japan, before the development of bureaucracy, was organized in this way. The same was undoubtedly true of China as well where, before the rationalization which took place in the territorial states, authority was in the hands of the "old families." Other types of examples are furnished by the caste system in India, and by Russia before the *Mjestnitschestvo* was introduced. Indeed, all hereditary social classes with established privileges belong in the same category.

3. The administrative staff may seek and achieve the creation and appropriation of individual positions and the corresponding economic advantages for its members. In that case, according to whether the tendency is to traditionalization or legalization, there will develop (*a*) benefices, (*b*) offices, or (*c*) fiefs. In the first case a prebendal organization will result; in the second, patrimonialism or bureaucracy; in the third, feudalism. These become appropriated in the place of the type of provision from gifts or booty without settled relation to the everyday economic structure.

Case (*a*), benefices, may consist in rights to the proceeds of begging, to payments in kind, or to the proceeds of money taxes, or finally, to the proceeds of fees. Any one of these may result from the regulation of provision by free gifts or by "booty" in terms of a rational organization of finance. Regularized begging is found in Buddhism; benefices in kind, in the Chinese and Japanese "rice rents"; support by money taxation has been the rule in all the rationalized conquering states. The last case is common everywhere, especially on the part of priests and judges and, in India, even the military authorities.

Case (*b*), the transformation of the charismatic mission into an office, may have more of a patrimonial or more of a bureaucratic character. The former is much the more common; the latter is found principally in Mediterranean Antiquity and in the modern Western World. Elsewhere it is exceptional.

In case (*c*), only land may be appropriated as a fief, whereas the position as such retains its originally charismatic character. On the other hand, powers and authority may be fully appropriated as fiefs. It is difficult to distinguish the two cases. It is, however, rare that orientation to the charismatic character of the position disappears entirely; it did not do so in the Middle Ages.

For charisma to be transformed into a permanent routine structure, it is necessary that its antieconomic character should be altered. It must be adapted to some form of fiscal organization to provide for the needs of the group and hence to the economic conditions necessary for raising taxes and contributions. When a charismatic movement develops in the direction of prebendal provision, the "laity" become differentiated from the "clergy"; that is, the participating members of the charismatic administrative staff which has now become routinized. These are the priests of the developing "church." Correspondingly, in a developing political body the vassals, the holders of benefices, or officials are differentiated from the "taxpayers." The former, instead of being the "followers" of the leader, become state officials or appointed party officials. This process is very conspicuous in Buddhism and in the Hindu sects. The same is true in all the states resulting from conquest which have become rationalized to form permanent structures; also of parties and other movements which have originally had a purely charismatic character. With the process of routinization the charismatic group tends to develop into one of the forms of everyday authority, particularly the patrimonial form in its decentralized variant or the bureaucratic. Its original peculiarities are apt to be retained in the charismatic standards of honor attendant on the social status acquired by heredity or the holding of office. This applies to all who participate in the process of appropriation, the chief himself, and the members of his staff. It is thus a matter of the type of prestige enjoyed by ruling groups. A hereditary monarch by "divine right" is not a simple patrimonial chief, patriarch, or sheik; a vassal is not a mere household retainer or official. Further details must be deferred to the analysis of social stratification.

As a rule the process of routinization is not free of conflict. In the early stages personal claims on the charisma of the chief are not easily forgotten and the conflict between the charisma of office or of hereditary status with personal charisma is a typical process in many historical situations.

1. The power of absolution—that is, the power to absolve from mortal sins—was held originally only by personal charismatic martyrs or ascetics, but became transformed into a power of the office of bishop or priest. This process was much slower in the Orient than in the Occident because in the latter case it was influenced by the Roman conception of office. Revolutions under a charismatic leader, directed against hereditary charismatic powers or the powers of office, are to be found in all types of corporate groups, from states to trade unions. The more highly developed the interdependence of different economic units in a monetary economy, the greater the pressure of the everyday needs of the followers of the charismatic movement becomes. The effect of this is to strengthen the tendency to routinization, which is everywhere operative, and as a rule has rapidly won out. Charisma is a phenomenon typical of prophetic religious movements or of expansive political movements in their early stages. But as soon as the position of authority is well established, and above all as soon as control over large masses of people exists, it gives way to the forces of everyday routine.

2. One of the decisive motives underlying all cases of the routinization of charisma is naturally the striving for security. This means legitimization, on the one hand, of positions of authority and social prestige, on the other hand, of the economic advantages enjoyed by the followers and sympathizers of the leader. Another important motive, however, lies in the objective necessity of adaptation of the patterns of order and of the organization of the administrative staff to the normal, everyday needs and conditions of carrying on administration. In this connection, in particular, there are always points at which traditions of administrative practice and of judicial decision can take hold; since these are needed both by the

normal administrative staff and by those subject to its authority. It is further necessary that there should be some definite order introduced into the organization of the administrative staff itself. Finally, as will be discussed in detail below, it is necessary for the administrative staff and all its administrative practices to be adapted to everyday economic conditions. It is not possible for the costs of permanent, routine administration to be met by "booty," contributions, gifts, and hospitality, as is typical of the pure type of military and prophetic charisma.

3. The process of routinization is thus not by any means confined to the problem of succession and does not stop when this has been solved. On the contrary, the most fundamental problem is that of making a transition from a charismatic administrative staff, and the corresponding principles of administration, to one which is adapted to everyday conditions. The problem of succession, however, is crucial because through it occurs the routinization of the charismatic focus of the structure. In it, the character of the leader himself and of his claim to legitimacy is altered. This process involves peculiar and characteristic conceptions which are understandable only in this context and do not apply to the problem of transition to traditional or legal patterns of order and types of administrative organization. The most important of the modes of meeting the problem of succession are the charismatic designation of a successor and hereditary charisma.

4. As has already been noted, the most important historical example of designation by the charismatic leader of his own successor is Rome. For the *rex,* this arrangement is attested by tradition; while for the appointment of the "dictator" and of the co-emperor and successor in the principate, it has existed in historical times. The way in which all the higher magistrates were invested with the *imperium* shows clearly that they also were designated as successors by the military commander, subject to recognition by the citizen army. The fact that candidates were examined by the magistrate in office and that originally they could be excluded on what were obviously arbitrary grounds shows clearly what was the nature of the development.

5. The most important examples of designation of a successor by the charismatic followers of the leader are to be found in the election of bishops, and particularly of the Pope, by the original system of designation by the clergy and recognition by the lay community. The investigations of U. Stutz have made it probable that, though it was later altered, the election of the German emperor was modeled on that of the bishops. He was designated by a group of qualified princes and recognized by the "people," that is, those bearing arms. Similar arrangements are very common.

6. The classical case of the development of hereditary charisma is that of caste in India. All occupational qualifications, and in particular all the qualifications for positions of authority and power, have there

come to be regarded as strictly bound to the inheritance of charisma. Eligibility for fiefs, involving governing powers, was limited to members of the royal kinship group, the fiefs being granted by the eldest of the group. All types of religious office, including the extraordinarily important and influential position of *guru,* the *directeur de l'âme,* were treated as bound to hereditary charismatic qualities. The same is true of all sorts of relations to traditional customers and of all positions in the village organization, such as priest, barber, laundryman, watchman, etc. The foundation of a sect always meant the development of a hereditary hierarchy, as was true also of Taoism in China. Also in the Japanese "feudal" state, before the introduction of a patrimonial officialdom on the Chinese model, which then led to prebends and a new feudalization, social organization was based purely on hereditary charisma.

This kind of hereditary charismatic right to positions of authority has been developed in similar ways all over the world. Qualification by virtue of individual achievement has been replaced by qualification by birth. This is everywhere the basis of the development of hereditary aristocracies, in the Roman nobility, in the concept of the *stirps regia,* which Tacitus describes among the Germans, in the rules of eligibility to tournaments and monasteries in the late Middle Ages, and even in the genealogical research carried on on behalf of the parvenu aristocracy of the United States. Indeed, this is to be found everywhere where a differentiation of hereditary social classes has become established.

The following is the principal relation to economic conditions: The process of routinization of charisma is in very important respects identical with adaptation to the conditions of economic life, since this is one of the principal continually operating forces in everyday life. Economic conditions in this connection play a leading role and do not constitute merely a dependent variable. To a very large extent the transition to hereditary charisma or the charisma of office serves in this connection as a means of legitimizing existing or recently acquired powers of control over economic goods. Along with the ideology of loyalty, which is certainly by no means unimportant, allegiance to hereditary monarchy in particular is very strongly influenced by the consideration that all inherited property and all that which is legitimately acquired would be endangered if subjective recognition of the sanctity of succession to the throne were eliminated. It is hence by no means fortuitous that hereditary monarchy is more acceptable to the propertied classes than, for instance, to the proletariat.

Beyond this, it is not possible to say anything in general terms, which would at the same time be substantial and valuable, on the relations of the various possible modes of adaptation to the economic order. This must be reserved to a special investigation. The development of a prebendal structure, of feudalism and the appropriation of all sorts of advantages on a hereditary charismatic basis, may in all cases have the same stereo-

35

typing effect on the economic order if they develop from charismatic starting points as if they developed from patrimonial or bureaucratic origins. The immediate effect of charisma in economic as in other connections is usually strongly revolutionary; indeed, often destructive, because it means new modes of orientation. But in case the process of routinization leads in the direction of traditionalism, its ultimate effect may be exactly the reverse.

Oligarchy

Robert Michels

Introductory—The Need for Organization

Democracy is inconceivable without organization. A few words will suffice to demonstrate this proposition.

A class which unfurls in the face of society the banner of certain definite claims, and which aspires to the realization of a complex of ideal aims deriving from the economic functions which that class fulfills, needs an organization. Be the claims economic or be they political, organization appears the only means for the creation of a collective will. Organization, based as it is upon the principle of least effort, that is to say, upon the greatest possible economy of energy, is the weapon of the weak in their struggle with the strong.

The chances of success in any struggle will depend upon the degree to which this struggle is carried out upon a basis of solidarity between individuals whose interests are identical. In objecting, therefore, to the theories of the individualist anarchists that nothing could please the employers better than the dispersion and disaggregation of the forces of the workers, the socialists, the most fanatical of all the partisans of the idea of organization, enunciate an argument which harmonizes well with the results of scientific study of the nature of parties.

We live in a time in which the idea of cooperation has become so firmly established that even millionaires perceive the necessity of common action. It is easy to understand, then, that organization has become a vital principle of the working class, for in default of it their success is *a priori* impossible. The refusal of the worker to participate in the collective life of his class cannot fail to entail disastrous consequences. In respect of culture and of economic, physical, and physiological conditions, the proletarian is the weakest element of our society. In fact, the isolated member of the working classes is defenseless in the hands of those who are eco-

SOURCE: *Political Parties,* translated by Eden and Cedar Paul, pp. 61–62, 65–73, 167–68, 170–71, 172–73, 364–71. Copyright © 1962 by The Crowell-Collier Publishing Company. Reprinted with permission of Macmillan Publishing Co., Inc.

nomically stronger. It is only by combination to form a structural aggregate that the proletarians can acquire the faculty of political resistance and attain to a social dignity. The importance and the influence of the working class are directly proportional to its numerical strength. But for the representation of that numerical strength organization and coordination are indispensable. The principle of organization is an absolutely essential condition for the political struggle of the masses.

Yet this politically necessary principle of organization, while it overcomes that disorganization of forces which would be favorable to the adversary, brings other dangers in its train. We escape Scylla only to dash ourselves on Charybdis. Organization is, in fact, the source from which the conservative currents flow over the plain of democracy, occasioning there disastrous floods and rendering the plain unrecognizable.

•   •   •

It is obvious that such a gigantic number of persons belonging to a unitary organization cannot do any practical work upon a system of direct discussion. The regular holding of deliberative assemblies of a thousand members encounters the gravest difficulties in respect of room and distance; while from the topographical point of view such an assembly would become altogether impossible if the members numbered ten thousand. Even if we imagined the means of communication to become much better than those which now exist, how would it be possible to assemble such a multitude in a given place, at a stated time, and with the frequency demanded by the exigencies of party life? In addition must be considered the physiological impossibility even for the most powerful orator of making himself heard by a crowd of ten thousand persons. There are, however, other persons of a technical and administrative character which render impossible the direct self-government of large groups. If Peter wrongs Paul, it is out of the question that all the other citizens should hasten to the spot to undertake a personal examination of the matter in dispute, and to take the part of Paul against Peter. By parity of reasoning, in the modern democratic party, it is impossible for the collectivity to undertake the direct settlement of all the controversies that may arise.

Hence the need for delegation, for the system in which delegates represent the mass and carry out its will. Even in groups sincerely animated with the democratic spirit, current business, the preparation and the carrying out of the most important actions, is necessarily left in the hands of individuals. It is well known that the impossibility for the people to exercise a legislative power directly in popular assemblies led the democratic idealists of Spain to demand, as the least of evils, a system of popular representation and a parliamentary state.[1]

1. Cf. the letter of Antonio Quiroga to King Ferdinand VII, dated January 7, 1820 (Don Juan van Halen, *Mémoires,* Renouard, Paris, 1827, Part II, p. 382).

Originally the chief is merely the servant of the mass. The organization is based upon the absolute equality of all its members. Equality is here understood in its most general sense, as an equality of like men. In many countries, as in idealist Italy (and in certain regions in Germany where the socialist movement is still in its infancy), this equality is manifested, among other ways, by the mutual use of the familiar "thou," which is employed by the most poorly paid wage-laborer in addressing the most distinguished intellectual. This generic conception of equality is, however, gradually replaced by the idea of equality among comrades belonging to the same organization, all of whose members enjoy the same rights. The democratic principle aims at guaranteeing to all an equal influence and an equal participation in the regulation of the common interests. All are electors, and all are eligible for office. The fundamental postulate of the *Déclaration des Droits de l'Homme* finds here its theoretical application. All the offices are filled by election. The officials, executive organs of the general will, play a merely subordinate part, are always dependent upon the collectivity, and can be deprived of their office at any moment. The mass of the party is omnipotent.

At the outset, the attempt is made to depart as little as possible from pure democracy by subordinating the delegates altogether to the will of the mass, by tieing them hand and foot. In the early days of the movement of the Italian agricultural workers, the chief of the league required a majority of four-fifths of the votes to secure election. When disputes arose with the employers about wages, the representative of the organization, before undertaking any negotiations, had to be furnished with a written authority, authorized by the signature of every member of the corporation. All the accounts of the body were open to the examination of the members, at any time. There were two reasons for this. First of all, the desire was to avoid the spread of mistrust through the mass, "this poison which gradually destroys even the strongest organism." In the second place, this usage allowed each one of the members to learn bookkeeping, and to acquire such a general knowledge of the working of the corporation as to enable him at any time to take over its leadership.[2] It is obvious that democracy in this sense is applicable only on a very small scale. In the infancy of the English labor movement, in many of the trade unions, the delegates were either appointed in rotation from among all the members, or were chosen by lot.[3] Gradually, however, the delegates' duties became more complicated; some individual ability becomes essential, a certain oratorical gift, and a considerable amount of objective knowledge. It thus becomes impossible to trust to blind chance, to the fortune of alphabetic

2. Egidio Bernaroli, *Manuale per la constituzione e il funzionamento delle leghe dei contadini,* Libreria Soc. Ital., Rome, 1902, pp. 20, 26, 27, 52.
3. Sidney and Beatrice Webb, *Industrial Democracy* (German edition), Stuttgart, 1898, vol. i, p. 6.

succession, or to the order of priority, in the choice of a delegation whose members must possess certain peculiar personal aptitudes if they are to discharge their mission to the general advantage.

Such were the methods which prevailed in the early days of the labor movement to enable the masses to participate in party and trade-union administration. Today they are falling into disuse, and in the development of the modern political aggregate there is a tendency to shorten and stereotype the process which transforms the led into a leader—a process which has hitherto developed by the natural course of events. Here and there voices make themselves heard demanding a sort of official consecration for the leaders, insisting that it is necessary to constitute a class of professional politicians, of approved and registered experts in political life. Ferdinand Tönnies advocates that the party should institute regular examinations for the nomination of socialist parliamentary candidates, and for the appointment of party secretaries.[4] Heinrich Herkner goes even farther. He contends that the great trade unions cannot long maintain their existence if they persist in entrusting the management of their affairs to persons drawn from the rank and file, who have risen to command stage by stage solely in consequence of practical aptitudes acquired in the service of the organization. He refers, in this connection, to the unions that are controlled by the employers, whose officials are for the most part university men. He foresees that in the near future all the labor organizations will be forced to abandon proletarian exclusiveness, and in the choice of their officials to give the preference to persons of an education that is superior alike in economic, legal, technical, and commercial respects.[5]

Even today, the candidates for the secretaryship of a trade union are subject to examination as to their knowledge of legal matters and their capacity as letter-writers. The socialist organizations engaged in political action also directly undertake the training of their own officials. Everywhere there are coming into existence "nurseries" for the rapid supply of officials possessing a certain amount of "scientific culture." Since 1906 there has existed in Berlin a Party-School in which courses of instruction are given for the training of those who wish to take office in the socialist party or in trade unions. The instructors are paid out of the funds of the socialist party, which was directly responsible for the foundation of the school. The other expenses of the undertaking, including the maintenance of the pupils, are furnished from a common fund supplied by the party and the various trade unions interested. In addition, the families of the pupils, in so far as the attendance of these at the school deprives the families of their breadwinners, receive an allowance from the provincial

4. Ferdinand Tönnies, *Politik und Moral,* Neuer Frankf. Verl., Frankfort, 1901, p. 46.
5. Heinrich Herkner, *Die Arbeiterfrage,* Guttentag, Berlin, 1908, 5th ed., pp. 116, 117.

branch of the party or from the local branch of the union to which each pupil belongs. The third course of this school, from October 1, 1908, to April 3, 1909, was attended by twenty-six pupils, while the first year there had been thirty-one and the second year thirty-three. As pupils, preference is given to comrades who already hold office in the party or in one of the labor unions.[6] Those who do not already belong to the labor bureaucracy make it their aim to enter that body, and cherish the secret hope that attendance at the school will smooth their path. Those who fail to attain this end are apt to exhibit a certain discontent with the party which, after having encouraged their studies, has sent them back to manual labor. Among the 141 students of the year 1910–11, three classes were to be distinguished: one of these consisted of old and tried employees in the different branches of the labor movement (fifty-two persons); a second consisted of those who obtained employment in the party or the trade unions directly the course was finished (forty-nine persons); the third consisted of those who had to return to manual labor (forty persons).[7]

In Italy, *L'Umanitaria,* a philanthropic organization run by the socialists, founded at Milan in 1905 a "Practical School of Social Legislation," whose aim it is to give to a certain number of workers an education which will fit them for becoming factory inspectors, or for taking official positions in the various labor organizations, in the friendly societies, or in the labor exchanges.[8] The course of instruction lasts for two years, and at its close the pupils receive, after examination, a diploma which entitles them to the title of "Labor Expert." In 1908 there were two hundred and two pupils, thirty-seven of whom were employees of trade unions or of cooperative societies, four were secretaries of labor exchanges, forty-five employees in or members of the liberal professions, and a hundred and twelve working men.[9] At the outset most of the pupils came to the school as a matter of personal taste, or with the aim of obtaining the diploma in order to secure some comparatively lucrative private employment. But quite recently the governing body has determined to suppress the diploma, and to institute a supplementary course open to those only who are already employed by some labor organization or who definitely intend to enter such employment. For those engaged upon this special course of study there will be provided scholarships of £2 a week, the funds for this purpose being supplied in part by *L'Umanitaria* and in part by the labor organizations which wish to send their employees to the school.[10] In the year 1909, under the auspices of the *Bourse du Travail,* there was founded

6. *Protokoll des Parteitags zu Leipzig,* 1909, "Vorwärts," Berlin, 1909, p. 48.
7. Heinrich Schulz, *Fünf Jahre Parteischule,* "Neue Zeit," anno xxix, vol. ii, fasc. 49, p. 807.
8. *Scuola Prat. di Legislaz. Sociale* (Programma e Norme), anno iii, Soc. Umanitaria, Milan, 1908.
9. Ibid., anno iv, Milan, 1909, p. 5.
10. Rinaldo Rigola, *I funzionari delle organizzazioni,* "Avanti," anno xiv, No. 341.

at Turin a similar school (*Scuola Pratica di Cultura e Legislazione Sociale*), which, however, soon succumbed.

In England the trade unions and cooperative societies make use of Ruskin College, Oxford, sending thither those of their members who aspire to office in the labor organizations, and who have displayed special aptitudes for this career. In Austria it is proposed to found a party school upon the German model.

It is undeniable that all these educational institutions for the officials of the party and of the labor organizations tend, above all, towards the artificial creation of an *élite* of the working class, of a caste of cadets composed of persons who aspire to the command of the proletarian rank and file. Without wishing it, there is thus effected a continuous enlargement of the gulf which divides the leaders from the masses.

The technical specialization that inevitably results from all extensive organization renders necessary what is called expert leadership. Consequently the power of determination comes to be considered one of the specific attributes of leadership, and is gradually withdrawn from the masses to be concentrated in the hands of the leaders alone. Thus the leaders, who were at first no more than the executive organs of the collective will, soon emancipate themselves from the mass and become independent of its control.

Organization implies the tendency to oligarchy. In every organization, whether it be a political party, a professional union, or any other association of the kind, the aristocratic tendency manifests itself very clearly. The mechanism of the organization, while conferring a solidity of structure, induces serious changes in the organized mass, completely inverting the respective position of the leaders and the led. As a result of organization, every party or professional union becomes divided into a minority of directors and a majority of directed.

It has been remarked that in the lower stages of civilization tyranny is dominant. Democracy cannot come into existence until there is attained a subsequent and more highly developed stage of social life. Freedoms and privileges, and among these latter the privilege of taking part in the direction of public affairs, are at first restricted to the few. Recent times have been characterized by the gradual extension of these privileges to a widening circle. This is what we know as the era of democracy. But if we pass from the sphere of the state to the sphere of party, we may observe that as democracy continues to develop, a backwash sets in. With the advance of organization, democracy tends to decline. Democratic evolution has a parabolic course. At the present time, at any rate as far as party life is concerned, democracy is in the descending phase. It may be enunciated as a general rule that the increase in the power of the leaders is directly proportional with the extension of the organization. In the various parties and labor organizations of different countries the influence of the leaders is mainly determined (apart from racial and individual grounds) by the varying development of organization. Where organization is stronger, we find that there is a lesser degree of applied democracy.

Every solidly constructed organization, whether it be a democratic state, a political party, or a league of proletarians for the resistance of economic oppression, presents a soil eminently favorable for the differentiation of organs and of functions. The more extended and the more ramified the official apparatus of the organization, the greater the number of its members, the fuller its treasury, and the more widely circulated its press, the less efficient becomes the direct control exercised by the rank and file, and the more is this control replaced by the increasing power of committees. Into all parties there insinuates itself that indirect electoral system which in public life the democratic parties fight against with all possible vigor. Yet in party life the influence of this system must be more disastrous than in the far more extensive life of the state. Even in the party congresses, which represent the party-life seven times sifted, we find that it becomes more and more general to refer all important questions to committees which debate *in camera*.

As organization develops, not only do the tasks of the administration become more difficult and more complicated, but, further, its duties become enlarged and specialized to such a degree that it is no longer possible to take them all in at a single glance. In a rapidly progressive movement, it is not only the growth in the number of duties, but also the higher quality of these, which imposes a more extensive differentiation of function. Normally, and according to the letter of the rules, all the acts of the leaders are subject to the ever vigilant criticism of the rank and file. In theory the leader is merely an employee bound by the instruction he receives. He has to carry out the orders of the mass, of which he is no more than the executive organ. But in actual fact, as the organization increases in size, this control becomes purely fictitious. The members have to give up the idea of themselves conducting or even supervising the whole administration, and are compelled to hand these tasks over to trustworthy persons specially nominated for the purpose, to salaried officials. The rank and file must content themselves with summary reports, and with the appointment of occasional special committees of inquiry. Yet this does not derive from any special change in the rules of the organization. It is by very necessity that a simple employee gradually becomes a "leader," acquiring a freedom of action which he ought not to possess. The chief then becomes accustomed to dispatch important business on his own responsibility, and to decide various questions relating to the life of the party without any attempt to consult the rank and file. It is obvious that democratic control thus undergoes a progressive diminution, and is ultimately reduced to an infinitesimal minimum. In all the socialist parties there is a continual increase in the number of functions withdrawn from the electoral assemblies and transferred to the executive committees. In this way there is constructed a powerful and complicated edifice. The principle of division of labor coming more and more into operation, executive authority undergoes division and subdivision. There is thus constituted a rigorously defined and hierarchical bureaucracy. In the catechism of party duties, the strict observance of hierarchical rules becomes the first article. The hierarchy comes into existence as the outcome of technical conditions, and its constitution is an essential postulate of the regular functioning of the party machine.

It is indisputable that the oligarchical and bureaucratic tendency of party organization is a matter of technical and practical necessity. It is the inevitable product of the very principle of organization. Not even the most radical wing of the various socialist parties raises any objection to this retrogressive evolution, the contention being that democracy is only a form of organization and that where it ceases to be possible to harmonize democracy with organization, it is better to abandon the former than the latter. Organization, since it is the only means of attaining the ends of socialism, is considered to comprise within itself the revolutionary content of the party, and this essential content must never be sacrificed for the sake of form.

In all times, in all phases of development, in all branches of human activity, there have been leaders. It is true that certain socialists, above all the orthodox Marxists of Germany, seek to convince us that socialism knows nothing of "leaders," that the party has "employees" merely, being a democratic party, and the existence of leaders being incompatible with democracy. But a false assertion such as this cannot override a sociological law. Its only result is, in fact, to strengthen the rule of the leaders, for it serves to conceal from the mass a danger which really threatens democracy.

For technical and administrative reasons, no less than for tactical reasons, a strong organization needs an equally strong leadership. As long as an organization is loosely constructed and vague in its outlines, no professional leadership can arise. The anarchists, who have a horror of all fixed organization, have no regular leaders. In the early days of German socialism, the *Vertrauensmann* (homme de confiance) continued to exercise his ordinary occupation. If he received any pay for his work for the party, the remuneration was on an extremely modest scale, and was no more than a temporary grant. His function could never be regarded by him as a regular source of income. The employee of the organization was still a simple workmate, sharing the mode of life and the social condition of his fellows. Today he has been replaced for the most part by the professional politician, *Berzirksleiter* (U.S. ward-boss), etc. The more solid the structure of an organization becomes in the course of the evolution of the modern political party, the more marked becomes the tendency to

replace the emergency leader by the professional leader. Every party organization which has attained to a considerable degree of complication demands that there should be a certain number of persons who devote all
their activities to the work of the party. The mass provides these by
delegations, and the delegates, regularly appointed, become permanent
representatives of the mass for the direction of its affairs.

For democracy, however, the first appearance of professional leadership marks the beginning of the end, and this, above all, on account of
the logical impossibility of the "representative" system, whether in parliamentary life or in party delegation.

• • •

The Struggle between the Leaders and the Masses

Those who defend the arbitrary acts committed by the democracy,
point out that the masses have at their disposal means whereby they can
react against the violation of their rights. These means consist in the right
of controlling and dismissing their leaders. Unquestionably this defense
possesses a certain theoretical value, and the authoritarian inclinations of
the leaders are in some degree attenuated by these possibilities. In states
with a democratic tendency and under a parliamentary regime, to obtain
the fall of a detested minister it suffices, in theory, that the people should
be weary of him. In the same way, once more in theory, the ill-humor and
the opposition of a socialist group or of an election committee is enough
to effect the recall of a deputy's mandate, and in the same way the hostility
of the majority at the annual congress of trade unions should be enough
to secure the dismissal of a secretary. In practice, however, the exercise
of this theoretical right is interfered with by the working of the whole
series of conservative tendencies to which allusion has previously been
made, so that the supremacy of the autonomous and sovereign masses is
rendered purely illusory. The dread by which Nietzsche was at one time
so greatly disturbed, that every individual might become a functionary of
the mass, must be completely dissipated in face of the truth that while all
have the right to become functionaries, few only possess the possibility.

With the institution of leadership there simultaneously begins, owing
to the long tenure of office, the transformation of the leaders into a closed
caste.

Unless, as in France, extreme individualism and fanatical political
dogmatism stand in the way, the old leaders present themselves to the
masses as a compact phalanx—at any rate whenever the masses are so
much aroused as to endanger the position of the leaders.

The election of the delegates to congresses, etc., is sometimes regulated by the leaders by means of special agreements, whereby the masses are in fact excluded from all decisive influence in the management of their affairs. These agreements often assume the aspect of a mutual insurance contract. In the German Socialist Party, a few years ago, there came into existence in not a few localities a regular system in accordance with which the leaders nominated one another in rotation as delegates to the various party congresses. In the meetings at which the delegates were appointed, one of the big guns would always propose to the comrades the choice as delegate of the leader whose "turn" it was. The comrades rarely revolt against such artifices, and often fail even to perceive them. Thus competition among the leaders is prevented, in this domain at least; and at the same time there is rendered impossible anything more than passive participation of the rank and file in the higher functions of the life of that party which they alone sustain with their subscriptions.[11] Notwithstanding the violence of the intestine struggles which divide the leaders, in all the democracies they manifest vis-à-vis the masses a vigorous solidarity. "They perceive quickly enough the necessity for agreeing among themselves so that the party cannot escape them by becoming divided." [12] This is true above all of the German social democracy, in which, in consequence of the exceptional solidity of structure which it possesses as compared with all the other socialist parties of the world, conservative tendencies have attained an extreme development.

When there is a struggle between the leaders and the masses, the former are always victorious if only they remain united. At least it rarely happens that the masses succeed in disembarrassing themselves of one of their leaders.

•   •   •

There is no indication whatever that the power possessed by the oligarchy in party life is likely to be overthrown within an appreciable time. The independence of the leaders increases concurrently with their indispensability. Nay more, the influence which they exercise and the financial security of their position become more and more fascinating to the masses, stimulating the ambition of all the more talented elements to enter the privileged bureaucracy of the labor movement. Thus the rank and file becomes continually more impotent to provide new and intelligent forces capable of leading the opposition which may be latent among the

---

11. Similar phenomena have been observed in party life in America (Ostrogorsky, *La Démocratie, etc.,* ed. cit., vol. ii, p. 196).
12. Antoine Elisée Cherbuliez, *Théorie des Garantis constitutionelles,* Ab. Cherbuliez, Paris, 1838, vol. ii, p. 253.

masses.[13] Even today the masses rarely move except at the command of their leaders. When the rank and file does take action in conflict with the wishes of the chiefs, this is almost always the outcome of a misunderstanding. The miners' strike in the Ruhr basin in 1905 broke out against the desire of the trade-union leaders, and was generally regarded as a spontaneous explosion of the popular will. But it was subsequently proved beyond dispute that for many months the leaders had been stimulating the rank and file, mobilizing them against the coal barons with repeated threats of a strike, so that the mass of the workers, when they entered on the struggle, could not possibly fail to believe that they did so with the full approval of their chiefs.

It cannot be denied that the masses revolt from time to time, but their revolts are always suppressed. It is only when the dominant classes, struck by sudden blindness, pursue a policy which strains social relationships to the breaking-point, that the party masses appear actively on the stage of history and overthrow the power of the oligarchies. Every autonomous movement of the masses signifies a profound discordance with the will of the leaders. Apart from such transient interruptions, the natural and normal development of the organization will impress upon the most revolutionary of parties an indelible stamp of conservatism.

The Struggle among the Leaders Themselves

The thesis of the unlimited power of the leaders in democratic parties, requires, however, a certain limitation. Theoretically the leader is bound by the will of the mass, which has only to give a sign and the leader is forced to withdraw. He can be discharged and replaced at any moment. But in practice, as we have learned, for various reasons the leaders enjoy a high degree of independence. It is none the less true that if the Democratic Party cannot dispense with autocratic leaders, it is at least able to change these. Consequently the most dangerous defect in a leader is that he should possess too blind a confidence in the masses. The aristocratic leader is more secure than the democratic against surprises at the hands of the rank and file. It is an essential characteristic of democracy that every private carries a marshal's baton in his knapsack. It is true that the mass is always incapable of governing; but it is no less true that each individual in the mass, in so far as he possesses, for good or for ill, the qualities which are requisite to enable him to rise above the crowd, can attain to

13. Thus Pareto writes: "If B [the new élite] took the place of A [the old élite] by slow infiltration, and if the social circulation is not interrupted, C [the masses] are deprived of the leaders who could incite them to revolt." (Trans. from Vilfredo Pareto, *Les Systèmes socialistes,* Giard and Brière, Paris, 1892, vol. i, p. 35).

the grade of leader and become a ruler. Now this ascent of new leaders always involves the danger, for those who are already in possession of power, that they will be forced to surrender their places to the newcomers. The old leader must therefore keep himself in permanent touch with the opinions and feelings of the masses to which he owes his position. Formally, at least, he must act in unison with the crowd, must admit himself to be the instrument of the crowd, must be guided, in appearance at least, by its goodwill and pleasure. Thus it often seems as if the mass really controlled the leaders. But whenever the power of the leaders is seriously threatened, it is in most cases because a new leader or a new group of leaders is on the point of becoming dominant, and is inculcating views opposed to those of the old rulers of the party. It then seems as if the old leaders, unless they are willing to yield to the opinion of the rank and file and to withdraw, must consent to share their power with the new arrivals. If, however, we look more closely into the matter, it is not difficult to see that their submission is in most cases no more than an act of foresight intended to obviate the influence of their younger rivals. The submission of the old leaders is ostensibly an act of homage to the crowd, but in intention it is a means of prophylaxis against the peril by which they are threatened—the formation of a new élite.

The semblance of obedience to the mass which is exhibited by the leaders assumes, in the case of the feebler and the more cunning among them, the form of demagogy. Demagogues are the courtesans of the popular will. Instead of raising the masses to their own level, they debase themselves to the level of the masses. Even for the most honest among them, the secret of success consists in "knowing how to turn the blind impulsiveness of the crowd to the service of their own ripely pondered plans."[14] The stronger leaders brave the tempest, well-knowing that their power may be attacked, but cannot be broken. The weak or the base, on the other hand, give ground when the masses make a vigorous onslaught; their dominion is temporarily impaired or interrupted. But their submission is feigned; they are well aware that if they simply remain glued to their posts, their quality as executants of the will of the masses will before long lead to a restoration of their former dominance. One of the most noted leaders of German socialism said in a critical period of tension between the leaders and the masses, that he must follow the will of the masses in order to guide them.[15] A profound psychological truth is hidden in this sarcasm. He who wishes to command must know how to obey.

• • •

14. Kochanowski, *Urzeitklänge, und Wetterleuchten Geschichtlicher Gesetze in den Ereignissen der Gegenwart,* Wagner, Innsbruck, 1910, p. 10.
15. "Ich bin ihr Führer, also muss ich ihnen folgen." (Cf. Adolf Weber, *Der Kampf zwischen Kapital u. Arbeit,* ed. cit., p. 369.)

Final Considerations

Leadership is a necessary phenomenon in every form of social life. Consequently it is not the task of science to inquire whether this phenomenon is good or evil, or predominantly one or the other. But there is great scientific value in the demonstration that every system of leadership is incompatible with the most essential postulates of democracy. We are now aware that the law of the historic necessity of oligarchy is primarily based upon a series of facts of experience. Like all other scientific laws, sociological laws are derived from empirical observation. In order, however, to deprive our axion of its purely descriptive character, and to confer upon it that status of analytical explanation which can alone transform a formula into a law, it does not suffice to contemplate from a unitary outlook those phenomena which may be empirically established; we must also study the determining causes of these phenomena. Such has been our task.

Now, if we leave out of consideration the tendency of the leaders to organize themselves and to consolidate their interests, and if we leave also out of consideration the gratitude of the led towards the leaders, and the general immobility and passivity of the masses, we are led to conclude that the principal cause of oligarchy in the democratic parties is to be found in the technical indispensability of leadership.

The process which has begun in consequence of the differentiation of functions in the party is completed by a complex of qualities which the leaders acquire through their detachment from the mass. At the outset, leaders arise SPONTANEOUSLY; their functions are ACCESSORY and GRATUITOUS. Soon, however, they become PROFESSIONAL leaders, and in this second stage of development they are STABLE and IRREMOVABLE.

It follows that the explanation of the oligarchical phenomenon which thus results is partly PSYCHOLOGICAL; oligarchy derives, that is to say, from the psychical transformations which the leading personalities in the parties undergo in the course of their lives. But also, and still more, oligarchy depends upon what we may term the PSYCHOLOGY OF ORGANIZATION ITSELF, that is to say, upon the tactical and technical necessities which result from the consolidation of every disciplined political aggregate. Reduced to its most concise expression, the fundamental sociological law of political parties (the term "political" being here used in its most comprehensive significance) may be formulated in the following terms: "It is organization which gives birth to the dominion of the elected over the electors, of the mandataries over the mandators, of the delegates over the delegators. Who says organization, says oligarchy."

Every party organization represents an oligarchical power grounded upon a democratic basis. We find everywhere electors and elected. Also we find everywhere that the power of the elected leaders over the electing

49

masses is almost unlimited. The oligarchical structure of the building suf-
focates the basic democratic principle. That which is oppresses THAT
WHICH OUGHT TO BE. For the masses, this essential difference between the
reality and the ideal remains a mystery. Socialists often cherish a sincere
belief that a new *élite* of politicians will keep faith better than did the old.
The notion of the representation of popular interests, a notion to which
the great majority of democrats, and in especial the working-class masses
of the German-speaking lands, cleave with so much tenacity and confidence, is an illusion engendered by a false illumination, is an effect of
mirage. In one of the most delightful pages of his analysis of modern
Don Quixotism, Alphonse Daudet shows us how the "brav' commandant"
Bravida, who has never quitted Tarascon, gradually comes to persuade
himself, influenced by the burning southern sun, that he has been to
Shanghai and has had all kinds of heroic adventures.[16] Similarly the modern proletariat, enduringly influenced by glib-tongued persons intellectually
superior to the mass, ends by believing that by flocking to the poll and
entrusting its social and economic cause to a delegate, its direct participation in power will be assured.

The formation of oligarchies within the various forms of democracy
is the outcome of organic necessity, and consequently affects every organization, be it socialist or even anarchist. Haller long ago noted that in
every form of social life relationships of dominion and of dependence are
created by Nature herself.[17] The supremacy of the leaders in the democratic and revolutionary parties has to be taken into account in every historic situation present and to come, even though only a few and exceptional minds will be fully conscious of its existence. The mass will never
rule except *in abstracto*. Consequently the question we have to discuss is
not whether ideal democracy is realizable, but rather to what point and in
what degree democracy is desirable, possible, and realizable at a given
moment. In the problem as thus stated we recognize the fundamental
problem of politics as a science. Whoever fails to perceive this must, as
Sombart says, either be so blind and fanatical as not to see that the democratic current daily makes undeniable advance, or else must be so inexperienced and devoid of critical faculty as to be unable to understand that
all order and all civilization must exhibit aristocratic features.[18] The great
error of socialists, an error committed in consequence of their lack of adequate psychological knowledge, is to be found in their combination of
pessimism regarding the present, with rosy optimism and immeasurable

16. Alphonse Daudet, *Tartarin de Tarascon,* Marpon et Flammarion, Paris, 1887,
p. 40.
17. Ludwig von Haller, *Restauration der Staatswissenschaften,* Winterthur, 1816, vol.
i, pp. 304 et seq.
18. Werner Sombart, *Dennoch!,* ed. cit., p. 90. Cf. also F. S. Merlino, *Pro e contro
Socialismo,* ed. cit., pp. 262 et seq.

confidence regarding the future. A realistic view of the mental condition of the masses shows beyond question that even if we admit the possibility of moral improvement in mankind, the human materials with whose use politicians and philosophers cannot dispense in their plans of social reconstruction are not of a character to justify excessive optimism. Within the limits of time for which human provision is possible, optimism will remain the exclusive privilege of utopian thinkers.

The socialist parties, like the trade unions, are living forms of social life. As such they react with the utmost energy aganist any attempt to analyze their structure or their nature, as if it were a method of vivisection. When science attains to results which conflict with their apriorist ideology, they revolt with all their power. Yet their defense is extremely feeble. Those among the representatives of such organizations whose scientific earnestness and personal good faith make it impossible for them to deny outright the existence of oligarchical tendencies in every form of democracy, endeavor to explain these tendencies as the outcome of a kind of atavism in the mentality of the masses, characteristic of the youth of the movement. The masses, they assure us, are still infected by the oligarchic virus simply because they have been oppressed during long centuries of slavery, and have never yet enjoyed an autonomous existence. The socialist regime, however, will soon restore them to health, and will furnish them with all the capacity necessary for self-government. Nothing could be more antiscientific than the supposition that as soon as socialists have gained possession of governmental power it will suffice for the masses to exercise a little control over their leaders to secure that the interests of these leaders shall coincide perfectly with the interests of the led. This idea may be compared with the view of Jules Guesde, no less antiscientific than anti-Marxist (though Guesde proclaims himself a Marxist), that whereas Christianity has made God into a man, socialism will make man into a god.[19]

The objective immaturity of the mass is not a mere transitory phenomenon which will disappear with the progress of democratization *au lendemain du socialisme*. On the contrary, it derives from the very nature of the mass as mass, for this, even when organized, suffers from an incurable incompetence for the solution of the diverse problems which present themselves for solution—because the mass *per se* is amorphous, and therefore needs division of labor, specialization, and guidance. "The human species wants to be governed; it will be. I am ashamed of my kind," wrote Proudhon from his prison in 1850.[20] Man as individual is by nature predestined to be guided, and to be guided all the more in proportion as the functions of life undergo division and subdivision. To an enormously greater degree is guidance necessary for the social group.

19. Jules Guesde, *La Problème et la Solution,* Libr. du Parti Socialiste, Paris, p. 17.
20. Charles Gide et Charles Rist, *Histoire des Doctrines économiques depuis les Physiocrates jusquà nos jours,* Larose et Tenin, Paris, 1909, p. 709.

From this chain of reasoning and from these scientific convictions it would be erroneous to conclude that we should renounce all endeavors to ascertain the limits which may be imposed upon the powers exercised over the individual by oligarchies (state, dominant class, party, etc.). It would be an error to abandon the desperate enterprise of endeavoring to discover a social order which will render possible the complete realization of the idea of popular sovereignty. In the present work, as the writer said at the outset, it has not been his aim to indicate new paths. But it seemed necessary to lay considerable stress upon the pessimist aspect of democracy which is forced on us by historical study. We had to inquire whether, and within what limits, democracy must remain purely ideal, possessing no other value than that of a moral criterion which renders it possible to appreciate the varying degrees of that oligarchy which is immanent in every social regime. In other words, we have had to inquire if, and in what degree, democracy is an ideal which we can never hope to realize in practice. A further aim of this work was the demolition of some of the facile and superficial democratic illusions which trouble science and lead the masses astray. Finally, the author desired to throw light upon certain sociological tendencies which oppose the reign of democracy, and to a still greater extent oppose the reign of socialism.

The writer does not wish to deny that every revolutionary working-class movement, and every movement sincerely inspired by the democratic spirit, may have a certain value as contributing to the enfeeblement of oligarchic tendencies. The peasant in the fable, when on his death-bed, tells his sons that a treasure is buried in the field. After the old man's death the sons dig everywhere in order to discover the treasure. They do not find it. But their indefatigable labor improves the soil and secures for them a comparative well-being. The treasure in the fable may well symbolize democracy. Democracy is a treasure which no one will ever discover by deliberate search. But in continuing our search, in laboring indefatigably to discover the undiscoverable, we shall perform a work which will have fertile results in the democratic sense. We have seen, indeed, that within the bosom of the democratic working-class party are born the very tendencies to counteract which that party came into existence. Thanks to the diversity and to the unequal worth of the elements of the party, these tendencies often give rise to manifestations which border on tyranny. We have seen that the replacement of the traditional legitimism of the powers-that-be by the brutal plebiscitary rule of Bonapartist parvenus does not furnish these tendencies with any moral or aesthetic superiority. Historical evolution mocks all the prophylactic measures that have been adopted for the prevention of oligarchy. If laws are passed to control the dominion of the leaders, it is the laws which gradually weaken, and not the leaders. Sometimes, however, the democratic principle carries with it, if not a cure, at least a palliative, for the disease of oligarchy. When Victor Considérant formulated his "democratico-pacificist" socialism, he declared that social-ism signified, not the rule of society by the lower classes of the popula-tion, but the government and organization of society in the interest of all, through the intermediation of a group of citizens; and he added that the numerical importance of this group must increase *pari passu* with social development.[21] This last observation draws attention to a point of capital importance. It is, in fact, a general characteristic of democracy, and hence also of the labor movement, to stimulate and to strengthen in the indi-vidual the intellectual aptitudes for criticism and control. We have seen how the progressive bureaucratization of the democratic organism tends to neutralize the beneficial effects of such criticism and such control. None the less it is true that the labor movement, in virtue of the theoretical postulates it proclaims, is apt to bring into existence (in opposition to the will of the leaders) a certain number of free spirits who, moved by prin-ciple, by instinct, or by both, desire to revise the base upon which au-thority is established. Urged on by conviction or by temperament, they are never weary of asking an eternal "Why?" about every human institution. Now this predisposition towards free inquiry, in which we cannot fail to recognize one of the most precious factors of civilization, will gradually increase in proportion as the economic status of the masses undergoes improvement and becomes more stable, and in proportion as they are admitted more effectively to the advantages of civilization. A wider edu-cation involves an increasing capacity for exercising control. Can we not observe every day that among the well-to-do the authority of the leaders over the led, extensive though it be, is never so unrestricted as in the case of the leaders of the poor? Taken in the mass, the poor are powerless and disarmed vis-à-vis their leaders. Their intellectual and cultural inferiority makes it impossible for them to see whither the leader is going, or to estimate in advance the significance of his actions. It is, consequently, the great task of social education to raise the intellectual level of the masses, so that they may be enabled, within the limits of what is possible, to counteract the oligarchical tendencies of the working-class movement.

In view of the perennial incompetence of the masses, we have to recognize the existence of two regulative principles:

1. The *ideological* tendency of democracy towards criticism and control;
2. The *effective* counter-tendency of democracy towards the creation of parties ever more complex and ever more differentiated— parites, that is to say, which are increasingly based upon the competence of the few.

21. Victor Considérant, *Principes du Socialisme. Manifeste de la Démocratie au xix Siècle,* Librairie Phalanstérienne, Paris, 1847, p. 53.

To the idealist, the analysis of the forms of contemporary democracy cannot fail to be a source of bitter deceptions and profound discouragement. Those alone, perhaps, are in a position to pass a fair judgment upon democracy who, without lapsing into dilettantist sentimentalism, recognize that all scientific and human ideals have relative values. If we wish to estimate the value of democracy, we must do so in comparison with its converse, pure aristocracy. The defects inherent in democracy are obvious. It is none the less true that as a form of social life we must choose democracy as the least of evils. The ideal government would doubtless be that of an aristocracy of persons at once morally good and technically efficient. But where shall we discover such an aristocracy? We may find it sometimes, though very rarely, as the outcome of deliberate selection; but we shall never find it where the hereditary principle remains in operation. Thus monarchy in its pristine purity must be considered as imperfection incarnate, as the most incurable of ills; from the moral point of view it is inferior even to the most revolting of demagogic dictatorships, for the corrupt organism of the latter at least contains a healthy principle upon whose working we may continue to base hopes of social resanation. It may be said, therefore, that the more humanity comes to recognize the advantages which democracy, however imperfect, presents over aristocracy, even at its best, the less likely is it that a recognition of the defects of democracy will provoke a return to aristocracy. Apart from certain formal differences and from the qualities which can be acquired only by good education and inheritance (qualities in which aristocracy will always have the advantage over democracy—qualities which democracy either neglects altogether, or, attempting to imitate them, falsifies them to the point of caricature), the defects of democracy will be found to inhere in its inability to get rid of its aristocratic scoriæ. On the other hand, nothing but a serene and frank examination of the oligarchical dangers of democracy will enable us to minimize these dangers, even though they can never be entirely avoided.

The democratic currents of history resemble successive waves. They break ever on the same shoal. They are ever renewed. This enduring spectacle is simultaneously encouraging and depressing. When democracies have gained a certain stage of development, they undergo a gradual transformation, adopting the aristocratic spirit, and in many cases also the aristocratic forms, against which at the outset they struggled so fiercely. Now new accusers arise to denounce the traitors; after an era of glorious combats and of inglorious power, they end by fusing with the old dominant class; whereupon once more they are in their turn attacked by fresh opponents who appeal to the name of democracy. It is probable that this cruel game will continue without end.

Scientific Management

Frederick W. Taylor

The writer has found that there are three questions uppermost in the minds of men when they become interested in scientific management.

First. Wherein do the principles of scientific management differ essentially from those of ordinary management?

Second. Why are better results attained under scientific management than under the other types?

Third. Is not the most important problem that of getting the right man at the head of the company? And if you have the right man cannot the choice of the type of management be safely left to him?

One of the principal objects of the following pages will be to give a satisfactory answer to these questions. . . .

Before starting to illustrate the principles of scientific management, or "task management" as it is briefly called, it seems desirable to outline what the writer believes will be recognized as the best type of management which is in common use. This is done so that the great difference between the best of the ordinary management and scientific management may be fully appreciated.

In an industrial establishment which employs say from 500 to 1000 workmen, there will be found in many cases at least twenty to thirty different trades. The workmen in each of these trades have had their knowledge handed down to them by word of mouth, through the many years in which their trade has been developed from the primitive condition, in which our far-distant ancestors each one practised the rudiments of many different trades, to the present state of great and growing subdivision of labor, in which each man specializes upon some comparatively small class of work.

The ingenuity of each generation has developed quicker and better methods for doing every element of the work in every trade. Thus the methods which are now in use may in a broad sense be said to be an

SOURCE: *Scientific Management,* pp. 30–48, 57–60. Copyright © 1911 by Frederick W. Taylor; renewed 1939 by Louise M.S. Taylor; renewed 1947 by Harper & Row, Publishers, Inc. Reprinted by permission of the publisher.

evolution representing the survival of the fittest and best of the ideas which have been developed since the starting of each trade. However, while this is true in a broad sense, only those who are intimately acquainted with each of these trades are fully aware of the fact that in hardly any element of any trade is there uniformity in the methods which are used. Instead of having only one way which is generally accepted as a standard, there are in daily use, say, fifty or a hundred different ways of doing each element of the work. And a little thought will make it clear that this must inevitably be the case, since our methods have been handed down from man to man by word of mouth, or have, in most cases, been almost unconsciously learned through personal observation. Practically in no instances have they been codified or systematically analyzed or described. The ingenuity and experience of each generation—of each decade, even, have without doubt handed over better methods to the next. This mass of rule-of-thumb or traditional knowledge may be said to be the principal asset or possession of everyday tradesman. Now, in the best of the ordinary types of management, the managers recognize frankly the fact that the 500 or 1000 workmen, included in the twenty to thirty trades, who are under them, possess this mass of traditional knowledge, a large part of which is not in the possession of the management. The management, of course, includes foremen and superintendents, who themselves have been in most cases first-class workers at their trades. And yet these foremen and superintendents know, better than any one else, that their own knowledge and personal skill falls far short of the combined knowledge and dexterity of all the workmen under them.. The most experienced managers therefore frankly place before their workmen the problem of doing the work in the best and most economical way. They recognize the task before them as that of inducing each workman to use his best endeavors, his hardest work, all his traditional knowledge, his skill, his ingenuity, and his goodwill—in a word, his "initiative," so as to yield the largest possible return to his employer. The problem before the management, then, may be briefly said to be that of obtaining the best *initiative* of every workman. And the writer uses the word "initiative" in its broadest sense, to cover all of the good qualities sought for from the men.

On the other hand, no intelligent manager would hope to obtain in any full measure the initiative of his workmen unless he felt that he was giving them something more than they usually receive from their employers. Only those among the readers of this paper who have been managers or who have worked themselves at a trade realize how far the average workman falls short of giving his employer his full initiative. It is well within the mark to state that in nineteen out of twenty industrial establishments the workmen believe it to be directly against their interests to give their employers their best initiative, and that instead of working hard to do the largest possible amount of work and the best quality of work for their employers, they deliberately work as slowly as they dare while they at the same time try to make those over them believe that they are working fast.[1]

The writer repeats, therefore, that in order to have any hope of obtaining the initiative of his workmen the manager must give some *special incentive* to his men beyond that which is given to the average of the trade. This incentive can be given in several different ways, as, for example, the hope of rapid promotion or advancement; higher wages, either in the form of generous piecework prices or of a premium or bonus of some kind for good and rapid work; shorter hours of labor; better surroundings and working conditions than are ordinarily given, etc., and, above all, this special incentive should be accompanied by that personal consideration for, and friendly contact with, his workmen which comes only from a genuine and kindly interest in the welfare of those under him. It is only by giving a special inducement or "incentive" of this kind that the employer can hope even approximately to get the "initiative of this workmen. Under the ordinary type of management the necessity for offering the workman a special inducement has come to be so generally recognized that a large proportion of those most interested in the subject look upon the adoption of some one of the modern schemes for paying men (such as piece work, the premium plan, or the bonus plan, for instance) as practically the whole system of management. Under scientific management, however, the particular pay system which is adopted is merely one of the subordinate elements.

Broadly speaking, then, the best type of management in ordinary use may be defined as management in which the workmen give their best *initiative* and in return receive some *special incentive* from their employers. This type of management will be referred to as the management of *"initiative and incentive"* in contradistinction to scientific management, or task management, with which it is to be compared.

The writer hopes that the management of "initiative and incentive" will be recognized as representing the best type in ordinary use, and in fact he believes that it will be hard to persuade the average manager that anything better exists in the whole field than this type. The task which the writer has before him, then, is the difficult one of trying to prove in a thoroughly convincing way that there is another type of management which is not only better but overwhelmingly better than the management of "initiative and incentive."

The universal prejudice in favor of the management of "initiative and incentive" is so strong that no mere theoretical advantages which can be pointed out will be likely to convince the average manager that any

1. The writer has tried to make the reason for this unfortunate state of things clear in a paper entitled "Shop Management," read before the American Society of Mechanical Engineers.

other system is better. It will be upon a series of practical illustrations of the actual working of the two systems that the writer will depend in his efforts to prove that scientific management is so greatly superior to other types. Certain elementary principles, a certain philosophy, will however be recognized as the essence of that which is being illustrated in all of the practical examples which will be given. And the broad principles in which the scientific system differs from the ordinary or "rule-of-thumb" system are so simple in their nature that it seems desirable to describe them before starting with the illustrations.

Under the old type of management success depends almost entirely upon getting the "initiative" of the workmen, and it is indeed a rare case in which this initiative is really attained. Under scientific management the "initiative" of the workmen (that is, their hard work, their good-will, and their ingenuity) is obtained with absolute uniformity and to a greater extent than is possible under the old system; and in addition to this improvement on the part of the men, the managers assume new burdens, new duties, and responsibilities never dreamed of in the past. The managers assume, for instance, the burden of gathering together all of the traditional knowledge which in the past has been possessed by the workmen and then of classifying, tabulating, and reducing this knowledge to rules, laws, and formulæ which are immensely helpful to the workmen in doing their daily work. In addition to developing a *science* in this way, the management take on three other types of duties which involve new and heavy burdens for themselves.

These new duties are grouped under four heads:

First. They develop a science for each element of a man's work, which replaces the old rule-of-thumb method.

Second. They scientifically select and then train, teach, and develop the workman, whereas in the past he chose his own work and trained himself as best he could.

Third. They heartily cooperate with the men so as to insure all of the work being done in accordance with the principles of the science which has been developed.

Fourth. There is an almost equal division of the work and the responsibility between the management and the workmen. The management take over all work for which they are better fitted than the workmen, while in the past almost all of the work and the greater part of the responsibility were thrown upon the men.

It is this combination of the initiative of the workmen, coupled with the new types of work done by the management, that makes scientific management so much more efficient than the old plan.

Three of these elements exist in many cases, under the management of "initiative and incentive," in a small and rudimentary way, but they are, under this management, of minor importance, whereas under scientific management they form the very essence of the whole system.

The fourth of these elements, "an almost equal division of the responsibility between the management and the workmen," requires further explanation. The philosophy of the management of "initiative and incentive" makes it necessary for each workman to bear almost the entire responsibility for the general plan as well as for each detail of his work, and in many cases for his implements as well. In addition to this he must do all of the actual physical labor. The development of a science, on the other hand, involves the establishment of many rules, laws, and formulæ which replace the judgment of the individual workmen and which can be effectively used only after having been systematically recorded, indexed, etc. The practical use of scientific data also calls for a room in which to keep the books, records,[2] etc., and a desk for the planner to work at. Thus all of the planning which under the old system was done by the workman, as a result of his personal experience, must of necessity under the new system be done by the management in accordance with the laws of the science; because even if the workman was well suited to the development and use of scientific data, it would be physically impossible for him to work at his machine and at a desk at the same time. It is also clear that in most cases one type of man is needed to plan ahead and an entirely different type to execute the work.

The man in the planning room, whose specialty under scientific management is planning ahead, invariably finds that the work can be done better and more economically by a subdivision of the labor; each act of each mechanic, for example, should be preceded by various preparatory acts done by other men. And all of this involves, as we have said, "an almost equal division of the responsibility and the work between the management and the workman."

To summarize: Under the management of "initiative and incentive" practically the whole problem is "up to the workman," while under scientific management fully one-half of the problem is "up to the management."

Perhaps the most prominent single element in modern scientific management is the task idea. The work of every workman is fully planned out by the management at least one day in advance, and each man receives in most cases complete written instructions, describing in detail the task which he is to accomplish, as well as the means to be used in doing the work. And the work planned in advance in this way constitutes a task which is to be solved, as explained above, not by the workman alone,

2. For example, the records containing the data used under scientific management in an ordinary machine-shop fill thousands of pages.

but in almost all cases by the joint effort of the workman and the management. This task specifies not only what is to be done but how it is to be done and the exact time allowed for doing it. And whenever the workman succeeds in doing his task right, and within the time limit specified, he receives an addition of from 30 per cent to 100 per cent to his ordinary wages. These tasks are carefully planned, so that both good and careful work are called for in their performance, but it should be distinctly understood that in no case is the workman called upon to work at a pace which would be injurious to his health. The task is always so regulated that the man who is well suited to his job will thrive while working at this rate during a long term of years and grow happier and more prosperous, instead of being overworked. Scientific management consists very largely in preparing for and carrying out these tasks.

The writer is fully aware that to perhaps most of the readers of this paper the four elements which differentiate the new management from the old will at first appear to be merely high-sounding phrases; and he would again repeat that he has no idea of convincing the reader of their value merely through announcing their existence. His hope of carrying conviction rests upon demonstrating the tremendous force and effect of these four elements through a series of practical illustrations. It will be shown, first, that they can be applied absolutely to all classes of work, from the most elementary to the most intricate; and second, that when they are applied, the results must of necessity be overwhelmingly greater than those which it is possible to attain under the management of initiative and incentive.

The first illustration is that of handling pig iron, and this work is chosen because it is typical of perhaps the crudest and most elementary form of labor which is performed by man. This work is done by men with no other implements than their hands. The pig-iron handler stoops down, picks up a pig weighing about 92 pounds, walks for a few feet or yards and then drops it on to the ground or upon a pile. This work is so crude and elementary in its nature that the writer firmly believes that it would be possible to train an intelligent gorilla so as to become a more efficient pig-iron handler than any man can be. Yet it will be shown that the science of handling pig iron is so great and amounts to so much that it is impossible for the man who is best suited to this type of work to understand the principles of this science, or even to work in accordance with these principles without the aid of a man better educated than he is. And the further illustrations to be given will make it clear that in almost all of the mechanic arts the science which underlies each workman's act is so great and amounts to so much that the workman who is best suited actually to do the work is incapable (either through lack of education or through insufficient mental capacity) of understanding this science. This is announced as a general principle, the truth of which will become apparent as one illustration after another is given. After showing these four elements in the handling of pig iron, several illustrations will be given of their application to different kinds of work in the field of the mechanic arts, at intervals in a rising scale, beginning with the simplest and ending with the more intricate forms of labor.

One of the first pieces of work undertaken by us, when the writer started to introduce scientific management into the Bethlehem Steel Company, was to handle pig iron on task work. The opening of the Spanish War found some 80,000 tons of pig iron placed in small piles in an open field adjoining the works. Prices for pig iron had been so low that it could not be sold at a profit, and it therefore had been stored. With the opening of the Spanish War the price of pig iron rose, and this large accumulation of iron was sold. This gave us a good opportunity to show the workmen, as well as the owners and managers of the works, on a fairly large scale the advantages of task work over the old-fashioned day work and piece work, in doing a very elementary class of work.

The Bethlehem Steel Company had five blast furnaces, the product of which had been handled by a pig-iron gang for many years. This gang, at this time, consisted of about seventy-five men. They were good, average pig-iron handlers, were under an excellent foreman who himself had been a pig-iron handler, and the work was done, on the whole, about as fast and as cheaply as it was anywhere else at that time.

A railroad switch was run out into the field, right along the edge of the piles of pig iron. An inclined plank was placed against the side of a car, and each man picked up from his pile a pig of iron weighing about 92 pounds, walked up the inclined plank and dropped it on the end of the car.

We found that this gang were loading on the average about 12½ long tons per man per day. We were surprised to find, after studying the matter, that a first-class pig-iron handler ought to handle between 47 and 48 long tons per day, instead of 12½ tons. This task seemed to us so very large that we were obliged to go over our work several times before we were absolutely sure that we were right. Once we were sure, however, that 47 tons was a proper day's work for a first-class pig-iron handler, the task which faced us as managers under the modern scientific plan was clearly before us. It was our duty to see that the 80,000 tons of pig iron was loaded on to the cars at the rate of 47 tons per man per day, in place of 12½ tons, at which rate the work was then being done. And it was further our duty to see that this work was done without bringing on a strike among the men, without any quarrel with the men, and to see that the men were happier and better contented when loading at the new rate of 47 tons than they were when loading at the old rate of 12½ tons.

Our first step was the scientific selection of the workman. In dealing with workmen under this type of management, it is an inflexible rule to talk to and deal with only one man at a time, since each workman has his own special abilities and limitations, and since we are not dealing with men in masses, but are trying to develop each individual man to his highest state of efficiency and prosperity. Our first step was to find the proper workman to begin with. We therefore carefully watched and studied these seventy-five men for three or four days, at the end of which time we had picked out four men who appeared to be physically able to handle pig iron at the rate of 47 tons per day. A careful study was then made of each of these men. We looked up their history as far back as practicable and thorough inquiries were made as to the character, habits, and the ambition of each of them. Finally we selected one from among the four as the most likely man to start with. He was a little Pennsylvania Dutchman who had been observed to trot back home for a mile or so after his work in the evening about as fresh as he was when he came trotting down to work in the morning. We found that upon wages of $1.15 a day he had succeeded in buying a small plot of ground, and that he was engaged in putting up the walls of a little house for himself in the morning before starting to work and at night after leaving. He also had the reputation of being exceedingly "close," that is, of placing a very high value on a dollar. As one man whom we talked to about him said, "A penny looks about the size of a cart-wheel to him." This man we will call Schmidt.

The task before us, then, narrowed itself down to getting Schmidt to handle 47 tons of pig iron per day and making him glad to do it. This was done as follows. Schmidt was called out from among the gang of pig-iron handlers and talked to somewhat in this way:

"Schmidt, are you a high-priced man?"

"Vell, I don't know vat you mean."

"Oh yes, you do. What I want to know is whether you are a high-priced man or not."

"Vell, I don't know vat you mean."

"Oh, come now, you answer my questions. What I want to find out is whether you are a high-priced man or one of these cheap fellows here. What I want to find out is whether you want to earn $1.85 a day or whether you are satisfied with $1.15, just the same as all those cheap fellows are getting."

"Did I vant $1.85 a day? Vas dot a high-priced man? Vell, yes, I vas a high-priced man."

"Oh, you're aggravating me. Of course you want $1.85 a day—everyone wants it! You know perfectly well that that has very little to do with your being a high-priced man. For goodness' sake answer my questions, and don't waste any more of my time. Now come over here. You see that pile of pig iron?"

"Yes."

"You see that car?"

"Yes."

"Well, if you are a high-priced man, you will load that pig iron on that car tomorrow for $1.85. Now do wake up and answer my question. Tell me whether you are a high-priced man or not."

"Vell—did I got $1.85 for loading dot pig iron on dot car tomorrow?"

"Yes, of course you do, and you get $1.85 for loading a pile like that every day right through the year. That is what a high-priced man does, and you know it just as well as I do."

"Vell, dot's all right. I could load dot pig iron on the car tomorrow for $1.85, and I get it every day, don't I?"

"Certainly you do—certainly you do."

"Vell, den, I vas a high-priced man."

"Now, hold on, hold on. You know just as well as I do that a high-priced man has to do exactly as he's told from morning till night. You have seen this man here before, haven't you?"

"No, I never saw him."

"Well, if you are a high-priced man, you will do exactly as this man tells you tomorrow, from morning till night. When he tells you to pick up a pig and walk, you pick it up and you walk, and when he tells you to sit down and rest, you sit down. You do that right straight through the day. And what's more, no back talk. Now a high-priced man does just what he's told to do, and no back talk. Do you understand that? When this man tells you to walk, you walk; when he tells you to sit down, you sit down, and you don't talk back at him. Now you come on to work here tomorrow morning and I'll know before night whether you are really a high-priced man or not."

This seems to be rather rough talk. And indeed it would be if applied to an educated mechanic, or even an intelligent laborer. With a man of the mentally sluggish type of Schmidt it is appropriate and not unkind, since it is effective in fixing his attention on the high wages which he wants and away from what, if it were called to his attention, he probably would consider impossibly hard work.

What would Schmidt's answer be if he were talked to in a manner which is usual under the management of "initiative and incentive"? say, as follows:

"Now, Schmidt, you are a first-class pig-iron handler and know your business well. You have been handling at the rate of 12½ tons per day. I have given considerable study to handling pig iron, and feel sure that you could do a much larger day's work than you have been doing. Now don't you think that if you really tried you could handle 47 tons of pig iron per day, instead of 12½ tons?"

What do you think Schmidt's answer would be to this?

Schmidt started to work, and all day long, and at regular intervals, was told by the man who stood over him with a watch, "Now pick up a pig and walk. Now sit down and rest. Now walk—now rest," etc. He worked when he was told to work, and rested when he was told to rest, and at half-past five in the afternoon had his 47½ tons loaded on the car. And he practically never failed to work at this pace and do the task that was set him during the three years that the writer was at Bethlehem. And throughout this time he averaged a little more than $1.85 per day, whereas before he had never received over $1.15 per day, which was the ruling rate of wages at that time in Bethlehem. That is, he received 60 per cent higher wages than were paid to other men who were not working on task work. One man after another was picked out and trained to handle pig iron at the rate of 47½ tons per day until all of the pig iron was handled at this rate, and the men were receiving 60 per cent more wages than other workmen around them.

The writer has given above a brief description of three of the four elements which constitute the essence of scientific management: first, the careful selection of the workman, and, second and third, the method of first inducing and then training and helping the workman to work according to the scientific method. Nothing as yet been said about the science of handling pig iron. The writer trusts, however, that before leaving this illustration the reader will be thoroughly convinced that there is a science of handling pig iron, and further that this science amounts to so much that the man who is suited to handle pig iron cannot possibly understand it, nor even work in accordance with the laws of this science, without the help of those who are over him.

• • •

The law is confined to that class of work in which the limit of a man's capacity is reached because he is tired out. It is the law of heavy laboring, corresponding to the work of the cart horse, rather than that of the trotter. Practically all such work consists of a heavy pull or a push on the man's arms, that is, the man's strength is exerted by either lifting or pushing something which he grasps in his hands. And the law is that for each given pull or push on the man's arms it is possible for the workman to be under load for only a definite percentage of the day. For example, when a pig iron is being handled (each pig weighing 92 pounds), a first-class workman can only be under load 43 per cent of the day. He must be entirely free from load during 57 per cent of the day. And as the load becomes lighter, the percentage of the day under which the man can remain under load increases. So that, if the workman is handling a half pig weighing 46 pounds, he can then be under load 58 per cent of the day, and only has to rest during 42 per cent. As the weight grows lighter the man can remain under load during a larger and larger percentage of the day, until finally a load is reached which he can carry in his hands all day long without being tired out. When that point has been arrived at this law ceases to be useful as a guide to a laborer's endurance, and some other law must be found which indicates the man's capacity for work.

When a laborer is carrying a piece of pig iron weighing 92 pounds in his hands, it tires him about as much to stand still under the load as it does to walk with it, since his arm muscles are under the same severe tension whether he is moving or not. A man, however, who stands still under a load is exerting no horse-power whatever, and this accounts for the fact that no constant relation could be traced in various kinds of heavy laboring work between the foot-pounds of energy exerted and the tiring effect of the work on the man. It will also be clear that in all work of this kind it is necessary for the arms of the workman to be completely free from load (that is, for the workman to rest) at frequent intervals. Throughout the time that the man is under a heavy load the tissues of his arm muscles are in process of degeneration, and frequent periods of rest are required in order that the blood may have a chance to restore these tissues to their normal condition.

To return now to our pig-iron handlers at the Bethlehem Steel Company. If Schmidt had been allowed to attack the pile of 47 tons of pig iron without the guidance or direction of a man who understood the art, or science, of handling pig iron, in his desire to earn his high wages he would probably have tired himself out by eleven or twelve o'clock in the day. He would have kept so steadily at work that his muscles would not have had the proper periods of rest absolutely needed for recuperation, and he would have been completely exhausted early in the day. By having a man, however, who understood this law, stand over him and direct his work, day after day, until he acquired the habit of resting at proper intervals, he was able to work at an even gait all day long without unduly tiring himself.

Now one of the very first requirements for a man who is fit to handle pig iron as a regular occupation is that he shall be so stupid and so phlegmatic that he more nearly resembles in his mental make-up the ox than any other type. The man who is mentally alert and intelligent is for this very reason entirely unsuited to what would, for him, be the grinding monotony of work of this character. Therefore the workman who is best suited to handling pig iron is unable to understand the real science of doing this class of work. He is so stupid that the word "percentage" has no meaning to him, and he must consequently be trained by a man more intelligent than himself into the habit of working in accordance with the laws of this science before he can be successful.

The writer trusts that it is now clear that even in the case of the most elementary form of labor that is known, there is a science, and that when the man best suited to this class of work has been carefully selected, when the science of doing the work has been developed, and when the carefully selected man has been trained to work in accordance with this science, the results obtained must of necessity be overwhelmingly greater than those which are possible under the plan of "initiative and incentive."

Human Relations

Fritz J. Roethlisberger
William J. Dickson

An Industrial Organization As a Social System

We shall now attempt to state more systematically than was possible in a chronological account the results of the research and some of their implications for practice. Each stage of the research contributed to the development of a point of view in terms of which the data could be more usefully assessed. In presenting the studies, this aspect of the research program was given primary emphasis and an effort was made to show how each successive step in the research resulted in the discovery of new facts which in turn brought forth new questions and new hypotheses and assisted in the development of more adequate methods and a more adequate conceptual scheme. The point of view which gradually emerged from these studies is one from which an industrial organization is regarded as a social system. In this chapter a statement of this point of view will be made. . . . Various management problems which have been discussed in connection with the various research studies will be restated in terms of this new point of view. . . . The application of the concept of an industrial concern as a social system to problems of personnel practice will be considered.

The study of the bank wiremen showed that their behavior at work could not be understood without considering the informal organization of the group and the relation of this informal organization to the total social organization of the company. The work activities of this group, together with their satisfactions and dissatisfactions, had to be viewed as manifestations of a complex pattern of interrelations. In short, the work situation of the bank wiring group had to be treated as a social system; moreover, the

SOURCE: *Management and the Worker,* Cambridge, Mass.: Harvard University Press, pp. 551–68. Copyright © 1939 by the President and Fellows of Harvard College; copyright © 1967 by F. J. Roethlisberger and William J. Dickson. Reprinted by permission of the publishers.

industrial organization of which this group was a part also had to be treated as a social system.

By "system" is meant something which must be considered as a whole because each part bears a relation of interdependence to every other part.[1] It will be the purpose of this chapter to state this conception of a social system, to specify more clearly the parts of the social system of which account has to be taken in an industrial organization, and to consider the state of equilibrium which obtains among the parts.

The Two Major Functions of an Industrial Organization

An industrial organization may be regarded as performing two major functions, that of producing a product and that of creating and distributing satisfactions among the individual members of the organization. The first function is ordinarily called economic. From this point of view the functioning of the concern is assessed in such terms as cost, profit, and technical efficiency. The second function, while it is readily understood, is not ordinarily designated by any generally accepted word. It is variously described as maintaining employee relations, employee good will, cooperation, etc. From this standpoint the functioning of the concern is frequently assessed in such terms as labor turnover, tenure of employment, sickness and accident rate, wages, employee attitudes, etc. The industrial concern is continually confronted, therefore, with two sets of major problems: (1) problems of external balance, and (2) problems of internal equilibrium. The problems of external balance are generally assumed to be economic; that is, problems of competition, adjusting the organization to meet changing price levels, etc. The problems of internal equilibrium are chiefly concerned with the maintenance of a kind of social organization in which individuals and groups through working together can satisfy their own desires.

Ordinarily an industrial concern is thought of primarily in terms of its success in meeting problems of external balance, or if the problems of internal equilibrium are explicitly recognized they are frequently assumed to be separate from and unrelated to the economic purpose of the enterprise. Producing an article at a profit and maintaining good employee relations are frequently regarded as antithetical propositions. The results of the studies which have been reported indicated, however, that these two sets of problems are interrelated and interdependent. The kind of social organization which obtains within a concern is intimately related to the

1. "The interdependence of the variables in a system is one of the widest inductions from experience that we possess; or we may alternatively regard it as the definition of a system." Henderson, L. J., *Pareto's General Sociology*, Harvard University Press, 1935, p. 86.

effectiveness of the total organization. Likewise, the success with which the concern maintains external balance is directly related to its internal organization.

A great deal of attention has been given to the economic function of industrial organization. Scientific controls have been introduced to further the economic purposes of the concern and of the individuals within it. Much of this advance has gone on in the name of efficiency or rationalization. Nothing comparable to this advance has gone on in the development of skills and techniques for securing cooperation, that is, for getting individuals and groups of individuals working together effectively and with satisfaction to themselves. The slight advances which have been made in this area have been overshadowed by the new and powerful technological developments of modern industry.

The Technical Organization of the Plant

In looking at an industrial organization as a social system it will first be necessary to examine the physical environment, for this is an inseparable part of any organization. The physical environment includes not only climate and weather, but also that part of the environment which is owned and used by the organization itself, namely, the physical plant, tools, machines, raw products, and so on. This latter part of the factory's physical environment is ordered and organized in a certain specified way to accomplish the task of technical production. For our purposes, therefore, it will be convenient to distinguish from the human organization this aspect of the physical environment of an industrial plant and to label it the "technical organization of the plant." This term will refer only to the logical and technical organization of material, tools, machines, and finished product, including all those physical items related to the task of technical production.

The two aspects into which an industrial plant can be roughly divided—the technical organization and the human organization—are interrelated and interdependent. The human organization is constantly molding and re-creating the technical organization either to achieve more effectively the common economic purpose or to secure more satisfaction for its members. Likewise, changes in the technical organization require an adaptation on the part of the human organization.

The Human Organization of the Plant

In the human organization we find a number of individuals working together toward a common end: the collective purpose of the total organization. Each of these individuals, however, is bringing to the work situation a different background of personal and social experiences. No two individuals are making exactly the same demands of their jobs. The demands a particular employee makes depend not only upon his physical needs but upon his social needs as well. These social needs and the sentiments associated with them vary with his early personal history and social conditioning as well as with the needs and sentiments of people closely associated with him both inside and outside of work.

The Individual

It may be well to look more closely at the sentiments the individual is bringing to his work situation. Starting with a certain native organic endowment the child is precipitated into group life by the act of birth. The group into which the child is born is not the group in general. The child is born into a specific family. Moreover, this specific family is not a family in isolation. It is related in certain ways to other families in the community. It has a certain cultural background—a way of life, codes and routines of behavior, associated with certain beliefs and expectations. In the beginning the child brings only his organic needs to this social milieu into which he is born. Very rapidly he begins to accumulate experience. This process of accumulating experience is the process of assigning meanings to the socio-reality about him; it is the process of becoming socialized. Much of the early learning period is devoted to preparing the child to become capable of social life in its particular group. In preparing the child for social participation the immediate family group plays an important role. By the particular type of family into which the child is born he is "conditioned" to certain routines of behavior and ways of living. The early meanings he assigns to his experience are largely in terms of these codes of behavior and associated beliefs. As the child grows up and participates in groups other than the immediate family his meanings lose, although never quite entirely, their specific family form. This process of social interaction and social conditioning is never-ending and continues from birth to death. The adult's evaluation of his surroundings is determined in a good part by the system of human interrelations in which he has participated.

The Social Organization of the Plant

However, the human organization of an industrial plant is more than a plurality of individuals, each motivated by sentiments arising from his own personal and private history and background. It is also a social organization, for the members of an industrial plant—executives, technical specialists, supervisors, factory workers, and office workers—are interacting daily with one another and from their associations certain patterns of relations are formed among them. These patterns of relations, together with the objects which symbolize them, constitute the social organization of the industrial enterprise. Most of the individuals who live among these patterns come to accept them as obvious and necessary truths and to react as they dictate. Both the kind of behavior that is expected of a person and the kind of behavior he can expect from others are prescribed by these patterns.

If one looks at a factory situation, for example, one finds individuals and groups of individuals who are associated at work acting in certain accepted and prescribed ways toward one another. There is not complete homogeneity of behavior between individuals or between one group of individuals and another, but rather there are differences of behavior expressing differences in social relationship. Some relationships fall into routine patterns, such as the relationship between superior and subordinate or between office worker and shop worker. Individuals conscious of their membership in certain groups are reacting in certain accepted ways to other individuals representing other groups. Behavior varies according to the stereotyped conceptions of relationship. The worker, for example, behaves toward his foreman in one way, toward his first-line supervisor in another way, and toward his fellow worker in still another. People holding the rank of inspector expect a certain kind of behavior from the operators—the operators from the inspectors. Now these relationships, as is well known from everyday experiences, are finely shaded and sometimes become complicated. When a person is in the presence of his supervisor alone he usually acts differently from the way he acts when his supervisor's supervisor is also present. Likewise, his supervisor acts toward him alone quite differently from the way he behaves when his own supervisor is also there. These subtle nuances of relationship are so much a part of everyday life that they are commonplace. They are taken for granted. The vast amount of social conditioning that has taken place by means of which a person maneuvers himself gracefully through the intricacies of these finely shaded social distinctions is seldom explicitly realized. Attention is paid only when a new social situation arises where the past social training of the person prevents him from making the necessary delicate interpretations of a given social signal and hence brings forth the "socially wrong" response.

In the factory, as in any social milieu, a process of social evaluation is constantly at work. From this process distinctions of "good" and "bad," "inferior" and "superior," arise. This process of evaluation is carried on with simple and ready generalizations by means of which values become attached to individuals and to groups performing certain tasks and operations. It assigns to a group of individuals performing such and such a task a particular rank in the established prestige scale. Each work group becomes a carrier of social values. In industry with its extreme diversity of occupations there are a number of such groupings. Any noticeable similarity or difference, not only in occupation but also in age, sex, and nationality, can serve as a basis of social classification, as, for example, "married women," the "old-timer," the "white-collared" or clerical worker, the "foreign element." Each of these groups, too, has its own value system.

All the patterns of interaction that arise between individuals or between different groups can be graded according to the degree of intimacy involved in the relationship. Grades of intimacy or understanding can be arranged on a scale and expressed in terms of "social distance." Social distance measures differences of sentiment and interest which separate individuals or groups from one another. Between the president of a company and the elevator operator there is considerable social distance, more for example than between the foreman and the benchworker. Social distance is to social organization what physical distance is to physical space. However, physical and social distance do not necessarily coincide. Two people may be physically near but socially distant.

Just as each employee has a particular physical location, so he has a particular social place in the total social organization. But this place is not so rigidly fixed as in a caste system. In any factory there is considerable mobility or movement. Movement can occur in two ways: the individual may pass from one occupation to another occupation higher up in the prestige scale; or the prestige scale itself may change.

It is obvious that these scales of value are never completely accepted by all the groups in the social environment. The shop worker does not quite see why the office worker, for example, should have shorter hours of work than he has. Or the newcomer, whose efficiency on a particular job is about the same, but whose hourly rate is less than that of some old-timer, wonders why service should count so much. The management group, in turn, from the security of its social elevation, does not often understand what "all the fuss is about."

As was indicated by many of the studies, any person who has achieved a certain rank in the prestige scale regards anything real or imaginary which tends to alter his status adversely as something unfair or unjust. It is apparent that any move on the part of the management may alter the existing social equilibrium to which the employee has grown accustomed and by means of which his status is defined. Immediately this disruption will be expressed in sentiments of resistance to the real or imagined alterations in the social equilibrium.

From this point of view it can be seen how every item and event in the industrial environment becomes an object of a system of sentiments. According to this way of looking at things, material goods, physical events, wages, hours of work, etc., cannot be treated as things in themselves. Instead they have to be interpreted as carriers of social value. The meanings which any person in an industrial organization assigns to the events and objects in his environment are often determined by the social situation in which the events and objects occur. The significance to an employee of a double-pedestal desk, of a particular kind of pencil, or of a handset telephone is determined by the social setting in which these objects appear. If people with double-pedestal desks supervise people with single-pedestal desks, then double-pedestal desks become symbols of status or prestige in the organization. As patterns of behavior become crystallized, every object in the environment tends to take on a particular social significance. It becomes easy to tell a person's social place in the organization by the objects which he wears and carries and which surround him. In these terms it can be seen how the introduction of a technical change may also involve for an individual or a group of individuals the loss of certain prestige symbols and, as a result, have a demoralizing effect.

From this point of view the behavior of no one person in an industrial organization, from the very top to the very bottom, can be regarded as motivated by strictly economic or logical considerations. Routine patterns of interaction involve strong sentiments. Each group in the organization manifests its own powerful sentiments. It is likely that sometimes the behavior of many staff specialists which goes under the name of "efficiency" is as much a manifestation of a very strong sentiment—the sentiment or desire to originate new combinations—as it is of anything strictly logical.

This point of view is far from the one which is frequently expressed, namely, that man is essentially an economic being carrying around with him a few noneconomic appendages. Rather, the point of view which has been expressed here is that noneconomic motives, interests, and processes, as well as economic, are fundamental in behavior in business, from the board of directors to the very last man in the organization. Man is not merely—in fact is very seldom—motivated by factors pertaining strictly to facts or logic. Sentiments are not merely things which man carries around with him as appendages. He cannot cast them off like a suit of clothes. He carries them with him wherever he goes. In business or elsewhere, he can hardly behave without expressing them. Moreover, sentiments do not exist in a social vacuum. They are the product of social behavior, of social interaction, of the fact that man lives his life as a member of different groups. Not only does man bring sentiments to the business situation because of his past experiences and conditioning outside of business, but also as a member of a specific local business organization with a particular social place in it he has certain sentiments expressing his particular relations to it.

According to this point of view, every social act in adulthood is an integrated response to both inner and outer stimuli. To each new concrete situation the adult brings his past "social conditioning." To the extent that this past social conditioning has prepared him to assimilate the new experience in the culturally accepted manner, he is said to be "adjusted." To the extent that his private or personal view of the situation is at variance with the cultural situation, the person is called "maladjusted."

73

The Formal Organization of the Plant

The social organization of the industrial plant is in part formally organized. It is composed of a number of strata or levels which differentiate the benchworker from the skilled mechanic, the group chief from the department chief, and so on. These levels are well defined and all the formal orders, instructions, and compensations are addressed to them. All such factors taken together make up the formal organization of the plant. It includes the systems, policies, rules, and regulations of the plant which express what the relations of one person to another are supposed to be in order to achieve effectively the task of technical production. It prescribes the relations that are supposed to obtain within the human organization and between the human organization and the technical organization. In short, the patterns of human interrelations, as defined by the systems, rules, policies, and regulations of the company, constitute the formal organization.

The formal organization of an industrial plant has two purposes: it addresses itself to the economic purposes of the total enterprise; it concerns itself also with the securing of co-operative effort. The formal organization includes all the explicitly stated systems of control introduced by the company in order to achieve the economic purposes of the total enterprise and the effective contribution of the members of the organization to those economic ends.

The Informal Organization of the Plant

All the experimental studies pointed to the fact that there is something more to the social organization than what has been formally recognized. Many of the actually existing patterns of human interaction have no representation in the formal organization at all, and others are inadequately represented by the formal organization. This fact is frequently forgotten when talking or thinking about industrial situations in general. Too often it is assumed that the organization of a company corresponds to a blueprint plan or organization chart. Actually, it never does. In the formal organization of most companies little explicit recognition is given to many social distinctions residing in the social organization. The blueprint plans of a company show the functional relations between working units, but they do not express the distinctions of social distance, movement, or equilibrium previously described. The hierarchy of prestige values which tends to make the work of men more important than the work of women, the work of clerks more important that the work at the bench, has little representation in the formal organization; nor does a blueprint plan ordinarily show the primary groups, that is, those groups enjoying daily face-to-face relations. Logical lines of horizontal and vertical coordination of functions replace the actually existing patterns of interaction between people in different social places. The formal organization cannot take account of the sentiments and values residing in the social organization by means of which individuals or groups of individuals are informally differentiated, ordered, and integrated. Individuals in their associations with one another in a factory build up personal relationships. They form into informal groups, in terms of which each person achieves a certain position or status. The nature of these informal groups is very important, as has been shown in the Relay Assembly Test Room and in the Bank Wiring Observation Room.

It is well to recognize that informal organizations are not "bad," as they are sometimes assumed to be. Informal social organization exists in every plant, and can be said to be a necessary prerequisite for effective collaboration. Much collaboration exists at an informal level, and it sometimes facilitates the functioning of the formal organization. On the other hand, sometimes the informal organization develops in opposition to the formal organization. The important consideration is, therefore, the relation that exists between formal and informal organizations.

To illustrate, let us consider the Relay Assembly Test Room and the Bank Wiring Observation Room. These two studies offered an interesting contrast between two informal working groups; one situation could be characterized in almost completely opposite terms from the other. In the Relay Assembly Test Room, on the one hand, the five operators changed continuously in their rate of output up and down over the duration of the test, and yet in a curious fashion their variations in output were insensitive to many significant changes introduced during the experiment. On the other hand, in the Bank Wiring Observation Room output was being held relatively constant and there existed a hypersensitivity to change on the part of the worker—in fact, what could almost be described as an organized opposition to it.

It is interesting to note that management could draw from these studies two opposite conclusions. From the Relay Assembly Test Room experiment they could argue that the company can do almost anything it wants in the nature of technical changes without any perceptible effect on the output of the workers. From the Bank Wiring Observation Room they could argue equally convincingly that the company can introduce hardly any changes without meeting a pronounced opposition to them from the workers. To make this dilemma even more striking, it is only necessary to recall that the sensitivity to change in the one case occurred in the room where no experimental changes had been introduced whereas the insensitivity to change in the other case occurred in the room where the operators had been submitted to considerable experimentation. To settle this question by saying that in one case the situation was typical and in the other case atypical of ordinary shop conditions would be to beg the question, for the essential difference between the two situations would again be missed. It would ignore the social setting in which the changes occurred and the meaning which the workers themselves assigned to the changes.

Although in both cases there were certain informal arrangements not identical with the formal setup, the informal organization in one room was quite different from that in the other room, especially in its relation to the formal organization. In the case of the Relay Assembly Test Room there was a group, or informal organization, which could be characterized as a network of personal relations which had been developed in and through a particular way of working together; it was an organization which not only satisfied the wishes of its members but also worked in harmony with the aims of management. In the case of the Bank Wiring Observation Room there was an informal organization which could be characterized better as a set of practices and beliefs which its members had in common —practices and beliefs which at many points worked against the economic purposes of the company. In one case the relation between the formal and informal organization was one of compatibility; in the other case it was one of opposition. Or to put it in another way, collaboration in the Relay Assembly Test Room was at a much higher level than in the Bank Wiring Observation Room.

The difference between these two groups can be understood only by comparing the functions which their informal organizations performed for their members. The chief function of the informal group in the Bank Wiring Observation Room was to resist changes in their established routines of work or personal interrelations. This resistance to change, however, was not the chief function of the informal group in the Relay Assembly Test Room. It is true that at first the introduction of the planned changes in the test room, whether or not these changes were logically in the direction of improvement, was met with apprehension and feelings of uneasiness on the part of the operators. The girls in the beginning were never quite sure that they might not be victims of the changes.

In setting up the Relay Assembly Test Room with the object of studying the factors determining the efficiency of the worker, many of the methods and rules by means of which management tends to promote and maintain efficiency—the "bogey," not talking too much at work, etc.— were, in effect, abrogated. With the removal of this source of constraint and in a setting of heightened social significance (because many of the changes had differentiated the test room girls from the regular department and as a result had elevated the social status within the plant of each of the five girls) a new type of spontaneous social organization developed. Social conditions had been established which allowed the operators to develop their own values and objectives. The experimental conditions allowed the operators to develop openly social codes at work and these codes, unhampered by interference, gave a sustained meaning to their work. It was as if the experimenters had acted as a buffer for the operators and held their work situation steady while they developed a new type of social organization. With this change in the type of social organization there also developed a new attitude toward changes in their working environment. Toward many changes which constitute an unspecified threat in the regular work situation the operators became immune. What the Relay Assembly Test Room experiment showed was that when innovations are introduced carefully and with regard to the actual sentiments of the workers, the workers are likely to develop a spontaneous type of informal organization which will not only express more adequately their own values and significances but also is more likely to be in harmony with the aims of management.

Although all the studies of informal organization at the Hawthorne Plant were made at the employee level, it would be incorrect to assume that this phenomenon occurs only at that level. Informal organization appears at all levels, from the very bottom to the very top of the organization.[2] Informal organization at the executive level, just as at the work level, may either facilitate or impede purposive cooperation and communication. In either case, at all levels of the organization informal organizations exist as a necessary condition for collaboration. Without them formal organization could not survive for long. Formal and informal organizations are interdependent aspects of social interaction.

The Ideological Organization of the Plant

There is one aspect of social organization in an industrial plant which cuts across both the formal and informal organizations: the systems of ideas and beliefs by means of which the values residing in the total organization are expressed and the symbols around which these values are organized. Both the formal and informal organizations of a plant have systems of ideas and beliefs. Some are more capable of logical and systematic expression than others. Those of the formal organization in general are more logically explicit and articulate than those of the informal organization, but they are not for that reason more powerful in their effects than those of the informal organization. The sentiments underlying the beliefs and ideas of informal organizations are often very powerful determinants of overt behavior.

Some of these systems of ideas and beliefs represent what the organization should be; that is, what the relations of people to one another should be or how people should behave. Some express the values of one part of the total organization, for each specialist tends to see the total or-

2. Barnard, C. I., *The Functions of the Executive,* Harvard University Press, 1938, pp. 223–24.

ganization from the point of view of the logic of his own specialty. Still others express the values residing in the interhuman relations of the different social groups involved.

Some of these ideas and beliefs represent more closely the actual situation than others. In all cases, however, they are abstractions from the concrete situation. In this respect they are to the concrete situation as maps are to the territories they represent.[3] And like maps these abstractions may be either misleading or useful. They may be misleading because sometimes the person using them fails to realize they are representing only one part of the total organization. Sometimes in the minds of certain individuals these abstractions tend to become divorced from the social reality and, in effect, lead an independent existence.

In their studies the investigators frequently ran into these different systems of ideas and beliefs. Although they were never made the object of systematic study, three general systems which seemed to cling together could be discerned.

The logic of cost. In the industrial plant there is a certain set of ideas and beliefs by means of which the common economic purposes of the total organization are evaluated. This we shall call the "logic of cost." Although the logic of cost is applied mostly to the technical organization, it is also sometimes applied to the human organization. When applied to the human organization it is frequently done under the label of "efficiency."

The word "efficiency" is used in at least five different ways, two of which are rather vague and not clearly differentiated: (*a*) sometimes when talking about a machine it is used in a technical sense, as the relation between output and input; (*b*) sometimes when talking about a manufacturing process or operation it is used to refer to relative unit cost; (*c*) sometimes when referring to a worker it is used to indicate a worker's production or output in relation to a certain standard of performance; (*d*) sometimes its reference becomes more vague and it is used as practically synonymous with "logical coordination of function"; (*e*) sometimes it is used in the sense of "morale" or "social integration."

We shall use the term "logic of cost" to refer only to the system of ideas and beliefs which are explicitly organized around the symbol of "cost" and are applied to the human organization from this point of view.[4] This logic represents one of the values of the formal organization: the system of ideas and beliefs which relates the human organization to the task of technical production.

3. This distinction has been borrowed from Korzybski, A., *Science and Sanity,* The Science Press Printing Co., New York, 1933.
4. According to this definition, "logic of cost" does not conform to any single one of the above uses of the word "efficiency" but conforms most closely to a combination of (*b*) and (*c*).

The logic of efficiency. Closely associated with the logic of cost is another system of ideas and beliefs by means of which the collaborative efforts of the members of an organization are evaluated. This we shall call the "logic of efficiency." [5] This system of ideas and beliefs, which is organized around the symbol of "cooperation," represents another value of the formal organization. It is addressed primarily to the problem of how cooperation between individuals and groups of individuals can be effectively secured and is manifested in plans, such as wage payment plans, designed to promote collaboration among individuals.

A system of beliefs and ideas such as this is usually based upon certain assumptions about employee behavior. In the case of the wage payment plan in the Bank Wiring Observation Room, for example, it was assumed that the employee was a logical being and therefore could see the system, as its creators saw it, as a logical, coherent scheme which he could use to his economic advantage. It was assumed that, given the opportunity, the employee would act in such a way as to obtain the maximum of earnings consistent with his physical capacity. Carrying this basic assumption still further, it followed that the slower workers, who would interfere with the logical functioning of that system, would be disciplined by the faster workers and that daywork claims would be kept at a minimum. It was assumed that the division of labor would permit the employees to increase production through specialization. The possibility that division of labor might result in social stratification, which in turn might generate nonlogical forces that would interfere with the logical functioning of that system, was unforeseen. Practically every aspect of the wage plan followed from the basic assumption that nothing would interfere with the economic motives. It is such assumptions as these that go to make up the "logic of efficiency."

The logic of sentiments. There is another system of ideas and beliefs which we shall give the label "the logic of sentiments." It represents the values residing in the interhuman relations of the different groups within the organization. Examples of what is meant here are the arguments employees give which center around the "right to work," "seniority," "fairness," "the living wage." This logic, as its name implies, is deeply rooted in sentiment and feeling.

Management and employee logics. At first glance it might seem that the logics of cost and efficiency are the logics of management groups, whereas the logic of sentiments is the logic of employee groups. Although in one sense this may be accurate, in another sense it is an oversimplification. All groups within the industry participate in these different logics, although some participate to a greater or less extent than others. One has only to interview a supervisor or executive to see that he has a logic of

---

5. The "logic of efficiency" conforms most closely to a combination of uses (*c*), (*d*), and (*e*) of the word "efficiency" as given in the previous section.

sentiments which is expressing the values residing in his personal inter-relations with other supervisors or executives. Employee groups, moreover, are not unknown to apply the logic of cost.

However, it is incorrect to assume that these different logics have the same significance to different groups in an industrial plant. The logics of cost and efficiency express the values of the formal organization; the logic of sentiments expresses the values of the informal organization. To management groups and technical specialists the logics of cost and efficiency are likely to be more important than they are to employee groups. In form the logic of sentiments expressed by an executive is indistinguishable from that expressed by a worker, but in content it is quite different. As anyone knows who has had industrial experience, much time is spent in industry in debating the relative weights attaching to the logics of cost, efficiency, and sentiments when they are applied to a particular concrete situation.

Definition of Terms

For convenience, it may be well to summarize the different parts into which the industrial plant as a social system can be divided and the way in which the labels attaching to them will be used. . . . The following outline will help the reader to see the levels of abstraction of the different parts of the system:

1. Technical Organization
2. Human Organization
   2.1. Individual
   2.2. Social Organization
      2.21. Formal Organization
         2.211. Patterns of Interaction
         2.212. Systems of Ideas and Beliefs
            (Ideological Organization)
            2.2121. Logic of Cost
            2.2122. Logic of Efficiency
      2.22. Informal Organization
         2.221. Patterns of Interaction
         2.222. Systems of Ideas and Beliefs
            (Ideological Organization)
            2.2221. Logic of Sentiments

1. The term "technical organization" will refer to the logical and technical organization of materials, tools, machines, and finished products, including all those physical items related to the task of technical production.

2. The term "human organization" will refer, on the one hand, to

the concrete individual with his rich personal and soical background and, on the other hand, to the intricate pattern of social relations existing among the various individuals and groups within the plant.

2.1. The term "individual" will refer to the sentiments and values which the person is bringing to the work situation because of his past social conditioning and present social situation outside of the plant; i.e., the past and present patterns of interaction in which he has participated or is participating outside of work.

2.2. The term "social organization" will refer to the actual patterns of interaction existing within and between employee groups, supervisory groups, and management groups in a plant here and now. It will include those relations that remain at a common human level (friendships, antagonisms, etc.), those that have been built up into larger social configurations (social codes, customs, traditions, routines, and associated ideas and beliefs), as well as those patterns of relations formally prescribed by the rules, regulations, practices, and policies of the company.

2.21. The term "formal organization" will refer to those patterns of interaction prescribed by the rules and regulations of the company as well as to the policies which prescribe the relations that obtain, or are supposed to obtain, within the human organization and between the human organization and the technical organization.

2.22. The term "informal organization" will refer to the actual personal interrelations existing among the members of the organization which are not represented by, or are inadequately represented by, the formal organization.

2.212 and 2.222. The term "ideological organization" will refer to the systems of ideas and beliefs by means of which the values of both the formal and informal aspects of the social organization are expressed and the symbols around which these values are organized.

2.2121. The term "logic of cost" will refer to that system of ideas and beliefs by means of which the common economic purposes of the total organization are evaluated.

2.2122. The term "logic of efficiency" will refer to that system of ideas and beliefs by means of which the collaborative efforts of the members of the organization are evaluated.

2.2221. The term "logic of sentiments" will refer to that system of ideas and beliefs which expresses the values residing in the interhuman relations of the different groups within the plant.

A Condition of Equilibrium

The parts of the industrial plant as a social system are interrelated and interdependent. Any changes in one part of the social system are accompanied by changes in other parts of the system. The parts of the system can be conceived of as being in a state of equilibrium, such that "if a small (not too great) modification different from that which will otherwise occur is impressed on the system, a reaction will at once appear tending toward the conditions that would have existed if the modification had not been impressed.[6]

Some parts of the system can change more rapidly than others. The technical organization can change more rapidly than the social organization; the formal organization can change more rapidly than the informal; the systems of beliefs and ideas can change more rapidly than the patterns of interaction and associated sentiments, of which these beliefs and ideas are an expression. In the disparity in the rates of change possible there exists a precondition for unbalance which may manifest itself in many forms.

In their studies the investigators identified two such possibilities of unbalance. One was the disparity in the rates of change possible in the technical organization, on the one hand, and the social organization, on the other. This condition was manifested in the workers' behavior by distrust and resistance to change. This resistance was expressed whenever changes were introduced too rapidly or without sufficient considerations of their social implications; in other words, whenever the workers were being asked to adjust themselves to new methods or systems which seemed to them to deprive their work of its customary social significance. In such situations it was evident that the social codes, customs, and routines of the worker could not be accommodated to the technical innovations introduced as quickly as the innovations themselves, in the form of new machines and processes, could be made. The codes, customs, and traditions of the worker are not the product of logic but are based on deeply rooted sentiments. Not only is any alteration of the existing social organization to which the worker has grown accustomed likely to produce sentiments of resistance to the change, but too rapid interference is likely to lead to feelings of frustration and an irrational exasperation with technical change in any form.

Another possibility of unbalance lies in the relation of the ideological organization to the actual work situation. The logics of the ideological organization express only some of the values of the social organization. They frequently fail to take into account not only the feelings and sentiments of people within the plant but also the spontaneous informal social groups which form at all levels of the organization. Thus they tend to become divorced from the concrete situation and to lead an independent existence. As a result of failing to distinguish the human situation as it is from the way it is formally and logically represented to be, many human

6. For a discussion of equilibrium, see Pareto, V., *The Mind and Society,* Harcourt, Brace & Co., New York, 1935, pp. 1435–42. The quotation used above is Dr. L. J. Henderson's adaptation of Pareto's definition of equilibrium.

problems are stated either in terms of the perversities of human nature or in terms of logical defects in the formal organization. The facts of social organization are ignored, and consequently the result in terms of diagnosis or remedy is bound to be inadequate.

It became clear to the investigators that the limits of human collaboration are determined far more by the informal than by the formal organization of the plant. Collaboration is not wholly a matter of logical organization. It presupposes social codes, conventions, traditions, and routine or customary ways of responding to situations. Without such basic codes or conventions, effective work relations are not possible.

Cooperation

Chester I. Barnard

The Theory of Formal Organization

An organization comes into being when (1) there are persons able to communicate with each other (2) who are willing to contribute action (3) to accomplish a common purpose. The elements of an organization are therefore (1) communication; (2) willingness to serve; and (3) common purpose. These elements are necessary and sufficient conditions initially, and they are found in all such organizations. The third element, purpose is implicit in the definition. Willingness to serve, and communication, and the interdependence of the three elements in general, and their mutual dependence in specific cooperative systems, are matters of experience and observation.

For the continued existence of an organization either *effectiveness* or *efficiency* is necessary; [1] and the longer the life, the more necessary both are. The vitality of organizations lies in the willingness of individuals to contribute forces to the cooperative system. This willingness requires the belief that the purpose can be carried out, a faith that diminishes to the vanishing point as it appears that it is not in fact in process of being attained. Hence, when effectiveness ceases, willingness to contribute disappears. The continuance of willingness also depends upon the satisfactions that are secured by individual contributors in the process of carrying out the purpose. If the satisfactions do not exceed the sacrifices required, willingness disappears, and the condition is one of organization inefficiency. If the satisfactions exceed the sacrifices, willingness persists, and the condition is one of efficiency of organization.

SOURCE: *The Functions of the Executive*, Cambridge, Mass.: Harvard University Press, pp. 82–95, 165–71. Copyright © 1938 by the President and Fellows of Harvard College; copyright © 1966 by Grace F. N. Barnard. Reprinted by permission of the publishers.

1. Editors' note: "An action is effective if it accomplishes its specific aim . . . it is efficient if it satisfies the motives of that aim, whether it is effective or not, and the process does not create offsetting dissatisfactions. We shall say that an action is inefficient if the motives are not satisfied, or offsetting dissatisfactions are incurred, even if it is effective" (*The Functions of the Executive*, p. 20).

In summary, then, the initial existence of an organization depends upon a combination of these elements appropriate to the external conditions at the moment. Its survival depends upon the maintenance of an equilibrium of the system. This equilibrium is primarily internal, a matter of proportions between the elements, but it is ultimately and basically an equilibrium between the system and the total situation external to it. This external equilibrium has two terms in it: first, the effectiveness of the organization, which comprises the relevance of its purpose to the environmental situation; and, second, its efficiency, which comprises the interchange between the organization and individuals. Thus the elements stated will each vary with external factors, and they are at the same time interdependent; when one is varied compensating variations must occur in the other if the system of which they are components is to remain in equilibrium, that is, is to persist or survive.

• • •

I

I. Willingness to Cooperate

By definition there can be no organization without persons. However, as we have urged that it is not persons, but the services or acts or action or influences of persons, which should be treated as constituting organizations, it is clear that *willingness* of persons to contribute efforts to the cooperative system is indispensable.

There are a number of words and phrases in common use with reference to organization that reach back to the factor of individual willingness. "Loyalty," "solidarity," *"esprit de corps,"* "strength" of organization, are the chief. Although they are indefinite, they relate to intensity of attachment to the "cause," and are commonly understood to refer to something different from effectiveness, ability, or value of personal contributions. Thus "loyalty" is regarded as not necessarily related either to position, rank, fame, remuneration, or ability. It is vaguely recognized as an essential condition of organization.

Willingness, in the present connection, means self-abnegation, the surrender of control of personal conduct, the depersonalization of personal action. Its effect is cohesion of effort, a sticking together. Its immediate cause is the disposition necessary to "sticking together." Without this there can be no sustained personal effort as a contribution to cooperation. Activities cannot be coordinated unless there is first the disposition to make a personal act a contribution to an impersonal system of acts, one in which the individual gives up personal control of what he does.

The outstanding fact regarding willingness to contribute to a given specific formal organization is the indefinitely large range of variation in its intensity among individuals. If all those who may be considered potential contributors to an organization are arranged in order of willingness to serve it, the scale gradually descends from possibly intense willingness through neutral or zero willingness to intense unwillingness or opposition or hatred. The *preponderance of persons in a modern society always lies on the negative side* with reference to any particular existing or potential organization. Thus of the possible contributors only a small minority actually have a positive willingness. This is true of the largest and most comprehensive formal organizations, such as the large nations, the Catholic Church, etc. Most of the persons in existing society are either indifferent to or positively opposed to any single one of them; and if the smaller organizations subordinate to these major organizations are under consideration the minority becomes of course a much smaller proportion, and usually a nearly negligible proportion, of the conceivable total.

A second fact of almost equal importance is that the willingness of any individual cannot be constant in degree. It is necessarily intermittent and fluctuating. It can scarcely be said to exist during sleep, and is obviously diminished or exhausted by weariness, discomfort, etc., a conception that was well expressed by the saying, "The spirit is willing, but the flesh is weak."

A corollary of the two propositions just stated is that for any given formal organization the number of persons of positive willingness to serve, but near the neutral or zero point, is always fluctuating. It follows that the aggregate willingness of potential contributors to any formal cooperative system is unstable—a fact that is evident from the history of all formal organizations.

Willingness to cooperate, positive or negative, is the expression of the net satisfactions or dissatisfactions experienced or anticipated by each individual in comparison with those experienced or anticipated through alternative opportunities. These alternative opportunities may be either personal and individualistic or those afforded by other organizations. That is, willingness to cooperate is the net effect, first, of the inducements to do so in conjunction with the sacrifices involved, and then in comparison with the practically available net satisfactions afforded by alternatives. The questions to be determined, if they were matters of logical reasoning, would be, first, whether the opportunity to cooperate grants any advantage to the individual as compared with independent action; and then, if so, whether that advantage is more or less than the advantage obtainable from some other cooperative opportunity. Thus, from the viewpoint of the individual, willingness is the joint effect of personal desires and reluctances; from the viewpoint of organization it is the joint effect of objective inducements offered and burdens imposed. The measure of this net result, however, is entirely individual, personal, and subjective. Hence, organizations depend upon the motives of individuals and the inducements that satisfy them.

II. Purpose

Willingness to cooperate, except as a vague feeling or desire for association with others, cannot develop without an objective of cooperation. Unless there is such an objective it cannot be known or anticipated what specific efforts will be required of individuals, nor in many cases what satisfactions to them can be in prospect. Such an objective we denominate the "purpose" of an organization. The necessity of having a purpose is axiomatic, implicit in the words "system," "coordination," "cooperation." It is something that is clearly evident in many observed systems of cooperation, although it is often not formulated in words, and sometimes cannot be so formulated. In such cases what is observed is the direction or effect of the activities, from which purpose may be inferred.

A purpose does not incite cooperative activity unless it is accepted by those whose efforts will constitute the organization. Hence there is initially something like simultaneity in the acceptance of a purpose and willingness to cooperate.

It is important at this point to make clear that every cooperative purpose has in the view of each cooperating person two aspects which we call (*a*) the cooperative and (*b*) the subjective aspect, respectively.

(*a*) When the viewing of the purpose is an *act of cooperation,* it approximates that of detached observers from a special position of observation; this position is that of the interests of the organization; it is largely determined by organization knowledge, but is personally interpreted. For example, if five men are cooperating to move a stone from A to B, the moving of the stone is a different thing in the organization view of each of the five men involved. Note, however, that what moving the stone means to each man personally is not here in question, but what he thinks it means to the organization *as a whole.* This includes the significance of his own effort as an element in cooperation, and that of all others, in his view; but it is not at all a matter of satisfying a personal motive.

When the purpose is a physical result of simple character, the difference between the purpose as objectively viewed by a detached observer and the purpose as viewed by each person cooperating *as an act of cooperation* is ordinarily not large or important, and the different cooperative views of the persons cooperating are correspondingly similar. Even in such cases the attentive observer will detect differences that result in disputes, errors of action, etc., even though no *personal* interest is implicated. But when the purpose is less tangible—for example, in religious cooperation—the difference between objective purpose and purpose as cooperatively viewed by each person is often seen ultimately to result in disruption.

We may say, then, that a purpose can serve as an element of a cooperative system only so long as the participants do not recognize that there are serious divergences of their understanding of that purpose as the object of cooperation. If in fact there is important difference between the aspects of the purpose as objectively and as cooperatively viewed, the divergencies become quickly evident when the purpose is concrete, tangible, physical; but when the purpose is general, intangible, and of sentimental character, the divergencies can be very wide yet not be recognized. Hence, an objective purpose that can serve as the basis for a cooperative system is one that is *believed* by the contributors (or potential contributors) to it to be the determined purpose of the organization. The inculcation of belief in the real existence of a common purpose is an essential executive function. It explains much educational and so-called morale work in political, industrial, and religious organizations that is so often otherwise inexplicable.

(*b*) Going back to the illustration of five men moving a stone, we have noted "that what moving the stone means to each man personally is not here in question, but what he thinks it means to the *organization as a whole*." The distinction emphasized is of first importance. It suggests the fact that every participant in an organization may be regarded as having a dual personality—an organization personality and an individual personality. Strictly speaking, an organization purpose has directly no meaning for the individual. What has meaning for him is the organization's relation to him—what burdens it imposes, what benefits it confers. In referring to the aspects of purpose as cooperatively viewed, we are alluding to the *organization* personality of individuals. In many cases the two personalities are so clearly developed that they are quite apparent. In military action individual conduct may be so dominated by organization personality that it is utterly contradictory of what personal motivation would require. It has been observed of many men that their private conduct is entirely inconsistent with official conduct, although they seem completely unaware of the fact. Often it will be observed that participants in political, patriotic, or religious organizations will accept derogatory treatment of their personal conduct, including the assertion that it is inconsistent with their organization obligations, while they will become incensed at the slightest derogation of the tenets or doctrines of their organization, even though they profess not to understand them. There are innumerable other cases, however, in which almost no organization personality may be said to exist. These are cases in which personal relationship with the cooperative system is momentary or at the margin of willingness to participate.

In other words we have clearly to distinguish between organization purpose and individual motive. It is frequently assumed in reasoning about organizations that common purpose and individual motive are or should be identical. With the exception noted below, this is never the case; and under modern conditions it rarely even appears to be the case. Individual motive is necessarily an internal, personal, subjective thing; common purpose is necessarily an external, impersonal, objective thing even though the individual interpretation of it is subjective. The one exception to this general rule, an important one, is that the accomplishment of an organization purpose becomes itself a source of personal satisfaction and a motive for many individuals in many organizations. It is rare, however, if ever, and then I think only in connection with family, patriotic, and religious organizations under special conditions, that organization purpose becomes or can become the *only* or even the major individual motive.

Finally it should be noted that, once established, organizations change their unifying purposes. They tend to perpetuate themselves; and in the effort to survive may change the reasons for existence. I shall later make clearer that in this lies an important aspect of executive functions.

III. Communication

The possibility of accomplishing a common purpose and the existence of persons whose desires might constitute motives for contributing toward such a common purpose are the opposite poles of the system of cooperative effort. The process by which these potentialities become dynamic is that of communication. Obviously a common purpose must be commonly known, and to be known must be in some way communicated. With some exceptions, verbal communication between men is the method by which this is accomplished. Similarly, though under crude and obvious conditions not to the same extent, inducements to persons depend upon communication to them.

The method of communication centers in language, oral and written. On its crudest side, motions or actions that are of obvious meaning when observed are sufficient for communication without deliberate attempt to communicate; and signaling by various methods is an important method in much cooperative activity. On the other side, both in primitive and in highly complex civilization "observational feeling" is likewise an important aspect of communication.[2] I do not think it is generally so recognized. It

2. The phrase "observational feeling" is of my coining. The point is not sufficiently developed, and probably has not been adequately studied by anyone. I take it to be at least in part involved in group action not incited by any "overt" or verbal communication. The cases known to me from the primitive field are those reported by W. H. R. Rivers on pp. 94–97 of his *Instinct and the Unconscious* (2nd edition, Cambridge University Press, 1924), with reference to Polynesia and Melanesia. One case is summarized by F. C. Bartlett, in *Remembering* (Cambridge University Press, 1932), at p. 297. Rivers states in substance that in some of the relatively

is necessary because of the limitations of language and the differences in the linguistic capacities of those who use language. A very large element in special experience and training and in continuity of individual association is the ability to understand without words, not merely the situation or conditions, but the *intention*.

The techniques of communication are an important part of any organization and are the preeminent problems of many. The absence of a suitable technique of communication would eliminate the possibility of adopting some purposes as a basis for organization. Communication technique shapes the form and the internal economy of organization. This will be evident at once if one visualizes the attempt to do many things now accomplished by small organizations if each "member" spoke a different language. Similarly, many technical functions could hardly be carried on without special codes; for example, engineering or chemical work. In an exhaustive theory of organization, communication would occupy a central place, because the structure, extensiveness, and scope of organization are almost entirely determined by communication techniques. . . .

II

I. Effectiveness of Cooperation

The continuance of an organization depends upon its ability to carry out its purpose. This clearly depends jointly upon the appropriateness of its action and upon the conditions of its environment. In other words, effectiveness is primarily a matter of technological processes. This is quite obvious in ordinary cases of purpose to accomplish a physical objective, such as building a bridge. When the objective is non-physical, as is the case with religious and social organizations, it is not so obvious.

It should be noted that a paradox is involved in this matter. An organization must disintegrate if it cannot accomplish its purpose. It also destroys itself by accomplishing its purpose. A very large number of successful organizations come into being and then disappear for this reason. Hence most continuous organizations require repeated adoption of new purposes. This is concealed from everyday recognition by the practice of generalizing a complex series of specific purposes under one term, stated to be "*the* purpose" of this organization. This is strikingly true in the case

---

small groups decisions are often arrived at and acted upon without having ever been formulated by anybody.

I have observed on innumerable occasions apparent unanimity of decision of equals in conferences to quit discussion without a word to that effect being spoken. Often the action is initiated apparently by someone's rising; but as this frequently occurs in such groups *without* the termination of the meeting, more than mere rising is involved. "Observational feeling," I think, avoids the notion of anything "occult."

of governmental and public utility organizations when the purpose is stated to be a particular kind of service through a period of years. It is apparent that their real purposes are not abstractions called "service" but specific acts of service. A manufacturing organization is said to exist to make, say, shoes; this is its "purpose." But it is evident that not making shoes in general but making specific shoes from day to day is its series of purposes. This process of generalization, however, provides in advance for the approximate definition of new purposes automatically—so automatically that the generalization is normally substituted in our minds for the concrete performances that are the real purposes. Failure to be effective is, then, a real cause of disintegration; but failure to provide for the decisions resulting in the adoption of new purposes would have the same result. Hence the generalization of purpose which can only be defined concretely by day-to-day events is a vital aspect of permanent organization.

II. Organization Efficiency

It has already been stated that "efficiency" as conceived in this treatise is not used in the specialized and limited sense of ordinary industrial practice or in the restricted sense applicable to technological processes. So-called "practical" efficiency has little meaning, for example, as applied to many organizations such as religious organizations.

Efficiency of effort in the fundamental sense with which we are here concerned is efficiency relative to the securing of necessary personal contributions to the cooperative system. The life of an organization depends upon its ability to secure and maintain the personal contributions of energy (including the transfer of control of materials or money equivalent) necessary to effect its purposes. This ability is a composite of perhaps many efficiencies and inefficiencies in the narrow senses of these words, and it is often the case that inefficiency in some respect can be treated as the cause of total failure, in the sense that if corrected success would then be possible. But certainly in most organization—social, political, national, religious—nothing but the absolute test of survival is significant objectively; there is no basis for comparison of the efficiencies of separate aspects.

. . . The emphasis now is on the view that efficiency of organization is its capacity to offer effective inducements in sufficient quantity to maintain the equilibrium of the system. It is efficiency in this sense and not the efficiency of material productiveness which maintains the vitality of organizations. There are many organizations of great power and permanency in which the idea of productive efficiency is utterly meaningless because there is no material production. Churches, patriotic societies, scientific societies, theatrical and musical organizations, are cases where the original flow of *material* inducements is toward the organization, not from it—a flow necessary to provide resources with which to supply material inducements to the small minority who require them in such organizations.

In those cases where the primary purpose of organization is the production of material things, insufficiency with respect to the nonmaterial inducements leads to the attempt to substitute material inducements for the nonmaterial. Under favorable circumstances, to a limited degree, and for a limited time, this substitution may be effective. But to me, at least, it appears utterly contrary to the nature of men to be sufficiently induced by material or monetary considerations to contribute enough effort to a cooperative system to enable it to be productively efficient to the degree necessary for persistence over an extended period.

If these things are true, then even in purely economic enterprises efficiency in the offering of noneconomic inducements may be as vital as productive efficiency. Perhaps the word efficiency as applied to such noneconomic inducements as I have given for illustration will seem strange and forced. This, I think, can only be because we are accustomed to use the word in a specialized sense.

The noneconomic inducements are as difficult to offer as others under many circumstances. To establish conditions under which individual pride of craft and of accomplishment can be secured without destroying the material economy of standardized production in cooperative operation is a problem in real efficiency. To maintain a character of personnel that is an attractive condition of employment involves a delicate art and much insight in the selection (and rejection) of personal services offered, whether the standard of quality be high or low. To have an organization that lends prestige and secures the loyalty of desirable persons is a complex and difficult task in efficiency—in all-round efficiency, not one-sided efficiency. It is for these reasons that good organizations—commercial, governmental, military, academic, and others—will be observed to devote great attention and sometimes great expense of money to the noneconomic inducements, because they are indispensable to fundamental efficiency, as well as to effectiveness in many cases.

The theory of organization set forth in this chapter is derived from the study of organizations which are exceedingly complex, although it is stated in terms of ideal simple organizations. The temptation is to assume that, in the more complex organizations which we meet in our actual social life, the effect of complexity is to modify or qualify the theory. This appears not to be the case. Organization, simple or complex, is always *an impersonal system of coordinated human efforts;* always there is purpose as the coordinating and unifying principle; always there is the indispensable ability to communicate, always the necessity for personal willingness, and for effectiveness and efficiency in maintaining the integrity of purpose and the continuity of contributions. Complexity appears to modify the quality and form of these elements and of the balance between them; but fundamentally the same principles that govern simple organizations may be conceived as governing the structure of complex organizations, which are composite systems.

•   •   •

The Theory of Authority

The necessity of the assent of the individual to establish authority *for him* is inescapable. A person can and will accept a communication as authoritative only when four conditions simultaneously obtain: (*a*) he can and does understand the communication; (*b*) *at the time of his decision* he believes that it is not inconsistent with the purpose of the organization; (*c*) *at the time of his decision,* he believes it to be compatible with his personal interest as a whole; and (*d*) he is able mentally and physically to comply with it.

a)   A communication that cannot be understood *can* have no authority. An order issued, for example, in a language not intelligible to the recipient is no order at all—no one would so regard it. Now, many orders are exceedingly difficult to understand. They are often necessarily stated in general terms, and the persons who issued them could not themselves apply them under many conditions. Until interpreted they have no meaning. The recipient either must disregard them or merely do anything in the hope that that is compliance.

Hence, a considerable part of administrative work consists in the interpretation and reinterpretation of orders in their application to concrete circumstances that were not or could not be taken into account initially.

b)   A communication believed by the recipient to be incompatible with the purpose of the organization, as he understands it, could not be accepted. Action would be frustrated by cross purpose. The most common practical example is that involved in conflicts of orders. They are not rare. An intelligent person will deny the authority of that one which contradicts the purpose of the effort as *he* understands it. In extreme cases many individuals would be virtually paralyzed by conflicting orders. They would be literally unable to comply—for example, an employee of a water system ordered to blow up an essential pump, or soldiers ordered to shoot their own comrades. I suppose all experienced executives know that when it is necessary to issue orders that will appear to the recipients to be contrary to the main purpose, especially as exemplified in prior habitual practice, it is usually necessary and always advisable, if practicable, to explain or demonstrate why the appearance of conflict is an illusion. Otherwise the orders are likely not to be executed, or to be executed inadequately.

c) If a communication is believed to involve a burden that destroys the net advantage of connection with the organization, there no longer would remain a net inducement to the individual to contribute to it. The existence of a net inducement is the only reason for accepting *any* order as having authority. Hence, if such an order is received it must be disobeyed (evaded in the more usual cases) as utterly inconsistent with personal motives that are the basis of accepting any orders at all. Cases of voluntary resignation from all sorts of organizations are common for this sole reason. Malingering and intentional lack of dependability are the more usual methods.

d) If a person is unable to comply with an order, obviously it must be disobeyed, or, better, disregarded. To order a man who cannot swim to swim a river is a sufficient case. Such extreme cases are not frequent; but they occur. The more usual case is to order a man to do things only a little beyond his capacity; but a little impossible is still impossible.

Naturally the reader will ask: How is it possible to secure such important and enduring cooperation as we observe if in principle and in fact the determination of authority lies with the subordinate individual? It is possible because the decisions of individuals occur under the following conditions: (*a*) orders that are deliberately issued in enduring organizations usually comply with the four conditions mentioned above; (*b*) there exists a "zone of indifference" in each individual within which orders are acceptable without conscious questioning of their authority; (*c*) the interests of the persons who contribute to an organization as a group result in the exercise of an influence on the subject, or on the attitude of the individual, that maintains a certain stability of this zone of indifference.

a) There is no principle of executive conduct better established in good organizations than that orders will not be issued that cannot or will not be obeyed. Executives and most persons of experience who have thought about it know that to do so destroys authority, discipline, and morale.[3] For reasons to be stated shortly, this principle cannot ordinarily

3. Barring relatively few individual cases, when the attitude of the individual indicates in advance likelihood of disobedience (either before or after connection with the organization), the connection is terminated or refused before the formal question arises.

It seems advisable to add a caution here against interpreting the exposition in terms of "democracy," whether in governmental, religious, or industrial organizations. The dogmatic assertion that "democracy" or "democratic methods" are (or are not) in accordance with the principles here discussed is not tenable. As will be more evident after the consideration of objective authority, the issues involved are much too complex and subtle to be taken into account in *any* formal scheme. Under many conditions in the political, religious, and industrial fields democratic processes create artificial questions of more or less logical character, in place of the real questions, which are matters of feeling and appropriateness and of informal organization. By oversimplification of issues this may destroy objective authority. No doubt in many situations formal democratic processes may be an important element in the maintenance of authority, i.e., of organization cohesion, but may in

be formally admitted, or at least cannot be professed. When it appears necessary to issue orders which are initially or apparently unacceptable, either careful preliminary education, or persuasive efforts, or the prior offering of effective inducements will be made, so that the issue will not be raised, the denial of authority will not occur, and orders will be obeyed. It is generally recognized that those who least understand this fact—newly appointed minor or "first line" executives—are often guilty of "disorganizing" their groups for this reason, as do experienced executives who lose self-control or become unbalanced by a delusion of power or for some other reason. Inexperienced persons take literally the current notions of authority and are then said "not to know how to use authority" or "to abuse authority." Their superiors often profess the same beliefs about authority in the abstract, but their successful practice is easily observed to be inconsistent with their professions.

b) The phrase "zone of indifference" may be explained as follows: If all the orders for actions reasonably practicable be arranged in the order of their acceptability to the person affected, it may be conceived that there are a number which are clearly unacceptable, that is, which certainly will not be obeyed; there is another group somewhat more or less on the neutral line, that is, either barely acceptable or barely unacceptable; and a third group unquestionably acceptable. This last group lies within the "zone of indifference." The person affected will accept orders lying within this zone and is relatively indifferent as to what the order is so far as the question of authority is concerned. Such an order lies within the range that in a general way was anticipated at time of undertaking the connection with the organization. For example, if a soldier enlists, whether voluntarily or not, in an army in which the men are ordinarily moved about within a certain broad region, it is a matter of indifference whether the order be to go to A or B, C or D, and so on; and goings to A, B, C, D, etc., are in the zone of indifference.

The zone of indifference will be wider or narrower depending upon the degree to which the inducements exceed the burdens and sacrifices

---

other situations be disruptive, and probably never could be, in themselves, sufficient. On the other hand the solidarity of some cooperative systems (General Harbord's army, for example) under many conditions may be unexcelled, though requiring formally autocratic processes.

Moreover, it should never be forgotten that authority in the aggregate arises from *all* the contributors to a cooperative system, and that the weighting to be attributed to the attitude of individuals varies. It is often forgotten that in industrial (or political) organizations measures which are acceptable at the bottom may be quite unacceptable to the substantial proportion of contributors who are executives, and who will no more perform their essential functions than will others, if the conditions are, to them, impossible. The point to be emphasized is that the maintenance of the contributions necessary to the endurance of an organization requires the authority of *all* essential contributors.

which determine the individual's adhesion to the organization. It follows that the range of orders that will be accepted will be very limited among those who are barely induced to contribute to the system.

c) Since the efficiency of organization is affected by the degree to which individuals assent to orders, denying the authority of an organization communication is a threat to the interests of all individuals who derive a net advantage from their connection with the organization, unless the orders are unacceptable to them also. Accordingly, at any given time there is among most of the contributors an active personal interest in the maintenance of the authority of all orders which to them are within the zone of indifference. The maintenance of this interest is largely a function of informal organization. Its expression goes under the names of "public opinion," "organization opinion," "feeling in the ranks," "group attitude," etc. Thus the common sense of the community informally arrived at affects the attitude of individuals, and makes them, as individuals, loath to question authority that is within or near the zone of indifference. The formal statement of this common sense is the fiction that authority comes down from above, from the general to the particular. This fiction merely establishes a presumption among individuals in favor of the acceptability of orders from superiors, enabling them to avoid making issues of such orders without incurring a sense of personal subserviency or a loss of personal or individual status with their fellows.

Thus the contributors are willing to maintain the authority of communications because, where care is taken to see that only acceptable communications in general are issued, most of them fall within the zone of personal indifference; and because communal sense influences the motives of most contributors most of the time. The practical instrument of this sense is the fiction of superior authority, which makes it possible normally to treat a personal question impersonally.

The fiction[4] of superior authority is necessary for two main reasons:

1. It is the process by which the individual delegates upward, or to the organization, responsibility for what is an organization decision—an action which is depersonalized by the fact of its coordinate character. This means that if an instruction is disregarded, an executive's risk of being wrong must be accepted, a risk that the individual cannot and usually will not take unless in fact his position is at least as good as that of another with respect to correct appraisal of the relevant situation. Most persons are disposed to grant authority because they dislike the personal responsibility which they otherwise accept, especially when they are not in a good position to accept it. The practical difficulties in the operation of organization seldom lie in the excessive desire of individuals to assume responsibility

4. The word "fiction" is used because from the standpoint of logical construction it merely explains overt acts. Either as a superior officer or as a subordinate, however, I know nothing that I actually regard as more "real" than "authority."

for the organization action of themselves or others, but rather lie in the reluctance to take responsibility for their own actions in organization.

2. The fiction gives impersonal notice that what is at stake is the good of the organization. If objective authority is flouted for arbitrary or merely temperamental reasons, if, in other words, there is deliberate attempt to twist an organization requirement to personal advantage, rather than properly to safeguard a substantial personal interest, then there is a deliberate attack on the organization itself. To remain outside an organization is not necessarily to be more than not friendly or not interested. To fail in an obligation intentionally is an act of hostility. This no organization can permit; and it must respond with punitive action if it can, even to the point of incarcerating or executing the culprit. This is rather generally the case where a person has agreed in advance in general what he will do. Leaving an organization in the lurch is not often tolerable.

Social Systems

Talcott Parsons

For the purposes of this article the term "organization" will be used to refer to a broad type of collectivity which has assumed a particularly important place in modern industrial societies—the type to which the term "bureaucracy" is most often applied. Familiar examples are the governmental bureau or department, the business firm (especially above a certain size), the university, and the hospital. It is by now almost a commonplace that there are features common to all these types of organization which cut across the ordinary distinctions between the social science disciplines. Something is lost if study of the firm is left only to economists, of governmental organizations to political scientists, and of schools and universities to "educationists."

The study of organization in the present sense is thus only part of the study of social structure as that term is generally used by sociologists (or of "social organization" as ordinarily used by social anthropologists). A family is only partly an organization; most other kinship groups are even less so. The same is certainly true of local communities, regional subsocieties, and of a society as a whole conceived, for example, as a nation. On other levels, informal work groups, cliques of friends, and so on, are not in this technical sense organizations.

The Concept of Organization

As a formal analytical point of reference, *primacy of orientation to the attainment of a specific goal* is used as the defining characteristic of an organization which distinguishes it from other types of social systems. This criterion has implications for both the external relations and the internal structure of the system referred to here as an organization.

The attainment of a goal is defined as a *relation* between a system

SOURCE: *Structure and Process in Modern Societies,* Chapter 1, "A Sociological Approach to the Theory of Organizations," pp. 16–19, 22–28, 41–47, 56–58. Copyright © 1960 by The Free Press of Glencoe. Reprinted with permission of Macmillan Publishing Co., Inc.

(in this case a social system) and the relevant parts of the external situation in which it acts or operates. This relation can be conceived as the maximization, relative to the relevant conditions such as costs and obstacles, of some category of *output* of the system to objects or systems in the external situation. These considerations yield a further important criterion of an organization. An organization is a system which, as the attainment of its goal, "produces" an identifiable something which can be utilized in some way by another system; that is, the output of the organization is, for some other system, an input. In the case of an organization with economic primacy, this output may be a class of goods or services which are either consumable or serve as instruments for a further phase of the production process by other organizations. In the case of a government agency the output may be a class of regulatory decisions; in that of an educational organization it may be a certain type of "trained capacity" on the part of the students who have been subjected to its influence. In any of these cases there must be a set of consequences of the processes which go on within the organization, which make a difference to the functioning of some other subsystem of the society; that is, without the production of certain goods the consuming unit must behave differently, i.e., suffer a "deprivation."

The availability, to the unit succeeding the organization in the series, of the organization's output must be subject to some sort of terms, the settlement of which is analyzable in the general framework of the ideas of contract or exchange. Thus in the familiar case the economic producer "sells" his product for a money prize which in turn serves as a medium for procuring the factors of production, most directly labor services, necessary for further stages of the productive process. It is thus assumed that in the case of all organizations there is something analogous to a "market" for the output which constitutes the attainment of its goal (what Chester I. Barnard calls "organization purpose"); and that directly, and perhaps also indirectly, there is some kind of exchange of this for entities which (as inputs into it) are important means for the organization to carry out its function in the larger system. The exchange of output for input at the boundary defined by the attainment of the goal of an organization need not be the only important boundary-exchange of the organization as a system. It is, however, the one most directly involved in defining the primary characteristics of the organization. Others will be discussed later.

The existence of organizations as the concept is here set forth is a consequence of the division of labor in society. Where both the "production" of specialized outputs and their consumption or ultimate utilization occur within the same structural unit, there is no need for the differentiation of specialized organizations. Primitive societies, in so far as their units are "self-sufficient" in both economic and other senses, generally do not have clear-cut differentiated organizations in the present sense.

In its internal reference, the primacy of goal-attainment among the functions of a social system gives priority to those processes most directly involved with the success or failure of goal-oriented endeavors. This means essentially the decision-making process, which controls the utilization of the resources of the system as a whole in the interest of the goal, and the processes by which those responsible for such decisions can count on the mobilization of these resources in the interest of a goal. These mechanisms of mobilization constitute what we ordinarily think of as the development of power in a political sense.

What from the point of view of the organization in question is its specified goal is, from the point of view of the larger system of which it is a differentiated part or subsystem, a specialized or differentiated function. This relationship is the primary link between an organization and the larger system of which it is a part, and provides a basis for the classification of types of organization. However, it cannot be the only important link.

This article will attempt to analyze both this link and the other principal ones, using as a point of departure the treatment of the organization as a social system. First, it will be treated as a system which is characterized by all the properties which are essential to any social system. Secondly, it will be treated as a functionally differentiated subsystem of a larger social system. Hence it will be the other subsystems of the larger one which constitute the situation or environment in which the organization operates. An organization, then, will have to be analyzed as the special type of social system organized about the primacy of interest in the attainment of a particular type of system goal. Certain of its special features will derive from goal-primacy in general and others from the primacy of the particular type of goal. Finally, the characteristics of the organization will be defined by the kind of situation in which it has to operate, which will consist of the relations obtaining between it and the other specialized subsystems of the larger system of which it is a part. The latter can for most purposes be assumed to be a society.

• • •

The Mobilization of Fluid Resources

The resources which an organization must utilize are, given the social structure of the situation in which it functions, the factors of production as these concepts are used in economic theory. They are land, labor, capital, and "organization" in a somewhat different sense from that used mainly in this paper. This possibly confusing terminological duplication is retained here because organization as a factor is commonly referred to in economic theory.

The factor of land stands on a somewhat different level from the other three. If we treat an organization, for purposes of analysis, as an already established and going concern, then, like any other social system, we can think of it as being in control of certain facilities for access to which it is not dependent on the maintenance of short-run economic sanctions. It has full ownership of certain physical facilities such as physical land and relatively nondepreciating or nonobsolescing building. It may have certain traditions, particularly involving technical know-how factors which are not directly involved in the market nexus. The more fully the market nexus is developed, however, the less can it be said that an organization has very important assets which are withdrawn from the market. Even sites of long operation can be sold and new locations found and even the most deeply committed personnel may resign to take other positions or retire, and in either case have to be placed through the labor market. The core of this aspect of the "land" complex is thus a set of commitments of resources on value grounds.

The two most fluid factors, however, are labor and capital in the economic sense. The overwhelming bulk of personal service takes place in occupational roles. This means that it is *contracted for* on some sector of the labor market. It is not based on ascription of status, through kinship or otherwise, but depends on the specific terms settled between the management of the organization and the incumbent. There are, of course, many types of contract of employment. Some variations concern the agents involved in the settlement of terms; for example, collective bargaining is very different from individual bargaining. Others concern the duration of commitment, varying all the way from a casual relation terminable at will, to a tenure appointment.

But most important, only in a limiting case are the specific *ad hoc* terms—balancing specifically defined services against specific monetary remuneration—anything like exhaustive of the empirically important factors involved in the contract of employment. The labor market cannot, in the economic sense, closely approach being a "perfect market." It has different degrees and types of imperfection according to whether the employer is one or another type of organization and according to what type of human service is involved. A few of these differences will be noted in later illustrations. Here the essential point is that, with the differentiation of functionally specified organizations from the matrix of diffuse social groupings, such organizations become increasingly dependent on explicit contracts of employment for their human services.

Attention may be called to one particularly important differentiation among types of relation existing between the performer of services and recipients of the ultimate "product." In the typical case of manufacturing industry the typical worker works within the organization. The end result is a physical commodity which is then sold to consumers. The worker has no personal contact with the customer of the firm; indeed no representative of the firm need have such contact except to arrange the settlement of the terms of sale. Where, however, the "product" is a personal service, the situation is quite different; the worker must have personal contact with the consumer during the actual performance of the service.

One way in which service can be organized is the case where neither performer nor "customer" belongs to an organization. Private professional practice is a type case, and doctor and patient, for example, come to constitute a small-scale solidary collectivity of their own. This is the main basis of the sliding scale as a pattern of remuneration. A second mode of organization is the one which assimilates the provision of service to the normal pattern involved in the production of physical commodities; the recipient is a "customer" who pays on a value-of-service basis, with prices determined by commercial competition. This pattern is approached in the case of such services as barbering.

But particularly in the case of professional services there is another very important pattern, where the recipient of the service becomes an operative member of the service-providing organization. The school, university, and hospital are type cases illustrating this pattern. The phrase "member of the university" definitely includes students. The faculty are in a sense dually employed, on the one hand by their students, on the other by the university administration. The transition is particularly clear in the case of the hospital. In private practice the patient is unequivocally the "employer." But in hospital practice the hospital organization employs a professional staff on behalf of the patients, as it were. This taking of the customer *into* the organization has important implication for the nature of the organization.

In a society like ours the requirements of an organization for fluid resources are in one sense and on one level overwhelmingly met through financing, i.e., through the provision of money funds at the disposal of the organization (cf. Weber, *Theory of Social and Economic Organization* [1947], ch. iii). This applies both to physical facilities, equipment, materials, buildings, and to the employment of human services—indeed also to cultural resources in that the rights to use patented processes may be bought. Hence the availability of adequate financing is always a vital problem for every organization operating in a monetary economy no matter what its goal-type may be; it is as vital for churches, symphony orchestras, and universities as it is for business firms.

The mechanisms through which financial resources are made available differ enormously, however, with different types of organization. All except the "purest" charitable organizations depend to some extent on the returns they receive for purveying some kind of a product, be it a commodity, or a service like education or music. But even within this range there is an enormous variation in the adequacy of this return for fully meeting financial needs. The business firm is at one pole in this respect. Its normal expectation is that in the long run it will be able to finance itself adequately from the proceeds of sales. But even here this is true only in the long run; investment of capital in anticipation of future proceeds is of course one of the most important mechanisms in our society.

Two other important mechanisms are taxation and voluntary contributions. In a "free enterprise" economy the general principle governing financing by taxation is that organizations will be supported out of taxation (1) if the goal is regarded as important enough but organizations devoted to it cannot be made to "pay" as private enterprises by providing the service on a commercial basis, e.g., the care of large numbers of persons from the lower income groups who (by current standards) need to be hospitalized for mental illnesses, or (2) if the *ways* in which the services would be provided by private enterprise might jeopardize the public interest, e.g., the provision of military force for the national defense might conceivably be contracted out, but placing control of force to this degree in private hands would constitute too serious a threat to the political stability of the society. Others in these categories are left to the "voluntary" principle, if they are publicly sanctioned, generally in the form of "nonprofit" organizations.

It is important to note that financing of organizations is in general "affected with a public interest" and is in some degree to be regarded as an exercise of political power. This consideration derives from the character of an organization as a goal-directed social system. Every subgoal within the society must to some degree be integrated with the goal-structure of the society as a whole, and it is with this societal goal-structure that political institutions are above all concerned.[1]

The Concept of Organization

The last of the four factors of production is what certain economists, notably Alfred Marshall, have called "organization" in the technical sense referred to above. This refers to the function of *combining* the factors of production in such ways as to facilitate the effective attainment of the organization's goal (in our general sense, in its "economic" or factor-consuming aspects). Its input into the organization stands on a level

1. This general thesis of the relation between financing and political power and the public interest has been developed by Parsons and Smelser, *Economy and Society* (1956), especially in chapters ii and iii.

different from that of labor services and financing since it does not concern the direct facilities for carrying out defined functions in a relatively routine manner, but instead concerns readjustment in the patterns of organization itself. It is, therefore, primarily significant in the longer run perspective, and it is involved in processes of structural change in the organization. In its business reference it is in part what J. A. Schumpeter (cf. *The Theory of Economic Development* [1934]) referred to as "entrepreneurship." Organization in this economic sense is, however, an essential factor in *all* organizational functioning. It necessarily plays a central part in the "founding" stages of any organization. From time to time it is important in later stages, since the kinds of adjustments to changing situations which are possible through the routine mechanisms of recruitment of labor services, and through the various devices for securing adequate financial resources, prove to be inadequate; hence a more fundamental structural change in the organization becomes necessary or desirable. This change would, in the present frame of reference, require a special input of the factor of organization in this technical sense.

The more generalized equivalent of the land factor is treated, except for the longest-run and most profound social changes, as the most constant reference point of all; its essential reference base is the stability of the value system in terms of which the goal of the organization is defined and the commitments involved in it are legitimized. It is from this reference base that the norms defining the broadly expected types of mechanism in the other respects will be derived, particularly those most actively involved in short-run operations, namely the recruitment of human services through the labor market and the financing of the organization.

•   •   •

The Problem of Power

As seen in the analysis in the first section of this paper, the development of organizations is the principal mechanism by which, in a highly differentiated society, it is possible to "get things done," to achieve goals beyond the reach of the individual and under conditions which provide a relative maximization of effectiveness, in Chester Barnard's sense. Subject to the over-all control of an institutionalized value system in the society and its subsystems, the central phenomenon of organization is the mobilization of *power* for the attainment of the goals of the organization. The value system *legitimizes* the organization's goal, but it is only through power that its achievement can be made effective.

Seen in these terms, power is the generalized capacity to mobilize resources in the interest of attainment of a system goal. The generation and utilization of power constitutes one of the fundamental functional imperatives of any social system. Like any other major system function, except in the simplest systems, power becomes the focus of a set of specialized mechanisms. So far as these mechanisms themselves become organized to constitute a distinct subsystem of the society, we can speak of the "polity" as the system oriented to the generation and allocation of power.[2] The polity in this sense is parallel to the economy as that concept is ordinarily used in economic theory.

The generation and exercise of power is most conspicuous in relation to a goal which is dramatically and unequivocally a common goal for a whole society, such as victory in war. But in more everyday terms, the goal of the society can be said to be to "get the things done" which are approved in terms of its values as "worth doing" (the term "worth" may of course, signify varying degrees of urgency). Hence we may speak of power as a generalized societal resource which is allocated to the attainment of a wide range of subgoals and to organizations as the agents of the attainment of such subgoals. Power is comparable to wealth, which, as a generalized societal resource, is allocated to many different societal subsystems for "consumption" or for "capital" use.

The power exercised in and by an organization is generated both outside and within the organization. Every organization, whatever the nature of its functional primacy—for example, manufacturing, or medical care—is part of the polity and a generator of power, but is also a recipient of the power generated at higher echelons in the polity.

The generation of power on any given level depends, as we see it, on four fundamental conditions. The first condition is the institutionalization of a value system which legitimizes both the goal of the organization and the principal patterns by which it functions in the attainment of that goal. The second condition is the regulation of the organization's procurement and decision-making processes through adherence to universalistic rules and to such institutions as authority and contract. It is on these bases that the organization establishes generalized claims to the loyal cooperation of its personnel and of persons outside the organization on whose cooperation it depends. The third condition is the command of the more detailed and day-to-day support of the persons whose cooperation is needed. The fourth is the command of necessary facilities, of which the primary category in our society is financial.

In our society the first condition has frequently become formalized through the privilege and practice of incorporation. This establishes a

---

2. The polity in this sense is *not* identical with government, which we interpret to be a complex of *organizations*. Government has other than political functions, and other organizations participate in the polity. We conceive of the relation of polity and government as approximately parallel to that between economy and business. Cf. Talcott Parsons and Neil Smelser, *Economy and Society* (*op. cit.*) ch. ii.

direct positive link with government and the legal system. Organization for the purpose at hand is formally "authorized," and certain powers and privileges are thereby conferred. The second condition is partly met by the legal regulation of all organizational activity, and partly by an informal reputation for integrity and "good practice" which in itself often becomes an organizational asset. The third and fourth conditions are met by the operative mechanisms of procurement of resources and the operative code previously described. Certain variations in the mechanisms by which this occurs in different types of organizations will be discussed presently.

The mobilization and utilization of power is the central focus of the operation of organizations, but by virtue of the fact that an organization is a social system, it is also dependent on all the other exigencies of such a system. The value component has already been discussed. The other two components are economic resources (centering on the problem of financing) and the command of loyalties (which underlies efficiency in Barnard's sense). Power helps to *command* these essentials, but their availability is not a function only of power but also of the ways in which the cognate activities of the organization mesh with the relevant features of the situation in which it functions. Thus the organization always to some extent "produces" economically valuable goods or services; the marketability of these products constitutes one central set of conditions of its operation. Similarly, the organization is always, through "informal" organization and otherwise, a focus of the relatively noncontingent loyalties of its personnel. The extent to which this is true and the basis on which it rests form another essential condition of the organization's functioning. Power as a factor operates to exploit advantages on these levels and to make up deficits; power never operates alone.

The scheme we have presented is characterized by a certain formal symmetry. The value system of the organization is treated as defining and legitimizing its goal. Each of the other three aspects, the adaptive mechanisms and those mechanisms of operative goal-attainment and the integration of the organization, is regulated by subvalues governing each of these three aspects of organizational functioning. Each primary type of resource input is regulated by a type of contractual pattern, e.g., employment and investment. Each part of the operative code is governed in turn by an aspect of authority, and finally each context of institutionalization is a way of defining, for those participating, the extent of "loyalty" owing to the organization as compared with other commitments.

Classification of Types of Organization

Organizations are of course always part of a larger social structure of the society in which they occur. There is necessarily a certain variability among organizations which is a function of this wider societal matrix; an American organization is never quite like a British one even though they are nearly cognate in function. Discounting this type of variability, however, organizations may in the first instance be classified in terms of the *type of goal or function* about which they are organized. The same basic classification can be used for goal types which has been used earlier in dealing with the functions of a social system. Thus we may speak of adaptive goals, implementive goals, integrative goals, and pattern-maintenance goals. The reference is always to function in the *society* as a system.

Seen in these terms the principal broad types of organization are:

1. *Organizations oriented to economic production.* The type case in this category is the business firm. Production should be understood in the full economic sense as "adding value"; it is by no means confined to physical production, e.g., manufacturing. It has been emphasized several times that every organization contributes in some way to every primary function (if it is well integrated in the society); hence we can speak only of economic *primacy,* never of an organization as being exclusively economic. This applies also to the other categories.

2. *Organizations oriented to political goals*, that is, to the attainment of valued goals and to the generation and allocation of power in the society: This category includes most organs of government, but in a society like ours, various other organizations are involved. The allocation of purchasing power through credit creation is an exercise of power in this sense; hence a good part of the banking system should be treated as residing in primarily political organizations. More generally, it seems legitimate to speak of incorporation as an allocation of power in a political sense; hence the corporate aspect of formal organizations generally is a political aspect.

3. *Integrative organizations.* These are organizations which on the societal level, contribute primarily to efficiency, not effectiveness. They concern the adjustment of conflicts and the direction of motivation to the fulfillment of institutionalized expectations. A substantial part of the functions of the courts and of the legal profession should be classed here. Political parties, whose function is the mobilization of support for those responsible for government operations, belong in this category, and, to a certain extent, "interest groups" belong here, too. Finally, those organizations that are primarily mechanisms of social control in the narrower sense, for example hospitals, are mainly integrative.

4. *Pattern-maintenance organizations.* The principal cases centering here are those with primarily "cultural," "educational," and "expressive" functions. Perhaps the most clearcut organizational examples are churches and schools. (Pattern maintenance is not here conceived to preclude creativity; hence research is included.) The arts so far as they

give rise to organization also belong here. Kinship groups are ordinarily not primarily organizations in our technical sense, but in a society so highly differentiated as our own the nuclear family approaches more closely the characteristics of an organization than in other societies. As such it clearly belongs in the pattern-maintenance category.

This primary basis of classification can be used as the point of departure for a more detailed one, by further subdividing each of the primary types into lower other subsystems. Thus in the economic case the main basis of subclassification would include specialization in adaptive functions for the economy (financing), in goal attainment (production and marketing in a narrower sense), etc. Similar considerations will apply in the cases of the other primary types. In each of these cases a primary determinant of the type of organization is the kind of boundary interchange operating between the societal system in which the organization is primarily anchored and the contiguous subsystem. Thus from the point of view of the economy, production and marketing are the sources of the ultimate production of goods and services to the consumer and of the input of labor services into the economy. Both consumer and worker are anchored in the first instance in the household as part of the pattern-maintenance system. Organizations oriented primarily to consumption interests are necessarily different from those oriented primarily to the financing of capital expansion.

• • •

Conclusion

The principal aim of this paper has been to relate the analysis of "formal organizations" more closely than is customary to some categorizations available in general sociological theory. There is a tendency in our society to consider different types of organizations as belonging in the fields allocated to different academic disciplines; thus students of business organization are likely to be economists, those of governmental and military organization, political scientists, and so forth. This tendency to divide the field obscures both the importance of the common elements, and the *systematic* bases of the variations from one type to another.

The procedure of this paper has been first to attempt to define an organization by locating it systematically in the structure of the society in relation to other categories of social structure. It seemed appropriate to define an organization as a social system which is organized for the attainment of a particular type of goal; the attainment of that goal is at the same time the performance of a type of function on behalf of a more inclusive system, the society.

It proved possible to bring to bear a general classification of the functional imperatives of social systems and with this to identify the principal mechanisms necessary to bring about the attainment of the goal or the organization purpose. The classification used has proved its applicability both for the level of the total society and for that of the small group. The present application to an intermediate level further increases confidence in its generality.

The classification distinguishes four main categories: the value system which defines and legitimizes the goals of the organization, the adaptive mechanisms which concern mobilization of resources, the operative code concerned with the mechanisms of the direct process of goal implementation, and finally the integrative mechanisms. These four categories are specifications of categories which, as noted, have been used in a variety of other contexts for the analysis of structural differentiation and phases of process over time in social systems.

These categories were first used to analyze the main components in the structure of an organization—its value system defining the societal commitments on which its functioning depends; its mechanisms of procurement of resources; its operative mechanisms centering about decision making in the field of policy, allocation, and integration; and its institutional patterns which link the structure of the organization with the structure of the society as a whole. It has proved possible to spell out these considerations in ways which link directly with the well-known ways of dealing with the problems of organization in the relevant literature.

The same basic classification of the functional problems of social systems was used to establish points of reference for a classification of types of organization, and the broadest outline of a proposed classification was sketched. The capacity of the conceptual scheme to account for variations in the important features of organizations was then tested in a preliminary, illustrative way by a rapid survey of some of the principal features of business, military, and academic organizations.

In the nature of the case this essay has been subject to severe limitations. Such limitations are partly involved in the space available. More important, however, is the fact that the essay constitutes a preliminary attempt to approach this range of problems systematically in terms of this order of general theoretical analysis. The results seem to justify the hope that carrying such analysis further will help to codify our knowledge of organizations more systematically than has been the case before, and to link it more closely with knowledge of other types of social systems and of the social environment within which formal organizations must operate in a society like our own.

The Comparative Study of Organizations

Peter M. Blau

The comparative method, in the broadest sense of the term, underlies all scientific and scholarly theorizing. If we mean by theory a set of generalizations that explains courses of events or situations on the basis of the conditions and processes that produce them, every theory must rest on comparisons of contrasting cases; for to explain a state of affairs requires that the difference between it and some other state of affairs be accounted for—why democratic institutions developed in some countries but not in others, or what political processes distinguish democracies with multiparty systems from those with two-party systems. Usually, however, the term "comparative method" is used in a much narrower sense, though by no means a consistent one. Spencer and Durkheim, for example, referred by it to virtually opposite methodological principles. The former's comparative method involves collecting descriptions of the same institution in many different societies to demonstrate "laws" of social evolution,[1] whereas Durkheim, who rejected this procedure of the evolutionists, employed the same term to refer to the establishment of concomitant variations or correlations between two social phenomena.[2]

Although every analysis of organizations entails some explicit or implicit comparisons, the comparative method in the study of organizations is defined here more narrowly as the systematic comparison of a fairly large number of organizations in order to establish relationships between their characteristics. In short, the term is used here to refer to quantitative comparisons that make it possible to determine relationships between

SOURCE: *Industrial and Labor Relations Review* 18, no. 3 (April 1965): 323–38. Copyright © 1965 by Cornell University. All rights reserved. Reprinted by permission of the author and the publisher.

1. See the discussion of Spencer's comparative method in Howard Becker and Harry E. Barnes, *Social Thought from Lore to Science*, 2nd ed., vol. 1 (Washington: Harren Press, 1952), pp. 748–49.
2. Emile Durkheim, *The Rules of Sociological Method* (Chicago: University of Chicago Press, 1930), pp. 125–40.

110

attributes of organizations, for example, what other differences are generally associated with variations in an organization's size, or the degree of its bureaucratization, or its functions. Lest this emphasis on quantitative research be misconstrued, let me hasten to add that it is not meant to imply a concern with mathematical models or advanced statistical techniques. These are not at all the focus of interest. The point made is rather that theoretical generalizations about organizations are necessarily rooted in comparisons of many that differ in relevant respects, regardless of how impressionistic the data on which the analysis is based. Since some quantitative comparisons are inherent in the method of constructing theories, such comparisons should be built into the research procedures from which the theories derive.

The distinctive nature of the comparative approach to the study of organizations, as defined, can be highlighted in juxtaposition with the case-study approach. Most empirical investigations in the field are case studies of single organizations. The rationale for this approach is that large modern organizations, which often contain many thousands of members, are too complex to permit studying more than one or two at a time. While this statement is obviously correct if the aim is to investigate the attributes and behavior of the individual members of organizations, it is highly questionable if the aim is to investigate the characteristics and operations of the organizations themselves. Many characteristics of organizations can be ascertained quite easily and without the time and effort required for a survey of a large part of the membership. In any case, to derive theoretical generalizations from the study of a single organization, either the conditions in this organization must be compared to those in others known from the literature, which means that most of the systematic information collected in the case study are ignored, or the analysis must center on internal comparisons of the various units within the organization.[3] The latter procedure tends to constrain the investigator to focus on principles about the structure of work groups and the behavior of individual members *within* organizations rather than on principles that govern the functioning and developing *of* organizations. As a result of these tendencies, empirical studies in the field of organizations have contributed more to our knowledge of human relations and group structures in the context of organizations than to the theory of organizations as distinct social systems. To be sure, the intensive analysis of internal processes possible in case studies can greatly enrich the theory of organization, but only as a complement to inquiries based on comparative studies.

An organization is a system for mobilizing and coordinating the efforts of various, typically specialized, groups in the pursuit of joint objectives. Although an organization could not exist without the individuals

3. On the method of internal comparison, see Seymour M. Lipset, *et al., Union Democracy* (New York: Free Press, 1956), pp. 425–27.

who compose its membership, it has characteristics that do not pertain to characteristics of its individual members, such as its size, to name only the most obvious example. The sociological theory of organizations, the economic theory of the firm, and the political theory of the state or government constitute important potential links for interdisciplinary cross-fertilization and comparative research, inasmuch as they deal with diverse kinds of organizations, the organized government in a society being a particular kind of organization, namely, the one with the largest scope.[4] But there is actually little cross-fertilization on this level, in part because the theory of organization is in such a rudimentary state.

The objectives of this article are to conceptualize various dimensions that can be distinguished in the analysis of organizational life, to outline the comparative approach to the study of organizations, and to indicate the theoretical significance of this approach.

Three Foci of Analysis

Three foci of analysis may be distinguished in organizational research, whether concern is with government agencies or industrial concerns, labor unions or political parties, armies or hospitals.[5] The focus of the analysis can be (1) the individual in his specific role as a member of the organization who occupies a certain position in it; (2) the structure of social relations among individuals in the various groups within the organization; or (3) the system of interrelated elements that characterizes the organization as a whole.

First, many studies carried out in organizations center attention on the attitudes and behavior of individual members insofar as they pertain to the functions of the organization. The application of survey techniques

4. This may well be at least as important a distinctive characteristic of the state as the usually emphasized monopoly over the use of force; see Max Weber, *The Theory of Social and Economic Organization* (New York: Oxford University Press, 1947), p. 156.
5. The conceptualization presented is a revision of one suggested in Blau, "Formal Organization," *American Journal of Sociology*, vol. 63, 1957, pp. 63–69. (Processes of development are not included as one of the three foci in the reconceptualized version because they belong to a different dimension which cuts across the three distinguished here, *not* because I consider them any less important.) A related schema of levels of analysis is presented in Stanley H. Udy, "The Comparative Analysis of Organizations," in James G. March, *Handbook of Organizations* (Chicago: Rand McNally, 1965), and a somewhat different schema is developed in W. Richard Scott, "Theory of Organizations," in Robert E. L. Faris, *Handbook of Sociology* (Chicago: Rand McNally, 1964). My ideas on this subject were clarified by the discussions of a work group in the Third Ford Seminar in the Social Science of Organizations, University of Pittsburgh, Summer 1964. The participants in this group were, in addition to Udy, Scott, and myself, Vaughn Blankenship, Tom Burns, Lyman W. Porter, and Stanton Wheeler, and I want to acknowledge the many stimulating ideas the discussion in this group provided for my reconceptualization.

to research in organizations invites this focus, especially if representative samples are used, because sampling surveys make individuals the independent units of analysis. This type of analysis is illustrated by investigations of the attitudes of soldiers in combat, of the career patterns of civil servants and their implications for commitment to the organization, of the influence of the background characteristics of the labor force on performance of tasks and turnover, or of the conditions that promote work satisfaction. Studies of voting exemplify the same type in respect to the political organization of the government. These studies deal with processes that occur in the context of organizations and often show how the context modifies these processes—for instance, how the composition of work groups affects conduct—but they are not studies of organizations and the principles that govern their character and development. *The American Soldier* examines sociopsychological processes, such as those manifesting relative deprivation, but it tells us little about the organization of the army,[6] *Voting* analyzes political processes, such as the crystallization of voting decisions under cross pressure, but it has little to say about the ways in which governments are organized;[7] and *Management and the Worker* deals with behavior in work groups but not the organization of the factory.[8]

A second type of analysis focuses upon the structures of social relations that emerge in the groups and segments in the organization. Since interest centers on networks of social relations and characteristics of group structures in this case, data are typically obtained from every member of selected subgroups rather than from a sample of individuals dispersed throughout the organization. Examples of this type are studies of the informal organization of work groups (*Management and the Worker* being a pioneering one), of union solidarity among factory workers, of consultation among officials, or of the differentiation of informal status that emerges in social interaction. Here concern is with the social processes that govern the development of group structures and the effects of these structures on patterns of conduct. The aim is to discover the principles that characterize group life, and the organizational context within which the work groups exist is considered as a set of limiting conditions for the emergence of group structure. The conditions in the larger organization, therefore, are treated as given rather than as problematical; that is, they are not made the subject of the inquiry that needs to be explained.

Third, the analysis may focus on the attributes of organizations themselves, the interrelations between these attributes, and the processes that produce them. In order to determine the relationships between various

6. Samuel A. Stouffer, *et al., The American Soldier,* 2 vols. (Princeton: Princeton University Press), 1949.
7. Bernard R. Berelson, *et al., Voting* (Chicago: University of Chicago Press, 1954).
8. F. J. Roethlisberger and William J. Dickson, *Management and the Worker* (Cambridge, Mass.: Harvard University Press, 1959).

characteristics of organizations, as an initial step in tracing the processes that give rise to them and explaining them, it is necessary to compare a large number of organizations which are similar in many respects but different in some. Studies on the connections between the size of organizations, their complexity, and the degree of bureaucratization within them illustrate this type, as do investigations of the impact of automation on the division of labor in factories, of the conditions that foster oligarchy in unions, of the implications of dispersed ownership for centralized control in corporations, or of the impact of the shape of the hierarchical pyramid on operations. The focus of interest now is the system of interrelated elements that characterize the organization as a whole, not its component parts. The aim is to discover the principles that govern the functioning system, although the processes and connections observed must often be inferred in the absence of detailed information on the internal structures and how they operate.

Implications

It is evident that the three foci lead to the analysis of quite different, though by no means unrelated, problems. The phenomena that are made the central subject of the inquiry in one kind of analysis are assumed to be given in the others. In the first case, the role attributes and performances of the individual members of organizations are investigated, and the context of the organization and even that of the work group are considered given conditions or stimuli that may affect the roles of individuals. In the second case, social relations and, particularly, the structures of social relations in groups are analyzed, and the characteristics of the individuals who compose these groups as well as the organizational context are treated as limiting conditions for the emergence of these social structures. In the third case, the combinations of attributes that characterize organizations as such and the development of these systems of organizing the efforts of various groups in joint endeavors are studied, and both the individual behavior and the group processes that underlie these systems are taken for granted.

The specific criterion for differentiating the three foci—role analysis, structural analysis, and organizational analysis—is whether the variables under consideration describe individuals, groups of interrelated individuals, or organized systems of interrelated groups. Thus, seniority, professional expertness, socioeconomic status, commitment to an organization, and political preference are attributes of individual human beings. But the strength of the cohesive bonds that unite group members and the extent of differentiation of status that emerges among them are variables that refer to groups as such and not to their individual members. Correspondingly, the division of labor among various groups, the degree of centralization of control in an organization, the age of the organization, and its size are characteristics of the organization as a whole that cannot be attributed either to its subgroups or to its individual members.

A complication arises, however, because the variables that *pertain* to a collectivity may be based on data *obtained* either by measuring a property of the collectivity itself or a property of all of its members. Lazarsfeld and Menzel have referred to the former as global properties, such as whether a factory is automated, uses assembly lines, or neither, and to the latter as analytical properties of collectivities, such as the proportion of older workers in a company.[9] The turnover rate in a factory, the average productivity of its labor force, and the proportion of its personnel in administrative positions are analytical properties that clearly refer to the organized collectivity but that are based on data derived from the behavior of individuals. For every analytical attribute that describes an organized collectivity there is a parallel attribute that distinguishes the members within it—the productivity of a worker, or whether an employee occupies an administrative position—but there are no such individual parallels for the global properties of collectivities—only factories can be distinguished by the degree of mechanization, not the individual workers within a factory. A simple illustration of this contrast is the difference between the age of a firm and the average age of its employees.

Focus on Organizational Attributes

The use of analytical properties—averages, proportions, or rates—as independent variables in organizational or structural analysis raises special problems. Let us assume that a comparative study of welfare agencies found that professionalization, that is, the proportion of caseworkers who have graduate training in social work, is associated with more extensive service to clients. Three interpretations of this finding are possible, depending on whether the focus is on roles, on group structures, or on the organization of the agencies. First, professionally trained individuals may provide more service to clients than untrained caseworkers. Second, the structure of work groups with a high proportion of professionals, perhaps by making informal status dependent on the way clients are treated, may encourage caseworkers, regardless of their own training, to extend more service to clients. Third, agencies with a high proportion of professionals on their staff may be better organized to serve clients, which would be reflected in improved service by individual caseworkers independent of these individuals' own training or the work groups to which they belong.

9. Paul F. Lazarsfeld and Herbert Menzel, "On the Relation between Individual and Collective Properties," in Amitai Etzioni, *Complex Organizations* (New York: Holt, Rinehart and Winston, 1961), pp. 426–35. The other two types of properties they distinguish can be considered special cases of the two noted in the text.

To determine which one of these three different interpretations is correct, or whether more than one or all three are, it is necessary to separate three distinct influences on treatment of clients, that of the individual's own training, that of the professional composition of his work group, and that of the professionalization of the agency in which he works. Statistical procedures for accomplishing this separation have been outlined elsewhere.[10]

It should be noted that the technical criterion by which organizational analysis is distinguished from the two other types is an analytical one that applies to all kinds of organized collectivities, not alone to formal organizations. Crosscultural comparisons or studies of the relationship between the stage of technological development and the stratification system in different societies involve organizational analysis in the technical sense, although they do not deal with formal organizations. To speak of a formal organization there must exist explicit procedures for organizing the subgroups in a collectivity to further some joint ends. On the basis of this definition, the political system in a society is a formal organization, while the stratification system is not, and neither is the economy, though a firm, of course, is one.

To advance the theory of formal organizations, a focus on organizational analysis is essential. This is not to say that role analysis and structural analysis of the members and work groups in organizations are unimportant, because they can supply evidence on the social processes that account for the systems that emerge in organizations, but this evidence can be used to explain organizational systems only in combination with comparative studies that focus on the relationships between various attributes of organizations themselves.

Social Processes in Organizations

The study of social processes is often contrasted with the study of social structures or that of the interrelations between factors in a system, but it is not always entirely clear what the specific distinguishing marks of the analysis of social processes are. One implication of the term is that processes occur over time and that their investigation, therefore, must be diachronic rather than synchronic. Whereas the synchronic study of the interrelations between attributes in a system takes the emergence of these attributes for granted, the diachronic study of social processes traces the sequence of events or occurrences that led to the development of these

10. Blau, "Structural Effects," *American Sociological Review,* vol. 25, 1960, pp. 178–93. The procedure there described for isolating the effects of social structure from those of role attributes can also be used to isolate the effects of organizational attributes from those of the other two.

attributes. An illustration of this difference would be an inquiry into the status structure in a group and the various characteristics associated with superior status, on the one hand, and an inquiry into the processes of differentiation that produced the status structure, on the other. Taking time into account, however, is only a necessary and not a sufficient condition for the analysis of social processes. Thus, panel studies that compare opinions or states of affairs at two points in time do not directly deal with social processes, although they make it easier to infer them than does research at a single point of time.

Analysis of Intervening Links

The analysis of social processes requires the specification of a series of intervening links between an earlier state and a system or structure that subsequently develops. Thus, the investigation of the process of socialization seeks to trace the many steps that link the behavior and attitudes of parents to the internalized values and personalities that their children ultimately develop. Similarly, the investigation of the process of bureaucratization seeks to trace the sequence of typical events stimulated by the large size and complexity of an organization and eventuating in a formalized system of procedures and hierarchical authority. In brief, the examination of social processes entails the specification of intervening variables that connect initial conditions with their effects in a time sequence.

External as well as internal social processes affect organizations. Research on processes that occur outside the framework of organizations must not make organizations the unit of analysis but must find another more appropriate one. Thus, the study of the processes that give rise to technological advancements and the chain of implications of technological innovations must compare different cultures and not merely different organizations in one society. To investigate the processes that govern career patterns, the occupational roles and career lines must be the focus of the analysis and the occupational experiences of individuals must be followed as they move into and out of various organizations. The student of organizations is not primarily concerned with these external processes but only with the results they produce, which constitute conditions that affect organizations, for instance, the limits set by the state of technological knowledge for organizational developments, or the influence career experiences have for the performance of organizational responsibilities.

The internal processes in organizations include the processes of social interaction among members that find expression in the emergent group structures and the processes through which the interrelated elements in the total system become organized. The analysis of processes of interaction may deal with the ways in which first impressions affect role expectations

117

and how these in turn affect the conduct of interacting persons, with the exchanges of rewards in the form of advice, help, approval, and respect that shape the relations among group members, and with the modifications in these exchange patterns produced by differences in the complexity of the task or in the style of supervision. The aim of the analysis is to explain the differentiated social structures that arise as the result of these processes of interaction among individuals. Whereas this anlysis exemplifies the structural focus, the organizational focus calls attention to such problems as the processes of increasing specialization, mechanization, professionalization, centralization, or bureaucratization, the conditions that give rise to these processes, and the interparlay between them. The aim here is to explain the systems of interrelated characteristics that evolve in various organizations. These are the processes that are of immediate concern to the student of organizations, because they constitute the intervening links that explain the connections between the inputs and outputs of the organizations, between the initial conditions and the system that develops.

Compass of Social Systems

Social systems are typically part of broader ones that encompass them and simultaneously constitute the environment of narrower systems they encompass. Work groups are the environment in which individuals act out their roles; the organization of the department is the context within which work groups develop their structure; the total organization sets limits to the ways in which departments can be organized; and the society, including the political order, other institutions, and the state of the technology, provides the social setting that conditions the character of the organizations in its boundaries. Whereas the larger system restricts the developments of those it encompasses, there are also feedback effects from the subsystems to the more encompassing ones, because subsystems are not infinitely pliable but tend to have a minimum of autonomy to which the encompassing system must adjust.[11] Thus, the occupational experiences and professional values of the members of an organization condition the performance of tasks, the informal structures of work groups modify the impact of the incentive system, and the professional requirements of the department of psychiatry set limits to the administrative requirements the hospital administration can impose on it.

Even in comparative studies only those characteristics of the units under consideration in respect to which the *differ* can be systematically investigated, whereas the characteristics all have in common must be allocated to the next higher level as part of the constant environment. If all

11. See Alvin W. Gouldner, "Reciprocity and Autonomy in Functional Theory," in Llewellyn Gross, *Symposium on Sociological Theory* (Evanston: Row, Peterson), pp. 254–66.

work groups under investigation consist of six workers under a supervisor, size cannot be treated as a variable in the analysis of group structure but the existence of work units of this size must be considered part of the organizational context that conditions the emerging group structures. Similarly, if computers are used in some organizations but not in others, the significance of this aspect of mechanization for other characteristics of the organization can be examined, but if secretaries in all the organizations studied use typewriters, it must be inferred that this aspect of mechanization is part of the technological state of the society that is invariably reflected in its organizations. Whether this inference is correct or not depends on the representativeness of the organizations included in the sample. Regardless of whether the inference about all organizations is warranted, however, the fact that a certain characteristic reveals no variation among all the organizations examined necessitates that it be treated as a given condition of organizational life in this particular research.

Whereas factors that cannot be explained within the framework of a specific investigation must be allocated to a more encompassing system, a full explanation of relationships between factors tends to involve references to a less encompassing system. A theoretical interpretation of an observed relationship between two variables, an antecedent and its effect, entails subsuming it under a general proposition that connects two abstract concepts of which the observed variables are specific manifestations and, in addition, specifying intervening variables that account for the connection.[12] Thus, Durkheim explained the relationship between religion and suicide rates by suggesting that an individualistic belief system, by lessening social integration, promotes an egoistic mentality, which affords weak protection against crises.[13]

To explain the correlation between an independent and a dependent variable, the intervening processes that account for the connection are specified, and to explain the principles that govern these processes, intervening processes on a more fundamental level are indicated. For example, the relationship between the composition of a group and the status structure that develops in it is explained by taking into account the processes of social interaction that lead to differentiation of status, and patterns of social interaction and exchange are explained in terms of the psychological processes that underlie them. An explanation of psychological principles, in turn, refers back to the underlying physiological processes, and these physiological processes can be further explicated in terms of chemical ones. Serious scientific explanations typically confine themselves to ad-

12. On the latter, see Patricia L. Kendall and Lazarsfeld, "Problems of Survey Analysis," in Robert K. Merton and Lazarsfeld, *Continuities in Social Research* (New York: Free Press, 1950), pp. 147–62.
13. Durkheim, *Suicide* (New York: Free Press, 1951), pp. 152–70.

jacent levels and do not skip across many. Physiological principles do not help to account for group structures and social processes, and nuclear physics does not aid in clarifying learning theory, though there are undoubtedly indirect connections.

Case Study and Comparative Approach

The aim of organizational analysis is to explain the systems of interrelated elements that characterize various kinds of organizations. For this purpose the interdependence between different attributes of organizations must be established—their size, complexity, specialization, authority structure, professionalization, bureaucratization, and so forth. To clarify this constellation of attributes requires an understanding of the social processes through which the different attributes develop and the connections between them evolve. Since the structures of social relations among the members of the organization affect the processes of its development, a knowledge of these structures further contributes to the understanding of the development of the organizational system. Research has shown, for instance, that the informal organization of work groups exerts important influences on performance, the exercise of authority, and the significance of the incentive system for operations, which indicates that the study of the relationships between these and other factors must take the impact of informal structures into account.

A major contribution of case studies on organizations has been that they have called attention to these informal structures and investigated them intensively. This intensive investigation involved the analysis of the social processes through which the informal structures emerged, such as the process of cooptation that modifies the leadership structure,[14] the sanctioning processes in which output becomes regulated,[15] or the process of exchange of advice that gives rise to status differentiation.[16] Comparative studies of organizations, however, need not repeat such intensive analysis of informal processes, since it suffices for them to take account of the results of these processes that find expression in group structures. Indeed, even the role of informal structures will probably have to be inferred rather than directly investigated in most comparative studies of organizations, for systematic organizational analysis—analogous to all systematic analysis—cannot possibly take all factors that indirectly

14. Philip Selznick, *TVA and the Grass Roots* (Berkeley: University of California Press, 1949), pp. 85–213.
15. Roethlisberger and Dickson, *op. cit.*, pp. 379–524.
16. Blau, *The Dynamics of Bureaucracy,* 2nd ed. (Chicago: University of Chicago Press, 1963), pp. 121–64.

influence organizational life into account but must treat some as given conditions while inquiring into the interrelations of the basic features of organizations.

Theoretical interpretations of the relationships between antecedent conditions and their consequences remain inevitably somewhat inferential, it would seem, not only because they subsume relations under propositions on a higher level of abstraction that cannot be directly confirmed in research, but also because they typically conceptualize the connecting process as a series of links too complex for direct empirical testing. The proposition that the antecedent A promotes the occurrence B can be empirically confirmed, provided that operational measures for the two factors exist, by showing that B is more prevalent under condition A than under non-A. If the analysis of social processes means the specification of the intervening variables that link A and B in a time sequence, multivariate analysis should make it possible to test whether the process occurs as specified by ascertaining the relationships between A, all intervening variables, and B. Although this is correct in principle, it is usually impossible to implement such a test in actual practice, because so many intervening links tend to be indicated in process analysis that it is virtually impossible to examine the interrelations between all of them simultaneously.[17] Computers facilitate the simultaneous analysis of many variables, but the capacities of the human mind still limit the number of interrelated concepts that can be simultaneously taken into account in a theory.[18] Although theoretical explanations couched in terms of complex social processes cannot be directly tested, precise specification of these processes makes it possible to predict what combinations of organizational features the processes produce under varying conditions, and these predictions serve as indirect tests for the theory.

Organizational Theory

A theory of organizations, whatever its specific nature, and regardless of how subtle the organizational processes it takes into account, has as its

17. The principle is the same as that of a game in its normal form, as I understand it. Although game theory does not deal with processes or sequential steps but with single choices between strategies, sequential steps can be taken into account in advance by translating all possible sequences into a game in its normal form and then treating it as one choice between all these possibilities. In actual fact, however, the number of alternatives for games with any degree of complexity is virtually infinite, which makes the formalistic solution of translating successive steps into a game in its normal form useless for practical purposes.
18. It is, of course, much easier to clarify many successive situations, one at a time, than all of them simultaneously. Even a very good chess player can anticipate only a few moves ahead.

central aim to establish the constellations of characteristics that develop in organizations of various kinds. Comparative studies of many organizations are necessary, not alone to test the hypotheses implied by such a theory, but also to provide a basis for initial exploration and refinement of the theory by indicating the conditions on which relationships, originally assumed to hold universally, are contingent. Strict impersonal detachment, for instance, may well promote efficiency only under some conditions and not at all under others.[19] Systematic research on many organizations that provides the data needed to determine the interrelations between several organizational features is, however, extremely rare. The main reason is that the investigation of the internal structure of a complex organization is so costly in time and effort to make the inclusion of many organizations in a single study design impracticable. One way out of this impasse is to study the major attributes of many organizations and sacrifice any detailed information on their internal structures.

The approach to comparative research on organizations proposed, therefore, would be explicitly restricted to those data that can be obtained from the records of organizations and interviews with key informants, without intensive observation or interviewing of most members, which would make it possible to collect the same data on one hundred or more organizations of a given type in one study. In other words, the research design sacrifices depth of information to achieve sufficient breadth to permit a minimum of quantitative comparison. The very limitation imposed by lack of extensive data on internal structures has a latent function, so to speak, inasmuch as it forces the investigator to focus on the neglected area of organizational analysis rather than on the repeatedly studied role relations and group structures within organizations. It is suggested that this approach, though prompted by methodological necessity, has the potential to contribute greatly to organizational theory. To illustrate the theoretical significance of the comparative approach to organizational research, let us examine how it could help refine Weber's theory of bureaucracy.[20]

Weber's Theory

Weber's analysis of bureaucracy is part of his general theory of types of political order and authority, and it is simultaneously a crucial case of the most pervasive theme in all his writings, namely, the increasing rationalization of modern life. The major characteristics Weber attributed to

19. See Eugene Litwak, "Models of Bureaucracy which Permit Conflict," *American Journal of Sociology,* vol. 67, 1962, pp. 177–84.
20. Weber, *op. cit.,* pp. 324–41, and *From Max Weber: Essays in Sociological Theory* (New York: Oxford University Press, 1946), pp. 196–244.

the typical bureaucracy will first be outlined, and his analysis of their functional interdependence will then be summarized.[21]

The large *size* of an organization and the great *complexity* of its responsibilities promote bureaucratization, according to Weber. One aspect of bureaucratization is the elaboration of the *administrative* apparatus in the organization. Bureaucracies also are characterized by a high degree of *specialization*, and their members are trained as specialized *experts* in the tasks assigned to them. Furthermore, official positions are organized in a *hierarchy* with clear lines of authority, the scope of which is precisely circumscribed by impersonal rules. Operations generally are governed by a consistent system of *rules* and regulations. *Impersonal* detachment is expected to prevail in the performance of duties and in official relations. Personnel and promotion policies, too, are governed by impersonal criteria, such as merit or seniority, which assures officials stable *careers* with some advancement in the organization. Weber held that this combination of characteristics tends to evolve because it is necessary for and furthers administrative efficiency.

In analyzing the processes that produce this interdependence among characteristics, Weber implicitly presents a functional analysis of bureaucracy, with rational decision making and administrative efficiency as the criteria of function. The requirement to discharge *complex* responsibilities effectively creates pressures to divide them into *specialized*, more easily manageable tasks and to appoint professionally qualified *experts* to perform the various specialized tasks. The pronounced division of labor, particularly in *large* organizations, creates special problems of coordination. An *administrative* apparatus tends to develop to maintain channels of communication and coordination, and a *hierarchy* of authority and responsibility is needed actually to effect the coordination of diverse tasks in the pursuit of organizational objectives by enabling superiors on sucessive levels to guide, directly or indirectly, the performance of increasingly wider circles of subordinates. But detailed supervision of all decisions by superiors is most inefficient and produces serious strains. The system of *rules* and official procedures is designed to standardize performance and restrict the need for direct supervisory intervention largely to extraordinary cases. Professional training and official rules notwithstanding, however, strong emotions or personal bias may interfere with rational decision making; the emphasis on *impersonal* detachment has the function of precluding the intrusion of such irrational factors into official decisions. Lest the strict impersonal discipline under which the members of a bureaucracy must operate alienate them, stable *careers* promote loyalty to the organization and counteract these burdens. In short, the problems created by one organizational feature stimulate processes that give rise to another,

21. Italics are used for the nine major concepts which are first presented, then related to one another, and finally operationalized.

and many interdependent processes of this kind produce the constellation of features characteristic of the typical bureaucracy as conceptualized by Weber.

Operational Measures

Operational measures for the characteristics of bureaucratic organizations described by Weber can be obtained by the comparative method here advocated, and it would be sheer waste in most cases to employ more intensive methods to obtain these data. This is evidently the case for the *size* of an organization. Whether size is measured by number of employees of a factory, number of voters for a party, number of beds in a hospital, or total assets of a firm, there is evidently no need to interview all members of the organization to ascertain this information. One index of *complexity* is the number of basic objectives or responsibilities of an organization—a university with graduate and professional schools has more complex responsibilities than a college without them—and another index of it is the number of different locations where the organization operates. Still another aspect of complexity is the degree of *specialization* in an organization, which might be measured by the number of different occupational positions, or by the distribution of the members among various occupational specialities, or by the number of functionally specialized departments. The amount of training required for various positions could serve as an indicator of professional *expertness,* as could the proportion of personnel with a given amount of professional education.

An index of bureaucratization that has been used in previous research is the relative size of the *administrative* component; that is, the proportion of personnel in administrative or staff positions.[22] Three related measures of the *hierarchy* of authority, which refer to the shape of the pyramid, would be the number of levels in the hierarchy, the average span of control, and the proportion of personnel in managerial positions. The extent to which procedures have been made explicit in formal *rules* is indicated by the existence and size of written procedure manuals and by the specificity of the prescriptions contained in them. Two other measures of an emphasis on uniform standards of performance are whether decisions are routinely reviewed for correctness and the amount of statistical information on operations that is kept in the organization as a basis for

22. See, for example, Theodore R. Anderson and Seymour Warkov, "Organizational Size and Complexity," *American Sociological Review,* vol. 26, 1961, pp. 23–28; Alton W. Baker and Ralph C. Davis, *Ratios of Staff to Line Employees and Stages of Differentiation of Staff Functions* (Columbus: Bureau of Business Research, Ohio State University, 1954); Reinhard Bendix, *Work and Authority in Industry* (New York: Wiley, 1956), pp. 221–22; and Seymour Melman, "The Rise of Administrative Overhead in the Manufacturing Industries of the United States, 1899–1947," *Oxford Economic Papers,* vol. 3, 1951, pp. 64–66, 89–90.

executive decisions. The use of such statistical records for the evaluation of the performance of subordinates can be considered an indication of *impersonality,* and so can precisely stipulated personnel policies, as exemplified by civil service regulations. The degree of *career* stability, finally, is manifest in membership turnover and average length of service.

This listing makes evident that the empirical data needed for research on the major characteristics of bureaucratic organizations included in Weber's theory are easily enough accessible to make it possible to obtain them for large numbers of organizations in brief visits to each. To be sure, to examine the various facets of each concept, as Weber does, would require more extensive data than those outlined. To cite only one example, an analysis of organizational authority should not be confined to the shape of the hierarchical pyramid but include other aspects of hierarchical control, such as the degree of centralization in the organization. There is no reason to assume, however, that additional measures suitable for comparative studies, which would complement the original ones and thus allow refinement of the analysis, cannot be devised; for instance, information could be obtained about the level in the hierarchy on which various important budgetary and personnel decisions are made to provide measures of centralization. The crucial point is that intensive investigations of internal structures and processes are neither needed nor appropriate for obtaining the data that pertain most directly to theories of organization.

Empirical data of this kind about a fairly large sample of comparable organizations would make it possible to test numerous hypotheses implied by Weber's theory, such as that the processes of specialization, professionalization, and bureaucratization tend to occur together in organizations. Chances are that research findings would reveal that many hypotheses must be revised, thereby directing attention to needed reformulations and specifications in the theory. Thus, impressionistic observation leads one to suspect that increasing specialization is indeed accompanied by increasing professionalization in some types of organizations, such as hospitals, but that a high degree of specialization reduces the need for an expertly trained working force in other types, such as assembly-line factories. If this impression should be correct, it would raise the question of the conditions that determine whether or not an extensive division of labor is associated with a highly trained working force.

Refining Theory

Systematic exploration of the empirical relationships between organizational features would provide a basis for refining the theory of bureaucracy by indicating the conditions on which the concurrence of various bureaucratic characteristics is contingent, by helping to answer some questions Weber did not resolve, and by clarifying problems and issues his theory raises. For example, Weber considers both seniority and merit impersonal criteria of bureaucratic advancement. An important question which he never answers is what conditions determine whether promotions are largely based on seniority or primarily on merit, a difference that undoubtedly has significant implications for careers and for the organization. Properly designed comparative studies of organizations could help answer this question.

Whereas Weber implies that the large size of an organization as well as its complexity promotes bureaucratization, recent comparative research indicates that size is unrelated or inversely related to bureaucratization as measured by the proportion of the organization's personnel in administrative positions.[23] It appears that complexity is associated with a disproportionately large administrative apparatus, and large size often goes together with a high degree of complexity, but increasing size as such does not lead to a disproportionate expansion of the administrative apparatus. The question these conclusions raise is whether other aspects of bureaucratization, such as extensive written rules, detailed statistical controls, or impersonal personnel procedures, are associated with both size and complexity independently, in accordance with Weber's assumption, or only with one of the two or possibly with neither.

An important issue that has been raised concerns the relationship between professional competence and bureaucratic authority. Several authors, including notably Parsons, Gouldner, and Stinchcombe,[24] have criticized Weber's contention that professional expertness is a typical characteristic of bureaucracies which goes together with such other bureaucratic characteristics as strict lines of hierarchical authority that require disciplined compliance with the commands of superiors. It has been held that professional principles often conflict with the principles that govern hierarchical administration and that the two are not complementary, as Weber assumes, but rather alternative mechanisms of control and coordination. The empirical question is under which conditions professionalization and bureaucratization, especially as revealed in centralized hierarchical control, are associated in organizations and under which conditions they are not. Comparative research might explore, for instance, whether the association between professionalization and bureaucratization depends on the degree of specialization in the organization, because professional standards facilitate coordination among men in similar fields, reducing the need for bureaucratic mechanisms, whereas they make coordination be-

23. See references cited in preceding footnote.
24. Talcott Parsons, "Introduction," to Weber, *The Theory of Social and Economic Organization,* pp. 58–60 (fn.); Gouldner, *Patterns of Industrial Bureaucracy* (New York: Free Press, 1954), pp. 22–24; and Arthur L. Stinchcombe, "Bureaucratic and Craft Administration of Production," *Administrative Science Quarterly,* vol. 4, 1959, pp. 168–87.

tween widely diverse fields more difficult, increasing the need for administrative mechanisms of coordination.

A related issue of even broader theoretical significance is posed by Weber's implicit assumption that strict hierarchical authority and discipline are universally most effective in achieving efficiency in administrative organizations. One might well wonder whether the Prussian army, which sometimes seems to have served Weber inadvertently as the prototype, is really the ideal model for all organizations, whatever the nature of their responsibilities, the composition of their personnel, and the culture in which they operate.[25] In a democratic culture where subordination under authoritative commands tends to be negatively valued, strict hierarchical control and close supervision may well be less effective methods of operation than delegating responsibilities and permitting subordinates some discretion in their exercise. The greater the professionalization of the staff, moreover, the less effective is control through directives from superiors likely to be. The most effective method for organizing an army, finally, is probably not identical with the most effective method for organizing a research laboratory. Comparative studies of organizations could throw some light on these broad issues too.

Conclusions

Three foci of analysis have been distinguished in the study of organizational life: (1) role analysis is concerned with individual members of organizations, their attitudes, and their behavior; (2) structural analysis focuses upon groups of interrelated individuals in organizations and the patterns of social associations that develop in these groups and give them their form; (3) organizational analysis centers attention on systems of interrelated groups explicitly organized to achieve some joint ends and the constellations of attributes that characterize these organizations. The differentiating criterion is whether the unit of analysis whose characteristics are being compared, and of which, therefore, a fairly large number must be examined, is the individual member, the work group, or the entire organization.

In terms of this criterion, a case study of an organization cannot make the organization the unit of systematic analysis but only the structures of subgroups or the roles of individuals. By the same token, the study of the influence of the environment on organizations would have to employ a research design that includes organizations in a variety of different en-

25. According to Carl J. Friedrich, Weber's "very words vibrate with something of the Prussian enthusiasm for the military type of organization"; "Some Observations on Weber's Analysis of Bureaucracy," in Merton, *et al., Reader in Bureaucracy* (New York: Free Press, 1952), p. 31.

vironments, and since hardly any studies do so, the complaint often heard that we know virtually nothing about the impact of the social setting on organizations is quite justified. Whereas more than three foci of analysis are possible—as just noted, the social setting could be the focus—the three outlined are the major ones in the study of organizational life. The most appropriate method for role analysis is the interviewing survey, for structural analysis, intensive observation of all members of selected groups, and for organizational analysis, the comparative study of many organizations.

A theory of organization seeks to explain the systems of relationships between elements in a structure that characterize organizations. Such explanations involve, like all theoretical explanations, subsuming observed relationships between characteristics under more general propositions and specifying the intervening processes responsible for the connections. A major contribution of case studies that investigate the internal structures of organizations is that they provide specific evidence on these underlying processes, which otherwise must be inferred in organizational analysis. But this is only a potential contribution to organizational theory as long as it stands by itself and is not yet a supplement to the data on constellations of organizational features provided by comparative studies of organizations, which must furnish the main foundation of such a theory. Only systematic comparisons of many organizations can establish relationships between characteristics or organizations and stipulate the conditions under which these relationships hold, thereby providing the material that needs to be explained by theoretical principles and important guides for deriving these principles. Although comparative research on a fairly large number of organizations is necessarily restricted to data easily accessible without time-consuming intensive investigations, these are the very data most relevant for organizational theory; for example, Weber's theory of bureaucracy.

PART TWO

Current Theoretical Perspectives

Organization theory is one of the most diverse and intellectually exciting areas in the field. In this part the reader will encounter widely divergent views and recommendations for approaching the study of organizations. For example, one can compare the rational model proposed in the first selection with the nonrational model proposed in the last selection. Or one might compare the formal theory of organizational structure proposed by Blau with Benson's dialectical approach, which is critical of such attempts. Finally, one might compare the population ecology model of Hannan and Freeman, and its reliance upon populations of organizations as the unit of analysis, with the coalitional/bargaining approach advocated by Pfeffer, with its focus upon internal political processes in organizations.

In the first selection, March and Simon focus upon the organizational member as a decision maker and problem solver. Their thesis is that the basic features of organizational structure are derived from the characteristics of human problem solving and rational choice. Central to the argument is the concept of "performance program," which refers to a highly complex and organized set of responses evoked from the organizational member by some organizational stimulus. In such situations, search and choice processes involved in problem solving are very much abridged (the example is given of the sounding of a gong in a fire station and the resulting responses on the part of the firemen). The importance of performance programs for understanding organizational behavior results from the fact that such situations account for a very large part of the behavior of all organizational participants, particularly those persons in lower-level and relatively routine positions. March and Simon conclude that knowledge of the performance programs

129

of organizations (which is relatively easily obtained through conventional research methods) permits one to understand and predict in considerable detail the behaviors of large numbers of organizational members.

In the second selection, Blau provides a deductive theory to explain the relationships among major structural characteristics of organizations based upon data obtained from government bureaus, private firms, universities and colleges, and hospitals. Three organizational characteristics—size, differentiation, and administrative apparatus—are central to Blau's theory. He argues that increasing organizational size gives rise to dialectical forces having opposite organizational effects. For example, large size leads to both greater differentiation and a proportionately smaller administrative apparatus. However, increased differentiation expands the proportion of the administrative apparatus. Large size, therefore, has opposite effects on the administrative apparatus, reducing it because of economy of scale, and raising it indirectly because of the differentiation of large organizations. Thus the complex structures of very large organizations counteract the economy of scale in administrative apparatus that large size makes possible. Two hypotheses are offered to explain these processes. First, differentiation shapes the organization's social structure by transforming its employees from a collection of individuals with little in common into a unified and coherent social enterprise. Second, the initial investments in administrative time and effort required to organize and control these differentiated operations reduce the proportion of administrators needed as the volume of such operations increases. Blau interprets the declining influence of size on both differentiation and administrative apparatus in terms of feedback processes that result from the administrative problems created by differentiation. The result is that the feedback processes keep the amount of differentiation produced by increasing organizational size below the level at which the additional administrative costs of coordination and control would equal the administrative savings realized by the larger scale of operations.

In the third selection Hannan and Freeman propose a population ecology perspective on organization-environment relations as an alternative to the dominant adaptation perspective. They identify a number of limitations on the ability of organizations to adapt to their environments stemming from both internal and external constraints. In order to deal effectively with this structural inertia, these authors believe that the adaptation perspective must be supplemented with a selection orientation. An important advantage of this orientation is a necessary shift in the unit of analysis. Whereas the most common focus has been upon a single organization and its relationships to its environment. Hannan and Freeman argue for a population level of analysis that deals with aggregates of organizations that are alike in some respect. With such a focus, their approach seeks to understand the distribution of organizations across environmental conditions. According to this perspective, the central question of interest is: why are there so many kinds of organizations? The answer, according to Hawley (*Human Ecology* [New York: Ronald Press, 1950]), is that the diversity of organizational forms is isomorphic to the diversity of environments. Only one particular organizational form is optimally adapted to the demands of a particular environmental configuration. Hannan and Freeman modify and extend Hawley's perspective by incorporating competition models to specify the processes producing isomorphism and by utilizing niche theory to deal with dynamic environments. In this way, classical population ecology theory has been modified to make it applicable to the study of organizations, and the way is thus prepared for increased theoretical stimulation from two heretofore widely isolated traditions within the field of sociology.

In the fourth selection, Benson proposes a dialectical approach to the study of organizations that challenges the theoretical and methodological approaches currently prevalent in the field. Benson believes that the dominant theoretical view has uncritically accepted existing organizational arrangements and adapted itself to the interest of administrative elites, with the result that much of current organizational theory has been dominated by issues of administrative concern. In contrast to this approach, Benson argues that the dialectical view offers an explanation of the processes involved in the production, reproduction, and destruction of particular organizational forms. Moreover, the dialectical view sees the social world as being in a continuous state of becoming. Attention is focused upon the transformation through which one set of arrangements gives way to another. Four principles of dialectical analysis are identified and discussed and then applied directly to the study of organizations. The organization is viewed as beset by contradictions that continually undermine its existing features. Its directions depend upon the interests of the people involved and upon the power of these interests to transform the organization. Benson argues that all theories neglect the social context in which they were created and one must therefore examine the relationship between organizational theories and organizational realities. The task of the dialectician is to understand the connection between theory and reality by analyzing the social context. Finally, dialectical analysis is concerned with the active reconstruction of organizations in such a way that human potentialities can be realized.

CURRENT THEORETICAL PERSPECTIVES

The two remaining selections bear some relationship to one another because of their common interest in social structure and power and their relative deemphasis of organizational goals. Pfeffer in "Who Governs?" (a passage from his book *Organizational Design* [1978]) elaborates the coalitional/bargaining approach to the study of organizational behavior. The central focus is social control. As Pfeffer notes: "Our central theme is simple. Organizations make choices, and the bases for these organizational decisions—who makes them and why—is an important analytical question to be asked about organizations" (p. 4). This perspective contrasts sharply with the traditional management emphasis on organizational objectives, which typically assumes consensus regarding goals. Instead, Pfeffer calls attention to the many conflicts that exist among the various interests in the organization, conflicts not only about the relative priority of various goal-related issues, but also concerning the allocation of scarce resources. These conflicts stem from differential access to information, as well as differences in social experiences and background. To understand the way an organization works one must comprehend its power structure, who controls the organization's resources, and who has access to and control over the key channels of communication. It is when decisions are of crucial importance to the organization that social influence processes become most meaningful. Despite the fundamental simplicity of the formulation, its application is not at all simple, since, as Pfeffer points out, the real wielders of power often prefer to remain hidden. As a result, unobtrusive methods of research are typically required.

March and Olsen, in the selection from their book *Ambiguity and Choice in Organizations* (1976) entitled "Organizational Choice under Ambiguity," present a new model of decision processes that differs from conventional approaches by its stress on nonrational considerations. Organizational choice is heavily constrained by ambiguity. Objectives are unclear and ill-defined. Technologies are vague. The environment is hard to understand. The past is misty, misconceived, and frequently misunderstood regarding the lessons it reveals. Moreover, participation in decision making in organizations varies from decision to decision and from one time to the next. A rational model of organizational choice fails to give these sources of ambiguity and uncertainty their rightful due. Therefore, the authors and their collaborators have developed a "garbage can" model (Michael D. Cohen, James G. March, and Johan P. Olsen, "A Garbage Can Model of Organizational Choice," *Administrative Science Quarterly,* 17, 1 [March 1972], 1–25) of choice processes in which four loosely coupled decision components are mixed: problems or issues, solutions, participants, and choice opportunities (matching a solution to a problem so as to form a decision). But the process of coming to a decision is neither random nor anarchical. Among other factors, social structure, norms, and values constrain participation in decision making in important ways. The present selection is devoted to demonstrating the need for an uncertainty model. It calls attention to the necessity for looking at decisions as "occasions" for a variety of activities, such as having fun, determining truth, and socializing, in addition to considering the business at hand. Moreover, despite the wishes of some members of the organization to think otherwise, some decisions are largely externally controlled. The March/Olsen perspective emphasizes context and, in so doing, blends the social psychology of learning and attention with the sociology of culture and social structure.

Decision-Making Theory

James G. March
Herbert A. Simon

The Concept of Rationality

How does the rationality of "administrative man" compare with that of classical "economic man" or with the rational man of modern statistical decision theory? The rational man of economics and statistical decision theory makes "optimal" choices in a highly specified and clearly defined environment:

1. When we first encounter him in the decision-making situation, he already has laid out before him the whole set of alternatives from which he will choose his action. This set of alternatives is simply "given"; the theory does not tell how it is obtained.

2. To each alternative is attached a set of consequences—the events that will ensue if that particular alternative is chosen. Here the existing theories fall into three categories: (*a*) *Certainty:* theories that assume the decision maker has complete and accurate knowledge of the consequences that will follow on each alternative. (*b*) *Risk:* theories that assume accurate knowledge of a probability distribution of the consequences of each alternative. (*c*) *Uncertainty:* theories that assume that the consequences of each alternative belong to some subset of all possible consequences, but that the decision maker cannot assign definite probabilities to the occurrence of particular consequences.

3. At the outset, the decision maker has a "utility function" or a "preference-ordering" that ranks all sets of consequences from the most preferred to the least preferred.

4. The decision maker selects the alternative leading to the preferred set of consequences. In the case of *certainty,* the choice is unambiguous. In the case of *risk,* rationality is usually defined as the choice of that alternative for which the expected utility is greatest. Expected utility is defined here as the average, weighted by the probabilities of occurrence,

SOURCE: *Organizations,* pp. 137–50, 169–71. Copyright © 1958 by John Wiley & Sons, Inc. Reprinted by permission of the authors and John Wiley & Sons, Inc.

of the utilities attached to all possible consequences. In the case of *uncertainty,* the definition of rationality becomes problematic. One proposal that has had wide currency is the rule of "minimax risk": consider the worst set of consequences that may follow from each alternative, then select the alternative whose "worst set of consequences" is preferred to the worst sets attached to other alternatives. There are other proposals (e.g., the rule of "minimax regret"), but we shall not discuss them here.

Some Difficulties in the Classical Theory

There are difficulties with this model of rational man. In the first place, only in the case of certainty does it agree well with common-sense notions of rationality. In the case of uncertainty, especially, there is little agreement, even among exponents of statistical decision theory, as to the "correct" definition, or whether, indeed, the term "correct" has any meaning here (Marschak, 1950).

A second difficulty with existing models of rational man is that it makes three exceedingly important demands upon the choice-making mechanism. It assumes (1) that all the alternatives of choice are "given"; (2) that all the consequences attached to each alternative are known (in one of the three senses corresponding to certainty, risk, and uncertainty respectively); (3) that the rational man has a complete utility-ordering (or cardinal function) for all possible sets of consequences.

One can hardly take exception to these requirements in a normative model—a model that tells people how they *ought* to choose. For if the rational man lacked information, he might have chosen differently "if only he had known." At best, he is "subjectively" rational, not "objectively" rational. But the notion of objective rationality assumes there is some objective reality in which the "real" alternatives, the "real" consequences, and the "real" utilities exist. If this is so, it is not even clear why the cases of choice under risk and under uncertainty are admitted as rational. If it is not so, it is not clear why only limitations upon knowledge of consequences are considered, and why limitations upon knowledge of alternatives and utilities are ignored in the model of rationality.

From a phenomenological viewpoint we can only speak of rationality relative to a frame of reference; and this frame of reference will be determined by the limitations on the rational man's knowledge. We can, of course, introduce the notion of a person observing the choices of a subject, and can speak of the rationality of the subject relative to the frame of reference of the observer. If the subject is a rat and the observer is a man (especially if he is the man who designed the experimental situation), we may regard the man's perception of the situation as objective and the rat's as subjective. (We leave out of account the specific difficulty that the rat presumably knows his own utility function better than the man does.) If, however, both subject and observer are men—and particularly if the situation is a natural one not constructed for experimental purposes by the observer—then it becomes difficult to specify the objective situation. It will be safest, in such situations, to speak of rationality only relative to some specified frame of reference.

The classical organization theory . . ., like classical economic theory, failed to make explicit this subjective and relative character of rationality, and in so doing, failed to examine some of its own crucial premises. The organizational and social environment in which the decision maker finds himself determines what consequences he will anticipate, what ones he will not; what alternatives he will consider, what ones he will ignore. In a theory of organization these variables cannot be treated as unexplained independent factors, but must themselves be determined and predicted by the theory.

Routinized and Problem-Solving Responses

The theory of rational choice put forth here incorporates two fundamental characteristics: (1) Choice is always exercised with respect to a limited, approximate, simplified "model" of the real situation. We call the chooser's model his "definition of the situation." (2) The elements of the definition of the situation are not "given"—that is, we do not take these as data of our theory—but are themselves the outcome of psychological and sociological processes, including the chooser's own activities and the activities of others in his environment (Simon, 1947, 1955; March, 1955; Cyert and March, 1955, 1956; Newell, Shaw, and Simon, 1958).

Activity (individual or organizational) can usually be traced back to an environmental stimulus of some sort, e.g., a customer order or a fire gong. The responses to stimuli are of various kinds. At one extreme, a stimulus evokes a response—sometimes very elaborate—that has been developed and learned at some previous time as an appropriate response for a stimulus of this class. This is the "routinized" end of the continuum, where a stimulus calls forth a performance program almost instantaneously.

At the other extreme, a stimulus evokes a larger or smaller amount of problem-solving activity directed toward finding performance activities with which to complete the response. Such activity is distinguished by the fact that it can be dispensed with once the performance program has been learned. Problem-solving activities can generally be identified by the extent to which they involve *search*: search aimed at discovering alternatives of action or consequences of action. "Discovering" alternatives may involve inventing and elaborating whole performance programs where these are not already available in the problem solver's repertory (Katona, 1951).

When a stimulus is of a kind that has been experienced repeatedly in the past, the response will ordinarily be highly routinized. The stimulus will evoke, with a minimum of problem-solving or other computational activity, a well-structured definition of the situation that will include a repertory of response programs, and programs for selecting an appropriate specific response from the repertory. When a stimulus is relatively novel, it will evoke problem-solving activity aimed initially at constructing a definition of the situation and then at developing one or more appropriate performance programs.

Psychologists (e.g., Wertheimer, Duncker, de Groot, Maier) and observant laymen (e.g., Poincaré, Hadamard) who have studied creative thinking and problem-solving have been unanimous in ascribing a large role in these phenomena to search processes. Search is partly random, but in effective problem-solving it is not blind. The design of the search process is itself often an object of rational decision. Thus, we may distinguish substantive planning—developing new performance programs—from procedural planning—developing programs for the problem-solving process itself. The response to a particular stimulus may involve more than performance—the stimulus may evoke a spate of problem-solving activity—but the problem-solving activity may itself be routinized to a greater or lesser degree. For example, search processes may be systematized by the use of check lists.

Satisfactory versus Optimal Standards

What kinds of search and other problem-solving activity are needed to discover an adequate range of alternatives and consequences for choice depends on the criterion applied to the choice. In particular, finding the optimal alternative is a radically different problem from finding a satisfactory alternative. An alternative is *optimal* if: (1) there exists a set of criteria that permits all alternatives to be compared, and (2) the alternative in question is preferred, by these criteria, to all other alternatives. An alternative is *satisfactory* if: (1) there exists a set of criteria that describes minimally satisfactory alternatives, and (2) the alternative in question meets or exceeds all these criteria.

Most human decision-making, whether individual or organizational, is concerned with the discovery and selection of satisfactory alternatives; only in exceptional cases is it concerned with the discovery and selection of optimal alternatives. To optimize requires processes several orders of magnitude more complex than those required to satisfice. An example is the difference between searching a haystack to find the *sharpest* needle in it and searching the haystack to find a needle sharp enough to sew with.

In making choices that meet satisfactory standards, the standards themselves are part of the definition of the situation. Hence, we need not regard these as given—any more than the other elements of the definition of the situation—but may include in the theory the processes through which these standards are set and modified. The standard-setting process may itself meet standards of rationality: for example, an "optimizing" rule would be to set the standard at the level where the marginal improvement in alternatives obtainable by raising it would be just balanced by the marginal cost of searching for alternatives meeting the higher standard. Of course, in practice the "marginal improvement" and the "marginal cost" are seldom measured in comparable units, or with much accuracy. Nevertheless, a similar result would be automatically attained if the standards were raised whenever alternatives proved easy to discover, and lowered whenever they were difficult to discover. Under these circumstances, the alternatives chosen would not be far from the optima, if the cost of search were taken into consideration. Since human standards tend to have this characteristic under many conditions, some theorists have sought to maintain the optimizing model by introducing cost-of-search considerations. Although we doubt whether this will be a fruitful alternative to the model we are proposing in very many situations, neither model has been used for predictive purposes often enough to allow a final judgment.

Performance Programs

We have seen that under certain circumstances the search and choice processes are very much abridged. At the limit, an environmental stimulus may evoke immediately from the organization a highly complex and organized set of responses. Such a set of responses we call a *performance program,* or simply a *program.* For example, the sounding of the alarm gong in a fire station initiates such a program. So does the appearance of a relief applicant at a social worker's desk. So does the appearance of an automobile chassis in front of the work station of a worker on the assembly line.

Situations in which a relatively simple stimulus sets off an elaborate program of activity without any apparent interval of search, problem-solving, or choice are not rare. They account for a very large part of the behavior of all persons, and for almost all of the behavior of persons in relatively routine positions. Most behavior, and particularly most behavior in organizations, is governed by performance programs.

The term "program" is not intended to connote complete rigidity. The content of the program may be adaptive to a large number of characteristics of the stimulus that initiates it. Even in the simple case of the fire gong, the response depends on the location of the alarm, as indicated by the number of strokes. The program may also be conditional on data that are independent of the initiating stimuli. It is then more properly called a *performance strategy*. For example, when inventory records show that the quantity on hand of a commodity has decreased to the point where it should be reordered, the decision rule that governs the behavior of the purchasing agent may call upon him to determine the amount to be ordered on the basis of a formula into which he inserts the quantity that has been sold over the past twelve months. In this case, search has been eliminated from the problem, but choice—of a very routinized kind, to be sure—remains.

We will regard a set of activities as routinized, then, to the degree that choice has been simplified by the development of a fixed response to defined stimuli. If search has been eliminated, but a choice remains in the form of a clearly defined and systematic computing routine, we will still say that the activities are routinized. We will regard activities as un-routinized to the extent that they have to be preceded by program-developing activities of a problem-solving kind.

Performance Programs in Organizations

There are several ways to determine what programs a particular organization uses:

1. Observing the behavior of organization members. In relatively routine positions, where the same situations recur repetitively and are handled in terms of fairly definite programs, it is easy to infer the program from behavior. This is a common method for inducting new members of an organization into its procedures.

2. Interviewing members of the organization. Most programs are stored in the minds of the employees who carry them out, or in the minds of their superiors, subordinates, or associates. For many purposes, the simplest and most accurate way to discover what a person does is to ask him.

3. Examining documents that describe standard operating procedures. Programs may be written down, more or less completely and more or less accurately. The relation of a written operating procedure to the actual program that is carried out is complex, for the program may have been written down: (*a*) as an instruction to initiate a new program and communicate it to those who will carry it out; (*b*) as a description of an existing program to instruct new organization members; or (*c*) as an exposition (with or without amendments) of an existing program to legitimize or "formalize'" it. There are other possibilities besides these three. In any event, when a document is used as a source of information about a program, the purposes for which it was prepared are relevant to its interpretation.

A person who has been trained in the observation of organizations can extract by these and other techniques a large part of the program that governs routine behavior. This is such a common-sense fact that its importance has been overlooked: Knowledge of the program of an organization permits one to predict in considerable detail the behavior of members of the organization. And the greater the *programming* of individual activities in the organization, the greater the *predictability* of those activities.

To be sure, prediction of behavior from the knowledge of a program has none of the element of "surprise" that we commonly associate with scientific prediction—any more than prediction of the lines that will be uttered by a Hamlet on the stage. It is no less important for its common-sense obviousness.

In general, we would anticipate that programs will be generated by past experience and in expectation of future experience in a given situation. Thus, the greater the *repetitiveness* of individual activities, the greater the programming. From this one would predict that programming will be most complete for clerical and factory jobs, particularly when the work is organized largely by process.

The prediction of behavior from a program when tasks are relatively simple and routine is illustrated by findings of Guetzkow and Simon (1955) using five-man experimental groups in the Bavelas network. Employing methods-analysis techniques, they were able to predict average trial times of groups to within 10 per cent from a knowledge of the methods the groups were using to perform the task.

If the program determines in some detail the behavior of individuals and groups performing relatively routine tasks, then we can predict behavior to the extent that we can answer the following questions: (1) What motivates members of the organization to accept a program as a determinant of their behavior? What processes, other than motivation, are involved in implementation of programs? This question has already been examined in earlier chapters. (2) What determines the content of a program? To what extent can the program be predicted uniquely from the requirements of the task? How are programs invented and developed, and what are the determinants of this process? (3) What are the consequences of programs, as developed and executed, for the goal and subgoal structure of the organization? (4) What are the predictors of behavior in areas that are not routinized and are unprogrammed? This question will be taken up in the next chapter.

We turn now to the second and third of these questions.

Program Content

The extent to which many human activities, both manual and clerical, can be programmed is shown by the continuing spread of automation to encompass a wider and wider range of tasks. In order to substitute automatic processes for human operatives, it is necessary to describe the task in minute detail, and to provide for the performance of each step in it. The decomposition of tasks into their elementary program steps is most spectacularly illustrated in modern computing machines which may carry out programs involving thousands of such steps. The capabilities of computers have now been extended to many tasks that until recently have been thought to be relatively complex, involving problem-solving activities of a fairly high order. Some examples are several existing computer programs for the automatic design of small electric motors and transformers, a program that enables a computer to discover proofs for certain kinds of mathematical theorems, and a program for translating languages.

Even on routine jobs, *program content* varies. We have already mentioned the extreme case: the detailed specification of output, methods, and pace in a man-paced assembly operation. But not all programs are of this type. They may not contain detailed time specifications (e.g., in typical machine-paced operations). In fact, programs usually specify the content of an activity more closely than its timing. They may specify the properties of the product (e.g., in blueprints, tolerances, etc.) rather than the detail of the methods to be used. We need propositions that will explain variations in program content along these dimensions:

a) The extent to which pacing rules are built into the program.
b) The extent to which work activities are detailed in the program.
c) The extent to which product specifications are detailed in the program.

Since performance programs are important aspects of the organizational system, their content will presumably tend to be related to the functions they perform. We can identify two major functions that such programs fulfill, or at least are intended to fulfill. First, they are a part of the control system in the organization. Organizations attempt to control employees by specifying a standard operating procedure and attaching organizational rewards and penalties to it. Second, performance programs are important parts of the coordination system in the organization. They help fulfill the needs for interdepartmental predictability (Blau, 1955).

Insofar as they are to function as controls, the programs must be linked to variables that are observable and measurable. We would expect program content to be a function of the *ease of observing job activities, the ease of observing job output,* and the *ease of relating activities to output.* Thus, we would predict that programs will contain activity specifications in preference to product specifications to the extent that: (*a*) the activity pattern is easily observed and supervised; (*b*) the quantity and quality of output are not easily observed and supervised; (c) the relations between activity pattern and output are highly technical, and are matters of scientific and engineering knowledge, better known to specialists in the organization than to the operatives (Ridley and Simon, 1938).

Conversely, programs will contain specifications of quality and quantity of output to the extent that: (a) the activity pattern is difficult to observe and supervise; (b) the quantity and quality of output are easily observed and supervised; (c) the relations between activity pattern and output are matters of common sense, are matters of skill in the specific occupation for which the operatives are trained, or are highly variable, depending upon circumstances of the individual situation that are better known to the operatives than to supervisors and specialists.

For performance programs to serve as coordinative devices, they must be linked to the coordination needs that are felt by the organization. Consequently, we would hypothesize that program content will be a function of the *need for activity coordination* and the *need for output coordination*. The more minutely other members of the organization need to synchronize or coordinate their activities with the activities of a particular member, the more completely will the program specify the activity pattern and/or the pacing of those activities. But to the extent that the activities of the former depend on the characteristics of the output of the latter, rather than on his activities, the program will specify product characteristics.

These propositions about program content are derived from the assumption that the program will be rationally adapted to the organization's objectives. To the extent that this assumption actually determines program, program content becomes a technological question in exactly the same way as the form of the production function is a technological question. In the experiment with the Bavelas network, mentioned previously, determining the most efficient program for performing the task is an exercise in methods study resting upon knowledge of human physiological constants—the times required to perform certain simple acts. If we assume that over some period of time an organization will actually arrive at an efficient program, we can predict its long-run behavior from our technical analysis.

Suppose, however, that we substitute for the maximizing assumption implicit in this method of prediction the assumption that behavior is rational in the more limited sense described earlier: that programs are sought that will operate "satisfactorily," and that the "best" program is not necessarily sought or found. In this case, predicting the program becomes more difficult. Which of the (presumably numerous) satisfactory potential programs the organization will adopt depends, under these circumstances, upon the procedures it employs to construct new programs and to improve existing ones.

143

The Structure of Programs

To illustrate further the structure of programs for handling recurrent events, we will describe some formal procedures often used by business concerns for controlling inventory. We will analyze first the common "two-bin" system of inventory control, then a more elaborate system.

In the two-bin system of inventory control, two quantities are established for each item kept in stock: (1) the order quantity (the amount to be purchased on a single order), (2) the buffer stock (the amount that should be on hand when a new order is placed). The program is very simple:

1. When material is drawn from stock, note whether the quantity that remains equals or exceeds the buffer stock. It not:
2. Write a purchase order for the specified order quantity.

Let us call the first step the "program-evoking" step, and the second step the "program-execution" step. The bifurcation is characteristic of programs—a program includes a specification of the circumstances under which the program is to be evoked. In the example just cited, the program specifies certain observations, which are to be made (whether the buffer stock is intact) whenever a certain event occurs (withdrawal of material from stock). A decision to act or not to act (to apply or not to apply the program) is based on the result of the observation.

The program-evoking step may involve only observation auxiliary to some other activity (as in this example), or it may invoke systematic scanning of some part of the environment (e.g., the activity of a quality inspector). Further, a program-execution step by one member of an organization may serve as a program-evoking step for another member. In the example above, the receipt of a purchase order from the inventory clerk is a program-evoking step for the purchasing department.

In our very simple example, the program-execution step requires neither discretion nor problem-solving. In more complicated situations, the program will be a strategy; i.e., action will be contingent on various characteristics of the situation. For example, in a more elaborate inventory control scheme, the purchase quantity may depend on a forecast of sales. Then the program might look like this:

1. When material is drawn from stock, note whether the quantity that remains equals or exceeds the buffer stock. If not:
2. Determine from the sales forecast provided by the sales department the sales expected in the next k months.
3. Insert this quantity in the "order quantity formula," and write a purchase order for the quantity thus determined.

This program, although it is contingent on certain changing facts (the sales forecast), does not allow discretion to the person who executes it—at least in ordinary meanings of the word "discretion." If, however, the organization does not provide the inventory clerk with an official sales forecast, or does not establish a specific order quantity, we would say that the clerk's activity was, to that extent, discretionary. We might discover by observation and interview that the clerk was in fact following a very definite and invariable program, but one stored in his own memory and not recorded in official instructions.

The Nature of Discretion

The amounts and kinds of *discretion* available to the organizational participant are a function of his performance program and in particular the extent to which the program specifies activities (means) and the extent to which it specifies product or outcome (ends). The further the program goes in the latter direction, the more discretion it allows for the person implementing the program to supply the means-end connections. Compare the programs cited earlier with the following alternative program:

1. It is the duty of the inventory clerk to determine when each item should be recorded and in what quantity, and to place orders with the purchasing department. He should perform this function with attention to the costs of holding inventories, the costs of shortages, and the economies associated with bulk orders.

If we interpret the last sentence as enjoining the clerk to minimize the sum of the specified costs, we see that this program specifies a goal, but leaves the means undetermined. To construct a "rational" program starting from these premises requires the following steps: (1) defining the total cost function in specific terms; (2) estimating the coefficients that appear in the cost function; (3) deriving a formula or "strategy" that specifies the ordering rules as functions of: (*a*) the coefficients that appear in the cost function, (*b*) the sales forecasts (i.e., finding the policy that minimizes step 1), and (4) inserting in the formula the coefficients estimated in step 2, and the sales forecasts.

It is difficult to find a place for discretion within the framework of traditional theories of rational behavior. In the present theory, however, a whole host of phenomena fall under this heading.

First, when a program involves search activities, the actual course of action depends on what is found. We may regard the choice of a course of action after search as discretionary.

Second, when a program describes a strategy, application of the strategy to specific circumstances requires forecasts or other estimates of data. We may regard the application of the strategy to select a course of action as discretionary.

Third, a program may exist in the memory of the individual who is to apply it, having arrived there either as a result of extraorganizational training (e.g., professional training or apprenticeship), or as a product of learning from experience rather than as a result of formal instructions. Under these circumstances we often regard him as behaving in a discretionary fashion.

In all of the cases listed above, the decision process may in fact be highly routinized—the term "discretionary" referring in these instances to the form of the performance program or the source from which it was acquired. These cases need to be distinguished from a fourth meaning of "discretionary": A program may specify only general goals, and leave unspecified the exact activities to be used in reaching them. Moreover, knowledge of the means-ends connections may be sufficiently incomplete and inexact that these cannot be very well specified in advance. Then "discretion" refers to the development and modification of the performance program through problem-solving and learning processes. Although it is difficult to draw a perfectly sharp line between changing a program and changing a datum in applying a strategy, we have already argued that there is an important difference of degree here. With these several meanings of the term "discretionary" in mind, we do not need separate propositions about the amount of discretion, for these will be subsumed under the propositions already noted that specify the form, content, and completeness of programs.

Interrelation of Programs

A program, whether simple or complex, is initiated when it is evoked by some stimulus. The whole pattern of programmed activity in an organization is a complicated mosaic of program executions, each initiated by its appropriate program-evoking step.

Insofar as the stimuli that evoke programs come from outside the organization, the individual pieces of this mosaic are related to each other only in making claims on the same time and resources, and hence in posing an allocation problem. Nevertheless, if the goal of optimizing is taken seriously, this allocation problem will usually complicate the problem-solving process greatly, for it requires the marginal return from activity in response to any particular stimulus to be equated with the marginal return from activities in response to all other stimuli. Hence, all programs must be determined simultaneously.

When the goal is to respond to stimuli in a satisfactory, but not necessarily optimal, fashion, choice is much simpler; for the standards may be set at levels that permit a satisficing response to each stimulus without concern for the others. The organization, under these circumstances, normally has some slack that reduces the interdependence among its several performance programs.

Apart from resource-sharing, there may be other and more integral connections among programs. Program A may be a *higher-level* program, i.e., a problem-solving activity whose goal is to revise other programs, either by constructing new ones, reconstructing existing ones, or simply modifying individual premises in existing programs. In this case, the *content* of the lower-level programs that are related to A will depend on A. Or, program A may be a program one of whose execution steps serves as an initiating stimulus for program B.

The inventory example illustrates both possibilities. As to the first, program A may be a forecasting program, or a program for periodic revision of the coefficients in the cost function. As to the second possibility, the order that goes from the inventory clerk to the purchasing department serves to initiate one of the purchasing programs of the latter.

Program and Organization Structure

In organizations there generally is a considerable degree of parallelism between the hierarchical relations among members of the organization and the hierarchical relations among program elements. That is to say, the programs of members of higher levels of the organization have as their main output the modification or initiation of programs for individuals at lower levels.

Any organization possesses a repertory of programs that, collectively, can deal in a goal-oriented way with a range of situations. As new situations arise, the construction of an entirely new program from detailed elements is rarely contemplated. In most cases, adaptation takes place through a recombination of lower-level programs that are already in existence. An important objective of standardization is to widen as far as possible the range of situations that can be handled by combination and recombination of a relatively small number of elementary programs.

Limitation of high-level action to the recombination of programs, rather than the detailed construction of new programs out of small elements, is extremely important from a cognitive standpoint. Out treatment of rational behavior rests on the proposition that the "real" situation is almost always far too complex to be handled in detail. As we move upwards in the supervisory and executive hierarchy, the range of interrelated matters over which an individual has purview becomes larger and larger, more and more complex. The growing complexity of the problem can only be matched against the finite powers of the individual if the problem is dealt with in grosser and more aggregative form. One way in which this is accomplished is by limiting the alternatives of action that are considered to the recombination of a repertory of programs (Simon, 1953).

We may again illustrate this point with the inventory example. Top management decides upon the total dollar inventories without controlling the distribution of inventories among individual items. Specific inventory control programs are found at lower levels of the organization.

• • •

Organization Structure and the Boundaries of Rationality

It has been the central theme of this chapter that the basic features of organization structure and function derive from the characteristics of human problem-solving processes and rational human choice. Because of the limits of human intellective capacities in comparison with the complexities of the problems that individuals and organizations face, rational behavior calls for simplified models that capture the main features of a problem without capturing all its complexities.

The simplifications have a number of characteristic features: (1) Optimizing is replaced by satisficing—the requirement that satisfactory levels of the criterion variables be attained. (2) Alternatives of action and consequences of action are discovered sequentially through search processes. (3) Repertories of action programs are developed by organizations and individuals, and these serve as the alternatives of choice in recurrent situations. (4) Each specific action program deals with a restricted range of situations and a restricted range of consequences. (5) Each action program is capable of being executed in semi-independence of the others— they are only loosely coupled together.

Action is goal-oriented and adaptive. But because of its approximating and fragmented character, only a few elements of the system are adaptive at any one time; the remainder are, at least in the short run, "givens." So, for example, an individual or organization may attend to improving a particular program, or to selecting an appropriate program from the existing repertory to meet a particular situation. Seldom can both be attended to simultaneously.

The notion that rational behavior deals with a few components at a time was first developed extensively in connection with economic behavior by John R. Commons, who spoke of "limiting factors" that become the foci of attention and adaptation. Commons' theory was further developed by Chester I. Barnard, who preferred the term "strategic factor."

This "one-thing-at-a-time" or *"ceteris paribus"* approach to adaptive behavior is fundamental to the very existence of something we can call "organization structure." Organization structure consists simply of those aspects of the pattern of behavior in the organization that are relatively stable and that change only slowly. If behavior in organizations is "intendedly rational," we will expect aspects of the behavior to be relatively stable that either (*a*) represent adaptations to relatively stable elements in the environment, or (*b*) are the learning programs that govern the process of adaptation.

An organization is confronted with a problem like that of Archimedes: in order for an organization to behave adaptively, it needs some stable regulations and procedures that it can employ in carrying out its adaptive practices. Thus, at any given time an organization's programs for performing its tasks are part of its structure, but the least stable part. Slightly more stable are the switching rules that determine when it will apply one program, and when another. Still more stable are the procedures it uses for developing, elaborating, instituting, and revising programs.

The matter may be stated differently. If an organization has a repertory of programs, then it is adaptive in the short run insofar as it has procedures for selecting from this repertory a program appropriate to each specific situation that arises. The process used to select an appopriate program is the "fulcrum" on which short-run adaptiveness rests. If, now, the organization has processes for adding to its repertory of programs or for modifying programs in the repertory, these processes become still more basic fulcra for accomplishing longer-run adaptiveness. Short-run adaptiveness corresponds to what we ordinarily call problem-solving, long-run adaptiveness to learning.

There is no reason, of course, why this hierarchy of mechanisms should have only three levels—or any specified number. In fact, the adaptive mechanisms need not be arranged hierarchically. Mechanism A may include mechanism B within its domain of action, and vice versa. However, in general there is much asymmetry in the ordering, so that certain elements in the process that do not often become strategic factors (the "boundaries of rationality") form the stable core of the organization structure.

We can now see the relation between Commons' and Barnard's theories of the "limiting" or "strategic" factor and organization structure. Organization will have structure, as we have defined the term here, insofar as there are boundaries of rationality—insofar as there are elements of the situation that must be or are in fact taken as givens, and that do not enter into rational calculations as potential strategic factors. If there were not boundaries to rationality, or if the boundaries varied in a rapid and unpredictable manner, there could be no stable organization structure. Some aspects of structure will be more easily modified than others, and hence we may need to distinguish short-run and long-run structure.

In this chapter, we have been concerned mostly with short-run structure—with programs to respond to sequences of situations requiring adaptive action. The "boundaries of rationality" that have been the source of our propositions have consisted primarily of the properties of human beings as organisms capable of evoking and executing relatively well-defined programs but able to handle programs only of limited complexity.

References

BLAU, P. M. *The Dynamics of Bureaucracy.* Chicago, 1955.

CYERT, R. M., and J. G. MARCH. "Organizational Structure and Pricing Behavior in an Oligopolistic Market." *American Economic Review* 45 (1955), 129–39.

———. "Organizational Factors in the Theory of Oligopoly." *Quarterly Journal of Economics* 70 (1956), 44–64.

GUETZKOW, H., and H. A. SIMON. "The Impact of Certain Communication Nets upon Organization and Performance in Task-oriented Groups." *Management Science* 1 (1955), 233–50.

KATONA, G. *Psychological Analysis of Economic Behavior.* New York, 1951.

MARCH, J. G. "An Introduction to the Theory and Measurement of Influence." *American Political Science Review* 49 (1955), 431–51.

MARSCHAK, J. "Rational Behavior, Uncertain Prospects, and Measurable Utility." *Econometrica* 18 (1950), 111–41.

NEWELL, A., J. C. SHAW, and H. A. SIMON. "Elements of a Theory of Human Problem Solving." *Psychological Review* 65 (1958), 151–66.

RIDLEY, C. E., and H. A. SIMON. *Measuring Municipal Activities.* Chicago, 1938.

SIMON, H. A. *Administrative Behavior,* New York, 1947.

———. "Birth of an Organization: The Economic Cooperation Administration." *Public Administration Review* 13 (1953), 227–36.

———. "A Behavioral Model of Rational Choice." *Quarterly Journal of Economics* 69 (1955), 99–118.

Interdependence
and Hierarchy
in Organizations

Peter M. Blau

The two objectives of this paper are to present empirical findings from a large number of organizations of several different types and to suggest a theory to explain these findings. A previous publication advanced a theory of differentiation in organizations based on data from employment security agencies and their local branches (Blau, 1970). But findings from one type of organization, even if based on quantitative data, cannot sustain a theory presumably applicable to work organizations in general. Hence the earlier analysis is replicated here with data from several very different types of organizations. Then some theoretical principles to explain the empirical findings are suggested. Whereas the previous formulation concentrated on organizing the empirically supported propositions into a deductive system, the new one focuses on underlying theoretical principles that can account for the observed regularities.

Empirical Regularities

Concern is primarily with three characteristics of work organizations, that is, organizations with employees responsible for accomplishing work: their size, their internal differentiation, and their administrative apparatus. Six sets of quantitative data collected in five studies of five different types of organizations are analyzed. It is impossible to discuss in detail the research procedures of these five large projects carried out over the last 6 years, which were concerned with many factors besides the three here considered.[1] A brief indication of procedures must suffice.

SOURCE: *Social Science Research* 1 (1972): 1–24. Copyright © 1972 by Academic Press, Inc. Reprinted by permission of the author and the publisher.
1. The research has been supported by Grants GS-553, GS-1528, GS-27073, and GS-28646X from the National Science Foundation to the Comparative Organization

Procedures. (1) Data on the 53 employment security agencies in this country (one in every state and one each in Puerto Rico, the Virgin Islands, and the District of Columbia) were obtained by three research assistants in personal visits to these agencies from informants and records. All the data under consideration, in the other studies as well as this one, consist of objective information derived from personnel records and detailed organizational charts constructed specifically for the research during the interview, which were checked against one another. (2) Data on the local branches of these agencies—1201 of them when the smallest and simplest are excluded—were collected during the same visits from information available at the headquarters. To ensure that the measures of branch characteristics are independent of those of corresponding agency characteristics, the latter are based on the structure and the administrative personnel at the agency headquarters, excluding branches. (3) Data on the 416 government finance departments of nearly all larger American cities, counties, and states were gathered in two different ways. N.O.R.C. interviewers visited the 256 larger and more complex ones, and self-administered mail questionnaires were returned by the rest.

In addition to these government agencies, research has been conducted on three other kinds of organizations. (4) Data on 124 department stores were obtained in visits by N.O.R.C. interviewers. These firms constitute two thirds of the largest department stores west of the Mississippi and north of the Mason-Dixon Line. Economic considerations led to the geographical restriction, and refusals are largely responsible for the fact that not all large northeastern department stores are included. (5) Data on 115 universities and colleges were collected in personal visits by research assistants. A weighting formula was applied to the analysis of this stratified sample, in which larger and higher-quality institutions are overrepresented, to make the results representative of the universe of the more than 1000 4-year liberal arts institutions in the country. (6) Data on the 1279 American teaching hospitals (the superior hospitals, specifically, all that have some residents, most of which have no direct university affiliation) were made available by the American Hospital Association, for which I am grateful. Although these data, secured for administrative purposes, furnish only crude indications of the organizational characteristics of interest, the large number of cases makes it tempting to use them nevertheless.

Size is conceptualized as the scope of an organization and its responsibilities; the measure is its number of employees (except in academic

Research Program, which I gratefully acknowledge. This paper is C.O.R.P. report No. 16. For full discussions of research procedures, see Blau and Schoenherr (1971), Meyer (1972), Goldman (1972), and future publications on academic institutions and hospitals.

institutions, where it is the number of faculty members). Methodological, theoretical, and empirical considerations dictated the choice of this measure of organizational size. Whereas the number of employees can be compared among different types, this is not the case for other measures of scope, such as sales in stores and beds in hospitals. Besides theoretical concern is with the way people—not assets or products—are organized and with the resulting structure of subgroupings of employees. Finally, there is a close empirical association between an organization's volume of responsibilities and its number of employees. The correlation between the number of insured unemployed in a state, whose needs the employment security agency is responsible to serve, and the agency's number of employees is .98; that between total sales and employees in a department store is .95; that between number of students and number of faculty in an institution of higher learning is .94.[2] As a matter of fact, an organization's personnel is quite highly correlated even with such indirect indications of its scope of operations as the population in a government finance department's jurisdiction (.62) and a hospital's total assets (.59).[3]

Organizations are differentiated in several dimensions, and the degree of differentiation in each is measured by the number of subunits. The number of hierarchical levels represents vertical differentiation. The number of major divisions under top management and of sections per division are two indicators of horizontal differentiation among subgroups with different functions.[4] The subdivision of work into occupational specialties is reflected by the number of official job titles or positions in government agencies and by the number of different departments in academic institutions and department stores. Two of the five types are geographically differentiated into branches, but since the branches of employment security agencies are analyzed separately, only those of department stores are treated as an independent measure of differentiation. The information from teaching hospitals furnished merely a single crude index of structural differentiation, the number of different types of residences, which is indicative of the number of the major, but not of all, medical divisions in the hospitals.

The basic measure of administrative apparatus is the proportion of managerial personnel, including managers and supervisors on all levels.

2. If both variables are logarithmically transformed ($\log_{10}$). Without transformation their correlation is .84.
3. No indication of the volume of operation of the local branches of employment security agencies is available. Community size does not provide a valid indirect measure of their work load, because there is more than one branch office in most larger cities.
4. Data on sections per division have been obtained only for employment security agencies and for department stores, since different sections in small organizations often are work groups performing essentially the same responsibilities. The average number of employees in these agencies (1195) and stores (1867) is substantially higher than the averages in the four other types.

Inasmuch as academic and medical work is not supervised by managers in the way work in government bureaus and business concerns is, somewhat different, though conceptually analogous, variables are used for universities and colleges and for hospitals, namely, the ratio of administrators (not including clerical personnel) to faculty, and the proportion of nurses in administration, respectively. Two supplementary indicators of the ratio of administrative manpower to operating personnel are the proportion of employees in staff rather than line positions (only available for employment security agencies) and the average span of control of first-line supervisors (available for three types).

Regression analysis is used to discern direct and indirect effects of one condition in organizations on another.[5] A regression coefficient must exceed twice its standard error when other relevant factors are held constant to be considered indicative of an effect. The assumption of causal order is: size—differentiation—administration. The nature of an organization's responsibilities is roughly controlled, since each type is analyzed separately.

Effects of size. The larger an organization the more differentiated it is along various lines. Whether we look at hierarchical levels, functional divisions, sections within them, occupational specialties, or geographical branches, organizations become differentiated into a larger number of them with increasing size, and this is the case for very different kinds of organizations. The findings from employment security agencies and their local branches are replicated, with minor variations, not only in other government bureaus and in private firms but also in universities and colleges and in teaching hospitals, as Table 1 indicates. Most of the correlations are high, and nearly all increase further when size is logarithmically transformed (using $\log_{10}$). On the average, size (log) accounts for more than two fifths of the variation in hierarchical levels, nearly two fifths of the variation in functional divisions, and more than half of the variation in occupational specialization. These findings challenge the conclusions of previous investigators that size does "not appear to affect organization as much as might have been expected" (Woodward, 1965, p. 31) and that "size and organizational structure are not closely related" (Hall *et al.*, 1967, p. 712).

Increasing organizational size promotes differentiation, but it does so at a declining rate. The scatter diagrams reveal that the regression lines of size (untransformed) on the various measures of differentiation for all six sets of data have declining positive slopes. As size increases, the number of subunits into which an organization becomes differentiated in any one dimension increase at first very rapidly and then more and more gradually.

5. The regression coefficients for employment security agencies reported are somewhat higher than those in Blau and Schoenherr (1971), because a different computer program has been used to derive the former (SPSS).

It is impossible to present this score of scatter diagrams here.[6] However, some indication of this curvature of the regression lines is provided by the fact that the logarithmic transformation of size raises its correlation with measures of differentiation (in 16 of 19 instances), as Table 1 shows. Some of the curves are shallow, so that logarithmic transformation of size produces a curve in the opposite direction (an accelerating positive slope) and improves the correlation little, and in three cases the curve in the opposite direction is so pronounced that the correlation decreases slightly.[7] Thus the addition of 100 employees stimulates much differentiation in organizations with fewer than 1000 employees but only little in those with several thousand. While increasing size has a pronounced impact on differentiation along various lines in work organizations regardless of type,

TABLE 1. Zero-order correlations between size and measures of differentiation

	ES [a]	LB [b]	FD [c]	DS [d]	U AND C [e]	TH [f]
Levels						
Size	.60	.68	.55	.51	.37	
Log size	.72	.69	.66	.66	.51	
Divisions [g]						
Size	.38	.61	.50	.28	.80	.52
Log size	.54	.67	.73	.33	.82	.50
Sec./div.						
Size	.16			.43		
Log size	.43			.62		
Occup. Spec. [h]						
Size	.78	.51	.81	.60	.83	
Log size	.82	.62	.80	.66	.79	
Branches						
Size	.94			.55		
Log size [i]				.62		

a. Employment security agencies ($N = 53$).
b. Local branches of ES agencies ($N = 1201$).
c. Finance departments ($N = 416$).
d. Department stores ($N = 124$).
e. Universities and colleges ($N = 115$).
f. Teaching hospitals ($N = 1279$).
g. In U and C, schools and colleges; in TH, types of residencies.
h. In DS and U and C, departments; otherwise, job titles.
i. Correlation with branches not available for ES.

6. A number of them are shown in Blau and Schoenherr (1971).
7. The scatter diagram for one of these three cases is presented in Blau and Schoenherr (1971), page 333. It shows that the regression curve (of size on occupational specialties in finance departments) has a declining slope, even though logarithmic transformation of size reduces the correlation.

the marginal influence of a given increment in size declines with increasing size.

Contrary to the stereotype of the proliferation of bureaucratic machinery in large organizations, the administrative apparatus is proportionately smaller in large than in small organizations. Different though government bureaus and retail businesses are from universities and hospitals, the proportion of personnel responsible for administering the organization declines in all of them with increasing size, as the negative correlations in Table 2 indicate. These results confirm those of Melman (1951), Anderson and Warkov (1961), Hawley et al. (1965), and Indik (1964). The span of control of supervisors is, correspondingly, wider in large than in small organizations. The correlations between size (log) and average number of subordination per first-line supervisor are .66 for the 1201 branches of employment security agencies, .51 for the 416 finance departments, and .34 for the 124 department stores. Despite the more complex structure of larger organizations produced by differentiation, they apparently can be administered with proportionately less manpower than small ones.

Organizations exhibit an economy of scale in administration. But this economy of scale declines with increasing organizational size. The savings in managerial and other administrative personnel that the large size of organizations seems to make possible diminish with their increasing size. Table 2 shows that logarithmic transformation of size increases its correlations with the measures of administration in all types of organization for which data are available. This implies that the regression line of size on administration has a declining negative slope, and the scatter diagrams confirm this inference. With increasing organizational size, the proportion of administrative personnel decreases sharply at first but less and less thereafter. The large size of organizations appears to reduce both the proportion of administrative personnel needed and the savings in administrative personnel that further increases size permit. Thus the negative mar-

TABLE 2. Zero-order correlations between size and measures of administrative apparatus

	ES	LB	FD	DS	U AND C	TH
% Managers [a]						
Size [b]	−.42	−.46		−.24	−.17	−.30
Log size	−.45	−.64	−.28	−.53	−.28	−.48
% Staff						
Size	−.44					
Log size	−.60					

a. Administration-faculty ratio in U and C; % admin. nurses in TH.
b. Not available for FD.

ginal influence of a given increment in organizational size on administration, just as its positive marginal influence on differentiation, declines with increasing size.

Effects of differentiation. Although size and differentiation tend to vary together in work organizations, they have opposite implications for the administrative apparatus. Whereas large size reduces the proportion of administrative personnel, pronounced structural differentiation expands it. Interestingly enough, the division of labor among individual roles (number of occupational specialties) has no such effect,[8] only differentiation that produces a structure of interdependent subgroups does. Specifically, what enlarges the administrative apparatus are the number of levels into which the hierarchy is differentiated, the number of divisions and that of sections per division among which functions are subdivided, and the number of geographical branches. But this effect is evident only when organizational size is controlled, because size produces spurious negative associations between measures of structural differentiation and administrative apparatus, which conceal the positive direct nexus between them. Table 3 presents six separate regression analyses which dissect the effects of size and differentiation on administration.

The negative standardized regression coefficients in the first row of

TABLE 3. Regression analysis of proportion of administrative personnel[a] on size and differentiation

	ES	LB	FD	DS	U and C	TH
Size (log)	−1.13	−1.47	−1.29	−.46	−.55	−.54
Levels	.47	.61	.94	.32	.25 [e]	
Divisions [b]	.36	.62	.53	.21	.12 [e]	.13
Sec./div. [c]	.33					
Branches				.53		
Ind. effect of size [d]	.68	.83	1.01	.61	.27	.06

a. Percentage of managerial personnel, except: (1) excluding buyers in DS, who are included in DS in Table 2 (see fn. 9); (2) administration-faculty ratio in U and C; (3) percentage of admin. nurses in TH.
b. In U and C, schools and colleges; in TH, types of residencies.
c. Excluded from regression analysis in DS, since it has no appreciable effect ($b^* = .05$).
d. The figures in this row are not part of the regression equation but provided for supplementary information; they are the difference between the r and the b^* of size (log).
e. Not twice its standard error.

8. The regression coefficients of number of occupational specialities, with size controlled, on the percentage of the personnel in administration are insignificantly small in all types (not available for hospitals). The zero-order correlations are negative and spurious, owing to the influence of size.

Table 3 reveal that large size as such, independent of differentiation, effects considerable more savings in administrative personnel than the zero-order correlations (in Table 2) indicate.[9] This is the case in all types of organizations examined, notwithstanding their diverse nature, though the strength of the direct relationship between size and administration varies among types (which is in part an artifact of the difference in the measures of differentiation that are controlled). But the large size of organizations is accompanied by differentiation in their structure, as we have seen, and this differentiation enlarges the administrative apparatus, as the positive regression coefficients in rows 2–5 of Table 3 show.[10] Hence, the indirect effect of large organizational size, mediated by the greater differentiation in the structure it generates, expands the administrative apparatus, counteracting its direct effect of reducing it. Row 6 presents these indirect effects of size $(r - b^*)$. The pattern of influences can be represented in a simple path diagram: [11]

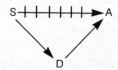

These findings raise a methodological question, however. The indicators of differentiation, particularly number of hierarchical levels, necessarily increase the number of managers in organizations of a given size. Are the observed relationships between differentiation and proportion of

9. In department stores, managerial personnel in Table 3 excludes buyers, who are part-time managers, while the figure in Table 2 includes buyers, making the two figures not comparable. The comparable figure—the zero order correlation for store size (log) and managers excluding buyers—is .15. If buyers were included in the regression analysis presented in Table 3, insignificantly small regression coefficients for levels. (.10) and divisions (.07) would be observed. Thus, the effect of structural differentiation in department stores increases primarily the number of "pure" managers who are not also buyers, whereas the administrative economies of large-scale operations are only evident if these part-time managers, the buyers, are included in the measure and largely result from a reduction in the proportion of these part-time managers. (The zero-order correlation between size (log) and percentage of buyers in the store is −.79.)

10. In universities and colleges, the regression coefficients for levels and divisions fail to exceed twice their standard error, probably because the measure of size is confined to faculty while students and other employees also effect administrative loads and structural differentiation. If number of students (log) is substituted for number of faculty (log) as the measure of size, all three standardized regression coefficients are greater than twice their standard error; they are −.75 (size), .26 (levels), and .30 (divisions).

11. The actual path diagram for each of the six sets of data can be completed with the information provided in Tables 3 and 1. Table 3 supplies the path coefficients between A and S (row 1) and those between several measures of D and S (rows 2–5). Table 1 supplies the path coefficients between these measures of D and S (rows 2, 4, 6, and 10).

administrative personnel merely the result of this mathematical connection? To answer this question, regression analyses are carried out substituting a measure of the ratio of administrative to operating personnel that is mathematically independent of the differentiation measures, namely, the average span of control of first-line supervisors, data on which are available for three types.[12] The same independent variables are, of course, expected to have the opposite effects on this ratio of operating personnel to lowest-level managers from those they have on the proportion of managers. Table 4 confirms this expectation in two of three cases. Large size increases, and differentiation decreases, the number of subordinates per first-line supervisor in the branches of employment security agencies and in finance departments but not in department stores, possibly because buyers there are often part-time supervisors.[13] The same pattern is observable in department stores if the span of control of middle managers instead of that of first-line supervisors is considered (column 4). Initial results are sufficiently corroborated to place some confidence in the conclusion that the relationships reflect empirical forces and not the confounding of empirical measures.

TABLE 4. Regression analysis of average span of control of supervisors on size and differentiation

	LB	FD	DS	DS [a]
Size (log)	1.31	1.08	.44	.50
Levels	−.49	−.25	−.18 [d]	−.35
Divisions [b]	−.46	−.55	.06 [d]	−.26
Ind. effect of size [c]	−.65	−.57	−.10	−.32

a. Mean span of control of managers who supervise buyers.
b. In U and C, schools and colleges; in TH, types of residencies.
c. These figures are not part of the regression equation (see Table 3, fn. d).
d. Not twice its standard error.

12. Regression analysis using the alternative measure for administrative apparatus in employment security agencies, percentage staff, yields another replication of the findings in Table 3. While this measure is not confounded with number of levels, it is probably affected by number of divisions and sections per division, because some of these subunits are staff units. Interestingly, however, the standardized regression coefficient for levels (.41) is greater than twice its standard error, whereas those for divisions (.28) and sections per division (.22) are not; the one for size (log) is −1.20.
13. Branches are not used as independent variables in department stores because the mean span of control *in the main store only* is the dependent variable. (Using them alters results little.) The somewhat different findings in department stores may have several reasons: the existence of many part-time managers (the buyers); the lesser reliability of the data from this project; distinctive patterns in profit-making enterprises, of which these stores are the only representative in the research program so far. No detailed interpretation of the distinctive features of department stores is offered in this paper concerned with the similarities in different types of organizations.

In organizations established to further academic pursuits or medical treatment as well as those explicitly designed for the efficient performance of work, large size produces very great savings in administrative manpower, other conditions being equal. But other conditions are not the same in large and in small organizations. The large size of organizations is accompanied by greater differentiation in their structure, which in turn leads to the expansion of administrative manpower. The complex structure of large organizations thereby counteracts the economy of scale in administration, without completely eliminating it. It appears as if increasing organizational size gave rise to dialectical forces having opposite effects, and decomposition in regression analysis can reveal these conflicting influences. Processes seem to arise with the increasing size of organizations that lessen needs for administrative personnel, and so do processes that generate a complex structure and consequently magnify needs for administrative personnel.

The consistent empirical regularities observed in quite different types of organizations pose several questions a theory should answer. Why do large organizations have a so much more differentiated structure than small ones? Why have large organizations, despite their greater complexity, and contrary to the bureaucratic stereotype, a relatively smaller administrative apparatus than small ones? One hardly needs to ask why a differentiated complex structure increases the proportion of administrative personnel in an organization, since a plausible interpretation readily comes to mind. But can this positive effect of differentiation on administration and the negative effect of size on it be explained by the same theoretical principle? Finally, what accounts for the decline in the influence of size on both differentiation and administration with increasing size? Theoretical answers to these questions will be suggested by advancing generalizations that logically imply and thus explain the empirical findings.

Functional Differentiation

In work organizations the terms "functional differentiation" and "functional interdependence" have quite specific meanings. There is no implicit assumption of mythical forces that create an equilibrium among diverse institutions and assure that each makes positive contributions to the others. Functional differentiation in organizations refers simply to the fact that a common enterprise has become differentiated into subunits with distinct responsibilities or functions, for example, that an automobile factory consists of a division manufacturing motors, a chassis division, a body division, and a sales division. The functions of these divisions are, of course, interdependent, and so are all functions or specialized duties that result from the subdivision of a given job, such as that for which a work organization is responsible.

Interdependence. For large numbers of persons to be integrated in a common enterprise requires either that they share distinctive values or interests that unite them or that they perform complementary functions that make them interdependent. Reference is to Durkheim's (1933) famous distinction between mechanical and organic solidarity, except that these concepts are applied, not to types of societies, but to associations within a society. The radical idealogy creates the bond of solidarity among the members of a revolutionary movement. Common economic interests unify workers in a labor union. Distinctive beliefs about morality and supernatural powers make a religious sect a highly cohesive body, and as the strength of religious convictions wanes, so does the social integration in the church.

The employees of an organization have no such distinctive common values or interests. To be sure, they have in common the basic cultural values and an interest in earning a living, but both of these they share with the employees of other organizations in the society. Besides the members of most work organizations, except very small ones, do not share the more specific value orientations individuals have, such as those reflecting their ethnic subculture, religious affiliation, and political allegiance. Even when such orientations are common to all or most employees of a work organization, they are not a distinctive bond, because they are shared with many other people. Occupational interests similarly tend not to be the same for all employees of an organization, and whether or not they are, many others outside share these interests. But are not the goals of an organization those of its members, furnishing a bond of common solidarity? Not in the case of work organizations. People join social movements or clubs because they are identified with their goals. But they do not work for General Motors because they are interested in raising its profits; or for a city finance department because they are interested in the fiscal welfare of the town; or for Columbia University because they are interested in *its* ability to advance knowledge and transmit it to students. Employees join organizations and make contributions to their goals because they are interested in receiving financial rewards, utilizing occupational skills, and, particularly in the case of some occupations, enhancing their professional reputation. The goals of the organization are not goals of its employees, at least not initially, though secondary identification with them and with the organization itself often tends to develop in the course of working for it.

What transforms an aggregate of individuals who happen to have the same employer into an integrated collective body is their functional interdependence produced by the subdivision of work in the organization. The employees of an organization perform complementary roles, that is, duties that have no instrumental significance unless complemented by other duties, such as those of the buyer of dresses in a department store, which require complementation by the work of sales ladies. The subdivisions of the work needed to pursue the organization's goals among subunits with different functions necessarily makes these subunits (for example, the division collecting unemployment taxes and that paying unemployment benefits), and hence their employees, instrumentally interdependent.[14]

In sum, the employees of a work organization are engaged in a common enterprise, which requires that they become an integrated social unit, but they do not have strong feelings of common solidarity, like those permeating the members of religious or political sects, for they lack the profound values shared only by the ingroup that create such firm bonds of solidarity and unite individuals in a cohesive group. The subdivision of work in organizations, however, has the result that its employees perform complementary roles and belong to subunits with complementary functions, and their consequent instrumental interdependence fuses employees into a distinctive coherent social organism. The differentiation of functions in an organization, developing for instrumental reasons, shapes its social structure and converts its employees from a collection of individuals with no distinctive common values or interests into a unified social entity.

Process of integration. The process of social integration of individuals in a large collectivity always involves direct social contacts in small groups. The kinship system of simple societies illustrates this. It is an institution that divides the society into small subunits which are interconnected in several ways. The intimate and frequent social interaction in small families makes it possible for individuals to be socialized, to acquire the common language and cultural values, to receive emotional support, and thereby to attain social integration. These social processes make individuals integrated members not only of small families but also of larger clans and the entire society, because families are linked together in the kinship system and transmit to children the cultural and subcultural values of the larger collectivities of which they are part. Another illustration of this principle is de Tocqueville's (1945) thesis that the integration of people into the political life of a large democracy depends on widespread participation in many voluntary associations, which are relatively small and serve as me-

14. The degree of interdependence in work organizations varies. At one extreme, illustrated by the assembly line, the work of one individual or group cannot be performed until that of another is. At the other extreme, illustrated by different sales departments, the work of one subunit can proceed regardless of that in others, but the significance of the various functions for the organization makes them interdependent. It takes a number of different sales departments to make up a department store; heart surgery can be performed whether or not orthopedic surgery is, but both are required in a general hospital, just as instructions in both natural sciences and humanities is needed in a college. Extensive differentiation of an organization's responsibilities intensifies the degree of interdependence among the functions of subunits and makes the performance of at least some directly contingent on that of others.

diaries between individual citizens and the state. There is no direct way individuals can relate themselves to a society or any other large collectivity. Their social integration requires subunits small enough for regular personal contacts among members.

The differentiation of instrumental functions along various lines has implications for social integration in work organizations analogous to those of the kinship system in simple societies, because it too creates small interlocking subunits in which stable social relations can develop. The recurrent social interaction among colleagues in these small groups socializes newcomers to informal as well as official procedures, furnishes continuing advice on problems of the job and social support, and consequently fosters integration in the immediate work group, and in the organization as well. The groupings are interlocking inasmuch as many employees belong to several of them—for example, with colleagues in the same specialty from different departments, with others in the same location regardless of specialty, and with fellow managers on the same level. Since these interdependent interlocking subgroups form a tight web as constituent elements of the organization's structure, employees who become integrated in subgroups are thereby enmeshed in the larger social structure and become integral members of the organization.

The larger an organization is, the more differentiation is required to produce the small subunits in which regular personal contacts further social intergration. But an explanation of the increasing differentiation with increasing organization size in these terms is subject to the criticism, often made of functional interpretations, that the existence of a social pattern is accounted for by the beneficial consequences it has for the social system, as if a benign "unseen hand" governed human existence. In work organizations, however, the existence of social patterns that make contributions to operations need not be attributed to an "unseen hand," because a specific agency exists to institute such patterns. Organizations have a management that is responsible for effective operations, rewarded for discharging this responsibility successfully, and empowered to implement its interest in efficient operations. Given the assumption that managers are interested in effective operations, conditions (such as large organizational size) that require certain structural arrangements for effective operations can be expected to constrain managers to institute these arrangements if possible.[15]

15. Another assumption is implied here: the prevailing characteristics of organizations, as distinguished from those in particular organizations, can be explained in terms of the influences of antecedent conditions in organizations (or their environment) without reference to the psychological preferences or decisions of individual managers, because these social conditions greatly restrict the options of managers who pursue an interest in efficient operations. This principle derives from Durkheim (1938:110): "The determining cause of a social fact should be sought among the social facts preceding it and not among the states of individual consciousness."

CURRENT THEORETICAL PERSPECTIVES

But does management's interest in efficient operations necessarily make it interested in the existence of highly integrated work groups? This can by no means be taken for granted, inasmuch as the social cohesion of work groups, which may strengthen the informal enforcement of output restrictions, is not consistently associated with superior performance (see, for example, Seashore, 1954, pp. 63–80). To be sure, management has an interest in the integration of employees in the work organization, which depends on their integration in its subgroups, but it is doubtful that managers are aware of differentiation's significance for this integration, even if the conjecture that it has such significance is correct. However, the differentiation of work into specialized responsibilities also makes instrumental contributions to operations, of which management is unlikely to remain unaware, and which furnish incentives for managerial decisions that promote differentiation.

Specialization. A large volume of work requires a large number of persons to accomplish it. For many people to collaborate on common endeavors, their work must be organized. Organizing work involves subdividing it into component parts. Even a single individual organizes his work by dividing it into parts and doing one at a time. The more complex the job, the more important it is to divide it into more homogeneous tasks that can be performed separately, because homogeneous tasks are easier than heterogeneous ones. If the volume of work is too large for an individual and requires a group, it can be subdivided among group members. Only in the most primitive collaboration of individuals, exemplified by log rolling, does every one perform the same tasks. Work in a group is typically subdivided, with different individuals performing different tasks, which makes the job of each more homogeneous and thus simplifies it. The subdivision of work in social space, therefore, complements its subdivision by time periods in most cases of collaboration in a group.

If a still larger volume of work requires many persons to accomplish it and not merely a small group, it can be divided among subgroups, enabling entire subgroups to concentrate on relatively homogeneous tasks. Whereas work in small groups tends to become organized, subdivided, and coordinated in the course of direct social interaction without formalized procedures, explicit formal procedures are necessary to organize and coordinate the work of a collectivity too large for every member to have direct contacts with all others. A work organization is simply an explicit system for organizing the work of many persons in a common enterprise. A sheer increase in the volume of work, by determining whether its accomplishment requires only one person or a small group or a large collectivity, alters the principle in terms of which the work is organized (by subdivision in time, among individuals, or among subgroups).

Organizations accomplish jobs of staggering complexity as well as magnitude, jobs far too complex for an individual or any number of individuals who are not organized, because the subdivision of work facilitates that of every individual and that of every subunit by making their tasks more homogeneous. This may be illustrated by the division of labor among specialized roles of individuals. In its absence, every employee would have to perform all the tasks involved in the discharge of the organization's responsibilities and would have to have all the requisite skills. For instance, all patient care in hospitals would have to be provided by G.P.'s. The division of labor segregates tasks into homogeneous jobs ranging usually from quite routine to very difficult ones. Less training suffices for the comparatively routine jobs. In the example of hospitals, nurses relieve physicians of some duties, and much patient care can be performed by aides. At the same time, greater specialized training can be required for the various difficult jobs, as exemplified by the substitution of surgeons and internists and other specialists for G.P.'s in hospitals. The division of labor consequently has a double advantage. It makes it possible to fill many positions with less trained personnel, which facilitates recruitment and achieves economies, and to fill the most difficult jobs with more highly trained experts, which improves the quality of performance. By reducing the range and enhancing the homogeneity of the tasks in any given position, the division of labor promotes specialized expertness as well as routinization. The brain surgeon's job encompasses, strictly speaking, a narrower range of more homogeneous duties than the G.P.'s, but this very fact enables the former successfully to perform tasks the latter cannot undertake.

In short the division of labor enables an organization to perform more complex work better and with less skilled personnel. It is a mechanism that translates quantitative changes into qualitative ones. A purely quantitative increase in the volume of work, without any initial changes in the nature of responsibilities, increases the number of persons engaged in the work and the division of labor among them, and it thereby gives rise to the performance of jobs that were not originally undertaken and could not have been, that is, to a change in the nature of the work. Thus jobs are performed in large organizations that do not exist in similar small ones.

Work is subdivided in organizations not only among positions occupied by individuals but also among organizational subunits. There are the major divisions under top management with different functions, and the sections within them with varying responsibilities. Sometimes organizations have geographical branches, and these also may have specialized functions. The subdivision of work among organizational segments is the organizational form of the division of labor, and it makes important instrumental contributions to operations. An entire group can concentrate on more homogeneous tasks and gain experiences and expertise in carrying them out. Consultation among colleagues engaged in similar work, which supplies advice when needed and social recognition for good advice, probably improves performance. The manager of a unit with relatively homogeneous tasks can have expert knowledge of most or all of them.

Another dimension of differentiation in work organizations is that between operations and administration. Operations involve the production of goods or the provision of services that is the organization's basic responsibility, be it furnishing services to the unemployed, retail selling, or treating the sick. Administration entails organizing the work of others and maintaining the organization, broadly conceived, including recruitment, guidance, coordination, and management. The subdivision of work in administration has the same advantages as that in operations, permitting some administrative jobs to be performed by less skilled personnel and others to be filled by specialized experts in various administrative responsibilities, including that of management. Before extending the analysis of administration, the principles of differentiation advanced should be concisely formulated.

The differentiation of instrumental functions in work organizations makes important contributions to effective operations. These exert compelling constraints on management, given its interest in effective operations, to make the administrative decisions required for the development of differentiation. But the degree of feasible differentiation in an organization is limited by its size, particularly inasmuch as differentiation occurs in several intersecting dimensions. An organization must be large for operating responsibilities to be much subdivided, and it must be still larger for administrative responsibilities to be much subdivided. Large size is a necessary condition for extensive differentiation, but not a sufficient one, and differentiation's instrumental contributions create the pressures that promote it to the degree size permits. If the increasing size of work organizations not only makes the social integration of employees dependent on extensive differentiation but also provides the opportunities for improving operations through progressive differentiation of functions, which gives management incentives to promote such differentiation, it follows that increasing organizational size is accompanied by increasing differentiation. Thus the theory can explain the first set of empirical findings. This does not prove the theory, of course.

Administrative Hierarchy

Work organizations have been briefly defined as explicit systems for organizing the work of many persons in a common enterprise. But they are specifically hierarchical control systems for doing so. An administrative hierarchy through which control over operations is exercised is a basic trait of organizations, as Weber (1946, p. 197) has emphasized. Whether hierarchical control is a necessary prerequisite for organizing work on a large scale is a moot question. Management has the responsibility for organizing and directing the work of other employees, has the authority that enables it to do so, and has command over resources, on which employees depend, to back up its authority. Although there is interdependence among subunits in organizations, it is asymmetrical. Functionally, every subunit is dependent on others, including management, which could not administer operations without employees to perform them. Existentially, however, the dependence of lower ranks on higher ones is unilateral, inasmuch as superiors have authority and sanctioning power over subordinates.

Economy of scale in administration. The large size of an organization expands management's power, both internally, by increasing the scope of its authority, and externally, by increasing the influence of the organization in the community and thereby management's. Many employees also enlarge the volume of administrative work. The principles suggested for operations also apply to administration. A large volume of work requires a large number of persons to perform it, in administration as elsewhere. For large numbers to work together on administering an organization, their administrative work must be organized, and organizing work entails subdividing it.

The subdivision of administrative work takes two forms. First, administrative duties that do not depend on managerial authority, such as recruitment and bookkeeping, are separated from the rest. These staff functions are in turn subdivided among positions and organizational subunits, exemplified by personnel divisions, training sections, comptroller offices, and typing pools. The slogan that staff advises but does not command expresses that these functions are divested of official authority, though staff experts often have much influence in organizations. Second, administrative responsibilities for management and supervision are differentiated into hierarchical levels, which vary in scope of authority and hence in the nature of major duties, ranging from responsibilities for assisting with and checking on operations to those for long-range planning, fundamental policy, and the organization's viability and success. Lower managerial levels are under the authority of higher ones, and official authority is ultimately rooted entirely in the hands of top management, which has command over resources, and which delegates authority to other managers. Hierarchical differentiation crosscuts the subdivision of work in operations and that within the staff. Whereas management is merely one of many functions in purely instrumental terms, its authority distinguishes it fundamentally from the rest. The differentiation of managerial levels obscures the fundamental distinction between management and other employees without making it any less important.

In contrast to its absolute amount, the proportionate amount of administrative work decreases with increases in the volume of operations and the number of employees to be organized. The reason is that organizing work entails initial investments largely independent of the volume of work to be carried out. The time and effort spent in setting up a computer program differs little whether one tabulation is made or several hundreds. Once a procedure for processing unemployment insurance checks has been designed, possibly after extensive investigation of alternatives, it can be used to issue any number of checks. The work involved in selecting the styles of dresses with most sales appeal hardly depends on the number of dresses to be bought for a store and offered for sale. To design a new procedure is a time-consuming task, whether it is applicable to the work of few employees or that of many.[16]

In short the investment of administrative time required for organizing operations is not proportionate to their volume, increasing far less than the volume of operations increases. To be sure, not all administrative duties involve such time investments. Personnel interviews with 100 job applicants take twice the time needed for interviews with 50, and closely supervising and reviewing the work of subordinates requires substantially more time if there are eight than if there are six. But even such administrative efforts permit savings with increasing size, which makes more efficient utilization of administrative personnel possible. A personnel officer may not be fully occupied in a small organization. Fewer employees with identical than with different duties can be supervised by one person. This makes it necessary for small organizations, which have only very few employees in some job categories, to assign fewer subordinates to supervisors than can large organizations.

The principle that the time involved in organizing the work of others is independent of limited differences in the amount of work being organized, though not of extreme differences, can explain the economy of scale in administration. If the volume of administrative work increases less than proportionately as the volume of operations increases; and if the volume of work governs the number of persons needed to accomplish it, in administration as well as in operations; it follows that the number of persons in administration increases less than that in operations; and hence that the proportion of administrative personnel decreases as the total number of employees increases, which is what the data show. The great power of top management of large organizations is an extreme instance of the same principle. A small handful of persons commanding large resources and empowered to formulate basic policies and to make the basic organizing

---

16. The time management spends in external relations—negotiating with suppliers, unions, or the I.R.S.—is also affected relatively little by the organization's size, but the focus here is on internal administrative responsibilities.

decisions is able to direct the work of hundreds of thousands of employees and to exercise tremendous influence in the society.[17]

Significance of heterogeneity. The complex structure of interdependent parts resulting from differentiation creates problems of coordination and communication in work organizations. The horizontal differentiation of functions among subunits produces especially problems of coordination, because interdependent responsibilities must be integrated, and the vertical differentiation of authority intensifies primarily problems of communication, because differences in authority impede the free flow of communication. The administrative attention these problems of coordination and communication demand furnish a plausible reason for the empirical finding that more differentiated organizations employ more administrative personnel than less differentiated ones of the same size.

The question arises whether the influence of structural differentiation on administration cannot be explained by a principle consistent with that advanced to explain the influence of organizational size on administration. This principle—that the administrative effort of organizing work increases much less than in proportion to increases in the volume of work—makes an implicit assumption, namely, that the work being organized is fairly homogenous. For the same organizing procedures cannot be applied to entirely dissimilar responsibilities. Different problems are involved in organizing the collection of unemployment taxes from employers, the disbursement of employment benefits to those entitled to them, and the provision of employment services. A single incentive system may not be suitable for clerical and for professional workers. The same procedure cannot be used to organize the manufacture of products and their sale.

A minimum of homogeneity characterizes work organizations. Department stores only sell retail merchandise, they do not collect taxes, instruct students, or treat the sick. What is more important, the larger an organization, the larger are its subunits with relatively homogeneous responsibilities.[18] The large segments with fairly homogeneous responsibilities in large work organizations are what reduces the proportion of administrative personnel in them, because the same procedures can be used to administer a large volume of responsibilities that are homogeneous. But if homogeneity lessens needed administrative effort, heterogeneity must expand it. Since structural differentiation increases the heterogeneity of responsibilities in an organization—among managerial levels as well as func-

17. The earlier statement that the structural constraints of conditions in the organization greatly restrict the options of managers referred to decisions pertaining to the way work is organized and does not imply that management lacks power in determining basic policies and courses of action.
18. This is the case despite the greater number of subunits in larger organizations. The positive correlations between total organizational size and average size of subunits are discussed below and presented in Table 5.

tional divisions and sections—it therefore is expected to enlarge its administrative personnel, which is what the data indicate.

Large size gives a work organization two instrumental advantages: a reduction in the proportion of personnel needed for administration, and an opportunity for extensive subdivision of work along various lines which facilitates operations. The subdivision of work that develops in large organizations produces simultaneously greater homogeneity within subunits of any given kind and greater heterogeneity among them. According to the theory, the former is expected to decrease and the latter to increase the administrative apparatus. Can be prediction of such opposite effects of one factor on another be empirically tested? It can, provided one is willing to make the assumption that organizational size, with number of different subunits in several dimensions controlled, represents within-unit homogeneity (as well as larger mean size of subunits) and that number of subunits, with size controlled, represents among-unit heterogeneity. Under these assumptions the empirical findings in Tables 3 and 4 conform to the predictions implied by the theory.

Dialectical processes seem to develop in work organizations with increasing size, which effect their administration in opposite ways. The progressive differentiation of functions accompanying increasing size, which makes it possible for many employees to be organized and integrated in the common enterprise, increases both the homogeneity within and the heterogeneity among subunits. Since the administrative effort needed for organizing work depends on its heterogeneity, large organizational size, by promoting differentiation and thus homogeneity in one respect and heterogeneity in another, has opposite effects on administration, one mediated by the greater homogeneity within larger subunits, and the other by the heterogeneity among subunits. Thus processes of differentiation can be considered dialectical forces through which increasing organizational size, which generates these processes, reduces the administrative apparatus proportionately, on the one hand, and expands it, on the other. The process of administration, inasmuch as it involves organizing work by differentiating responsibilities, creates new administrative problems in the course of solving others, because differentiation engenders dialectical forces. The differentiation of functions in work organizations must be kept within bounds lest the administrative problems it creates outweigh the instrumental advantages it produces.

Feedback. The administrative problems in the complex structures to which differentiation in organizations gives rise seem to have feedback effects that modify the influence of size on differentiation and on administration. One can think of these problems, from which feedback processes engendered by the heterogeneity among organizational subunits are inferred, in economic terms—the cost of large administrative overhead—or in sociological ones—the difficulty of coordinating many diverse subgroups. The reaction to administrative problems may be either resistance to the conditions that create them or adjustment to these conditions. Both apparently occur, perhaps in different organizations, perhaps in the same ones at different times or in different parts.

If administrative problems produced by differentiation along various lines in work organizations evoke resistance against further differentiation, the pressure of increasing size promoting differentiation must overcome increasing counterpressure from this resistance, similar to the growing counterpressure the force of a piston in a cylinder compressing a gas must overcome. Given the principle that the effect of increasing organizational size on differentiation arouses increasing resistance, it follows that the influence of a unit increment in size (say 500 employees) on differentiation declines as size, and with it differentiation, increases. This is what the data show, for all measures of differentiation, in all types of organizations under examination. A further implication is deducible. If the number of subunits (the measure of differentiation in any dimension) increases less rapidly than the total size of the organization, the average size of subunits (the ratio of total size to their number) must increase with increasing size. The data reveal very high positive correlations between total size and average subunit size in all cases (Table 5).

Instead of resisting differentiation, because it creates administrative problems, it can be adjusted to in organizations by enlarging the administrative apparatus. Since increasing organizational size effects reductions in the proportionate size of the administrative apparatus, such adjustments to the progressive differentiation it fosters must increasingly counteract these reductions. This implies that the effect of a given increment in size on the administrative apparatus, decreasing its proportionate size, declines as size increases, and with it differentiation, which is the pattern empirically observed. Thus the declining marginal influence of organizational size on

TABLE 5. Zero-order correlations between total size and mean size of certain subunits

	ES	LB	FD	DS	U and C	TH [a]
Divisions	.96	.76	.94	.76	.32	
Sections	.95			.51		
Levels [b]	.99	.98	.94	.98	.99	
Occup. spec. [c]	.94	.85	.30	.84	.77	
Branches	.65			.74		

a. Not available.
b. The number of personnel per level has no concrete meaning.
c. In DS and U and C, departments; otherwise, job titles.

both differentiation and administration can be interpreted in terms of feedback processes assumed to result from administrative problems differentiation causes.

Resistance to differentiation in organizations, which has been inferred to explain the diminishing influence of size on differentiation, can also help explain the economy of scale in administration, the net effect of large size reducing the proportion of administrative personnel. For the strong associations between total size and mean subunit size are attributable to this resistance. The greater the size of subunits among which responsibilities are divided, the larger are the segments of employees with relatively homogeneous duties. Inasmuch as homogeneity lessens the need for administrative personnel, according to the theory, the larger subunits with comparatively homogeneous duties resulting from the resistance that keeps the differentiation in large organizations within limits can be considered to be responsible for the proportionately smaller administrative apparatus in large than in small organizations.[19]

Conclusions

The major propositions of the theory advanced are summarized in deductive form. In doing so, explications and refinements of the theoretical propositions are ignored, and so are definitions and purely tautological statements. (For example, not included are such self-evident propositions as, "if a is virtually constant and b increases substantially, $a/(a+b)$ must decrease.") Nine theoretical assumptions or axioms (which are numbered) are used to deduce seven theorems or empirical propositions (designated by numbers preceded by a T). One additional empirically supported theorem is introduced for the derivations (T–0).

T–0. The larger the volume of work of a certain kind, the larger is the number of persons needed to perform it.

1. If a common enterprise, including a work organization, depends on the social integration of its members.
2. And if social integration of employees in a work organization, who do not share distinctive basic values or interests, requires the interdependence among heterogeneous small subunits of them.

19. Problems of multicollinearity (note the very high correlations in Table 5) make it meaningless to perform regression analyses of size on both mean size and number of subunits, which would provide a direct test of the theoretical assumption. All zero-order correlations between mean subunit size and the index of administrative apparatus are negative, but this is simply the result of the correlation of both variables with total size.

3. And if management is interested and capable of furthering effective operations.
4. And if effective operations are promoted by the homogeneity of tasks within subunits.
5. And if more homogeneity within subunits, more heterogeneity and interdependence among them, and their reduced size are all results of the progressive differentiation of functions.
6. And if the degree of differentiation is limited by the organization's size (or number of employees, many being a necessary though not sufficient condition for much differentiation).

   T–1. It follows that increasing organizational size promotes differentiation.

7. If the administrative investments involved in organizing work are largely independent of the amount of similar work being organized, so that the volume of administrative work, of which these investments are a part, increases less than proportionately as the volume of operation increases.

T–0. And if the number of employees depends on the volume of work (in administration as well as in operations).

   T–2. It follows that increasing size reduces the proportion of personnel in administration.

T–0. If the number of employees needed depends on the volume of work.
8. And if the volume of administrative work depends on the heterogeneity of responsibilities (for example, the heterogeneity among subunits, other things being equal).
5. And if heterogeneity among interdependent subunits (as well as other conditions) results from differentiation.

   T–3. It follows that differentiation, independent of other conditions, expands the proportion of personnel in administration.

T–0. If the number of employees needed depends on the volume of work.
8. And if the volume of administrative work depends on the heterogeneity of responsibilities (and hence inversely on their homogeneity).
5. And if both homogeneity within the heterogeneity among interdependent subunits results from differentiation.
T–1. And if the degree of differentiation depends on organizational size.

T–4. It follows that increasing organizational size influences the proportion of administrative personnel in opposite ways: effecting reductions in it, mediated by the greater homogeneity within (larger)[20] subunits; and effecting expansions of it, mediated by the greater heterogeneity among more subunits.

9. If differentiation creates administrative problems that arouse resistance and require adjustment to it.

T–1. And if increasing size promotes differentiation.

T–5. It follows that the influence of increasing size on differentiation must overcome increasing resistance and hence declines.

9. If differentiation creates administrative problems that arouse resistance and require adjustment to it.

T–3. And if (adjustment to) differentiation expands administrative personnel.

T–1. And if increasing size promotes differentiation.

T–2. And if increasing size reduces the proportion of personnel in administration.

T–6. It follows that the influence of increasing size on reductions in administrative personnel is more and more counteracted by the expansion of such personnel in the increasingly differentiated structure, and hence declines.

T–5. If the number of relatively homogeneous subunits—the indicator of differentiation in a given dimension—increases at a declining rate with increasing size.

T–7. It follows that the mean size of these comparatively homogeneous subunits increases as the size of the organization does (which has been previously assumed, and which is a basic reason for the economy of scale in administration).

References

ANDERSON, T. R., and WARKOV, S. (1961), Organizational size and functional complexity, *American Sociological Review* 26, 23–28.

BLAU, P. M. (1970), A formal theory of differentiation in organization, *American Sociological Review* 35, 210–218.

20. The larger size of subunits in larger organizations is for the time being assumed in the deductive formulation, since it has not yet been made part of it, but this theorem will be formally derived, and empirical evidence in support of it has been presented (Table 5).

BLAU, P. M., and SCHOENHERR, R. A. (1971), "The Structure of Organizations," Basic Books, New York:

DURKHEIM, E. (1933), "The Division of Labor in Society," Macmillan, New York.

DURKHEIM, E. (1938), "The Rules of Sociological Method," University of Chicago Press, Chicago.

GOLDMAN, P. (1972), The organization of department stores, Ph.D. Dissertation, University of Chicago.

HALL, R. H., HAAS, J. E., and JOHNSON, N. J. (1967), Organizational size, complexity, and formalization, *American Sociological Review* 32, 903–912.

HAWLEY, A. H., BOLAND, W., and BOLAND, M. (1965), Population size and administration in institutions of higher education, *American Sociological Review* 30, 252–255.

INDIK, B. P. (1964), The relationship between organization size and supervisory ratio, *Administrative Science Quarterly* 9, 301–312.

MELMAN, S. (1951), The rise of administrative overhead in the manufacturing industries of the United States, 1899–1947, *Oxford Economic Papers* 3, 61–112.

MEYER, M. W. (1972), "Bureaucratic Structure and Authority," Harper, New York.

SEASHORE, S., (1954), "Group Cohesiveness in the Industrial Work Group," Institute for Social Research, University of Michigan, Ann Arbor.

TOCQUEVILLE, A. DE (1945), "Democracy in America," Knopf, New York.

WEBER, M. (1946), "Essays in Sociology," Oxford University Press, New York.

WOODWARD, J. (1965), "Industrial Organization," Oxford University Press, London.

The Population Ecology of Organizations[1]

Michael T. Hannan
John Freeman

I. Introduction

Analysis of the effects of environment on organizational structure has moved to a central place in organizations theory and research in recent years. This shift has opened a number of exciting possibilities. As yet nothing like the full promise of the shift has been realized. We believe that the lack of development is due in part to a failure to bring ecological models to bear on questions that are preeminently ecological. We argue for a reformulation of the problem in population ecology terms.

Although there is a wide variety of ecological perspectives, they all focus on selection. That is, they attribute patterns in nature to the action of selection processes. The bulk of the literature on organizations subscribes to a different view, which we call the adaptation perspective.[2]

SOURCE: *American Journal of Sociology* 82, no. 5 (March 1977): 929–40, 946–49, 955–64. Copyright © 1977 by The University of Chicago. Reprinted by permission of the authors and the publisher.

1. This research was supported in part by grants from the National Science Foundation (GS-32065) and the Spencer Foundation. Helpful comments were provided by Amos Hawley, François Nielsen, John Meyer, Marshall Meyer, Jeffrey Pfeffer, and Howard Aldrich.

2. There is a subtle relationship between selection and adaptation. Adaptive learning for individuals usually consists of selection among behavioral responses. Adaptation for a population involves selection among types of members. More generally, processes involving selection can usually be recast at a higher level of analysis as adaptation processes. However, once the unit of analysis is chosen there is no ambiguity in distinguishing selection from adaptation. Organizations often adapt to environmental conditions in concert and this suggests a systems effect. Though few theorists would deny the existence of such systems effects, most do not make them a subject of central concern. It is important to notice that, from the point of view embraced by sociologists whose interests focus on the broader social system, selection in favor of organizations with one set of properties to the disfavor of those with others is often an adaptive process. Societies and communities which consist in part of formal organizations adapt partly through processes that adjust the mixture of various kinds of organizations found within them. Whereas a complete theory of organization and environment would have to consider both adaptation and selection, recog-

According to the adaptation perspective, subunits of the organization, usually managers or dominant coalitions, scan the relevant environment for opportunities and threats, formulate strategic responses, and adjust organizational structure appropriately.

The adaptation perspective is seen most clearly in the literature on management. Contributors to it usually assume a hierarchy of authority and control that locates decisions concerning the organization as a whole at the top. It follows, then, that organizations are affected by their environments according to the ways in which managers or leaders formulate strategies, make decisions, and implement them. Particularly successful managers are able either to buffer their organizations from environmental disturbances or to arrange smooth adjustments that require minimal disruption of organizational structure.

A similar perspective, often worded differently, dominates the sociological literature on the subject. It plays a central role in Parson's (1956) functional analysis of organization-environment relations and it is found in the more strictly Weberian tradition (see Selznick, 1957). It is interesting to note that, while functionalists have been interested in system effects and have based much of the logic of their approach on survival imperatives, they have not dealt with selection phenomena. This is probably a reaction against organization theory which reflects social Darwinism.

Exchange theorists have also embraced the adaptation perspective (Levine and White 1961). And it is natural that theories emphasizing decision making take the adaptation view (March and Simon 1958; Cyert and March 1963). Even Thompson's (1967) celebrated marriage of open-systems and closed-systems thinking embraced the adaptation perspective explicitly (see particularly the second half of Thompson's book).

Clearly, leaders of organizations do formulate strategies and organizations do adapt to environmental contingencies. As a result at least some of the relationship between structure and environment must reflect adaptive behavior or learing. But there is no reason to presume that the great structural variability among organizations reflects only or even primarily adaptation.

There are a number of obvious limitations on the ability of organizations to adapt. That is, there are a number of processes that generate structural inertia. The stronger the pressures, the lower the organizations' adaptive flexibility and the more likely that the logic of environmental selection is appropriate. As a consequence, the issue of structural inertia is central to the choice between adaptation and selection models.

The possibility that organization structure contains a large inertial

nizing that they are complementary processes, our purpose here is to show what can be learned from studying selection alone (see Aldrich and Pfeffer [1976] for a synthetic review of the literature focusing on these different perspectives).

component was suggested by Burns and Stalker (1961) and Stinchcombe (1965). But, on the whole the subject has been ignored. A number of relevant propositions can be found in the organizations literature, however.

Inertial pressures arise from both internal structural arrangements and environmental constraints. A minimal list of the constraints arising from internal considerations follows.

1. An organization's investment in plant, equipment, and specialized personnel constitutes assets that are not easily transferable to other tasks or functions. The ways in which such sunk costs constrain adaptation options are so obvious that they need not be discussed further.

2. Organizational decision makers also face constraints on the information they receive. Much of what we know about the flow of information through organizational structures tells us that leaders do not obtain anything close to full information on activities within the organization and environmental contingencies facing the subunits.

3. Internal political constraints are even more important. When organizations alter structure, political equilibria are disturbed. As long as the pool of resources is fixed, structural change almost always involves redistribution of resources across subunits. Such redistribution upsets the prevailing system of exchange among subunits (or subunit leaders). So at least some subunits are likely to resist any proposed reorganization. Moreover, the benefits of structural reorganization are likely to be both generalized (designed to benefit the organization as a whole) and long-run. Any negative political response will tend to generate short-run costs that are high enough that organizational leaders will forego the planned reorganization. (For a more extensive discussion of the ways in which the internal political economy of organizations impedes change or adaptation, see Downs [1967] and Zald [1970].)

4. Finally, organizations face constraints generated by their own history. Once standards of procedure and the allocation of tasks and authority have become the subject of normative agreement, the costs of change are greatly increased. Normative agreements constrain adaptation in at least two ways. First, they provide a justification and an organizing principle for those elements that wish to resist reorganization (i.e., they can resist in terms of a shared principle). Second, normative agreements preclude the serious consideration of many alternative responses. For example, few research-oriented universities seriously consider adapting to declining enrollments by eliminating the teaching function. To entertain this option would be to challenge central organizational norms.[3]

The external pressures toward inertia seem to be at least as strong. They include at least the following factors.

3. Meyer's (1970) discussion of an organization's charter adds further support to the argument that normative agreements arrived at early in an organization's history constrain greatly the organization's range of adaptation to environmental constraints.

1. Legal and fiscal barriers to entry and exit from markets (broadly defined) are numerous. Discussions of organizational behavior typically emphasize barriers to entry (state licensed monopoly positions, etc.). Barriers to exit are equally interesting. There are an increasing number of instances in which political decisions prevent firms from abandoning certain activities. All such constraints on entry and exit limit the breadth of adaptation possibilities.

2. Internal constraints upon the availability of information are paralleled by external constraints. The acquisition of information about relevant environments is costly particularly in turbulent situations where the information is most essential. In addition, the type of specialists employed by the organization constrains both the nature of the information it is likely to obtain (see Granovetter 1973) and the kind of specialized information it can process and utilize.

3. Legitimacy constraints also emanate from the environment. Any legitimacy an organization has been able to generate constitutes an asset in manipulating the environment. To the extent that adaptation (e.g., eliminating undergraduate instruction in public universities) violates the legitimacy claims, it incurs considerable costs. So external legitimacy considerations also tend to limit adaptation.

4. Finally, there is the collective rationality problem. One of the most difficult issues in contemporary economics concerns general equilibria. If one can find an optimal strategy for some individual buyer or seller in a competitive market, it does not necessarily follow that there is a general equilibrium once all players start trading. More generally, it is difficult to establish that a strategy that is rational for a single decision maker will be rational if adopted by a large number of decision makers. A number of solutions to this problem have been proposed in competitive market theory, but we know of no treatment of the problem for organizations generally. Until such a treatment is established we should not presume that a course of action that is adaptive for a single organization facing some changing environment will be adaptive for many competing organizations adopting a similar strategy.

A number of these inertial pressures can be accommodated within the adaptation framework. That is, one can modify and limit the perspective in order to consider choices within the constrained set of alternatives. But to do so greatly limits the scope of one's investigation. We argue that in order to deal with the various inertial pressures the adaptation perspective must be supplemented with a selection orientation.

We consider first two broad issues that are preliminary to ecological modeling. The first concerns appropriate units of analysis. Typical analyses of the relation of organizations to environments take the point of view of a single organization facing an environment. We argue for an explicit focus on populations of organizations. The second broad issue concerns the applicability of population ecology models to the study of human social organization. Our substantive proposal begins with Hawley's (1950, 1968) classic statement on human ecology. We seek to extend Hawley's work in two ways: by using explicit competition models to specify the process producing isomorphism between organizational structure and environmental demands, and by using niche theory to extend the problem to dynamic environments. We argue that Hawley's perspective, modified and extended in these ways, serves as a useful starting point for population ecology theories of organizations.

II. Population Thinking in the Study of Organization-Environment Relations

Little attention is paid in the organizations literature to issues concerning proper units of analysis (Freeman 1975). In fact, choice of unit is treated so casually as to suggest that it is not an issue. We suspect that the opposite is true—that the choice of unit involves subtle issues and has far-reaching consequences for research activity. For instance, in the case at hand, it determines which of several ecological literatures can be brought to bear on the study of organization-environment relations.

The comparison of unit choice facing the organizational analyst with that facing the bioecologist is instructive. To oversimplify somewhat, ecological analysis is conducted at three levels: individual, population, and community. Events at one level almost always have consequences at other levels. Despite this interdependence, population events cannot be reduced to individual events (since individuals do not reflect the full genetic variability of the population) and community events cannot be simply reduced to population events. Both the latter employ a population perspective which is not appropriate at the individual level.

The situation faced by the organizations analyst is more complex. Instead of three levels of analysis, he faces at least five: (1) members, (2) subunits, (3) individual organizations, (4) populations of organizations, and (5) communities of (populations of) organizations. Levels 3–5 can be seen as corresponding to the three levels discussed for general ecology, with the individual organization taking the place of the individual organism. The added complexity arises because organizations are more nearly decomposable into constituent parts than are organisms. Individual members and subunits may move from organization to organization in a manner which has no parallel in nonhuman organization.

Instances of theory and research dealing with the effects of environments on organizations are found at all five levels. For example, Crozier's well-known analysis of the effects of culture on bureaucracy focuses on the cultural materials members bring to organizations (1964). At the other end of the continuum we find analyses of "organizational fields"

(Turk 1970; Aldrich and Reiss 1976). But, the most common focus is on *the* organization and *its* environment. In fact, this choice is so widespread that there appears to be a tacit understanding that individual organizations are the appropriate units for the study of organization-environment relations.

We argue for a parallel development of theory and research at the population (and, ultimately, the community) level. Because of the differing opinions about levels of analysis, "population" has at least two referents. Conventional treatments of human ecology suggest that the populations relevant to the study of organization-environment relations are those aggregates of members attached to the organization or, perhaps, served by the organization. In this sense, the organization is viewed as analogue to a community: it has collective means of adapting to environmental situations. The unit character of a population so defined depends on shared fate. All members share to some extent in the consequences of organizational success or failure.

We use the term population in a second sense: to refer to aggregates of organizations rather than members. Populations of organizations must be alike in some respect, that is, they must have some unit character. Unfortunately, identifying a population of organizations is no simple matter. The ecological approach suggests that one focus on common fate with respect to environmental variations. Since all organizations are distinctive, no two are affected identically by any given exogenous shock. Nevertheless, we can identify classes of organizations which are relatively homogeneous in terms of environmental vulnerability. Notice that the populations of interest may change somewhat from investigation to investigation depending on the analyst's concern. Populations of organizations referred to are not immutable objects in nature but are abstractions useful for theoretical purposes.

If we are to follow the lead of population biologists, we must identify an analogue to the biologist's notion of species. Various species are defined ultimately in terms of genetic structure. As Monod (1971) indicates, it is useful to think of the genetic content of any species as a blueprint. The blueprint contains the rules for transforming energy into structure. Consequently all of the adaptive capacity of a species is summarized in the blueprint. If we are to identify a species analogue for organizations, we must search for such blueprints. There will consist of rules or procedures for obtaining and acting upon inputs in order to produce an organizational product or response.

The type of blueprint one identifies depends on substantive concerns. For example, Marschak and Radner (1972) employ the term "organizational form" [4] to characterize the key elements of the blueprint as seen

4. The term "organizational form" is used widely in the sociological literature (see Stinchcombe 1965).

within a decision-making framework. For them the blueprint or form has two functions: an information function that describes the rules used in obtaining, processing, and transmitting information about the states of external environments, and an activity function that states the rules used in acting on received information so as to produce an organizational response. To the extent that one can identify classes of organizations that differ with regard to these two functions, one can establish classes or forms of organization.

Since our concerns extend beyond decision making, however, we find Marschak and Radner's definition of forms too limiting. In fact, there is no reason to limit a priori the variety of rules or functions that may define relevant blueprints. So for us, an organizational form is a blueprint for organizational action, for transforming inputs into outputs. The blueprint can usually be inferred, albeit in somewhat different ways, by examining any of the following: (1) the formal structure of the organization in the narrow sense—tables of organization, written rules of operation, etc.; (2) the patterns of activity within the organization—what actually gets done by whom; or (3) the normative order—the ways of organizing that are defined as right and proper by both members and relevant sectors of the environment.

To complete the species analogue, we must search for qualitative differences among forms. It seems most likely that we will find such differences in the first and third areas listed above, formal structure and normative order. The latter offers particularly intriguing possibilities. Whenever the history of an organization, its politics, and its social structure are encoded in a normative claim (e.g., professionalization and collegial authority), one can use these claims to identify forms and define populations for research.

Having defined the organizational form, we can provide a more precise definition of a population of organizations. Just as the organizational analyst must choose a unit of analysis, so must he choose a system for study. Systems relevant to the study of organization-environment relations are usually defined by geography, by political boundaries, by market or product considerations, etc. Given a systems definition, a population of organizations consists of all the organizations within a particular boundary that have a common form. That is, the population is the form as it exists or is realized within a specified system.

Both uses of the term population (and the ecological theories implied thereby) are likely to prove beneficial to the study of organizational structure. The first, more common, view suggests that organizational structure ought to be viewed as an outcome of a collective adaptive process. According to this view, structure and change ought to depend on the adaptiveness of subunits and on the differential access of subunits to environmental resources. The second view ignores the adaptive activities of elements within the organization except as they constitute organizational structure. It focuses on the organization as an adapting unit. Certainly both perspectives are needed. We are concerned here only with the latter, however.

Finally, we would like to identify the properties of populations most interesting to population ecologists. The main concern in this regard was expressed clearly by Elton (1927): "In solving ecological problems we are concerned with *what animals do* in their capacity as whole, living animals, not as dead animals or as a series of parts of animals. We have next to study the circumstances under which they do those things, and, most important of all, the limiting factors which prevent them from doing certain other things. By solving these questions it is possible to discover the reasons for *the distribution and numbers of animals in nature.*" Hutchinson (1959) in the subtitle to his famous essay, "Homage to Santa Rosalia," expressed the main focus even more succinctly: "Why Are There So Many Kinds of Animals?" Taking our lead from these distinguished ecologists, we suggest that a population ecology of organizations must seek to understand the distributions of organizations across environmental conditions and the limitations on organizational structures in different environments, and more generally seek to answer the question, Why are there so many kinds of organizations?

III. Discontinuities in Ecological Analysis

Utilization of models from ecology in the study of organizations poses a number of analytic challenges involving differences between human and nonhuman organizations with regard to their essential ingredients. Consider, first, the nongenetic transmission of information. Biological analyses are greatly simplified by the fact that most useful information concerning adaptation to the environment (which information we call structure) is transmitted genetically. Genetic processes are so nearly invariant that extreme continuity in structure is the rule. The small number of imperfections generates structural changes, which, if accepted by the environment, will be transmitted with near invariance. The extreme structural invariance of species greatly simplifies the problem of delimiting and identifying populations. More important, the adaptiveness of structure can be unambiguously identified with net reproduction rates. When a population with given properties increases its net reproduction rate following an environmental change, it follows that it is being selected for. This is why modern biologists have narrowed the definition of fitness to the net reproductive rate of population.

Human social organization presumably reflects a greater degree of learning or adaptation. As a result it is more difficult to define fitness in a precise way. Under at least some conditions, organizations may undergo such extreme structural change that they shift from one form to another. As a result, extreme adaptation may give rise to observed changes that mimic selection. This is particularly problematic when the various organizational forms are similar on many dimensions.

We have argued previously (Hannan and Freeman 1974) for a composite measure of fitness that includes both selection (actual loss of organizations) and mobility among forms (extreme adaptation). Fitness would then be defined as the probability that a given form of organization would persist in a certain environment. We continue to believe that such an approach has value, but we now believe that it is premature to combine adaptation and selection processes. The first order of business is to study selection processes for those situations in which inertial pressures are sufficiently strong that mobility among forms is unlikely.

Furthermore, it is worth noting that the capacity to adapt is itself subject to evolution (i.e., to systematic selection). As we argue below, organizations develop the capacity to adapt at the cost of lowered performance levels in stable environments. Whether or not such adaptable organizational forms will survive (i.e., resist selection) depends on the nature of the environment and the competitive situation. Therefore, a selection point of view treats high levels of adaptability as particular evolutionary outcomes.

There is a second sense in which human ecology appears to differ from bioecology. Blau and Scott (1962) point out that, unlike the usual biological situation, individual organizations (and populations of organizations) have the potential to expand almost without limit. The expandability of primitive elements is a problem because of our focus on the distribution of organizational forms over environments. A given form (e.g., formal bureaucracy) can expand throughout some system, market, or activity, either because one bureaucracy grows or because many bureaucracies are founded. Either process will generate an increase in the prevalence of bureaucratic organizational activity. A literal application of population ecology theory to the problem of organizational change would involve simply counting relative numbers in populations. Such a procedure may miss a phenomenon of central interest to the organizational analyst. Winter (1964), in discussing the analytic problem raised here, suggests distinguishing between survival, which describes the fate of individual organizations, and viability, which describes the "share of market" of a given organizational form.

We find at least as much merit in another perspective on the issue of size. Many theorists have asserted that structural change attends growth; in other words, a single organization cannot grow indefinitely and still maintain its original form. For instance, a mouse could not possibly maintain the same proportion of body weight to skeletal structure while growing as big as a house. It would neither look like a mouse nor operate physiologically like a mouse. Boulding (1953) and Haire (1959) argue that the same is true for organizations. Caplow (1957), building on work by Graicunas (1933) and others, argues that the ability of each member of an organization to carry on face-to-face interactions with each of the others declines with the number of organizational participants. This creates a shift in the nature of interactions such that they assume a more impersonal, formal style. Blau and a number of coauthors have argued for similar causal effects of size on structure (Blau and Scott 1962, pp. 223–42; Blau and Schoenherr 1971; Blau 1972). If it is true that organizational form changes with size, selection mechanisms may indeed operate with regard to the size distribution. When big organizations prevail it may be useful to view this as a special case of selection, in which the movement from "small form" to "large form" is theoretically indistinguishable from the dissolution ("death") of small organizations and their replacement by (the "birth" of) large organizations.

In sum, we have identified a number of challenges. The first concerns the two sources of change, selection and adaptive learning. We feel that the organizations literature has overemphasized the latter at the expense of the former. Much more is known about decision-making practices, forecasting, and the like than about selection in populations of organizations. The second challenge involves the distinction between selection and viability. Whether such a distinction is necessary depends on the results of research on size which is currently being pursued by many organization researchers.

IV. The Principle of Isomorphism

In the best developed statement of the principles of human ecology, Hawley (1968) answers the question of why there are so many kinds of organizations. According to Hawley, the diversity of organizational forms is isomorphic to the diversity of environments. In each distinguishable environmental configuration one finds, in equilibrium, only that organizational form optimally adapted to the demands of the environment. Each unit experiences constraints which force it to resemble other units with the same set of constraints. Hawley's explanation places heavy emphasis on communication patterns and structural complements of those patterns: "[organization units] must submit to standard terms of communication and to standard procedures in consequence of which they develop similar internal arrangements within limits imposed by their respective sizes" (1968, p. 334).

While the proposition seems completely sound from an ecological perspective, it does not address a number of interesting considerations. There are at least two respects in which the isomorphism formulation must be modified and extended if it is to provide satisfactory answers to the question posed. The first modification concerns the mechanism or mechanisms responsible for equilibrium. In this respect, the principle of isomorphism must be supplemented by a criterion of selection and a competition theory. The second modification deals with the fact that the principle of isomorphism neither speaks to issues of optimum adaptation to changing environments nor recognizes that populations of organizations often face multiple environments which impose somewhat inconsistent demands. An understanding of the constraints on organizational forms seems to require modeling of multiple, dynamic environments. Of course, we cannot fully extend Hawley's principle here. We attempt only to outline the main issues and suggest particular extensions.

V. Competition Theory

The first of the needed extensions is a specification of the optimization process responsible for isomorphism. We have already discussed two mechanisms: selection and adaptive learning. Isomorphism can result either because nonoptimal forms are selected out of a community of organizations or because organizational decision makers learn optimal responses and adjust organizational behavior accordingly. We continue to focus on the first of these processes: selection.

Consideration of optimization raises two issues: Who is optimizing, and what is being optimized? It is quite commonly held, as in the theory of the firm, that organizational decision makers optimize profit over sets of organizational actions. From a population ecology perspective, it is the environment which optimizes.[5] Whether or not individual organizations are consciously adapting, the environment selects out optimal combinations of organizations. So if there is a rationality involved, it is the "rationality" of natural selection. Organizational rationality and environmental rationality may coincide in the instance of firms in competitive markets. In this case, the optimal behavior of each firm is to maximize profit and the rule used by the environment (market, in this case) is to select out profit maximizers. Friedman (1953) makes use of this observation to propose a justification of the theory of the firm in terms of the principles of evolution. However, Winter (1964) has argued convincingly that the actual situation is much more complicated than this and that it is most unusual for individual rationality and environmental or market rationality

5. In biological applications, one assumes that power (in the physical sense) is optimized by natural selection in accordance with the so-called Darwin-Lotka law. For the case of human social organization, one might argue that selection optimizes the utilization of a specific set of resources including but not restricted to the power and the time of members.

to lead to the same optima. When the two rationalities do not agree, we are concerned with the optimizing behavior of the environment.

A focus on selection invites an emphasis on competition. Organizational forms presumably fail to flourish in certain environmental circumstances because other forms successfully compete with them for essential resources. As long as the resources which sustain organizations are finite and populations have unlimited capacity to expand, competition must ensue.

Hawley (1950, pp. 201–3) following Durkheim (1947) among others, places a heavy emphasis on competition as a determinant of patterns of social organization. The distinctive feature of his model is the emphasis on the indirect nature of the process: "The action of all on the common supply gives rise to a reciprocal relation between each unit and all the others, if only from the fact that what one gets reduces by that amount what the others can obtain . . . without this element of indirection, that is, unless units affect one another through affecting a common limited supply, competition does not exist" (Hawley 1950, p. 202). In Hawley's model, competition processes typically involve four stages: (1) demand for resources exceeds supply; (2) competitors become more similar as standard conditions of competition bring forth a uniform response; (3) selection eliminates the weakest competitors; and (4) deposed competition differentiate either territorially or functionally, yielding a more complex division of labor.

It is surprising that there is almost no reliance on competitive mechanisms in Hawley's later work. In particular, as we noted above, the rationale given for the isomorphism principle uses an adaptation logic. We propose to balance that treatment by adding an explicit focus on competition as a mechanism producing isomorphism. In so doing, we can bring a rich set of formal models to bear on the problem.

• • •

VI. Niche Theory

The principle of isomorphism implies that social organizations in equilibrium will exhibit structural features that are specialized to salient features of the resource environment. As long as the environment is stable and certain, we see no difficulty with this proposition. But does it hold when the environment shifts either predictably or unpredictably among several alternative configurations? Though the issues raised by attempting to answer this question are complex, doing so is crucial to developing adequate models of organizational-environment relations.

Intuition suggests that isomorphism holds as a good approximation only in stable environments. Faced with unstable environments, organizations ought to develop a generalist structure that is not optimally adapted to any single environmental configuration but is optimal over an entire set of configurations. In other words, we ought to find specialized organizations in stable and certain environments and generalist organizations is unstable and uncertain environments. Whether or not this simple proposition holds for social organizations, only empirical research will tell. However, a variety of population ecology models suggests that it is too simplistic. We cannot hope in one paper to develop fully the arguments involved. Instead we indicate the main lines of development with reference to one rather evocative perspective developed by Levins (1962, 1968): the theory of niche width.

The concept of "niche," initially borrowed by biologists from early social science, plays a central role in ecological theory. This is not the place for an extended discussion of the multiple uses of the concept (see Whittaker and Levin 1976). The model which follows uses Hutchinson's (1957) formulation. From this point of view the (realized) niche of a population is defined as that area in constraint space (the space whose dimensions are levels of resources, etc.) in which the population outcompetes all other local populations. The niche, then, consists of all those combinations of resource levels at which the population can survive and reproduce itself.

Each population occupies a distinct niche. For present purposes it suffices to consider cases where pairs of populations differ with respect to a single environmental dimension, E, and are alike with respect to all others. Then relative competitive positions can be simply summarized as in Figure 1. As we have drawn this figure, one population, A, occupies a very broad niche, whereas the other, B, has concentrated its fitness, denoted W, on a very narrow band of environmental variation. This distinction, which is usually referred to as generalism versus specialism, is crucial to biological ecology and to a population ecology of organizations.

In essence, the distinction between specialism and generalism refers to whether a population of organizations flourishes because it maximizes its exploitation of the environment and accepts the risk of having that environment change or because it accepts a lower level of exploitation in return for greater security. Whether or not the equilibrium distribution of organizational forms is dominated by the specialist depends, as we will see, on the shape of the fitness sets and on properties of the environment.

Part of the efficiency resulting from specialism is derived from the lower requirements for excess capacity. Given some uncertainty, most organizations maintain some excess capacity to insure the reliability of performance. In a rapidly changing environment, the definition of excess capacity is likely to change frequently. What is used today may become

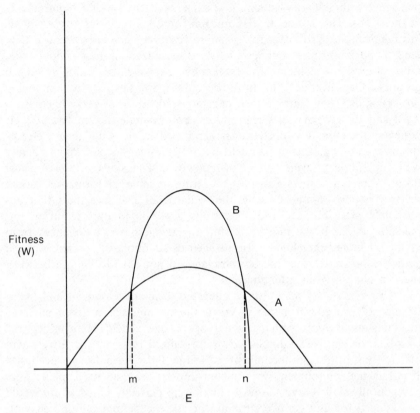

FIGURE 1. Fitness functions (niches) for specialists and generalists.

excess tomorrow, and what is excess today may be crucial tomorrow. Organizations operating in environments where the transition from state to state is less frequent will (in equilibrium) have to maintain excess capacity in a given allocational pattern for longer periods of time. Whereas those charged with assessing performance will be tempted to view such allocations as wasteful, they may be essential for survival. Thompson (1967) has argued that organizations allocate resources to units charged with the function of insulating core technology from environmentally induced disruption. So, for example, manufacturing firms may retain or employ legal staffs even when they are not currently facing litigation.

The importance of excess capacity is not completely bound up with the issue of how much excess capacity will be maintained. It also involves the manner in which it is used. Organizations may insure reliable performance by creating specialized units, as Thompson (1967) suggests, or they may allocate excess capacity to organizational roles, by employing personnel with skills and abilities which exceed the routine requirements of their jobs. This is one of the important reasons for using professionals in organizations. Professionals use more resources not only because they tend to be paid more, but also because organizations must allow them more discretion (including the freedom to respond to outside reference groups). Organizations, in turn, become more flexible by employing professionals. They increase their capacity to deal with a variable environment and the contingencies it produces. For example, hospitals and their patients often employ obstetricians and pediatricians in their delivery rooms even though the normal delivery of babies can be performed equally well, and perhaps even better, by midwives. The skills of the medical doctor represent excess capacity to insure reliable performance should delivery not be normal. Usually, the pediatrician examines the infant immediately after birth to see if there is any abnormality requiring immediate action. If the mother is suffering dangerous consequences from giving birth, and the child is also in need of attention, the presence of the pediatrician insures that the obstetrician will not have to choose between them in allocating his attention.

Excess capacity may also be allocated to the development and maintenance of procedural systems. When the certainty of a given environmental state is high, organizational operations should be routine, and coordination can be accomplished by formalized rules and the investment of resources in training incumbents to follow those formalized procedures. If in fact the environment were unchanging ($p = 1$), all participants were procedurally skilled, and the procedures were perfectly tuned, there would be no need for any control structure at all, except to monitor behavior. However, when certainty is low, organizational operations are less routine. Under these circumstances, a greater allocation of resources to develop and maintain procedural systems is counterproductive and optimal organizational forms will allocate resources to less formalized systems capable of more innovative responses (e.g., committees and teams). In this case, excess capacity is represented by the increased time it takes such structures to make decisions and by increased coordination costs.

The point here is that populations of organizational forms will be selected for or against depending upon the amount of excess capacity they maintain and how they allocate it. It may or may not be rational for any particular organization to adopt one pattern or another. What would seem like waste to anyone assessing performance at one time may be the difference between survival and failure later. Similarly, organizations may survive because high levels of professionalization produce coordination by mutual adjustment despite a somewhat chaotic appearance. Others, in which everyone seems to know precisely what he is doing at all times, may fail. Under a given set of environmental circumstances the fundamental ecological question is: which forms thrive and which forms disappear.

• • •

Consider an example. In his analysis of bureaucratic and craft administration or production, Stinchcombe (1959) argued that construction firms do not rely upon bureaucratically organized administrative staffs because of seasonal fluctuations in demand. Administrative staffs constitute an overhead cost which remains roughly constant over the year. The advantage of the otherwise costly (in terms of salaries) craft administration is that coordination of work is accomplished through a reliance upon prior socialization of craftsmen and upon organization. Since employment levels can more easily be increased or decreased with demand under a craft system, administrative costs are more easily altered to meet demand.

The fundamental source of this pattern is the seasonal variation in construction. In ecological terms, the demand environment is coarse-grained. In addition, the two states defined by season are quite different, resulting in a concave fitness curve. Craft-administered housing construction firms are probably quite inefficient when demand is at its peak and when the kind of housing under construction is standardized. In such situations, we would expect this form of organization to face stiff competition from other firms. For instance, in regions where housing construction is less seasonal, modular housing, mobile homes, and prefabricated housing are more likely to flourish and we would expect the construction business to be more highly bureaucratized.

Another variation in demand is to be found in the business cycle. While seasonal fluctuations are stable (uncertainty is low), interest rates, labor relations, and materials costs are more difficult to predict. Variations of this sort should favor a generalist mode of adaptation. That is, when environments are coarse-grained, characterized by concave fitness curves, and uncertain, populations of organizations will be more likely to survive if they hedge their bets by seeking a wider variety of resource bases. For this reason, we think, craft-administered construction organizations are frequently general contractors who not only build houses but engage in other kinds of construction as well (shopping plazas, office buildings, etc.). In comparison, modular housing is cheaper and the units are installed on rented space. Consequently, interest rates are less important. Since organizations producing this kind of housing do not employ craftsmen but use the cheapest and least skilled labor they can obtain, labor relations are less problematical. It may be that their reliance on different materials (e.g., sheet aluminum) contributes to a lower level of uncertainty. In consequence, we would expect this form of organization to be more highly specialized in its adaptation (of course there are technical factors which also contribute to this as well).

Craft-administered construction firms are set up in such a way that they can adapt rapidly to changes in demand, and they can adapt to different construction problems by varying the mix of skills represented in their work force. Bureaucratically administered construction firms are more specialized and as a result they are efficient only when demand is high, and very inefficient when it is low. We also believe that they tend to be more specialized with regard to type of construction. Craft-administered organizations sacrifice efficient exploitation of their niche for flexibility. Bureaucratic organizations choose the opposite strategy. This formulation is an extension of Stinchcombe's and serves to show that his argument is essentially ecological.

VII. Discussion

Our aim in this paper has been to move toward an application of modern population ecology theory to the study of organization-environment relations. For us, the central question is, why are there so many kinds of organizations? Phrasing the question in this way opens the possibility of applying a rich variety of formal models to the analysis of the effects of environmental variations on organizational structure.

We begin with Hawley's classic formulation of human ecology. However, we recognize that ecological theory has progressed enormously since sociologists last systematically applied ideas from bioecology to social organization. Nonetheless, Hawley's theoretical perspective remains a very useful point of departure. In particular we concentrate on the principle of isomorphism. This principle asserts that there is a one-to-one correspondence between structural elements of social organization and those units that mediate flows of essential resources into the system. It explains the variations in organizational forms in equilibrium. But any observed isomorphism can arise from purposeful adaptation of organizations to the common constraints they face or because nonisomorphic organizations are selected against. Surely both processes are at work in most social systems. We believe that the organizations literature has emphasized the former to the exclusion of the latter.

We suspect that careful empirical research will reveal that for wide classes of organizations there are very strong inertial pressures on structure arising both from internal arrangements (e.g., internal politics) and the environment (e.g., public legitimation of organizational activity). To claim otherwise is to ignore the most obvious feature of organizational life. Failing churches do not become retail stores; nor do firms transform themselves into churches. Even within broad areas of organizational action, such as higher education and labor union activity, there appear to be substantial obstacles to fundamental structural change. Research is needed on this issue. But until we see evidence to the contrary, we will continue to doubt that the major features of the world of organizations arise through learning or adaptation. Given these doubts, it is important to explore an evolutionary explanation of the principle of isomorphism. That is, we wish to embed the principle of isomorphism within an explicit selection framework.

In order to add selection processes we propose a competition theory using Lotka-Volterra models. This theory relies on growth models that appear suitable for representing both organizational development and the growth of populations of organizations. Recent work by bioecologists on Lotka-Volterra systems yields propositions that have immediate relevance for the study of organization-environment relations. These results concern the effects of changes in the number and mixture of constraints upon systems with regard to the upper bound of the diversity of forms of organization. We propose that such propositions can be tested by examining the impact of varieties of state regulation both on size distributions and on the diversity of organizational forms within broadly defined areas of activity (e.g., medical care, higher education, and newspaper publishing).

A more important extension of Hawley's work introduces dynamic considerations. The fundamental issue here concerns the meaning of isomorphism in situations in which the environment to which units are adapted is changing and uncertain. Should "rational" organizations attempt to develop specialized isomorphic structural relations with one of the possible environmental states? Or should they adopt a more plastic strategy and institute more generalized structural features? The isomorphism principle does not speak to these issues.

We suggest that the concrete implication of generalism for organizations is the accumulation and retention of varieties of excess capacity. To retain the flexibility of structure required for adaptation to different environmental outcomes requires that some capacities be held in reserve and not committed to action. Generalists will always be outperformed by specialists who, with the same levels of resources, happen to have hit upon their optimal environment. Consequently, in any cross-section the generalists will appear inefficient because excess capacity will often be judged waste. Nonetheless, organizational slack is a pervasive feature of many types of organizations. The question then arises: what types of environments favor generalists? Answering this question comprehensively takes one a long way toward understanding the dynamic of organization-environment relations.

We begin addressing this question in the suggestive framework of Levin's (1962, 1968) fitness-set theory. This is one of a class of recent theories that relates the nature of environmental uncertainty to optimal

193

levels of structural specialism. Levins argues that along with uncertainty one must consider the grain of the environment or the lumpiness of environmental outcomes. The theory indicates that specialism is always favored in stable or certain environments. This is no surprise. But contrary to the view widely held in the organizations literature, the theory also indicates that generalism is not always optimal in uncertain environments. When the environment shifts uncertainly among states that place very different demands on the organization, and the duration of environmental states is short relative to the life of the organization (variation is fine-grained), populations of organizations that specialize will be favored over those that generalize. This is because organizations that attempt to adapt to each environmental outcome will spend most of their time adjusting structure and very little time in organizational action directed at other ends.

Stated in these terms, the proposition appears obvious. However, when one reads the literature on organization-environment relations, one finds that it was not so obvious. Most important, the proposition follows from a simple explicit model that has the capacity to unify a wide variety of propositions relating environmental variations to organizational structure.

We have identified some of the leading conceptual and methodological obstacles to applying population ecology models to the study of organization-environment relations. We pointed to differences between human and nonhuman social organization in terms of mechanisms of structural invariance and structural change, associated problems of delimiting populations of organizations, and difficulties in defining fitness for populations of expandable units. In each case we have merely sketched the issues and proposed short-run simplifications which would facilitate the application of existing models. Clearly, each issue deserves careful scrutiny.

At the moment we are frustrated at least as much by the lack of empirical information on rates of selection in populations of organizations as by the unresolved issues just mentioned. Census data are presented in a manner that renders the calculation of failure rates impossible; and little longitudinal research on populations of organizations has been reported. We do, however, have some information on rates of selection. We know, for example, that failure rates for small businesses are high. By recent estimates upwards of 8% of small business firms in the United States fail each year (Hollander 1967; Bolton 1971; see also Churchill 1955).

In part this high failure rate reflects what Stinchcomb (1965) called the liability of newness. Many new organizations attempt to enter niches that have already been filled by organizations that have amassed social, economic, and political resources that make them difficult to dislodge. It is important to determine whether there is any selective disadvantage of smallness not of newness.

We doubt that many readers will dispute the contention that failure rates are high for new and/or small organizations. However, much of the sociological literature and virtually all of the critical literature on large organizations tacitly accepts the view that such organizations are not subject to strong selection pressures. While we do not yet have the empirical data to judge this hypothesis, we can make several comments. First, we do not dispute that the largest organizations individually and collectively exercise strong dominance over most of the organizations that constitute their environments. But it does not follow from the observation that such organizations are strong in any one period that they will be strong in every period. Thus, it is interesting to know how firmly embedded are the largest and most powerful organizations. Consider the so-called Fortune 500, the largest publicly owned industrial firms in the United States. We contrasted the lists for 1955 and 1975 (adjusting for pure name changes). Of those on the list in 1955, only 268 (53.6%) were still listed in 1975. One hundred twenty-two had disappeared through merger, 109 had slipped off the "500," and one (a firm specializing in Cuban sugar!) had been liquidated. The number whose relative sales growth caused them to be dropped from the list is quite impressive in that the large number of mergers had opened many slots on the list. So we see that, whereas actual liquidation was rare for the largest industrial firms in the United States over a 20-year period, there was a good deal of volatility with regard to position in this pseudodominance structure because of both mergers and slipping sales.[6]

Second, the choice of time perspective is important. Even the largest and most powerful organizations fail to survive over long periods. For example, of the thousands of firms in business in the United States during the Revolution, only 13 survive as autonomous firms and seven as recognizable divisions of firms (*Nation's Business* 1976). Presumably one needs a longer time perspective to study the population ecology of the largest and most dominant organizations.

Third, studying small organizations is not such a bad idea. The sociological literature has concentrated on the largest organizations for obvious design reasons. But, if inertial pressures on certain aspects of structure are strong enough, intense selection among small organizations may greatly constrain the variety observable among large organizations. At least some elements of structure change with size (as we argued in Section III) and the pressure toward inertia should not be overemphasized. Nonetheless we see much value in studies of the organizational life cycle that would inform us as to which aspects of structure get locked in during which

6. From at least some perspectives, mergers can be viewed as changes in form. This will almost certainly be the case when the organizations merged have very different structures. These data also indicate a strong selective advantage for a conglomerate form of industrial organization.

phases of the cycle. For example, we conjecture that a critical period is that during which the organization grows beyond the control of a single owner/manager. At this time the manner in which authority is delegated, if at all, seems likely to have a lasting impact on organizational structure. This is the period during which an organization becomes less an extension of one or a few dominant individuals and more an organization per se with a life of its own. If the selection pressures at this point are as intense as anecdotal evidence suggests they are, selection models will prove very useful in accounting for the varieties of forms among the whole range of organizations.

The optimism of the previous paragraph should be tempered by the realization that when one examines the largest and most dominant organizations, one is usually considering only a small number of organizations. The smaller the number, the less useful are models that depend on the type of random mechanisms that underlie population ecology models.

Fourth, we must consider what one anonymous reader, caught up in the spirit of our paper, called the anti-eugenic actions of the state in saving firms such as Lockheed from failure. This is a dramatic instance of the way in which large dominant organizations can create linkages with other large and powerful ones so as to reduce selection pressures. If such moves are effective, they alter the pattern of selection. In our view the selection pressure is bumped up to a higher level. So instead of individual organizations failing, entire networks fail. The general consequences of a large number of linkages of this sort is an increase in the instability of the entire system (Simon 1962, 1973; May 1973), and therefore we should see boom and bust cycles of organizational outcomes. Selection models retain relevance, then, even when the systems of organizations are tightly coupled (see Hannan 1976).

Finally, some readers of earlier drafts have (some approvingly, some disapprovingly) treated our arguments as metaphoric. This is not what we intend. In a fundamental sense all theoretical activity involves metaphoric activity (although admittedly the term "analogue" comes closer than does "metaphor"). The use of metaphors or analogues enters into the formulation of "if . . . then" statements. For example, certain molecular genetic models draw an analogy between DNA surfaces and crystal structures. The latter have simple well-behaved geometric structures amenable to strong topological (mathematical) analysis. No one argues that DNA proteins are crystals; but to the extent that their surfaces have certain crystal-like properties, the mathematical model used to analyze crystals will shed light on the genetic structure. This is, as we understand it, the general strategy of model building.

We have, for example, used results that rely on the application of certain logistic differential equations, the Lotka-Volterra equations. No known population (of animals, or of organizations) grows in exactly the manner specified by this mathematic model (and this fact has caused numerous naturalists to argue that the model is biologically meaningless). What the equations do is to model the growth path of populations that exist on finite resources in a closed system (where population growth in the absence of competition is logistic and the presence of competing populations lowers carrying capacities in that system). To the extent that the interactions of populations of *Paramecium aureilia* and *P. caudatum* (Gause's experiment) meet the conditions of the model, the model explains certain key features of population dynamics and the relationship of environmental variations to structure. To the extent that the interactions of populations of rational-legal bureaucracies and populations of patrimonial bureaucracies also meet the conditions of the model, the model explains the same important phenomena. Neither the protozoa nor the bureaucracies behave exactly as the model stipulates. The model is an abstraction that will lead to insight whenever the stated conditions are approximated.

Throughout we make a strong continuity-of-nature hypothesis. We propose that, whenever the stated conditions hold, the models lead to valuable insights regardless of whether the populations under study are composed of protozoans or organizations. We do not argue "metaphorically." That is, we do *not* argue as follows: an empirical regularity is found to hold for certain protozoans; because we hypothesize that populations of organizations are like populations of protozoans in essential ways, we propose that the generalizations derived from the latter will hold for organizations as well. This is the kind of reasoning by which biological propositions have most often entered sociological arguments (e.g., the famous—or infamous—organismic analogy advanced by Spencer).

Instead of applying biological laws to human social organization, we advocate the application of population ecology theories. As we have indicated at a number of points, these theories are quite general and must be modified for any concrete application (sociological *or* biological). Our purpose has been twofold. First, we sketched some of the alterations in perspective required if population ecology theories are to be applied to the study of organizations. Second, we wished to stimulate a reopening of the lines of communication between sociology and ecology. It is ironic that Hawley's (1944, p. 399) diagnosis of some 30 years ago remains apt today: "Probably most of the difficulties which beset human ecology may be traced to the isolation of the subject from the mainstream of ecological thought."

References

ALDRICH, HOWARD E., and JEFFREY PFEFFER. 1976. "Environments of Organizations." *Annual Review of Sociology* 2:79–105.

ALDRICH, HOWARD E., and ALBERT J. REISS. 1976. "Continuities in the Study of Ecological Succession: Changes in the Race Composition of Neighborhoods and Their Businesses." *American Journal of Sociology* 81 (January): 846–66.

BLAU, PETER M. 1972. "Interdependence and Hierarchy in Organizations." *Social Science Research* 1 (April): 1–24.

BLAU, PETER M., and RICHARD A. SCHOENHERR. 1971. *The Structure of Organizations*. New York: Basic.

BLAU, PETER M., and W. RICHARD SCOTT. 1962. *Formal Organizations*. San Francisco: Chandler.

BOLTON, J. E. 1971. *Small Firms*. Report of the Committee of Inquiry on Small Firms. London: Her Majesty's Stationery Office.

BOULDING, KENNETH. 1953. "Toward a General Theory of Growth." *Canadian Journal of Economics and Political Science* 19:326–40.

BURNS, TOM, and G. M. STALKER. 1961. *The Management of Innovation*. London: Tavistock.

CAPLOW, THEODORE. 1957. "Organizational Size." *Administrative Science Quarterly* 1 (March): 484–505.

CHURCHILL, BETTY C. 1955. "Age and Life Expectancy of Business Firms." *Survey of Current Business* 35 (December): 15–19.

CROZIER, MICHEL. 1964. *The Bureaucratic Phenomenon*. Chicago: University of Chicago Press.

CYERT, RICHARD M., and JAMES G. MARCH. 1963. *A Behavioral Theory of the Firm*. Englewood Cliffs, N.J.: Prentice-Hall.

DOWNS, ANTHONY. 1967. *Inside Bureaucracy*. Boston: Little, Brown.

DURKHEIM, E. 1947. *The Division of Labor in Society*. Translated by G. Simpson. Glencoe, Ill.: Free Press.

ELTON, C. 1927. *Animal Ecology*. London: Sidgwick & Jackson.

FREEMAN, JOHN. 1975. "The Unit Problem in Organizational Research." Presented at the annual meeting of the American Sociological Association, San Francisco.

FREEMAN, JOHN, and JACK BRITTAIN. 1977. "Union Merger Processes and Industrial Environments." *Industrial Relations*, in press.

FRIEDMAN, MILTON. 1953. *Essays on Positive Economics*. Chicago: University of Chicago Press.

GAUSE, G. F. 1934. *The Struggle for Existence*. Baltimore: Williams & Wilkins.

GRAICUNAS, V. A. 1933. "Relationship in Organizations." *Bulletin of the International Management Institute* (March), pp. 183–87.

GRANOVETTER, MARK S. 1973. "The Strength of Weak Ties." *American Journal of Sociology* 78 (May): 1360–80.

HAIRE, MASON. 1959. "Biological Models and Empirical Histories of the Growth of Organizations." Pp. 272–306 in *Modern Organization Theory*, edited by Mason Haire. New York: Wiley.

HANNAN, MICHAEL T. 1975. "The Dynamics of Ethnic Boundaries." Unpublished.

———. 1976. "Modeling Stability and Complexity in Networks of Organizations." Presented at the annual meeting of the American Sociological Association, New York.

HANNAN, MICHAEL T., and JOHN FREEMAN. 1974. "Environment and the Structure of Organizations." Presented at the annual meeting of the American Sociological Association, Montreal.

HAWLEY, AMOS H. 1944. "Ecology and Human Ecology." *Social Forces* 22 (May): 398–405.

——. 1950. *Human Ecology: A Theory of Community Structure.* New York: Ronald.

——. 1968. "Human Ecology." Pp. 328–37 in *International Encyclopedia of the Social Sciences,* edited by David L. Sills, New York: Macmillan.

HOLLANDER, EDWARD O., ed. 1967. *The Future of Small Business.* New York: Praeger.

HUMMON, NORMAN P., PATRICK DOREIAN, and KLAUS TEUTER. 1975. "A Structural Control Model of Organizational Change." *American Sociological Review* 40 (December): 812–24.

HUTCHINSON, G. EVELYN. 1957. "Concluding Remarks." *Cold Spring Harbor Symposium on Quantitative Biology* 22:415–27.

——. 1959. "Homage to Santa Rosalia, or Why Are There So Many Kinds of Animals?" *American Naturalist* 93:145–59.

LEVIN, SIMON A. 1970. "Community Equilibrium and Stability: An Extension of the Competitive Exclusion Principle." *American Naturalist* 104 (September–October): 413–23.

LEVINE, SOL, and PAUL E. WHITE. 1961. "Exchange as a Framework for the Study of Interorganizational Relationships." *Administrative Science Quarterly* 5 (March): 583–601.

LEVINS, RICHARD. 1962. "Theory of Fitness in a Heterogeneous Environment. I. The Fitness Set and Adaptive Function." *American Naturalist* 96 (November–December): 361–78.

——. 1968. *Evolution in Changing Environments.* Princeton, N.J.: Princeton University Press.

MACARTHUR, ROBERT H. 1972. *Geographical Ecology: Patterns in the Distribution of Species.* Princeton, N.J.: Princeton University Press.

MACARTHUR, ROBERT H., and RICHARD LEVINS. 1964. "Competition, Habitat Selection and Character Displacement in Patchy Environment." *Proceedings of the National Academy of Sciences* 51:1207–10.

MARCH, JAMES G., and HERBERT SIMON. 1958. *Organizations.* New York: Wiley.

MARSCHAK, JACOB, and ROY RADNER. 1972. *Economic Theory of Teams.* New Haven, Conn.: Yale University Press.

MAY, ROBERT M. 1973. *Stability and Complexity in Model Ecosystems.* Princeton, N.J.: Princeton University Press.

MEYER, JOHN W. 1970. "The Charter: Conditions of Diffuse Socialization in Schools." Pp. 564–78 in *Social Processes and Social Structures,* edited by W. Richard Scott. New York: Holt, Rinehart & Winston.

MONOD, JACQUES. 1971. *Chance and Necessity.* New York: Vintage.

Nation's Business. 1976. "America's Oldest Companies." 64 (July): 36–37.

NIELSEN, FRANÇOIS, and MICHAEL T. HANNAN. 1977. "The Expansion of National Educational Systems: Tests of a Population Ecology Model." *American Sociological Review,* in press.

CURRENT THEORETICAL PERSPECTIVES

PARSONS, TALCOTT. 1956. "Suggestions for a Sociological Approach to the Theory of Organizations, I." *Administrative Science Quarterly* 1 (March): 63–85.

PENROSE, EDITH T. 1959. *The Theory of the Growth of the Firm.* New York: Wiley.

SELZNICK, PHILIP. 1957. *Leadership in Administration.* New York: Row, Peterson.

SIMON, HERBERT A. 1962. "The Architecture of Complexity." *Proceedings of the American Philosophical Society* 106 (December): 467–82.

———. 1973. "The Organization of Complex Systems." Pp. 1–28 in *Hierarchy Theory: The Challenge of Complex Systems,* edited by H. Patee. New York: Braziller.

SIMON, HERBERT A., and C. P. BONINI. 1958. "The Size Distribution of Business Firms." *American Economic Review* 48 (September): 607–17.

STINCHCOMBE, ARTHUR L. 1959. "Bureaucratic and Craft Administration of Production." *Administrative Science Quarterly* 4 (June): 168–87.

———. 1965. "Social Structure and Organizations." Pp. 153–93 in *Handbook of Organizations,* edited by James G. March. Chicago: Rand McNally.

TEMPLETON, ALAN R., and EDWARD A. ROTHMAN. 1974. "Evolution in Heterogenous Environments." *American Naturalist* 108 (July–August): 409–28.

THOMPSON, JAMES D. 1967. *Organizations in Action.* New York: McGraw-Hill.

TURK, HERMAN. 1970. "Interorganizational Networks in Urban Society: Initial Perspectives and Comparative Research." *American Sociological Review* 35 (February): 1–19.

WHITTAKER, ROBERT N., and SIMON LEVIN, eds. 1976. *Niche: Theory and Application.* Stroudsberg, Pa.: Dowden, Hutchinson & Ross.

WINTER, SIDNEY G., JR. 1964. "Economic 'Natural Selection' and the Theory of the Firm." *Yale Economic Essays* 4:224–72.

ZALD, MAYER. 1970. "Political Economy: A Framework for Analysis." Pp. 221–61 in *Power in Organizations,* edited by M. N. Zald. Nashville, Tenn.: Vanderbilt University Press.

Organizations: A Dialectical View

J. Kenneth Benson

The study of complex organizations has been guided by a succession of rational and functional theories and by positivist methodology.[1] These efforts have proceeded on the basis of an uncritical acceptance of the conceptions of organizational structure shared by participants. The distinctions between divisions, departments, occupations, levels, recruitment and reward strategies, and so forth, through which participants arrange their activities have become scientific categories. Likewise, the participants' explanations for the structure of the organization have been formalized as scientific theories.

As a result of these tendencies the sociology of organizations has failed to develop a critical posture. The theoretical constructs of the field are tied to and tend to affirm the present realities in organizations. Radical transformations of organizations would undermine the corresponding theories.

The basic problem may be seen clearly considering two divergent assessments of the future of organizational life in industrial societies. Howton (1969) envisioned the extension of the core processes of rationalization and functionalization to whole societies; thus, in his view the society would become a large organization with carefully articulated parts contributing to overall objectives. Such a development would permit the continued relevance of rational-functional theories of organizations, indeed would extend the range of those theories. Yet, the process through which this new organizational society emerges would remain outside rational-

SOURCE: *Administrative Science Quarterly* 22, no. 3 (September 1977): 1–21. Reprinted by permission of the author and the publisher.
1. Revision of a paper presented at the Sixty-eighth Annual Meeting of the American Sociological Association, New York, N.Y., August, 1973. I gratefully acknowledge comments on earlier drafts of this paper by Howard Aldrich, Eliot Freidson, Peter M. Hall, Wolf Heydebrand, James Mulherin, Charles Perrow, Richard Riddle, Stephen Turner, Robert A. Day, Mayer Zald, and students in my bureaucracy and theory seminars at the University of Missouri-Columbia. In preparation of this draft I have particularly benefited from extensive conversations with Mark Wardell and Robert Hagan. None of these are to be blamed for flaws remaining in the argument, and some have disagreed substantially with my position.

functional theories, although these theories may describe adequately the operation of such a society.

Simpson (1972) provided an opposing assessment of the future which raises the same theoretical problem. He suggested the possibility of the demise of rationality in organizations and a resurgence of emotional and moralistic bases of decision. The demise of organizational rationality would also spell the end of theories tied to it. As with the Howton example, the process giving rise to and/or undermining the realities to which the theories refer remains outside the theories. Dialectical analysis provides a way of reaching beyond these limits.

Dialectical theory, because it is essentially a processual perspective, focuses on the dimension currently missing in much organizational thought. It offers an explanation of the processes involved in the production, the reproduction, and the destruction of particular organizational forms. It opens analysis to the processes through which actors carve out and stabilize a sphere of rationality and those through which such rationalized spheres dissolve. Thus, dialectical theory can explain the empirical grounding of conventional organization theories because it deals with the social processes which conventional theories ignore.[2]

This article draws upon a general Marxist perspective on social life to develop a dialectical view of organizational theory. This approach to organizational studies has few close parallels. (For related efforts see Heydebrand, 1977; Goldman and Van Houten, 1977.) Marxists have rarely been interested in organizational analysis except to criticize the entire field; and organization scientists, for their part, have made minimal use of Marxist thought.

The dialectical view challenges the theoretical and methodological orthodoxies currently prevalent in the field. The established approaches, although varying in details, share a structure of reasoning or problematic which has been characterized as the "rational selection model" (Benson, 1971), the "goal paradigm" (Georgiou, 1973), and the "tool view" (Perrow, 1972). According to this problematic, much of what occurs in the organization is understood as a result of goal pursuit and/or need fulfillment. This view has been coupled with a methodological stance which accepts the conventionally understood components of the organization as scientific categories. The combination has uncritically accepted existing organizational arrangements and adapted itself to the interests of administrative elites. As a consequence organizational analysis has been

2. There have been a few efforts to develop dialectical analyses of organizational phenomena. Blau and Scott (1962: 222–253) for example devoted a chapter to ongoing processes through which dilemmas are confronted and partly resolved only to be confronted again in modified form. Also see Weinstein, Weinstein, and Blau (1973) and Lourenço and Gildewell (1975).

dominated by issues of administrative concern. Its primary research questions have been administrative issues one step removed.

Despite this, all existing work will not be categorically rejected. Even work thoroughly within the conventional mode may be valuable. More important, a substantial amount of prior work has remained partially free of the dominant model—focusing on such phenomena as alternative power structures, strategic contingencies, political economy, negotiated order, and co-optative mechanisms—and may be usefully incorporated in a dialectical analysis. Thus, this article builds upon existing work while going beyond it at certain crucial points.

The Dialectic As Social Process

The dialectical view is a general perspective on social life which can be extracted from the Marxist analysis of economic structure and its ramifications.[3] Marx's analysis of the capitalist economy is an application of the general perspective. The general perspective is, then, expressed through Marx's analyses of capitalism but not locked into the specific categories and arguments of that analysis. Rather, a more general perspective running through Marx's work may be discerned.[4]

A dialectical view is fundamentally committed to the concept of process. The social world is in a continuous state of becoming—social arrangements which seem fixed and permanent are temporary, arbitrary patterns and any observed social pattern are regarded as one among many possibilities. Theoretical attention is focused upon the transformation through which one set of arrangements gives way to another. Dialectical analysis involves a search for fundamental principles which account for the emergence and dissolution of specific social orders.

There are four principles of dialectical analysis—social construction/ production, totality, contradiction, praxis. These constitute a perspective

3. In formulating a position I have been influenced most heavily by proponents of a dialectical Marxism, specifically Lukács (1971), Lefebvre (1968, 1971), Markovíc (1974), Goldmann (1969), Birnbaum (1969, 1971), and Habermas (1970, 1971, 1973). In addition, I have drawn occasional insights from such structural Marxists as Althusser (1970; Althusser and Balibar, 1970) and Godelier (1972). Finally, there are a number of places where I have drawn upon phenomenological sociologies, especially Berger and Luckmann (1966). I have consciously tried to work within a dialectical Marxist problematic and to draw upon other perspectives selectively where they provide insights which may be assimilated to the dialectical position.

4. My procedure is not one of relying upon dialectical laws of nature such as the transformation of quantity into quality, the interpenetration of opposites, and the like. The notion of dialectical laws located in nature and expressed both in society and in physical phenomena has been rightly criticized by Mills (1962: 129–130) and many others. Rather I have tried to utilize some general features of Marx's model and method of analysis, as did Mills himself (1962: 36–40).

on the fundamental character of social life. A dialectical view of any particular field of study must be guided by an application of these principles.

Social Construction/Production

The transformation of the social world is rooted in fundamental characteristics of human social life. People are continually constructing the social world. Through their interactions with each other social patterns are gradually built and eventually a set of institutional arrangements is established. Through continued interactions the arrangements previously constructed are gradually modified or replaced.

The construction of social arrangements is not a wholly rational-purposeful process, although the Marxist vision is that someday it might be. Social arrangements are created from the basically concrete, mundane tasks confronting people in their everyday life. Relationships are formed, roles are constructed, institutions are built from the encounters and confrontations of people in their daily round of life. Their production of social structure is itself guided and constrained by the context.

An important constraint is, of course, the existing social structure itself. People produce a social world which stands over them, constraining their actions. The production of social structure, then, occurs within a social structure. There are powerful forces which tend to occasion the reproduction of the existing social structure. These include, as prominent elements, the interests of particular groups of people and their power to defend their interests within an established order. Nevertheless, the efforts of people to transcend their present limits bring them eventually into conflict with the established arrangements and lead to social change. Sometimes the process is not planned and coherent, for example, where in reaching for higher levels of material productivity people go beyond the limits of present social arrangements. Sometimes, however, people may come to understand the limits of social structure and purposely rearrange it, a process termed "negation of the negation" (Marković, 1974: 24).

Totality

Another important commitment of dialectical thought is that social phenomena should be studied relationally, that is, with attention to their multiple interconnections. Any particular structure is always seen as part of a larger, concrete whole rather than as an isolated, abstract phenomenon.

The basis for this claim lies in the concept of social construction/production itself. People produce social structure, and they do so within a social context. The produced social world always constitutes a context which influences the ongoing process of production. Components of the social structure then become intertwined in complex ways. Divisions between components are not clear-cut or clean. Analysis must deal with the complex interlocking through which components are built into each other. This involves a search for dominant forces or components without resort to a deterministic argument.

The linkages between components are not complete nor wholly coherent. Rather, the processes of social construction take place in unique, partially autonomous contexts. These varying contexts are not centrally controlled and regulated except in rare cases. Thus, dialectical analysis, while looking at wholes, stresses the partial autonomy of the components. The principle of totality, then, expresses a commitment to study social arrangements as complex, interrelated wholes with partially autonomous parts. Analysis pursues the major breaks or divisions of the social structure which occasion divergent, incompatible productions, and the relations of dominance between sectors or layers of the social structure.

Because social construction is an emergent, partially autonomous process, the realities accepted by participants at any particular time may be continually undermined by ongoing acts of social construction. Even powerful actors may be unable to maintain an orderly, rationalized system of social relations in the face of this ongoing process. The totality, conceived dialectically then, includes newly emerging social arrangements as well as those already in place.

Contradiction

Contradiction in the social order is a third principle of a Marxist dialectical view. The social order produced in the process of social construction contains contradictions, ruptures, inconsistencies, and incompatabilities in the fabric of social life. Radical breaks with the present order are possible because of *contradictions*. Some of these are necessary features of a particular order. For example, an integral part of capitalist social formations is that they are antithetical to the interests of labor, yet the functioning system maintains or reproduces this contradiction.

Other contradictions, by contrast ,are system-destructive, that is, their presence undermines the system and destroys it. In classical Marxist analysis, the contradiction between the forces of production and economic relations is of this type. The advancement of the productive forces brings these into contradiction with the established system of economic relations. Economic systems pass from the scene as a consequence of this contradiction. (See Godelier, 1972.)

The ongoing process of social construction produces social formations. Once produced, these develop a seemingly autonomous, determinate structure. The structure may be studied and orderly relations between its components may be observed as if it were not a human product. Hence, conventional, theoretical approaches and positivistic methodologies may contribute to the description of these orderly patterns.

The dialectical approach differs from conventional strategies in treating these orderly patterns as created, produced arrangements with latent possibilities which can be transformed. The dialectical vision of the future is not one of continuous, predictable development through an extension or consolidation of the present order; rather, the future has many possibilities and the final determination depends upon human action or praxis (Markovíc, 1974: 210).

Contradictions grow out of social production in two ways. First, there is in any social setting a contradiction between ongoing production and the previously established social formation. The production of new patterns must always go against these established interests.

Second, the production process is carried out in differentiated social contexts producing multiple and incompatible social forms. The contexts vary in regard to the conditions affecting and limiting the process of production. There is in most instances little coordination between the multiple contexts within which construction takes place. Attempts to tightly regulate the process through authoritative direction or ideological manipulation are only partly successful, whether in political empires or organizational regimes. At the societal level the production processes in separate institutional sectors are partially autonomous. Likewise, at the level of organizations, the multiple levels and divisions form differentiated contexts within which social production proceeds in a partially autonomous manner. As a result the fabric of social life is rent with contradictions growing out of the unevenness and disconnectedness of social production.

Social contradictions have important effects upon production. (1) They may occasion dislocations and crises which activate the search for alternative social arrangements; (2) they may combine in ways which facilitate or in ways which thwart social mobilization; (3) they may define the limits of change within a particular period or within a given system. Consciousness of these limits may permit the ultimate negation of the limits; but in the interim the contradictions may be quite constraining.

Praxis

The final principle is praxis or the free and creative reconstruction of social arrangements on the basis of a reasoned analysis of both the limits and the potentials of present social forms.

The commitment to praxis is both a description—that is, that people under some circumstances can become active agents reconstructing their own social relations and ultimately themselves on the basis of rational analysis—and an ethical commitment—that is, that social science should contribute to the process of reconstruction, to the liberation of human potential through the production of new social formations.

Dialectical analysis contributes to this process in part by dereifying established social patterns and structures—points out their arbitrary character, undermines their sense of inevitability, uncovers the contradictions and limits of the present order, and reveals the merchanisms of transformation.

An important dimension of such analysis is the critique of theories which affirm the present order or which deal only with minor adjustments or variations upon that order. From a dialectical perspective, the practice of social science is, like other human activities, a process of production imbedded in a social context. The social scientist uses the tools and raw materials at hand to construct realities.

The next section explores the implications of each of the general principles for the analysis of organizational phenomena. This involves the formulation of a conceptual apparatus and a methodology appropriate to the dialectical study of complex organizations.

The Social Production of Organizational Reality

An organization as part of the social world is always in a state of becoming; it is not a fixed and determinate entity. Its major features—goals, structural arrangements, technology, informal relations, and so on—are the outcroppings of the process of social construction. The dialectical perspective focuses attention upon this process through which a specific organizational form has been produced, the mechanisms through which an established form is maintained (or reproduced), and its continuous reconstruction.

The organization is a product of past acts of social construction. As a product, it has some orderly, predictable relationships among its components at any particular point in time. These relationships may be studied scientifically and empirical generalizations may be framed to describe the order. In fact, this is the focus of much sociological research on organizations—for example, Perrow (1967), Woodward (1965; 1970), Zwerman (1970), and others found correlations between the technologies and the power structures of organizations. The demonstration of such relations, however, is not the end of inquiry but the beginning. Rather than treating such relationships as determinate, causal connections, for instance, arguing that technology determines social structure, the dialectician investigates the social process through which the orderly, predictable relations have been produced and reproduced.

There is a tendency in much organizational research to interpret observed correlations in terms of a hypothetical social process. For example, Blau and Schoenherr (1971) formulated some possible processes through which executives decide to increase organizational differentiation. Actual historical research tracing the sequence of events, however, has been rare. (See Chandler, 1962, for an exception.) The usual explanatory strategy, as with Blau and Schoenherr, is to formulate a hypothetical sequence involving actors who make rational or functional decisions, for example, fitting structure to technology in order to achieve efficiency.

Dialectical explanations observe or reconstruct sequences on the basis of historical evidence. The alernatives conceived by actors are explored; the constraints upon their decisions discovered; and the power bases of various actors uncovered. Once a pattern of organizational life is discovered, the processes through which it is maintained and/or modified are studied. Thus, an orderly pattern is taken to be a crystallized but temporary outcome of the process of social construction whose emergence and maintenance demands explanation. Several principles of social construction may be ventured as tentative guidelines for such investigations.

Ideas and Actions

The consciousness of organizational participants is partially autonomous from the contextual situations in which they exist (Murphy, 1971). They are not in any simple sense captives of the roles, official purposes, or established procedures of the organization. The participants fill these "forms" with unique "content." Sometimes they may so so in an automatic, unreflective way; in other periods they may become very purposeful in trying to reach beyond the limits of their present situation, to reconstruct the organization in accord with alternative conceptions of its purposes, structures, technologies, and other features. Zald and McCarthy (1975) and Strauss and others (Strauss *et al.,* 1964; Bucher and Stelling, 1969; Bucher, 1970) have provided examples of this phenomenon.

Interests

The process of social construction proceeds through the mediation of interests in which the participants' perspectives are affected by the present structure of advantages and disadvantages built into the organization. This is not to say that a perfect correspondence between interests and ideas will prevail at all times—rather, over time the structure of interests will gradually influence the formation of ideas. In crisis periods, when thoroughgoing change is possible, participants may see their interests more clearly and conform their ideas and actions closely to them.

208

Power

The ideas which guide the construction of the organization depend upon the power of various participants, that is, their capacity to control the direction of events. Some parties are in dominant positions permitting the imposition and enforcement of their conceptions of reality. Others are in positions of relative weakness and must act in conformity with the definitions of others. (See Silverman, 1971, for a similar analysis.)

Power in the organization derives to some extent from the official authority structure. Those occupying positions of authority have power to establish and enforce a model. They can design the organization as an instrument in the service of specific purposes. They can articulate its parts, adjust its technology and motivate its participants with certain ends in view. Once the organization is stabilized, they can use their power to maintain it as a rationally articulated structure by resisting interference from outside and opposing sources of resistance inside. (See Bendix, 1956, for a particularly valuable documentation of such processes.)

In most organization theories this state of affairs is assumed and is outside the area of inquiry. The organization is assumed to be an instrument designed for a purpose, and research focuses on the structural consequences flowing from that and on the technical adjustments necessary to enhance goal pursuit. The power base of the leadership is not examined; alternative systems based on different power bases are not considered. Perrow (1972) explicitly recognized that the organization is a tool in the hands of powerful actors; but he did not provide a framework for analyzing the struggle to control the tool. Rather, he asserted that organizational analysis should permit us to assess the effectiveness of organizational instruments for reaching specific objectives.

An examination of the power base of authority figures would generally extend beyond the boundaries of the organization itself and this is perhaps why most organization theorists have avoided the problem. The grounding of organizational authority in larger systems—interorganizational networks, political-economic power blocs, legal systems, and the like—is important to the dialectical approach. Crises in the universities in the late 1960s and the ultimate reliance of university administrators upon military and police forces to maintain order have demonstrated the importance of such investigations.

The sources of power to resist and ultimately to overturn the official authority structure of organizations are also important foci of dialectical analysis. How are some groups better able than others to extract advantages and privileges from the organization? How are some groups better able than others to influence the major decisions affecting the direction of the organization? Analyses of control over uncertainty by Crozier (1964; 1972; 1973); Pfeffer (1972; 1973; Pfeffer and Leblebici, 1973; Pfeffer and Salancik, 1974; Salancik and Pfeffer, 1974; Pfeffer, Salancik, and Leblebici, 1976) and Hickson (Hickson *et al.,* 1971; Hinings *et al.,* 1974) have provided important beginnings on such questions. Yet, these insightful analyses must be placed within a more encompassing framework with a critical-reflexive component, otherwise, this line of investigation breaks down easily into a technocratic effort to reduce irrational bases of resistance to authority. Also, analyses of "negotiated order" by Strauss, Bucher, and others (Strauss *et al.,* 1963; Bucher, 1970) may provide valuable elements of an explanation, even though their efforts are faulty in giving the impression that everything of importance is currently negotiable. (See Benson and Day, 1976, for a critique.) Likewise, the arguments of Bell (1973), Galbraith (1967), and Touraine (1971) stressing the centrality of occupations to the core technology of the organization as a basis of power should be explored, being careful not to accept the deterministic, functional explanations implicit in some of these analyses (particularly those of Bell and Galbraith).

The mobilization of participants to pursue their interests and to reach out for alternative structural arrangements is also a significant component of a dialectical analysis of power. Occupational groups, racial groups, social classes, and others may envision alternatives and become actively committed to their achievement. Such mobilization of commitment and resources will greatly enhance their power in the organization. It is intriguing that mobilization has been given little thought in organizational theory despite its obvious significance in the labor movement. Although mobilization has been prominent in other fields such as collective behavior, race relations, and politics, it seems to lie outside the paradigm of organizational studies. A few observers with analytical roots in these other fields have analyzed mobilization in organizations (Gamson, 1975; Bachrach and Baratz, 1970), as have students of social movement organizations (Zald and Ash, 1966). These efforts, however, are clearly outside the mainstream of organizational studies.

The Organization As a Totality

In a dialectical analysis the organization must be studied as a whole with multiple, interpenetrating levels and sectors. This means conceptualizing the organization as a concrete total phenomenon and attending to the intricate ways in which its components are tied together. The conventional, taken-for-granted distinctions should be rejected as the boundaries of inquiry. For example, abstracting a "formal structure" from the flux of ongoing social life is an unacceptable move for the dialectician; for concrete social life consists of an intricate interplay between form and content, between structure and process, and the like. Similarly, abstracting a sphere of "rational action" from the daily round of events is an equally serious error. Organizational phenomena must be understood as wholes in all of their interpenetrating complexity.

The principle of totality also directs us to see the intricate ties of organizations to the larger society—not only to macrostructural features such as economic and political systems but also to the everyday activities of people. Again, the arbitrary but conventional boundaries between phenomena must be distrusted. The conventional separation between organization and environment must be critically examined. The essential continuity, the relational character of social life must itself be analyzed and not overlooked in a search for analytical boundaries and units of analysis. The processes through which such conventional boundaries are produced and sustained must be pursued. The interests and power relations on which the conventional boundaries rest must be examined.

The presently established approaches to organization theory, by contrast, rely upon abstraction. Their abstractions correspond closely to the conventional administrative view and function as an ideology justifying, rationalizing administrative actions as well as a normative model or goal of administrative actions. That the model corresponds to our experience and seems reasonable is an indicator of our indoctrination with the administrative perspective and of the success of administrators in constructing a world in this image.

The history of organization theory may be seen, in part, as a process in which a series of "nonrational factors" have been conjured up only to be subdued by the rationalizing core. Thus, in the 1930s human relations theory arose as a champion of the informal structure. The thrust of human relations theory, however, was to harness and control the informal in the interest of rationality. Later, the environment emerged as an important challenge in the work of Selznick (1949) and others. Yet through the years the trend has been toward extending the tentacles of rationalization to this sphere as well. Thus, recent theorists like March and Simon (1958), Lawrence and Lorsch (1967), and the school termed "neo-Weberians" by Perrow (1972) espouse a refined rationalism in which the sources of irrationality internal and external to the organization can be contained. This corresponds, incidentally, with an era of organizational monsters which Perrow (1972) warns control their environments and in which principles of rationalization and functionalization are being extended to wider spheres of social life (Howton, 1969).

Dialectical analysis is not to be restricted to the narrow, limited, conventional reality promulgated by administrators. Its focus is the total organization from which this limited segment has been wrenched. It analyzes the intricate ways in which the organization as a rationally articulated structure is linked to its unrationalized context; it explores and uncovers the social and political processes through which a segmental view becomes

211

dominant and is enforced; and, it anticipates the emergence of new ar-rangements based on shifting power relations. Thus, the dialectical view takes the rationalized organization as an arbitrary model unevenly im-posed upon events and insecure in its hold. The strategy for developing this kind of analysis here includes the recognition of two levels of organi-zational reality—morphology and substructure.

Organizational Morphology

Morphology refers to the officially enforced and conventionally ac-cepted view of the organization. It refers to the organization as abstracted from its concrete, intricate relations with other aspects of social life. This is the administrators' vision of the organization, the form which they try to impose upon events. Since they are partly successful, the morphology may also be somewhat accurate as a description of organizations.

Four aspects of organizational reality at the level of morphological analysis must be distinguished.

1. The paradigm commitments of an organization—specifically, its commitments to a domain, a technology, and an ideology. These commitments provide, respectively, a definition of the objectives of the organization, a specific set of techniques for pursuing objec-tives, and a set of ideas interpreting and justifying the organiza-tion's activities.
2. The officially recognized and legitimate structural arrangements of the organization—specifically, the network of social roles and role sets in the organization. This includes characteristics such as differentiation, centralization, bureaucratization, and so on.
3. The constitution of the organization—specifically, the bases of participation and involvement in the organization. These concern the terms on which participation and compliance of individuals and groups are effected. (On organization "constitutions" see Zald, 1970a, 1970b.)
4. The organization-environment linkages—specifically, the pattern-ing or structuring of relations with organizations and individuals external to the focal organization.

One may, of course, construct organizational analysis on the corre-lated variability between morphological components like most organiza-tion theorists. Their efforts generally proceed by: (1) demonstrating an empirical regularity in organizations, such as a correlation between num-ber of hierarchical levels and number of separate divisions, (2) establish-ing the types of organizations within which the relationship holds, and (3) inferring a rational or functional linkage between the correlated factors (for example, see Etzioni, 1961; Perrow, 1967; Blau and Schoenherr, 1971).

The research undertaken by Blau and associates (Blau, 1968, 1973; Blau, Heydebrand and Stauffer, 1966; Blau and Schoenherr, 1971) in the Comparative Organization Research Program exemplifies the pattern. The research relies upon summary indicators of structural patterns based on documents such as organization charts and on interview reports of structural patterns. From these data measures for structural features such as hierarchy, differentiation, and so forth are derived. These are correlated with each other and with other factors such as size and technology. The pattern of correlations is then explained as a result of a rational or functional arrangement of the organization's parts. The actual process of adjustment, the sequence of events producing the pattern has not been observed but has been inferred to be one of rational or functional adjustment. Thus, the entire explanatory effort remains within the confines of an abstracted organization ripped from its historical roots and societal context and innocent of its deeper-lying power struggles and negotiations. Thus, the research itself is drawn into the presuppositions of the order under study. The extra-rational processes—internal and external to the rationally conceived organization—remain out of focus, beyond the periphery of the investigators' vision. (See Turner, 1977, for a related critique.)

A dialectical analysis, by contrast, should attend to the underlying process which produced and sustained the observed regularities. The systematic relationships among parts of the organization's morphology must be explained by reference to a more fundamental substructure such as a power structure which generates changes within the morphology. This too involves finding an empirical base for organizational measurement, that is, continuously analyzing how the primary data sources such as organization charts are produced and sustained.[5]

This does not mean that morphological research is worthless. On the contrary, the description of regularities at this level is a necessary step in a dialectical analysis. These efforts must, however, be integrated in a larger explanatory program. Most important, morphological studies should not be allowed to define the parameters of the field and thereby limit its explanatory capacity.

Even appeals to rational or functional selection processes may have a continuing importance. One certainly cannot argue a priori that such processes are of no consequence. Such processes, however, should not be

5. The substructure consists of the network of social relations through which the morphology is produced and reproduced. Here one encounters the bases of power, the dominance relations which establish and maintain the morphology of the organization. The orderly sequences of development, the predictable relations between components at the morphological level are grounded in and ultimately explained by this substructure.

213

invoked as final arbiters, as the ultimate basis of organizational analysis; rather, actual event sequences must be examined. When rational or functional processes appear to be operating, such processes must themselves be grounded, that is, one must inquire about the production process through which rational or functional selection criteria are established and maintained. This, of course, may lead us beyond the conventional boundaries of the organization to larger systems of dominance.

Organizational Substructure

The substructural network provides the basis for transformation of the organization's morphology. The substructure is in part a nonrationalized sphere of organizational action, a complex network of relations linking participants to each other and to the larger social world in a multiplicity of unregulated ways. Administrative rationalizers try and have been partly successful at containing or harnessing the energy flowing from these ties. Much of organizational analysis, of course, has been supportive of such rationalizing moves by élites. Because it is only partly rationalized, the substructure provides the social basis for a latent social system forming within the established order and threatening its hegemony. For example the cleavage between sexual or racial groups, where coterminous with administrative divisions, could provide a cutting edge for consciousness formation (Gordon, 1972; Crozier, 1964). On the basis of substructural linkages people may act to overthrow the established morphology.

The substructure includes linkages to the larger societal system. These include the bases of recruitment of organizational élites; the framework of interests in the larger society setting limits upon the operations of the organization; the power structure controlling the flow of resources into organizations and through interorganizational networks; the ties of the organization to social classes, racial groups, ethnic groups, sexual groups, and others in the society; the institutionalized dominance patterns of professions in their spheres of practice; and so on. Developments within the organization often appear to be intricately related to events occurring in the larger society. In many ways the organization is a part of these larger patterns. Yet, the prevailing analytical strategy is to abstract the organization from these relations and treat it as if it were autonomous or at least capable of channeling or filtering the environment through its input-output orifices. (For exceptions see especially Zald, 1970a, 1970b; Warren, Rose, and Bergunder, 1974.) Dialectical analysis, by contrast, focuses attention upon the relations.

The substructure also includes bases of dominance that are intra-organizational. Included here are structures of control over strategic resources giving some departments, divisions, occupations, and so forth, advantages vis-à-vis others. The centrality of an occupation to the core technology of an organization or the capacity of some departments to control uncertainty affecting significantly the welfare of other departments might provide leverage for exercising power in the main reality-defining arenas of the organization. These and other sources of power might be explored within a dialectical framework.

There is a large body of literature dealing with these issues that may be incorporated in a dialectical analysis. This includes the work of Crozier (1964, 1972, 1973), Hickson and others (Hickson *et al.*, 1971; Hinings *et al.*, 1974) on strategic contingencies, Pfeffer (1972, 1973; Pfeffer and Salancik, 1974; Salancik and Pfeffer, 1974; Pfeffer, Salancik, and Leblebici, 1976) and Aldrich (1972, 1976; Whetten and Aldrich 1975) on resource dependence, and that of Zald and Wamsley (Zald, 1970a, 1970b; Wamsley and Zald, 1973) on political economy. While none of these works are cast within a dialectical framework, they grapple with the underlying, non-rationalized bases of control within the organization. There is a tendency within some of these efforts, especially those of Zald and Wamsley, to see these underlying power-dependence relations as the foundation of organizational goals paradigmatic commitments, and authority structures.[6]

6. Since some of my argument here has been anticipated in the work on strategic contingencies, resource dependencies, and political economy, it seems important to suggest the ways in which a dialectical perspective incorporates but goes beyond these earlier efforts. The major difference is that these contributions represent partial perspectives which can be incorporated in a variety of more encompassing arguments. The dialectical view is instead a more nearly complete explanatory framework into which the more limited theories may be drawn. Work on strategic contingencies, for example, has been framed at times within an overall functionalist framework by assuming that the organization will grant power to those segments most crucial to its work (see especially Hickson *et al.*, 1971). The recent work by Pfeffer and Aldrich on resource dependence has produced a set of testable propositions floating free of any larger analytical system. In fact, they (Aldrich and Pfeffer, 1976) have recently tried to integrate their work with an evolutionary model. Thus, both the theoretical and practical connections of this body of thought are indeterminate. Drawing it into a dialectical framework provides a more general set of principles to guide analysis. We are directed to the role of contradictions, to the larger totality, to the importance of praxis, reflexivity, and the like. Thus, the tendency to fall into evolutionist, functionalist, or positivist stances is counteracted.

The work of Zald, Wamsley, and others within a political economy perspective presents a more difficult problem. Clearly, I have been heavily influenced by the political economy view; my previous work on interorganizational networks (Benson, 1975) takes a political economy stance. Further, the work of Zald (1970a, 1970b) and Wamsley and Zald (1973) constitute a very ambitious effort to grapple with the issues addressed in the present paper. Their work grounds goals, technologies, constitutions, and other features of the organization in more basic power relations. They are sensitive to the latent, unregulated social networks (termed substructure here) beneath the superficial realities addressed by most conventional theories. Overall, their work constitutes the closest parallel within the existing literature. Yet, they do not characterize their work as dialectical or Marxian. In part my effort is to

Organizational Contradictions

The organizational totality, as conceived dialectically, is character-ized by ruptures, breaks, and inconsistencies in the social fabric. To these we apply the general term "contradiction," while recognizing that such rifts may be of many different types. Many theorists see the organization as a reasonably coherent, integrated system, rationally articulated or func-tionally adjusted. This view, of course, is an abstraction. If one looks at the organization concretely and pays attention to its multiple levels and varied relations to the larger society, contradictions become an obvious and important feature of organizational life. (See Heydebrand, 1977.)

The Production of Contradictions

Social construction-production is not a rationally guided, centrally controlled process. Despite the efforts of administrations to contain and channel the process, some elements in the organization and outside of it remain beyond the reach of rationalization. Beyond this, the rationaliza-tion process produces structures which then resist further rationalization.

Some contradictions are generated within the organization—growing out of the divisions, reward structures, control structures, and other separation points in the organization. These define distinct, semi-autono-mous spheres of social action, which are divergent contexts for social construction-production. The people occupying particular locations will

---

establish a link suggesting how this important body of work may be incorporated in a dialectical view.

Beyond this, however, there are some important differences. The proponents of political economy, resource dependence, strategic contingencies, and the like remain committed to a basically positivist methodology. They have adopted an un-critical, unreflexive stance toward organizational realities. They fail to see or at least to grapple with the tentativeness, the arbitrariness of the phenomena they describe. They do not examine how these phenomena are produced. Instead they pursue the description and analysis of a particular kind of order—characterized by resource dependencies. Dialectical analysis must go beyond this to deal with the processes through which this kind of order is produced and maintained. Clearly the political economy model is historically and contextually limited. Its accuracy, pre-dictive utility, and so on are contingent. This complication cannot be ignored by the dialectician.

As with other theories we must seek the connection between interests and theoretical orientations. In some instances work of this type has been funded exten-sively by government agencies with an apparent interest in smoothing interorganiza-tional coordination, overcoming resistance to change, and creating more flexible organizational apparatuses. Thus, we must pursue the possibility that such work formalizes a perspective and interest that are institutionally isolable and limited. This may involve a program of technocratic rationalization through planning for, bargaining with, and manipulating organizations.

tend to develop models of organizational structure based on their peculiar priorities and problems—from a specific occupational or departmental standpoint. Thus, across a range of sectoral divisions or levels the organization generates opposing models or images of organizational morphology. Beyond this, the subgroups created by sectoral divisions, levels, and the like may be sufficiently autonomous to implement their opposing models to some degree. In any case, a large, complex organization is likely at any given time to harbor a number of structural inconsistencies, for example, some departments organized along professional lines; others, more bureaucratized. Many sociologists have analyzed inconsistencies of this kind, but few have recognized their basis as being a fundamental social process.[7]

Beyond this, the ongoing process of social construction in all sectors of the organization will continually generate alternatives to the presently established morphology. This may occur at all stratified levels. Even authorities may frequently generate innovations which are contradictory to the established patterns. Increased use of computers for purposes of coordination and control, new budgeting procedures, and other innovations from above may stand in opposition to previously constructed arrangements. Thus, the organization as established constitutes a structure which may resist its own further development. This should not be seen as a mysterious occurrence, but as a result of the rooting of present arrangements in a concrete structure of advantages, interests, commitments, and the like.

Contradictions may be generated also in the larger society and imposed upon the organization. An organization may be charged with multiple, contradictory functions, for instance, the prison's dual purposes of rehabilitation and protection. This may produce inconsistent moves within the organization yielding contradictory structures, competing interest groups, and occasional periods of crisis. Or, an organization may be made dependent upon support or cooperation from opposing sources. For example, a manpower program might be dependent both upon employers with a conservative ideology regarding work and militant advocacy groups with a radical ideology. The manpower agency may internalize the conflict by developing contradictory components to deal with those opposed publics (Schmidt and Kochan, 1976).

Some contradictions within the organization may directly reflect the fundamental features of the larger economic-political system. Management-conflict, for example, is a basic feature of capitalist societies which is reproduced by the workings of those societies. This conflict leads to the production of contradictory arrangements inside all of the work organizations

---

7. Benson (1973) for an analysis of bureaucratic-professional conflict which elaborates this point.

in the society. This sets limits upon structural innovations, ideological formulations, morale levels, and other features within the organizations (Krupp, 1961).

The Structure of Contradictions

The organization is typically the scene of multiple contradictions. The ongoing processes of social construction internal and external to the organization produce a complex array of interrelated contradictions. The combinations are contingent upon the ways in which components of the organization and the society are engaged. Contradictions become overlaid in unique clusters or patterns depending upon the ways in which different groups become involved in their production. Every organization is, then, a unique case because of the contingencies affecting social construction-production.[8]

Consider, as an example, the knitting together of authority level and racial status as bases of social construction. Where a racial minority is subordinate in the organization's authority structure, the resulting patterns of contradiction may be different from otherwise comparable situations lacking the overlay of race upon authority. Recent crises in some state prisons have reflected the overlay of race and authority. The largely black populations of the prisons have increasingly seen the organization as an instrument of white oppression. Black inmates have created structures based upon racial antagonism, used a racial ideology, and linked their cause to that of racial liberation in the larger society.

Contradictions may be combined in ways which exacerbate conflict or in ways which contain it. Some combinations may constitute what Althusser (1970) terms a "ruptural unity," that is, a combination that permits a drastic reorganization of the system. Other combinations may tend to fragment the organization in a series of overlapping, partially competitive interest groups.

Participants may try to reach their objectives by managing or manipulating the combinations of contradictions. It has been argued, for example, that corporate élites have purposely created secondary labor markets for minorities and women as a device for maintaining control over jobs and dividing the labor movement (Gordon, 1972). Of course, combinations produced for one purpose may later produce perverse outcomes. The coincidence of race and occupation produced heightened racial tensions in the 1960s.

8. It is not possible in a programmatic statement of this kind to specify a catalogue of contradictions weighted according to their importance. This is because (1) the combinations of contradictions operating in a particular organization is a unique, contingent structure; and (2) the ongoing process of social production continuously generates new contradictions.

The Production of Change

Contradictions feed into the social construction-production process in several ways. (1) Contradictions provide a continuing source of tensions, conflicts, and the like which may, under some circumstances, shape consciousness and action to change the present order. (2) Contradictions set limits upon and establish possibilities for reconstruction at any given time. (3) Contradictions may produce crises which enhance possibilities for reconstruction. (4) Contradictions are important, finally, as defining limits of a system. Some contradictions may be crucial features of a particular organizational order. Other contradictions of lesser significance may be eroded without changing the fundamental character of the organization. The fundamental contradictions tend to be reproduced in the organization by its normal operation as a system and by its linkages to a larger network. These contradictions define limits which must be exceeded in order to transform an organization.

The most basic, generic contradiction is that between the constructed social world and the ongoing process of social construction. The reification of the organization as a determinate thing standing over against people is contradictory to the ongoing process of production. This contradiction is the essence of social and political alienation. As people become conscious of this contradiction and act to overcome it, they rationally reconstruct the present order and overcome its limitations. Thus, we arrive at praxis.

Toward Organizational Praxis

Dialectical theory attends to the interplay between practical interests and scholarship. The study of organizations is seen as a product of social construction—that is, theories has been produced by particular groups of people acting within a limited context on the basis of their practical concerns. Theories, then, reflect the social context in which they were created and the practical concerns of their creators (not simply the authors but the larger group of people whose actions produced the theories). In turn, theories are inextricably involved in the construction of organizations. Theories guide actors in their efforts to understand and control the organization. Theories provide models to be implemented, illuminate problems to be solved, reveal controls to be exercised, and so on. There is, then, a dialectical relation between organizational arrangements and organizational theories. The use of theories as guidelines for administrative control and as programs for organizational revolutions should be the object of study. This involves a "reflexive" moment within dialectical analysis and parallels the kind of analysis proposed by Gouldner (1970), Friedrichs (1970), and others.

The Critique of Limited Perspectives

Many theories of organizations can be understood as formalized solutions of certain actors (usually administrators or other dominant figures) to the technical, practical problems posed by the organization's dialectical character. Such a theory formalizes a way of dealing with (controlling or adjusting to) the multilevel, contradictory complexity of the organization. Devices such as socializing, monitoring, rewarding, adjusting, structuring, and negotiating provide solutions to concrete problems encountered by participants. Theorists pull these devices together into coherent systems which then may be adopted within organizations, sometimes as a result of aggressive social movements. Such theories provide sets of procedures, movements, routines which may be employed to pursue an objective by cancelling, controlling, or capitalizing upon the contradictory complexity of organizational life.

From a dialectical perspective, then, specific theories are not in any simple sense to be set aside. Rather, they are to be superseded in a more encompassing framework. Human relations, structural-functional, decision, and open systems theories may each provide accurate predictive statements about some aspects of organizational structure and process within delimited time periods and institutional locations. The dialectician goes beyond such formulations to inquire into the relationships between organization theories and organizational realities—considering the "reality-defining" potential of a theory of administration, the linkage between administrator and theoretician, and the connection of social theories movements of various kinds. Such issues have been raised regarding human relations theories (see Carey, 1967; Krupp, 1961; Perrow, 1972; Mills, 1970) but, this type of critique must be broadened to include other theories as well. For example, open systems theories appear to be linked in time to the growing prominence of administrative circles of cybernation and its application to the organization structure and not merely to production technology. In this situation, the open systems theories have considerable intuitive appeal and have provided the intellectual foundation for a number of textbooks on management, industrial sociology, and complex organizations. Indeed, such theories may have some predictive power within this new institutional setting. However, it is important from dialectical perspective to recognize that open systems theories and theorists are deeply enmeshed in the social process creating the new administrative situation. The new administrative realities and the new administrative theories have emerged hand-in-hand. The theories and theorists are, then, part of the reality they describe. Their plausibility and predictive power may be derived from and circumscribed by this historically and institutionally delimited phenomenon. Furthermore, the entire "package" of events may be linked inextricably to larger and more fundamental processes of societal transformation such as the emergence of dominance patterns within which technology and science serve as legitimating ideologies (cf. Habermas, 1970; Karpik, 1972).

Similarly, theories of "negotiated order," which the author finds intuitively more appealing than open systems theory, must be subjected to the same mode of unrelenting critical examination. This perspective has been the creation of analysts working mainly in professional organizations (mostly medical settings). The perspective does seem intuitively to have a high degree of correspondence to events in those settings, particularly to the interactional patterns characterizing everyday life among professional staff members (Strauss *et al.,* 1963; Strauss *et al.,* 1964; Bucher and Stelling, 1969). Some questions that should be pursued about this perspective include the following: Is "negotiated order" a general theory of order or a theory of a specific kind of order existing within a narrowly delimited class of organizational settings? What issues are generally non-negotiable and thus ignored by or taken a defining boundaries by negotiated order theorists? Are the proponents of negotiated order theory engaged in dispensing its insights to practitioners in professional organizations? Do negotiated order theorists merely articulate and conceptualize the perspectives of insightful actors in the settings under study? (See Benson and Day, 1976.)

The task of the dialectician, then, is neither to reject these theories out of hand nor to accept their accuracy uncritically. Rather, it is to understand the connection between theory and reality by analyzing the social context.

The Construction of Alternatives

Dialectical analysis must go beyond reflexivity; it has an active as well as reflexive moment. It must be concerned with the active reconstruction of organizations. This reconstruction is aimed toward the realization of human potentialities by the removal of constraints, limitations upon praxis. This task involves both the critique of existing organizational forms and the search for alternatives. The search for alternatives is based on the view that the future is not necessarily a projection of the present order; rather, the future is full of possibilities and one of them has to be made. This is not an unrealistic or utopian task; rather, it must be tied to an empirically grounded understanding of limits and possibilities in the present.

The commitment to social reconstruction is toward the freeing of the process of social construction from blockages and limitations occasioned by dominance. The larger objective is the realization of a social situation in which people freely and collectively control the direction of change on the basis of a rational understanding of social process (Marković, 1974; Habermas, 1971, 1973).

A dialectical analysis of organizations, then, should be concerned with conditions under which people may reconstruct organizations and establish social formations in which continuous reconstruction is possible. This provides guidance regarding the selection of research questions. Some important issues are the humanization of work processes, the development of systems of participation (self-management), the discovery of alternatives to bureaucracy, the removal of systems of dominance, the provision for the utilization of expert knowledge without creating technocratic élites, removing the resistance of organizations to more rational arrangements (for example, overcoming resistance to the development of rationally arranged systems of organization). These are, of course, difficult problems and the task is complicated by the possibility that contradictions will develop between them, for example, creating rational systems may undermine self-management. Thus, the prospect is for a continuous process of reconstruction.

Conclusion

Organizations constitute important instruments of domination in the advanced industrial societies. Any effort to change these societies must deal with the organizational dimension. Likewise, efforts to construct alternative social arrangements within or in the place of the present order must grapple with the problem of organization. (See Schurman, 1968, for an examination of the organizational problems posed in Communist China.)

Despite the central importance of organizations to thoroughgoing social reconstruction, the study of organizations has not developed a capacity to deal with fundamental change. Instead, established approaches tend to affirm present organizational realities and to deal with relatively minor adjustments within the present order.

This article has attempted to begin the process of constructing an emancipatory alternative approach by proposing a dialectical view of organizations committed to the centrality of process. Four basic principles of dialectical analysis—social production, totality, contradiction, and praxis—are developed and applied to organizational studies. The principles of dialectical analysis provide a guiding perspective for organizational studies grounded in a view of human social life. The principles do not constitute a developed substantive theory of organizations nor a conceptual framework to guide research. The dialectical view provides instead a critical-emancipatory stance toward organizational studies. Much work remains to be done in developing the implications of this perspective within substantively based theory and research.

References

ALDRICH, HOWARD
1972 "An organization-environment perspective on cooperation and conflict in the manpower training system." In A. Negandhi (ed.), Interorganization Theory: 49–70. Kent, Ohio: Center for Business and Economic Research.
1976 "Resource dependence and interorganizational relations: local employment service offices and social services sector organizations." Administration and Society 7:4: 419–454.
ALDRICH, HOWARD, and JEFFREY PFEFFER
1976 "Environments of organizations." The Annual Review of Sociology, 2: 79–106.
ALTHUSSER, LOUIS
1970 For Marx. Trans. by Ben Brewster. New York: Vintage, a division of Random House.
ALTHUSSER, LOUIS, and ETIENNE BALIBAR
1970 Reading Capital. Trans. by Ben Brewster. New York: Pantheon.
BACHRACH, PETER S., and MORTON S. BARATZ
1970 Power and Poverty, Theory and Practice. New York: Oxford University Press.
BELL, DANIEL
1973 The Coming of Post-Industrial Society: A Venture in Social Forecasting. New York: Basic Books.
BENDIX, REINHARD
1956 Work and Authority in Industry. New York: Harper and Row.
BENSON, J. KENNETH
1971 Models of Structure Selection in Organizations: On the Limitations of Rational Perspectives. Paper presented at the Annual Meeting of the American Sociological Association, Denver, Colorado, August.
1973 "The analysis of bureaucratic-professional conflict: functional versus dialectical approaches." The Sociological Quarterly, 14: 376–394.
1975 "The interorganizational network as a political economy." The Administrative Science Quarterly, 20: 229–249.
BENSON, J. KENNETH, and ROBERT A. DAY
1976 On the Limits of Negotiation: a Critique of the Theory of Negotiated Order." Paper presented at the 71st Annual Meeting of the American Sociological Association, New York, New York, September.
BERGER, PETER L., and THOMAS LUCKMAN
1966 The Social Construction of Reality. Garden City, N.Y.: Doubleday.
BIRNBAUM, NORMAN
1969 The Crisis of Industrial Society. New York: Oxford University Press.
1971 Toward a Critical Sociology. New York: Oxford University Press.

CURRENT THEORETICAL PERSPECTIVES

BLAU, PETER M.
1968 "The hierarchy of authority in organizations." The American Journal of Sociology, 73: 453–467.
1973 The Organization of Academic Work. New York: Wiley.

BLAU, PETER M., WOLF V. HEYDEBRAND, and ROBERT E. STAUFFER
1966 "The structure of small bureaucracies." The American Sociological Review, 31:2: 179–191.

BLAU, PETER M., and RICHARD A. SCHOENHERR
1971 The Structure of Organizations. New York and London: Basic Books.

BLAU, PETER M., and RICHARD SCOTT
1962 Formal Organizations. San Francisco: Chandler.

BUCHER, RUE
1970 "Social process and power in a medical school." In Mayer N. Zald (ed.), Power in Organizations: 3–48. Nashville, Tenn.: Vanderbilt University Press.

BUCHER, RUE, and J. STELLING
1969 "Characteristics of professional organizations." The Journal of Health and Social Behavior, 10: 3–15.

CAREY, A.
1967 "The Hawthorne studies: a radical criticism." The American Sociological Review, 32:3: 403–416.

CHANDLER, ALFRED D., JR.
1962 Strategy and Structure: Chapters in the History of the Industrial Enterprise. Cambridge, MA: MIT Press.

CROZIER, MICHEL
1964 The Bureaucratic Phenomenon. Chicago: University of Chicago Press.
1972 "The relationship between micro and macrosociology, a study of organizational systems as an empirical approach to problems of macrosociology." Human Relations, 25:3: 239–251.
1973 The Stalled Society. New York: Viking Press.

ETZIONI, AMITAI
1961 A Comparative Analysis of Complex Organizations. New York: Free Press.

FRIEDRICHS, ROBERT W.
1970 A Sociology of Sociology. New York: Free Press.

GALBRAITH, JOHN KENNETH
1967 The New Industrial State. Boston: Houghton-Mifflin.

GAMSON, WILLIAM A.
1975 The Strategy of Social Protest. Homewood, IL: Dorsey Press.

GEORGIOU, PETRO
1973 "The goal paradigm and notes towards a counter paradigm." The Administrative Science Quarterly, 18: 291–310.

GODELIER, MAURICE
1972 "Structure and contradiction in capital." In Robin Blackburn (ed.), Ideology in Social Science: 334–368. New York: Vintage Books.

GOLDMAN, PAUL, and DONALD R. VAN HOUTEN
1977 "Managerial strategies and the worker: a Marxist analysis of bureaucracy." The Sociological Quarterly, 18: in press.

GOLDMANN, LUCIEN
1969 The Human Sciences and Philosophy. Trans. by Hayden V. White and Robert Anchor. London: Jonathan Cape.
GORDON, DAVID M.
1972 Theories of Poverty and Underemployment. Toronto and London: D.C. Heath.
GOULDNER, ALVIN W.
1970 The Coming Crisis in Western Sociology. New York: Basic Books.
HABERMAS, JÜRGEN
1970 Toward a Rational Society. Trans. by Jeremy J. Shapiro. Boston: Beacon Press.
1971 Knowledge and Human Interests. Trans. by Jeremy J. Shapiro. Boston: Beacon Press.
1973 Theory and Practice. Trans. by John Viertel. Boston: Beacon Press.
HEYDEBRAND, WOLF
1977 "Organizational contradictions in public bureaucracies: toward a Marxian theory of organizations." The Sociological Quarterly 18:1: in press.
HICKSON, D. J., C. R. HININGS, C. A. LEE, R. E. SCHNECK, and J. M. PENNINGS
1971 "A Strategic contingencies' theory of intraorganizational power." The Administrative Science Quarterly, 16: 216–229.
HININGS, C. R., D. J. HICKSON, J. M. PENNINGS, and R. E. SCHNECK
1974 "Structural conditions of intraorganizational power." The Administrative Science Quarterly, 19: 22–44.
HOWTON, F. WILLIAM
1969 Functionaries. Chicago: Quadrangle Books.
KARPIK, LUCIEN
1972 Le Capitalisme. Technologique 1: 2–34.
KRUPP, SHERMAN
1961 Pattern in Organization Analysis. New York: Holt, Rinehart and Winston.
LAWRENCE, PAUL R., and JAY W. LORSCH
1967 Organization and Environment. Boston: Graduate School of Business Administration, Harvard University.
LEFEBVRE, HENRI
1968 Dialectical Materialism. Trans. by John Sturrock. London: Jonathan Cape.
1971 Everyday Life in the Modern World. Trans. by Sacha Rabinovitch. New York: Harper and Row.
LOURENÇO, SUSAN V., and JOHN C. GILDEWELL
1975 "A dialectical analysis of organizational conflict." The Administrative Science Quarterly, 20: 489–508.
LUKÁCS, GEORG
1971 History and Class Consciousness. Studies in Marxist Dialectics. Trans. by Rodney Livingstone. Cambridge, MA: MIT Press.
MARCH, JAMES, and HERBERT SIMON
1958 Organizations. New York: Wiley.
MARKOVÍC, MIHAILO
1974 From Affluence to Praxis. Ann Arbor: University of Michigan Press.

MILLS, C. WRIGHT
1962 The Marxists. New York: Dell.
1970 "The contribution of sociology to studies of industrial relations." Berkeley Journal of Sociology, 15:11–32.
MURPHY, ROBERT F.
1971 The Dialectics of Social Life. New York: Basic Books.
PERROW, CHARLES
1967 "A framework for the comparative analysis of organizations." The American Sociological Review, 32:3: 194–208.
1972 Complex Organizations: A Critical Essay. Glenview, IL: Scott, Foresman.
PFEFFER, JEFFREY
1972 "Size and composition of corporate boards of directors: the organization and its environment." The Administrative Science Quarterly. 17: 218–228.
1973 "Size, composition, and function of hospital boards of directors: a study of organization-environment linkage." The Administrative Science Quarterly, 18: 349–364.
PFEFFER, JEFFREY, and HUSEYIN LEBLEBICI
1973 "Executive recruitment and the development of interfirm organizations." The Administrative Science Quarterly, 18: 449–461.
PFEFFER, JEFFREY, and GERALD R. SALANCIK
1974 "Organizational decision-making as a political process: the case of a university budget." The Administrative Science Quarterly, 19: 135–151.
PFEFFER, JEFFREY, GERALD R. SALANCIK, and HUSEYIN LEBLEBICI
1976 "The effect of uncertainty on the use of social influence in organizational decision-making." The Administrative Science Quarterly, 21: 227–245.
SALANCIK, GERALD R., and JEFFREY PFEFFER
1974 "The bases and use of power in organizational decision-making: the case of a university." The Administrative Science Quarterly, 19: 453–473.
SCHMIDT, STUART M., and THOMAS A. KOCHAN
1976 "An application of a 'political economy' approach to effectiveness. Employment service-employer exchanges." Administration and Society, 7: 455–474.
SCHURMAN, FRANZ
1968 Ideology and Organization in Communist China: enlarged Edition. Berkeley and Los Angeles: University of California Press.
SELZNICK, PHILLIP
1949 TVA and the Grass Roots. Berkeley, California: University of California Press.
SILVERMAN, DAVID
1971 The Theory of Organizations, a Sociological Framework. New York: Basic Books.
SIMPSON, RICHARD L.
1972 "Beyond rational bureaucracy: changing values and social integration in post-industrial society." Social Forces, 51: 1–6.

226

STRAUSS, ANSELM, LEONARD SCHATZMAN, RUE BUCHER,
DANUTA EHRLICH, and MELVIN SABSHIN
1964 Psychiatric Ideologies and Institutions. New York: Free Press.
STRAUSS, ANSELM, LEONARD SCHATZMAN, DANUTA EHRLICH,
RUE BUCHER, and MELVIN SABSHIN
1963 "The hospital and its negotiated order." In Eliot Friedson (ed.), The
Hospital in Modern Society: 147–169. London: Free Press of Glencoe.
TOURAINE, ALAIN
1971 The Post-Industrial Society. Trans. by Leonard F. X. Mayhew. New
York: Random House.
TURNER, STEPHEN P.
1977 "Blau's theory of differentiation: is it explanatory." The Sociological
Quarterly, 18: in press.
WAMSLEY, GARY, and MAYER N. ZALD
1973 The Political Economy of Public Organizations. Lexington, MA: Lex-
ington Books, D.C. Heath.
WARREN, ROLAND L., STEPHEN M. ROSE, and ANN F. BERGUNDER
1974 The Structure of Urban Reform. Community Decision Organizations in
Stability and Change. Lexington, MA: Lexington Books, D.C. Heath.
WEINSTEIN, MICHAEL, DEENA WEINSTEIN, and PETER M. BLAU
1972 "Blau's dialectical sociology and dialectical sociology: comments." Sociological Inquiry, 42: 173–189.
WHETTEN, DAVID, and HOWARD ALDRICH
1975 Predicting Organization Set Size and Diversity. Paper presented at the
Annual Meeting of the American Sociological Association, San Francisco, California.
WOODWARD, JOAN
1965 Industrial Organization: Theory and Practice. London: Oxford University Press.
1970 Industrial Organization: Behavior and Control. London: Oxford University Press.
ZALD, MAYER N.
1970a "Political economy: a framework for comparative analysis." In Mayer
N. Zald (ed.), Power in Organizations: 221–261. Nashville, Tenn.:
Vanderbilt University Press.
1970b Organizational Change: The Political Economy of the YMCA. Chicago: University of Chicago Press.
ZALD, MAYER N., and ROBERTA ASH
1966 "Social movement organizations: growth, decay, and change." Social
Forces, 44: 327–341.
ZALD, MAYER N., and JOHN D. MCCARTHY
1975 "Organizational intellectuals and the criticism of society." Social Service
Review, 49:3: 344–362.
ZWERMAN, WILLIAM L.
1970 New Perspectives on Organization Theory. Westport, Connecticut:
Greenwood Press.

Who Governs?

Jeffrey Pfeffer

There are two analytical questions that can be asked of any social group: (1) how resources, legitimacy, and effort are organized and directed to produce collective benefits or output; and (2) how the benefits, these outputs of the collective effort, are distributed. Gamson (1968) posed these two alternative questions as complementary perspectives for analyzing social power and influence. Each asks about a different aspect of organizations. One asks about how organizations are structured, managed, and controlled to produce goods or services. The second asks who gets what, when, and how (Lasswell, 1936) from the organization—who decides what to produce, and who gets the benefits of the collective effort. The issues are intertwined. The mobilization of collective effort is related to the issue of who benefits and how much from the effort.

Traditional approaches to organizational design have emphasized the creation-of-output problem. Studies focus on determining optimal organizational designs for various technological and environmental contingencies—optimal in the sense of being either: (a) more profitable, or (b) more productive. The fact that the goods or services should be produced at all—the organizational goal, if you will—is taken as given. The assumption of productivity or profit as the overriding concern implicitly takes the point of view of the ownership or managerial interests of the organization.

From this perspective, organizational design is like an engineering problem (Child, 1973). Organizational structure, the relationships among positions in the organization, is something to be adjusted, turned, or twisted until better results occur. Organizational design is a tool in the manager's tool kit, and the manager is presumed to be interested in effectiveness, profit, or outputs. A representative definition of organizational design is this: "Design is essentially the activity of constructing and changing organizational structure to achieve optimum effectiveness" (Calder, Rowland, and Leblebici, 1974, p. 1).

This view of organizational design takes the production of a collective output as the critical problem. Structures should be designed to maximize the organization's productivity. Thus, Miles has written, "The prime implication is that management must design a structure which, in contrast to the traditional hierarchy, is aimed more at facilitating positive contributions than at controlling deviant performance" (1975, p. 84). But Gamson (1968) noted that the problem of the authorities was control of behavior, and control is a central theme in much of the literature on bureaucracies and organizations. From Weber (1947) to Ouchi and Dowling (1974), the control of behavior in organizations has been viewed as an objective of organizational rules, systems of evaluation, and structure. The conflict between control of behavior and presumed individual needs has been commented on by Argyris (1957), and the techniques of control are prominent in the social, psychological, and sociological literature on organizations—socialization, social influence, conformity, social learning, and role behavior.

But the issue is not, as implied by Miles' comment quoted above, that the strategies of management are inappropriate. It is possible that control itself, not control as a means of ensuring the efficient production of output, becomes the objective of action. When there is conflict over goals and technology, the control of the organization is the problem confronted by the authorities. It is the theme of this book that the problems of organizational design are concerned with control, not merely with the best way to produce more output.

Governance and Organizational Choice

While organizational theorists may not, other persons understand quite clearly the central importance of the question of who governs. On the tenth anniversary of the Free Speech Movement,[1] an editorial under the title "Who Governs?" appeared in the Berkeley student newspaper.

---

1. The Free Speech Movement was a precursor of much of the political action on college campuses and led to a great deal of turmoil at Berkeley. It originated over the issue of placing tables of literature and leaflets on Sproul Plaza, situated between an administration building and the student union complex. Such literature, and associated speeches and rallies in the plaza, were frequently political, and as such, embarrassing to the university. With the subsequent history of demonstrations and riots on campuses over the Viet Nam war, conflict over the issue of distributing leaflets and speaking out seems almost impossible to comprehend. This illustrates the pace of social change in the past decade.

But another cause also motivated the Free Speechers—the question of who rightfully governs the University. A central issue in the Free Speech Movement was whether the aloof and historically conservative Board of Regents could unilaterally direct the affairs of the University, unmoved by the desires and opinions of those who attended, taught for, or worked for the institution (The *Daily Californian,* October 2, 1974, p. 5).

Many of the issues negotiated in labor-management disputes involve the question of who has the right to dictate the terms and conditions of employment and the conduct of workers on the job. In other words, the issues again frequently revolve around who controls, and what is the scope and operation of the control. At the opening of the 94th Congress there was a contest for the control of committee chairmanships, with the basis for allocation and the outcomes of this process being questioned by the less senior members, particularly in the House of Representatives. Consumers also have made claims for increased control over the activities of business organizations, demanding more say as to what the corporation's policies, products, and prices are. Indeed, it is difficult to think of any organization in which the issue of control is not problematic, and in which there are not contesting groups contending for control over the allocation and use of the organization's resources.

Our theme is simple. Organizations make choices, and the bases for these organizational decisions—who makes them and why—is an important analytical question to be asked about organizations. Since organizations are frequently large, and our society is, indeed, dominated by organizations (Boulding, 1953), the choices and decisions made by organizations are important. These decisions are important because of their effect on our lives as individuals working in or being served by organizations, and because of their effect on how society's resources are allocated and used.

The next logical question is, then, who benefits and who controls these organizations. It is only reasonable to assume that organizational benefits are not equally distributed. The question of control and governance becomes important in affecting what organizations do, and who benefits. Decisions must be made on the allocation of organizational resources. It is unreasonable to assume that people are disinterested observers of this process. Rather, organizational participants are in a contest for resources and their control. This contest is political and is fought in many contexts within organizations. One context is the structural arrangement of positions and persons within organizations. Design is an important factor affecting who controls organizations, who governs. Since there is a contest for control, there is a contest and conflict over organizational design. Organizational structure is, indeed, an important factor in organizational control, but control and design are the outcomes of power and influence operating within organizations.

230

A View of Organizations

It is appropriate to make explicit the conceptualization of organizations behind our discussion. There are two prominent perspectives on organizations. One sees organizations as having goals, and the problem of management is to recruit, train, control, and motivate organizational participants so as to achieve the organization's goal (or goals). This is the virtually universal perspective adopted in the management literature on organizations. The second view of organizations sees them as coalitions, composed of varying groups and individuals with different demands. Cyert and March (1963) developed this perspective in their critique of conventional economic treatments of the theory of the firm (see March, 1962). A coalition model of organizations posits that coalition participants must receive inducements from belonging greater than the contributions they are required to make. Coalition members, then, are continually calculating whether to remain in the organization, or whether they might fare better if they altered their participation. In addition to the allocation of resources, policies and policy commitments are important, and they are the objects of bargaining as well.

Since the organization is viewed as a coalition of many participants, the organization's goal becomes a concept with little meaning. As Cyert and March (1963, p. 30) pointed out, it makes as much sense to talk of the organization's goal as maximizing the janitor's salary as it does maximizing profits. Owners and janitors are both coalition participants. If either does not receive enough from coalition membership, withdrawal is likely. But speaking of the organization's goal as being the goal of the owners assumes a degree of control and acceptance of this control by other organizational participants that probably is infrequent.

The coalition view of organizations strongly implies that there will be conflict over objectives, rather than consensus over one or a few organizational goals. Since the organization is composed of persons with varying backgrounds and perspectives, occupying varying positions, it is only natural that differences in criteria for evaluating organizational actions develop. The shop floor worker, the personnel manager, the principal stockholder, and the foreman are not likely to have the same objectives or criteria for evaluating the organization's operations.

There is empirical evidence supporting the view that organizations serve many interests with conflicting criteria. Friedlander and Pickle (1968) examined the effectiveness of 96 small businesses in Texas, asking about organizational effectiveness from the perspectives of the owners, employees, creditors, suppliers, customers, and local and federal governments. The authors found that there were either small or slightly negative correlations among the assessments of how well an organization satisfied each of these seven groups. The authors concluded that organizations served many

231

interests, and moreover, could not simultaneously please all of them equally well.

There are also likely to be disagreements concerning the connections between actions and outcomes. Organizational technology is frequently as uncertain as organizational goals. A recent example illustrates what we mean. Early in 1975, there was general agreement on the goal of reducing energy use, and particularly gasoline consumption, in the United States. But differences of opinion existed concerning the connections between actions and results. Some believed that raising the price would restrict consumption, though there was uncertainty about how much reduction would be achieved for how much price increase (the elasticity of demand was unknown). Other effects were equally in dispute. Similarly, in organizations there may be agreement over the goal, perhaps to maximize profits, but there may be disagreements concerning strategies or actions to achieve these goals.

One source of disagreement is that different participants in the organization have access to different information. The information that a marketing manager has, and the data possessed by the production manager, are fundamentally different. Data differences may lead to differences in the interpretation of problems, as well as to differences in beliefs about solutions. Secondly, there are differences in training and socialization which orient managers to attend to different aspects of the situation, and to look to different strategies for solution. Dearborn and Simon (1958) illustrated this phenomenon nicely in a study conducted on businesses executives attending a training session. A business case was given to the executives, and the problem in the case was identified as a finance problem by the finance executives, a marketing problem by the marketing executives, a production problem by the production executives. Differences in background, socialization, training, and information all may cause differences in beliefs about the likely outcomes of organizational actions. Additionally, there may simply be not enough information to assess the connections between actions and results. Frequently, organizations confront novel situations and, lacking experience, are uncertain about the effectiveness of alternative decisions.

Where's Rationality?

Much of the organization and management literature is prescriptive in tone, and one of the criteria for evaluating decision-making that is frequently proposed is that of rationality. Rationality is linked to the process of choice (Friedland, 1974), and is generally construed to mean choosing that course of action which will maximize the chooser's expected utility. The concept of utility recognizes that outcomes may have different values to different persons, and the concept of expectation recognizes that decisions may be made under conditions of uncertainty. However, what this concept of rationality does not address is how to cope with conflicting standards of assessment, the fact that goals may not be shared among the organizational participants. Arrow (1951) showed that there is no general method of aggregating the ordinal preferences of individuals into a single ordered pattern of social preferences consistent with a number of assumptions used to describe rationality.

Simply put, since rationality is defined with respect to some preference for outcomes, when there is no consensus on outcome preferences it is difficult to speak of rationality. Thompson and Tuden (1959) have developed a useful typology of decision-making structures and situations. They wrote that when there is agreement on goals and on the beliefs about the connections between actions and results, a computational mode of decision-making could be employed. But when disagreements arose, some other form of decision-making, using judgment or compromise, was required. The computational mode of decision-making corresponds to the definitions of rationality, indicating that rationality is defined and achieved only in those instances where there is agreement over objectives and technology.

Thus, one problem in speaking of the rationality of organizational actions is caused by attributing a goal to an essentially diverse coalition of interests. Another difficulty with the concept of rational choice is a challenge posed to the concept of a goal at even the individual level of analysis. Weick (1969), following Schutz (1967), has argued that the meaning of action is inferred retrospectively, or after the action has occurred. In this formulation, goals and other attitude statements are attempts to make sense out of actions that have already occurred, rather than plans for the future. The similarity between this perspective and some elements of attribution theory (Kelley, 1971) should be apparent. In both cases, the argument is that meaning is inferred by the observer from the action, and since the action must have occurred in order for it to be examined, then meaning in both instances is inferred retrospectively.

The possibility that behavior is not goal-directed is one that is difficult for most people to accept. Yet all of us can think of everyday experiences in which we were able, after the fact, to explain—rationalize—our actions much better than we could before we engaged in them; similarly with planning. When I ask my students to develop a career plan, they have a great deal of difficulty, not only because of uncertainty concerning future events, but also because they cannot foresee how their preferences will change through experience. Conversely, they are very good at explaining their past behavior. Past action is real; the future is less concrete. It is not illogical, then, to expect the reality of our past behavior to have a major influence in shaping statements of our goals and opinions. We are assimilators of past experience, and meaning is at least partly inferred from retrospective examinations of our behavior.

Two Examples

Two examples illustrate how difficult it is to talk of rationality in real organizational decision-making situations. One is the construction of the Bay Area Rapid Transit System (BART). This is a well-publicized major effort to construct a new, modern, efficient transportation system for the San Francisco Bay Area. More complete histories of this system can be found in Homburger (1967) and Wolfe (1968). For the present, it is sufficient to note the following (1) the initial planning committees instrumental in planning for BART were dominated by companies that stood to benefit either directly from the work of the project or indirectly through their positions in real estate or their possible involvement as underwriters of the BART financing; (2) the appointed board of directors was generally unfamiliar with the engineering and technical aspects of the project; (3) the largest donors to the Citizens for Rapid Transit, the group that advertised in favor of the special bond election to finance BART in 1962, were the Bank of America, Wells Fargo, Crocker Bank, Tudor Engineering, Bechtel, Westinghouse Electric, Bethlehem Steel, Kaiser Industries, Perini Corporation (real estate), Westinghouse Air Brake, the Downtown Property Owner's Association, and Parsons, Brinckerhoff, Quade, and Douglas (engineering consulting) (Wolfe, 1968); (4) Parsons, in a joint venture with Tudor and Bechtel, was retained as the engineering consultant for system design and construction, with an open-ended fee arrangement which climbed from its initially expected $47 million to over $120 million; (5) BART was completed years late, at a cost of $1.6 billion rather than the originally estimated figure of about $900 million.

Our question is: Was this a rational organizational process, effective in serving its intended goals? It should be obvious that the answer to this question is very much dependent on where in the coalition one is. From the perspective of a taxpayer, burdened with both a special sales tax increment and property tax increments as well, many aspects of the system were not rational or effective. From the perspective of the contributors to Citizens for Rapid Transit, all of whom have enriched themselves enormously from the contracts involved in the construction, the project was both successful and rational. Indeed, the higher the costs and the greater the difficulties, the better for Bechtel and its joint venture associates, which could make fees designing the system, and would make additional fees fixing it when it did not work. The moral: What looks like irrational behavior, leading to inefficiency, is only irrational to those not profiting from the extra revenues generated.

Our second example involves the allocation of faculty positions to subject area groups within, say, a school of business. Further, let us assume that class enrollments are the only factor to be considered. Here, you might expect, is a computational decision situation if there ever was one. After all, a student is a student, and we can all count students and faculty. But, does an undergraduate student count the same as an M.B.A., or an M.B.A. the same as an advanced M.B.A. taking an elective, or a Ph.D. student? Is a course taught by an instructor the same as one taught by an assistant professor, or one by a full professor? And, how about students who take the courses from other departments? How should they be weighted in determining resource needs by the various subject areas? It is probably the case that in any real situation, the resource-allocation implications are altered greatly, depending upon how these weights are assigned. And while it is true that there are facts—the number of students of what types, and the composition of the faculty—it is far from a computational procedure to determine how varying students should be counted for purposes of allocating resources, although once the weightings are assigned, the actual decision-making appears to be routine. Here is an instance in which there is ostensible agreement on the criterion, allocating positions based on teaching loads, and there is plenty of objective data, and even so, the possibility remains of conflict and influence being associated with the decision.

It is difficult to think of situations in which goals are so congruent, or the facts so clear-cut that judgment and compromise are not involved. What is rational from one point of view is irrational from another. Organizations are political systems, coalitions of interests, and rationality is defined only with respect to unitary and consistent orderings of preferences.

A Model of Organizational Choice

That decisions are not made computationally or bureaucratically, that goals are hard to identify, does not mean that decisions are made in a random fashion. Rather, when consensually agreed upon, objective standards are missing from the situation, social power and influence affect the outcome of decisions. This statement is well supported by the literature from social psychology. Festinger (1954) noted that persons sought social referents for their beliefs and attitudes. Smith (1973) noted that ambiguity, because of this need for the social anchoring of beliefs, could lead to situations of informational social influence—social influence that derives from the reduction of uncertainty, not from hierarchical position or the possession of money or other inducements. In an ambiguous, uncertain situation, social influence is likely to operate to influence the decision's outcome.

Social power and influence are also more likely to operate when the resource being allocated is scarce or the decision being made is important (Salancik and Pfeffer, 1974). There is no point contending when the decision is not critical. And there is not a decision problem or a problem of allocation unless there is some element of scarcity. If every person can get all he wants, or what he wants, then there is no need to use social power and influence, because everyone can be satisfied simultaneously.

Finally, social power and influence can operate when decision processes are more hidden from public scrutiny. Most people instinctively sense this, wanting to know the criteria by which they are being evaluated, how these criteria are measured, and how they are combined. We distrust decision-making done in secret, suspecting that the process may not be equitable, particularly for those who are not participants.

Goal statements and objective criteria are used in the decision-making process as arguing points, and are used selectively depending on who benefits from their application. In interviews with 29 department heads at the University of Illinois, Salancik and Pfeffer (1974) reported that each head tended to favor basing budget allocations on criteria which tended to favor his own department. These authors concluded that power was used to affect the criteria for decisions. This is a reasonable position, since it is unlikely that in a meeting to make a decision a person will say, "Give more to my subunit because we are more powerful." Rather, social influence will be used to affect the goals or criteria so as to favor that subunit.

This view of organizational choice suggests that influence within the organization is an important factor in explaining variance in the decisions made. There is some empirical support for this position. Stagner (1969), in a survey of business executives, reported that the executives said that strong subunits within the organization were frequently able to get their way without regard for the welfare of the whole organization. And Pfeffer and Salancik (1974), examining budget allocations to departments in a university, reported that even after controlling for objective factors, social influence accounted for a significant amount of the variation in resource allocation. When computational modes of decision-making are impossible because of conflict over goals or uncertainty concerning technology, the power of participants in the coalition comes to affect the decisions made.

The coalition model of organizations seems to imply a continual contest for power and a continual process of conflict and negotiation. Such an outcome is only partially observed. Individuals enter and leave the contest as their strength and interests dictate, but some level of change and negotiation does continue as a process in the organization. Conflict is uncomfortable to most organizational participants, and moreover, to undertake long struggles over each decision would be too time-consuming. Consequently, precedent becomes very important in organizational decision-making. Once an acceptable basis for resource allocation is achieved or once a set of policies is adopted, precedent becomes the guide to future organizational decisions. This avoids reopening negotiations, which might reactivate the conflict and involve a lot of time and effort. Davis, Dempster, and Wildavsky (1966) noted that the best predictors of a U.S. government agency's current budget are its budget last year, its request for the current year, and factors that represent its growth and ability to obtain incremental budget from Congress. Incrementalism saves analytical effort and recognizes the cognitive and information-processing limitations of both persons and organizations. Incrementalism and precedent will operate as long as the existing balance of influence remains relatively stable. When, however, the distribution of influence within the organization shifts dramatically from what it had been when the initial set of bargains was reached, it is likely that those who have gained influence will attempt to reopen the negotiation, seeking to throw away precedent and to establish a new basis for future organizational actions.

Since there are fundamental disagreements over criteria, goals, and even the definition of the situation, control of the organization becomes an important issue. If there were agreement over objectives and technology, then control would be unimportant, because the decisions and policies would be identical, no matter who was in power. Because of the disagreements and uncertainty, control is critical in determining organizational actions.

Because of disagreements over goals, and because of the differences in backgrounds and information possessed by organizational participants, organizational decisions are affected by the location in the organization where they are made and where the problem is located. Cyert and March (1963) made this argument when they noted that the search for solutions tends to begin in a localized fashion, starting first by focusing on that part of the organization in which the problem was first noticed. So, if a company is losing its share of the market, if the problem is identified first by and in the marketing department, it will probably initially be viewed as a marketing problem. The advertising budget and strategy will be examined, and the organization and effectiveness of the sales force will be analyzed. Only later will the search be extended to examine other sources of the problem, such as delays in delivery caused by production, or by the inability to give competitive credit terms as a result of policies set in the finance department. The fact of localized search makes the organization's information-gathering and transmission structure very important in determining organizational actions. If problem definition determines the likely initial course of behavior, then where and by whom the problem is located accounts for much of the variance in possible responses.

Determinants of Social Power

We have argued that because of the coalitional nature of organizations, few decisions are made computationally, and most decisions are affected by subunit and individual power within the organization. The answer to the question of who controls or governs the organization is that person or group with the most power. It is relevant to our consideration of organizational design as an outcome and as a factor in the contest for control that dimensions of organizational structure have a great deal to do with the distribution and possession of power in organizations.

Formal Authority

There are few people who are not familiar with an organization chart, that formal representation of positions and their relationship to one another within the organization. Although we also know about informal organizations, and the fact that the chart does not tell everything about the organization's functioning, the formal structure of an organization does provide one determinant of power and control. Coupled with job descriptions delimiting responsibilities, the formal structure specifies who reports to whom and who has the authority to evaluate another person. The evaluation process is central in the process of cotrolling behavior within organizations (Scott, et al., 1967). These authority rights are conveyed through the formal hierarchy—it is typically, though not inevitably, the case that a person in a given level has the right to evaluate those persons who are immediately below him and linked to him in the hierarchy (see Simmons, 1978).

When a person goes to work, he implicitly enters into an agreement that involves receiving pay and other benefits in return for giving some control over his behavior to the organization, and more specifically, his designated supervisor. We make these bargains so often, trading money for our freedom of action on the job, that we seldom think about them. Nevertheless, the first and frequently the most important determinant of governance is the formal hierarchy of evaluation and authority existing in the organization.

Control Over Resources

Yet another basis for power in an organization is the possession of control over critical resources. Salancik and Pfeffer (1974) found that the best predictor of department power in a university was the amount of outside money the department brought in. Pfeffer and Leong (1977) examined the allocations of United Funds to member agencies in a number of cities, and found again that the ability to raise outside support was a principal determinant of power within the coalition. Organizations require resources for survival. Control over resources critical to the organization provides a person or subunit with power in the organization.

Control over resources is affected by the division of labor in the organization and one's position in the resultant social structure. For example, consider possible alternative methods of allocating university-funded scholarships. Under one system, suppose we create an Office of Scholarships and Financial Aid, and place in charge of that office a director with the responsibility of allocating scholarships to the individual departments. Alternatively, suppose we have a similarly titled office, but in this instance, the director is merely responsible for raising funds; allocations to the departments are based solely on the number of students enrolled. It is clear that, other things being equal, in the former case the occupant of the position of Director of Scholarships and Financial Aid will have more power in the organization. Similar examples readily come to mind for other organizational settings—job descriptions and the allocations of task leave the control of resources differentially distributed in the organization. Power and control accrue to those positions with the most discretionary control over critical and scarce resources.

Information and Access

One special resource is information, and access to and control of channels of communication. This resource is different enough from financial resources, however, to bear special discussion. One's position in the organizational structure profoundly affects the amount of information one possesses, and one's centrality in the communication network. Both of these factors, information and communication centrality, profoundly affect the ability of the position's occupant to wield power in the organization.

Once again, we shall provide some examples. Power can accrue to a person because of his position in the flow of communication, and therefore because of his ability to filter, summarize, and analyze information as it is passed. In one university, the head of a department resigned, and a search was instituted for a replacement. The department was a subunit in a college, and the college had an executive committee that advised the Dean. The appointment was the responsibility of the Dean. As is occasionally done, the Dean appointed a search committee to locate qualified candidates. The search committee was to report its recommendations to the executive committee, and through it, to the Dean. It so happened than one inside candidate for the job was appointed to the search committee, and was also on the college executive committee. Initially, this candidate had little support in either the search committee or the executive committee; however, as the months wore on, he emerged as the leading contender. This was accomplished by systematically providing information between the two committees that led to the elimination of our candidate's principal competitors from consideration. Since he was the only person serving on both committees, he reported between the two, and in the process served his own interests.

The importance of access gives power to many staff positions (Tuggle, 1978). The ability to buffer, filter, and selectively provide information enables one to control the information and even the premises on which decisions will be made. Access to and control of information comes from one's position in the social structure.

And then we have the case of using information to centralize control. Currently, many universities face financial difficulty. In times of resource scarcity, the argument goes, decisions concerning the use of resources must be made as carefully and as effectively as possible. In order to accomplish this, elaborate evaluation and information-gathering systems have been established on many university campuses, involving the expansion in both numbers and functions of the data-processing units. In the University of California system and on the campus level, such positions report directly to administrative officers of the highest level. The implications of all of this for control are evident by attending any meeting. While the faculty have opinions, values, beliefs, and eloquence, the vice chancellor (or the chancellor, or the president) has the computer output. "The facts" usually win, as many students have learned when they use elaborate presentations in case preparations to "snow" the instructor or the class. By controlling information, one controls the premises of the discussion and the outcome.

It is, therefore, not surprising that some of the most bitter fights have occurred in organizations over the placement or movement of the computer or information-processing department. Managers instinctively know that control of the information system is tantamount to control over the organization, and the contest for this function is intense.

Uncertainty Reduction

The most prominent current explanation for power in organizations is the ability to cope with critical organizational uncertainty. Crozier (1964) illustrated this with his example of the maintenance engineers in a French plant. Because the breakdown of machinery was the only remaining contingency faced by the organization, the maintenance engineers came to have extraordinary influence, particularly because they had the foresight to keep their expertise in their heads rather than on paper where others could acquire it. Thompson (1967) based his discussion of power also on the ability to deal with uncertainty, and the capability of coping with uncertainty is the central variable in Hickson et al.'s (1971) strategic contingencies' theory of intraorganizational power. Hickson and his colleagues also argued that power was increased to the extent that uncertainty was pervasive or important in the organization, and to the extent that the coping capability could not be easily replaced.

We noted earlier in this chapter that theories of informal social communication also emphasize the importance of coping with uncertainty. Smith (1973) explained that in conditions of uncertainty, informational social influence is possible as people seek to resolve the uncertainty, and Festinger (1954) demonstrated that uncertainty leads to increased social communication. Uncertainty, then, provides the subunit or group that can reduce it with the opportunity to obtain increased control in the organization.

The ability to reduce organizational uncertainty again depends on the position in the social structure. Clearly, the capability of reducing uncertainty is related to one's access to information, the position in the communication structure, and also the possession of resources valued by the organization. More specifically, roles and tasks can be restructured to give certain positions either more or less influence in the organization. As Thompson (1967, p. 129) has written, decentralization creates more power positions, but lessens the organization's dependence on any single one. Subdividing a task into very simple components makes it easier to substitute employees, lessening the power of any single employee. The routinization of functions such as production scheduling, financial analysis or other managerial tasks diminishes the influence of those employees whose tasks have been made less uncertain.

I once was interviewed for a summer job at a large food-manufacturing facility. On this occasion, I spoke with the executive in charge of one product division. It so happened that in this division, production scheduling was done by a man in his 60s not using the most sophisticated methods of operations research, occasionally with disastrous results. Nevertheless, the attempt to hire bright, young M.B.A.'s to update the forecasting technology was singularly unsuccessful. This man, scheduling by intuition, practice, and experience, resisted any attempts either to routinize or otherwise to change his function that might reduce his influence in the organization. More than occasionally, resistance to organizational change originates from those whose jobs are being redefined in such a way as to diminish the uncertainty and discretion associated with them, and consequently, the influence of the job holders.

Assessing Power in Social Structures

If power is important in determining organizational choice, including the choice of structures, then it is critical for organizational participants to be able to diagnose systems of organizational influence. To contend in a political process, one must at least be able to diagnose the distribution of power and the preferences and demands of the other participants. There are several approaches to assessing the power of various organizational actors.

One approach involves determining the sources of power in the system, and then assessing how much of each source each organizational actor (individual, actor, or subunit) possesses. This procedure is equivalent to Gamson's (1968) suggestion that since power derives from resources, one can assess power by assessing the resources controlled by various social actors. In the study of determinants of power in a university, Salancik and Pfeffer (1974) assessed how important various resources brought into the organization by subunits were to the total organization. One could then argue that those subunits that controlled or accounted for more critical resources would have the most power. If uncertainty reduction is important, then power should accrue to those subunits that can reduce the most critical uncertainty, and for which few substitutes are available. The first way of assessing power, then, is simply to determine what are sources of power, and see how much of these sources various participants possess.

Power is used in affective organizational decisions and thus becomes visible. In addition to examining the sources of power, systems of influence can be diagnosed by examining the outcroppings of the effects of power in organizations. For instance, power may be used to affect the choice of organizational leaders, the distribution of scarce and critical resources, and the implementation of favored rules, policies, and procedures. Pfeffer and Salancik (1974) argued that representation on important committees might be both a source of power and a reflection of the existing structure of influence in universities. Their committee-based measures of power accounted for more of the variance in budget allocations than did interview-derived measures, though both measures were highly correlated. The affiliation of the chief executive officer and other officials in major executive positions and on important committees frequently provides information about the distribution of power. This is true in both corporations, universities, and other organizations. If the chief executive in a corporation always comes from marketing, or if the dean of a business school is always an economist, in both instances there is a clue about power in the organization.

There are typically many possible outcroppings of the use of power, and the shrewd analyst will look for convergence in the measures, since any single indicator may be affected by random error or chance. In an assignment to diagnose the distribution of influence among subject areas in a school of business, an M.B.A. class came up with a large number of possible indicators, including the academic affiliations of chief administrative officers, the number of required courses in the various subjects, the relative teaching loads and student/faculty ratios, the representation on important committees, the success in obtaining promotions, and increments in total faculty positions. Important committees tend to be those associated with the allocation of resources, while unimportant committees can be discovered by determining which are easy to get on and which serve only ceremonial functions or have relatively less powerful functions, such as dealing with low-power clients.

The importance of using multiple measures cannot be overemphasized. One should look for convergence in indicators of subunit or personal power in making diagnoses of structures of organizational influence. It also helps to assess power as unobtrusively as possible. Since power is not a legitimate basis for organizational action, persons will likely be reluctant to provide honest and accurate assessments of power positions (see Pettigrew, 1973). Furthermore, asking about power may be perceived as threatening, illegitimate, or excessively naive. Reports from colleagues or outside observers about distributions of power should always be checked against the realities of the determinants and outcomes of power. It is, after all, in the interests of power holders to hinder the accurate diagnosis of actual systems of influence. Power is best exercised unobtrusively, and must, consequently, be diagnosed in a similar fashion.

What Is Organizational Design?

We have talked about one view of organizations, and how this way of thinking makes the issue of organizational control and governance very important for understanding the decisions and actions taken by organizations. We have briefly explored some determinants of power and influence in organizations, and have sketched how organizational structure may be related to these factors. It is now time to describe explicitly what is meant by organizational design and organizational structure.

Structure has been defined as the patterning of relationships or activities in organizations (Thompson, 1967, p. 51). As Weick (1969) has noted, structure is a picture, at a given time, of a continuing process of organizing. This theme has been developed by Mackenzie (1978) who describes the relationship between process and structure. We can look at activities such as the use or nonuse of various half-channels in a communication network to cope with a particular task, and represent these relationships in a structure. It is important to remember that structure is nothing more than the relationships among positions or roles in an organization, and since relationships change, structures change also.

Thompson (1967, ch. 5) argued that organizational structures developed in the following way. Activities within organizations are differentiated—different people do different parts of the task. Because the total

243

task is subdivided, the differentiated roles in the organization are inter-dependent. Interdependence requires coordination. In the case of designing an automobile, the size of the engine and the size of the hood are interdependent. In the case of the Chevrolet Monza 2+2, when Chevrolet decided not to introduce the rotary engine, but substitute a V-8 instead, someone forgot to take this into account in designing the engine compartment. Thus, Chevrolet produced a car in which, to change one of the eight spark plugs, it was necessary to unmount and partially lift the engine. Organizational structures are presumably developed to coordinate the interdependence among activities in organizations, and Thompson further hypothesized that structures would develop so as to minimize the costs of coordination and communication.

In this conception, organization design is the process of grouping activities, roles, or positions in the organization to coordinate effectively the interdependencies that exist. In the literature on organizational design (e.g., Galbraith, 1973), the implicit goal of the structuring process is achieving a more rationalized and coordinated system of activity.

As we have stated throughout, . . . it is not only tasks that are allocated and distributed throughout organizations. Control over resources, legitimate authority, and control of decision-making are also distributed. In addition to talking of the relationship between interdependent tasks, we can talk of the relationship between resource holders, between persons with varying authority rights, and between positions with varying degrees of decision-making authority.

Structure is a continuing process of activity, but change is not as frequent as one might expect. Weick (1969) cautioned that we should focus on the incredible regularities in behavior in organizations, and not just on episodic instances of change. Patterns of behavior are maintained by rules and procedures that may be formally written down, or by informally but strongly held norms about behavior. Mackenzie (1978) has referred to these as behavioral constitutions. Rules develop about changes in structure, and about the allocation of tasks and activities among group participants. These rules and norms are reinforced by systems of evaluation, frequently administered through the formal hierarchy of authority. Everyone in an organization is constantly evaluated, not only by his organizational supervisor, but also by his peers and his subordinates. Kahn et al. (1964) describe the set of persons a given occupant of a position interacts with as that person's role set. Everyone in the role set has expectations for the focal person's behavior, and evaluates on a more or less frequent basis the extent to which his expectations are being met. Evaluation, and the subsequent administration of rewards and punishments, help to maintain the stability of relationships and activities in the organization.

Structure involves relationships, including authorizations to evaluate, the differential distribution of the right to reward and punish, the unequal allocation of information, resources, and the capability of coping with uncertainty, and as a consequence, differences in power, influence, and control within organizations. Assuming conflicts over preferences and goals, as well as over beliefs about the consequences of actions, structures become one focus for the contest over control, and at a given time, provide differential governance to various organizational participants. There are, it appears, two perspectives for analyzing social structures. One asks the appropriateness of a given structure for the coordination of interdependence to achieve some task; the other asks why and how structure is a result of organizational influence processes and the consequences of a given structure for the distribution of control and power within organizations. It is likely that these are complementary rather than competing perspectives.

References

ANONYMOUS. "Who Governs?" *Daily Californian* (Berkeley: University of California), 2 October 1974, p. 5.

ARGYRIS, CHRIS. *Personality and Organization.* New York: Harper, 1957.

ARROW, KENNETH. *Social Choice and Individual Values.* New York: John Wiley, 1951.

BOULDING, KENNETH, E. *The Organizational Revolution.* New York: Harper, 1953.

CALDER, BOBBY J.; ROWLAND, KENDRITH M; and LEBLEBICI, HUSEYIN. "The Use of Scaling and Cluster Techniques in Investigating the Social Structure of Organization." Faculty Working Paper #212. Urbana, Ill.: College of Commerce and Business Administration, University of Illinois, 1974.

CHILD, JOHN. "Organization: A Choice for Man." In *Man and Organization,* edited by John Child, pp. 234–570. London: Halsted Press, 1973.

CROZIER, MICHEL. *The Bureaucratic Phenomenon.* Chicago: University of Chicago Press, 1964.

CYERT, RICHARD M., and MARCH, JAMES G. *A Behavioral Theory of the Firm.* Englewood Cliffs, N.J.: Prentice-Hall, 1963.

DAVIS, OTTO A.; DEMPSTER, M. A. H.; and WILDAVSKY, AARON. "A Theory of the Budgetary Process." *American Political Science Review 60* (1966): 529–47.

DEARBORN, D. C., and SIMON, H. A. "Selective Perception: A Note on the Departmental Identification of Executives." *Sociometry 21* (1958): 140–44.

FESTINGER, LEON. "A Theory of Social Comparison Processes." *Human Relations 7* (1954): 117–40.

FRIEDLAND, EDWARD I. *Introduction to the Concept of Rationality in Political Science.* Morristown, N.J.: General Learning Press, 1974.

FRIEDLANDER, F., and PICKLE, H. "Components of Effectiveness in Small Organizations." *Administrative Science Quarterly 13* (1968): 289–304.

245

GALBRAITH, JAY. *Designing Complex Organizations.* Reading, Mass.: Addison-Wesley, 1973.

GAMSON, WILLIAM A. *Power and Discontent.* Homewood, Ill.: Dorsey Press, 1968.

HICKSON, D. J.; HININGS, C. R.; LEE, C. A.; SCHNECK, R. E.; and PENNINGS, J. M. "A Strategic Contingencies Theory of Intraorganizational Power." *Adminstrative Science Quarterly 16* (1971): 216–29.

HOMBURGER, WOLFGANG S. "Case Study: San Francisco Bay Area Rapid Transit Planning and Development." In *Urban Mass Transit Planning,* edited by W. S. Homburger. Berkeley: Institute of Transportation and Traffic Engineering, University of California, 1967.

KAHN, ROBERT L.; WOLFE, DONALD M.; QUINN, ROBERT P.; and SNOEK, DIEDRICH J. *Organizational Stress: Studies in Role Conflict and Ambiguity.* New York: John Wiley, 1964.

KELLEY, HAROLD H. *Attribution in Social Interaction.* Morristown, N.J.: General Learning Press, 1971.

LASSWELL, HAROLD D. *Politics: Who Gets What, When, How.* New York: McGraw-Hill, 1936.

MACKENZIE, KENNETH D. *Organizational Structures.* Arlington Heights, Ill.: AHM Publishing Corporation, 1978.

MARCH, JAMES G. "The Business Firm as a Political Coalition." *Journal of Politics 24* (1962): 662–78.

MILES, RAYMOND E. *Theories of Management: Implications for Organizational Behavior and Development.* New York: McGraw-Hill, 1975.

OUCHI, WILLIAM G., and DOWLING, JOHN B. "Defining the Span of Control." *Administrative Science Quarterly 19* (1974): 357–65.

PETTIGREW, ANDREW M. *The Politics of Organizational Decision-Making.* London: Tavistock, 1973.

PFEFFER, JEFFREY, and LEONG, ANTHONY. "Resource Allocation in United Funds: Examination of Power and Dependence." *Social Forces 55* (1977): 775–790.

PFEFFER, JEFFREY, and SALANCIK, GERALD R. "Organizational Decision Making as a Political Process: The Case of a University Budget." *Administrative Science Quarterly 19* (1974): 135–51.

SALANCIK, GERALD R., and PFEFFER, JEFFREY. "The Bases and Use of Power in Organizational Decision Making: The Case of a University." *Administrative Science Quarterly 19* (1974): 453–73.

SCHUTZ, A. *The Phenomenology of the Social World.* Evanston, Ill.: Northwestern University Press, 1967.

SCOTT, W. R.; DORNBUSCH, S. M.; BUSCHING, B. C.; and LAING, J. D. "Organizational Evaluation and Authority." *Administrative Science Quarterly 12* (1967): 93–117.

SIMMONS, RICHARD E. *Managing Behavioral Processes: Applications of Theory and Research.* Arlington Heights, Ill.: AHM Publishing Corporation, 1978.

SMITH, PETER B. *Groups Within Organizations.* London: Harper and Row, 1973.

STAGNER, R. "Corporate Decision Making: An Empirical Study." *Journal of Applied Psychology 53* (1969): 1–13.

THOMPSON, JAMES D. *Organizations in Action.* New York: McGraw-Hill, 1967.

THOMPSON, J. D., and TUDEN, A. "Strategies, Structures, and Processes of Organizational Decision." In *Comparative Studies in Administration,* edited by J. D. Thompson, P. B. Hammond, R. W. Hawkes, B. H. Junker, and A. Tuden, pp. 195–216. Pittsburgh: University of Pittsburgh Press, 1959.

TUGGLE, FRANCIS D. *Organizational Processes.* Arlington Heights, Ill.: AHM Publishing Corporation, 1978.

WEBER, M. *Theory of Social and Economic Organization.* New York: Oxford, 1947.

WEICK, KARL E. *The Social Psychology of Organizing.* Reading, Mass.: Addison-Wesley, 1969.

WOLFE, BURTON H. "Bart Probe." *The Bay Guardian,* June 18, August 30, November 1, and December 24, 1968.

Organizational Choice under Ambiguity

James G. March
Johan P. Olsen

1.0 Introduction

Organizational choice often involves a curious paradox. The process is both surprising and not surprising. It is familiar to ordinary experiences; it is puzzling for many interpretations of that experience. Very few reports of organizational decision making strike experienced participants in organizations as unusual. At the same time, many common observations about organizations are pathological from the point of view of theories of organizations. What is mundane to experience frequently becomes unexplained variance in the theories. What is standard in the interpretation of organizations frequently becomes irrelevant to experience.

The observations reported in this book are not surprising. Organizations are often observed to do nothing to implement a decision after having devoted much time, energy, and enthusiasm to making it; or to make apparently major decisions with only minor participation by key administrators and significant constituents; or to combine a struggle over participation rights with an indifference to exercising them; or to make argument over ideology without affective action; or to separate the outcome of a major political dispute from the details of the political process involved. Though the examples are new, the stories are old.

Despite their familiarity, the observations are theoretically curious. They appear to be partly inconsistent with several fundamental ideas implicit in ordinary conversations about organizations and decisions in them, as well as several conventional, and highly useful, theoretical treatments of organizations: rational models of individual choice, microeconomic theory, social welfare theory, interest group theories of politics and bureaucracy, theories of power, democratic theories of politics,

Source: *Ambiguity and Choice in Organizations,* pp. 10–23. Copyright © 1976 by Universitetsforlaget, Oslo, Norway. Reprinted by permission of the authors and the publisher.

theories of negotiation and bargaining, theories of planning, management theory.

We wish to examine some aspects of those theoretical ideas and suggest modifications in them. The suggestions are relatively fundamental, but they are not comprehensive. Without attempting a complete reconstruction of ideas about decisions in organizations, we will try to outline some possible perspectives that may make ordinary experience in organizations somewhat more explicable.

Our emphasis is on decisions, but we are impressed by the ways in which the imagery of "decision making" confounds an understanding of organizational phenomena. We will examine below some problems with the standard conception of the choice cycle in organizations and some of the ways in which the organizational settings with which we will be concerned involve substantial elements of ambiguity that is not accommodated well within that conception; but we preface the discussion with the observation that the ideas of "decision" (as an outcome) and "decision making" (as a process) are already confused by a semantic presumption that the latter is connected to the former in some self-evident fashion.

Choice situations include law-making, price-setting, planning, and a host of other similar things. They are overtly concerned with the allocation of resources and burdens, selection of personnel, designing of new organizational arrangements, policy-programs and the like. Parliaments, courts, universities, firms, political parties, bureaucracies, and hospitals are involved in decision situations frequently. There are social expectations that the main thing taking place in such situations is "decision making."

Explicit decision activities in such situations may have much to do with the outcomes that occur. A choice situation may provide an occasion for problem-solving and conflict resolution, the aggregation of individual and group preferences and power into collective choices. But often the process of decision does not appear to be much concerned with making a decision. Indeed, the activities within a choice situation may be explicable only if we recognize the other major things that take place within the same arena at the same time.

A choice process provides an occasion for a number of other things, most notably:

- an occasion for executing standard operating procedures, and fulfilling role-expectations, duties, or earlier commitments.
- an occasion for defining virtue and truth, during which the organization discovers or interprets what has happened to it, what it has been doing, what it is doing, what it is going to do, and what justifies its actions.
- an occasion for distributing glory or blame for what has happened

249

in the organization; and thus an occasion for exercising, challenging or reaffirming friendship or trust relationships, antagonisms, power or status relationships.

• an occasion for expressing and discovering "self-interest" and "group interest," for socialization, and for recruiting (to organizational positions, or to informal groups).

• an occasion for having a good time, for enjoying the pleasures connected to taking part in a choice situation.

The several activities are neither mutually exclusive nor mutually inconsistent. They are aspects of most choice situations and illustrate their complexity. Decisions are a stage for many dramas.

The dramatic complexity is further elaborated by the pervasiveness of ambiguity. By the term *ambiguity* we intend to signify four major kinds of opaqueness in organizations. The first is the ambiguity of *intention*. Many organizations are characterized by inconsistent and ill-defined objectives. It is often impossible to specify a meaningful preference function for an organization that satisfies both the consistency requirements of theories of choice and the empirical requirements of describing organizational motive. The second lack of clarity is the ambiguity of *understanding*. For many organizations the causal world in which they live is obscure. Technologies are unclear; environments are difficult to interpret. It is hard to see the connections between organizational actions and their consequences. The third lack of clarity is the ambiguity of *history*. The past is important, but it is not easily specified or interpreted. History can be reconstructed or twisted. What happened, why it happened, and whether it had to happen are all problematic. The fourth lack of clarity is the ambiguity of *organization*. At any point in time, individuals vary in the attention they provide to different decisions; they vary from one time to another. As a result, the pattern of participation is uncertain and changing.

All organizations confront elements of ambiguity in decision making. For some organizations ambiguity is a dominant condition. In particular, ambiguity is a major feature of decision making in most public and educational organizations; it seems to characterize a wide variety of organizations when they are young or when their environments are changing.

1.1 Limitations in the Complete Cycle of Choice

In order to accommodate these concerns, it is necessary to reexamine some fundamental ideas about organizational choice. They are simple ideas, general in their appeal; but relative to the interplay of events within a decision situation, they are too simple and too seductive.

Consider what might be called the complete cycle of organizational choice. It is a familiar conception, and a useful one.[1]

> At a certain point in time some participants see a discrepancy between what they think the world ought to be (given present possibilities and constraints) and what the world actually is. This discrepancy produces individual behavior, which is aggregated into collective (organizational) action or choices. The outside world then "responds" to this choice in some way that affects individual assessments both of the state of the world and of the efficacy of the actions.

This conception of choice assumes a closed cycle of connections (Figure 1.0):

1. The cognitions and preferences held by individuals affect their behavior.
2. The behavior (including participation) of individuals affects organizational choices.
3. Organizational choices affect environmental acts (responses).
4. Environmental acts affect individual cognitions and preferences.

These basic ideas are fundamental to much of our understanding of decisions in organizations. Although frequently subject to criticism, the ideas are implicit in most ordinary conversations about organizations and about important events of policy making. They are the basis for many theoretical treatments, including our own. While we think this conception of choice illuminates choice situations significantly, we want to modify the details of that perspective and explore some specific limitations in a theory based on the closed sequence shown in Figure 1.0.

The limitations we will consider are of considerable significance under some situations, of little significance under others. The complete cycle of organizational choice assumes four simple relations. Each of those

FIGURE 1.0. The complete cycle of choice.

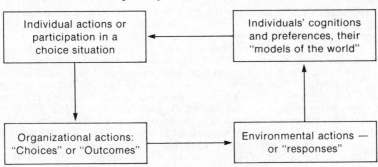

1. This section draws heavily on March and Olsen (1975).

relations is obviously more complex than the closed cycle represents them to be. More importantly, they are more complex in ways that lead to systematic limitations in the theory. The limitations are particularly important when the cycle is incomplete, when one or more of the connections are broken or confounded by exogenous factors. Under such circumstances, we require a theory of organizational choice that recognizes the loose coupling. We consider each of the four relations, in turn.

1.1.0 Individual Beliefs and Individual Action

Most organization theory is purposive. It assumes that behavior and attention[2] follow belief and attitude. Beliefs and attitudes, in turn, are stable enough so that attention is stable over the course of a choice; and differential levels of attention are predictable from the content of the decision. Decision making activity thus stems from self-interest and is generally attractive so long as the resources being allocated are significant.

Our observations suggest a modification of this view.[3] Instead of stable activity levels we find that people move in and out of choice situations. There is considerable variation among individuals, and over time for the same individual, in terms of the degree and form of attention to decision problems. A step toward understanding this flow of attention, and its connection to individual beliefs and attitudes, is to note that time and energy are scarce resources.

Involvement in decisions is not attractive for everyone in all relevant choice situations, all the time. The capacity for beliefs, attitudes, and concerns is larger than the capacity for action. Under such circumstances, we will observe beliefs and values without behavioral implications. Even given the time and energy, there are alternative choice situations where

2. The concept of participation is broad. We will use it with reference to activities like seeking information, discussing, proselyting, attending meetings, voting, making speeches, campaigning and competing for offices, with no references to the motivation for or the effect of the activities. The central criterion thus becomes presence or attendance.

3. Modifications have been suggested by a rather broad range of people. Weick (1969, p. 29) notes that the assumption in organization theory "that once the perceptions of organization members are affected, action consistent with these perceptions will follow automatically" has not been affected by recent work by psychologists interested in how beliefs and values get translated into action. Both Weick (ibid.) and Bem (1970) argue for theories assuming that cognition follows action. The primacy of behavior or praxis over ideas or theory is a classical theme in Marxist theory. Often the point of departure is the statement that life is not determined by consciousness, but consciousness by life (Marx and Engels, 1970). However, the debate between marxists and non-marxists has to some degree detracted attention from the debate among marxists on the role of ideas as a driving force in history. Ibsen reflected some of the complexity when he had Peer Gynt say (on observing a man chopping off a finger to avoid being drafted): "The thought, perhaps—the wish—the will. Those I could understand, but really to do the deed! Ah, no—that astounds me."

an individual can present his concerns. The flow of attention will not depend on the content of a single choice alone, but upon the collection of choice situations available. We should not expect that a set of beliefs and preferences will have behavioral implications in any specific choice situation independent of the available claims on attention.

A theory that recognizes time as a scarce resource (Becker, 1965; Linder, 1970) makes attention contextual, subject to resource constraints and alternative "consumption" possibilities. Such a conception assumes some hierarchy of beliefs and preferences, and some hierarchy of choice situations in terms of attractiveness. Individuals are seen to allocate available energy by attending to choice situations with the highest expected return. They do not act in one arena because they are acting in another.

Although it clarifies some aspects of decision involvement, even this contextual version of the connection between values and action is problematic in an organization. It ignores the importance of roles, duties, and standard operating procedures for determining behavior; and it underestimates the ambiguity of self-interest.

Any complex social structure has considerable capability for weakening the connection between individual behavior and individual beliefs and preferences. The potential has produced some affective ambivalence. It has been celebrated as an important device in fighting personal favoritism and establishing equity and equality. It has been portrayed as a major source of organizational inertia preventing progress. Here we are not primarily concerned with a normative evaluation, but with the simple fact that roles, duties, and obligations are behaviorally important to involvement. People attend to decisions not only because they have an interest at stake, but because they are expected to or obliged to. They act according to rules.

Even when they act in self-interest terms, participants in organizations do not appear to act in a way fully anticipated by self-interest theories. They have an abundance of preferences and beliefs. The complexity increases as one moves from interest in immediate, substantive outcomes to long-term effects and to various side agendas (e.g., status) involved in a decision situation. The architecture of these values does not easily lend itself to description in terms of well-behaved preference functions. The behavior apparently stemming from the values proceeds without concern about that fact. Not all values are attended to at the same time; attention focus rather than utility, seems to explain much of the behavior (Cyert and March, 1963). At the same time, beliefs and preferences appear to be the results of behavior as much as they are the determinants of it. Motives and intentions are discovered post factum (March, 1972).

We require a theory that takes into consideration the possibility that there may be attitudes and beliefs without behavioral implications, that there may be behavior without any basis in individual preferences, and that there may be an interplay between behavior and the definition (and redefinition) of "self-interest."

1.1.1 Individual Action and Organizational Choice

Organizational choices are ordinarily viewed as derivative of individual actions. A decision process transforms the behavior of individuals into something that could be called organizational action. Explorations into the nature of this "visible hand" comprise much of the literature; and most of the theoretical issues are questions of suitable metaphors for characterizing the process. It is sometimes captured by metaphors of deduction (organizational goals, sub-goals, efficiency); sometimes by metaphors of implicit conflict (markets, bureaucracy); sometimes by metaphors of explicit conflict (bargaining, political processes, power). Each of these metaphors accepts the basic notion that organizational choice is understandable as some consequence of individual action. They interpret organizations as instruments of individuals.

Our observations suggest that the connection between individual action and organizational action is sometimes quite loose. Sometimes we observe that the (internal) decision-making process is not strongly related to the organizational action, i.e., the policy selected, the price set, the man hired. Rather it is connected to the definition of truth and virtue in the organization, to the allocation of status, to the maintenance or change of friendship, goodwill, loyalty, and legitimacy; to the definition and redefinition of "group interest." In short, the formal decision-making process sometimes is directly connected to the maintenance or change of the organization as a social unit as well as to the accomplishment of making collective decisions and producing substantive results. A theory of organizational choice probably should attend to the interplay between these two aspects of the internal process.

Sometimes we observe a considerable impact on the process of the temporal flow of autonomous actions. We need a theory that considers the timing of different individual actions, and the changing context of each act. Most theories imply the importance of the context of an act. Typically, however, they have assumed that this context has stable properties that allow unconditional predictions. We observe a much more interactive, branching, and contextual set of connections among the participants, problems, and solutions in an organization.

Sometimes we observe an internal process swamped by external events of factors. Organizational action is conspicuously independent of internal process. The dramatic version—where some external actor intervenes directly, or where some external event completely changes the conditions under which the organization is operating, is well known. In a similar way, macro-theorists of social process rarely feel required to consider the details of organizational phenomena. Theories of the market or long-run social movements have identified important characteristics of the deep structure in which organizational phenomena occur; and it would be foolish for a theory of organizational choice situations not to recognize the extent to which the decision process is part of a broader stream of events. We need a theory of choice that articulates the connections between the environmental context of organizations and their actions in such a way that neither is simply the residual unexplained variance for the other.

In general, we need a theory of organizational choice that considers the connection between individual actions and organizational actions sometimes as variable. Organizational action may be determined, or strongly contained, by external forces. Internal process may be related to other phenomena than the organizational choice (i.e., allocating status, defining organizational truth and virtue). The structure of the internal process may be highly time-dependent; changing contexts of the individual acts may produce organizational actions not anticipated or desired by anyone.

1.1.2 Organizational Choice and Environmental Response

The complete cycle of choice assumes a connection between organizational actions and environmental actions. The latter are treated as responses to the choices made in the organization.[4] The notion is a simple one. We assume that there is an environment with a schedule of responses to alternative actions on the part of the organization. Voters respond to party platforms or candidate images. Consumers respond to produce quality and price. Competitors respond to challenges. Students respond to curricula. Citizens respond to social experiments. Out of such a paradigm come many of our ideas about organizational learning and natural selection (Cohen and March, 1973; Winter, 1964).

We need a theory of the environment which is less organization centered, a theory where the actions and events in the environment sometimes may have little to do with what the organization does. Environmental acts frequently have to be understood in terms of relationships among events, actors, and structures in the environment, not as responses to what the organization does. As a result, the same organizational action will have different responses at different times; different organizational actions will have the same response. The world of the absurd is some-

4. There are two versions of the theory: The strong organization making the environment adapt to its decisions, and the weak organization being "conditioned" by the environment.

times more relevant for our understanding of organizational phenomena than is the idea of a tight connection between action and response.

This independence of action and response is accentuated by our tendency to attempt to explain fine gradations in both. Organizations act within environmentally constrained boundaries. On the rare occasions on which they violate those constraints, the environment is likely to react unambiguously. Most of the time, however, the range of behavior is relatively small; and within that range very little of the variation in response is attributable to variations in the action. Insofar as we wish to explain variations in organizational behavior wihtin the range in which we observe it, we will require a theory that recognizes only a modest connection between environmental response and organizational decision.[5]

1.1.3 Environmental Response and Individual Beliefs

Classical theory offers two alternative versions of how environmental actions and events are connected to individual cognition. In the first version, the problem is assumed away. Organizational decision-makers are equipped with perfect information about alternatives and consequences. Since the full cycle is well understood ahead of any individual action there is no learning in the system. In the second version, the connection is understood in terms of a model of individual, rational adaption. Beliefs and models of the world are tied to reality through experience. Events are observed; the individual changes his beliefs on the basis of his experience; he improves his behavior on the basis of this feedback.

Our observations suggest a modification of this view. There is a need for introducing ideas about the process by which beliefs are constructed in an organizational setting. In many contexts the interpretation of an organizational choice process is as important as the immediate, substantive action we commonly consider.[6] Individuals, as well as organizations or nations, develop myths, fictions, legends, and illusions. They develop conflicts over myths and ideology. We need models of the development of belief which do not assume necessary domination by events or "objective reality."

Environmental actions and events frequently are ambiguous. It is not clear what happened, or why it happened. Ambiguity may be inherent

5. Participants in an organization are likely, under a variety of circumstances, to see the connection between action and response as tighter than it is. As a result, one of the major phenomena that we will need to comprehend is superstitious learning within organizations.
6. Vickers (1965, p. 15) is interested in both these two outcomes of choices: "events" and "ideas." He views the Royal Commissions as units which seldom are supposed to make direct choices, but to affect opinions and conceptions or "the appreciative setting" of a certain phenomenon.

in the events, or be caused by the difficulties participants have in observing them. The complexity of, and change in, the environment often overpower our cognitive capacity. Furthermore, our interpretations are seldom based only on our own observations; they rely heavily on the interpretations offered by others. Our trust in the interpretations are clearly dependent on our trust in the interpreters. The degree of ambiguity will be strongly dependent upon the efficiency of the channels through which interpretations are transmitted.

The elaboration of such a theory is particularly germane to the study of organizations. Much of what we know, or believe we know, is based on our interpretation of reports from participants. When we ask a participant to report what happened, we solicit his model of events. When we ask a participant to assess the relative power of various individuals or groups, we ask him to carry out a complex theoretical analysis (March, 1966). It is often true that participants differ in significant ways among themselves or differ in significant ways from the interpretations that we, as outside observers, report. In order to sort out the complications of developing an understanding of participant reports, we need to understand the development of belief structures in an organization under conditions of ambiguity.

This review of some of the limitations of the complete cycle of choice suggests that we can develop some kinds of theories that attend to complications in the relations between individual beliefs and individual action, between individual action and organizational choice, between organizational choice and environmental response, and between environmental response and individual beliefs. Such theories exist in preliminary form already. What might distinguish their use in the study of organizational choice is their linkage to generate some understanding of their interactions in choice situations.

1.2 Reality, Intention, and Necessity

The limitations on the complete cycle of choice also suggest a series of possible confusions in our ordinary ideas about organizational events. The first potential confusion is to assume that what appeared to happen did happen. We do not need to accept a rigidly subjective interpretation of reality to concede that most of what we believe we know about events within organizational choice situations as well as the events themselves, reflects an interpretation of events by organizational actors and observers. Those interpretations are generated within the organization in the face of considerable perceptual ambiguity. Organizational action requires a model of the world. That model itself becomes of interest to us, along with the process by which it is developed and changed.

The second potential confusion is to assume that what happened was intended to happen. It is common to understand organizational actions in terms of intentions, either organizational or individual, to imagine that individuals have intentions and that those intentions are translated into action in a way that makes organizational action some product of individual or group will. Although not everyone gets his way, the primary reason one person fails to achieve an intended outcome is because it is inconsistent with someone else's intended outcome. Thus, choices within an organization are produced by preferences. If something happened, someone wanted it to happen. Different intentions will produce different outcomes. Better intentions will produce better outcomes. The converse position is three fold: First, the flow of individual actions produces a flow of decisions that is intended by no one and is not related in a direct way to anyone's desired outcomes. The process by which individual intentional behavior combines to produce organizational behavior is not one in which shifts in intentions will produce consistent shifts in organizational action. Indeed, much organizational behavior is dominated by rules that exist and are followed without significant impact of individual intentions. Second, individual intent and individual action are sometimes only loosely connected. Much individual behavior is less understandable as a consequence of individual preferences than as a pattern of duty and obligation. Third, the simple process of decision within an organization is often easily swamped by exogenous factors that are much more compelling than are the intentional actions of participants in the process.

The third potential confusion is to assume that what happened had to happen. The presumption is one of classical understanding. Because the objective is taken as explaining why a particular organizational (decision) outcome occurred, the observed event is treated as having an exceptional status relative to events that did not occur. Differences between an observed outcome and alternative possible, but not realized, outcomes are seen as fundamental. In our judgment, this idea is a mistake. Substantial differences in final outcomes are sometimes produced by small (and essentially unpredictable) differences in intermediate events leading to the outcomes. Lawful processes operate subject to essentially chance variation.[7] As a result, an interpretation of an event should include an

7. The idea that some processes may be understandable only up to some distribution is a familiar one. It permeates much of modern physics, biology, and economics. What distinguishes the fields in which it is common is the extent to which they have substantial opportunities to study aggregate effects empirically. Much of the study of organizational decision making is closer to history or clinical practice. The data are more likely to take the form of individual outcomes. In such fields the inclination is strong to treat the outcome as understandable in itself rather than as an instance in a distribution. Yet, it seems unlikely that nature has so neatly divided the phenomena as to ensure that only those processes that generate large numbers of observations are subject to incomplete understanding.

interpretation of alternative events that could easily have occurred but did not.

All three potential confusions are particularly significant to the study of organizations because they affect both the methods of organizational research and the style of theory about organizations. If what is believed by participants in organizations is a construct subject to being understood in its own right, we require greater sophistication in understanding standard field data. The process by which people in an organization come to believe what they believe about organizational events is demonstrably powerful enough to confound any easy transmutation of beliefs into evidence for the phenomena to which they refer.

If what happened is seen as only one of a number of things that might tional, we are in theoretical trouble. Most organization theories begin with some kind of presumption that individuals and groups pursue objectives and that organizational outcomes reflect that pursuit in some fairly self-evident way. Thus, we are directed to discover who the participants are, what their intentions, beliefs, and resources are. We are encouraged to see revealed preference techniques for identifying intentions or resource distribution techniques for identifying power not as definitional tautologies but as reflection of structure underlying an intentional process. To the extent to which the underlying process is not intentional, the meaning and utility of such procedures shifts, as does our metaphor for understanding events.

If what happened is seen as only one of a number of things that might easily have happened, we require a different historical methodology. In common with most other historians, students of decisions tend to accept the convention that the precision of a realized outcome demonstrates a necessity in that outcome. Relatively few students of decision histories write those histories with an eye to alternative scenarios with prior likelihoods comparable to that of the observed events. The issue is, of course, not unique to studies of organizational decisions and includes a deep challenge to conventional ideology with respect to the relation between theory and data.

1.3 Conclusion

We remain in the tradition of viewing organizational participants as problem-solvers and decision-makers. However, we assume that individuals find themselves in a more complex, less stable, and less understood world than that described by standard theories of organizational choice; they are placed in a world over which they often have only modest control. Nevertheless, we assume organizational participants will try to understand what is going on, to activate themselves and their resources in order to solve their problems and move the world in desired directions. These attempts will have a less heroic character than assumed in the perfect cycle theories, but they will be real.

We have argued that any of the connections in the basic cycle of choice can be broken or changed so significantly as to modify the implications of the whole system. Intention does not control behavior precisely. Participation is not a stable consequence of properties of the choice situation or individual preferences. Outcomes are not a direct consequence of process. Environmental response is not always attributable to organizational action. Belief is not always a result of experience.

In addition, the cycle is frequently touched by exogenous factors outside the control of the internal process. The process is embedded in a larger system. Under relatively easily realized situations, any one of the connections may be overwhelmed by exogenous effects. External factors may dictate individual action without regard to individual learning, organizational action without regard to individual action, environmental action without regard to organizational action, or individual learning without regard to environmental action.

In order to respond to such concerns in a theory of organizations, we require three clusters of interrelated theoretical ideas:

First, we need a modified theory of organizational choice. Such a theory will need to be contextual in the sense that it reflects the ways in which the linkages in the complete cycle of choice are affected by exogenous events, by the timing of events, by the varieties of ways in which the participants wander onto and off the stage. It will need to be structural in the sense that it reflects ways in which stabilities can arise in a highly contextual system. We have tried to suggest the basis for such a theory elsewhere (Cohen, March, and Olsen, 1972).

Second, we need a theory of organizational attention. Such a theory should treat the allocation of attention by potential participants as problematic. Where will they appear? What are the structural limits on their decision activity? How do they allocate time within those limits? Such a theory must attend to the elements of rational choice in attention allocation, to the importance of learning to the modification of attention rules, and to the norms of obligation that affect individual attention to alternative organizational concerns.

Third, we need a theory of learning under conditions of organizational ambiguity. The complete cycle is implicitly a theory of learning. What happens when the cycle is incomplete? What is a possible perspective on the development and change of belief structures?

As we pursue these ideas, we will elaborate a numer of themes that are familiar to readers of the modern literature on organizational choice. The work we report has a parentage. We owe a particular debt to Allison (1969), Coleman (1957), Cohen and March (1973), Crecine (1969),

Cyert and March (1963), Edelman (1960), Heider (1958), Hirschman (1970), Jacobsen (1964), Lindblom (1965), Long (1958), March and Simon (1958), Schilling (1968), Steinbruner (1974), Stinchcombe (1974), Thompson (1967), Vickers (1965), and Weick (1969). Our intentions are conservative. We wish to continue a course of theoretical development, as illuminated by a series of studies of organizational choice situations.

References

ALLISON, G. T. "Conceptual Models and the Cuban Missile Crises," *American Political Science* Review, 63, no. 3, (September 1969).

BECKER, GARY S. "A Theory of the Allocation of Time," *Economic Journal,* 75 (September 1965): 493–517.

BEM, D. J. *Beliefs, Attitudes, and Human Affairs.* Belmont, Calif.: Brooks Cole Publishing Company, 1970.

COHEN, MICHAEL D., MARCH, JAMES G., and OLSEN, JOHAN P. "A Garbage Can Model of Organizational Choice," *Administrative Science Quarterly,* 17, no. 1. (March 1972): 1–25.

COHEN, MICHAEL D., and MARCH, JAMES G. *Leadership and Ambiguity: The American College President.* New York: McGraw-Hill, Carnegie Commission on the Future of Higher Education, 1974.

COLEMAN, J. S. *Community Conflict.* New York: Free Press, 1957.

CRECINE, J. P. *Governmental Problem Solving: A Computer Simulation of Municipal Budgeting.* Chicago: Rand McNally, 1969.

CYERT, R. M., and MARCH, J. G. *A Behavioral Theory of the Firm.* Englewood Cliffs, N.J.: Prentice-Hall, 1963.

EDELMAN, M. *The Symbolic Uses of Politics.* Urbana: University of Illinois Press, 1964.

HEIDER, F. *The Psychology of Interpersonal Relations.* New York: Wiley, 1958.

HIRSCHMAN, A. O. *Exit, Voice and Loyalty.* Cambridge, Mass.: Harvard University Press, 1970.

JACOBSEN, K. D. *Teknisk hjelp og politisk struktur.* Oslo: Universitetsforlaget, 1964.

LINDBLOM, C. E. *The Intelligence of Democracy.* New York: Free Press, 1965.

LINDER, STAFFAN B. *The Harried Leisure Class.* New York: Columbia University Press, 1970.

LONG, N. "The Local Community as an Ecology of Games," *American Journal of Sociology,* 44 (November 1958): 251–261.

MARCH, J. G. "The Power of Power," in *Varieties of Political Theory,* ed. David Easton, Englewood Cliffs, N.J.: Prentice-Hall, 1966.

MARCH, J. G. "Model Bias in Social Action," *Review of Educational Research,* 42 (Fall 1972): 413–429.

MARCH, J. G., and OLSEN, J. P. "The Uncertainty of the Past. Organizational

Learning under Ambiguity," *European Journal of Political Research,* 3 (1975).

MARCH, J. G., and SIMON, H. A. *Organizations.* New York: Wiley, 1958.

MARX, K., and ENGELS, F. *The German Ideology.* London: Lawrence and Wishare, 1970.

SCHILLING, W. R. "The H-Bomb Decision: How to Decide Without Actually Choosing," in W. R. Welson, *The Politics of Science.* London: Oxford University Press, 1968.

STEINBRUNER, JOHN D. *The Cybernetic Theory of Decision.* Princeton, N.J.: Princeton University Press, 1974.

STINCHOMBE, ARTHUR L. *Creating Efficient Industrial Administration.* New York, Academic Press, 1974.

THOMPSON, J. *Organizations in Action.* New York: McGraw-Hill, 1967.

VICKERS, GEOFFREY. *The Art of Judgment.* New York: Basic Books, 1965.

WEICK, K. E. *The Social Psychology of Organizing.* Reading, Mass.: Addison-Wesley, 1969.

PART THREE

The Person in the Organization

The studies in this part emphasize the characteristics of the persons in the organizations studied, such as the way they respond to leadership opportunities, the manner in which they adapt to the requirements of a total institutional setting, and the way in which theft can be used as a means of "solving" problems. The first article presents a general orientation stressing the dynamic interrelationship among the person, the organization, and the environment.

This first selection, "Enactment and Organizing," is from Karl Weick's *The Social Psychology of Organizing* (1979). Weick insists that organizations should not be viewed as "relative sensors of those things that happen outside," since organizations are simply constrained by their environment. In fact, they also can rearrange their environment. He wishes to replace the passive perspective on organizational members' behavior with one that sees persons as differentially active in constructing the very environment to which they must adapt.

Weber's approach to succession involved a focus on its implications for organizational control via the transfer of authority to the new leader. Gouldner's intensive case study of succession in a gypsum plant (from *Patterns of industrial Bureaucracy* [1954]) extends Weber's formulations, although the study is still based on the assumption that "the adaptation of an organization to a threat is mediated and shaped by powerful individuals" (p. 436). A number of new and important problems are highlighted: the effects of succession on the relationship between the new man and his subordinates, the problems of legitimacy that beset the new leader, the origin of challenges to his legitimacy, the importance of his commitments to higher-level management, and the relevance of changes in style of supervision.

THE PERSON IN THE ORGANIZATION

In the third selection Goffman provides ethnographic data describing the forms of secondary adjustments made by mental patients that constitute part of the "underlife of social establishments." Goffman first specifies the organizational conditions necessary for the existence of this underlife and then describes such techniques as "working the system," make-do's," "places," "stashes," and "removal activities."

The final selection by Dalton examines the normative structure of business organization and reveals the intricate relationship between official and implicit understanding. The detailed analysis of theft not only demonstrates how the formal structure of the business system guides the particular pattern of theft behavior, but also shows how the organization's effectiveness can deteriorate under certain conditions if the system is unduly disturbed.

Enactment and Organizing

Karl E. Weick

The essence of enactment is found in these three exhibits:

1. "Experience is not what happens to a man. It is what a man does with what happens to him" (Huxley, cited in Auden and Kronenberger 1966, p. 54).
2. "Our so-called limitations, I believe,
   Apply to faculties we don't apply.
   We don't discover what we can't achieve
   Until we make an effort not to try"
   (Hein 1968, p. 33).
3. Imagine that you are playing a game of charades, and that you must act out the title of a movie. Imagine that you are given, as your title, the movie *Charade*. As the presenter, you probably would try somehow to get "outside" of the present game and point to it so that the observers would see that the answer is the very activity they are now engaged in. Alas, the observers are likely to miss this subtlety and instead to shout words like, "pointing," "finger," "excited," "all of this," and so forth.

One of the ironies in organizational analysis is that managers are described as "all business," "doers," "people of action," yet no one seems to understand much about the fine grain of their acting. "If we knew more about the normative theory of acting before you think, we could say more intelligent things about the function of management and leadership in organizations where organizations or societies do not know what they're doing" (March and Olsen 1976, p. 79). This study is about acting that sets the stage for sense-making. In each case enactment served to bracket and construct portions of the flow of experience. Bracketing and construction are visible in the three comments that begin this study.

SOURCE: *The Social Psychology of Organizing*, 2d ed., pp. 147–48, 149–54, 157–60, 164–65, 168–69. Copyright © 1979 by Addison-Wesley, Reading, Massachusetts. Reprinted with permission of the author and the publisher.

Examples of Enactment

The Enactment of Experience

There is no such thing as *experience* until the manager does something. Passive reception of a shower of inputs is not synonymous with having an experience (Simmel 1959). Experience is the consequence of activity. The manager literally wades into the swarm of "events" that surround him and actively tries to unrandomize them and impose some order. The manager acts physically in the environment, attends to some of it, ignores most of it, talks to other people about what they see and are doing (Braybrooke 1964). As a result the surroundings get sorted into variables and linkages and appear more orderly.

• • •

The Enactment of Limitations

Perceptions of personal "limitations," in Piet Hein's view, turn out to be a failure *to act* rather than a failure *while acting.* Limitations are deceptive conclusions but, unfortunately, people don't realize this. What they don't realize is that limitations are based on presumptions rather than action. Knowledge of limitations is not based on tests of skills but rather on an *avoidance* of testing.

On the basis of avoided tests, people conclude that constraints exist in the environment and that limits exist in their repertoire of responses. Inaction is justified by the implantation, in fantasy, of constraints and barriers that make action "impossible." These constraints, barriers, prohibitions then become prominent "things" in the environment. They also become self-imposed restrictions on the options that managers consider and exercise when confronted with problems. Finally, these presumed constraints, when breached by someone who is more doubting, naive, or uninformed, often generate sizable advantages for the breacher.

As a laboratory exercise, Harold Garfinkel (1967) had some of his students go into a department store and offer a small fraction of the list price for some item. The students were apprehensive in advance about doing this, since an explicit rule presumed to exist in most American stores is that things must be bought for the list price. Much to their surprise, the students discovered that once they actually began to bargain for items, they were able to get rather substantial reductions in price. The interesting thing about the list price "rule" is that it seems to have force because everyone expects it to be followed and no one challenges it.

Garfinkel takes that observation and expands it to a more general statement about knowledge based on avoided tests:

266

If upon the arousal of troubled feelings persons avoid tinkering with these "standardized" expectancies (in the example above the standardization would be the rule that things must be bought for the list price) the standardization could consist of an *attributed* standardization that is supported by the fact that persons avoid the very situations in which they might learn about them. Lay as well as professional knowledge of the nature of rule governed actions and the consequences of breaching the rules is prominently based on just such procedure. Indeed, the more important the rule, the greater is the likelihood that knowledge is based on avoided tests. Strange findings must certainly await anyone who examines the expectancies that make up routine backgrounds of commonplace activities for they have rarely been exposed by investigators even to as much revision as an imaginative rehearsal of their breach would produce (1967, p. 70).

Even though organizations appear to be quite solid, in fact much of their substance may consist of spurious knowledge based on avoided tests. While Garfinkel does not formulate propositions about avoided tests, it *is* possible to speculate about the form such propositions would take. For example, implicit in his analysis is the suggestion that avoided tests may occur because people fear the experience of failure. Transformed into a proposition, it might be predicted that the greater the fear of failure, the greater the likelihood that a person's knowledge of the world is based on avoided tests.

Notice that if one were to fail while attempting a test, the results might or might not be reversible. In other words, a person might be able to undo the damage or might never be able to normalize the event. This suggests that the greater the difficulty of undoing an outcome, the more likely it is for a person to engage in avoided tests.

There appears to be a cognitive side to the avoidance of tests. So far it has been argued that immediate outcomes of pleasure or pain may control the choice to test or not. Notice, however, that there are subtleties in the interpretation of outcomes. If you go into a store, try to buy a 49-cent toothbrush for 40 cents, fail, and experience some embarrassment, you might interpret that outcome as one of those little stresses in life that "builds character." Thus, if individuals in organizations believe in such things as the cleansing power of suffering, the school of hard knocks, or the saneogenesis proposition that it is too little rather than too much stress that causes breakdown (Scher 1962), then those individuals will be more likely to attempt tests rather than to avoid them.

There is a parallel between avoided tests and the Ziergarnik Effect. An avoided test is like an unfiinished task, especially if the person has wondered repeatedly whether a barrier is fictional or substantial. There is a distinct quality of unfinished business in avoided tests. This suggests that people should be more aware of their avoided tests than of their nonavoided tests.

Not very much is known about avoided tests, but it seems likely that they could be the basis for a substantial portion of the knowledge that organizations retain. The question of interest for organization epistemologists would be, "What precedes and is the occasion for an avoided versus an attempted test?"

A variation of the point that the ingenuous shall coopt the environment is the idea that people who seem backward historically are, in fact, privileged (Sahlins and Service 1960). Their privilege lies in the fact that they can benefit from the mistakes and oversights of pioneers. The "backward" group is able to leapfrog the pioneer and employ neglected actions to locate opportunities that prove beneficial. With both avoided tests and privileged backwardness it is inaction (a failure to enact) propped up by the fiction of constraints that erects trappings which, when treated irreverently, vanish abruptly.

A presumption throughout this book is that managers often know much less about their environments and organizations than they think. One reason for this imperfect knowing is that managers unwittingly collude among themselves to avoid tests. And they build elaborate explanations of why tests should be avoided, why one shouldn't/couldn't act within settings presumed to be dangerous. The disbeliever, the unindoctrinated, the newcomer, all being less influenced by a cause map dotted with noxiants, wade in where avoiders fear to tread. Having waded in they find either that the avoider's fear is unfounded or that it is valid, in which case their demise provides vicarious learning for the avoiders.

The point is that the enormous amount of talk, socializing, consensus-building, and vicarious learning that goes on among managers often results in pluralistic ignorance (Shaw and Blum 1965) about the environment. Stunted enactment is the reason. Each person watches someone else avoid certain procedures, goals, activities, sentences, and pastimes and concludes that this avoidance is motivated by "real" noxiants in the environment. The observer profits from that "lesson" by himself then avoiding those acts and their presumed consequences. As this sequence of events continues to be repeated, managers conclude that they know more and more about something that none of them has actually experienced firsthand. This impression of knowing becomes strengthened because everyone seems to be seeing and avoiding the same things. And if everyone seems to agree on something, then it must exist and be true.

If people want to change their environment, they need to change themselves and their actions—not someone else. Repeated failures of organizations to solve their problems are partially explained by their failure to understand their own prominence in their own environments. Problems that never get solved, never get solved because managers keep tinkering with everything *but* what they do.

The Enactment of Charades

As the final example, Jencks and Silver (1973) provide a perfect description of charades when they call it an "acted out rebus." A rebus is a representation of original words or symbols by means of some other pictures or symbols that sound like the original. For example, ICURYY4me is a rebus for "I see you are too wise for me." Charades involve the same kind of representation. An object is symbolized by other objects that sound the same. According to Jencks and Silver, one of the all-time best (or worst?) solutions for a charade occurred when a person was given the name Salvador Dali and acted out the three words, "saliva," "tore," and "doily."

There are several interesting features of enactment in charades. The person doing the gesturing knows what he is perceived as enacting only after he hears the observers' guesses. That is, the actor produces a soliloquy, the punctuation of which is done by others. The actor produces an enacted environment as an output, but the observers are faced with a display that they can punctuate and connect in numerous ways. The actor imposes meanings on his environment that come back and organize his activities, except that the observers see these implanted meanings as puzzles rather than certainties. If the actor has enacted a puzzling or complicated or subtle environment, that enactment comes back and organizes him in the sense that he has to do enormous work to salvage, patch up, and redirect the observers' efforts to invent plausible constructions for his subtleties.

The image of a rebus is relevant for organizations because it captures the essence of enactment. People in organizations need to act to find out what they have done, and the person enacting a rebus needs to play out his version of the charade to see what he really is conveying to interested observers. The person acting out a charade enacts most of the environment for observers. And what we are arguing is that it isn't that much different in organizations. The environment that the organization worries over is put there by the organization.

Conclusion

The reciprocal linkage between ecological change and enactment in the organizing model is intended to depict the subjective origin of organizational realities (Israel 1972). People in organizations repeatedly impose that which they later claim imposes on them. Farmers with heavy tractors enact the packed earth (ecological change), which requires heavier tractors, more fuel, deeper plows, and/or wider tires to work. The presence of elaborate multitrack mixers in recording studios has compelled engineers to produce increasingly elaborate effects on recordings, which leads to demands for even more elaborate mixing equipment, and so on. Many listeners, however, have become fed up with this meddling and are now purchasing direct-to-disc music that bypasses the engineer, his busy hands, his passion for remixing, his elaborate technology, and his precious output (McDonough 1978). Nevertheless, engineers have enacted the environment of contrived music that now organizes and threatens to disorganize their jobs. Physicians, through nonsubtle diagnostic procedures ("hmmm, when did you start holding your head at that angle?"), often implant maladies that *weren't* there when the examination began. Their procedures consolidate numerous free-floating symptoms into the felt presence of a single, more specific, more serious problem. Physician-induced disease (*iatrogenics*) is a perfect example of people creating the environment that confronts them (Scheff 1965). Firemen on steam locomotives enacted the pattern of hot and cold spots within the boiler by their method of shoveling coal into it, which then constrained their subsequent attempts to preserve steam pressure (Withuhn 1975).

Examples like this are plentiful. The point is, much current work on the relationships between organizations and their environments tends to downplay the extent to which the boundaries between the two are blurred (Starbuck 1976, p. 1070) and the extent to which organizations produce their environments.

Characteristics of Enactment

Enactment As Bracketing

We have described enactment as a bracketing activity. To visualize what this means, imagine that the major input to be processed by employees is either a stock market tickertape with no spaces between symbols, or a teletype machine whose output contains no punctuation into sentences or paragraphs. In the unpunctuated output one does not know where one "story" leaves off and another story begins, or even whether a story is a reasonable unit of analysis. The same thing is true in the case of the unpunctuated stock market tickertape. In both cases there is a mass of data, without any hints concerning their importance. It's the job of the employee to tear off portions of the tickertape or teletype for further study. Those activities of tearing are crude kinds of enactments. Once something has been isolated, then that *is* the environment momentarily for the organization and that environment has been put into place by the very actions of the employees themselves.

To get a feeling for the phenomenon we're interested in, think back to times when you have read the verbatim protocol of some important speech. When these speeches are printed verbatim, the columns of type often continue uninterrupted without any indications of how the speech is structured. When a reader confronts this display of uninterrupted type he wonders such things as, "Where were the good parts?" "What was said that is new?" "What's different?" "What's surprising?" "What's the news?" As you read, these questions become frustrating because you basically have to decide for yourself what's new and different and good without any prompting from commentators. Confronted with an unpunctuated speech, you're in precisely the same position as an employee who confronts a flow of experience and has no one around to coach him on which are the good parts, the bad parts, the interesting parts, and the trivia. Those are all decisions involving bracketing.

When you pull out some portion of the text of the speech from its surrounding context, then the environment that you have bracketed for inspection is a different environment than the original one that contained intonations, facial expressions, and surrounding text. The reader of the extracted portion does see part of herself because her own interests influenced the process of extracting. And this is true whether those biases suggest that speeches are better at the end than at the beginning, or that paragraphs starting with personal pronouns are better than those that don't. The "chaos" of the speech transcript has been dealt with by breaking it into chunks, by ignoring portions of it, and by trying to figure out on the basis of the extracted chunk what kinds of decisions and situations on the part of the speaker would have generated those particular words (in other words, the bracketed portion is analyzed in terms of potential antecedents and consequences).

A suggestion of the way in which bracketing might operate is found in Neisser's (1976) recent discussion of the perceptual cycle. Neisser casts his discussion of perceptual cycles in terms of schemas used to aid interpretation. A schema is an abridged, generalized, corrigile organization of experience that serves as an initial frame of reference for action and perception. A schema is the belief in the phrase, "I'll see it when I believe it." Schemata constrain seeing and, therefore, serve to bracket portions of experience.

• • •

Enactment As Deviation Amplification

In many instances of enactment there is a deviation-amplifying causal structure that contains an even number of negative signs. The importance of this observation is that minor disturbances, when they are embedded in a deviation-amplifying loop, can grow into major happenings with major consequences. When it is argued that organizations enact their environments, some readers may assume that these enactments have always been present on about the scale they now exhibit. That implication is not intended. The modest origins of consequential enactments are illustrated by efforts to desegregate the schools in San Francisco (Weiner 1976).

In trying to figure out how desegregation should be implemented in San Francisco, a Citizens Advisory Committee consisting of 67 citizens was appointed by the board of education. Over time this committee became increasingly influential in deciding how the desegregation order would be implemented. The fascinating point for our analyses is the differential frequency with which these 67 people attended meetings.

The committee began its deliberations on February 16, 1971, and concluded them on June 2, 1971. During this time they held 70 meetings, or approximately one meeting every two days. This implies the obvious point that all members could not attend all meetings. This minor difference in participation rates soon became amplified:

> Deadlines led to a domination of the decision making process by middle and upper class white women, who had available time during the day because they were not employed and could arrange care for their children, and by other participants whose employers permitted them to devote daytime hours to the decision making process (Weiner 1976, pp. 234–35).

As a result, black members of the committee did not participate actively in developing the desegregation plan. But the issue here is not just one of time. There is the further issue of differential competence produced by differential attendance:

> As high participation rates continue the most active members become a relatively small group processing a near monopoly position concerning the competencies required in decision making. The joint operation of these factors constitutes a positive feedback loop where activity causes greater competence and greater competence leads to increased activity. . . . Thus, one effect associated with the sharply increased participation rates by some participants in the choice is that the most active participants gain a much higher share of the competence and experience necessary to deal with the remaining problems. As they become substantially more competent it becomes more difficult for other potential participants to gain access to the decision making process (Weiner 1976, p. 247).

Weiner labels this phenomenon the *competence multiplier*. The participants who show up repeatedly produce an environment of sophisticated analyses that requires more participation from them, which makes them even more informed to deal with the issues that are presented. A vicious circle is created in which the regular participants of the advisory council enact the very sophisticated and subtle issues that their new-found competence enables them to deal with. People who attend less often feel less informed, increasingly unable to catch up, and more reluctant to enter the conversation at the level of sophistication voiced by the persistent participants. The relatively less informed people select themselves out of the decision-making process, and this elevates the level of desegregation planning to an even more detailed and complicated level where even fewer people can comprehend it. Over time the combination of high and low participation rates, a minor deviation in the beginning, changes the issues, plans, and environment that confronts the Citizens Advisory Committee.

The question of desegregation and how to implement it is not an external problem that is handed to the committee for its action. Instead, the issue that gets handed to them is an issue partly of their own making. The density of detail in the solution, the subtlety of the issues addressed, and the interests that are accommodated are all influenced by the patterns of participation at the meetings.

Once again we have a clear example of a deviation-amplifying loop. People with time to spend on a problem transformed that problem into something that only people with time to spend on the problem can manage. The resulting discussion is one from which infrequent attendees become more and more alienated because they understand fewer of its intricacies. Thus the mundane activity of simply showing up at meetings generates an environment that only those who show up at meetings are able to manage and control. Several iterations through the cycle are necessary for this consequence to occur, but again, its plausibility is evident and its relevance to enactment processes should be apparent.

Enactment As Self-fulfilling Prophecies

Enactment could be described as efferent sense-making. The modifier *efferent* means centrifugal or conducted outward. The person's idea is extended outward, implanted, and then rediscovered as knowledge. The discovery, however, originated in a prior invention by the discoverer. In a crude but literal sense, one could talk about efferent sense-making as thinking in circles. Action, perception, and sense--making exist in a circular, tightly coupled relationship that resembles a self-fulfilling prophecy (e.g., Archibald 1974; G. W. Bateson 1951; James 1956; Kelley and Stahelski 1970; Henshel and Kennedy 1973; R. A. Jones 1977).

A self-fulfilling phophecy involves

> behavior that brings about in others the reaction to which the behavior would be an appropriate reaction. For instance, a person who acts on the premise that "nobody likes me" will behave in a distrustful, stiff, defensive, or aggressive manner to which others are likely to react unsympathetically, thus bearing out his original premise. What is typical about this sequence and makes it a problem of punctuation is that the individual

concerned conceives of himself only as reacting to, but not as provoking, those attitudes (Watzlawick, Beavin, and Jackson 1967, pp. 98–99).

A related phenomenon has been described by music critic Leonard Meyer as the presumption of logic and was noted briefly in Chapter 5. Meyer assumes that the persumption of logic is important in comprehending new music (that is, an equivocal input). Essentially Meyer argues that whenever individuals try to comprehend new music, their success or failure at this activity depends on their prior belief in the seriousness, purposefulness and logic of the artist, and the work:

> The presumption that nothing in art happens without a reason and that any given cause should be sufficient and necessary for what takes place is a fundamental condition for the experience of art. . . . Without this basic belief the listener would have no reason for suspending judgement, revising opinion, and searching for relationships; the divergent, the less probable, the ambiguous would have no meaning. There would be no progression, only change. Without faith in the purposefulness and rationality of art, listeners would abandon their efforts to understand, to reconcile deviants to what has gone before or to look for their raison d'etre in what is still to come (Meyer 1956, p. 75).

Notice that the presumption of logic resembles a self-fulfilling prophecy. The listener presumes that the music about to be played will have made sense, exerts effort to make the music sensible, postpones premature judgments on whether it makes sense or not, and thereby makes his own contribution toward inventing a sensible, complete work of music. The presumption of logic is slightly more content-free than is a self-fulfilling prophecy. Self-fulfilling prophecies typically contain specific content such as the expectations that students will be bright or stupid (Rosenthal and Jacobson 1968), that people will like me or dislike me (James 1956, pp. 23–25), that the bank is about to become insolvent (Merton 1948), or that this is a fatalistic world (G. W. Bateson 1951). Each of those prophecies is quite explicit, whereas the presumption of logic is more general (a metaprophecy) and says essentially that there *is* an order of some kind there and that it's simply up to the listener to extract/create that order.

When managers confront equivocality and try to reduce it, they too often operate on the presumption of logic. They assume that their views of and actions toward the world are valid, they assume that other people in the organization will see and do the same things, and it is rare for the managers to check these assumptions. Having presumed that the environment is orderly and sensible, managers make efforts to impose order, thereby enacting the orderliness that is "discovered." The presumption of nonequivocality provides the occasion for managers to see and do those things that transform the environment into something that is unequivocal.

●   ●   ●

Enactment As Social Construction of Reality

The concept of an *enacted environment* is not synonymous with the concept of a *perceived environment,* even though citations of the concept would suggest that it is. If a perceived environment were the essence of enactment then, as Lou Pondy suggested, the phenomenon would have been called enthinkment, not enactment.

We have purposely labeled the organizational equivalent of variation en*act*ment to emphasize that managers construct, rearrange, single out, and demolish many "objective" features of their surroundings. When people act they unrandomize variables, insert vestiges of orderliness, and literally create their own constraints. This holds true whether those constraints are created in fantasy to justify avoided tests or created in actuality to explain tangible bruises (Simmel 1959).

People have talked for some time about the fact that reality is constructed (e.g., MeLeod and Chaffee 1972; R. A. Jones and Day 1977; Berger and Luckmann 1967; Ball 1972). These views stress that reality is selectively perceived, rearranged cognitively, and negotiated interpersonally. In most cases it is assumed that something tangible is the target of these efforts and that what is required to locate this target is that one be clever enough to choose both a good partner and a good procedure to uncover this underlying order. Analyses of the social construction of reality emphasize that actors attain at least a partial consensus on the meaning of their behavior and that they look for patterns that underlie appearances, actions, events. These patterns are assumed to have an existence independent of the interpretation procedures (e.g., Goffman 1974, pp. 1–2; Gonos 1977).

A more extreme position is that the social order exists precariously and has no existence at all independent of the members' accounting and describing practices (e.g., Mehan and Wood 1975). The organizing model is based on the view that order is imposed rather than discovered, on the grounds that action defines cognition. The basic sense-making device used within organizations is assumed to be talking to discover thinking. How can I know what I think until I see what I say? In that sequence, the action of talking is the occasion for defining and articulating cognitions. When it is argued that organizational members spend much of their time uttering soliloquies, we are describing a crucial feature of enactment. The soliloquies are action soliloquies because it is action that leads and defines cognition. G. W. Bateson uses a similar image: "an explorer can never know what he is exploring until it has been explored" (1972, p. xvi).

The notion that reality is a product of social construction does have some connotation of action conveyed by the word *construction*. But this construction is usually thought to involve activities of negotiation between people as to what is out there. Less prominent in these analyses is the idea that people, often alone, actively *put* things out there that they then perceive and negotiate about perceiving. It is that initial implanting of reality that is preserved by the word *enactment*.

• • •

A major caution implicit here is that analysts should be wary of asserting that they know what *the* environment consists of and should be eager to assert that environments are plural and that there is always *an* environment. Environments are multiple, exist in the eye of the beholder, and are more prone to breakage and reassembly than is often realized. A reasonable question is, "So what?"

Whenever an organization tries to position itself to "see" the environment better, those actions should be examined from a different standpoint. The question should be, in positioning itself to see the environment, "What is the organization doing that might create the very displays it will see?" When an organization wants to see things, it usually positions itself so that in seeing things it is also seen. The environment that "knows" it is being watched is thereby rearranged and gives off different raw data than if it were blind. Under these conditions it is obvious that the organization sees much of itself when it wades into a data collection effort.

The enactment perspective implies that people in organizations should be more self-conscious about and spend more time reflecting on the actual things they *do*. If people imagine that the environment is separate from the organization and lies out there to be scanned so that effective responses can be produced, then they will spend their resources outfitting themselves with the equivalents of high-powered binoculars to improve acuity. If people recognize that they create many of their own environments, then all of that effort to improve acuity is irrelevant. The organization concerned about its own enactment needs to discover ways to partial out the effects of its own interventions from effects that would have happened had the observer never obtruded in the situation in the first place. An organization that is sensitive to the fact that it produces enacted environments will be less concerned with issues of truth and falsity and more concerned with issues of reasonableness. If environments are enacted then there is no such thing as a representation that is true or false, there simply are versions that are more and less reasonable. Thus, endless discussion of questions about whether we see things the way they really are, whether we are right, or whether something is true will be replaced by discussions that focus on questions such as What did we do? What senses can we make of those actions? What didn't we do? What next step best preserves our options and does least damage to our repertoire? What do these bruises mean? How did we ruin that equipment.

References

ALDRICH, H., and D. HERKER. 1977. Boundary spanning roles and organization structure. *Academy of Management Review* 2: 217–230.

ALLISON, G. T. 1971. *Essence of decision: Explaining the Cuban missile crisis.* Boston: Little, Brown.

ARCHIBALD, W. P. 1974. Alternative explanations for self-fulfilling prophecy. *Psychological Bulletin* 31: 74–84.

AUDEN, W. H., and L. KRONENBERGER. 1966. *The Viking book of aphorisms.* New York: Viking.

AXELROD, R. (ed.), 1976. *Structure of decision: The cognitive maps of political elites.* Princeton, N.J.: Princeton University Press.

BALL, D. W. 1972. "The definition of situation": Some theoretical and methodological consequences of taking W. I. Thomas seriously. *Journal for the Theory of Social Behavior* 2: 61–82.

BATESON, G. W. 1951. Conventions of communications: Where validity depends on belief. In J. Ruesch and G. Bateson (eds.), *Communication, the social matrix of society.* New York: Norton, pp. 212–227.

———. 1972. *Steps to an ecology of mind.* New York: Ballentine.

BERGER, P. L., and T. LUCKMAN. 1967. *The social construction of reality.* Garden City, N.Y.: Doubleday, Anchor Books.

BOUGON, M., K. E. WEICK, and D. BINKHORST. 1977. Cognition in organizations: An analysis of the Utrecht Jazz Orchestra. *Administrative Science Quarterly* 22: 606–639.

BRAYBROOKE, D. 1964. The mystery of executive success re-examined. *Administrative Science Quarterly* 8: 533–560.

CAMPBELL, D. T. 1975. On the conflicts between biological and social evolution and between psychology and moral tradition. *American Psychologist* 30: 1103–1126.

GARFINKEL, H. 1967. *Studies in ethnomethodology.* Englewood Cliffs, N.J.: Prentice-Hall.

GOFFMAN, E. 1974. *Frame analysis.* New York: Harper.

GONOS, G. 1977. "Situation" versus "frame": The "interactionist" and the "structuralist" analyses of everyday life. *American Sociological Review* 42: 854–867.

GRUBER, H. E., and J. J. VONÉCHE (eds.). 1977. *The essential Piaget.* New York: Basic Books.

HALL, R. J. 1977. *Organizations: Structure and process* (2nd ed.). Englewood Cliffs, N.J.: Prentice-Hall.

HEIDER, F. 1959. Thing and medium. *Psychological Issues* 1, No. 3: 1–34.

HEIN, P. 1968. *Grooks II*. Cambridge, Mass.: MIT Press (Borgens Billigböger).

HENSHELL, R. L., and L. W. KENNEDY, 1973. Self-altering prophecies: Consequences for the feasibility of social prediction. *General Systems Yearbook* 18: 119–126.

ISRAEL, J. 1972. Stipulations and construction in the social sciences. In J. Israel and H. Tajfel (eds.), *The context of social psychology*. New York: Academic, pp. 123–211.

JAMES, W. 1950. *The principles of psychology* (Vols. 1 and 2), New York: Dover.

———. 1956. Is life worth living? In W. James, *The will to believe*. New York: Dover, pp. 32–62.

JANIS, I. R. 1972. *Victims of groupthink*. Boston: Houghton Mifflin.

JENCKS, C., and N. SILVER. 1973. *Adhocism*. Garden City, N.Y.: Doubleday, Anchor Books.

JONES, R. A. 1977. *Self-fulfilling prophecies*. Hillsdale, N.J.: Erlbaum.

JONES, R. A., and R A. DAY. 1977. Social psychology as symbolic interaction. In C. Hendrick (ed.), *Perspectives on social psychology*. Hillsdale, N.J.: Erlbaum, pp. 75–136.

JORDAN, N. 1968. *Themes in speculative psychology*. London: Tavistock.

KELLEY, H. H., and A. J. STAHELSKI. 1970. Social interaction basis of cooperators' and competitors' beliefs about others. *Journal of Personality and Social Psychology* 16, No. 1: 66–91.

KLEIN, L. 1976. *A social scientist in industry*. New York: Wiley.

LEIFER, R., and A. DELBECQ. 1978. Organizational/environmental interchange: A model of boundary spanning activity. *Academy of Management Review* 3: 40–50.

MARCH, J. G., and J. P. OLSEN. 1976. *Ambiguity and choice in organizations*. Bergen, Norway: Universitetsforlaget.

MARTIN, M. 1977. The philosophical importance of the Rosethal effect. *Journal for the Theory of Social Behavior* 7: 81–97.

MCDONOUGH, J. 1978. Review of *The King James Version* by Harry James. *Downbeat,* June 15, 1978, pp. 23–29.

MCLEOD, J., and S. H. CHAFFEE. 1972. The construction of social reality. In J. T. Tedeschi (ed.), *The social influence processes*. Chicago: Aldine, pp. 50–99.

MEHAN, H., and H. WOOD. 1975. *The reality of ethnomethodology*. New York: Wiley.

MERTON, R. K. 1948. The self-fulfilling prophecy. *Antioch Review* 8: 193–210.

MEYER, L. B. 1956. *Emotion and meaning in music*. Chicago: University of Chicago Press.

NEISSER, U. 1976. *Cognition and reality*. San Francisco: W. H. Freeman.

ROSENTHAL, R., and L. JACOBSON. 1968. *Pygmalion in the classroom: Teacher expectation and pupils' intellectual development*. New York: Holt, Rinehart and Winston.

ROSS, L. 1977. The intuitive psychologist and his shortcomings: Distortions in the attribution process. In L. Berkowitz (ed.), *Advances in experimental social psychology* (Vol. 10) New York: Academic, pp. 173–220.

SAHLINS, M. D., and E. R. SERVICE (eds.). 1960. *Evolution and culture*. Ann Arbor: University of Michigan Press.

SCHEFF, T. J. 1965. Decision rules, types of error, and their consequences in medical diagnosis. In F. Massarik and P. Ratoosh (eds.), *Mathematical explorations in behavioral science*. Homewood, Ill.: Dorsey, pp. 66–83.

SCHER, J. M. 1962. Mind as participation. In J. M. Scher (ed.), *Theories of the mind*. New York: Free Press, pp. 354–375.

SHAW, M. E., and J. M BLUM. 1965. Group performance as a function of task difficulty and the group's awareness of member satisfaction. *Journal of Applied Psychology* 49: 151–154.

SIMMEL, G. 1959. On the nature of philosophy. In K. H. Wolff (ed.), *Essays on sociology, philosophy and aesthetics*. New York: Harper, pp. 282–309.

STARBUCK, W. H. 1976. Organizations and their environments. In M. D. Dunnette (ed.), *Handbook of industrial and organizational psychology*. Chicago: Rand, pp. 1069–1123.

WARWICK, D. P. 1975. *A theory of public bureaucracy: Politics, personality, and organization in the State Department*. Cambridge, Mass.: Harvard University Press.

WATZLAWICK, P., J. H. BEAVIN, and D. D. JACKSON. 1967. *Pragmatics of human communication*. New York: Norton.

WEINER, S. S. 1976. Participation, deadlines, and choice. In J. G. March and J. P. Olsen, *Ambiguity and choice in organizations*. Bergen, Norway: Universitetsforlaget, pp. 225–250.

WITHUHN, B. 1975. A primer for coal shovelers. *Trainline*. Spring 1975, No. 6, pp. 5–6.

Succession and the Problem of Bureaucracy

Alvin W. Gouldner

With Peele's promotion to plant manager, the growth of bureaucratic organization became pronounced. How can this be explained? As a first step, though by no means as a complete answer, it is helpful to consider Peele as a man playing a peculiar role—the role of a "successor." Instead of examining Peele's unique personality, let us begin by identifying the kinds of pressures and problems which beset him because of this role. Peele's psychological "traits" will be considered only to the extent that they relate to conditions of sociological importance.

Before proceeding further, however, one other feature of Peele's behavior deserves emphasis; these are changes which he made among middle management personnel. As already shown, Peele brought in a new personnel director, Jack Digger, from the "outside." Digger had come from the plant at which Peele formerly had been manager, a plant also owned by the Company. Beyond this, four other replacements were made to supervisory positions which had been newly opened. This rapid change in supervisory personnel, following a succession, is so common that it should be given a distinctive label—we shall call it "strategic replacements."

The problem of the present chapter can now be formulated as follows: In what ways does the role of a successor conduce to increasing bureaucratization and to an increased rate of strategic replacements?

The Successor's Sentiments

Before being handed the reins at the Oscar Center plant, Peele was called to the main office for a "briefing." The main office executives told Peele of his predecessor's shortcomings, and expressed the feeling that

SOURCE: *Patterns of Industrial Bureaucracy*, pp. 70–101. Copyright © 1954 by The Free Press of Glencoe. Reprinted with permission of Macmillan Publishing Co., Inc.

things had been slipping at the plant for some time. They suggested that Old Doug, the former manager who had recently died, had grown overindulgent with his advancing years, and that he, Peele, would be expected to improve production. As Peele put it, "Doug didn't force the machine. I had to watch it. Doug was satisfied with a certain production.[1] But the Company gave me orders to get production up."

With the renewed pressure of postwar competition, the main office expected things to start humming; traditional production quotas were about to be rationalized. A "briefing," it will be seen, does more than impart technical data. It also serves to crystallize *attitudes* toward an assignment and to raise the salience of *values* considered appropriate to the situation.

Peele, therefore, came to the plant sensitized to the rational and impersonal yardsticks which his superiors would use to judge his performance.

As a successor, Peele had a heightened awareness that he could disregard top management's rational values only at his peril, for his very promotion symbolized the power which they held over him. Since he was now on a new assignment, Peele also realized that he would be subject to more than routine observation by the main office. As a successor, he was "on trial" and, therefore, he was anxious, and anxious to "make good." Comments about Peele's anxiety were made by many main office personnel, as well as by people in the plant, who spoke repeatedly of his "nervousness."

In turn, this anxiety spurred Peele to perform his new role according to main office expectations. As one of the main office administrative staff said, "Peele is trying hard to arrive. He is paying more attention to the plant." Peele also accepted top management's view of the plant out of *gratitude* for having been promoted from the smaller plant at which he had been, to the larger one at Oscar Center. "I appreciate their confidence in me," he said, "and I want to show it."

By virtue of his succession, Peele was, at the very least, new to his specific position in the Oscar Center plant's social system. As it happened, he had come from the "outside" and was new to the entire plant. He was all the more a stranger among strangers, as yet untied by bonds of friendship to people in his new plant. He was, therefore, able to view the plant situation in a comparatively dispassionate light and was, further, freer to put his judgments into practice. Unhampered by commitments to the informal understandings established in the plant, the successor came with a sharpened propensity for rational, efficiency-centered action.

---

1. Roethlisberger and Dickson have emphasized the tendency of informal cliques of workers to limit their output in a traditionalistic way, through their beliefs concerning a "fair day's work." But restriction of output, or "sabotage" as Veblen referred to it, is not manifested solely by operatives; it is found also among managerial personnel. Veblen, of course, has long since noted this; he tended, however, to focus on the rational motives for "sabotage" among managers, neglected the traditionalistic component.

Even before setting foot in the plant, then, Peele had an intimation that there would be things which needed "correction." He began to define the plant as one needing some "changes," changes oriented to the efficiency-maximizing values of top management, and he tentatively began shaping policies to bring about the requisite changes.

The Old Bunch

When a successor's promotion is announced, he may, however, be subjected to pressures which can introduce another, potentially conflicting, element into his frame of reference. On his way up, he is likely to have incurred obligations and to have made some friends whose loyalty and help expedited his ascent. Since a succession is often a time of promotion and enhanced power, it becomes the moment of reckoning awaited by friends, when their past favors to the successor can be reciprocated.

In a succession entailing a promotion, such as this, the successor is subjected, therefore, to somewhat contradictory pressures. On the one hand, his superiors expect him to conform to rational values and to act without "fear or favor" for any individuals in accomplishing his new mission. His old friends, however, are simultaneously exerting counterpressures, expecting him to defer to their claims for personal preferment. The outcome of these conflicting pressures cannot be predicted without considering the distinctive problems that succession engenders for the new manager.

It might be imagined that the successor would quickly resolve this conflict in favor of the demands and outlook of top management. After all, the main office has far more power over him than his friends can muster. Moreover, the successor might evade his old obligations if he is no longer among the friends to whom he owes them. (He might say, as the newly crowned Henry the Fifth said to Falstaff, "I know thee not, old man: fall to thy prayers . . . Presume not that I am the thing I was. . . .")

But when the successor enters and tries to become a part of his new plant, he faces another difficulty which soon leads him to look with favor upon the claims of his old friends. The difficulty is that, as a new manager, he is left with a heritage of promises and obligations that his *predecessor* has not had an opportunity to fulfill. For example, when a mechanic was asked about his chances of becoming a foreman, he answered unhappily:

> I don't know what the chances are here. I wasn't approached last time. But when Doug was here, he asked me, and I said I would like it very much and would appreciate it. . . . He asked me, but then he died and we got this new man, Mr. Peele.

The successor finds that his predecessor has left behind him a corps of lieutenants who were personally close and loyal to him. When the old lieutenants find that the successor, either because of ignorance or deliberate decision, fails to respect these old obligations and their informally privileged position, they begin to resist.[2]

One expression of this was found in the behavior of the old office manager, Joe Cook. Cook had been with Doug for a long while and had worked closely with him. When Peele came, Cook continued on as office manager. But to Cook, Peele was not the man that Doug had been, and he proceeded to make Peele "look bad" in the eyes of the main-office executives.

For example, when the main office would telephone the plant, Cook frequently would take the call in Peele's absence. When asked to put Peele on the phone Cook would make some effort to find him, but would finally report that he couldn't contact Peele. Instead of *"covering up"* for Peele— as he had for Doug—by pretending that Peele was in some inaccessible part of the mine, Cook would intimate that Peele had not let him know where he could be found. The main office was allowed to draw the inference that Peele was acting irresponsibly.

Since they are often placed in strategic positions, the old lieutenants are able to do substantial damage to the successor—if they want to. Another of the reasons why they were willing to do so was the old lieutenants' belief that the new manager was not the legitimate heir. In this plant, there was a widespread conception of the proper line of succession to the position of plant manager; the supervisor of the "board building" was commonly viewed as "next in line" for promotion to manager. The old lieutenants, therefore, considered one of their own group, Johnson, the board building super, as the legitimate heir to the managership. When deprived of what he felt to be his just aspirations, Johnson became disaffected and hostile to Peele.

On one occasion, for example, Peele had to be hospitalized during a heated siege of wage negotiations. Johnson was then appointed as acting plant manager, with responsibility for conducting discussions with the union. From management's point of view, he played an extremely ineffectual role in the negotiations, not attempting to "handle" or "control" the situation even when it headed toward a strike. For these reasons, Peele became particularly critical of Johnson, disparaging him as the "least strict" of all the supervisors in the plant.

2. Other industrial studies have also emphasized that succession periods often induce widespread tensions. For example, "A new boss inevitably disrupts (established informal understandings). . . . The employees feel held off and frustrated in trying to find out what is wanted and in trying to secure the customary satisfaction of their wants. Inevitably this prevents them from relying with confidence upon a new superior. . . ." *Technology and Labor,* by Elliott Dunlap Smith with Richmond Carter Nyman, Yale University Press, New Haven, p. 125. Instead of dealing only with the responses of "employees" in general to the successor, we have found it useful to distinguish the responses made by rank and file operatives, on the one hand, and the "old lieutenants" or supervisory staff, on the other.

The old lieutenants are, also, often in a position to mobilize rank and file sentiment against the successor. An illustration of this involved Ralph Byta. Byta was a neighbor of Doug and had been induced by him to come to work at the plant. Doug had promised Byta quick advancement which, because of Doug's sudden death, did not materialize.

About four months after Peele's arrival, Byta was elected president of the plant's union. Byta's new position was now much more invulnerable than those of the other old lieutenants who held supervisory offices. He could not be replaced or fired, but had to be "dealt with." As Byta stated with disarming frankness:

> The good men know that a union's the best way to get ahead. You can't walk into the Company and ask them for a raise yourself. It's different, though, if you represent 150 men. *Then, too, if the Company sees you're a leader—and the Company sees it!—well, maybe you can get yourself a raise.*

Nor was Byta's expectation a fanciful one; it had solid justification in the Company's previous actions. As a member of the main-office staff explained:

> Some of our foremen are ex-union presidents. . . . The union can pick out a good man for president. If you want a good man, pick the president of the union. If you have good morale, the men elect responsible people to union leadership.

When first elected, Byta played the role of a militant and was characterized by management as "bitter." Some months following his election Peele had a "man to man" talk with him, after which Byta was viewed by management as much more "reasonable." Byta's case, then, is another example of the resistance of the old lieutenants to the successor. For his part, Peele quickly detected this mounting resistance. As he put it:

> Every foreman had set ways. When I wanted to make some changes (in procedure), the supervisors told me, "Doug used to do this and that." I didn't make many changes and I'm satisfied with the changes I've made. The foremen are getting smoothed off now.

Peele needed to bring the resisting old lieutenants "into line" in some way; it is partly for this reason that the successor's old friends cease to be a source of embarrassment to him and become, instead, a reserve of possible allies. For it is among them that he first looks for loyal and willing subordinates with whom he can replace the intractable old lieutenants. If he fulfills his friends' claims, he can now justify this as a means of securing personnel enabling him to satisfy top management's demands for heightened efficiency.

The Workers' Resistance

The old lieutenants' resistance finds its counterpart among rank and file operatives, when the successor's new measures are put into effect. As the discussion of the "Rebecca Myth" will indicate later, the operatives resist because they resent the dissolution of their old prerogatives and the crumbling of the indulgency pattern.

Like their supervisors, the workers too may challenge and deny the legitimacy of the new manager. Whether or not this occurs depends, in part, on the specific yardsticks used to evaluate a manager's "right" to hold office. In general, though, a succession provides a suitable occasion when threatening questions about the legitimacy of a successor will be generated and entertained most readily. In a society such as ours, with its accent on achieved, rather than ascribed, status, especially in the industrial sphere, the manner in which a manager obtains and then uses his office is a crucial measure of his legitimacy. In this plant, if a manager accepted workers' traditional privileges, if he did not "act superior," workers were disposed to accept his authority as legitimate. If, moreover, the manager showed a readiness to "stand on his own feet," without obsequious dependence on the main office, he would, all the more quickly, be taken to the workers' hearts.

Influenced by his main office briefing, however, the successor prejudged some of the workers' established privileges as impediments to efficiency. He was, too, inclined to wait for the main office to resolve the plant's problems. Main office administrators recognized that Peele's dependent and procrastinating behavior was, in some measure, compelled by his status as a successor. As one of them said, "A new plant manager is more prone to lean on the top administration than a more experienced one."

Workers viewed this pattern of behavior as "unmanly." It created a situation in which they did not know where they stood, and in which they felt powerless. For example, a mechanic remarked:

> The main office reads the labor law for its own benefit and Vincent Peele doesn't dare to read it any other way. The workers get hooked in any deal like this. *We got nobody out here to give you a down-and-out yes and no. Nobody here has any say-so.*

A supervisor concurred, saying:

> Vincent is a stickler for running the plant according to the main office. Vincent says that if that's the way they want it, that's the way they get it.

These were almost exactly the words of Digger, Peele's new aide:

I'm not interested in what went on before. The way the Company wants it, that's the way it's going to be.

A union officer summed up the workers' contemptuous feelings about Peele's behavior by saying:

Peele can't do too much without getting Lakeport permission. . . . The saying around here is that Vincent can't take a s—— without calling Lakeport first. We come in and ask him for something and he tells us to *wait* while he thinks it over. Then we come back in *several days* and he has the answer. He's telephoned Lakeport in the meanwhile.

For these reasons, therefore, workers challenged Peele's legitimacy. Since any human relationship is stable to the extent that the behavior of each party is adjusted to the expectations of the other, and "rewarded" by his responses, it is clear that the succession had shaken the stability of the worker-manager relationship at its very foundations. For by virtue of his preoccupation with *top management* expectations, the successor acted with little regard for the expectations of the *workers in his plant*. Since the successor primarily sought the approval of the main office, the workers' ability to "control" him and influence their relationship was impaired. If, in effect, the successor would not accept the workers' approval as "legal tender," it became necessary for them to buy what they wanted from him, namely the restoration of the indulgency pattern, by minting a more compelling coin, disapproval and resistance.

The Rebecca Myth

A common indication of the degree and source of workers' resistance to a new manager is the prevalence of what may be called the "Rebecca Myth." Some years ago Daphne DuMaurier wrote a novel about a young woman who married a widower, only to be plagued by the memory of his first wife, Rebecca, whose virtues were still widely extolled. One may suspect that many a past plant manager is, to some extent, idealized by the workers, even if disliked while present.

Bill Day, for example, had made many complimentary remarks about Old Doug, but another supervisor who had overheard him, said sourly:

Sure, that's today. But you should have heard Day talk when Doug was *here*. My wife used to know his, and the things Day's wife used to say were plenty.

Day's idealized image of Doug was typical of many; for the workers' reminiscences about the regime of "Old Doug" were scarcely less than a modern version of "Paradise Lost." [3]

3. In another connection the Lynds have commented on this phenomenon. "Middletown is wont to invoke old leaders against new leaders who threaten to leave the

Though the world of mythology has a weakness for heroes all shining, and villains all fearsome, nonetheless, even myths are instructive things. For the many-threaded stereotypes of Doug and Peele, which the workers wove, reveal the sharp impact which the successor's policies had upon them.

Almost to a man, workers in the plant were in the spell of a backward-looking reverie. They overflowed with stories which highlighted the differences between the two managers, the leniency of Doug and the strictness of Peele. One tale contrasted the methods which Peele and Doug used to handle the problem of absenteeism. In the words of one worker:

> Among other things, Vincent is cracking down on absenteeism. He really lays the law down on this issue. Usually there are some who take off after payday for a day or so; mostly among the miners. But Vincent doesn't stand for it anymore. Doug used to go right out and get the men. It was funny. If a man or a couple of men were out, the foremen called Doug about it. He would hop into his car, drive down to their house and tell the men that he needed them. And nine times out of ten, they would go back with him. Vincent doesn't stand for it, and he has let it be known that any flagrant violations will mean that the man gets his notice.

An edge man complained about Peele's method of "checking up" on workers:

> Some of the men were saying that he was snooping around at three in the morning, but what probably happened was that he broke up a crap game. . . . Old Doug never used to come around much and when he did, you could just see him puffing to get back to the office.

"Peele's the opposite of Doug," said a laborer.

> He's always around checking on the men and standing over them. As long as production was going out Doug didn't stand over them. Peele is *always around* as though *he doesn't have faith* in the men like Doug.

Peele's impersonal attitudes were widely thought to be inappropriate. An electrician put it this way:

> When Doug was here, it was like one big happy family. Peele is *all business.*

A car operator in the mine adds:

> Doug was a little more *intimate* with his men. Peele is a little stricter.

'safe and tried middle of the road.' " Robert S. Lynd and Helen M. Lynd, *Middletown in Transition,* New York, 1937; cf., W. Lloyd Warner and J. O. Low, *The Social System of the Modern Factory,* New Haven, 1947, for a pithy account of the functioning of the Rebecca Myth during a strike.

In other words, Peele's withdrawal from informal interaction with the workers was experienced as a deprivation. A foreman, fumbling for words, explains:

> I don't mean that Vincent wouldn't stop and pass the time of day with a man in the shop, if they should happen to meet. But it was different with Doug. All the men liked Doug, but most of them don't get very *close* to Vincent.

A car trimmer in the mine also said:

> Doug was more friendly. Every time he'd see me he'd say, 'Hi'ya, Jack.' Doug was more friendly than Peele.

"I'll give you an illustration about the difference between Doug and Peele," said another worker:

> When Doug was here, all you had to say to Doug was, "Say, Doug, I need some board for the house." "Take a truck or a box car and fill 'er up," he would say. "But git it the hell out of here." With Peele, you have to pay for any board you take.

Nor did the men feel that Peele gave them a "second chance." Even one of the mine foremen recognized this:

> Doug and Vincent just had entirely different ways. Doug always gave the men more of a chance in the plant. If he had any problems he wanted straightened out, he would go down to the mine and ask them what they thought about it. . . . He wouldn't go directly to the foremen like Vincent does . . . Vincent backs up the foremen, doesn't deal with the men.

A catalogue of Doug's virtues reads as follows: Never came around much; "ran the plant by phone"; gave the workers free board; related to everyone in a friendly and personal way; didn't punish men for their absences; but he was especially appreciated, perhaps, because he "knew how to handle the front office." The men noticed that he had entertained and had been on "drinking terms" with the president of the Company. They chuckled over stories that Doug used his deafness as a cover-up, pretending he couldn't hear things, when he did not want to take the main office's advice.

The men saw that Peele, by contrast, was "nervous" in his dealings with the Lakeport office; they felt he was stingy, coldly impersonal or "businesslike," and much too strict about the rules.

This, then, was the content of the "Rebecca Myth" at the Oscar Center Plant. The myth seems to have served as a means of demonstrating that Doug had accepted the workers' criteria of a "good plant" and of expressing the grievances which Peele's behavior had aroused. Since, as seen earlier, so many of the workers' standards of a good plant were of dubious validity, it would not be easy to complain openly of their violation. The myth of Old Doug was an effort to legitimate the indulgency pattern; by transforming Peele's attack on the indulgency pattern into an attack on Old Doug, the workers' grievances could be given voice. The issue need no longer be "This is what *we* want"; it could be stated, "Old Doug did thus and so, and he was a good man."

The "Rebecca Myth" also had bearing on the bureaucratic system which was developing in the plant. As shown, the very things for which Doug was extolled were his informality, his lack of emphasis on formal hierarchy and status, his laxness with the rules, his direct interaction with the workers. These, typically, are traits which are the antithesis of bureaucratic administration. The one unfriendly comment heard about Doug came from a mechanic who remarked:

> Doug used to say that any fellow was a mechanic to some extent . . . and he didn't want maintenance to come in on a thing until the men had tried to fix it. . . .

This, though, only reinforces the picture; for Doug's rejection of distinctly separated and limited spheres of competence also violates bureaucratic principles of organization. On the other hand, the nicest compliments heard about Peele were that he "comes to the point" and was "businesslike"—in other words, that he behaved with bureaucratic impersonality.

"Sits not so easy on me"

The new manager was caught in a tangle of interrelated problems: (1) Implementation of the efficiency goals set for him by top management and which he himself accepted. (2) As a necessary condition for solution of this first problem, he needed to control or eliminate the resistance to his plans by the "old lieutenants"; in Peele's words, "straightening out shirkers." (3) As another condition for successful solution of the first problem, he needed to handle the resistance developing among rank-and-file workers. (4) Finally, Peele experienced a problem, more accurately, perhaps, a diffuse "tension," on a totally different, a psychological, level. This was the necessity to cope with his mounting anxiety, which, situationally aroused by the definition of his succession as a "test," was exacerbated by the resistance he met.

Broadly speaking, the successor had two major avenues of solution available to him: (a) He could act upon and through the informal system of relations. (b) He could utilize the formal system of organization in the plant. Stated differently, Peele could attempt to solve his problems and ease his tensions either by drawing upon his resources as a "person," or by bringing into operation the authority invested in his status as plant manager.

To consider the first tactic, the utilization of informal relations in the plant: Peele could have attempted to mobilize informal solidarity and group sentiment and harness them to his goals. Such an approach might be exemplified by the appeal, "Come on, men, let's all pitch in and do a job!" He could offer his friendship to the men, or at least pretend to,[4] hoping that in return the workers would support his program. Peele did, for example, take pains to contact the men. "I talk with them," he explained, "I congratulate them about births and things like that, *if I can only get an inkling of it. Personal touches here and there help.*"

But in this case, mobilization of the informal system was a difficult, if not impossible, task for several reasons:

1. The very program for which Peele sought to enlist the aid of informal relations by his "personal touches" was a program that violated the workers' informal sentiments. He could not very well use the informal system to uproot customs that it was organized to express and defend.

Informal solidarity premises a greater consensus of ends and sentiments than existed. Because of his role as a successor, Peele was particularly concerned with cutting costs and raising productivity. The workers, though, were much less interested in these ends and were more concerned about defending the old indulgency pattern. Peele was oriented to the future and indifferent to the past; he symbolized the initiation of new and better ways. The workers, however, stood for the preservation of the old and time-honored paths. It is difficult to maintain, and especially to create, informal solidarity in pursuit of ends which are so differently valued by group members.

2. Even if a successor is wise to the ways of manipulation and pretended friendship, he is tongue-tied by his sheer *ignorance*. As Peele indicated, in his last comment above, his efforts to be friendly with the men were snarled by his inability to get "an inkling" of the things which personally concerned them. Successful manipulation of the informal network requires knowledge of the intimate events and sentiments which they communicate. Peele, though, was a successor knowing little of the subtle, but all too concrete, arrangements and understandings comprising the plant's informal system; because he was ignorant of the magic words of condolence and congratulation, the doors to the informal system remained unyielding. In fact, he even had grave difficulties with the informal group nearest his own level, the "old lieutenants."

The new manager, therefore, found that he had no social "connective tissue," that is, no informal social relations, between himself and the lower echelons. As he became more isolated at this point, he was increasingly

4. This, in brief, is Robert K. Merton's concept of "pseudo-gemeinschaft." That is, "the feigning of personal concern with the other fellow in order to manipulate him the better." *Mass Persuasion,* by Robert K. Merton with the assistance of Marjorie Fiske and Alberta Curtis, Harper and Bros., New York, 1946, p. 142.

aware of his own inadequate supply of news and information. A communication problem, to be considered in the next chapter, is added to those he already had.

The Successor's Defenses

These cumulated pressures channeled Peele's anxiety, focusing it into a suspicion of what was happening down below. One worker assessed the situation acutely.

> When Doug was here, it was all like one big happy family. . . . Why, Doug could *get on the phone,* call up the foremen and have the situation well in hand. *Peele has to come around and make sure things are all right.* Maybe that's why he's bringing in his own men.

These remarks suggest that "strategic replacement" served to bridge the communication gap between Peele and the rest of the plant and, thereby, to alleviate his own suspicions and anxieties. They also indicate another mechanism used to mend poor upward communications; Peele goes out and "sees for himself," and engages in "close supervision." [5]

Close Supervision

Peele's practice of flitting around the plant released a vicious cycle which only intensified his problems; for the men resented his continual presence, feeling it to be an expression of distrust. A sample worker stated this succinctly:

> Doug *trusted* his men to do a job. Vincent doesn't. Doug didn't come around so much. He *relied* on the men.

Close supervision, which served as a substitute for informal upward communication, violated workers' beliefs that they should be little checked upon, and resulted in even greater exclusion of the successor from the informal system and its communication networks. Mere visitations to the plant, though, did little to dissolve Peele's tensions. He was well aware that the men modified their behavior upon his approach. Peele, therefore, soon took to showing up at what he hoped would be unexpected times and places. In a mechanic's words:

> Peele is like a mouse in a hole. You don't know when he will pop out.

But Peele could not be truly ubiquitous; try as he might, he could not be everywhere at once personally checking up on everyone. He was

5. This term is borrowed from Daniel Katz and Robert L. Kahn, "Human Organization and Worker Motivation," in *Industrial Productivity,* edited by L. Reed Tripp, Industrial Relations Research Association, 1951.

compelled, therefore, to resort to methods more congruent with his role. Although as a successor he had no secure position in the system of informal relations and communications, and could not infuse it with his goals, he still had unimpaired use of his official powers as plant manager. He could, therefore, make changes in the formal organization of the plant and move about, or remove, certain of the key personnel.

Strategic Replacements

Peele could deal with the problem of the resistant "old lieutenants" in a limited number of ways: (1) He might get rid of the "old lieutenants" and replace them with his own; (2) he could open up new or additional supervisory posts which he could staff, thereby affecting the "balance of power" among the middle managers; or (3) he might decide to "pay off" the inherited obligations to the "old lieutenants."

These three solutions are not equally useful to the successor, nor are they all equally available to him. If, for example, the new manager employs the last tactic, the "old lieutenants" may simply view this as "squaring accounts." The "old lieutenants" may feel that the successor has only given them something which they had long since earned and they, therefore, may believe they owe him nothing in return.

Thus, when Peele did promote some of the older men in the plant to new supervisory positions, they were not especially appreciative. "They don't feel very good about it," said a supervisor:

> You see they have felt that *their having worked here for a long time should have earned them promotions anyhow.* . . . They feel that they are being given the jobs now only because there are no experienced men left to take them. They are taking them all right, but there is still that tongue-in-cheek feeling against the higher-ups.

This "ungrateful" reaction, among men who feel entitled to their rewards, directs the successor away from choosing replacements who would be legitimate, and hence acceptable, supervisors, in terms of the plant workers' values. By the very nature of the case, the legitimate replacements will often feel that they have merely been given their due, and will not tend to respond as the new manager hopes.

The successor finds himself constrained, therefore, to choose as replacements those whose appointment is more likely to make the workers resentful. The pressures are such that he inclines toward replacements either from among plant workers whose claim to advancement is not strongly legitimate, or else from among men he has known outside the plant. As a result, he tends to handle his problems by replacing the recalcitrant supervisors or by opening up new supervisory positions.

The successor's ability to create new positions is, however, definitely limited. As a new manager he is especially hesitant to initiate anything that would require main office approval, particularly if it entails increased costs. Yet this is involved in opening up new supervisory positions.

An escape from the above difficulty is possible if new equipment and machinery are being installed in the plant. The simultaneous introduction of new machinery and new managers probably occurs with a frequency greater than that due solely to chance.[6]

In this plant, about a million and a half dollars worth of new equipment was being installed in the board building, at just this time. With the anticipated increase in scope and speed of operations, a case was made out, in pure efficiency terms, to expand the supervisory staff. For example, it was pointed out that the increased speed of the new machines made for greater waste if a breakdown occurred, and thus more supervisors were needed to prevent this. The addition of "know-how" and "do-how" foremen was justified in this way.

It is not being suggested that the successor merely "rationalized" his status-generated needs for additional supervisors in terms made convenient by the technological innovations.[7] Regardless of the new manager's motives for requesting additional supervisors, the introduction of new machinery did allow for the expansion of the supervisory staff, which consequently helped the successor to handle the "old lieutenants."

The gains which accrue to the successor, if he solves the problem of the "old lieutenants" by replacing them with new ones, are now clear. No budgetary increase is required and, in consequence, main office sanction, if needed at all, is less complicated. It is hard for the main office to judge from its distance whether or not a man at a local plant deserves to be fired; it is comparatively easy for them to estimate whether an increased dollar outlay is justified. A decision about the former problem is, for this reason, more likely to be left to the discretion of the plant manager. Thus replacement of the old with new supers, as a method of handling the "old lieutenants," is a more reliable and controllable solution for the successor.

Nor need he replace the entire group of "old lieutenants," even if this were feasible; for by firing some he creates anxiety among those who remain and extracts conformity from them. As Peele noted when asked:

6. This is partially supported by the findings of Smith and Nyman, *ibid.* For example, "An extensive labor-saving installation commonly involves the elimination of some unfit employees and even executives" (p. 68). In this case Peele's succession was due to Doug's death; it just so happened, however, that new machinery was also introduced shortly prior to Doug's death and heightened main-office concern with efficiency, in order to make the new machinery pay.
7. The role of technological and market pressures in inducing tensions will be examined in *Wildcat Strike,* Yellow Springs, Ohio: Antioch Press, 1954.

You had some difficulty with the supervisors . . . ?
Yes, I had some trouble straightening out shirkers. Some of them thought they were going to get fired. *I could work on these guys.* But others, who didn't expect to get fired, were. Each foreman is just a little bit *on edge* now. They don't know whether they're doing right. A new plant manager is going to make some changes—to suit my own way. I had to watch them. I made those changes.

In short, the use of replacements enables the successor to accomplish several things: (1) He gets rid of some of those who were "shirking"; (2) he silences others and forces acquiescence from them, and (3) he can create new lieutenants, from among those he brings up, who will be grateful and loyal to him. This can be seen from an interview with one of Peele's replacements:

Who was the plant manager at the time you began working here?
Why, Fier was top man then and after him Farr, Doug Godfrey, and now Vincent.
How would you compare the four men as bosses?
They were all good men if you did the job.
Would you say any was a little more strict than the other?
Oh, maybe a little, one way or the other, but you expect that. Vincent comes around more than Godfrey did, but none of them was really strict.
How would you say the men generally felt about them?
I don't think there was any feelings against any of them. I've never heard a word against Vincent.
Would you say then that the men feel the same way about Vincent as they did about Doug?
I think that maybe the men think a little *more* of Vincent because he really sticks up for the men, and I don't mean only the foremen, but all the men.

Unlike his references to the preceding plant managers, this supervisor called Peele by his first name; he was reluctant to give voice to the near-universal criticisms of Peele's strictness; he imagined that Peele was better liked than Doug. Evidently his appointment to a supervisory position by the successor made him a staunch adherent of the new manager.[8]

8. The connection between succession and strategic replacements has not gone unnoticed by other industrial sociologists. There has, however, been a tendency to explain strategic replacements primarily as a consequence of efficiency needs and the technical inadequacy of the old supervisors. For example: "The new manager did all in his power to develop sufficient ability in the supervisory force to measure up to the new requirements. But as these requirements were raised, first one supervisor then another proved incapable of being developed to meet them. . . . (Therefore) in the long run nearly the entire original staff was dismissed. . . ." Smith and Nyman, *ibid.,* p. 128. This analysis omits consideration of two things which we have held focal: (1) The function of strategic replacements in resolving the new manager's status problems, which are generated by his role as a *successor;* (2) the existence of certain elements in the situation which constrain the successor to meet his problems by dismissing the old supervisors, rather than utilizing other problem solu-

The New Informal Group

In obligating new lieutenants to himself, through the use of strategic replacements, the successor establishes extra-formal ties with them which he can draw upon to implement his goals. In effect, strategic replacement enables the new manager to form a new informal social circle, which revolves about himself and strengthens his status. It provides him with a new two-way communication network; on the one hand, carrying up news and information that the formal channels exclude; on the other hand, carrying down the meaning or "spirit" of the successor's policies and orders.[9] Beyond its purely communication functions, the new informal group also enables the successor to control the plant more fully; for the new lieutenants can be depended on to enforce the new manager's changes and punish deviations from them.

Finally, the new informal group also served to ease Peele's personal anxieties. A new manager commonly becomes very friendly with one of his strategic replacements. This became Digger's role and, soon after his arrival, he was known to be Pcele's confidant. Digger and Peele's relationship was widely resented in the plant and became one of the men's most outspoken grievances. Disturbed by Peele's failure to establish friendly connections with them, the workers, with more than a touch of envy, complained: "Digger and Peele are as thick as thieves."

Digger provided Peele with an opportunity to unburden himself at a time when few men wanted to have anything to do with him. Digger gave Peele support and approval when most of those near to him "hated his guts." In this way, Digger played an important cathartic function for Peele, serving to ease his fears and anxieties. Digger helped Peele, but at the cost of heightening the workers' awareness of Peele's impersonal and unfriendly behavior toward them. Moreover, since he felt confident of Peele's favor, Digger could behave in an "arrogant" manner, leading the workers to complain that "he acted as if he owned the plant." This, in turn, only swelled the workers' hostility toward Peele.

---

tions. Smith and Nyman recognize that "to attempt to meet the situation by replacement is perilous. Extensive or unjust discharges cause the remaining management and employee body to fear the changes and in secret to work against it" (ibid., p. 129). If this is typically or at least frequently the case, as Smith and Nyman suggest, then strategic replacements frustrate the intended improvement of efficiency. We must, therefore, attempt to account for the repeated coincidence of succession and strategic replacements in terms other than the utilitarian emphasis on efficiency consequences.

9. This last point deserves emphasis, for, no matter how model a bureaucratic structure the successor may finally create, its formal rules will be enmeshed in and in need of reinforcement by a framework of supporting sentiments and attitudes. Cf., Reinhard Bendix, "Bureaucracy: The Problem and Its Setting," American Sociological Review, Oct., 1947, for a discussion of this point.

Succession and Bureaucracy

Disposing of the "old lieutenants" takes time. If the new manager is at all sensitive to what is going on, he does not wish to be accused of failing to give the "old lieutenants" a "chance," nor of seeking to install his favorites with indecent haste. He has to spend some time looking for possible allies and lining up replacements. In the meanwhile, the breakdown of upward communications to the new manager grows more acute. It is, in part, as an outgrowth of this crisis that the successor elaborates the system of "paper reports," the better to "keep his finger on things," and to check up on the unreliable "old lieutenants."

At this time, he also began to introduce and emphasize adherence to the "rules." Barred from effective use of the informal system of controls, the successor was compelled to rely more heavily upon the formal system. As an observant main office executive noticed: "Peele will follow along in *organizational* lines, while Doug handled things on a *personal* basis." The comments of the Company's labor relations director provide a clue about the role of succession in this change:

> *New* managers always tend to rely more on the rules. They call us up and ask us if we have lists of rules which they can use. *They are unsure of themselves and they need something to lean on.* After they're on the job somewhat longer they're less worried about the rules.

These remarks tend to reinforce the contention that there is a close connection between succession and a surge of bureaucratic development, particularly in the direction of formal rules.

To appreciate why this is so, it is necessary to consider another of the dilemmas in which the successor finds himself. It has been shown that the new manager's role disposes him to a great dependence on the main office. Yet his position is such that he must attempt to conceal this dependence, and attempt to act with a semblance of autonomy.

Some of the latter pressures stem from workers' feeling that a manager should "stand on his own feet." The main office staff, too, is ambivalent about the successor's dependence on them. The main office prefers a manager who will heed its advice on matters of major policy; but within these limits they want a manager to be independent. "We have about twenty-five plants to handle," explained a Lakeport administrator. "We just can't spend all of our time on any one plant." Nor does the main office especially esteem a manager who "doesn't talk back once in a while."

Thus the new manager must, somehow, seek techniques whereby he can be sure that his decisions are in conformity with main-office expectations; techniques which will, at the same time, allow him to make these decisions with a minimum of contact with main office people, quickly, and with the appearance of independence. These appear, in part, to be the specific functions performed by the rules which the successor seeks from his main office. Once he has the rules, he need no longer telephone it about every problem that arises in the plant. The rules, further, provide a framework which he can use to justify his decisions should the main office ever examine or challenge them.

Nor are the rules useful only in the successor's dealings with the main office; they also help to make his behavior a bit more palatable to people in the plant. When Peele did something which he knew the workers would not like, he often justified it as due to main office requirements. The workers would then criticize the main office for the new pattern, blaming Peele only because he "didn't have guts enough to fight back." Thus one worker commented:

> . . . it has always been the plant policy not to have men who are relations, especially father-and-son teams. But while Doug was here we did that quite a bit. He was pretty easygoing on that. But now that Vincent is here, it isn't being done.
> *Why do you suppose that this is so?*
> Vincent is more strict on conforming to Company rules than Doug was.

In other words, Peele was seen as bringing the plant into line with established Company rules. Some of the aggression that would have been directed at Peele was thereby deflected onto the main office. In general, the Lakeport office was aware of this and accepted it as a way of relaxing relationships between plant workers and local management, encouraging the latter to "put the blame on us."

Like all other solutions which Peele adopted to handle the problems of his succession, the development of formal rules also had an anxiety-allaying function. The rules define the new situation into which the successor has entered, allowing him to make decisions with a minimum of uncertainty and personal responsibility. Moreover, there is reason to believe that the rules had, more specifically, a guilt-relieving role for Peele. Some of the things which Peele had done could not be easily condoned, even by himself. His failure to give Day a warning before he demoted him, or an explanation afterwards, involved the infraction of values which Peele had never deliberately set out to violate, and to which he was still oriented. The belief that he was only doing what he must, softened Peele's doubts about his own behavior. As he remarked:

> Some of the men probably think I'm a mean cuss, but I've got to follow our Company policy like everyone else. If I don't, someone else will.

The Rate of Succession

The Oscar Center plant had about six managers from the time of its inception, an average of about one for every four years of its existence.

These changes suggest the importance of another specific dimension of succession, the rate of turnover among plant managers. In a case study such as this, however, since it extends over only a small period in the plant's lifetime, it is impossible to do more than allude to the possible significance of varying rates of succession and their effects on patterns of administration.

Even a cursory contrast with previous societies suggests that the rate of succession in the modern factory is "high." In part, this high rate of succession, particularly in the pinnacles of authority, is made possible by the development of the corporative form.[10] In fact, the corporation was, in some measure, deliberately designed to enable business organizations to persist beyond the life of their founders.

Where authority may have to be transferred frequently, personalized loyalties to those in office may impede succession, as noted in the discussion of the "Rebecca Myth." Contrariwise, it is easier to transfer authority when workers' loyalties are attached to the office, and the rules of which it is composed, rather than to the person who occupies the position. Bureaucratization is, therefore, functional to a group subjected to an institutionally compelled "high" rate of succession while, in turn, a high rate of succession operates as a selecting mechanism sifting out or disposing to bureaucratic modes of organization.[11]

As this was a plant with a history of some twenty-five years, it was not totally lacking in bureaucratic procedures. Nor was Peele devoid of bureaucratic intentions prior to his arrival. On the contrary, the plant had experienced a degree of bureaucratization before Peele came. Moreover, the new manager was oriented to values which might, in any event, have led him in a bureaucratic direction, regardless of the circumstances of his succession.

The role of a successor, however, confronted Peele with distinctive

10. It is interesting to note that the problem of succession in strategic offices appears to be becoming a matter of conscious and public interest among business executives. Apparently, though, pressures are being exerted to define this problem primarily in terms of its pecuniary consequences, rather than in its impact on the organization as a social system. Thus in the November, 1949, *Fortune,* The Mutual Benefit Life Insurance Company had the following advertisement:
"Am I really that old?" was my first thought.
"Jim, you're too valuable to lose. The firm's going to insure your life. . . ."
"Don't let these gray hairs fool you, J. D.," I quipped half-heartedly.
"They don't, Jim," he reassured me. "But this is a special kind of insurance that's going to do both of us a lot of good. . . . This plan protects our company against the loss of valuable key men like yourself. It provides cash to attract a capable replacement, and it cushions our possible losses while he's breaking in."
11. Some of John Commons' writings suggest the connection between the rate of succession and rules on a more general level; he spoke, for example, of the "set of working rules which keep on working regardless of the incoming and outgoing of individuals." *The Legal Foundations of Capitalism,* Macmillan Co., 1932, New York, p. 135.

problems. He had to solve these problems if he wished to hold his job as manager. In the process of solving them, the successor was compelled to use bureaucratic methods. Peele intensified bureaucracy not merely because he wanted to, not necessarily because he liked bureaucracy, nor because he valued it above other techniques, but also because he was constrained to do so by the tensions of his succession.

Underlying Assumptions

The assumptions underlying the analysis thus far can be summarized as follows: Bureaucratic behavior was conceived of as a problem-solving type of social action. This led to an inquiry about the nature of these problems; how were they conceived or formulated? We then had to specify who formulated these problems; that is, what was this person's status, and how did his status influence his formulation of problems and choice of problem-solutions?

Since groups possess forms of stratification, it cannot be tacitly assumed that all individuals, or all positions in the system of stratification, exert equal influence on those decisions from which bureaucratization emerges as planned or unanticipated consequence. Pedestrian as this point is, Weber's analysis of bureaucracy largely ignores it. But bureaucratic behavior in a factory must either be initiated by the manager, or at least finally ratified by him or his superiors. What has here been essayed is an analysis of some institutionally derived pressures, convergent on the position of a new plant manager, which made him accept and initiate bureaucratic patterns.

Thus the relevance of *status*-generated tensions and perspectives is accentuated. Instead of assuming that bureaucracy emerged in direct response to threats to the *organization as a homogeneous whole,* the analysis proceeded from a different premise; namely, that the adaptation of an organization to a threat is mediated and shaped by powerful individuals. It was assumed, further, that to the degree these powerful individuals perceived the "needs" of the organization, they became "problems" which were molded in specific ways by status tensions. As a result, the adaptive efforts which are made may be divergent from the "needs" of the organization as a whole.

Peele's bureaucratic innovations cannot be understood in terms of their contribution to the stability of the plant as a whole. Nor were "strategic replacements" or "close supervision" mechanisms that brought the entire plant into equilibrium. At the very least, each of these three defense mechanisms did as much to disturb, as to defend, the integration of the plant. These paradoxical consequences were explained by taking into account the dilemmas and tensions engendered by the peculiar role of a successor.

Growing Points

If Peele's bureaucratic behavior, especially his development of bureaucratic rules, is usefully viewed as a problem-solution, what was the nature of the problem as he perceived it? A brief recapitulation of the plant situation, as Peele first came upon it, will reveal this.

When he arrived, Peele found that some workers preferred to punch in early and accumulate a little overtime, or punch out early on special occasions. He discovered that the miners believed that a certain amount of absenteeism was permissible, and, in fact, was a customary way of showing that "down here we are our own bosses." The resistance to Peele grew wider and more acute when he attempted to eliminate these practices.

As his "mouse-in-the-hole" behavior attests, Peele began to lose "faith" in workers and middle management, commencing to "check up" closely on both groups. He did not "trust" his subordinates, and he doubted whether they would perform their roles in accordance with his expectations. In fact, as he said explicitly of the "old lieutenants," they were "shirkers."

So much, for the present, concerning the orientation and outlook of those who initiate or ratify bureaucratic measures. Aside from this point of departure, analysis of the succession process also brought into view certain aspects of the organizational *situation* out of which the bureaucratic patterns grew. These, too, provide growing points for subsequent expansion, indicating a range of specific variables important in the later discussion.

From the standpoint of their effects on the plant as a social system, the following seem to be the most crucial tension-provoking features of the succession situation:

1. *Interaction of bearers of different values.* The successor was oriented to rational, efficiency-enhancing values, while workers were oriented mainly to the traditional, custom-honored sentiments of the indulgency pattern. The successor's outlook was structured by the main office's emphasis on rational administration; thus there was a value-cleavage emerging along status lines, that is, between top managers and the workers.

2. *Ambiguous canons of legitimacy.* Whether or not the expectations held by workers were legitimate, or were properly applicable to the plant situation, was uncertain even in the workers' view. They were not so sure that their expectations were a solid and justifiable basis for action.

3. *Unrequited expectations.* The workers expected the new manager to conform to the indulgency pattern, even though unsure that this expecta-

tion was legitimate. The successor, though, was more concerned about his superiors' efficiency-centered expectations and, therefore, was not responsive to subordinates.

4. *Decline of informal interaction across status lines.* The new manager had fewer personal ties with workers.

5. *Hiatus in the chain of command.* The successor could not rely upon the "old lieutenants" in supervisory positions to support and enforce his new policies.

6. *Shortcircuited communications.* Because of the inaccessibility of the informal system to the successor, as well as the hiatus in the chain of command, the new manager's sources of information were meager.

7. *Challenge to managerial legitimacy.* Both the "old lieutenants" and the rank and file of workers doubted the legitimacy of the successor. They did not merely resist him because they thought they could get away with it, that is, on purely expedient grounds, but because they felt that he was not a "proper" manager and did not *deserve* to be supported.

8. *Degeneration of motives for obedience.* Both supervisors and workers had fewer sentiments of loyalty to Peele than they had to Doug. They resisted his program of changes and the policies he formulated.

The Underlife of a Public Institution: A Study of Ways of Making Out in a Mental Hospital

Erving Goffman

An "instrumental formal organization" may be defined as a system of purposely coordinated activities designed to produce some overall explicit ends. The intended product may be material artifacts, services, decisions, or information, and may be distributed among the participants in a great variety of ways. I will be mainly concerned with those formal organizations that are lodged within the confines of a single building or complex of adjacent buildings, referring to such a walled-in unit, for convenience, as a social establishment, institution, or organization.

Some qualifications might be suggested to my traditional approach. Formal organizations may have a multiplicity of conflicting official goals, each with its own special adherents, and some doubt as to which faction is to be the spokesman for the organization. Further, while a goal like cost reduction or asepsis can be objectively applied as a detailed standard for many of the minor activities occurring within some organizations, other establishments, such as some clubs and community recreation centers, do not have the kind of goals that provide a clear-cut standard against which to examine details of life within the establishment. In still other formal organizations the official goal may be of small importance, the main issue being the conservation or survival of the organization itself. Finally, physical boundaries such as walls may in the last analysis be an incidental feature of organizations, not an analytical one.[1]

Walled-in organizations have a characteristic they share with few other social entities: part of the individual's obligation is to be *visibly* engaged at appropriate times in the activity of the organization, which entails a mobilization of attention and muscular effort, a bending of oneself to the

SOURCE: *Asylums* (Garden City, N.Y.: Doubleday, 1961), pp. 175–80, 188–93, 201–203, 207–212, 227–30, 248–51, 298–300, 308–312, 318–20.
1. Amitai Etzioni has suggested this argument in personal conversation.

activity at hand. This obligatory engrossment in the activity of the organization tends to be taken as a symbol both of one's commitment and one's attachment, and, behind this, of one's acceptance of the implications of participation for a definition of one's nature. Any study, then, of how individuals adapt to being identified and defined is likely to focus on how they deal with exhibiting engrossment in organizational activities.

An instrumental formal organization survives by being able to call forth usable contributions of activity from its members; stipulated means must be employed, stipulated ends must be achieved. However, as Chester Barnard has suggested, an organization, acting through its management, must recognize limits upon the degree to which a member can be relied upon to contribute suitable activity.[2] The human vessel is defined as notoriously weak; compromises must be made, consideration must be shown, protective measures must be taken. The particular way in which these limitations to the use of participants are formulated in a given culture would seem to be a very important characteristic of it.[3]

Our Anglo-American imagery for delineating these limits appears to be something like the following, as expressed from the point of view taken here, which identifies an organization with its managers.

First, the participant is granted certain "standards of welfare" while he is engaged in the activity of the organization, these being above the minimum required to keep the human organism going. Standards here pertain to: levels of comfort, health, and safety; limits on the kind and amount of effort required; consideration for the member's participation in other organizations that have a legitimate claim upon him; rights regarding retirement and vacations; expression of grievances and even legal review; and, at least at the level of public pronouncements, a right to dignity, self-expression, and opportunities for creativity.[4] These standards of welfare clearly acknowledge that a human being is something more than just a member of the particular organization.

Second, the imagery of our society suggests that the member of an organization may voluntarily cooperate because of "joint values" through which the interests of the organization and the individual member coalesce, intrinsically as well as strategically. In some cases it is presumably the individual who identifies himself with the organization's goals and fate, as when someone takes personal pride in his school or place of work. In other

2. Chester Barnard, *The Functions of the Executive* (Cambridge: Harvard University Press, 1947), ch. xi, "The Economy of Incentives."
3. For economic institutions this has recently been summarized by Talcott Parsons and Neil J. Smelser, *Economy and Society* (New York: The Free Press, 1956), ch. iii, "The Institutional Structure of the Economy." A detailed treatment regarding industrial organizations may be found in Reinhard Bendix, *Work and Authority in Industry* (New York: Wiley, 1956).
4. Bendix, *op. cit.,* "Managerial Conceptions of 'The Worker,' " pp. 288–97.

cases the organization appears to become involved in the personal fate of a particular member, as when a hospital staff becomes genuinely excited over a patient's recovery. In most organizations some of both kinds of joint value serve to motivate the member.

Third, it is sometimes recognized that "incentives" may have to be provided, these being rewards or side payments that frankly appeal to the individual in his capacity as someone whose ultimate interests are not those of the organization.[5] Some of these incentives are externally relevant, being rewards that the recipient can carry off the premises and use at his own discretion without implicating other members of the organization; money payments, training, and certification are the three principal instances. Some incentives are internally relevant, being perquisites that require the organization's own stage setting for their realization; important here are increases in rank and improvement in one's allotment of institutional conveniences. Many incentives carry both types of relevance, as in the case of occupational titles such as "executive."

Finally, it is perceived that participants may be induced to cooperate by threats of punishment and penalty if they do not. These "negative sanctions" can involve an eventful decrease in usual rewards or in usual levels of welfare, but something other than mere reduction in reward seems to be involved. The notion that punishment can be an effective means of calling forth desired activity is one that requires assumptions about the nature of human nature different from those needed to account for the motivating effect of incentives. Fear of penalization seems adequate to prevent the individual from performing certain acts, or from failing to perform them; but positive rewards seem necessary if long-range, sustained, personal effort is to be obtained.

In our society, then, as presumably in some others, a formal instrumental organization does not merely use the activity of its members. The organization also delineates what are considered to be officially appropriate standards of welfare, joint values, incentives, and penalties. These conceptions expand a mere participation contract into a definition of the participant's nature or social being. These implicit images form an important element of the values which every organization sustains, regardless of the degree of its efficiency or impersonality.[6] Built right into the social arrangements of an organization, then, is a thoroughly embracing conception of

5. Our way of thinking easily distinguishes between organizational goals and payments to employees, when in fact these may coincide. It is possible to define the goal of the organization as the allocation of privately consumable rewards to its employees, the janitor's pay having the same status as an organizational goal as the stockholder's profits. See R. M. Cyert and J. G. March, "A Behavioral Theory of Organizational Objectives," in Mason Haire, ed., *Modern Organization Theory* (New York: Wiley, 1959), p. 80.
6. For a consideration of the value tasks of economic organizations, see Philip Selznick, *Leadership in Administration* (Evanston, Ill: Row, Peterson & Co., 1957).

the member—and not merely a conception of him *qua* member, but behind this a conception of him *qua* human being.[7]

We can readily see these organizational conceptions of man in those radical political movements and evangelical religious groups that stress Spartan standards of welfare and joint values that are at once intense and pervasive. Here the member is expected to place himself at the disposal of the current needs of the organization. In telling him what he should do and why he should want to do this, the organization presumably tells him all that he may be. There will be many ways of backsliding, and even where backsliding does not occur frequently, concern that it may happen may be great, clearly pointing to the question of identity and self-definition.[8]

• • •

Primary and Secondary Adjustments

A concept can now be introduced. When an individual cooperatively contributes required activity to an organization and under required conditions—in our society with the support of institutionalized standards of welfare, with the drive supplied through incentives and joint values, and with the promptings of designated penalties—he is transformed into a co-operator; he becomes the "normal," "programmed," or built-in member. He gives and gets in an appropriate spirit what has been systematically planned for, whether this entails much or little of himself. In short, he finds that he is officially asked to be no more and no less than he is prepared to be, and is obliged to dwell in a world that is in fact congenial to him. I shall speak in these circumstances of the individual having a *primary adjustment* to the organization and overlook the fact that it would be just as reasonable to speak of the organization having a primary adjustment to him.

I have constructed this clumsy term in order to get to a second one, namely, *secondary adjustments,* defining these as any habitual arrangement by which a member of an organization employs unauthorized means, or obtains unauthorized ends, or both, thus getting around the organization's assumptions as to what he should do and get and hence what he should be. Secondary adjustments represent ways in which the individual stands

7. For a case study see Alvin Gouldner, *Wildcat Strike* (London: Routledge & Kegan Paul, 1955), especially "The Indulgency Pattern," pp. 18–22, where he outlines workers' moral expectations of the organization which are not an official part of the work contract.
8. This is nicely portrayed in Isaac Rosenfeld's story, "The Party," *The Kenyon Review,* Autumn, 1947, pp. 572–607.

apart from the role and the self that were taken for granted for him by the institution. For example, it is currently assumed in America that prisoners are persons who should have library facilities, the minds of prisoners being something that can and ought to be allowed to profit from reading. Given this legitimate library activity, we can anticipate Donald Clemmer's finding that prisoners often order books not for self-edification but to impress the parole board, give trouble to the librarian, or merely receive a parcel.[9]

There are sociological terms that refer to secondary adjustments, but these also refer to other things. The term "informal" might be used, except that an organization can formally provide a time and place where members can be officially on their own, to create and enjoy recreational activity of their own choosing while exercising a behavioral style of locker-room informality: morning recess at school is an example. Informality here is part of primary adjustment. The term "unofficial" might be used, except that this concept tends to pertain only to what would ordinarily be the official part of activity in the organization, and in any case the term "unofficial" can properly be applied to those tacit understandings and uncodified activities through which the official aims of the organization can be furthered and the participants attain whatever primary adjustment is possible in the situation.[10]

I want to mention here some difficulties in using the concept of secondary adjustments. There are some secondary adjustments, such as a worker's practice of supplying his family's needs for the product he helps produce, that become so much an accepted part of the workings of an organization that they take on the character of "perquisites," combining

9. Donald Clemmer, *The Prison Community* (reissue; New York: Rinehart, 1958), p. 232.
10. In the classic Hawthorne study of informal or unofficial work groups, the main function of worker solidarity seems to have been to counter management's view of what workers ought to do and what they ought to be, in which case secondary adjustments and informal adjustments would refer to the same thing. However, later studies illustrated the fact that informal cliques at work might sustain activities perfectly compatible with, and even supportive of, the role established by management for workers. See Edward Gross, "Characteristics of Cliques in Office Organizations," *Research Studies,* State College of Washington, 19 (1951), especially p. 135; "Some Functional Consequences of Primary Controls in Formal Work Organizations," *American Sociological Review,* 28 (1953), pp. 368–73. Obviously, a choice of "substantive" rationality over "formal" rationality—the selective pursuit of some official goals over other conflicting official goals—may be exhibited by management as well as by subordinates. See, for example, Charles Page, "Bureaucracy's Other Face," *Social Forces,* 25 (1946), pp. 88–94; A. G. Frank, "Goal Ambiguity and Conflicting Standards: An Approach to the Study of Organization," *Human Organization,* 17 (1959), pp. 8–13. See also the very remarkable study by Melville Dalton, *Men Who Manage* (New York: Wiley, 1959), for example, p. 222: ". . . informal action may work for many ends: to change and preserve the organization, to protect weak individuals, punish erring ones, reward others, to recruit new personnel, and to maintain dignity of the formal, as well as, of course, to carry on power struggles, and to work for ends we would all frown on."

the qualities of being neither openly demanded nor openly questioned.[11] And some of these activities are not merely ones that are soon to be made legitimate but rather ones that must remain unofficial if they are to be effective. As Melville Dalton has shown, special capacities of a participant may have to be underwritten with rewards that no one else of his category receives. And what the courted participant may see as something he is getting away with—a secondary adjustment—may be deliberately allowed him by a conscientious official acting solely from a desire to see the over-all efficiency of the organization sustained.[12] Further, as previously suggested, there may be little agreement as to who are the spokesmen of the organization, and, where there is agreement, the spokesmen may be doubtful in their own minds as to where to draw the line between primary and secondary adjustments. For example, in many American colleges it would be considered a wrongheaded view of the nature of the student to curb too much the extracurricular "social" part of college experience. This is in line with current views as to the necessity of having "all-round" or "well-rounded" students. But there is less consensus about exactly how the student's time is to be divided between academic and extracurricular work. Similarly, it is understandable and widely accepted that some female students will meet their future husbands at college and, once married, feel it more appropriate to drop out of school than to complete work for a degree. But college deans show varying degrees of concern when a female student switches her major each year upon playing out the

11. See, for example, the discussion by Paul Jacobs, "Pottering about with the Fifth Amendment," *The Reporter*, July 12, 1956.
12. Dalton, *op. cit.,* especially ch. vii, "The Interlocking of Official and Unofficial Reward." Dalton argues (pp. 198–99) that, in industry, corresponding to a wide range of unofficial rewards there is a very wide range of unofficial services that the executive must somehow call forth from his men if the organization is to function smoothly:
> "Although informal reward ideally is given for effort and contribution beyond what is expected of a specific rank, it is also granted for many other purposes, often unexpected and formally taboo yet important for maintaining the organization and winning its ends. For example, it may be given (1) in lieu of a promotion or salary increase that could not be effected; (2) as a bonus for doing necessary but unpleasant or low-prestige things; (3) as an opiate to forget defeats in policy battles or status tiffs; (4) as a price for conciliating an irate colleague or making, in effect, a treaty with another department; (5) as a perquisite to key persons in clerical or staff groups to prevent slowdowns, and to bolster alertness against errors during critical periods; (6) as a frank supplement to a low but maximum salary; (7) for understanding and aid in the operation, and the defense, of the unofficial incentive system; (8) for great personal sacrifices. There are, of course, more subtle supports which may not be articulated but are intuitively recognized and rewarded where possible. These include: ability to maintain morale in the group or department; skill in picking and holding good subordinates; habitual tacit understanding of what superiors and colleagues expect but would not in some cases want to phrase, even unofficially; and expertness in saving the face of superiors and maintaining the dignity of the organization under adverse conditions."

field of men that the courses made accessible. Similarly, the managers of a commercial office may be clear about feeling it permissible for clerks and secretaries to select one another for personal relationships—provided that not too much working time is wasted in this way—and just as clearly disapprove of trainees who stay only long enough to check through the courting possibilities before going on to a fresh office and a new pasture. But management may be much more vague as to where between these two extremes the line is to be drawn separating the legitimate incidental use of an establishment as a convenience from illegitimately making a convenience of an institution.

Another problem associated with the distinction between primary and secondary adjustments is that these two modes of adaptation do not exhaust the possibilities; to get a rounded picture we may have to introduce another possibility. In whatever direction management presses the participants, it is possible for the participants to show more commitment and attachment to the entity than has been asked for or, sometimes, than is desired by management. A parishioner may try to live too much in and for the church; a housewife can keep her domain too clean; a junior officer can insist on going down with the ship. I do not think we have a major social problem here, except perhaps for those inmates of jails, mental hospitals, barracks, colleges, and parental homes who decline to use their discharge; analytically, however, we must see that just as there will always be persons who are felt not to embrace sufficiently a social entity to which they belong, so we will always find at least a few who may embarrass an organization by embracing it too warmly.

Finally, as we shall see later, the official doctrine according to which an institution is run may be so little honored in practice, and a semiofficial perspective may be so firmly and fully established, that we must analyze secondary adjustments relative to this authorized-but-not-quite-official system.

•　•　•

We can begin to look at secondary adjustments—at the pratices comprising the underlife of social establishments—by noting that they occur with different frequency and in different forms according to the location of the practitioner in the hierarchy of the organization. Persons at the bottom of large organizations typically operate in drab backgrounds, against which higher-placed members realize their internal incentives, enjoying the satisfaction of receiving visible indulgences that others do not. Low-placed members tend to have less commitment and emotional attachment to the organization than higher-placed members. They have jobs, not careers. In consequence they seem more likely to make wide use of secondary adjustments. Although people toward the top of organizations are likely to be appreciably motivated by joint values, their special duties as representatives of the organization are also likely to lead to travel, entertaining, and ceremonials—that special class of secondary adjustments recently publicized in descriptions of the "expense account" round of life. Perhaps secondary adjustments are least found in the middle range of organizations. It is here, perhaps, that people most closely approach what the organization expects them to be, and it is from here that models of good conduct can be drawn for the edification and inspiration of those lower down.[13]

At the same time, of course, the character of primary adjustments will differ according to rank. Workers at the bottom may not be expected to throw themselves into the organization or "take it home" with them, but high officers are likely to have these identificatory obligations. For example, an attendant in a state mental hospital who leaves work as soon as his shift is over may be acting in a way that has been legitimated for him, expressing the nature the organization accords him; if a head of a service gives this nine-to-five impression, however, he may be considered dead wood by management—someone who is not living up to the standards of devotion expected of a real doctor. Similarly, an attendant who reads a magazine during working hours on the ward may be considered within his rights as long as no immediate duty calls him; a nurse who thus conducts herself is more likely to offend because this is "unprofessional" conduct.

The undergrowth of secondary adjustments also differs in extent according to the type of establishment.

Presumably the shorter the period of continuous time that a given category of participant spends on the premises, the more possible it will be for management to maintain a program of activity and motivation that these participants accept. Thus, in those establishments whose purpose is the sale of a minor standardized item such as cigarettes, customers will usually complete the purchase cycle without deviating very far from the role programmed for them—except, perhaps, in demanding or declining a moment's sociability. Establishments that oblige the participant to "live in" will presumably be rich in underlife, for the more time that is programmed by the organization, the less likelihood of successfully programming it.

So also in those organizations where recruitment is involuntary, we can expect that, at least initially, the recruit will not be in harmony with the self-definitions officially available for persons like himself and will therefore orient himself to unlegitimized activities.

Finally, as previously suggested, establishments that do not provide appreciable external incentives, not having made their peace with what is seen as the Adam in man, are likely to find that some external incentives are unofficially developed.

All of the conditions that are likely to promote active underlife are

13. Suggested by Paul Wallin.

present in one institution that is receiving considerable attention today: the mental hospital. In what follows I want to consider some of the main themes that occur in the secondary adjustments I recorded in a year's participant observation study of patient life in a public mental hospital of over 7000 patients, hereafter called "Central Hospital."

• • •

Sources

I turn now to consider the sources of materials that patients employ in their secondary adjustments.

The first thing to note is the prevalence of *make-do's*. In every social establishment participants use available artifacts in a manner and for an end not officially intended, thereby modifying the conditions of life programmed for these individuals. A physical reworking of the artifact may be involved, or merely an illegitimate context of use, in either case providing homely illustrations of the Robinson Crusoe theme. Obvious examples come from prisons, where, for example, a knife may be hammered from a spoon, drawing ink extracted from the pages of *Life* magazine,[14] exercise books used to write betting slips,[15] and cigarettes lit by a number of means—sparking an electric-light outlet,[16] a homemade tinderbox,[17] or a match split into quarters.[18] While this transformation process underlies many complex practices, it can be most clearly seen where the practitioner is not involved with others (except in learning and teaching the technique), he alone consuming what he just produced.

In Central Hospital many simple make-do's were tacitly tolerated. For example, inmates widely used freestanding radiators to dry personal clothing that they had washed, on their own, in the bathroom sink, thus performing a private laundry cycle that was officially only the institution's concern. On hard-bench wards, patients sometimes carried around rolled-up newspapers to place between their necks and the wooden benches when lying down. Rolled-up coats and towels were used in the same way. Patients with experience in other imprisoning institutions employed an even more effective artifact in this context, a shoe.[19] In transferring from one

14. Cantine and Rainer, *op. cit.,* p. 42.
15. Frank Norman, *Bang to Rights* (London: Secker and Warburg, 1958), p. 90.
16. *Ibid.,* p. 92.
17.George Dendrickson and Frederick Thomas, *The Truth About Dartmoor* (London: Gollancz, 1954), p. 172.
18. *Ibid.,* pp. 172–73.
19. Compare the naval equivalent (Melville, *op. cit.,* p. 189): ". . . the hard, unyielding, and ponderous man-of-war and Navy regulation tarpaulin hat which, when new, is stiff enough to sit upon, and indeed, in lieu of his thumb, sometimes serves the common sailor for a bench."

ward to another, patients would sometimes carry their belongings in a pillow slip knotted at the top, a practice which is semi-official in some jails.[20] The few aging patients fortunate enough to have a private sleeping room would sometimes leave a towel underneath their room washstand, transforming the stand into a reading desk and the towel into a rug to protect their feet from the cold floor. Older patients who were disinclined or unable to move around sometimes employed strategies to avoid the task of going to the toilet; on the ward, the hot steam radiator could be urinated on without leaving too many long-lasting signs; during twice-weekly shaving visits to the basement barbershop, the bin reserved for used towels was used for a urinal when the attendants were not looking. Back-ward patients of all ages sometimes carried around paper drinking cups to serve as portable spittoons and ash trays, since attendants were sometimes more concerned about keeping their floors clean than they were in suppressing spitting or smoking.[21]

In total institutions make-do's tend to be focused in particular areas. One area is that of personal grooming—the fabrication of devices to facilitate presenting oneself to others in a seemly guise. For example, nuns are said to have placed a black apron behind a window pane to create a mirror—a mirror being a means of self-examination, correction, and approval ordinarily denied the sisterhood.[22] In Central Hospital, toilet paper was sometimes "organized"; neatly torn, folded, and carried on one's person, it was apologetically used as Kleenex by some fastidious patients. So, too, during the hot summer months a few male patients cut and tailored their hospital-issue khaki pants into neat-appearing summer shorts.

The simple make-do's I have cited are characterized by the fact that to employ them one need have very little involvement in and orientation to the official world of the establishment. I consider now a set of practices that imply somewhat more aliveness to the legitimated world of the institution. Here the spirit of the legitimate activity may be maintained but is carried past the point to which it was meant to go; we have an extension and elaboration of existing sources of legitimate satisfactions, or the exploitation of a whole routine of official activity for private ends. I shall speak here of "working" the system.

20. For a British example, see Dendrickson and Thomas, *op. cit.,* p. 66.
21. In Central Hospital many patients remained entirely mute, were incontinent, hallucinated, and practiced other classic symptoms. However, very few patients, as far as I could see, had the temerity purposely and persistently to drop ashes on the linoleum floor, just as few declined to line up for food, take their shower, go to bed, or get up on time. Behind a ward show of frank psychosis was a basic ward routine that was quite fully adhered to.
22. Kathryn Hulme, *The Nun's Story* (London: Muller, 1956), p. 33. Norman, *op. cit.,* p. 87, states that during Christmas-day relaxation of discipline at the British prison, Camp Hill, homosexuals made their faces up with white tooth powder and reddened their lips with dye obtained by wetting the covers of books.

Perhaps the most elementary way of working the system in Central Hospital was exhibited by those patients on back wards who went on sick call or declined to comply with ward discipline in order, apparently, to trap the attendant or physician into taking notice of them and engaging them in social interaction, however disciplinarian.

Most hospital techniques for working the system did not seem to be closely connected with mental illness, however. An example of such techniques is the elaborate set of practices associated with food-getting. For example, in a large cafeteria where the 900 patients of a male chronic service [23] ate in shifts, some would bring their own condiments so as to season their own food to their own taste; sugar, salt, pepper, and catsup were brought in for this purpose in small bottles carried in jacket pockets. When coffee was served in paper cups, patients sometimes protected their hands by inserting their cup in a second paper cup. On days when bananas were made available, a few of the patients would spirit away a cup of milk from the jug meant for those who required milk on their diet, and would cut their bananas up in slices, put on some sugar, and expansively eat a "proper" dessert. On days when the food was both liked and portable, for example when frankfurters or liver were served, some patients would wrap up their food in a paper napkin and then go back for "seconds," taking the first serving back to the ward for a night snack. A few patients brought empty bottles on days when milk was served, taking some of this back to the ward, too. If more of a given item on the menu was desired, one device was to eat just that item, dump the remainder of one's serving in the slop pail, and return (when this was allowed) for a full course of seconds. A few of the paroled patients assigned to eat in this cafeteria would, for the evening meal in summer, put their cheese between two slices of bread, wrap up what had now become a sandwich, and eat in peace outside the patient canteen, buying a cup of coffee. Patients with town parole would sometimes top this off by buying pie and ice cream at the local drugstore. In a smaller dining room in a different hospital service, patients who (rightly) feared that seconds would not be available for long would sometimes take their portion of meat from their plate, put it between two pieces of bread, leave this by their place, and immediately return to the line to get seconds. These farsighted patients would sometimes return to

23. Residentially speaking, American mental hospitals are typically organized officially by wards and services. A ward usually consists of sleeping quarters (which often can be locked off), a day room, a nurses' station with a view of the day room, various maintenance and administrative offices, a row of isolation cells, and sometimes a dining-room area. A service consists of a set of these wards filling one or more separate buildings, involving a common administration, and having some basis of patient homogeneity—age, sex, race, chronicity, etc. This homogeneity allows the service to evolve wards of differentiated character and function, roughly providing a ladder of privilege, up and down which any patient in the service can be shifted with minimum bureaucratic effort. The hospital as a whole tends to repeat through its services what, in miniature, each service does through its wards.

their places to find that a fellow inmate had made off with the first serving, cheating the cheaters at the cost of very little effort.

In order to work a system effectively, one must have an intimate knowledge of it; [24] it was easy to see this kind of knowledge put to work in the hospital. For example, it was widely known by parole patients that at the end of charitable shows at the theater hall cigarettes or candy would probably be given out at the door, as the patient audience filed out. Bored by some of these shows, some patients would come a few minutes before closing time in order to file out with the others; still others would manage to get back into the line several times and make the whole occasion more than ordinarily worthwhile. Staff were of course aware of these practices, and latecomers to some of the hospital-wide patient dances were locked out, the assumption being that they timed their arrival so as to be able to eat and run. The Jewish Welfare women apparently served brunch after the weekly morning service and one patient claimed that "by coming at the right time you can get the lunch and miss the service." Another patient, alive to the little-known fact that the hospital had a team of seamstresses to keep clothes in repair, would take his own clothes there and get shirts and pants tailored to a good fit, showing his gratitude by a package or two of cigarettes or a small sum of money.

•   •   •

Places

Some of the elementary sources of material for secondary adjustments in Central Hospital have been considered. I turn now to the question of the setting, for if these activities of underlife are to occur, they must occur in some place or region.[25]

In Central Hospital, as in many total institutions, each inmate tended to find his world divided into three parts, the partitioning drawn similarly for those of the same privilege status.

First, there was space that was off limits or out of bounds. Here mere

24. Knowledge of a guard's routine figures in many fictional escape stories. Desperation and knowledge of routines are also linked in real experience as Kogon (*op. cit.,* p. 180) illustrates in discussing the response of Buchenwald prisoners to reduction and withdrawal of rations: ". . . When an inmate had died in the tents, the fact was concealed and the dead man was dragged or carried by one or two men to the bread issue point, where the ration was issued to the 'helpers.' The body was then simply dumped anywhere in the roll-call area."
25. The study of the social use of space has recently been restimulated by the work of animal ethologists such as H. Hediger and Konrad Lorenz. See, for example, the very interesting paper by Robert Sommer, "Studies in Personal Space," *Sociometry,* 22 (1959), pp. 247–60, and H. F. Ellenberger, "Zoological Garden and Mental Hospital," *Canadian Psychiatric Association Journal,* 5 (1960), pp. 136–49.

presence was the form of conduct that was actively prohibited—unless, for example, the inmate was specifically "with" an authorized agent or active in a relevant service role. For example, according to the rules posted in one of the male services, the grounds behind one of the female services were out of bounds, presumably as a chastity measure. For all patients but the few with town parole, anything beyond the institution walls was out of bounds. So, too, everything outside a locked ward was off limits for its resident patients, and the ward itself was off limits for patients not resident there. Many of the administrative buildings and administrative sections of buildings, doctors' offices, and, with some variations, ward nursing stations were out of bounds for patients. Similar arrangements have of course been reported in other studies of mental hospitals:

> When the charge [attendant] is in his office, the office itself and a zone of about 6 square feet outside the office is off limits to all except the top group of ward helpers among the privileged patients. The other patients neither stand nor sit in this zone. Even the privileged patients may be sent away with abrupt authority if the charge or his attendants desire it. Obedience when this order occurs—usually in a parental form, such as "run along, now"—is instantaneous. The privileged patient is privileged precisely because he understands the meaning of this social space and other aspects of the attendant's position.[26]

Second, there was *surveillance space,* the area a patient needed no special excuse for being in, but where he would be subject to the usual authority and restrictions of the establishment. This area included most of the hospital for those patients with parole. Finally, there was space ruled by less than usual staff authority; it is the varieties of this kind of space that I want to consider now.

The visible activity of a particular secondary adjustment may be actively forbidden in a mental hospital, as in other establishments. If the practice is to occur, it must be shielded from the eyes and ears of staff. This may involve merely turning away from a staff person's line of vision.[27] The inmate may smile derisively by half-turning away, chew on food without signs of jaw motion when eating is forbidden, cup a lighted cigarette in the hand when smoking is not permitted, and use a hand to conceal cigarette chips during a ward poker game when the supervising nurse passes through

26. Ivan Belknap, *Human Problems of a State Mental Hospital* (New York: McGraw-Hill, 1956), pp. 179–80.
27. An American prison example may be cited from Alfred Hassler's *Diary of a Self-Made Convict* (Chicago: Regnery, 1954), p. 123: "A few minutes later the guard makes his 'count,' at which time each man is supposed to be standing, fully dressed, at his door. Since the hack simply glances in at the window, however, it is a simple enough matter to slip one's shirt on and, by standing close to the door, give the desired impression."

the ward. These were concealment devices employed in Central Hospital. A further example is cited from another mental institution:

> My total rejection of psychiatry, which had, after coma, become a fanatical adulation, now passed into a third phase—one of constructive criticism. I became aware of the peripheral obtuseness and the administrative dogmatism of the hospital bureaucracy. My first impulse was to condemn; later, I perfected means of maneuvering freely within the clumsy structure of ward politics. To illustrate, my reading matter had been kept under surveillance for quite some time, and I had at last perfected a means of keeping *au courant* without unnecessarily alarming the nurses and attendants. I had smuggled several issues of *Hound and Horn* into my ward on the pretext that it was a field-and-stream magazine. I had read Hoch and Kalinowski's *Shock Therapy* (a top secret manual of arms at the hospital) quite openly, after I had put it into the dust jacket of Anna Balakian's *Literary Origins of Surrealism*.[28]

In addition, however, to these temporary means of avoiding hospital surveillance, inmates and staff tacitly cooperated to allow the emergence of bounded physical spaces in which ordinary levels of surveillance and restriction were markedly reduced, spaces where the inmate could openly engage in a range of tabooed activities with some degree of security. These places often also provided a marked reduction in usual patient population density, contributing to the peace and quiet characteristic of them. The staff did not know of the existence of these places, or knew but either stayed away or tacitly relinquished their authority when entering them. Licence, in short, had a geography. I shall call these regions *free places*. We may especially expect to find them when authority in an organization is lodged in a whole echelon of staff instead of in a set of pyramids of command. Free places are backstage to the usual performance of staff-inmate relationships.

● ● ●

In everyday life, legitimate possessions employed in primary adjustments are typically stored, when not in use, in special places of safekeeping which can be gotten to at will, such as footlockers, cabinets, bureau drawers, and safe deposit boxes. These storage places protect the object from damage, misuse, and misappropriation, and allow the user to conceal what he possesses from others.[29] More important, these places can repre-

28. Carl Solomon, "Report from the Asylum," in G. Feldman and M. Gartenberg, eds., *The Beat Generation and the Angry Young Men* (New York: Dell Publishing Co., 1959), pp. 177–78.
29. Personal places of safekeeping are, of course, known in cultures not our own. See, for example, John Skolle, Azalaï (New York: Harper & Bros., 1956), p. 49:

sent an extension of the self and its autonomy, becoming more important as the individual forgoes other repositories of selfhood. If nothing can be kept only for oneself, and everything one uses is used by others, too, then little protection from social contamination by others is possible. Further, some of the things one must give up are those with which one has become especially identified and which one employs for self-identification to others. It is thus that a man in a monastery may be concerned about his one privacy, his letterbox,[30] and a man on a frigate about his canvas clothes bag.[31]

Where such private storage places are not allowed, it is understandable that they will be illicitly developed, if one is to possess an object illicitly, then the place in which it is stored may itself have to be concealed. A personal storage space that is concealed and/or locked not merely to thwart illegitimate interlopers but also legitimate authority is sometimes called a *stash* in the criminal and near-criminal world, and will be called this here.[32] It may be noted that these illicit storage places represent a more complex matter, organizationally, than do simple make-do's, since a stash can ordinarily safeguard more than one kind of illicit possession. I would like to add that one important object that may be stashed is the human body (dead or alive), giving rise to special terms such as hideout, stowaway, laying low, and to one of the inevitable scenes of detective fiction.

When patients entered Central Hospital, especially if they were excited or depressed on admission, they were denied a private, accessible place to store things. Their personal clothing, for example, might be stored in a room that was beyond their discretionary use. Their money was kept in the administration building, unobtainable without medical and/or their legal

---

"The Tuareg carried all their possessions in leather bags. Those containing valuables they would lock with their native *cadenas,* three keys sometimes being required to work the combination. The system seemed singularly ineffectual as a measure of precaution because every man carried a dagger and anyone who so desired could ignore the lock and slash the leather bag. But no one thought of doing this. The lock was universally respected as a symbol of privacy."

30. Thomas Merton, *The Seven Storey Mountain* (New York: Harcourt, Brace and Company, 1948), p. 384.

31. Melville, *op. cit.,* p. 47.

32. An American prison example may be cited from Hassler, *op. cit.,* pp. 59–60:

"Directly across from me is the dormitory's most illustrious tenant—'Nocky' Johnson, erstwhile political boss of Atlantic City and, if my memory serves, concessionaire for most of the more sordid activities in that resort. Nocky is a tall, heavily built man in his sixties. His standing in the prison hierarchy is evident, at first glance, in the half-dozen fine woollen blankets stacked on his cot (the rest of us have two of much poorer quality) and the lock on his tin cabinet—definitely *de trop* among the lesser fry. My embezzler neighbor tells me the hacks never examine Nocky's possessions as they do everyone else's. The glimpse I had of the interior of his cabinet showed it to be jammed with cartons of cigarettes—the principal medium of exchange in this moneyless sanctuary."

agents' permission. Valuables or breakables, such as false teeth, eyeglasses, wrist watches, often an integral part of body image, might be locked up safely out of their owners' reach. Official papers of self-identification might also be retained by the institution.[33] Cosmetics, needed to present oneself properly to others, were collectivized, being made accessible to patients only at certain times. On convalescent wards, bed boxes were available, but since they were unlocked they were subject to theft from other patients and from staff, and in any case were often located in rooms locked to patients during the day.

If people were selfless, or were required to be selfless, there would of course be a logic to having no private storage place, as a British ex-mental patient suggests:

> I looked for a locker, but without success. There appeared to be none in this hospital; the reason soon abundantly clear; they were quite unnecessary—we had nothing to keep in them—everything being shared, even the solitary face cloth which was used for a number of other purposes, a subject on which my feelings became very strong.[34]

But all have some self. Given the curtailment implied by loss of places of safekeeping, it is understandable that patients in Central Hospital developed places of their own.

It seemed characteristic of hospital life that the most common form of stash was one that could be carried around on one's person wherever one went.[35] One such device for female patients was a large handbag; a parallel technique for a man was a jacket with commodious pockets, worn even in the hottest weather. While these containers are quite usual ones in the wider community, there was a special burden placed upon them in the hospital: books, writing materials, washcloths, fruit, small valuables, scarves, playing cards, soap, shaving equipment (on the part of men), containers of salt, pepper, and sugar, bottles of milk—these were some of the objects sometimes carried in this manner. So common was this practice that one of the most reliable symbols of patient status in the hospital was bulging pockets. Another portable storage device was a shopping bag lined with another shopping bag. (When partly full, this frequently employed stash also served as a cushion and back rest.) Among men, a small stash was sometimes created out of a long sock: by knotting the open end and twisting this end around his belt, the patient could let a kind of moneybag

---

33. It should be clearly stated that there are many strong clinical and administrative arguments for denying particular patients their personal possessions. The question of the desirability of such denials is not here at issue.
34. Johnson and Dodds, *op. cit.,* p. 86.
35. In the light literature on criminal activity there are well-known portable stashes: false heels, false-bottomed suitcases, anal suppositories, etc. Jewels and narcotics are the favorite items stashed in this manner. More fanciful stashes are described in espionage fiction.

inconspicuously hang down inside his trouser leg. Individual variations of these portable containers were also found. One young engineering graduate fashioned a purse out of discarded oilcloth, the purse being stitched into separate, well-measured compartments for comb, toothbrush, cards, writing paper, pencil, soap, small face cloth, toilet paper—the whole attached by a concealed clip to the underside of his belt.

●   ●   ●

I want to raise two general questions about underlife in Central Hospital.

First, it should be clear that a description of underlife in an institution can provide a systematically biased picture of life in it. To the degree that members confine themselves to primary adjustments (whether out of satisfaction or incapacity to build a different world), underlife may be unrepresentative and even unimportant. Moreover, the secondary adjustments most easily observed may be ones that are elaborate and colorful, and these, as in the case of Central Hospital, may be practised mainly by a handful of well-connected informal leaders. Their conduct may be of great importance to the student if he wants to learn how the particular institution can be worked and how institutions in general might be worked; but in searching for the range and scope of secondary adjustments, the student may fail to see how the average member lives. This report necessarily focuses on the activity of manipulative paroled patients, giving an over-rosy view both of the life of patients as a whole in Central Hospital and of the efficiency of their techniques for unofficially altering their life conditions.

The second general question I want to raise has to do with social control and bond formation.

The social arrangements which make economic and social exchange possible obviously function to ensure that the individual will be able to incorporate into his own plan of action the efforts of others, increasing many times the efficacy of secondary adjustments he makes by himself on his own behalf. Now it is plain that if these social arrangements are to be sustained, some form of social control will have to be exerted to keep people in line, to make them live up to their bargains and their obligation to perform favors and ceremonies for others. These forms of social control will constitute secondary adjustments of a very special class—a class of adjustments which underlie and stabilize a vast complex of other unofficial, undercover practices. And from the point of view of inmate underlife in total institutions, these controls will have to be exerted over both inmates and staff.

Inmate control of staff in total institutions takes traditional forms, for example: arranging for "accidents" to occur to a staff person,[36] or the massed rejection of a particular item of food,[37] or the slowing-down of work production, or the sabotaging of plumbing, lighting, and communication systems, all of which are readily vulnerable to inmate action.[38] Other inmate sanctions of staff may take the form of "collective" or individual teasing and more subtle forms of ritual insubordination, such as the military technique of saluting a troublesome officer from too great a distance, or with too much precision, or with too slow a tempo. A staff threat to the whole system of undercover arrangements may be answered with extreme action such as strikes or riots.

• • •

Of the many different kinds of secondary adjustment, some are of particular interest because they bring into the clear the general theme of involvement and disaffection, characteristic of all these practices.

One of these special types of secondary adjustment is "removal activities" (or "kicks"), namely, undertakings that provide something for the individual to lose himself in, temporarily blotting out all sense of the environment which, and in which, he must abide. In total institutions a useful exemplary case is provided by Robert Stroud, the "Birdman," who, from watching birds out his cell window, through a spectacular career of finagling and make-do, fabricated a laboratory and became a leading ornithological contributor to medical literature, all from within prison.[39] Language courses in prisoner-of-war camps and art courses in prisons [40] can provide the same release.

Central Hospital provided several of these escape worlds for inmates.[41] One, for example, was sports. Some of the baseball players and a few tennis players seemed to become so caught up in their sport, and in the daily record of their efforts in competition, that at least for the summer months this became their overriding interest. In the case of baseball this was further strengthened by the fact that, within the hospital, parole patients could follow national baseball as readily as could many persons

36. For example, Dendrickson and Thomas, *op. cit.,* p. 130.
37. Cantine and Rainer, *op. cit.,* p. 4.
38. *Ibid.,* p. 10.
39. Gaddis, *op. cit.*
40. J. F. N., *op. cit.,* pp. 17–18.
41. Behind informal social typing and informal group formation in prisons there is often to be seen a removal activity. Caldwell, *op. cit.,* pp. 651–53, provides some interesting examples of prisoners on such kicks: those involved in securing and using drugs; those focused on leatherwork for sale; and "Spartans," those involved in the glorification of their bodies, the prison locker room apparently serving as a muscle beach; the homosexuals; the gamblers, etc. The point about these activities is that each is world-building for the person caught up in it, thereby displacing the prison.

on the outside. For some young patients, who never failed to go, when allowed, to a dance held in their service or in the recreation building, it was possible to live for the chance of meeting someone "interesting" or remeeting someone interesting who had already been met—in much the same way that college students are able to survive their studies by looking forward to the new "dates" that may be found in extracurricular activities. The "marriage moratorium" in Central Hospital, effectively freeing a patient from his marital obligations to a nonpatient, enhanced this removal activity. For a handful of patients, the semi-annual theatrical production was an extremely effective removal activity: tryouts, rehearsals, costuming, scenery-making, staging, writing and rewriting, performing—all these seemed as successful as on the outside in building a world apart for the participants. Another kick, important to some patients—and a worrisome concern for the hospital chaplains—was the enthusiastic espousal of religion. Still another, for a few patients, was gambling.[42]

Portable ways of getting away were much favored in Central Hospital, paper-back murder mysteries,[43] cards, and even jigsaw puzzles being carried around on one's person. Not only could leave be taken of the ward and grounds be taken leave of through these means, but if one had to wait for an hour or so upon an official, or the serving of a meal, or the opening of the recreation building, the self-implication of this subordination could be dealt with by immediately bringing forth one's own world-making equipment.

Individual means of creating a world were striking. One depressed, suicidal alcoholic, apparently a good bridge player, disdained bridge with almost all other patient players, carrying around his own pocket bridge player and writing away occasionally for a new set of competition hands. Given a supply of his favorite gumdrops and his pocket radio, he could

---

42. Melville, op. cit., devotes a whole chapter, ch. lxxiii, to illicit gambling aboard his frigate.
43. The getaway role of reading in prison is well described in Behan, op. cit.; see also Heckstall-Smith, op. cit., p. 34: "The prison library offered a fairly good selection of books. But as time went by I found myself reading merely to kill time—reading everything and anything I could lay my hands on. During those first weeks, reading acted as a soporific and on the long early summer evenings I often fell asleep over my book."
  Kogon, op. cit., pp. 127–28, provides a concentration-camp example:
  "In the winter of 1942–43 a succession of bread thefts in Barracks 42 at Buchenwald made it necessary to establish a nightwatch. For months on end I volunteered for this duty, taking the shift from three to six o'clock in the morning. It meant sitting alone in the day room, while the snores of the comrades came from the other end. For once I was free of the ineluctable companionship that usually shackled and stifled every individual activity. What an experience it was to sit quietly by a shaded lamp, delving into the pages of Plato's *Dialogues,* Galsworthy's *Swan Song,* or the works of Heine, Klabund, Mehring! Heine? Klabund? Mehring? Yes, they could be read illegally in camp. They were among books retrieved from the nation-wide wastepaper collections."

pull himself out of the hospital world at will, surrounding all his senses with pleasantness.

In considering removal activities we can again raise the issue of over-commitment to an establishment. In the hospital laundry, for example, there was a patient worker who had been on the job for several years. He had been given the job of unofficial foreman, and, unlike almost all other patient workers, he threw himself into his work with a capacity, devotion, and seriousness that were evident to many. Of him, the laundry charge attendant said:

> That one there is my special helper. He works harder than all the rest put together. I would be lost without him.

In exchange for his effort, the attendant would bring from home something for this patient to eat almost every day. And yet there was something grotesque in his adjustment, for it was apparent that his deep voyage into the work world had a slightly make-believe character; after all, he was a patient, not a foreman, and he was clearly reminded of this off the job.

Obviously, as some of these illustrations imply, removal activities need not be in themselves illegitimate; it is the function that they come to serve for the inmate that leads us to consider them along with other secondary adjustments. An extreme here, perhaps, is individual psychotherapy in state mental hospitals; this privilege is so rare in these institutions,[44] and the resulting contact with a staff psychiatrist so unique in terms of hospital status structure, that an inmate can to some degree forget where he is as he pursues his psychotherapy. By actually receiving what the institution formally claims to offer, the patient can succeed in getting away from what the establishment actually provides. There is a general implication here. Perhaps every activity that an establishment obliges or permits its members to participate in is a potential threat to the organization, for it would seem that there is no activity in which the individual cannot become overengrossed.

• • •

It would be easy to account for the development of secondary adjustments by assuming that the individual possessed an array of needs, native or cultivated, and that when lodged in a milieu that denied these needs the individual simply responded by developing makeshift means of satisfaction. I think this explanation fails to do justice to the importance of these under-cover adaptations for the structure of the self.

The practice of reserving something of oneself from the clutch of an

44. Of approximately 7000 patients in Central Hospital, I calculated at the time of the study that about 100 received some kind of individual psychotherapy in any one year.

institution is very visible in mental hospitals and prisons but can be found in more benign and less totalistic institutions, too. I want to argue that this recalcitrance is not an incidental mechanism of defense but rather an essential constituent of the self.

Sociologists have always had a vested interest in pointing to the ways in which the individual is formed by groups, identifies with groups, and wilts away unless he obtains emotional support from groups. But when we closely observe what goes on in a social role, a spate of sociable interaction, a social establishment—or in any other unit of social organization—embracement of the unit is not all that we see. We always find the individual employing methods to keep some distance, some elbow room, between himself and that with which others assume he should be identified. No doubt a state-type mental hospital provides an overly lush soil for the growth of these secondary adjustments, but in fact, like weeds, they spring up in any kind of social organization. If we find, then, that in all situations actually studied the participant has erected defenses against his social bondedness, why should we base our conception of the self upon how the individual would act were conditions "just right"?

The simplest sociological view of the individual and his self is that he is to himself what his place in an organization defines him to be. When pressed, a sociologist modifies this model by granting certain complications: the self may be not yet formed or may exhibit conflicting dedications. Perhaps we should further complicate the construct by elevating these qualifications to a central place, initially defining the individual, for sociological purposes, as a stance-taking entity, a something that takes up a position somewhere between identification with an organization and opposition to it, and is ready at the slightest pressure to regain its balance by shifting its involvement in either direction. It is thus *against something* than the self can emerge. This has been appreciated by students of totalitarianism:

> In short, Ketman means self-realization *against* something. He who practices Ketman suffers because of the obstacles he meets; but if these obstacles were suddenly to be removed, he would find himself in a void which might perhaps prove much more painful. Internal revolt is sometimes essential to spiritual health, and can create a particular form of happiness. What can be said openly is often much less interesting than the emotional magic of defending one's sanctuary.[45]

I have argued the same case in regard to total institutions. May this not be the situation, however, in free society, too?

45. Czeslaw Milosz, *The Captive Mind* (New York: Vintage Books, 1955), p. 76.

Without something to belong to, we have no stable self, and yet total commitment and attachment to any social unit implies a kind of selflessness. Our sense of being a person can come from being drawn into a wider social unit; our sense of selfhood can arise through the little ways in which we resist the pull. Our status is backed by the solid buildings of the world, while our sense of personal identity often resides in the cracks.

The Interlocking of Official and Unofficial Reward

Melville Dalton

Use of materials and services for personal ends, individual or group, is, of course, officially forbidden, for in both plant theory and popular usage this is *theft*. But our concern to pinpoint the informal phases of administration where possible requires scrutiny of this generally known but taboo subject.

Such practices are as delicate to discuss as they are to apply. For as long as rivalries can generate "reasons" there will be double talk around the concept of "reward," especially in organizations that stress "fair-dealing," "job evaluation," "merit-rated salaries," etc. The dynamics of individual and group action do not require that one agree fully with those who say that no word [1] ever has the same meaning twice, but they do demand that one recognize the difficulties of assigning absolute meanings to terms describing the kinds of situations we are dealing with.[2] What in some

SOURCE: *Men Who Manage*, pp. 194–217. Copyright © 1959 by John Wiley & Sons, Inc. Reprinted by permission of John Wiley & Sons, Inc.

1. S. I. Hayakawa, *Language and Thought in Action*, Harcourt, Brace and Co., New York, 1949, pp. 60–62.
2. Even in the physical sciences there are disputes about the definition, perception, and nature of matter. See the comments of two *physicists:* Martin Johnson, *Art and Scientific Thought*, Columbia University Press, New York, 1949; and J. Bronowski, "Science and Human Values," *The Nation*, 183: 550–66, December 29, 1956, and *The Common Sense of Science*, Wm. Heinemann, Ltd., London, 1951, especially chaps. 6–8. Disputes increase in the biological sciences. For example, because they combine both plant and animal characteristics, we find such organisms as *Euglena viridis* and the slime-fungi studied by both zoologists and botanists. Books from satirical to scientific levels debate the nature of *truth, fact,* and *meaning.* In the opening pages of his *Ethics*, Aristotle notes the difficulty of expecting a mathematician to see facts as *probable*, or a politician to see them as *precise.* For himself he believed that different subject matters admit of different degrees of precision in handling. See also the two works of T. V. Smith, "In Accentuation of the Negative," *The Scientific Monthly*, 63: 463–69, December, 1946 and *The Ethics of Compromise*, Starr King Press, Boston, 1956; and the numerous articles in L. Bryson et al., *Symbols and Values*, Harper and Brothers, New York, 1954, *Symbols and Society*, Harper and Brothers, New York, 1955; Anthony Standen, *Science Is a Sacred Cow*, E. P. Dutton and Co., New York, 1950; S. I. Hayakawa, ed., *Language, Meaning and Maturity*, Harper and Brothers, New York, 1954; H. Hoijer, ed., *Language in*

sense is theft, may, in the context of preserving the group and solving present problems, lose much or all of its odious overtones. We only need note the gradations of terms referring to theft to suspect this. As theft requires more ingenuity, becomes larger in amount, and is committed by more distinguished persons (whose power is often related to their importance in the operation of society), its character is correspondingly softened by such velvety terms as *misappropriation, embezzlement,* and *peculation,* which often require special libraries to define. To spare the living [3] and some of the recent dead, and to ignore differences in time and place, we can point to Cellini—and remember Pope Paul III's judgment of him that "men like Benvenuto, unique in their profession, are not bound by the laws"—Aretino, Casanova, and even Voltaire. These men were all scoundrels of a kind who, nevertheless, were esteemed for their commendable contributions to society.

Always there are genuine transitional nuances, with debatable margins, between covert internal theft and tacit inducement or reward. Immemorially the esteemed personality who also performs unique services can move closer to "theft" than others without censure.

Managerial Motivation

To talk of rewarding is to talk of motivation, and students declare, and show by their disagreement, that little is known of managerial motivation.[4] Distinguished executives and specialized students admit that the whole subject of reward is so dynamic that attempts either rigidly to de-

Culture, University of Chicago Press, 1954; E. A. Burtt, *The Metaphysical Foundations of Modern Science,* Doubleday and Co., Garden City, N.Y., 1955; Howard Becker, *Through Values to Social Interpretation,* Duke University Press, Durham, N.C., 1950; Boris B. Bogoslovsky, *The Technique of Controversy,* Harcourt, Brace and Co., New York, 1928, especially chaps. 4–9; Kenneth Burke, *Attitudes Toward History,* 2 vols., The New Republic, New York, 1937, especially vol. 2, pp. 52–256.
3. See Edwin H. Sutherland, *White Collar Crime,* The Dryden Press, New York, 1949; *The Autobiography of Lincoln Steffens,* Harcourt, Brace and Co., New York, 1931; John T. Flynn, *Graft in Business,* The Vanguard Press, New York, 1931, pp. 103–6.
4. Summer Slichter, "Report on Current Research: Economics," *Saturday Review,* 36: 24, April 4, 1953; Arthur H. Cole, "An Approach to the Study of Entrepreneurship," *Journal of Economic History* 6, Supplement 1–15 (1946); Robert A. Gordon, *Business Leadership in the Large Organization,* Brookings Institution, Washington, D.C., 1945; Clare E. Griffin, *Enterprise in a Free Society,* R. D. Irwin, Chicago, 1949, chap. 5; John K. Galbraith, *American Capitalism,* Houghton Mifflin, Boston, 1952; Albert Lauterbach, *Man, Motives and Money,* Cornell University Press, Ithaca, New York, 1954; George Katona, *Psychological Analysis of Economic Behavior,* McGraw-Hill Book Co., New York, 1951; *Business Week,* "A Tempo Shapes a Type," April 25, 1953, pp. 56, 58, 60; C. C. Abbott, J. D. Forbes, L. A. Thompson, *The Executive Function and Its Compensation,* Graduate School of Business Administration, The University of Virginia, Charlottesville, 1957.

fine motivation,[5] or specifically to reward managers [6] are both likely to go amiss.

Our data have shown that what is a reward for one man is not for another[7] . . . ; that the rank a manager craves at one time, he rejects at another . . . ; that the same inducements cannot be given to all on a given level because of differences in ability and demand for reward . . . ; uses of the office of assistant-to, etc.; [8] that the organization's contact with the community may demand greater reward for some managers than for others; that "power struggles" are forbidden but do occur and must be disguised; [9] and that more than financial reward is necessary.[10] We know that some managers are more venturesome and more inclined to "play the game" than others are.[11] This may mean unexpected errors, losses, and gains for the organization. In any case such managers must have greater resources and rewards than rigid planning will allow.[12] We saw . . . that Milo managers were concerned to maintain social as well as productive mechanisms, and that, in addition to the use of materials and services for this purpose, they juggled accounts to (a) allow full and part-time employment of the friends and relatives of plant and community associates, to (b) justify plush offices stemming from their rivalries, and to (c) keep a margin, or kind of "slush fund," in the naval sense, for emergencies—social and mechanical.

Although these pratices may vary among cultures and inside a given culture,[13] and with the size, age and financial state of a firm,[14] as well as by industry,[15] they nevertheless occur widely and point to further problems

---

5. C. I. Barnard, *Functions of the Executive,* Harvard University Press, Cambridge, 1938, pp. 138–60.
6. P. F. Drucker, *The Practice of Management,* Harper and Brothers, New York, 1954, p. 152; Abbott, Forbes, and Thompson, *op. cit.,* pp. 46–55.
7. See also Morris S. Viteles, *Motivation and Morale in Industry,* Norton, New York, 1953; Kornhauser, in Kornhauser, Dubin, and Ross, *op. cit.,* pp. 59–85; W. F. Whyte *et al., Money and Motivation,* Harper and Brothers, New York, 1955.
8. Also see C. I. Barnard, "Functions and Pathology of Status Systems in Formal Organizations" in W. F. Whyte, ed., *Industry and Society,* McGraw-Hill Book Co., New York, 1946, pp. 207–43.
9. The various struggles of Milo and Fruhling with their Offices. Also see Galbraith, *American Capitalism,* Houghton Mifflin, Boston, 1952, p. 28.
10. Barnard, *op. cit., pp.* 139–60.
11. Griffin, *op. cit.,* chap. 5; Gordon, *op. cit., pp.* 305–12. Geiger's "free-wheeling" bent is suggested by his remark that "The engineers aren't practical. They want everything to be exact. They can't see that in operation you've got to lie and steal and cheat a little." See also W. H. Knowles, *Personnel Management: A Human Relations Approach,* American Book Co., New York, 1955, p. 130; Robert B. Fetter and Donald C. Johnson, *Compensation and Incentives for Industrial Executives,* Indiana University, Bloomington, 1952, p. 57.
12. Abbott, Forbes, and Thompson, *op. cit.,* p. 41.
13. Lauterbach, *op. cit.,* chap. 1.
14. Katona, *op. cit.,* chap. 9.
15. *Business Week,* April 25, 1953, pp. 56, 58, 60.

for the manager who deals with other firms or other plants of his own corporation; we have but to recall Geiger's problems from having his unit compared with that of the Colloid plant.

As a result of these gaps between the inherent limitations of formal reward and the obscure complex of activities that must be rewarded, an organization's services and materials, designed for its official functioning, are repeatedly drawn on to fill the breach. Used injudiciously, this may lead to plunder.

Theft: Real and Questionable

Before we present cases, let us admit the probably universal existence of internal theft, individual and organized, that is more damaging than helpful to the firm and that would strain the term to be called reward for specific contributions. Various informants report almost incredible cases of empire-building with minimum functions or contributions for many members; of favors and perquisites granted to some for no obvious important service in return; organized pilfering rights—including regular paid frolics for some of the company's members as "representatives" or "spokesmen" at some "event"; and the purely personal use of plant resources under the guise of "community relations," and sometimes not honored with a pretext. This is reported as common in some of the large firms doing contracted work for various governmental bodies where . . . the pressure for economy is less.

There is, of course, widespread individual theft in which tools, clerical supplies, home fixtures, etc., are taken for personal use without the knowledge of superiors or concern for one's group or the organization, and which could not be justified in case of detection. Similar internal theft by subgroups and cliques, with lifting-license tied so closely to rank that stealing beyond one's station is punished by death, can occur even in sacred organizations.[16] Civic bodies of antiquity were similarly tapped by members.[17]

Theft may also be enforced in the group and occur systematically over a long period. For example, in a small cabinet factory in the Mobile Acres region, the employees of one department, on piece-rate pay, regularly turned in more pieces than they actually completed, and coerced newcomers to do the same to protect old hands.

Between theft and informal reward is the gray-green practice of expense-accounting, which is also related to rank. "Theft" is softened to "abuse of privilege," but the feeling of some companies is clear in their

16. Will Durant, *The Renaissance*, Simon and Schuster, New York, 1953, p. 401.
17. Article "Aqueducts," *Encyclopaedia Britannica*, vol. 2, 14th edition, 1932, p. 161.

demands for explanations. Others, however, including those sensitive to the tax factor, see large accounts as "part of the man's compensation," or as necessary to "attract and hold top men," or as a practice comparable to the "employee medical program." [18]

One organization reflects this attitude in its contract with a well-known top executive. After defining his duties and authority, the company says that:

> During the continuance of the employment of [the executive] hereunder he shall be paid a weekly salary of Twenty-five Hundred ($2500) Dollars, and in addition a weekly general expense allowance of Five Hundred ($500) Dollars which shall not include travelling expenses or other items generally related thereto, which shall also be paid by the Company. There shall be no abatement or diminution of the compensation or expense allowance of [the executive] during such time, if any, as he may fail to perform the services required to be performed by him hereunder solely because of illness or physical incapacity even though such illness or incapacity may prevent the performance by him of any duties whatsoever for a period up to six consecutive months. . . . [If the executive shall be required to change headquarters around the Company operating areas he shall receive] such suitable office accommodations and such clerical and other assistance as shall, from time to time, be reasonably required by him, and of such type, character and extent as shall be consistent with the position of Chief Executive Officer of the Company. . . . [He] shall receive fair and reasonable vacations with pay, commensurate with the position and duties undertaken by him hereunder.[19]

Coercion in expense-accounting can function as in the cabinet factory cited above. An informant from an optical company reports that lower-ranking, and obviously less imaginative, employees who rarely used expense accounts were not permitted by higher-ranking members to list their costs exactly. Rather they were forced to inflate the report, sometimes very much, so as not to "show-up the fat accounts" of the habitual users. Internal coercion to protect one's masquerade might at times be justified, but apparently was not in this case.

Though parallel cases only at times, featherbedding by labor, and the various professional and managerial practices embracing pay-backs, split-fees and rebates,[20] also lie in this twilight area.

18. *Newsweek*, "Those Big-Figure Expense Accounts," vol. 41, No. 20, pp. 87, 90–92, May 20, 1957; Seymour Mintz, "Executive Expense Accounts and Fringe Benefits: A Problem in Management, Morality and Revenue," *Journal of Taxation*, 1: 2–9, June, 1954; Abbott, Forbes, and Thompson, *op. cit.*, p. 41.
19. See various responses (public documents) to form 10-K of the Securities and Exchange Commission, Washington, D.C., for the Fiscal Year ended August 21, 1956.
20. Fred H. Colvin, *The Industrial Triangle*, Columbia Graphs, Columbia, Connecticut, 1955, pp. 95–96; Benjamin Aaron, "Governmental Restraints on Featherbedding," *Stanford Law Review*, 5: 680–721, 1953.

Unofficial Incentives

In crossing the middle ground between understood theft of materials and their controlled use of inducements and rewards, one must always fight the sheep-or-goat concept of truth. Responsible persons who succeed in this apparently broaden the system of rewards and are able to stimulate those not lured by standard appeals, or who also require other [21] incentives for greater effort.

Individual

Because of the tacit stress on flexibility and supplementation of the more common inducements, unofficial reward is naturally directed more toward specific contributions and situations than toward rank as such. But obviously if such reward is not confidential, or if it is known and not justified in the minds of others, it is likely to follow formal rank and become systematic theft of the kind we noted above.

Although informal reward ideally is given for effort and contribution beyond what is expected of a specific rank, it is also granted for many other purposes, often unexpected and formally taboo yet important for maintaining the organization and winning its ends. For example, it may be given (1) in lieu of a promotion or salary increase that could not be effected; (2) as a bonus for doing necessary but unpleasant or low-prestige things; (3) as an opiate to forget defeats in policy battles or status tiffs; (4) as a price for conciliating an irate colleague or making, in effect, a treaty with another department; (5) as a perquisite to key persons in clerical or staff groups to prevent slowdowns, and to bolster alertness against errors during critical periods; (6) as a frank supplement to a low but maximum salary; (7) for understanding and aid in the operation, and the defense, of the unofficial incentive system; (8) for great personal sacrifices. There are, of course, more subtle supports which may not be articulated but are intuitively recognized and rewarded where possible. These include: ability to maintain morale in the group or department; skill in picking and holding good subordinates; habitual tacit understanding of what superiors and colleagues expect but would not in some cases want to phrase, even unofficially; and expertness in saving the face of superiors and maintaining the dignity of the organization under adverse conditions. This last may be aptness in masking and supporting the fictions essential for regulation of error, and in perpetuating symbols considered necessary by the dominant group. [22]

21. See the theory of Abbott, Forbes, and Thompson, *op. cit.,* pp. 34–38.
22. See Havelock Ellis, *The Dance of Life,* The Modern Library, New York, 1923, pp. 89–98, and Robert Dubin, *Human Relations in Administration,* Prentice-Hall, New York, 1951, pp. 336–45.

These performances are not exhaustive and may overlap in the same person. There is no fixed tie either, of course, between services rendered and the kind of material reward or privilege granted. Though we are confining our discussion to positive rewards, there are also negative ones, such as exemptions from rules binding on others, which . . . was but one in the first-line foreman's repertory of inducements for production workers.

Though his general contributions were great, the Milo foreman, Kustis . . . illustrates the privileges given for personal sacrifice. Kustis dropped his Catholicism, from choice but with suffering, to become a Mason and thus demonstrate his fealty and fitness. . . . But with the knowledge of his superiors, he built a machine shop in his home, largely from Milo materials. He equipped his drill press, shaper, and lathe with cutters and drills from Milo. He supplemented these with bench equipment, such as taps, reamers, dies, bolts and screws. Finally, piece by piece and day by day he removed a retired grinder from his shop. Normally such tools were sent to another department or unit of the corporation.

Ted Berger, officially foreman of Milo's carpenter shop, was *sub rosa* a custodian and defender of the supplementary reward system. Loyal beyond question, he was allowed great freedom from formal duties and expected, at least through the level of department heads, to function as a clearinghouse for the system. His own reward was both social and material, but his handling of the system unintentionally produced a social glue that bound together people from various levels and departments. Not required to operate machines, Berger spent a minimum of six hours daily making such things as baby beds, storm windows, garage windows, doll buggies, rocking horses, tables, meat boards, and rolling pins. These objects were custom built for various managers. European-born[23] Berger was a craftsman and eager to display his skills. However, his American-born associates with their folklore of "one good turn deserves another," often gave him a "fee" for his work. Since everyone knew his thirst, these gifts[24] were usually wines, ranging from homemade "Dago Red" to choice imported varieties. But he also accepted dressed fowl, preferably duck and

23. In a study of production workers on piece rate in a plant of Mobile Acres, I earlier indicated some of the differences in feeling for craftsmanship between European-apprenticed and American-born workers. See "Worker Response and Social Background," *Journal of Political Economy*, 55: 323–32, August, 1947.
24. A colleague suggests that this "looks like bribery." It is hardly that. Rather these gifts were gestures of good will, and in some cases substitutes for favors due that could not be exchanged in the course of carrying out regular duties. One can argue that people were being persuaded to violate their official duties. With no more casuistry one can also argue that "bribes" of this kind contribute to the carrying out of official duties, and that, inside varying and debatable limits, they are a legitimate cost for the maintenance of solidarity. This is not to deny that bribery occurs in industry, as elsewhere (Flynn, *Graft in Business*, The Vanguard Press, New York, 1931, pp. 55–76), or that bestowal of gifts cannot be bribery. See "Should Companies Give?" *Newsweek*, December 24, 1956, pp. 59–60.

turkey. In some cases he made nothing, but used his influence to aid with a problem. In other cases he found a place in his department for the summer employment of someone's son, and again usually he received some unspoken favor. The transfer effect of these exchanges needs no elaboration.

Jim Speier, one of Peters' (formal chart) foremen, gave Peters great support in the latter's conflicts with Taylor. An understanding foreman and bulwark of the unofficial directorate, he made great use of both the structural and carpenter shops with Blanke's approval. He had a wood and steel archway for his rose garden prefabricated in the plant, and removed it piecemeal. Incentive-appliers estimated that exclusive of materials[25] the time spent on this object would have made its cost at least $400, in terms of the hourly charging rate. Also in Berger's shop, Speier had fourteen storm windows made, and a set of wooden lawn sprinklers cut in the form of dancing girls and brightly painted. For use on his farm, Speier had a stainless steel churn made that cost over a hundred and fifty dollars by the charging rate. In the same shop Speier had several cold-pack lifting pans made, also of stainless steel. According to self-styled experts on such matters, the design and workmanship of these pans was superior to anything obtainable on the market. Incentive-appliers declared that the welding, brazing, grinding, and polishing costs made the pans "worth their weight in gold."

Pete Merza, a general foreman in Springer's division, was given enough freedom in the use of building materials that his reward was seen by some—ignorant of his unofficial contributions—as approaching theft. Like Kustis, he had withdrawn from the Church to become a Mason, but this was more a gesture than a personal sacrifice for him. An inimitably warm and helpful person acceptable to all factions, he was really rewarded as Milo's peacemaker in the clashes between Operation and Maintenance. Informants stated that he "carried out several hundred dollars worth" of bricks and cement and used Milo bricklayers on company time to build much, or most, of his house.

In another Milo case, reorganization dropped two general foremen to the first-line level. At that time, salary decreases followed automatically. Since the two men did not wish to continue at Milo as first-line foremen, they were put in charge of warehouses as positions there opened. They understood that discreet use of nails, paint, brushes, plumbing and electric fixtures, safety shoes, etc., was acceptable as long as inventories balanced.

Unofficial rewards are of course given for uncovering *pure* theft and misuse of materials. But this calls for internal espionage, which is a harrowing and impossible role for some people. This informal role of theft intelligencer is essential in many organizations. House detectives, various

25. No estimate was made of the cost of materials, since many of these came from the scrap pile and would have been discarded anyway.

guards, and company police are the conventional guardians in business and industry. But this official role advertises itself. Everyone knows who to watch, and many resent the implications of being watched. Those who play the formal role of guard and investigator are not only likely to be compromised in various ways (see below), but they cannot function at the expected level of efficiency. For as they begin to accomplish official purposes they become the focus of informal attack and are made aware that they can be put in a bad light. . . . The theft intelligencer compensates for this defect. Simultaneously filling a formal role,[26] he must be one who has the tact and address to conceal his role of developing intimacies to discover misuse of materials.

At Milo, such investigations were usually carried on by selected persons in both staff and line. However as rule-makers and refiners who had to justify their existence, staff groups were especially eager to avoid blots on their professional escutcheons. Meeting this inherent perspective of the staff role limited the means of unofficially rewarding staff people. Materials and services would usually be inconsistent as a reward. Hence the staff agent who successfully carried out "intelligence" assignments was usually given his next promotion six months early, which admirably fitted *his* needs, and job logic.

Some inducements were both rewards and rights, but for different people. For example, what was at first a reward to some younger officer grew with his rank and seniority into a right which he in turn doled out judiciously as a reward to demanding subordinates.[27] Services and materials from the company garage, and long distance telephone calls were among the items spread along this axis of reward-rights. Line officers in good standing above the level of general foreman, and certain anointed staff figures including Rees at Milo and Reynolds at Attica, frequently, if not regularly, filled their gas tanks from company stock and received car servicing including washing and waxing. Rank was exercised, with the understanding for all that interference with garage personnel and use of materials culminating in defective operation or tie-up of company trucks and tractors, or accidents of any kind attributable to such interference, would threaten or even cut off reward-rights. As the balance of rewards and rights became too heavy with rights, inevitable crackdowns cut the

26. In diplomacy, the old role of papal *legatus a latere* was similar in the sense that a formal role, usually that of cardinal, embraced a confidential unofficial function.
27. Naturally, friendship was sometimes a consideration in meeting pressure from below. But where demands were made without significant contribution—and in the tone of "a right to share"—the "reward" given was sometimes a disguised penalty. At Attica one such aggressive person demanded a "share" of the house paint he knew others had received. He was given all the usual bulk-purchased and unmixed ingredients—except the drying fluid. Elated, he mixed and applied the paint. When it did not dry, the accumulations of dust and insects ruined his work. He became a laughing-stock without recourse.

rights and led higher executives to call on skilled machinists from the shops, instead of garage personnel, to give tune-ups, minor repairs, etc. Machinists in a sense shared these rewards and rights by (a) escape from repetitive work; (b) association with superiors whom they never met socially and seldom officially; (c) the privilege of taking Lincolns and Cadillacs out of the plant for "trialspins" after tune-ups, and driving home "on company time" to take their wives shopping and "be seen." All time of machinists in such activity was of course charged to their regular jobs.

The axis of reward-right has another common phase: some executives ambiguously feel a "right" to use materials and services whether granted or not, and if questioned would defend their practice as a due reward. These are the managers who put in much overtime (emergencies, meetings, etc.) without extra compensation, and who resent the time-and-a-half overtime pay of hourly-paid workers, and who assist in compiling and circulating lists of these workers whose annual incomes exceed, say, six thousand dollars. Frequently these are also the officers who angrily agree that the organization owns them and in turn, quite within the range of normal madness, protest a counter ownership of its resources. These managers would say, sociologically, that unofficial demands call for unofficial rewards. Where people have been "oversold" by higher management's attempt to win their identification, they may of course expect greater reward than they receive and resort to supplementation.

Use of materials to supplement low salary is apparently rather common in some of the smaller firms that are less formalized and less able to pay incomes comparable to those of larger companies. In the Argo Transit Company, a firm of two hundred employees, several of the office force were variously rewarded to keep them from moving elsewhere. One individual who had reached the top pay bracket, was given an extra day off each week with pay. Another person, considered as an indispensable secretary, was each week given any halfday off she desired with pay. Since she sewed much for her family and was the only secretary in that office, she did most of her handwork there in connection with sewing. She also did all her letter writing on the job and used company materials and stamps. Use of stamps at Christmas time amounted to a bonus. As she was expected to conceal her unofficial pay and to guard the box from other employees, she evidently also received a certain psychic reward. As a practice this is of course not new. Saintly Charles Lamb, known to have hated his job at the East India Company, used his employer's time and materials and franked letters to his friends, whom he requested to write collect to him. This was probably understood and acceptable, and was not a positive reward as in the case above.

An X-ray technician—of unknown quality—in a general hospital reported that his salary was so low he was "expected to steal hams and canned food" from the hospital supplies to supplement it. Though not in the same hospital, this may be related to the Midwestern hospital thefts nationally reported in October, 1953. There many additional items were taken, but the thefts may have started as an internal reward system and then have grown to a pilfering right extending to outside persons. The typical internal use of materials is suggested by the defense of one of the hospital attendants who allegedly said she had "never seen a hospital where they didn't take things," and the hospital administrator's apparent knowledge of the thefts and reluctance to intervene.

Evidently leaks of information at the technician's hospital transformed the plan of salary supplementation into a problem of theft. For one person rewarded by the informal plan was also unofficially paid for his suggestion for keeping the system in bounds. Despite its obvious complications, his proposal that nurses leave the hospital by the rear exit was accepted. As they passed through this door their clothing and bundles were inspected. But professional indignation and the rights of rank ended the inspection when one nurse objected that she had worked there "twenty years only to be reduced to sharing the scrub woman's entrance!"

Unofficial Incentives for the Group

Berger's remarks above indicated the private use of work groups by some Milo managers. As one of those referred to, Hardy's worth to the firm was unquestioned. Presumably Stevens knew of his more overt use of materials and services, which included the necessary labor and supplies for building a fireplace in his home under construction. Through Milo offices he also ordered a plate glass for his picture window and removed the glass from Milo on Sunday. He may have paid part of the cost of the glass since one reward-right in many firms is to allow elect members to buy through the company at wholesale prices, and less.

A recently retired Milo executive, who was a bird lover, had an eleven unit aviary built in Milo shops and installed on his large rear lawn. Each spring he sent carpenters from the plant—and continues to receive this service possibly as a phase of his pension—to remove, recondition, renovate, and re-install the bird houses. This person, who started the emphasis on Masonry as an unannounced requirement, frequently used the same carpenters for redecorating his home. Lack of comparable maintenance skills apparently checked this practice at Attica, but it occurred at Fruhling though documentary support is inadequate for that plant. As with the use of materials alone, this double employment of facilities and stores obviously may become abused "rights" that blur the line between theft and reward. However, managers in both firms raised defenses that fluctuated between double talk and sound argument. My bantering of intimates raised certain questions. For example, when unavoidable emergencies, errors in planning, and market changes made work shortages, was it better

334

to let "idle" men be seen by those who were busy, to reduce the work force, or to take the idle men out of the plant to do something else, something that was usually a lark for them? Management argued that unrest is promoted by "task inequities," and that men with nothing to do are pleased with a break in the monotony. Inquiries to Beemer, Brady, Spencer, and various maintenance workers usually elicited strong approval of this last alternative. For example, it was pointed out that "you get to sit down for twenty to forty minutes both ways" in traveling to and from an executive's home. Beemer saw this as equivalent to "several coffee breaks." Furthermore, the executive's wife "always gives us a lot of good eats." The president of the Milo union local supported the practice and held that it prevented layoffs. Management said essentially the same thing in noting that training costs and turnover were reduced, and at the same time there was no surplus of employees, for many of those "used on odd jobs" had to put in overtime at other periods. As with the machinists called on to service executive cars, those employees sporadically retained for out-plant work with some executive, derived both imponderable and concrete satisfactions. However, some first-line foremen and some workers saw the practice as "dirty," "unfair," and "taking advantage of your authority." And some people will call the practice high-level rationalization or collusion, but . . . it is more likely to be expediency periodically reclothed with new protective fictions.

Theft overlaps with reward-right where lower groups, foremen or workers, draw on plant resources, and higher management knows but dares not interfere, as in the hospital scandal. A European informant tells me of maintenance workers in railroad shops who drive their cars into the plant, rather than park outside as in our cases, and repair each other's cars on company time with company supplies. The cars are few and old and serve as busses as well as private vehicles. The practice is known to all, but since there is no fixed lunch hour, workers give the pretext if questioned that they work on the cars only during their lunch periods. Sometimes five to eight workers will be around one car for two or three hours at a stretch. With a short labor supply, and the practice apparently universal, management may officially protest, but usually looks the other way for fear the workers will seek jobs elsewhere.

The force of materials and services as unofficial incentives—internally for the company and externally for its ties with the community—was clearly visible in the activities of Magnesia's Yacht Club. As we saw in the preceding chapter, at least one hundred and fourteen members of Milo, and an unknown number from Fruhling, were active participants in the Club, at an individual annual fee of $50. Building additions to the Club and maintenance of its plant, as well as of privately owned boats, drew on the stores and services of Milo and Fruhling. Repair work was charged to various orders, which . . . was done with some regular work. Propeller shafts, bushings, fin keels, counterweights, pistons, hand railings, and the like, were made and/or repaired for boat owners among the managers as well as their friends in the community.

All of this was tied in with the prevailing practice here, and throughout industry, of doing "government jobs." These include original, as well as repair, work of many kinds usually done by maintenance forces—with plant materials and equipment on job time—as a "favor" for employees at all levels. At Milo, workers were singled out to aid the Club by doing miscellaneous government jobs. This was a compliment to their skills and a gesture of acceptance by higherups that appealed to the impulse to serve others, however weak this urge is according to cynics, or overpowering according to some theorists. Praise and minor perquisites were accepted as abundant rewards. And for some, inside and across all job divisions, old rifts born in the heat of past emergencies were often healed by shared work on these unofficial assignments. The opportunities offered by such work for exchange of obligations, for establishing warm understandings, and for blurring differences in official reward, needs no comment. Bureaucratic rationality is progressively, if unwittingly, reduced through these invasions by community recreational life. It can be argued that government jobs aid the survival of Maintenance, which is normally at conflict with Operation in their official functions.

We need more study on the ramifications of government jobs [28] and unofficial services, apart from understood rewards.

The Auditor's Dilemma

Together, theft and socially consumed materials cut into a firm's substance sufficiently to alarm auditors and staffs, committed as they are to compiling the statistics for detection, analysis, and control of all departures from the ideal, and to warrant their own pay.[29]

Above Milo's divisional level, concern was always shown when inventories turned up losses. The usual reaction was to state that nonsupervisory employees were to blame, and to order plant police to be more vigilant in their inspection of lunch buckets, bags, and bulging coats of outgoing personnel at the four gates.

The volume of materials "lost" was not known exactly. But cost

28. At least one large company outside this study sees government jobs as a problem unless limited to certain employees and done by specific people during given hours. In this case, only salaried people may take such work to a shop set up for that purpose which operates between 6 P.M. and 10 P.M., Monday through Friday.
29. Probably all organizational groups demand the stimulus of extra reward whether it be more of what they are already receiving or a greater share of those things having prestige value. The perquisite of staffs is usually the less material one of late arrival, early departure, and more socializing on the job, though additionally they, too, may participate in small government jobs.

analysts totaled and classified all incoming materials, then removed from the compilations all items, about 85 per cent of the total, that "could not possibly" be taken from the plant by persons on foot without detection. According to one analyst:

> It's not right on the nose, but about $15,000 of every $100,000 worth of material that *could* be taken out disappear—and never can be accounted for. Books can be juggled on some things but not much on this. Besides it's too damn constant. There's no question that it's carried out. If it's not, where the hell does it go to?

Some of the Milo managers and police suspected each other of carrying out materials or of collusively working with others to that end. Voicing his suspicions, the police chief was notified that his distrust was unfounded and insulting. On its side, management pointed to "statistical evidence" of police laxity. In delivering materials and removing the product, outside truckers had somehow sandwiched in forty-seven of some six hundred motors stored in an empty bay before the theft was discovered by the police. Management suspected some of the guards of bribed collaboration. Hardy set up a plan for unsystematic rotation of police around the circuit of gates. He believed this would prevent collusion between them and outsiders. Rotations were made monthly, but instead of moving all the men from one gate to the next nearest gate, only one man moved at a time and not in any sequence of gates or period of the month. This theory was not based on what had happened, and it was faulty in assuming that the major "nonproductive" consumption of materials was pure theft and was confined to production workers. Both in underestimating the ingenuity of lower ranking employees and in not seeing the nature of human association, the scheme did not prevent production workers from carrying out materials.

First, the theft of motors was accomplished by collusion of a few laborers with the truckers, but was concealed to protect a night supervisor. The suspected laborers were officially laid off for other reasons. The police were not participants. Second, we have seen that the major unofficial consumption of materials was by management itself, and in many cases was not pure theft. Finally, the theory ignored both the backgrounds of the police and the significance of government jobs. The police were not overpaid, and as company watchdogs they were, of course, persons for production workers to stand in well with. But as ex-workers, in most cases, the police also knew plant life and had need of government jobs for which they, too, were prepared to exchange favors. For example, when one of the gate guards knew that a friend wished to carry something from the plant, he told the friend which gate he was tending. At the gate, with a guard on each side, the friend making his exit approached his confidant who simulated an inspection and sent him through with a clap on the back.

In Department Stores

The use of internal materials and services as spurs and requitals of course is not confined to factories. Department stores, with their range of commodities, are a rich field for research in the use of implicit rewards.[30] The Rambeau Mart, member of a state chain, was one of the most flourishing department stores in the Mobile Acres area, and probably owed much of its solidarity to its flexible unofficial incentives.

Rambeau had a total of three hundred and seventy employees including the clerical force and three levels of management: the store chief and his assistants, the division heads, and the department heads. The store had the usual official structure—an auditing department with appropriate specialists, a quadruplicate reporting system, explicit rules against personal use of materials and services, and a budget allowance of ten per cent to cover shoplifting. Two store detectives supplemented the controls. They were gatetenders of a kind in seeing that only employees entered the store before opening time, and in checking the parcels of outgoing employees, at quitting time only, to see that they bore sales slips and the signature of a department head. Yet the managers of Rambeau tacitly adapted its resources to individual orientations, and in a showdown clearly approved the practice.

The unofficial incentive system took various forms. When conditions allowed, and within limits, some department heads privately altered the price of merchandise to fit the local market and to satisfy their own needs. Also, department heads aided each other, but in all cases they worked inside the dual requirement of having to show a profit and to pass the scrutiny of an annual audit. The latitude that ingenuity could establish inside these limitations showed that a brand of individual enterprise still exists and is rewarded in organizations that, at least unofficially, accent individual as well as group effort.

A common practice by department heads was to take items they wanted that were "shopworn" or "damaged" and mark them down "reasonably" for their own purchase. Some female heads regularly, but discreetly, gave certain items a "damaged" appearance. Division chiefs unofficially knew of this, and set no limit to the markdown that could be made, other things equal. However, those department heads who shrank from the ambiguities of exercising their authority and asked a division manager the limit for a markdown were usually told "30 per cent."

Heads of the various men's departments usually clothed themselves from each other's stocks at little or no cost. This might be accomplished, for example, by selling a bargain stock of two thousand pairs of socks not

30. For an intensive study of twenty salesgirls in the setting of a large department store, see George F. F. Lombard, *Behavior in a Selling Group,* Harvard University, Graduate School of Business Administration, Boston, 1955.

at the agreed 59 cents per pair, but at 69 cents, which accumulated to a fund of $200 above profit requirements. A given head could draw from this to cover the suits, shoes, shirts, etc., essential for his proper grooming. The markup, like the kind and volume of stock, might vary.

Normally, merchandise control demanded that each item, even when the stock and price were uniform, have its individual stock number and price tag. But as in the case of the socks, some commodities might be thrown on a table, without their separate labels, under one posted price. This of course allowed inclusion of some lower-priced items of similar quality which, as with the socks, contributed to the private trading fund. Detailed records of what he removed for himself or others in the interdepartmental trading, and careful balancing of the dollar value of total merchandise withdrawn against the dollar value of unofficial markups enabled the department chief to meet the inventory. If emergencies prevented this, he reported his stock as larger than it was at the time of inventory; for instance, he might report thirty suits on hand, when he had only twenty-seven. Help from assistants in the inventory allowed this, but no help could postpone judgment day beyond the next inventory when this particular stock would be double-checked. To prevent abuse of this elastic incentive, there was always the threat that auditors from another unit would be present to assist at some inventory.

Department heads reciprocated in their markdown of items sold to each other. When the transaction had to be written up, the heads sometimes used a fictitious name, or the names of their new employees as customers. This utilized the fact that the employees themselves were as yet still naive, and their names were still strange in the auditing and shipping departments. Obviously intended in part to forestall such practices, the quadruplicate form requiring a name and address meant little in these cases until the employee became widely known. Where the women in these interchanges usually got only clothing, the men fully utilized the system. For example, Joe, in plumbing, wanted furniture, so he talked with Bill, head of furniture, to see what Bill wanted in plumbing of about the same value that could be exchanged. The total of their trades and adjusted records, however, did not prevent them from showing a profit in the annual audit. Where such persons work together for years this becomes simple and so unofficially acceptable that it seems natural.[31] Like the

31. Favor-trading and adaptation of official procedures are likely to rise above any control. Even the outside organizations called in to assist in guaranteeing a certain conduct among given employees are simlarly used by cliques to protect the group and to maintain the informal status of its individual members. For example, Rambeau subscribed to the service of "Willmark," an organization that checks on the selling behavior of clerks. This is done by confidentially sending representatives to make purchases from employees and then formally scoring and reporting each person's sales behavior to the store office. However, at Rambeau—and doubtless elsewhere— when the "shoppers" registered in the manager's office, an upper member of the

skeletons in every family closet, these practices are not for public consumption but serve to unify the firm, as the skeletons do the family.

However, two department heads were dropped from this unit of Rambeau because of their use of company resources. Officially, one was released because of theft; the other, L. Nevers, because he wanted to transfer to another unit of the firm. The first head flagrantly took money from the tills of his salesmen, so that the following morning their cash and sales tallies did not match. This person was fired outright before he had taken a hundred dollars. But in Nevers' case light is thrown on what the internal use of materials and services meant in the context of incentives.

Nevers followed the procedures we have sketched and added his own refinements. In his accounting he was aided by one of his saleswomen whom he regularly befriended by ringing his sales on her cash drawer. However, her friendly relations with a saleswoman in another department led her to report Nevers' accounting methods and use of merchandise to the store manager and to name it as theft and malfeasance. Nevers' saleswoman, a "rate-buster," had worked with the other woman for years at Rambeau and elsewhere. Her friend's husband, shortly to return from the armed forces, had been head of a Rambeau department before being drafted. However there was uncertainty about his getting his old position back. So his wife, seeing the interpretation that could be made of Nevers' bookkeeping, and the consequences, hoped to have him fired and have her husband succeed him. She persuaded Nevers' saleswoman to report him in as bad a light as possible. The officially ignorant general manager knew roughly of Nevers' techniques and regarded him as "too good a man for the organization to lose." Forced to defend procedural dignity, he simulated a release but gave Nevers his choice of workplace among the statewide units, vigorously recommended him, and aided him in the successful transfer.

Two common merchandising policies encourage the use of goods as a supplementary incentive. First, the department head, as in other organizations, is expected to interpret policy. Second, all items are age-coded and regarded as having an approximate life expectancy. Some items of women's clothing may be "old" in less than four months, whereas some merchandise in hardware has an indefinite life. The age-code, or purchase date of items, is recorded at inventory. If too old, this advertises both the department head's poor judgment in making the original purchase, and his failure to "move" the goods. Hence in part to escape discredit he marks down older items for disposal among employees. Of course, he simul-

---

grapevine heard of it and whispered the phrase "shoppers today" to an intimate on the selling floor who passed the word. But only insiders were alerted; they in effect commanded deference and aid from new and fringe members of the sales force by tacit threat of not notifying them.

taneously sets up counter claims. In the phraseology of Rambeau department heads these items were "odds and ends of merchandise lying around
in the way that can't be sold anyhow." One of these heads declared that
the "paper and handling costs" of storing or returning some items for disposal elsewhere exceeded the worth of the merchandise many times over
and were, therefore, a drain on the firm.

The conditions attending demotion of a female department head support the existence of these policies. This person originally gained the post
through her brother's office at state headquarters. She "worried the life
out of" the division heads because only rarely could she "make decisions
on her own." She, too, desired "shopworn" items, including jewelry with
chipped stones, but she called on the merchandising chief for judgments on
the markdown she should make and was repeatedly given the official
"30 per cent." Knowing that others more than doubled this figure, she
caused trouble by her gossip and insinuations. She was eventually demoted
on the pretext that "store policy" demanded placement of a returning
veteran—actually from another unit of Rambeau—and that hers was the
logical post. Aware that the conditions of her original employment were
contrary to Rambeau's merit system, she offered no resistance and was
even "glad to get away from all that crazy paper work."

Thus inside the same unit, officially bureaucratic Rambeau could
adjust its incentives to satisfy both its enterprising and its less ambitious
managers. But in environments of this kind, the person who fits the ideal
of believing that his pay matches or exceeds his worth to the firm becomes a potential isolate and requires special attention, though his contribution is valued and utilized. Higher managers naturally wish to reward
this attitude, but since the employee may misinterpret any concrete informal reward as unacceptable "favoritism," the question is how? Rambeau had a female department head of this type. Of all the departments,
her inventory came nearest to the expected dollar value. It would have
been perfect except for the small surplus from single sales of three-for-a-
price items. (The surplus also indicated departmental alertness against
shoplifting.) Since she was a known devotee of bureaucratic procedure,
her department in effect selected personnel like herslf, and acquired a
reputation for this. When new heads for the candy counter were required
they were drawn from this woman's department because of the likelihood
that they would not be "free-loaders," nor tolerant of such people among
other employees. The only informal reward that Rambeau chiefs could
give this person and her kind was deference, and praise before others.

Rambeau's rule-devotee had a counterpart in one unit of a drugstore
chain near Mobile Acres. She managed the drugstore's soda fountain. A
problem arose from her consistently having the highest percentage of profits
among the chain's soda fountain managers. The matter was an issue among
fountain heads in neighboring units of the chain, who were in personal

rivalry with her. Her success was officially honored, for the situation was competitive and fountain supervisors received a percentage of profits above a given level. But a typical condition—which some students may mistakenly call "institutionalized theft"—existed among all the other units and worked to adversely interpret her achievement. Volume of business on the fountains was comparable in cities near the same size as was the seating capacity, facilities, and the margin of profits among all but the one fountain. The chief difference between practices in this fountain and the others—covertly charged by the woman and admitted by some of the store managers and pharmacists—was that the other fountain heads gave food and confections free to relatives and close friends, drinks to fountain employees, and variously bartered with nonfountain employees in much the manner of department heads at Rambeau. Unofficial reward, in the form of meals, to fountain employees was, of course, encouraged by the chain's wage rate which, while comparable to that of the local stores, was no higher than the minimum industrial rates. Most of the fountain heads covertly rewarded their "good workers" in this way to hold them.

The practices were engaged in up to the point of maintaining at least a narrow margin of profit for the store if not for the fountain heads. The latter were apparently guided more by concern to show a small profit for the fountain—which they did not share—than by a wish to achieve the higher departmental margin that would allow them a percentage of money profits from the fountain. Prices to the public, set by the chain's state-wide committee, were uniform throughout the system. Excepting the one, all fountain managers discreetly helped themselves to canned foods, dairy products, and meats from the departmental stock, with the knowledge of the store manager who received free meals, and coffee at any time. The one fountain chief allowed no gratis consumption to employees, friends, relatives, or herself. She kept the refrigerators locked and closely supervised the handling of stock. When emergencies prevented her from shopping for her family and she took a loaf of bread from the fountain stock, she deposited the price in the cash register. Married to a farmer-factory worker, she stressed loyalty to the store chief, customer service, and money profits for herself. Her superior could not condemn this, but he was disturbed by her boasting of her standing in the chain, and by the innuendoes from other store managers about her "pencil work." To minimize the woman's behavior, he backed his half-hearted praise of her with the logic that fountains are only a supplement to drug and cosmetic services, and that in total store profits his unit was sometimes second or lower in state rankings. But the resentment of other fountain managers—and of his own nonfountain employees against the woman's opposition to the perquisites usually allowed such personnel—forced him openly to check her records, to imply that she was making errors, and to withhold the praise she obviously craved. Higher chain officials also asked her to explain her unique performance and hinted that she could not be that much superior to other fountain managers. After two years of mounting resentments, she quit the firm. The store manager regarded her as a failure because she did not understand what he could not tell her—that her margin of profits was too high and that some social use of materials, not theft, was expected. In his mind, she was too little concerned with the system's internal harmony, and too devoted to formalities.

These practices at Rambeau and in the drugstore chain are doubtless common in many stores, but they are not made obvious to the students responsible for theory about organizational roles, job structure, resources, and pay. And they mean different things to the people involved.

Summary and Comment

The diversity and range of contributions required of an administrative or functional group cannot be exactly reflected in the official system of rewards. This is an inherent, not a diabolical, shortcoming. It springs largely from (1) the assumption that the total duties and essential skills for a given job are boxed in and paid for, and from (2) the impossibility of officially recognizing some of the extraordinary contributions made by various members—often out of role—during crises.

On the first point, not only must compensation be planned to maintain minimum harmony among personnel, but the limited resources of every firm require it. On the second point, open recognition of some essential contributions would advertise conditions that should not exist, promote rivalries,[32] hurt official dignity, and encourage disrespect for regulations. Hence recourse is had to semi-confidential use of materials and services as a supplement. This can be both inducement and requital to those who must receive great recognition to do their best, and to those who would move elsewhere without the increment.

Supplementation may be accompanied by abuse to the extent (1) that the reward becomes habitual and is unrelated to contribution; (2) that it

32. We earlier noted Barnard's analysis of democratic rivalries, and the need in decision making to anticipate and avoid their consequences. In the 1830s an acute French visitor commented on the always smoldering envy among Americans. Here officially to study our prison system, he remarked that "the hatred which men bear to privileges increases in proportion as privileges become more scarce . . . so that democratic passions . . . seem to burn most fiercely . . when they have least fuel." Americans, then as now, "dread all violent disturbance . . . and love public tranquillity." But in their mania for equality they attribute the success of an *equal* "mainly to some one of his defects" rather than "to his talents or virtues." For to do otherwise "is tacitly to acknowledge that they are themselves less virtuous and talented." See Alexis de Tocqueville, *Democracy in America* (trans. by Henry Reeve), 2 vols., The Cooperative Publication Society (The Colonial Press), New York, 1900, vol. 1, p. 229; vol. 2, pp. 307–8.

is shared by those who make no unusual contribution; or (3) that it expands and becomes coerced theft. The changing line between reward and abuse may be difficult to find and hold, but nothing can be done until the problems is faced. Evading it disposes nonparticipating personnel and the public to label all use of materials and services in this sense as theft. This cynicism cannot be eliminated by allocating 10 to 15 per cent of the budget to cover "shoplifting" by nonsupervisory employees and the public. Such allocation may of course enable some managers and subordinates to hide their own theft up to this limit. But it fails to distinguish theft from essential maintenance of the social mechanism. The problem is pervaded by our tradition of political spoils,[33] and our logic that service to the organization must have a one-to-one relation to rank and explicit compensation. We must note that absence of this neat balance induces supplementation, and inflicts moral suffering among members inversely to their capacity for automatic hypocrisy.

It is unlikely that a universally applicable system of informal rewards can be set up, but it is certain that where abuse of the practice develops it will not be eliminated by moral exhortations, elaborate paper forms, or rigid policing. These restraints all help, but as we all know, those who make and apply controls may be like Cellini. If so, their close associates are likely to share their privileges [34] and echo the general lament of abuse by "others."

Admitting the potential disruptiveness of implicit rewards, can we assure the full commitment of all abler members without them? And since we dare not preach what we practice, how do we know that we would have less disturbance and as much or more contribution without supplementation and some abuse? Can we show that the cost of, say 15 per cent, to cover theft and unofficial reward is excessive in lieu of other inducements which also cost? This is not to say that what exists is good, but to say that we do not know how bad it is until we can see it more closely.

Abuse is indefensible, but for the sake of a sharper focus on the issue let us say that as varieties of supplementation and limited abuse sap one brand of company resources, they protect other assets. For example, do they not in many cases also reduce disruptive conflict, break the monotony of routine, allow more personal expression, ease the craving for spon-

---

33. Walter Lippmann, *A Preface to Politics,* The Macmillan Company, New York, 1913, chap. 1; Charles A. and Mary Beard, *The Rise of American Civilization,* 2 vols. in one, The Macmillan Co., New York, 1937, vol. 1, pp. 547–57; V. O. Key, Jr., *Politics, Parties, and Pressure Groups,* 2nd edition, Thomas Y. Crowell Co., New York, 1947, pp. 316–39.

34. Again speaking timelessly, but referring to earlier Americans, de Tocqueville declared that, "Whatever may be the general endeavor of a community to render its members equal and alike, the personal pride of individuals will always seek to rise above the line, and to form somewhere an inequality to their own advantage." *Op. cit.,* vol. 2, p. 226.

taneity, and to some extent catch up all levels of personnel in a system of mutual claims so that aid can be requested and hardly denied?

However, even with revision of the sheep-or-goat outlook, the problem must mark time until serious students are able in many contexts to at least look at (1) the elusive nature of organization that requires unofficial performances; (2) the relation of reward to informal services given; and (3) the relation of all reward to organizational resources, material and social.

Our study of unofficial rewards is not an attempt to justify internal plunder or to say that theft by membership is inevitable. Both "theft" and "reward" derive their meaning from the social context. To insist that this context is constant—so that we can preserve the admitted convenience of fixed definitions—is to pervert meaning, block the issue, and deny that there are ethics in reward.

To repeat, the aim has been to show that however well defined official tasks may be, and however neatly we think we have fitted our personnel to these roles, the inescapably fluid daily situation distorts expected working conditions. Circumstances require various out-of-role and unplanned actions. Regardless of formal rankings, which are often only nominally based on potential for such action, some personnel more aptly do what is essential than do others. Tacitly or not, both they and their rewarders are aware of who solves problems and sustains the organization. Through time they are compensated as resources and situations allow. The process may seem to overlap with theft, or it may escape control and become theft, but able executives both utilize and contain unofficial rewards.

PART FOUR

Organizational Structure

The selections contained in this part illustrate major issues associated with the ways in which organizations are structured, such as the necessary structural arrangements to ensure democracy in voluntary organizations, the complexity and difficulties involved in devising a structure for social service delivery systems, the issues involved in the relationships between women and organizational structure, and the relative effects of different technologies in explaining differences in organizational structure.

All organizations are political entities and therefore, the complete analysis of organizational structure must include the distribution and exercise of power. The first selection applies and develops principles derived from Michels' classic analysis of *Political Parties,* an excerpt of which was presented in Part One. This study of a deviant case—the International Typographers Union, a democratic labor union—raises this fundamental question: to what extent can an organization of any kind in a democratic society both attain its official objectives and meet the emergent political requirements of its members? Lipset, Trow, and Coleman confront the problem of organizational democracy. The legitimacy of an opposition party within the organization's structure is shown to be one crucial structural element essential to the maintenance of the democratic process. The nature of large-scale organization itself and the learned orientations to power of its leaders, as well as the unique concatenation of historical events, are equally important.

In the second selection Aldrich presents an interesting example of some of the difficulties in understanding the complexities involved in organizational structure. His focus is social service delivery systems, with particular emphasis upon the manpower services system. Such systems illustrate very well the arguments for either a centralized or decentralized organizational structure. Of particular interest in this respect is the fact that Aldrich is able to demonstrate that neither argument seems to have won and most systems there-fore contain a mixture of both. Hence, structural contradictions are built into these systems. Aldrich reviews four common arguments in favor of centralized structures and four common arguments made in favor of decentralized structures. As he notes, "the arguments are so persuasive that planners who on one occasion argue strongly for centralization find themselves on other occasions defending the benefits of decentralization. Such is the appeal of the arguments that most human service delivery systems ultimately are designed with both sets of principles underlying them." A further complica-tion in understanding the nature of organizational structure is evi-denced in the level of analysis selected. Aldrich shows that one's conclusions regarding the benefits of centralized or decentralized systems depends greatly upon whether one is focusing upon clients, organizations, or the interorganizational field. Aldrich concludes that there is no one best way to design human service delivery systems and, indeed, such master plans are probably beyond our comprehension and competence at this point in time.

In the third selection Kanter provides a necessary corrective to current knowledge concerning organizational structure. Kanter demonstrates that very little research and theory have been con-cerned with the ways in which women affect and are affected by organizational structure. She argues that a "masculine ethic" of rationality and reason is easily identified in much of the early theory and research concerned with organizational structure. This mana-gerial viewpoint was congruent with the nearly exclusive male oc-cupancy of managerial and administrative positions. The focus upon managerial rationality also "justified" the absence of women from positions of power. In addition, most of this theory and research failed to address the larger issues of the relation between the differ-ential distributions of men and women in the larger society, and the consequences of this for understanding organizational structure. Kanter argues, therefore, for a structuralist perspective on women and organizations that will correct many of these earlier distortions, maintaining that the sexual composition of organizations and groups within organizations has an impact on behaviors related to a large number of issues, such as sexism, responses to "token women," and role entrapment of tokens. She then examines a number of signifi-cant theoretical and practical problems that arise from single-sixed groups, mixed-sex groups, and the effects of skewed sex ra-tios as illustrations of the type of research that could and should provide a better and more accurate understanding of organizational structure.

In the final selection, Blau and his colleagues evaluate the relative effects of differing types of technology in explaining differences in organizational structure. Specifically, they examine the relationships among technology and four dimensions of organizational structure—personnel components, spans of control, differentiation, and centralization—for a sample of 110 manufacturing organizations. They find that different types of technology have very different effects upon organizational structure. Degree of mechanization of production technology, for example, was not related to the dimensions of organizational structure. In contrast, organizational size was related to all of the dimensions of structure, which further confirms Blau's formal theory of organizational structure reported in Part Two. On the other hand, a curvilinear relationship is found between type of production technology and the four dimensions of organizational structure. This determination differs significantly from previous research findings in this area that focused upon linear relationships. Finally, Blau and his associates find that computer automation is related to the dimensions of organizational structure in ways that contradict many current speculations concerning the effects of computers on organizations. Of particular significance is the discovery that production technology and computer automation have very different effects upon centralization. Highly mechanized production technologies tend to provoke centralized structures, whereas computer automation encourages decentralized structures. The authors conclude that computer automation of administrative functions will continue with the increasing automation of the manufacturing process itself, and this growing automation of factories will raise both the level of skill and responsibility of the workers involved.

Why Democracy in the ITU?

Seymour M. Lipset
Martin A. Trow
James S. Coleman

In spite of the detailed nature of our analysis the reader may still legitimately raise the question: Why democracy in the ITU? Is it really a necessary consequence of the structural factors which have been examined? Is it not possible that even if a union possesses all the attributes that the ITU has, it will not develop nor sustain a democratic political system? To what extent could matters have developed differently in the ITU if certain events had occurred differently, or if at some crucial periods in its existence ruthless and powerful men had been at the helm of the union and had been willing to risk destruction of the union rather than lose power? In a real sense, these questions cannot be answered, for in the context of the study of a single case it is impossible to isolate completely all the potentially relevant factors and then specify which factors, either individually or in combination, account for the differences in internal political organization between the ITU and most other unions. We know, for example, that the particular pattern of ITU politics is not repeated in other printer unions in Europe, although there is evidence which suggests that as a group they are more democratic and less centralized than unions in other occupations.

Historical Analysis

The sociological analysis with which most of the book is concerned is an analysis of the factors which contribute to the continuation of the democratic political system at the present time. But it is important to recognize that this analysis gives only a static picture, a description which shows the processes at work within the going system, but not the processes which enabled the system to reach more or less stable equilibrium. At any point in time, the political system of an organization or a society has a certain degree of stability. That is, it has a certain probability of continuing in its present form, and a certain probability of changing. The political system of the ITU is always being supported by some factors and undermined by others. By thus viewing the system as being in an equilibrium which at any point in time has a certain stability, but which could have moved in different directions if some of the factors in the situation had occurred differently, we can see the need to deal with historical materials. It remains for the historical analysis of events which were unique to the ITU to indicate which factors favored the emergence and stability of ITU democracy at different points in time, and to specify the crucial junction points at which new elements entered the situation.

In this way we see that the existence of democracy in the ITU is largely the result of the convergence of a set of events, each of which contributes to or detracts from the continuing stability of the system. If some one event in the early history had turned the other way, then present-day democracy in the union would have been less likely. The existence of democracy at present may be likened to a series of successive outcomes of casting dice, dice which are with each favorable throw more heavily loaded toward a favorable outcome on the next throw.[1] Democracy in the ITU was thus no necessary consequence of a particular set of static factors, but rather was favored from the beginning by numerous factors and even more strongly favored as time went on and numerous events added to the system's stability.

The answer to our original question, Why democracy in the ITU? can be found only by combining the structural and historical analyses to determine the system's stability at each point in time. Thus, in conclusion we would like to examine again some of the crucial turning points in the union's early history.

Many of the factors which contribute to ITU's democracy were present when the union was organized. The printers' strong identification with the craft of printing, probably more pronounced then than now, meant that they were more likely to be involved in the affairs of their organization than workers in other occupations. This same identification, together with other factors such as the high status and irregular work hours of printing, also fostered a strong occupational community. This occupational community, in turn, stimulated the desire of printers to participate in their union. The borderline or marginal status of printing between the middle class and the working class insured the value cleavage which provided the content of politics and evenly split the union into "radical" and

---

1. See Max Weber: *The Methodology of the Social Sciences,* New York, Free Press, 1949, pp. 182–85, for a similar discussion, including this "dice-throwing" analogy.

moderate camps. Perhaps most important of all at this period was the fact that a large proportion of the printing trades was organized before the creation of a strong international union with a large treasury and paid full-time officials. Thus, the various large city locals of the ITU had a long history of complete autonomy and resisted efforts to create a centralized international structure.

The significance of this factor in the history of the union may be seen by comparing the implications of two ideal-type patterns through which organizations are created. One is organization from the top down, where the group which originally starts the association organizes other individuals and branches into a larger structure. In such a situation we may expect the existence from the start of a formal bureaucratic structure with the new subordinate officials and groups deriving their authority from the summits of the organization. On the other hand, a large national organization may come into existence as a federation through the combination of a number of existing groups. In such a federation the creation of a one-party bureaucratic hierarchy requires the reduction of once independent locals or groups of leaders to subordinate power and status position.

While the ITU illustrates the second pattern, which obviously has greater potential for internal conflict and politics, the International Printing Pressmen and Assistants' Union, the other large printing trades union, exemplifies the first pattern. There, George Berry became president of the union while it was a small, weak organization, and organizd the bulk of the trade into a highly centralized and dictatorial organization.[2] Thus the way in which the ITU came into existence and the late development of full-time international officers was not only a factor making for early democracy in the union, but also helped insure that the next throw of the dice would be loaded in favor of democracy and decentralization.[3]

2. See Carolyn A. Taylor: *The Emergence and Stabilization of Oligarchy in the International Printing Pressmen and Assistants Union of North America.* M.A. thesis, Columbia University, Department of Sociology, 1952.

3. A somewhat similar variation in organizational history accounts in large part for the differences in the political history of the United Automobile Workers and the United Steel Workers, two unions formed about the same time and affected by similar structural conditions. The Steel Workers was originally formed by the Steel Workers Organizing Committee under Philip Murray. With few exceptions, almost every local of this union was created *after* the initial power structure was established. From its inception there have been no serious factional disputes in the union which have given the members the right to choose among rival candidates for office. Any local center of disturbance was eliminated by Murray. On the other hand, the United Automobile Workers was formed out of an amalgamation of a number of existing automobile unions, and a number of its other local units were organized independently of national control and with relatively little aid from the national body. The subsequent bitter factional fights in the union have in part been a consequence of the attempt of various national administrations to set up a single bureaucratic hierarchy. Most of the factional leaders in the UAW were leaders in the early organizational period of the union, and the different factions have largely been coalitions of the groups headed by these different leaders jointly resisting efforts to sub-

A second important event affecting ITU politics was the formation of the secret societies which over the years endeavored to control both union offices and foremen's jobs. These societies, which were the first major challenges to the democracy of the printers' locals, contributed important elements to the union's democratic system. The autonomy of the locals, referred to above, helped prevent the secret societies from completely dominating the union, for the existence of local administrations opposed to the dominant secret society gave the ordinary printers a nucleus of organization and helped to expose the activities of the society. Also important is the fact that the intense identification of printers with their craft meant that the norms of brotherhood engendered by this identification made membership in an exclusive clique illegitimate in the eyes of many secret-society members as soon as the society lost its early legitimate function of protecting the union.

Thus the stability of ITU democracy was tested and found strong even before the institutionalization of the party system. The struggle over the secret societies, however, added another element which served to preserve the union. Large numbers of printers had a deep personal interest in the fight, since it affected their personal security of employment and opportunity to get work. At least two major cliques or factions developed in most locals, the adherents and the opponents of the secret societies, and these cleavages resulted in deep personal conflicts. The struggle, consequently, could not simply be solved by the victory of one group in an election and the subsequent disappearance of the defeated faction, a frequent development in other unions where the factionalism has not deeply involved the interests or values of the large majority of the members. In the ITU the opposing factions had their roots in a basic cleavage among the members themselves, a cleavage which outlived the tenure in office of a given group and provided the basis for continuing opposition.

Again, it is difficult to state why such secret societies developed only within the ITU; but one guess is that the factors making for an occupational community helped to sustain the secret societies. These groups (and their opponents as well) were not just power-politics groups, but social clubs which fulfilled many of the same functions as other clubs in the printers' community. The fact, however, that secret political societies were formed cannot be explained by the tendency of printers to mingle with fellow craftsmen, but rather must be seen as a fortuitous reaction to a crisis in the union's relation with employers. Had the union not required such instruments of defense in the 1870's, there was no necessary reason

---

ordinate them to the national organization. In spite of the fact that the structural conditions in a large industrial union like the UAW are not favorable to internal democracy and large-scale rank-and-file participation, it has taken close to two decades to approach a one-party structure, and the process is still not completed.

for the emergence of these groups nor for the subsequent development of bitter struggles to abolish them.

The struggle over the secret societies also facilitated the democratization of the ITU's political structure through providing a rationale (a) for making the election of international officers a popular election, replacing the then existing system of election-by-convention, which is more easily controllable by the administration even in the ITU; (b) for reserving the decision on many matters to popular referendum; and (c) for providing an easy method of rank-and-file initiation of referenda. These measures in turn enabled the ITU membership to hold down the salaries of their officers, since increases could only be secured with the approval of the membership in referenda, approval which usually was not given. The fact that the fight against the secret societies was defined as a struggle against domination by visible organized minority cliques, and not simply as a fight against an incumbent administration, helped give the membership a sophisticated awareness of structural dangers to democracy. Thus were instituted important legal elements which support the stability of ITU democracy today.

Again, the pressmen may be used as a comparative case. Although that union underwent a factional struggle early in its history which resulted in the overthrow of the incumbent administration in 1907, factionalism was not institutionalized and perpetuated. The Pressmen's Union had a typical factional fight organized around a specific issue—the conservative collective-bargaining policy followed by the union. Once the old administration was defeated, factionalism practically vanished, since it did not take on the deep intralocal and personal character of the early ITU fights. The new president, George Berry, was able to use his victory to change the constitution in ways which solidified the power of the administration.

These two important points in the early history of the ITU are part of a pattern of "favorable dice throws." Another example, the permanent institutionalization of a rigid priority system in the ITU, was a result of the desire by the members to restrict one of the sources of power of the secret societies and was made possible largely by the existence of the referendum. Without the secret societies and the referendum, the ITU might never have developed a rigid priority system, and one of the factors which safeguard the members' activity in politics against the administration would never have developed. The pressmen, for example, have never adopted a priority system, and its absence has been one of the major resources of the oligarchic rulers of that union.

One additional turning point in the ITU's history deserves mention because it involves the first coming to power of the opposition party. The institutionalization of the practice of gracefully giving up office to an opposition without attempting to use illegitimate means to retain office is one of the most important aspects of a democratic society, which those living in such a society take for granted, while citizens of many states and members of many trade unions know that it is not a simple and regular event. In many unions, administrations on the verge of defeat have resorted to various means, such as the expulsion of the opposition or its leaders, in order to retain power. It is not inconceivable that the Wahneta administration of 1919–1920 might have done the same thing. One factor, however, which served to prevent this from happening was the fact that the Progressives captured only one of the executive offices, the presidency, in the election, while the Administration Party retained its hold over the rest of the major offices and the Executive Council. Given its long-term rule of the union, it is clear that it expected to regain the presidency and retain control of the union once the temporary crisis occasioned by the 1919 New York strike was over. But the union remained more or less evenly divided between the two parties from 1920 to 1928. During these years each party could well hope that the next election would give it complete power. Thus, democratic practices continued through this critical period. Comparison may again be made with the Pressmen's Union, where evidence would suggest that George Berry was on the verge of defeat in the 1920s. He averted such a result by expelling opposition locals and leaders.

The 1920 election was important for the continuation of ITU democracy for another reason. As we pointed out earlier, Marsden Scott, the Wahneta president of the ITU, attempted to break the "vacationist" strike of the New York union. Had this not led to a defeat for Scott, primarily because the New York local voted overwhelmingly against him, the autonomy of the large locals would have been seriously impaired. The international officers would have felt free to manipulate the large locals at will. As it was, this event marked the first major victory of the Progressives, and served as a warning to future international officers not to treat lightly the wishes of large locals. This occurrence also may serve as another illustration of the way in which previous events help load the dice in one direction. The 1919 strike was a joint action of the New York pressmen and typographer locals against the orders of their internationals. When the IPP local disobeyed, Berry expelled the entire New York membership and brought in strikebreakers from outside the city. Scott limited his actions to calling publicly upon the men in Big Six to ignore their local leaders and return to work. Perhaps one reason why Berry and Scott acted differently was that the political consequences of their actions were predictably different. The pressmen's constitution, drawn up by Berry before he faced internal opposition, provided for elections through an electoral-college system in which large locals such as New York have a maximum of six votes while every small local has at least one electoral vote. Thus six locals with less than two hundred members among them, which supported Berry, could balance out the vote of the entire New York membership against him. In the ITU, however, every member votes individually. Scott, therefore, had to try to retain some support in New York if he hoped to be re-elected, and this fact may have operated to restrain his strikebreaking activities. The fact that the ITU decided in 1896 to elect officers by referendum may have been a crucial element in preserving its democracy in 1919–1920.

Without discussing other events chronologically, it is worth mentioning in this context the way in which the existence of an institutionalized party system operates to preserve and extend democratic institutions. At various points in ITU history the constitution has been amended at the initiative of the opposition or by a party just returned to office, in ways designed to weaken the power of the incumbents. The right of all candidates to print statements in the *Typographical Journal,* various elaborate controls over the spending of union monies, the creation of independent auditors elected in staggered six-year terms, and other similar legislation are examples of the ways in which ITU democracy has become incorporated in the law and mores.

These examples of different historical events which have strengthened the base for ITU democracy should serve to illustrate the point that social structure—using the term in this case to refer to the social system comprising the occupation, the industry, and union—defines the probabilities that given historical events can result in an enduring institutional pattern such as a two-party system. Social structure thus constitutes a *potential* for democracy, a potential which, however, may be realized only under certain historical circumstances. This potential can exist without bearing fruit if the initiating events do not occur, or if other abortive events happen. The history of the Pressmen's Union is perhaps a case in point. More often in American unions, one can find a pattern of events which might have initiated a party system had it not occurred in an organization whose social structure offered barren ground for democratic institutions. The United Automobile Workers is perhaps a case in point here.

Implications for Organizational Democracy

Observers have called the ITU an anachronism, much like some of the small Swiss cantons which still preserve the direct citizen-assembly control of government, and there is much truth in that view. The major trends in our society are all toward further rationalization of industry, the further concentration and centralization of economic units, and the increasing division of labor, with the substitution of automatic machine operations for skilled craftsmen. Technological developments in the printing industry point in the same direction, with the introduction of new mechanical processes which require little more than the skills of the typist.

Although the union is resisting efforts on the part of the employers to divide composing work into two skill levels, many union leaders and members are privately pessimistic about their ability to maintain the centuries-old principle of printers that every worker who sets type should have the same training and be regarded as of equal skill level. The threats to the union posed by new mechanical devices, plus the growing importance of international union policies which meet the need to protect past rights challenged by government legislation, seem to be gradually resulting in a decline of the autonomy of the larger locals. Identification with the craft, and the isolation of printers from interaction with people in higher or lower status levels than themselves also appears to be lessening with changes in the American status structure, and the evidence would seem to indicate that the occupational community of the late forties and early fifties, while still strong, is weaker than it was before World War II. The ITU is still one of the most powerful unions in America and may for some time absorb or cushion the impact of technological developments on the status, income, and skill definition of printing. But major changes in the structure of the industry such as are occurring could conceivably destroy the political system of the union by changing the social system in which it is rooted.

There are mitigating factors, however. The decline of democracy in the ITU is a prediction for the long run, and as John Maynard Keynes has said, in the long run we are all dead. In the meantime, those political institutions which were institutionalized as a consequence of the social conditions making for democracy may prolong for a considerable period the democracy which exists. The normative and legal safeguards to the stability of democracy which developed throughout the union's history can act to preserve democracy long after some of the factors which gave rise to them have vanished. Perhaps the most important democratic defense mechanism which has been institutionalized in the ITU is the two-party system itself. The sheer existence of a two-party system provides one of the principal opportunities and stimulations for participation in politics by the members of an organization or community. If one compares a party conflict to contests between different athletic organizations, one can see how this process operates in areas other than politics. In a city which has two baseball clubs, or two high-school football teams, many individuals who have no great interest in sports are exposed to pressures to identify with one or the other team by the fans of each one. Such identification once made and reinforced by personal relations with committed fans seems to lead many people to become strongly interested in who wins a given sports contest. Political identification, while more complicated, nevertheless takes on some of the aspects of team identification. Political parties, once in existence, attempt to activate the apathetic in order to keep alive and win power. This process undoubtedly leads more people to become interested and involved in the affairs of the community or organization than when no political conflict exists.[4]

As long as some men feel strongly about union issues and others are desirous of securing or retaining the status derivative from the role of union political leader, the party organizations will be maintained in the ITU, since they are the institutionalized mechanisms through which such men can express themselves.

In a one-party structure, on the other hand, politically interested or ambitious men have only one outlet for their activity, and that is involvement in the activities sponsored by the administration. In the absence of a democratic political arena in which men may learn the skills of politics outside the administration, union officers are usually faced with a paucity of skilled and capable prospective subordinate officials, and are usually willing and even anxious to coopt capable union activists into the administrative structure. In such one-party unions, apathy on the part of the membership is functional to the stability of the incumbent machine. The less the members know or desire to know about policy, the more secure the leaders are. The single-party organization in a trade union consequently acts to dampen participation, while in the ITU, membership interest and activity are the lifeblood of the party.[5]

This brief comparison of some of the ways in which one-party and two-party systems, once institutionalized, operate to perpetuate the existing system demonstrates again the link between the historical and the sociological levels of analysis. The historical analysis explains how the system, in this case two-party democracy, came into existence, while the socio-

4. Various election studies show that the closer the contest in a given electoral unit, the higher the rate of voting participation. See Herbert Tingsten, *Political Behaviour;* D. E. Butler: *The British General Election of 1951,* London, The Macmillan Co., Ltd., 1951; H. F. Gosnell: *Why Europe Votes,* Chicago, University of Chicago Press, 1930; and V. O. Key, *Southern Politics.*

5. There is one important exception to the generalization that leaders of one-party unions or dictatorships will not attempt to stimulate membership participation. In totalitarian states and in Communist-controlled labor unions, extreme efforts are made to secure the participation of citizens or members. The totalitarian leader is concerned with having his followers attend meetings, read political or union literature, listen to broadcasts, and engage in other similar activities, since this means that he can reach them with his point of view and attempt to indoctrinate them. If the members or citizens are not "politically" active, they are also removed from the influence of the controlling power. As a general hypothesis, one might suggest that the greater the changes in the structure of the society that a governing group is attempting to introduce, or the greater the changes in the traditional functions of unions that a union leadership is attempting to effect, the more likely a leadership is to desire and even require a high level of participation by citizens or members. The radical changes that accompany social revolution, or on a smaller scale, the transformation of a trade union into a political weapon, put severe strains on group loyalties and create the potential for strong membership hostility toward the leadership. A high level of controlled and manipulated rank-and-file participation is perhaps the only effective way, given the leadership's purposes, of draining off or redirecting the discontent which violent changes in traditional patterns and relationships engender.

359

logical analysis accounts for the ways in which structural factors, either those existing in the situation or those created by specific historical developments, operate to maintain it. The latter factors, those which are created by a unique series of events, may over the years turn out to be even more important in explaining why the system continues. An example drawn from economic history may help to illustrate the general significance of this methodological point.

Max Weber, in his classic studies of the relations between economic behavior and cultural values, attempted to demonstrate that the emergence of a unique cultural ethos in certain Protestant sects provided the effective set of economic values which made possible the development of a rational capitalist economic system.[6] Ascetic Protestantism, especially Calvinism, so defined the situation for its followers as to require their concentration on the maximization of economic wealth so as to assure themselves that they were predestined to go to heaven. The specific Protestant *religious* ethos have disappeared, however, in many countries in which the economic "spirit of capitalism" still exists. The religious system is no longer necessary in the United States, for example, to support the economic ethos of a going industrial society. Any attempt today to explain the continued existence of a secular "Protestant ethic," must locate the relationship between that ethic and the functional requirements of a going capitalist economic system. Such an analysis might point to the fact that in a capitalist social system the dominant roles through which social status is secured are best achieved or maintained by men acting in accordance with the "spirit of capitalism." Here we have an interdependent system in which status achievement requires adhering to certain values, and adhering to these values facilitates status achievement. Such a functional analysis, however, will not explain why this system is best developed in countries with an ascetic Protestant background rather than in Catholic or non-Christian countries. To deal with this problem, it would be necessary to go back to an analysis of the conditions under which the new system first came into existence.

Conclusions

The conclusions derived from theoretical analyses of the possibilities for democracy inherent in the structure of large-scale voluntary organiza-

6. See Max Weber: *The Protestant Ethic and the Spirit of Capitalism*, New York, Charles Scribner's Sons, 1930; *The Religion of China*, New York, Free Press, 1950; and *Ancient Judaism*, New York, Free Press, 1952; also see Talcott Parsons: *The Structure of Social Action*, New York, Free Press, 1949, for a discussion of Weber's method. Weber's conclusions have been challenged by many economic historians. In citing this example, however, we are not interested in who is right in this controversy, but rather in the method of analysis.

tions, from empirical descriptive analysis of what actually goes on in most trade unions and other voluntary organizations, and from specifying the conditions which are related to democracy in the most democratic large voluntary association, the International Typographical Union, suggest that the functional requirements for democracy cannot be met most of the time in most unions or other voluntary groups.

To recapitulate the major points in this analysis:

1. The structure of large-scale organization inherently requires the development of bureaucratic patterns of behavior. The conditions making for the institutionalization of bureaucracy and those making for democratic turnover in office are largely incompatible. While bureaucracy reduces the area which is political—the area subject to discussion and choice among the members—it also gives an incumbent administration great power and advantage over the rank and file or even an organized opposition. This advantage takes such forms as control over financial resources and internal communications, a large, permanently organized political machine, a claim to legitimacy, and a near monopoly over political skills.

2. The normal position of the trade-union member in modern urban society makes it likely that few individuals will ordinarily be actively interested in the affairs of the union. Leisure-time activities are centered around home and neighborhood rather than around one's vocation. The absence of membership participation facilitates the existence of one-party oligarchy.

3. While the power inherent in bureaucratic social organization and lack of membership participation would be enough to account for the absence of democracy in trade unions, various pressures on trade-union leaders act as further forces making them seek means of reducing democracy in their unions. In the trade-union movement, democracy—the possibility that an official can be defeated for re-election—means that the leader must be willing to move from a position of high status, power, and income to a much lower one if he is still to remain within the union. The institutionalization of such movement from high to low status would require the union leader to accept as probable a future sharp decline in his position in society. Given the great emphasis placed by the social structure on achieving and maintaining high status, it is clear that the norms of democracy in trade unions and those of achievement in the larger society are often in sharp conflict. This may help account for the fact that democracy is found mostly in unions in high-status occupations or in small local organizations in which the status differentiation between leaders and followers is very small. Where the status gap is large, the leader is under strain from his position to institutionalize dictatorial mechanisms which will reduce the possibility that he may lose his office.[7]

7. Instead of suggesting that power corrupts in all situations, this analysis suggests that such corruption is a consequence of specific social structures, where *conformity*

ORGANIZATIONAL STRUCTURE

Our analysis of the factors related to democracy in the ITU has pointed to conditions under which democracy may be institutionalized in large-scale private governments. Basically, however, it does not offer many positive action suggestions for those who would seek consciously to manipulate the structure of such organizations so as to make the institutionalization of democratic procedures within them more probable. We have shown that there is much more variation in the internal organization of associations than the notion of an iron law of oligarchy would imply, but nevertheless, the implications of our analysis for democratic organizational politics are almost as pessimistic as those postulated by Robert Michels.

It may be, however, that like Michels, we are too hard on trade unions and voluntary associations. Perhaps viewing such organizations in other perspectives may justify more optimistic conclusions. Before closing therefore, we should like to examine some of the alternative conceptions of the democratic potential inherent in trade unions.

One school of thought, the Marxist, has for obvious reasons been much concerned with the problem of oligarchy in labor organizations. Those Marxists who have written on the problem have tended to agree with Michels that trade unions are oligarchic, but have suggested that some of the factors making for oligarchy are inherent in the capitalist system of social relations, and that under a new social structure of socialism or communism, some of the factors making for oligarchy will be reduced, while those making for democracy will increase. Perhaps the most sophisticated presentation of this approach can be found in a book by Nikolai Bukharin, one of the major pre-Stalinist theoreticians of communism. Bukharin recognized the problem and even acknowledged that after the working class comes to power, "There will inevitably result a *tendency* to 'degeneration,' i.e., the excretion of a leading stratum." [8]

The answer to the problem posed by a "stratum of leaders" who would seek to control the institutions of a socialist society is, according to Bukharin, that "what constitutes an eternal category in Michels' presentation, namely, the 'incompetence of the masses' will disappear, for this incompetence is by no means an attribute of every social system; it likewise is a product of the economic and technical conditions, expressing themselves in the general cultural being and in the educational conditions. We may state that in the society of the future there will be a colossal overproduction of organizers, which will nullify the *stability* of the ruling groups." [9] Thus, interestingly, Bukharin posits that one of the conditions

---

to one norm necessarily involves violation of another norm. Cf. R. K. Merton: *Social Theory and Social Structure,* New York, Free Press, 1949, Chap. 4, "Social Structure and Anomie."

8. Nikolai Bukharin, *Historical Materialism,* pp. 310–11.
9. *Loc. cit.* (Bukharin's emphasis).

362

which will develop under socialism is similar to one which we have suggested already exists in the ITU, namely, a large group of men who are educated and skilled in the ways of politics, a group which is too large to be encompassed in the governing apparatus and which constitutes the base for an organized opposition to the dominant faction. On a theoretical level, however, Bukharin could not recognize that control over a "leading stratum" required an organized opposition group, a second party, since Marxian dogma prescribed that parties could only reflect class antagonism and within the working class there could be no such antagonism.[10]

We would be foolhardy to reject the possibility that major changes in the social structure will increase the potential for democracy within the labor movement. In fact, a number of the changes which are an outgrowth of the efforts for a more socialist or equalitarian society do point in the direction of reducing the factors making for oligarchy within the labor movement. Perhaps the most important of these are the efforts in Great Britain and the Scandinavian countries to reduce the income and presumably consequent status differentiation attached to various levels of skill. In addition, as trade unions assume the power to affect major national political questions such as foreign policy, national wage policy, local planning, and many others, the battles traditionally fought at the ballot box in democratic countries are increasingly becoming questions of controversy within British trade unions. Aneurin Bevan, for example, has recently threatened to work directly within the trade unions to challenge their leadership on issues which are far removed from collective-bargaining policies. Consequently the crucial way in which the emergence of socialism improves the conditions for democracy within labor unions is by legitimating internal controversies within labor organizations that are conducted on ideological lines and involve more than the bread-and-butter questions of "business unionism." By stating that a union should be concerned with matters beyond collective bargaining, socialist union leaders are unwittingly encouraging the possibility of political factionalism within their organization.

Conversely, it should be noted that business unionism, as a set of ideas justifying the narrowest definitions of a union's role in society, also helps to legitimate one-party oligarchy, for it implies that union leadership is simply the administration of an organization with defined, undebatable goals: the maximization of the member's income and general welfare. The more narrowly an organization defines its functions as fulfilling limited and

10. Friends of Bukharin have reported that, following his defeat by Stalin, he did recognize the need for a second party in the Soviet Union. It is interesting to note that even in 1923 when he first wrote this book, Bukharin, although a leading member of the ruling group in Russia, could write that the question of whether there would be a socialist democracy or the dictatorship of the leading stratum was not a settled question. "The outcome will depend on which tendencies turn out to be the strongest." *Ibid.*, p. 311.

specific needs, the narrower the range there is for controversy.[11] No one has attempted either a qualitative or quantitative analysis of the relationship between diffuse political or specific business-union ideologies and the presence or absence of political conflict within trade unions. The general proposition may be suggested, however, that the more diffuse the ideology of a trade union, the greater the likelihood of internal factionalism. Consequently, the more directly unions are involved in politics and the more important their political decisions are to power in the total society, the more likely that national political ideologies and movements will affect the internal politics of labor. This pattern might have developed in a more clear-cut fashion than it has if a part of the left wing of the labor movement had not been captured by a totalitarian political movement, the Communist Party. Before the emergence of the Communist Party, many European labor unions and socialist parties were divided between left and right wings, which battled for influence and power according to the rules of democracy, much as do supporters of Aneurin Bevan and Hugh Gaitskell in the present-day British Labour Party. The Communists, by refusing to play the democratic game, help to break down or prevent the institutionalization of internal democratic procedures within the more political European labor movement. It is, however, possible that a democratic socialist society, somehow blessed with the absence of the Communists, will have more democratic trade unions than now exist.

11. It should also be noted that limiting the functions of an organization helps to reduce the likelihood that a member will feel the need to participate in and influence the policies of the organization. People may belong to many organizations, such as the American Automobile Association, a local consumer's cooperative, a medical plan, a bowling congress, a national stamp club, and many others, without feeling any obligation to participate actively in the internal operations of the group and without feeling coerced by the fact that decisions are made without their having been consulted. In large measure, each of the various voluntary associations to which people may belong is judged on the basis of the ability to satisfy a limited need of its individual members. On the other hand, the more diffuse the functions of a group or organization, the more likely an individual is to find sources of disagreement with and desire to participate actively in its operation.

Applying the above analysis to trade unions, the union which simply operates as a business union may be placed in the category of specific, one-function organizations. Outside of the shop organization where there is normally the largest participation by workers, the single major task of the business union, collective bargaining, does not take place oftener than once a year, and in many unions only once every two or three years. The day-to-day administration of union affairs need not concern the average member any more than do the day-to-day activities that go into running a veterans' group or a medical plan. It is of course true that a union deals with the individual in his occupational role, and we might expect it to call forth more of his interest and concern than other voluntary organizations to which the individual relates through his less important roles. Nevertheless, the generalization should hold within the labor movement; the more specific the functions of the union, the less involvement of members; and the more diffuse its relations to the members, the more involvement. The latter situation may be a by-product either of an occupational community, as in the case of the ITU, or of a political ideology which widens the definition of the role of the union as occurs in many European countries.

A second school of thought, found most generally among supporters of existing trends in the labor movement, challenges the definition of democracy used by Michels and would presumably reject the one used in this book. These observers argue that trade unions are democratic in the sense that they represent the interests of their members in a struggle with the employers, regardless of whether internal opposition can exist within them. As V. L. Allen has put it:

> It has been argued by some that a voluntary society must provide for membership participation and install the checks and brakes on authority in the manner undertaken by the State in order to achieve and maintain democracy. This contention is misleading, for a voluntary society is not a State within a State; nor does it operate on the same scale or undertake the same functions. Its end and its means are different from those of the State. The government operates the supreme coercive power within a State and the necessity of preventing the use of that power contrary to the interests of the community is of immense over-riding importance in a political democracy. . . . None of this holds for voluntary societies, which by definition, cannot impose punitive measures on their members and which have no means of enforcing their regulations other than by persuasion and sound common sense. There is not in a voluntary society "the organized force which is the distinctive mark of the state (and which) so alters the nature of the political problems as to make any analogy between democracy in politics and in non-political societies only misleading."
>
> It is the voluntary nature of organizations within a State which is essential for the preservation of democracy within those organizations. . . .
>
> It is contended here, however, that trade union organization is not based on theoretical concepts prior to it, that is on some concept of democracy, but on the end it serves. In other words, the end of trade-union activity is to protect and improve the general living standards of its members and not to provide workers with an exercise in self-government.[12]

It is the general assumption of exponents of this school that trade unions, even when oligarchic and dictatorial, are representative of their members' interest in the general socio-economic struggle in the same sense that political parties, although not directly controlled by the social groups which give them electoral support, nevertheless represent these social groups in the government. Presumably unions or political parties which ceased to represent their constituents or members would lose their allegiance. In the most general sense of the term "represent," this assumption is probably valid. One can show that even the most dictatorial trade-

---

12. V. L. Allen: *Power in Trade Unions,* London, Longmans, Green and Company, Lt.., 1954, pp. 10–11, 15. The quotation is from A. D. Lindsay, *The Essentials of Democracy,* p. 49.

union leaders must be somewhat responsive to the economic needs of their members. A union oligarchy which does not defend the economic interests of the rank and file may find its membership disappearing either into another union or into nonmembership in any union, as John L. Lewis did in the twenties and early thirties. Lewis, then a trade-union as well as a political conservative, almost lost the United Mine Workers. Only after adopting the militant tactics for which he is now famous was he able to rebuild the union. A trade union which is not an economic defense organization has no function and will not long remain on the scene.

To recognize this fact does not involve declaring that a trade union is necessarily representative of its members' interests, or must be considered a democratic organization. Control over the organizational machinery enables the officialdom of a union to define the choices availabe to the organization and its members. Without a sophisticated organized opposition, the members have no way of discovering for themselves what is possible. A union may, for example, present a contract as containing substantial gains by engaging in statistical double talk, as the United Steel Workers did recently. The failure of the printing pressmen to win a priority system cannot be presented as the will of the membership in that completely dictatorial union. The divergencies in the national political action of the Amalgamated Clothing Workers and the International Ladies Garment Workers are clearly a product of the political ambitions and viewpoints of Sidney Hillman and David Dubinsky, not of the membership of the two unions. Communist-led unions have on occasion engaged in prolonged strikes which were unjustifiable by any collective-bargaining criteria, while other conservative unions have attempted to avoid strikes under almost all conditions. Some union leaders have engaged in programs to rationalize their industry, even though this meant a great decline in the total number of man-hours of work available to their members, while others have fought efforts to institute labor-saving devices. The West Coast longshoremen have instituted a rigid sharing of the work according to a numerical list, while the East Coast longshoremen have retained the shape-up system of hiring, which permits hiring bosses to discriminate among the men.[13] In the face of these differences, it would be hard to assert that unions represent their members' interests when the members have little control over policy formation.

The lack of internal democracy also tends to reinforce a factor which makes for both oligarchy and unrepresentativeness: the widening of the salary and status gap between the members and leaders. Without the presence of opposition groups, most American union leaders have raised their salaries far above those of the members. The history of the United Auto-

13. This system was legally abolished in 1954 by the states of New Jersey and New York, after the union refused to abolish it.

mobile Workers is a good example of this phenomenon. While major factional groups existed in the union, national officers, including the president, received less than $10,000 a year. Once Reuther consolidated his power, the salaries of officers gradually increased. Perhaps even more important than salaries, however, is the union officers' opportunity to receive perquisites in the form of expense accounts, union-purchased automobiles, vacation expenses, and the like, which do not appear in the records. In recent years, union welfare funds have provided a new source of extra income for some union leaders, their families or friends, through new pay rolls and insurance commissions. In the ITU or any union with an organized opposition, such financial manipulations would be impossible, since the opposition would make them an election issue.

As union leaders secure higher financial rewards from their jobs, their sense of identification with the men and the urgency of their problems must inevitably suffer. Hence lack of opposition makes for unrepresentative action both in the form of union policies which the membership probably would not approve if they had the power to affect them, and also by diminishing the leaders' sense of importance of members' economic problems.

The principal premise in the argument that oligarchic unions may be regarded as democratic rests, as Allen makes clear, on the assumption that trade unions are voluntary associations which members may leave much as they may quit a stamp club when they object to what it is doing. This assumption clearly does not apply to most American trade unions, although it may be applicable to many British and European labor organizations. Under the closed shop, and more recently the union shop, men cannot legally quit their union without losing their jobs. Where the union has power, even the legal right to resign from the union and keep one's job is relatively meaningless, since the union can effectively blacklist a man either by having the cooperation of the employer who seeks to keep on good terms with the union leadership, or through sanctions imposed by men who remain in the union. The development of union welfare funds has proved to be a new restriction on the rights of workers to choose their union. Recently, a minority group in the United Textile Workers, CIO, attempted to secede from that union and join the AFL textile union. A number of locals which were sympathetic with the secession move found that their welfare funds were tied up with the international union and that they would lose them if they left the CIO.[14]

The fact, therefore, that unions must to some extent represent their members' interests in the market must not be allowed to conceal the fact that union leaders possess great power to do things which would never be

14. It should be noted that Allen makes an exception in his argument about union democracy for unions which have compulsory membership.

approved if a democratic choice were available. As Howe and Widdick have pointed out:

> There is one decisive proof of democracy in a union (or any other institution): oppositionists have the right to organize freely into "parties," to set up factional machines, to circulate publicity and to propagandize among the members. . . . The presence of an opposition . . . is the best way of insuring that a union's democratic structure will be preserved. . . . To defend the right of factions to exist is not at all to applaud this or that faction. But this is the overhead (well worth paying) of democracy: groups one considers detrimental to the union's interest will be formed. The alternative is dictatorship.[15]

The emphasis in this book on the undemocratic character of most labor unions is not designed to negate the general proposition of the political pluralists that trade unions, like many other internally oligarchic organizations, serve to sustain political democracy in the larger society.[16] As many political observers have made clear, many internally dictatorial organizations operate to protect the interests of their members by checking the encroachments of other groups. Democracy in large measure rests on the fact that no one group is able to secure such a basis of power and command over the total allegiance of a majority of the population that it can effectively suppress or deny the claims of groups it opposes. The labor movement in particular has played a major role in fostering the institutions of political democracy in the larger society and in fostering the ideology of equalitarianism. Workers today can live and act with much less fear of the consequences of their acts than was generally true even three decades ago. There are few, although unfortunately some, unions which have as much potential power over the lives of their members as employers once held over their workers. In large measure, the chance that the collectivist society which is developing in most countries will be democratic rests on the possibility that trade unions, although supporters of socialist objectives, will maintain their independence of the state, and will act to protect their members and the citizenry in general against the tremendous state power inherent in a collectivist society. The behavior of the trade unions of the British Commonwealth and Scandinavian countries furnishes real evidence that trade unions, regardless of their internal structure, will continue to play the role of defenders of democracy and equalitarianism under collectivism.

Nevertheless, the extension of democracy in an industrial society requires the extension of control by men over those institutions they depend on. To the sympathetic student of the labor movement, the ITU stands as

15. Howe and Widdick, *The UAW and Walter Reuther*, pp. 262–63.
16. Cf. Franz L. Neumann: "Approaches to the Study of Political Power," *Political Science Quarterly*, 65: 161–80 (June, 1950).

a model of the trade union in a democratic society. In the ITU he sees the image of the democratic processes he prizes in the national body politic, in the organization through which printers exercise some control over the conditions of their livelihood. Although the events and conditions which have given rise to and sustained democracy in the ITU are unique and are rarely found in trade unions or other voluntary large social organizations generally, it would be foolhardy to predict that democratic processes cannot develop elsewhere. The specific factors which underlie ITU democracy are not likely to be duplicated elsewhere; but the very great variety of factors present in the situation suggests that democratic processes may develop under quite different conditions and take quite different forms.

If it is not to serve as a model, the ITU may well serve as a touchstone against which the internal political processes of other unions and of other voluntary groups, such as the American Legion or the American Medical Association, may be appraised and criticized. As Robert K. Merton has said in another connection:

> In the world laboratory of the sociologist, as in the more secluded laboratories of the physicist and chemist, it is the successful experiment which is decisive and not the thousand-and-one failures which preceded it. More is learned from the single success than from multiple failures. A single success proves it can be done. Thereafter, it is necessary only to learn what made it work. This, at least, is what I take to be the sociological sense of those revealing words of Thomas Love Peacock: "Whatever is, is possible." [17]

The ITU and its democratic political system *is:* to know what makes and has made it what it is may help make possible the development of organizational democracy elsewhere. Democracy, whether in national society or in private organizations, is not achieved by acts of will alone; but men's wills, through action, can shape institutions and events in directions that reduce or increase the chances for the development and survival of democracy. For men of good will, there is much to learn in the history, institutions, and arguments of American printers.

17. Robert K. Merton: *Social Theory and Social Research,* New York, Free Press, 1949, pp. 194–95.

Centralization Versus Decentralization in the Design of Human Service Delivery Systems: A Response to Gouldner's Lament*

Howard Aldrich

Gouldner's Lament

A commitment to a theory often occurs by a process other than one which its proponents believe and it is usually more consequential than they realize. A commitment to a theory may be made because the theory is congruent with the mood or deep-lying sentiments of its adherents, rather than merely because it has been cerebrally inspected and found valid.

So too is it with the theory of organization. Paradoxically enough, some of the very theories which promise to make man's own work more intelligible to himself and more amenable to his intelligence are infused with an intangible metaphysical pathos which insinuates, in the very midst of new discoveries, that all is lost. For the metaphysical pathos of much of the modern theory of group organization is that of pessimism and fatalism. (Gouldner, 1955: 498)

SOURCE: *The Management of Human Services,* edited by Rosemary Sarri and Yeheskel Hasenfeld, pp. 51–79. Copyright © 1978 by Columbia University Press. Reprinted by permission of the author and the publisher.

* As usual, Pat Reeves provided phenomenal last-minute assistance in the preparation of this paper, making possible its completion. In drawing up these arguments, I have been heavily influenced by Banfield and Grodzins' (1958) discussion of arguments concerning metropolitan reorganization. This paper builds upon ideas originally developed in a paper given at the International Institute of Management, Berlin, June 1975, and published as Aldrich (1977). I am indebted to Charles Perrow and Jane Weiss for their critical comments on an earlier version of this paper.

A dialectical tension exists in social service delivery systems between advocates of a strongly centralized structure and advocates of a strongly decentralized structure. Neither party has managed a clear-cut victory, and the strength of each has led to systems containing an unstable mixture of centralization *and* decentralization. Government agencies and other funding sources typically display an overarching policy concern for "interorganizational coordination" and elimination of "duplication of effort," and they are often joined by professionals and administrators in dominant agencies. Clients and local interest groups typically argue against the degree of centralization sought by the former, but there are many exceptions. I have investigated one system that has swung back and forth between the two positions and embodies characteristics of both—the manpower services system.

In 1973, the federal Comprehensive Employment and Training Act (CETA) upgraded the role of local communities in allocating funds for manpower training and substantially reduced the role of *direct* federal control. Categorical programs were eliminated in favor of local determination of services required, with local elected officials given control over the service delivery systems in their jurisdictions. The delegation of authority from the national to the local level was part of the general package of revenue sharing items enacted by the Nixon administration and proved very popular with local officials. Whether the changes created a more effective and efficient manpower training system is difficult to determine, as evaluations are still in progress. Nevertheless, it seems clear that program designers have concentrated on the technology of delivering and administering services, while ignoring the impact of organizational-level factors on the distribution of benefits.

I will review the centralization versus decentralization issue from the perspective of organizational as well as client needs. All human service delivery systems are products of compromises between centralizing and decentralizing forces, and I emphasize the contradictions structured into systems because of the irresolvable nature of the arguments. Examples are taken from a comparative field study of manpower organizations in New York State communities, as well as from the literature on social service organizations.

Levels of Analysis and Evaluations

Social service organizations face a situation of uncertain technologies, few resources, demand overload, and constant pressures from other organizations and groups to modify their activities in one way or another. Debates over the appropriate design for human service delivery systems are quite confusing because multiple constituencies, technologies, and operating paradigms are involved. Such issues come to the surface whenever authorities attempt to reorganize social service systems or to coordinate the actions of organizations to improve general public welfare. Authorities cannot escape the questions of relative power and resource allocation among organizations in these situations, although the fundamental issues are sometimes obscured because of the rhetoric used.

A central question in system design is the degree to which a population of organizations should be tightly or loosely coupled internally, with the major determinant of coupling being the degree of hierarchical control exercised by a central authority. "Coupling" refers to the strength of vertical or horizontal ties between organizations, to the generality or specificity of policy guidelines, to voluntary or mandated relations, and to the number of direct and indirect ties between organizations. Interorganizational systems are dynamic in part because of the mix of centralization and decentralization on the different dimensions of coupling.

Observers often mistake the new programs, new relationships, and new technologies in a system as indicating chaos or disorder. "Yet, when viewed from the inclusive level, the major domains, the division of labor, the legitimated technologies, the basic orientations to the social problems of the inner cities—all have shown, in their total configuration, an identifiable and specifiable stability" (Warren et al., 1974: 154). Choosing appropriate levels and units of analysis is thus a critical step in examining the coordination issue.

Three units of analysis in social services systems differ markedly in their roles and in their vulnerability to outside interventions: clients, organizations, and the interorganizational field. Clients are the raw material for people-processing and people-changing organizations, and they confront service bureaucracies as isolated individuals against powerful and professionalized staff. Organizations develop and apply service programs, and require an administrative structure organized according to a logic all its own. Access to external resources is an especially critical problem for social service organizations, as their market on the output side is not clearly defined and their product is difficult for consumers or supraorganizational authorities to evaluate. Most organizations are thus oriented toward the acquisition of resources through various forms of subsidization— the so-called "grants economy"—and varieties of interorganizational coordination. The resource dependence perspective has emerged as a conceptual scheme that incorporates these assumptions into a theory of administrators' behavior (Aldrich and Pfeffer, 1976).

The interorganizational field consists of the population of social service organizations, their organization sets, and the linkages among organizations and agencies. A comprehensive view of interorganizational fields includes not only organizations in local communities but also their links to state and federal agencies. If the vocabulary agency administrators use in describing their operations sounds slightly alien to clients caught up in local programs—"universe of need," "placements," "outreach"—that of system-level planners is even more bizarre. Planners are concerned with "delivery agents," "target populations," "prioritizing," and "trainable occupations."

Two criteria appear in most social service evaluation, whether made by agency administrators or system planners: Who benefits from programs, and the degree of adaptiveness and innovativeness of programs, given changing local needs. The distinction between the three units of analysis is manifestly apparent in the differential way benefits are distributed across clients, organizations, and fields by various structures. Adaptiveness and innovativeness are assessed in terms of a program's fit with target population needs and its ability to function effectively as needs change. I am assuming that meeting local needs is a high priority in the American political system.

The strength of arguments on both sides of the centralization-decentralization debate, and the discovery of structures that provide examples of each, shows the complexity of the design issue. Just as organization theorists have reconciled themselves to the realization that there is no "one best way" to organize, given the extent to which environments and tasks vary across occasions, so planners have discovered there is not one best way to design a "coordinated" human service delivery system. General points can be made about the tendency of centralization (tight coupling) or decentralization (loose coupling) to produce particular kinds of benefits, but master plans are beyond our comprehension or competence at this point. In reviewing four arguments on each side of the debate, I will introduce elements of the resource control and population ecology models of organizations.

Arguments for Centralization/Tight Coupling

Arguments in support of centralizing planning and control in human service delivery systems assert that tight coupling and hierarchical control must be used to negate the tendencies of organizations to pursue narrow sectarian interests. Services benefiting socially and economically heterogeneous populations are possible only in structures where special interests are held tightly in check. The equitable distribution of benefits is treated as more important than the adaptation of programs to local needs. Arguments for decentralization, on the other hand, emphasize adaptiveness and innovativeness while arguing that loose coupling is the most efficient way of allocating societal resources.

Indivisible Problems Require a Centralized Structure

Social service programs require extensive involvement with clients, long-term followup, contain unanticipated side-effects, and possess other complicating factors that make large-scale action necessary. The treatment of multi-problem families, the crime problem in metropolitan areas, and the provision of health care facilities cannot be carried out by small organizations acting on their own. If these large-scale problems are broken down into separate pieces and different organizations are allowed to work on problems from their own perspectives, the result is a series of incomplete solutions. Resources are wasted because each organization duplicates work done by others: intake, processing of clients, record or account keeping, revenue raising, and so forth.

The most common variation on the theme of indivisible problems is the argument for economies of scale. Advocates of centralization assert that it is uneconomical to attack certain problems on other than a tightly coordinated multi-organization scale. Planners contrast the wasted resources and duplication of effort resulting from market transactions with the efficiency and speed of transactions internalized under one hierarchical structure.

Whether defined as unemployment or underemployment, problems in the manpower sector are too widespread to be dealt with by small organizations. Manpower planners argue that coping with an unemployment rate of more than 6 percent requires the redistribution of massive resources. Without a large scale commitment of funds, local organizations only scratch the surface of the problems. For example, in one county manpower planners drew up a plan of service for 1976–77 that identified areas of need and what the local program could do. The resulting plan resembles a David and Goliath scenario: there were 5,800 welfare recipients with 165 to be served; 4,200 veterans in need of service were identified, with 38 to be served by the program, and so forth. The surge in unemployment in the past few years has swamped even the largest manpower services organizations.

The major reasoning behind the 1973 Comprehensive Employment and Training Act was that the resources of a local community would be assembled into one operation. The resulting organization would combine all the functions previously distributed among the autonomous manpower programs, each funded under its own categorical grant from the federal government. Local programs were sponsored by Community Action Agencies. Model Cities agencies, local school districts, associations of businessmen. and the Employment Service. Also, state Departments of Labor mounted their own programs. The new structure would combine the functions of intake, placement, counseling, and so forth in the same office; one administrative staff would be used to cover all sub-programs. The scale of the resulting organizations would allow new procedures to be introduced that could not be implemented in smaller organizations. For example, small organizations had great difficulty in coping with the problem of following up their clients; that is, what happened to clients after the processing period was over. Large operations were able to create specialized recordkeeping divisions to keep track of clients, with some information systems automated and computerized.

To counter arguments by decentralization advocates that the resulting structure was unwieldy and too far removed from local conditions, planners pointed out that a centralized structure still allowed for specialization within the system. Large corporations, especially multinationals, use a divisionalized structure that permits the adaptation of specialized divisions to local environments while at the same time retaining a centralized accounting and control structure. Divisions are guided by headquarter's policies, but have enough autonomy to respond to specialized opportunities. Planners argued that these same principles were applicable to the public sector.

Manpower regulations can be written to allow local flexibility and staff discretion. For example, one CETA operation uses the Employment Service to screen everyone for eligibility, the Urban League to recruit blacks and other minorities, an association of the aged to recruit older workers, and the community action agency to recruit and place low income and rural persons. All this is done through a series of subcontracts with the main CETA office.

The reasoning behind the CETA bill was that large metropolitan areas or rural counties comprise a single employment catchment area, and planning on a smaller level would fragment and damage the delivery of manpower services. Whether a problem is, in fact, "indivisible" depends upon the extent to which its causes are understood and an appropriate technology is available. A common characteristic of problems defined through the public policy-making process is that their boundaries are often arbitrary and are determined through bypassing technical analysis. Some problems are so complex as to defy reasoned analysis, such as the "poverty problem" of the 1960s in the United States. In these cases, the critical point is not in the structuring of a solution, but rather in defining a problem's boundaries.

Organization Autonomy Is a Barrier to System-Wide Solutions

Advocates for centralization assert that the existence of autonomous organizations and agencies, each with its own protective boundaries, fragments problems and creates nearly insurmountable obstacles to coordination. Administrators defend their agencies' domains and seek preservation of the integrity of their own organization's boundaries. The vested interests of administrators take precedence over any sentiments embodied in abstract declarations concerning interorganizational cooperation. A strong centralized authority is needed to override individual organizational boundaries. This is, of course, the familiar problem of the rationality of collective action. A mechanism has to be found to force organizations to cooperate, thus solving the "hold-out" problem. The hold-out problem can occur only when organizations have the autonomy and separate authority to reject proposed system-wide solutions.

Most social service agencies face demands far greater than they can possibly meet with their limited resources. A central characteristic of the services sector is that demand is nearly infinitely expandable because of subsidized costs and the lack of client contributions. Thus, faced with a potential overload of clients, staff can practice "creaming" and exercise their discretion in ways that benefit the agency but not necessarily the total system or clients in need. Attacks on the creaming process can be repelled by pointing out that, of course, clients *are* being served. It is, therefore, hard to fault an agency unless a critic can come up with a rigorous ranking of clients by priority of need.

A number of studies have shown the insidious effects of staff discretion, given agency autonomy and client overload. Gordon's (1975) research on the use of administrative discretion in welfare agencies found that staff were able to reward clients who had knowledge of the bureaucratic ropes and caused fewer problems than ignorant clients. Discretion was exercised in ways that favored the outcomes desired by knowledgeable clients. Roth (1972) found that medical practitioners systematically discriminated against certain classes of patients for purely organizational reasons. These same tendencies are also present in centralized structures, but they can be controlled through central monitoring and auditing units. A "welfare inspector" empowered to intervene in local agencies' operations has more influence than external resource groups not part of the authority structure.

In the manpower training sector, public service employment is rapidly becoming the largest single component. This component recruits and places individuals in jobs requiring a fairly high degree of competence in local government and non-profit agencies. Since training and socialization of underskilled employees is not a main orientation of the recipient departments and agencies, it is understandable that they seek the most competent and highly skilled clients. One consequence has been that manpower programs have moved away from service to the unskilled and disadvantaged populations originally served in the 1960s. Perhaps a stronger regional or national auditing agency is needed to reassert service priorities.

Autonomous agencies and organizations can use their autonomy to "hide" from public scrutiny. There is little need for them to advertise their existence, given the tremendous demand for their services and the fact that agencies can rely on other organizations for referrals. A common strategy is to lay low and avoid attracting attention. Experience with CETA shows that even "centralization" at the community-level may be too much "decentralization" if administrators aren't committed to a concern for constituency assessment of their program. A central component of the CETA program is the local Manpower Planning Advisory Council (MPAC) made up of representatives from the various important segments of the community. This body was designed as a review and consultation group giving advice to the CETA staff, suggesting new programs, and in general overseeing the policies of the program. Rather than serving as a review and advisory body, however, the MPAC has *internalized* the potential *external* evaluators of the program and thus coopted them. "Voice" has been muted by encouraging loyalty among persons and representatives who at one time might have been critical of CETA operations (Hirschman, 1972).

Some planners assert that a decentralized system fragments the client population and encourages agencies to deal with clients on a "professionalized" one-to-one basis. The large number of agencies and their autonomous status make it difficult for external pressure groups to mount an effective counter pressure. Opponents have to fight many small skirmishes instead of several big battles. A possible remedy to client powerlessness is the centralization of programs thus facilitating the formation and effectiveness of external pressure groups.

The MPAC, for example, is hampered because its members have an ideological commitment to the program but little time to follow up on issues. As non-paid, part-time members, they can't hope to compete with the full-time staff of CETA. If centralization were used to provide funds for pressure groups and organizations of clients, then perhaps the balance could be righted. At the very least, one could argue that the MPAC deserves a professional planning staff of its own. At present, under the decentralized CETA operation the major evaluator and pressure organization maintaining standards is the federal Department of Labor, by default. In spite of the fact that the system is much more decentralized than previously, a powerful central agency still plays a significant role, reinforcing the point that most delivery systems are a dynamic mix of centralized and decentralized components.

Information impactedness and opportunism are major problems in interorganizational fields organized on market principles (Williamson, 1975). Planners, wishing to take a system-wide view, can't get the accurate and timely information they need to draw up useful plans. Autonomous agencies withhold information or release inaccurate and misleading information. Centralizing a system by bringing agencies under one hierarchical structure internalizes former market transactions and substantially lessens the problems of acquiring valid information.

The resource dependence model treats authority as a resource that is sought by organizations seeking to control their environments. Authority over other organizations is sometimes achieved through deliberate strategies and tactics, but in the social services sector it is most often achieved through legislative mandates or bureaucratic directives from supraordinate authority. Research on the manpower training system has shown the importance of mandated relationships in bringing organizations together that otherwise would deal with each other only at arms length. Prior to the 1973 reorganization, the Employment Service occupied a central role in manpower training systems because many manpower organizations were mandated to use it for referrals and placements. Research showed that the scope and intensity of relations between the ES and manpower organizations formally linked to it were much greater than for organizations whose ties to the ES were based only on needs generated by the interorganizational division of labor.

Formalization of ties enhanced the prospect of complementary relations and increased the volume of contact, thus moving clients between organizations that had different services to offer. Formalization also smoothed interorganizational contacts, as interaction was more likely to be standardized and interagency rivalries were lessened (Aldrich, 1976a, 1976b). Research on relations between the ES and Social Services Department uncovered similar processes, as mandated interaction led to more intense interaction and an imbalance in favor of the ES, but lower perceived cooperation. Currently, mandated interaction between social services departments and the ES exists in the 131.5 Program, under which employable welfare recipients must pick up their checks at Employment Service offices. This brings clients into periodic contact with another important agency, even though in most cases this is a rather perfunctory visit.

Perhaps theorists have overlooked the importance of manipulating authority in interorganizational systems because they have taken it as one of the fixed parameters of a system. The resource dependence perspective, however, warns us that such relations should not be taken for granted. Mandating relations may be the only way to bring agencies together with complementary services to offer.

Normal Interorganizational Relations Focus on Organizational Rather Than System Needs

The resource dependence perspective posits that administrators seek their own organization's survival, privileged position, or dominance of the field. Such objectives would seem to be incompatible with the system-wide perspective that centralization is designed to achieve. Normal interorganizational transactions are conducted on too issue-specific a level to allow the achievement of coordination among organizations at the population level. The divergent objectives of organizations within decentralized systems mean that some attend closely to clients whereas others do not, resulting in inequitable treatment of the client population. There are exceptions—agencies where "client concern" shines through—but they don't cumulate to have system-wide consequences.

The behavior of social service organization adminstrators can be characterized in three empirical generalizations (Benson, 1975). First, administrators attempt to fulfill program requirements justifying their organizations' claims to a supply of funds and authority. This requires action with *visible* consequences, such as a high number of referrals, a large number of clients served, or the manipulation of a measurement and accounting system. Interorganizational behavior thus reflects a concern for the intensity of interaction with other organizations; that is, with the amount and frequency of resource flows.

Second, administrators attempt to maintain a clear domain that is societally legitimated. Given the general acceptance among organizations of the social service paradigm, there are few conflicts over domains. Thus, the extended application and defense of an organization's domain occurs sporadically and does not figure very heavily in day-to-day activities.

Third, administrators seek to maintain an orderly, reliable pattern of resource flow as free from uncertainty as is organizationally and technologically possible. The drive toward reducing uncertainty often takes the form of standardizing transactions to make them more predictable and manageable. Standardization can be achieved either by segmenting organizations into separate functional units, with each assigned a limited portion of a transaction, or through routinizing procedures and allowing them to be invoked upon recognition of a relatively small number of cues.

The resource dependence perspective's prediction that administrators will show a high concern for the volume of resource flows and attempt to routinize transactions is supported by several research findings (Aldrich, 1976a, 1976b). The greater the flow of resources between two social service agencies, the more likely transactions are to be standardized and the less likely it is that agency heads will desire still greater standardization. A high volume of interaction leads to a positive evaluation of the cooperativeness of another agency, and a high degree of standardization in transactions has a similar effect.

Minimizing uncertainty by standardizing transactions allows staff members to become skilled in the offering of certain specialized services and may free them from the needless duplication of effort occurring when each transaction is begun anew. The danger is that staff will become inflexible and unresponsive to the specific needs of clients not fitting into

379

prestandardized categories. Centralization partly overcomes this danger by allowing a high enough degree of internal differentiation to permit separate standardized and unstandardized boundary routines. Thus, in large organizations, staff members who cannot cope with a particular client's needs are able to route the client to the appropriate routine or unit. The small size of organizations in decentralized systems means that many of them are crisis oriented and are more vulnerable to short-term environmental fluctuations than larger organizations. Large, centralized organizations can differentiate internally, not only to offer a mix of standardized and unstandardized routines, but also to allow the creation of a planning department which enables them to avoid a crisis mentality.

Dominant Organizations Benefit the Most from Decentralization

Some theorists argue that, in the absence of authoritative and planned coordination, the flow of resources benefits the already dominant organizations in a system. Loose coupling favors the groups and organizations with the most resources and strongest lobbying efforts. They can push aside the smaller organizations and gain access to resources which they use to enhance their dominant position. New programs are simply absorbed by the pre-existing system, aided by the presence of an institutionalized thought structure (Warren et al., 1974).

Perhaps the already dominant organizations in a community *should* benefit because they are less parochial or particularistic than others. However, research on social services organizations is not cause for optimism in this regard. Agreement among dominant organizations on a common paradigm generally ensures that new organizations will not radically *challenge* existing ones. Powerful organizations subscribe to a shared paradigm that defines the nature of community problems and the form of acceptable solutions. For example, Model Cities organizations in the 1960s made little progress in changing patterns of interaction among social service oragnizations because the shared interorganizational paradigm diagnosed social problems as a failure of the individual rather than the social system.

The population ecology model of organizations posits that in loosely coupled interorganizational networks, a key role is played by linking pin organizations (Aldrich, 1979). Linking pin organizations have extensive and overlapping ties to different parts of a network and play a key role in integrating the population. Having ties to more than one subset or subnetwork, linking pin organizations are the nodes through which a network is loosely coupled. Three functions of linking pin organizations are particularly important: (1) They serve as communication channels between organizations; (2) They provide general services that link third parties to one another by transfering resources, information, or clients; and (3) If they are dominant or high status organizations, they serve as models to be imitated by other organizations or use the dependence of other organizations on themselves to actively direct network activities. Linking pin organizations help preserve the complexity of networks that would otherwise decay into isolated subnetworks.

Dominant or high status organizations would be expected to occupy the roles of linking pin organizations, as they achieve their position in the organizational hierarchy by strategic maneuvering into central positions and by manipulating interorganizational relations as a means of retaining power. Dominant employers in a local economy, for example, exercise power in a variety of contexts, with their influence extending from setting standards for wages down to the very subtle level of providing much of the leadership for voluntary associations. The community power literature emphasizes the coordinating role of organizations representing vested interests—such as the Chamber of Commerce, country clubs, or local economic development associations (Freeman, 1968).

Despite all the attention paid to "domains" and "domain consensus" in the social service organizations literature, it is difficult to find evidence of overt conflict in the field. Consensus, albeit implicit, reigns supreme. A multicity study of the Model Cities program found so little evidence for domain conflict that it was hardly worth analyzing (Warren et al., 1974). In my own research I found a high incidence of perceived domain overlap between manpower programs and the Employment Service with no apparent ill effects (Aldrich, 1976a, 1976b). Out of 48 manpower organizations, only 4 instances of genuine domain conflict in the previous year were recorded. In another study of 249 social service organizations, only two directors named the local Employment Service office as duplicating their own function. There was no overt evidence of any manifest battles over domain control in spite of the fact that the ES was the most visible target for critics of the manpower training system in the 1960s and early 1970s.

The resource dependence perspective predicts that these findings should by typical, as the network of interorganizational relations evolving at the community level is highly stable. Stability is promoted and conflict inhibited because of three factors. First, stability is supported at the level of individual agency administrators seeking certainty in relations with their environments. Second, vested interests are characteristic of relations between pairs of organizations through authoritative dominance, resource dependence, or complementarity of needs. Finally, at the level of institutional legitimacy, the overarching normative and legal order is supported by state and federal laws and by local community support from institutional elites. Thus, new programs placed in local communities can be expected to have little impact in terms of either increasing innovativeness or altering the existing distribution of benefits. Only a large scale centralized structure can overcome the bonds of dependence and dominance joining the components of the existing system.

Some evidence for these propositions may be found in comparing the pre- and post-CETA manpower systems in New York State communities. Under the old manpower system, funds for on-the-job training were provided to employers who could take a fairly large number of trainees, thus minimizing counseling and overhead costs. Expenditures for both on-the-job training and classroom training represented, to some extent, the externalization of the training function by large firms in the private sector. Private employers had their training costs subsidized by public funds. Perhaps this would make sense for jobs in the secondary labor market, where there is a high level of turnover and a great deal of mobility between fairly low skilled jobs. However, it makes less sense for jobs in the primary sector, which relies heavily upon training persons in highly firm-specific skills and promoting them up through an internal labor market. Turnover is much lower and skills are not as transferable between firms as in the secondary labor market. Under the new system, large employers are not as favored and some prime sponsors have a rule that only one training slot will be allocated to each employer. Others require firm evidence that a person taken on is being trained and that funds are not being used to substitute for the firm's normal training costs.

Centralization may protect programs that would otherwise face a debilitating opposition from special interest groups. Organizations that oppose social services such as "free" health clinics, legal aid, and abortion referrals are organized on a national scale and disseminate information about opposition tactics to their local affiliates. If social service programs are not partially insulated against these external pressures through their incorporation into a hierarchical structure, they are quite vulnerable. Thus there must be structural congruence between social service programs and their opponents, as in the labor relations sector, where unions attempt to organize on the same scale as employers.

Summary of Arguments for Centralizing

1. Indivisible problems require large-scale planned interaction of a magnitude not possible if social service organizations interact only to satisfy their own requirements.

2. The autonomy and separate authority of organizations impedes the development of a more encompassing solution to clients' problems, as parochial interests take precedence over system-wide interests. Differences in organizational objectives and commitment mean that a market solution at the organizational level may result in an inequitable distribution of benefits at the client level.

3. Normal interorganizational relations are focused on specific or-

ganizational needs rather than the common welfare. This leads to a concern for standardized and routinized transactions which may not be in the clients' best interest.

4. In a decentralized, loosely coupled system, the flow of resources tends to benefit the already well-off organizations.

Arguments for Decentralization/Loose Coupling

Most of the arguments for decentralization emphasize the increased adaptiveness and innovativeness that result from decentralization. Advocates argue that loose coupling is a more efficient means of allocating societal resources and that although equity is an important issue, a centralized system is inappropriate in situations where goals are ambiguous, technologies uncertain, and environmental conditions constantly changing. The four arguments reviewed below are not simply attempts to refute arguments for centralization. They stand on their own as substantive assertions of the benefits of decentralization and, by implication, the costs of centralization. Indeed, the arguments are so persuasive that planners who on one occasion argue strongly for centralization find themselves on other occasions defending the benefits of decentralization. Such is the appeal of the arguments that most human service delivery systems ultimately are designed with both sets of principles underlying them. These built-in contradictions manifest themselves in numerous ways, some of which will be pointed out in the examples given. The strength of arguments advanced for decentralization may mean that a resolution of conflicting stands—if such a result is desired—may be achieved only on a case-by-case basis, and then only after an explicit recognition that many design questions actually concern fundamental values rather than technical procedures.

Decentralization Allows for Maximum Organizational Responsiveness

One implication of highly centralized systems is that problems are indivisible and much the same for all the clients involved. A contrary argument, positing that many problems are not the same for all clients, is one basis for arguments in support of decentralization. An implicit assumption of this argument is that planners should place as high a value on allowing localized choice of means to ends as on the quality of outcomes themselves. The superiority of loosely coupled systems in an evolving environment lies in the freedom individual units have to adapt to local conditions.

Arguments for maximum responsiveness underlay the movement in the 1960s for community control and in the 1970s for governmental decentralization and revenue sharing. Advocates of decentralization argued that money saved by coordination and consolidation of individual agencies did not offset the costs added when additional layers of authority were imposed between decision makers and local environments. This was the basis for the argument over decategorization under the 1973 CETA bill. The Department of Labor Manpower Administration in Washington was attacked for being too far from local labor markets to design programs for them. Centralized coordination had made administrators unresponsive to idiosyncratic needs. It was assumed that local leaders with an ear to their political constituency know what's happening in their environments and what local needs actually are. Planners were frustrated over their inability to alter centralized regulations concerning how resources should be used. The inability of local planners to design unique programs reinforced a particular way of dealing with manpower services that critics saw as outdated.

Loose coupling is especially important in manpower planning, where information on labor market conditions is difficult to obtain. Federal and state data are often out of date and not detailed enough to be of much use for local planning. Instead planners rely on "general community knowledge" and informal sources. They still have access to federal and state information, but they supplement it with their own knowledge of the local community. In fact, the manpower planning system is remarkable for the large amount of money spent in an area with so little information available about existing conditions or the consequences of treatments used. This has changed very little since 1973 and probably won't until local planners are given enough resources to create community-based information systems.

Decentralization brings local *accountability* to systems by making visible the local leaders and administrators responsible for programs. Centralized and categorical programs, while allowing for centralized accountability. make administrators invisible to local populations. Under these conditions, it is not clear who should be held accountable for expenditures and the quality of services. Increased accountability is promoted only if a feedback mechanism is provided linking constituency evaluations to organizational rewards. Because of the non-market nature of most organization-client transactions and the tenuous link between individual citizen evaluations and agency funding, it has proved extremely difficult for planners to design effective feedback mechanisms.

Decentralization does not mean the absence of ties between organizations or the breakdown of delivery systems into chaos. Indirect ties—through third parties—serve a very important function in coordinating the behavior of independent organizations. Research on the manpower training systems of local communities prior to the 1973 act found that indirect ties between organizations increased the intensity of interaction between them over and above the level expected on the basis of individual organizational characteristics. For example, the greater the number of indirect linkages between social service organizations and local Employment Service offices, the larger the two-way flow of referrals. At that time the Employment Service stood near the center of the manpower training system referral process and had many direct ties to manpower programs. Therefore, it also had many indirect ties to social service organizations that were linked to manpower programs .These indirect ties were a link that drew the organizations closer together. These findings as well as others demonstrate the potential of network analysis for understanding relations within social service delivery systems (Aldrich, 1979).

Advocates assert that a loosely coupled structure is most appropriate under conditions of environmental change where decisions must be taken rapidly and where a high degree of responsiveness to citizen demands is desired. Advocates of centralization attack these arguments on the grounds that a decentralized system caters to local interests at the expense of societal interests and is more costly to administer because of duplication of administrative overhead across many semi-autonomous organizations.

Decentralization Allows Maximum Benefits from the Interorganizational Division of Labor

In a decentralized system, each organization can respond to a unique set of needs and can carve a niche for itself in an area where it is most competent. When problems are divisible, establishing centralized structures amounts to administrative overkill. Centralized structures are attacked for being only loosely tied to their markets and thus pursuing goals that are relevant to various internal procedural and administrative needs rather than client needs. Centralized structures wipe out the subtle differences between specialized organizations that are preserved in decentralized systems.

Centralization inhibits innovation by subunits if guidelines for regulations are tightly written or if innovation is not in the interest of dominant organizations. Extreme centralization thus prevents specialization and the division of labor from taking their natural course. The benefits of specialization and the division of labor have been commented upon by a number of investigators. Aiken and Alford (1970), in their study of innovation in urban renewal and public housing programs, argued that "The greater the number of centers of power in a community, and the more pervasive and encompassing the interfaces, the higher the probability of innovation in a given issue area." A large number of power centers in frequent interaction with one another lead to the introduction of innovations as the by-product of competitive strategies. The separate and autonomous power centers are quick to imitate their rivals' innovative behaviors or to join coalitions to support their own programs.

Advocates of centralization argue that allowing free reign to the division of labor and specialization will result in chaos and disorder at the interorganizational field level. However, decentralization proponents counter with the argument that a number of factors prevent chaos from resulting. First, there is a high degree of consensus among agencies and professionals on the service paradigm and this guides most organizational and staff actions. Radical departures from the paradigm are infrequent. Second, there is an extremely high degree of interchange of personnel between social service organizations. Quite a few boundary spanning personnel in the various agencies have extensive contacts with other social service organizations. For example, many CETA staff were taken from the Employment Service, Community Action Agencies, and other social service agencies concerned with manpower in one form or another.

·Maximizing responsiveness to local conditions and reaping the benefits of specialization are interrelated arguments. If local populations vary sufficiently in their needs, then programs tailored to those needs will eventually become highly specialized. Similarly, specialized programs linked to target populations by effective feedback procedures should become quite responsive to local needs. Whether either of these sequences develops in a particular program depends upon the ability of planners to establish a link between client satisfaction and organizational rewards.

Duplication and Overlap Increase System Reliability

Redundancy in human service delivery systems increases the possibility of detecting system errors and of occasionally hitting the target. The simplest way to grasp the importance of duplication or redundancy in a complex system is to consider the interpersonal communication process. If I avoid all repetition and redundancy in speaking to you, my message will be short but there will be no way for you to assess its reliability or whether you have truly understood it. It is only when I repeat the same message in different ways—speak in a redundant fashion—that the detection of error or misunderstanding is possible. A message with zero redundancy would not allow for the detection of error. This argument can be generalized to the situation of interorganizational relations in a complex system (Landau, 1969).

Traditional theories of public administration call for "each role to be perfected, each bureau to be exactly delimited, each linkage to articulate unfailingly and each line of communication to be noiseless—all to produce one interlocking system, one means ends chain which possesses the absolute minimum number of links, and which culminates at a central control point" (Landau, 1969: 354). In systems terms, this is a highly centralized, hierarchical, richly coupled system. This model is clearly a high risk one because the failure of a single component could shut down the entire system. A single failure breaks the system, just as a failure in an electrical circuit connected in series shuts down the entire circuit. Error introduced at one point is sent unchecked throughout the entire system.

The most appropriate environment for a richly coupled, highly centralized system appears to be one where the environmental conditions producing the problem treated by the social service agency are fully known and therefore uncertainty is low, where the goals of all the components are fixed and widely accepted, and where the technologies of the various components are well understood. Needless to say, these conditions don't obtain very often in most social service delivery systems. Economists are still trying to untangle the link between inflation and unemployment and educators still aren't certain why Johnny can't read. Most recent organizational research calls into question the usefulness of static models for understanding interorganizational relations.

One of the objectives of the redesigned manpower training system under CETA has been to eliminate redundancy. Under the old system, even though programs were categorically determined from Washington, a number of options were open to the unemployed. Each of the various programs had its own intake and placement operation. Now these functions are all centralized under CETA, although in many cases CETA has delegated them to other organizations. Nevertheless, the delegation process has generally been one of finding a single subcontractor to take a single function. A systems theorist could argue that eliminating all duplication and overlap may lead to lessened system performance in the long run.

Under certain conditions a system with individual elements that are unreliable can be formed into a system with a fairly high degree of reliability. Two conditions are that the failure of component parts must be random and statistically independent of one another. In such a system the probability of failure of the whole system decreases exponentially as redundancy factors increase arithmetically. For example, assume that in a metropolitan area there are three organizations performing roughly the same function. Each has a probability of failure of .20 over some specified time period. Failures occur at random and are not related. The probability of two organizations failing at the same time is .20 × .20 or .04. The probability of all three organizations failing at the same time is only .008. Thus, a one unit increase in redundancy from one to two or from two to three leads to a geometric increase in the system's reliability. This example is admittedly oversimplified and one would have to consider how rapidly the surviving organizations could expand their operations to take in the clients of failed organizations. Nonetheless, the general point is well taken: in an environment that is uncertain and somewhat unpredictable, where technologies used are incompletely understood, and where objectives are still evolving, duplication of effort and overlap between goals and domains is one way of increasing the probability of some organizations accomplishing their tasks.

Centralization and "Coordination" Tend to Reinforce Prior Patterns of Dominance

Decentralization advocates argue that centralization or "coordinated" strategies are thinly disguised attempts to further the interests of dominant organizations. They point out that if a coordination plan is administered by or through existing organizations, they gain a predominant voice in what is to be done (Warren, 1973). Gaining a major voice, in turn, benefits dominant organizations in several ways. The social service "problem" is defined in the organization's own terms, allowing it to use its existing staff and technology. Dominant organizations can reduce the threat of competition from new organizations in the name of "avoiding duplication of services." The problem can be defined as one requiring more services, especially of the kind offered by existing organizations. Defining the problem of poverty, medical care, legal services and manpower services, and so forth, as a problem of coordinating the behavior of existing organizations enables the affluent and influential sectors of the population to avoid more drastic change. In short, it enables the privileged to retain their positions.

The effect of turning CETA over to local governments has been to redistribute benefits into local government agencies and bureaus. The work experience program, designed to give disadvantaged and unemployed persons a taste of a real work experience, has become a supplemental labor force for local governments. This is in addition to the public service employment component which was explicitly designed to aid the public sector. Attaching CETA to existing political units has meant that in some cases it is nearly inseparable and indistinguishable from existing city or county departments. In these situations it is treated as simply another departmental resource. Continuing a trend apparent under the old system, the private business sector has been relatively neglected in favor of the public and non-profit sectors. The benefits to local non-profit agencies in particular have been phenomenal.

Indeed, one issue not raised explicitly up to now is the question of why programs are so seldom evaluated in terms of their benefits to the other organizations in a community. In the case of CETA, local CETA operations provide part- and full-time employees to dozens and in some cases hundreds of local non-profit agencies, such as the Red Cross, Salvation Army, YMCA, day care centers, alternate education operations, programs for the aged, and just about every social service imaginable. This is in addition to the employees provided to governmental bureaus and departments. Curiously enough, the program is never described in these terms. Rather, it is described in terms of benefits to clients in the program and in terms of a reduction in the unemployment rate resulting from trainees finding jobs in the private sector. It would seem equally important to point out the tremendous supplement that these subsidized workers provide to the social services sector.

Centralization in the manpower training system has meant that the allocation of manpower training funds has not become an issue in "partisan politics." Some planners see this as a decided plus for the system, while others decry the passing of an opportunity to debate crucial political priorities. For the latter group, the issue has become a "non-issue" (Bachrach and Baratz, 1962).

The issue has been de-politicized for a number of reasons. First, there is consensus on the social services paradigm. Neither major political party advocates major institutional change in the United States. Second, most staff positions within the various agencies are allocated on a merit basis. Thus, neither party sees any gain to be had from taking over the programs. Third, the program is designed so that issues can be defined as "getting more for our local constituency in the contest with other localities." This unites the two parties in the community against the other communities in a region. Finally, the public has no alternative source of information about programs and must rely upon announcements by public officials and administrators. The effect of these factors has been to keep CETA remarkably conflict free, at least with regard to the political arena.

Centralization allows dominant organizations to deal with potential dissent from community groups by coopting them. Establishing new plans or councils to achieve "better coordination" is a way of coopting protesting clients and interest groups. It gives the appearance of change and responsiveness to "voice" without requiring major changes in the traditional definition of problems or their solutions. Moreover, the resource pot available to centralized agencies is sizeable, and their legislatively enforced central position gives dominant organizations the right to distribute benefits so as to reward "cooperative" organizations.

In the 1960s, Community Action Agencies were among the most vocal critics of local social services operations. Many were highly critical of the way manpower programs were run, arguing that the poor and minority groups were being systematically neglected in favor of more skilled workers. Both Community Action Agencies and Model Cities agencies adopted what Warren et al. (1974) referred to as "Paradigm II." This is a paradigm which says that more services are not enough, and that major institutional change is required to improve the position of the poverty stricken and disadvantaged in American society. Many Community Action Agencies were funded under the old manpower training system, but they received money separately through the Office of Economic Opportunity HEW program for youth. In the reorganized system, Community Action Agencies have been coopted by CETA administrators giving them major roles to play. In a number of the cities studied in New York State, Community Action Agencies play important roles in running CETA programs. They have subcontracts to do intake counseling, placement, and in at least one large city, they run the entire program under subcontract from the county government. For example, in one county 25 percent of the Community Action Agency's budget comes from CETA and 30 of its staff positions are CETA funded. In another large upstate city, the CAA is the single largest contractor under CETA, with more than a million dollars in grant funds. Other groups and organizations that were potentially problematic for CETA have been coopted either by giving them subcontracts and placements or by their being given advisory voice: educational organizations. Chambers of Commerce, social service departments, organizations of minority groups, and so forth.

Centralization makes it easier for existing programs to survive *if* they're supported by major interests in a community. However, it is also easier to omit those not supported by major interests. What's difficult is the creation of new programs that go outside the existing set of services offered.

Centralization not only reinforces prior patterns of dominance, but also reinforces the trend toward the over-bureaucratization of social service organizations. Human service organizations lack a market test and tend to be over-administered, as authorities search for ways to control the behavior of staff members and administrators. Positions proliferate on the basis of *internal* evaluations of need and professionals lobbying for more of their own kind. Centralization simply enhances this tendency. Advocates of decentralization argue that instead of economies of scale resulting from centralization, what in fact happens is that centralization leads to an administrative explosion. It is better, they assert, to fund smaller organizations with one or two people performing a large number of functions and getting most of them right.

Given the different pattern of subcontracting among the CETA operations of the various cities studied, it is difficult to make direct comparisons of staff size, but some differences were striking. One county has 20 CETA staff and their plan of action for the last fiscal year said that they would achieve 83 direct placements (this means persons placed without going through training), 108 indirect placements (after training), with 28 clients obtaining their own placements in the course of a year's budget. Might it not be better to distribute these 20 staff positions across 5, 6, or even 9 separate organizations? In an adjacent county that is quite a bit larger and serves quite a few more clients, the CETA staff consists of only 13 persons, but this is partially due to the fact that this CETA agency uses the Employment Service and Community Action Agency extensively, whereas the first county does not. Thus, one agency has used its power and discretion to grow internally, whereas another has a relatively smaller staff and has subsidized other major community organizations.

390

The argument that centralization tends to benefit the already well-off organizations could, of course, be used to argue for either greater centralization or decentralization. Advocates of still greater centralization argue that centralized control should be strengthened, perhaps by giving higher authorities more control, so that dominant organizations are forced to subordinate their goals to those of a larger plan. Public choice theorists and system designers who value citizen autonomy and the benefits of a market mechanism might interpret the fourth argument to imply that small, less powerful, and unrepresented groups and organizations should be assisted and given preferential treatment so they can compete on an equal basis with dominant organizations. I am unsure as to how one would resolve debate of this kind by relying solely on technical analysis.

Summary of Arguments for Greater Decentralization

1. Decentralization allows organizations to be maximally responsive to heterogeneous client demands and to innovate when local conditions demand.

2. Decentralization allows the maximum benefits of the interorganizational division of labor and specialization to be realized.

3. Duplication and overlap of functions and domains increases overall system reliability.

4. Centralization favors the already well-off organizations and decentralization is a way of breaking up the existing flow of benefits.

Conclusions

Advocates of centralization and decentralization both claim that the "other" structure benefits dominant and well-established organizations. Both sets of arguments are compelling and it may be that this result—elite domination—is inescapable. The manipulation of authority to gain a dominant position or to avoid dominance by others in a network is a common tactic in interorganizational networks. Some centralized systems are obviously a result of such strategic moves by dominant organizations. Whether anything could or should be done about this is not obvious from the research findings available at present. Answering such questions requires research that correlates interorganizational system outputs with system characteristics, and knowledge on this score is woefully deficient. Moreover, undoubtedly the "best" systems combine elements of centralization *and* decentralization, and most of us are simply not clever enough to design such systems in the abstract.

Considering organizations as the relevant units of analysis and evaluation, it may be that smaller organizations actually benefit more from a centralized than a decentralized system. This seems to have been one result of the reorganization of manpower training under CETA. Programs are more visible in large centralized structures and the scale of administration is such that administrators can devote resources to assisting smaller organizations. In decentralized systems, it is probable that innovation is greater in response to specialized needs and organizational technologies, but smaller organizations have much more difficulty in gaining access to resources to follow up innovations. In centralized systems, new programs are sheltered from buffeting forces by protection under the wing of dominant organizations.

Richly coupled systems that are *not* hierarchies are inherently unstable (Simon, 1962), and heavy environmental pressure is required to preserve them. The failure of many voluntarily constituted richly coupled systems, such as coordinating councils, clearing house agencies, or human service coalitions, is due to the lack of either external pressure *or* an authority structure that could preserve the system. It is also easy for dominant organizations to sabotage such systems through non-cooperation. Planners desiring highly decentralized systems with weak central authority may have to accept a high degree of isolation of key units as the cost of local autonomy and responsiveness. Alternatively, planners concerned with the equitable treatment of clients may have to accept a high degree of centralization at supraordinate authority levels—state and federal—and also accept the inevitable marginality or demise of small local organizations.

A major problem in designing a human services delivery system lies in defining the boundaries of an ideal decision-making unit. Such a unit should include the causes of problems, the victims, and related externalities. In the social services sector, the focus of problems and the relevant catchment areas are ambiguous and open to manipulation. For example, in the manpower training realm, is the relevant unit a city, county, metropolitan area, region, or the entire economy? When technical analysis is unable to supply answers to these questions, the resulting uncertainty is resolved by turning to other bases for decision making: the prestige and power of persons or organizations proposing solutions, the convenience of using existing solutions, and so forth (Pfeffer, 1977).

Regardless of the boundaries of a system, the relation between benefits to component organizations and benefits to individuals is not obvious. Planners sometimes assume that any structure efficient in saving resources, by eliminating duplication of effort or administrative overhead or other means, results in more resources for clients or at least for other programs. However, social service organizations are labor intensive and it's very easy to add more persons to a staff. There is little or no investment in fixed assets and budgets can expand very quickly with little advance planning.

This shows up in two ways in the manpower planning system. First, local CETA administrators are asked to respond very quickly to requests for proposals from the Department of Labor, sometimes within thirty days, and many of their proposals contain allotments for new staff to be recruited in a very short period of time. Second, several times in the past few years money has been made available on very short notice for public service employment positions, and local governments as well as non-profit agencies have suddenly found room for new personnel as if by magic. My impression is that personnel sections of social service budgets have voracious appetites all their own which can greedily devour funds saved from other activities.

The biggest gap in assessing whether organizational advantages translate into benefits for clients is the tenuous link between clients' evaluations and organizational fate. Assessments of benefits to clients are usually made by professionals who have a vested interest in the survival of their programs. The manpower training system, for example, has not been able to work out a satisfactory evaluation system that includes clients. Manpower Planning Advisory Councils have not lived up to the expectations expressed in the 1973 legislation, as they've been dominated by CETA administrators and their staff.

The title to this paper was left deliberately ambiguous, reflecting my own feelings regarding Gouldner's lament.

> Wrapping themselves in the shrouds of nineteenth-century political economy, some social scientists appear to be bent on resurrecting a dismal science. Instead of telling men how bureaucracy might be mitigated, they insist that it is inevitable. Instead of explaining how democratic patterns may, to some extent, be fortified and extended, they warn us that democracy cannot be perfect. Instead of controlling the disease, they suggest that we are deluded, or more politely, incurably romantic, for hoping to control it. Instead of assuming responsibilities whenever they can, many social scientists have become morticians, all too eager to bury men's hopes. (Gouldner, 1955: 507)

On one side, I think the problem is more severe than Gouldner recognized, as I've tried to point out in these conclusions. On the other side, I think many social scientists are as eager as ever to make positive contributions. The question is, is anybody listening?

References

AIKEN, MICHAEL, and ROBERT ALFORD. 1970. "Community Structure and Innovation: The Case of Urban Renewal," *American Sociological Review,* 35:650–65.

ALDRICH, HOWARD. 1976a. "Resource Dependence and Interorganizational Relations: Local Employment Service Offices and Social Services Sector Organizations," *Administration and Society,* 7:419–54.

———. 1976b. "An Interorganization Dependency Perspective on Relations between the Employment Service and Its Organization Set." In R. Kilmann, L. Pondy, and D. Slevin, eds., *The Management of Organization Design,* pp. 231–66. Amsterdam: Elsevier.

———. 1977. "Visionaries and Villians: The Politics of Designing Interorganizational Relations," *Organization and Administrative Sciences,* 8:23–40.

———. 1979. *Organizations and Environments.* Englewood Cliffs, N.J.: Prentice Hall.

ALDRICH, HOWARD, and JEFFREY PFEFFER. 1976. "Environments of Organizations." In A. Inkeles, ed., *Annual Review of Sociology,* 2:79–106. Palo Alto: Annual Reviews.

BACHRACH, PETER, and MORTON BARATZ. 1962. "The Two Forces of Power," *American Political Science Review,* 57:947–52.

BANFIELD, EDWARD and MORTON GRODZINS. 1958. *Government and Housing in Metropolitan Areas.* New York: McGraw-Hill.

BENSON, J. KENNETH. 1975. "The Interorganizational Network as a Political Economy," *Administrative Science Quarterly,* 20:229–49.

FREEMAN, LINTON. 1968. *Patterns of Local Community Leadership.* Indianapolis: Bobbs-Merrill.

GORDON, LAURA. 1975. "Bureaucratic Competence and Success in Dealing with Public Bureaucracies," *Social Problems,* 23:197–208.

GOULDNER, ALVIN. 1955. "Metaphysical Pathos and the Theory of Bureaucracy," *American Political Science Review,* 49:496–507.

HIRSCHMAN, A. O. 1972. *Exit, Voice, and Loyalty.* Cambridge: Harvard University Press.

LANDAU, MARTIN. 1969. "Redundancy, Rationality, and the Problem of Duplication and Overlap," *Public Administration Review,* 39:346–58.

PFEFFER, JEFFREY. 1977. "Power and Resource Allocation in Organizations." In B. Staw and G. Salancik, eds., *New Directions in Organizational Behavior.* Chicago: St. Clair Press.

ROTH, JULIUS. 1972. "Some Contingencies of the Moral Evaluation and Control of Clientele: The Case of the Hospital Emergency Service," *American Journal of Sociology,* 77:839–56.

SIMON, H. A. 1962. "The Architecture of Complexity." *Proceedings of the American Philosophical Society,* 106:284–315.

WARREN, ROLAND. 1973. "Comprehensive Planning and Coordination—Some Functional Aspects," *Social Problems,* 20:355–64.

WARREN, ROLAND, STEPHEN ROSE, and ANN BERGUNDER. 1974. *The Structure of Urban Reform: Community Decision Organizations in Stability and Change.* Lexington, Mass.: D.C. Heath.

WILLIAMSON, O. 1975. *Markets and Hierarchies: Analysis and Antitrust Implications.* New York: Free Press.

Women and the Structure of Organizations: Explorations in Theory and Behavior

Rosabeth Moss Kanter

This is an "organizational" society. The lives of very few of us are untouched by the growth and power of large, complex organizations in the twentieth century. The consequences of decisions made in these organizations, particularly business enterprises, may affect the availability of goods and services, the distribution of wealth and privilege, and the opportunity for meaningful work. The distribution of functions within organizations affects the quality of daily life for a large proportion of working Americans: their opportunities for growth and self-expression, for good or poor health, as well as their daily social contacts. The distribution of power within organizations affects who benefits, and to what degree, from the things organizations make possible, and whose interests are served by the organization's decisions. Despite a prevalent image in social science of modern organizations as universalistic, sex-neutral tools, sex is a very important determinant of who gets what in and out of organizations.

The ways in which women have been connected to organizations and have operated within them, and whether these ways differ from those of men, have been underinvestigated in social research. While there is a relatively large and growing literature that documents the degree to which women are socialized to perform different kinds of activities from men

SOURCE: Marcia Millman and Rosabeth Moss Kanter, *Another Voice*, pp. 34–74. Copyright © 1975 by Sociological Inquiry. Reprinted by permission of the author and Doubleday & Company, Inc.

I wish to thank the following people for their critical comments and support: Nancy Chodorow, Susan Eckstein, Joan Huber, Barry Stein, Chris Argyris, Zick Rubin, William Form, William Torbert, Caroline Butterfield, and Joanna Hiss.

(often activities with less power and monetary reward), there has been less attention paid to the patterned relationships between women and men in organizations.

This paper is an attempt to define directions for an enlarged understanding of the sociology of organizations as it concerns women, and of the study of women as it contributes to a more comprehensive and accurate sociology of organizations. The focus throughout is solely on the United States and largely on the administrative levels of business organizations. In part, this was an attempt to place limits on an area with a vast amount of literature. But it is also because the administrative issues of business tended to provide the impetus for the early sociology of organizations. Business organizations, additionally, have great power in American society and, because they are successful, are assumed to be successfully managed, so that their organization and management has often served as a model for other systems. It is also in business organizations that women seem most conspicuously absent from positions of prestige and power.

Management: A Male Category

Women generally do not hold positions of power and authority in organizations, especially in American industry. Those few women in management tend to be concentrated in lower-paying positions, in selected fields, in staff rather than line positions, and in less powerful, less prestigious organizations. In 1969 U.S. Census figures indicate that women constituted only 3.25 per cent of the managers and administrators earning over $15,000 per year (before taxes), and 2.26 per cent of those earning over $30,000 per year. Women themselves may make the choice not to compete for managerial positions. Educated women, for example, tend not to enter fields that are linked to, and are preparation for, management. A substantially higher proportion of female college graduates than male become "professional, technical, and kindred" workers rather than managers and administrators, for instance (77.4 per cent as opposed to 58.9 per cent—Bureau of the Census, 1973a). Women with doctorates generally do not take them in management-related fields, as figures on earned doctorates in the United States between 1960 and 1969 indicate.[1]

1. Data are from HEW, via a University of Minnesota publication, reprinted by the Women's Equity Action League, Washington, D.C., in 1974. M.D.'s and other professional doctorates are not included. Women earned 11.63 per cent of the total doctorates reported, but only 2.82 per cent of the doctorates in business and commerce (a total of 86 women in 10 years), 5 per cent of those in hospital administration (1 woman out of 20 doctorates), and none of those in trade or industrial training. Women earned 11.10 per cent of all the social science doctorates but only 4.17 per cent of those in industrial relations and 8.13 per cent of those in public administration.

At least a portion of the evidence that women earn less than men can be accounted for by the fact that women hold jobs carrying less pay even in well-paid fields like management. Bureau of Labor Statistics figures indicate that in 1970 the median annual earnings of female managers and administrators (excluding farm administration) were around half of that for men, even in fields such as school administration and wholesale/retail trade, where female administrators are clustered. A recent national personnel survey of 163 U.S. companies discovered that the farther up the management ladder, even scarcer are the women. In over half of the companies, women held only 2 per cent or less of the first-level supervisory jobs (including such positions as manager of secretaries); in *three quarters* of the companies, women held 2 per cent or fewer of the middle-management jobs; and in *over three quarters* of the companies, they held *none* of the top-management jobs (*Personnel Policies Forum,* 1971).

The few management women are also clustered in particular kinds of organizations. The *Personnel Policies Forum* survey found that women were proportionately more represented in management in nonbusiness rather than in business organizations, and, within business, in nonmanufacturing rather than in manufacturing enterprises. A 1965 *Harvard Business Review* survey of 1,000 male and 900 female executives (the men were drawn from the *HBR* readership, but there were so few women among top executives that separate lists had to be used to locate them) found women disproportionately represented in the management of retail/wholesale trade (merchandising fields) and advertising, whereas men were disproportionately represented in the management of banking/investment/insurance companies (financial concerns) and industrial goods manufacturing (Bowman, Worthy, and Greyser, 1965). (Calculations based on 1969 U.S. Census figures confirm the clustering of women managers in retail trade and services, including stenographic services, and men in manufacturing.[2]) The *HBR* respondents, further, felt that opportunities for women in management lie only in: education, the arts, social services, retail trade, office management, personnel work, and nonmanagement positions. One third of the respondents felt, as of 1965, that there were *no* opportunities for women in the management of labor unions; construction, mining, and oil companies; industrial goods manufacturing; production; and top management in general (Bowman, Worthy, and Greyser, 1965). The *HBR* survey is also suggestive of the concentration of women in staff positions, where they tend not to have authority over subordinates, or in low-status areas. Women in the *HBR* study were heavily represented in

2. Of the managers and administrators earning over $15,000 per year, 26.1 per cent of the women vs. 17.2 per cent of the men are in retail trade, 25.8 per cent of the women vs. 8.5 per cent of the men are in "professional and related services," and 12.2 per cent of the women vs. 26.7 per cent of the men are in manufacturing. Women represent 9.3 per cent of the total managers in services but only 1.52 per cent of the total in manufacturing. Calculations from Census Bureau (1973b).

marketing and office management (39 per cent and 10 per cent of the female respondents, respectively, as opposed to 16 per cent and 3 per cent of the males, respectively) and underrepresented in general management (10 per cent of the women, compared with 40 per cent of the men falling into this category). Similarly, the women were disproportionately found in small (and hence less powerful or statusful) organizations.

These data suggest that women are virtually absent from the management of large industrial enterprises and present to only a slightly greater degree in the management of retail or business-support service organizations. Even in areas in which the workers are likely to be female, their managers are likely to be male. The number of male and of female bank tellers in the United States in 1969 was nearly equal, for example (255,549 men and 220,255 women), but "bank officers and financial managers" were largely male (82.48 per cent male and 17.52 per cent female). Office workers are largely female, yet office *managers,* a relatively low-status management position, are still more likely to be male than female (59.64 per cent male, 40.36 per cent female) (calculations based on figures of Bureau of the Census, 1973a).

We need to know the barriers to women in organizational leadership and also what difference their presence makes: how culture and behavior are shaped by the sex distribution of managers. The behavior and experiences of the few women in management and leadership positions should be considered as a function of membership in male-dominated settings. (Some of the findings of the few studies done to date are reported later.) The politics and informal networks of management as influenced by its male membership should be further studied—e.g., the degree to which managerial as well as worker behavior and culture is shaped in part by the traditions, emotions, and sentiments of male groups.[3] How the culture and behavior of management is affected by (or reflected in) the sex ratio of managers is also important (e.g., how retail or service organizations differ from manufacturers), as well as the influence of the sex composition of management on its relations with other organizational strata.

Office Work: Female Function

Women are to clerical labor as men are to management. According to Census Bureau data, there were over 10 million female "clerical and kindred workers" in the United States in 1969, 73.78 per cent of the total employed workers in this category. Men in the clerical labor force tend to be concentrated in a few, physically oriented occupations where they far

3. Several popularized accounts treat management as an expression of the instincts of male hunting bands and make management, indeed, seem charged with masculine culture and traditions. See Tiger (1969) and Jay (1967, 1971).

outnumber women (computer operators, messengers, mail carriers, shipping and receiving clerks, and stock clerks). The rest of the occupations, the core of office work, are heavily female. Women comprised 82.14 per cent of the bookkeepers, 81.84 per cent of the billing clerks, 68.96 per cent of the payroll and timekeeping clerks, and 82.08 per cent of the file clerks. In secretarial and related functions, men are as underrepresented as women are in management. Women comprised 93.46 per cent of the stenographers in 1969, 94.18 per cent of the typists, 94.65 per cent of the receptionists, and 97.71 per cent of the secretaries. In fact, these four positions account for nearly 40 per cent of the 1969 female "clerical and kindred workers"; secretaries alone account for 25 per cent of the 1969 female clerical labor force (calculations based on Bureau of the Census, 1973a). Labor Bureau statistics for 1970, calculated on a slightly different basis, show even fewer men in such positions: of the category "stenographers, typists, and secretaries," 98.6 per cent are female and only 1.40 per cent are male (Bureau of Labor Statistics, 1971). *Work in America* (1972), a task force report to HEW, has concluded that the job of secretary is symbolic of the status of female employment, both qualitatively and quantitatively. Office jobs for women have low status, little autonomy or opportunity for growth, and generally low pay.

Women did not always dominate the clerical labor force; office work in the nineteenth century was first a male job. The same turn-of-the-century period (1890–1910) that brought large organizations and the growth of the professional manager also witnessed the emergence of the modern office, with its invention of new roles for women. The three-person office of midnineteenth-century Dickens novels was socially reorganized into departments and functional areas headed by office managers, and this change—itself a product of bureaucraticization and machine technology—permitted the massive introduction of office machines. Though invented in the 1870s, the typewriter was not widely used until the twentieth century; but from 1900–20, office employment rose dramatically, and typing soon became women's work (Mills, 1951:192–93).

The rise in the employment of women in the office around the turn of the century was dramatic, and it corresponded to a large decrease in "household occupations" (servants, dressmakers and seamstresses outside of factories, and laundresses). In 1870 the "clerical group" (clerks, stenographers, typists, bookkeepers, cashiers, and accountants) accounted for less than 1 per cent of the women employed outside of agriculture; by 1920 it accounted for over 25 per cent of female nonagricultural employment (Hill, 1929:39). In 1880 the proportion of women in the clerical labor force as a whole was 4 per cent; in 1890, 21 per cent (Davies, 1974). By 1910, women were already 83.2 per cent of the stenographers and typists; by 1920, they were 91.8 per cent of the stenographers/typists and 48.8 per cent of the bookkeepers, cashiers, and accountants (Hill, 1929:

56–57). Between 1910 and 1920 the number of female clerks (excluding store clerks) quadrupled; female stenographers and typists more than doubled (Hill, 1929:33). Slightly more women were still employed in factory than in clerical jobs in 1920 (about 1.8 million and 1.5 million, respectively), but less than 1 per cent of those in industry could be classified as managers, superintendents, or officials (calculations based on Hill, 1929: Table 115). The growth of modern administration brought women into domination in the office but absent in management. Whereas factory jobs were divided between men and women (though often sex-typed), clerical jobs rapidly became the work almost exclusively of women.

To what extent was the nature of office work and the structural position of office workers in organizations shaped by the "feminization" of the clerical labor force? Did the nature of this organizational status come to be defined in sex-role-appropriate terms,[4] and did the emergent relations between office work and the management for which it was done reinforce the female caste of the former and the masculine caste of the latter? Did the sexual stratification of these two organizational categories constitute a barrier to mobility between them? Sociologists have tended to neglect these questions. Studies of the history of the office, the social relations it entailed, and the structural relations between and within categories of clerical and managerial personnel have generally not been included in studies of modern organizations (Miller, 1950:303; Crozier, 1965:15). (The few pioneering studies include C. Wright Mills' *White Collar* [1951], Nancy Morse [1953] on job satisfaction of white-collar workers, and Michel Crozier [1965] on Parisian insurance office workers. Margery Davies' work in progress [1974] considers the social implications of the feminization of the clerical labor force.)[5]

The secretary may be a prototypical and pivotal role to examine; research should consider the place of this job in the clerical hierarchy, its relations to management, and whether its role demands bar women from moving into management positions. Even though private secretaries represent only a small proportion of the female clerical labor force, this position is sometimes the highest to which a woman office worker may aspire—the best-paid, most prestigious, and for secretaries of executives, one with "reflected power" derived from the status of the manager. It is also the job in which there are the most clearly defined male-female relations—the private secretary has been called an "office wife" (Mills, 1951).[6]

4. Margery Davies (1974) discovered that a 1916 *Ladies' Home Journal* article was already glorifying the feminine traits of stenographers: radiating sympathetic interest, agreeableness, courtesy. In 1900, however, the same magazine was urging women to stay out of offices.
5. See also recent journalistic accounts by Garson (1973) and Langer (1970); on secretaries see Benet (1973) and Halter et al. (1973).
6. A New York corporation informant, a former executive secretary promoted into management, told me that leaving her boss was like getting a divorce. For the first

Women and the Structure of Organizations

My field work in a large New York-based corporation indicates that the traditional secretary-manager relationship has striking parallels to Weber's definition of "patrimonial rule" (Bendix, 1960:425), even though this relationship occurs within organizations that social scientists have assumed generally fit Weber's "bureaucratic" model. The relationship can be defined as "patrimonial" to the extent that managers make demands at their own discretion and arbitrarily recruit secretaries on the basis of appearance, personality, and other subjective factors rather than on skill, expect personal service, exact loyalty, and make secretaries part of their private retinue (e.g., expecting them to move when they move). Further, secretaries in many large organizations may derive their status from that of their boss, regardless of the work they do; a promotion for a secretary may mean moving on to a higher-status manager, whether or not her work changes or improves.[7] There may be no job descriptions, as there are for managerial positions, that help match the person's skills to the job or insure some uniformity of demands across jobs, so that there are often no safeguards to exploitation, no standards for promotion other than personal relationships, and no way of determining if a secretary can be moved to another job (all barriers to mobility out of the secretarial ranks for women).[8] The relation of the secretarial work force to management may be one of status in addition to function; e.g., secretaries may be chosen for the status they give their bosses in having educated, attractive secretaries, whether or not their skills are utilized, and acquisition of a secretary may be a status symbol in its own right in many organizations, signifying a manager's importance.[9]

Within the organizational structure secretarial positions are probably the most dramatic example of the much larger issue of the relationships

---

four months of her new job, she stopped in to see him every morning and hung her coat in her old office.

7. A manager of clerical employees told me that sometimes promotions mean that secretaries have *less* work to do and have trouble justifying their larger salaries to their peers. As with marriage, if a woman has the good fortune to be connected with a high-status male, she gets more money and does less work.

8. The large corporation in my research, beginning to design "upward mobility" programs for women, has discovered secretarial work to be arbitrary and particularistic. The change effort includes generating job descriptions and decoupling a secretary's status from her boss's so that she will no longer derive rank from him or necessarily move with him when he moves.

9. A chatty advice-to-managers book (Burger, 1964) devotes a chapter to "living with your secretary," with whom, the book declares, a man spends more of his waking hours than with his wife. She is a status symbol: "In many companies, a secretary outside your door is the most visible sign that you have become an executive; a secretary is automatically assigned to each executive, whether or not his work load requires one. . . . When you reach vice-presidential level, your secretary may have an office of her own, with her name on the door. At the top, the president may have two secretaries. . . . 'Miss Amy, please take a letter,' are words which have inwardly thrilled every young executive with a sense of his own importance . . . they symbolize power and status" (Burger, 1964:219, 220).

between sex-typed roles. But the whole problem has, nevertheless, been largely neglected in organization research. Let us turn to a re-examination of historical models of organizations to see why.

Early Models of Organizations: Managerialism and a "Masculine Ethic"

The period 1890–1910 brought what Daniel Bell (1957) has called "the breakup of family capitalism"—the beginnings of corporate mergers and finance capitalism (through bank intervention), which increasingly took (at least daily) control out of the hands of owners and put it in the domain of professional managers of large organizations. In 1941 James Burnham maintained that the character of twentieth-century economic organizational life was determined by this "managerial revolution" (Burnham, 1941). Whether or not capital owners actually did fade into the background, a point of some dispute (see Zeitlin, 1974), the rise of large organizations created a new and growing profession, with an internal decision-making monopoly and authority over those within the organization.

The advantages, authority, and control of the newly prominent managers required explanation and justification (Bendix, 1956). The new career managers lacked a class position buttressed by tradition that would provide grounds for legitimation, seeking it instead in the increasing professionalization of management, in the development of a "spirit of managerialism" that gave ideological coherence to the control of a relatively small and exclusive group of men over a large group of workers.[10] A

10. Even today management has legitimacy issues. The tasks of management are largely intangible, and the results of managerial efforts depend largely on products of the work of other people. Technical expertise, according to analysts from Chester Barnard on, plays only a small role; indeed, many sociologists assume an organizational conflict between expertise and authority—i.e., between professionals and managers. The necessity (in economic and social terms) for large cadres of managers has yet to be demonstrated definitively (cf. the conflicting results of the several studies in Heydebrand, 1974). Barry Stein (1974) has marshaled evidence to indicate that the presumed efficiencies of scale in large organizations are often instead inefficiencies, and administrative costs are one important cause. A recent study of 167 large corporations over a 20-year period concludes that much of the variance in sales, earnings, and profit margins can be explained by factors other than the impact of management (Lieberson and O'Connor, 1972). To some extent, then, management may still have the tasks of justifying its necessity, importance, numbers, and privileges, though of course management in the 1970s is already very different in character from management of earlier years.

A provocative analogy could be made between management and fatherhood: necessary for conception but not visibly connected to or necessary for production thereafter. The uncertainty of management's actual connection to the results is like the uncertainty of paternity—the biological father can never be definitively identified. Yet in both cases control and the product's legitimacy are vested in the paternal figure. (I am indebted to Nancy Jay for the insight about fatherhood.)

social science both of management and of organizations grew with the growth of large organizations. This early organization theory aided legitimation of managerialism in several ways: first, by accepting, more or less uncritically, management's definition of itself, its tasks, and its importance; second, by providing both concepts (through research and writing) and an academic base (through schools of administration) that confirmed the power and perquisites of managers as well as educating them to managerial theory.[11]

The class origins of early-to-midtwentieth-century top-business management—largely white, Protestant men from elite schools—and the connections of such a social base with managerial ideologies have been rather extensively documented (Burnham, 1941; Miller, 1950, 1952; Warner and Abegglen, 1955; Sutton et al., 1956). Given the virtually all-male occupancy of these positions, it is worth examining whether sexual status, in conjunction with class and ethnicity, was also reflected in managerial ideologies and models of organization, thus helping solidify the already apparent sex stratification of organizations.

A "masculine ethic" of rationality and reason can be identified in the early image of managers. This "masculine ethic" elevates the traits assumed to belong to men with educational advantages to necessities for effective organizations: a tough-minded approach to problems; analytic abilities to abstract and plan; a capacity to set aside personal, emotional considerations in the interests of task accomplishment; and a cognitive superiority in problem-solving and decision-making. These characteristics were assumed to belong to management in two early models of organizations. This view both supported managerial authority and served as intellectual blindfolds, limiting the utility of the models for social research.

Rational Models

Social science first came to define modern organizations as rational instruments oriented to the attainment of specific goals, in which the un-

---

11. The first school of business at an American university was the Wharton School, founded in 1884 at the University of Pennsylvania. Management as a separate field was not introduced until decades later, at the Harvard Business School. The connection between theory and practice is especially great in this field. Many social scientists consult to industry and teach at schools of administration. A great deal of the early research on organizations was done at the invitation of management. Both Frederick Taylor and Chester Barnard, influential early- and middle-organization theorists, had backgrounds in industry, Barnard as president of New Jersey Bell. In Reinhard Bendix's (1956) analysis of the development of American managerial ideology, social science was seen as playing a role in feeding concepts to management justifying authority and defining distance from workers. Alvin Gouldner goes even farther in connecting social science with legitimation of managerial authority (1959:414–15).

equal distribution of authority aided efficiency. (The classical "rational" models have already been critized from a variety of perspectives, so that few social scientists today would actually agree to such limited definitions of organizations. See especially Argyris, 1957, 1972, 1973.)

During the same turn-of-the-century period that generated the growth of large organizations and professional management, Frederick I. Taylor introduced his theories of "scientific management" (the label was applied by Louis D. Brandeis in 1910) to American audiences, becoming a business consultant and prime creator of "classical" administrative theory. Taylor's premise was the application of the systematic analysis of science to management methods, emphasizing routines, order, logic, production planning, and cost analysis (Taylor, 1947; Tillett, Kempner, and Wills, 1970). His ideas influenced task specialization, time-and-motion studies, and assembly-line philosophies. Taylor's work also supported professional management at a time when unions were gaining in strength and employers were waging militant antiunion campaigns (Cochran, 1957). Taylor separated technical ability to perform a limited task from cognitive ability to abstract, plan, and logically understand the whole process; the latter was the special ability of management. Later Chester Barnard (1938) modified the idea of rationality; his conception of the rational organization was based on information and decisions rather than on routines and the orderly structuring of positions. He stressed communication (including informal channels) rather than hierarchy per se, but the need for a class of decisionmakers was clear. Goals were the special responsibility of the manager, whose functions included abstract generalizing and long-range planning. Authority was a necessary by-product of these decision-making functions (Tillett, Kempner, and Wills, 1970). (Herbert Simon has continued this tradition.)

Early organization theory thus developed rationality as the central ideal of formal organizations and hierarchy as the central structural principle. Organizations were considered tools for generating rational decisions and plans. Workers were motivated to participate on utilitarian grounds and could contribute specific skills, but the real effectiveness of the organization was seen to lie in the efforts of management to design the best way for individuals to fit together in an overall scheme. The rationality of the formal organization was thought to arise not so much from the nature of its participants as from the superiority of its plan, but the plan depended on rational decisionmakers. The design could minimize the nonrational, efficiency-undermining features of human beings to the extent that the participants consented to authority up the line. The very design of organizations thus was oriented toward, and assumed to be capable of, suppressing irrationality, personality, and emotionality, and people who had these unfortunate characteristics were devalued and kept from influencing the otherwise flawless machine. For Weber this gave bureaucratic organizations their advantage of efficiency over other types of corporate groups; bureaucracy was the truly "passionless" organization (Gerth and Mills, 1958:215–16).[12]

The development of the classical rational model limited research and theory in several directions. The model assumed that it was possible to design or engineer efficient structures, given specific, measurable goals. In emphasizing the goal-directed features of modern organizations, a consideration that in itself posed analytic difficulties,[13] it in turn focused attention on the visible, public-role players, the officials with the power to "speak for" and decide for the organization. The focus on goals in part legitimized managerial authority on other than political grounds, for managers were conceptualized as the keepers of the "goals," while workers were seen as free to act in terms of their own self-interest alone. An extension of the concern with goals and measures of output and efficiency was that the relative importance of sectors of an organization were seen in terms of their connection with the specific goals and/or production plans, and that segments of the system contributing in other ways—e.g., internal service or maintenance—were generally ignored in analysis. Given the concentration of women in such maintenance-support functions as office work, it was likely that the position of women and other such workers, the demands of their roles, their particular structural situation, and their contribution to the system would be underexamined, as indeed these issues have been in the organizational literature. Much research in the rational-model tradition emphasizes either structural design features or systems analyses of such issues as communication channels and horizontal and vertical linkages. Wider issues of organizational stratification,

12. Weber's notion of the virtues of bureaucracy's exclusion of passion converges interestingly with Freud's argument that women—the bearers of passion and sexuality—must be excluded from the workaday world of men. Women, Freud wrote in *Civilization and Its Discontents* (1930), are driven by emotion and incapable of suppressing or sublimating their passions and sexual instincts as men could. Further, since the work of men in civilized societies removed them from their homes and families, women become hostile to the male world of organizations, constantly trying to lure men away from their higher, reasoned pursuits. Resisting female enticements, men carry on the burdens of government and rational thought; rationality is the male principle, in opposition to the female principle of emotionality. Men master their sexuality, in the Freudian view, while women cannot. It would be interesting to study the convergences of Weber and Freud, not only on male and female principles in organizational life but also on the origin and nature of authority.

13. The literature abounds with examples of the difficulties one encounters in the concept of organizational goals. According to familiar analyses, goals may be: unclear, undefined, utopian, or nonoperational; precarious; changeable, in a process of goal succession or changing external conditions; ignored and/or deflected. There may be multiple goals, unstated goals, professed vs. operating goals, "task" vs. "maintenance" goals, and subgroup goals. There may be conflicts about which goals are thought appropriate by various segments of the organization, depending on their organizational position, internal or external constituency, and primary reference group. And there may be a wide gap between the stated goals of an organization and its functions for members or for society. See also Etzioni (1964).

as opposed to narrower issues of the number and types of positions and their direct linkages, were generally not considered. Finally, the classical model also supported managerial authority and a masculine ethic of rationality. While organizations were being defined as sex-neutral machines, masculine principles were dominating their authority structures.

Human-relations Models

The 1930s and 1940s gave rise to another model of organizations. A group of researchers working with Elton Mayo at Harvard Business School, beginning in the mid-1920s, discovered the importance for productivity of primary, informal relations among workers in the Hawthorne experiments (discussed later in this article; see also Roethlisberger and Dickson, 1939; Mayo, 1933).[14] This generated the concept of "informal organization" to include the emotional, nonrational, and sentimental aspects of human behavior in organizations, the ties and loyalties that affected workers. "Formal organization" came to refer to those features studied by the classical model, i.e., the organizational pattern designed by management: positions, functions, division of labor, relationships as defined by the organization chart, distribution of material rewards and privileges, and the official rules; "informal organization" to the social relations developed among workers beyond the formal ones given by the organization or to the actual behavior resulting from working relations rather than rote obedience to official rules (see Etzioni, 1964:40). The human-relations model assumed that people were motivated by social as well as economic rewards and that their behavior and attitudes were a function of group memberships. The model emphasized the roles of participation, communication patterns, and leadership style in effecting organizational outcomes.

While introducing social considerations and focusing on the human side of organizations, the human-relations analysts supported the concept of managerial authority and managerial rationality. In Mayo's view, workers were controlled by sentiment, emotion, and social instincts, and this phenomenon needed to be understood and taken into account in organizational functioning. Managers, on the other hand, were rational, logical, and able to control their emotions in the interests of organizational design (Mayo, 1933:122). Though the emphasis on informal, social factors could not be further from the factors considered important by scientific management, the view of the role of management in an organization

14. Mary Parker Follett was among the influential figures in generating this more human approach to management and one of the only important female organization theorists. Her interest in management grew out of her experience with the administration of social-welfare organizations.

was strikingly similar (Bendix, 1956:312). If the human-relations school's metaphor was the "family" rather than the "machine" of classical models, the organization was still thought to require a rational controller at its head. A consequence of this perspective, Reinhard Bendix has indicated, was a simplified version, which viewed the successful manager as the man who could control his emotions, whereas workers could not. Bendix quotes a 1947 management manual: "He [the leader] knows that the master of men has physical energies and skills and intellectual abilities, vision and integrity, and he knows that, above all, the leader must have emotional balance and control. The great leader is even-tempered when others rage, brave when others fear, calm when others are excited, self-controlled when others indulge" (Bendix, 1956:332). He found a strikingly similar description of the superiority of the manager lying in the manager's ability to control his emotions, in a 1931 volume. One does not have to look too far beyond such statements for the basis of the viewpoint of some managers in a 1965 survey that women were "temperamentally unfit" for management because they are too emotional (Bowman, Worthy, and Greyser, 1965).

Further, the literature on informal organization derived from the human-relations model, though introducing "non-rational" elements into organizational behavior, in practice turned out largely to *support* the rational bias of the formal system. Roethlisberger and Dickson as well as Warner and Low distinguished in their writing between the managerial elite's logic of efficiency and the workers' logic of sentiment. Informal organization was studied more often among workers or between workers and supervisor, leaving the impression that only workers have informal ties—managers do not (see Gouldner, 1959:407). There seems to be some support in the human-relations model, too, then, for managerial authority and the association of characteristics of the "masculine ethic" with management.

Research and theory based on the human-relations model proved limited in other ways. They tended to focus on informal work group relations in an abstract sense—independent of task, functional, or structural relationship to other organizational units, power and status outside of the group, or historical/cultural backdrop. Thus, many studies considered to be organizationally relevant were conducted in the laboratory in artificial situations rather than in the field. Findings about group cohesion, or leaders and subordinates, for example, were assumed to be generalizable over large numbers of kinds of groups, regardless of the complexities of the structural situations in which relationships in real organizations might be embedded.

Such, then, was the historical legacy of American organization theory. The early rational and human-relations models tended to support a managerial viewpoint that, in turn, can be seen to have latent functions as a "masculine ethic," congruent with the nearly exclusively male occupancy of the newly prominent careers in management and administration. The focus on managerial rationality could also justify the absence of women—the bearers of emotion—from power. At the same time, these leanings of traditional organization theory also had intellectual consequences, limiting its analytic perspective. Larger issues of organizational structure and stratification and their relation to social placement in the larger society, the differential distributions of men and women, and the consequences of these for organizational behavior—these questions were largely unnoticed. If the status quo of power in organizations and women's disadvantaged position was supported, it was as much because of intellectual blinders as because of deliberate intent. Theorists did not necessarily *want* to neglect women or keep them in their place, but the theorists tended not to see them because of the limits of the early models, and the theorists tended to assume that women were doing just what they ought to be doing: the office housework.

A Structuralist Perspective on Women and Organizations

It is now time for use of a newer, more eclectic and integrated model, one that *can* examine structural issues in organizations and their consequences for behavior. This more recent model, which Amitai Etzioni has termed "structuralist" (1964:41) (though it also encompasses the work of Argyris, Katz and Kahn, neo-Marxists, and others), addresses itself to the weaknesses of the earlier theories and is capable of offering enlarged understanding of women's position and behavior in organizations. A structuralist perspective views the organization as a large, complex social unit in which many groups interact. These groups are defined both by their formal (task-related, functional) and informal connections and differentiations. The relative number and power of such organizational groupings, their tasks, and the ways in which they come into contact shape the nature of the organization. Groups may comprise different strata, like different social classes, with interests and values potentially in conflict, and integration between them limited by the potential for conflicts of interest. Those with power wield it in the interests of their own group as well as perhaps in the interests of the system as a whole (though in this model it is often difficult to define such collective interests). Self-interest, including material self-interest, is considered as potentially important as social needs, so that the formation of relationships should be seen in the more political sense of advantage to the person as well as in the human-relations sense of social satisfaction. Further, people are viewed as members of groups outside as well as inside of the organization, which both help to place them within the organization, give them status, define their involvement with it, and may or may not articulate with the organization's interests. Finally, the tasks of the organization and the tasks of those within it (the division of labor) are important because they define the number, interests, and relative arrangements of organizational classes as well as how informal relations may articulate with formal ones.

The "sex typing" of occupations and professions is relatively well known—the fact that many occupations are nearly exclusively filled by members of one sex and come to have a "gender," to be described in sex-role-appropriate terms. But to fully describe the position and behavior of women (and men) in organizations, we must understand not only their typical occupations (e.g., manager and secretary) but how these are *related* to one another and to the larger context of the organization as a social structure. Occupations carry with them membership in particular organizational classes. Each class may have its own internal hierarchy, political groupings and allegiances, interactional rules, ways of coming into contact with other classes, promotion rules, culture, and style, including demeanor and dress.[15] In many organizations, managers and clerical workers, for example, constitute two separate organizational classes, with separate hierarchies, rules, and reward structures, and practically no mobility between them. The managerial elite has the power and a group interest in retaining it. The position of clerical workers, on the other hand, is often anomalous: in contact with the organizational elite, dependent on, and in service to it, thus facilitating identification with it, but similar to other workers in subordination, lack of autonomy, and subjugation to routine (Crozier, 1965).

The economic concept of an "internal labor market" (Doeringer and Piore, 1971) is applicable here. When women enter an organization, they are placed not only in jobs but in an opportunity structure. Internal allocation of personnel is governed by hiring, promotion, and layoff rules within each structure, as well as by "suitability," as defined by the customs of each separate workplace. And ability in one workplace is not always transferable to others; what leads to success in one may even be dynsfunctional for mobility into another. The rules of the internal labor market, Doeringer and Piore theorize, may vary from rigid and internally focused to highly responsive to external economic forces; rules also vary among

15. In a discussion of labor women, Patricia Cayo Sexton defines dress and hair style as well as personal appearance as a barrier to upward mobility, since the styles of labor women are very different from those of more elite women (1974:392–93). Informants in a corporation told me that there was a "caste" barrier between secretaries and professional women visible in style differences: e.g., secretaries wore platform shoes while professional women wore pumps.

organizational strata. They argue, for example, that there is a tendency for managerial markets, in contrast with other internal labor markets, to span more than one part of a company, to carry an implicit employment guarantee, and to reward ability rather than seniority (1971:3). But women participate in a different labor market than men, even within the same organization. Their "typical jobs" in the office carry with them not only sex-role demands but also placement in a class and hierarchy that itself limits mobility into positions of power.

The issue, thus, is not a mere division of labor between women and men but a difference of organizational class, at least on the administrative levels of modern organizations. Simplistically, women are part of a class rewarded for routine service, while men compose a class rewarded for decision-making rationality and visible leadership, and this potential membership affects even those found outside their own sexual class. This phenomenon constitutes the structural backdrop for an understanding of the organizational behavior of women and men.

Even though it is largely ignored in the organizational behavior literature, sex can be seen to be an important variable affecting the lives of groups, given the significant differences in the positions and power of women and men in society and in organizations. The sexual composition of a group appears to have impact on behavior around issues of power and leadership, aspirations, peer relations, and the relative involvement visibility or isolation/invisibility of members.

Sex and Organizational Behavior: Female and Male Single-sexed Groups

Does a group of women behave differently from a group of men? The situations in which women and men find themselves are often so different that common-sense observation indicates a difference in both themes and process. Organizational research, on the other hand, has generally treated all groups of participants or workers alike, for the most part not distinguishing sex as a variable, and therefore implicitly assuming that gender does not make a difference in organizational behavior—reinforcing the mistaken idea that modern organizational life is universalistic and sex-neutral. Yet, even in the classic study that first discovered the importance of small, primary groups in worker behavior and opened the study of human relations in organizations, the sex of the groups studied varied and may have contributed to the different sets of specific findings. The experiments at the Hawthorne plant of Western Electric in the late 1920s and early 1930s developed the concept of informal organization by indicating how important a role the small group might play in worker productivity (cf. Roethlisberger and Dickson, 1939). These researchers have been examined and re-examined for all possible explanations of the findings, including, recently, operant conditioning (Parsons, 1974); sex composition is, to my knowledge, not mentioned among them. Three small groups were studied. In two sets of conditions, the Relay Assembly Test Room and the Mica Splitting Test Room, workers encouraged each other in raising productivity and believed that their efforts would be rewarded. In the third, the Bank Wiring Observation Room, workers developed an informal system that discouraged "rate busting" and kept productivity at an even keel, partly out of a mistrust in management—the belief that increased productivity would result in higher expectations, not higher rewards. There were differences among the three sets of conditions in size of group (fourteen in the third, vs. five or six in the first and second, depending on how the team is counted), nature of the task (a large number of units processed by individuals in the first two conditions, a small number of units in the third), experimental manipulations (like rest pauses), and "laboratory" vs. "natural" working conditions. But another striking difference is sex. The first two sets of groups, co-operative and trusting of management, were all female. The third, counterdependent, aggressively controlling, and suspicious, was all-male.

There is also evidence, if we reinterpret other studies not explicitly focused on sex, that women in female groups may be more oriented toward immediate relationships than men in male groups. Several studies of male professionals in organizations found a correlation between professionalism and a "cosmopolitan" rather than a local orientation. The exception was a study of nurses by Warren Bennis and colleagues. In this *female* group, the more professionally oriented nurses "did not differ from others in their loyalty to the hospital, and they were *more* apt than others, not less, to express loyalty to the local work group" (Blau and Scott, 1962:69). While Blau and Scott conclude that this is due to the limited visibility of the nurses' professional competence, other evidence indicates that this finding is consistent with a sex-linked interpretation. Constantini and Craik (1972) found, for example, that women politicians in California were oriented intraparty and locally rather than toward higher office, as men were.

Other evidence confirms that women in organizations, especially in the clerical class, limit their ambitions, prefer local and immediate relationships, and orient themselves to satisfying peer relationships. In a study of values of 120 occupational groups, secretaries, the only female group studied, were unique in placing their highest priorities on such values as security, love, happiness, and responsibility (Sikula, 1973). Female game-playing strategy in several laboratory studies was accommodative, including rather than excluding, and oriented toward others rather than toward winning, whereas the male strategy was exploitative and success-oriented (Vinacke, 1959; Uesugi and Vinacke, 1963). All-female group themes in a comparison of single-sex and mixed laboratory groups included affiliation, family, and conflicts about competition and leadership, self, and relationships, in contrast to the male themes: competition, aggression, violence, victimization, practical joking, questions of identity, and fear of self-disclosure (Aries, 1973). An earlier study compared all-male with all-female groups and found *no* significant differences in nine different conditions *except* persuasibility (higher in female groups) and level of aspiration (higher in male groups) (Cattell and Lawson, 1962).

In attitudinal studies distinguishing factors motivating increased performance as opposed to those merely preventing dissatisfaction ("hygiene" factors), attitudes toward interpersonal relations with peers constituted the only variable differentiating men and women. (The women in two studies included those in both high-level and low-level jobs.) For women, peer relationships were a motivational factor, whereas for men they were merely a hygiene factor (Davis, 1967:35–36). Structural factors can explain this. My field research in progress on a large New York-based corportation indicates that peer relations affect a woman's decision not to seek promotion into managerial ranks, where she will no longer be part of a group of women; for men, of course, peer relations are a given throughout managerial ranks, and therefore, perhaps, more easily "taken for granted."

Other differences in male and female behavior in single-sex settings fail to be consistently demonstrated, as the Cattell and Lawson (1962) research, above, indicates. (See also Mann, 1959.) In studies of sex differences in the "risky shift," for example (the tendency for groups to make riskier decisions than individuals), there were *no* significant differences between male and female college students in initial conservatism or in the shift to risky decisions in the single-sex groups (Wallach, Kogan, and Bem, 1968). Organizational comparisons are rare, but Crozier's data on forty groups of French office workers revealed no difference in an atmosphere between male and female work groups; both kinds of groups showed the same wide range (1965:111).

Thus it is reasonable to hypothesize that groups of women differ from groups of men primarily in orientations toward interpersonal relationships and level of aspiration. One might interpret this as consistent with the training of women for family roles and thus label it a sex-linked attribute. But such orientations could also be seen as *realistic responses* to women's structural situation in organizations, of the kinds of opportunities and their limits, of the role demands in the organizational strata occupied by women, and of the dependence of women on relationships for mobility.

Mixed-sex Groups

When men and women are together, in roughly equal numbers, as peers, tensions may emerge, and the behavior of each sex may be influenced. In Aries' laboratory study, people in two cross-sex groups were more tense, serious, self-conscious, and concerned with heterosexual attractiveness than those in the same-sex groups. Women generally spoke less than men (Aries, 1973). The sexual questions and "crosscultural" issues that can arise in mixed-sex groups are useful explanations for their tensions; William Foote Whyte has hypothesized, extrapolating from studies of the ethnic composition of groups, that "other things being equal, a one-sex work group is likely to be more cohesive" than a mixed-sex group (1961:511). Crozier's Parisian study found male-female conflicts when men and women worked in the same office (1965:110).

In addition to sexual and cultural issues, there are also status and power issues when men and women interact, a function of the structural positions and organizational class memberships of the sexes. Much social psychological research has indicated the importance of power and status in determining behavior in groups: e.g., those low in power tend to engage in more approval seeking, while those high in power engage in more influence attempts; those in low-status positions tend to communicate upward in a hierarchy, a form of "substitute locomotion" or "vicarious mobility." The differential behavior of the more and less powerful coincides with the observed group behavior of men and women. A field experiment tested more specifically the effects of high and low power on group relations, using thirty-two six-person groups at a one-day professional conference. Participants were labeled high-power or low-power on the basis of the prestige of their occupations, assumed to correlate with ability to influence. While the authors do not report the sex distribution of participants, it is likely from occupational sex-typing that men were found more often in the high-power category (psychiatrists, psychologists) and women in the low-power category (nurses, social workers, teachers). The researchers found that "highs" were liked more than "lows"; "highs" liked "lows" less than they liked other "highs"; "highs" talked more often than "lows"; "lows" communicated more frequently to "highs" than to other "lows"; and the amount of participation by "lows" was consistently overrated, as though people felt the "lows" talked too much (Hurwitz, Zander, and Hymovitch, 1968).

The interpretation is straightforward. In mixed groups of "peers," men and women may not, in fact, be equal, especially if their external statuses and organizational class memberships are discrepant. The resulting behavior, including frequency of participation, leadership, and conformity, may reflect status and power differences more than sex-linked personality traits.

413

The Effects of Skewed Sex Ratios: The Lone
Woman in the Male Group

The dynamic of interaction in settings with highly skewed sex ratios—numerical dominance by members of one sex and a "lone" or nearly alone member of the other sex—also deserves attention; in management and some professions, women are often one of very few women in a group of men. This makes "sex status" as important for interaction as occupational status (Epstein, 1970:1952).

Skewed sex ratios lend themselves, first, to cases of "mistaken identity"—to incorrect attributions. Lone women in male settings are sometimes initially misperceived as a result of their statistical rarity. The men with whom they come into contact may make a judgment about what a woman is doing in that particular situation, based on reasoning about the probabilities of various explanations, and may act toward her accordingly. This can be called "statistical discrimination" (Council of Economic Advisers, 1973:106), to distinguish it from prejudice; that is, an unusual woman may be treated as though she resembles women on the average. This may be the case every time someone assumes a female manager answering the telephone or sitting in an office is a secretary (cf. examples in Lynch, 1973; Epstein, 1970:191). Given the current occupational distribution, that person is likely to be correct a high proportion of the time. But the woman in question may still feel unfairly treated, as indeed she is, and there may be awkward exchanges while the woman's true identity is established.[16]

Attributions may also be made about the lone woman's expected informal role. These attributions put the woman in her place without challenging the male culture of the group. Field observations of lone women in male-dominated groups (including business meetings, academic conferences, sales training programs, and postprofessional training groups) have distinguished four kinds of roles attributed to lone women in male groups: "mother"; "sex object" or "seductress"; "pet" (group mascot); and "iron maiden" (militant and unapproachable) (Kanter, 1975). Such attributed roles affect both what the men in the group expect of the woman and how they interpret what she does. For her, the pressure is to confine her behavior to the limits of the role, whether or not it expresses her competence. Indeed, the roles provide a measure of security and uncertainty-reduction for some women, while others may devote time to struggling against the implications of the attributions. In either case, a woman's

16. Sometimes the categorical attributions have extreme and negative implications: e.g., a female manager having a drink with her boss and assumed by a neighbor to be his mistress (Lynch, 1973:136). In another example, a woman executive was the only female present at an executive cocktail party at a New York hotel, when a drunk male guest entered, accosted her, and tried to tear her clothes off, assuming she was a call girl (Lynch, 1973:137).

behavior in a situation like this is less likely to reflect her competencies, and it may take her longer to establish them, than at other times, when she is not a statistical rarity.

Several hypotheses are suggested. When a person is a statistical rarity, it may take her/him *more time* to untangle mistaken identities and establish a competence-based working relationship, particularly with members of the numerically dominant category. This may, in turn, generate a preference for minimizing change in work relations with peers, superiors/ subordinates, or clients. As Epstein argues, "status discrepancies make continuous role definition necessary during interactions that should be routine" (1970:194). Margaret Cussler's sample of female executives in the 1950s suggests that this hypothesis may have some validity, for the women apparently changed work situations much less often than would be expected of male counterparts. Thus there may be a longer time-span for the establishment of competence-based relationships and a conservatism about changing relationships among "lone" women in male-dominated organizations.

Isolation and invisibility, self- as well as group-imposed, are often consequences of status as a lone woman in an otherwise all-male collectivity. In one study, six small training groups with only one woman each in a group of eight to twelve men were observed: three sensitivity training groups for business school students, and three work groups of psychiatric residents. In each case, the woman was eventually isolated, failed to become a leader or ally herself with the emergent leaders, and was defined by the researchers as a "casualty" of the groups. The researchers felt that the six groups' productivity tended to be low, in part because of the problematic interactions around the solo woman (Wolman and Frank, 1975). While the results of this study should not be taken as definitive,[17] they do suggest directions for further inquiry.

The female executives studied by Margaret Hennig (1970) support the isolation hypothesis. They reported that their most difficult relationships were with male peers when they (the women) were in the early to middle career. The women had little contact or relationship with the men, tried to be unobtrusive or invisible, and practiced strategies of conflict avoidance, as did lone professional women in Cynthia Epstein's research (1970:176). Epstein also suggests that team membership may be harder for the lone woman among male professional peers than for a man, pointing to institutionalized isolation (such as barriers to membership in male clubs or associations) as well as interactional isolation. As a consequence, she proposes that women have been less likely to be successful

---

17. Aside from *post hoc* reasoning, one of the researchers, a woman, was also a group leader in some of the groups and does not discuss the impact of her own presence as another woman in a *powerful* position.

in fields that require participation on a team of peers as opposed to individual activity (1970:175).

Lone women may reinforce their own isolation by a series of accommodative strategies. The limiting of visibility ("taking a low profile") is one such accommodation to and reinforcement of isolation. Hennig's respondents reported early career strategies of trying to minimize their sexual attributes so as to blend unnoticeably into the predominant male culture:

> You dressed carefully and quietly to avoid attracting attention; you had to remember to swear once in a while, to know a few dirty jokes, and never to cry if you got attacked. You fended off all attempts of men to treat you like a woman; you opened doors before they could hold them, sat down before a chair could be held, and threw on a coat before it could be held for you [Hennig, 1970:vi–21].

In other reports, lone women managers have also participated in the limiting of the visibility of their competence by not taking credit for accomplishments or letting someone else take the credit (Lynch, 1973; Cussler, 1958). Some women, in interviews, even expressed pride that they could influence a group of men without the men recognizing the origin of the idea, or they rejoiced in the secret knowledge that they were responsible for their boss's success. (These reports match the Megaree finding reported below that high-dominance women may let a man assume official leadership while strongly influencing the decision.) Epstein (1970) points out that, in general, on elite levels women have less-visible jobs than men, promote themselves less often, feel the need to make fewer mistakes, and try to be unobstrusive.

With another context in mind, Seymour Sarason (1973) has argued that members of minority groups who have succeeded may try to limit the visibility of that success in fear of reprisals from the majority-dominant group, which might not be aware of the minority's success and might take action against it if known. He has reported a prevalent feeling among Jews that statistics about the high percentage of Jews in elite colleges such as Yale, for example, should not be broadcast. A concern like this, rather than a female sex-linked characteristic, could account for the woman manager's acceptance of the invisibility of her achievements. In the case of lone women, the pressure to adopt this stance must be even greater because of attributes like modesty assigned to the female stereotype.

This analysis suggests a re-examination of the "fear of success" in women hypothesis. Perhaps what has been called fear of success is really fear of visibility. In the original research by Matina Horner (1968) that identified this concept, women responded to a hypothetical situation in which a woman was at the top of her class in medical school—presumably a lone woman in a male peer group. Such a situation is the kind that creates pressure for a woman to make herself and her achievements invisible. When similar research was conducted using settings in which a woman is not a statistical rarity, "fear of success" imagery was greatly reduced (Tresemer, 1973).

Women and Leadership

If it's hard to demonstrate competence as a woman among men, it may be even harder to exercise leadership, given the current sex-stratification patterns in organizations. It is still an open question whether there are major sex differences in leadership *style* (Crozier, 1956:126, finds none); but the structural and interactional context is certainly different for women. Taking directives from a woman has been anathema to most men and some women. In a 1965 *Harvard Business Review* survey of 1,000 male and 900 female executives, over two thirds of the men and nearly one fifth of the women reported that they themselves would not feel comfortable working for a woman. Very few of either sex (9 per cent of the men and 15 per cent of the women) felt that *men* feel comfortable working for a woman; and a proportion of the male respondents said that women did not belong in executive positions. A total of 51 per cent of the men responded that women were "temperamentally unfit" for management, writing comments such as, "They scare male executives half to death. . . . As for an efficient woman manager, this is cultural blasphemy. . ." (Bowman, Worthy, and Greyser, 1965).

Male resentment of taking orders from a woman influenced the work flow and the interaction between waitresses and countermen in the restaurants studied by William Foote Whyte during World War II, a classic of organizational analysis· There were several devices in one restaurant by which countermen could avoid direct contact with waitresses (and hence direct orders) or could make their own decisions about the order in which to prepare food and drinks, thus taking initiative and forcing the waitresses to wait. Orders were written on slips and placed on a spindle, and a warming compartment imposed a high barrier between the waitresses and the countermen, thus eliminating face-to-face interaction. In a restaurant without these equalizing devices, satisfaction was low, and there was constant wrangling. Whyte's explanation is simple: People of higher status (men) like to do the directing for people of lower status (women) and resent reversals (1961:128).

Even if women have formal authority, then, they may not necessarily be able to exercise it over reluctant subordinates. Margaret Cussler's (1958) study of female executives provides several examples of this. In one case a woman had formal leadership of a group of men, but the men did not accept this, reporting informally to her male superior. The subordinates further met together at lunch to share information, excluding her. More formal meetings then developed, "conceived of by the woman as meetings of her staff, by the men as a mutual protection society for the interchange of ideas" (1958:76–77).

At the same time, women tend to assume visible leadership reluctantly, in keeping with the invisibility of the lone woman mentioned earlier. A creative laboratory study discovered that for women the situational context rather than a dominant personality tended to predict a woman's exercise of visible leadership. Same-sex and cross-sex dyads were paired by scores on a "dominance" measure and given a task in which one member had to lead and one to follow. Assumption of leadership by high-dominance women paired with a low-dominance man was significantly lower than in any other pairing. The greatest assumption of leadership by high-dominance subjects occurred when a high-dominance man was paired with a low-dominance woman; the high- and low-dominance single-sex pairings showed about the same intermediate distribution of leadership. However, in the situation in which a high-dominance woman was paired with a low-dominance man, the *woman* made the final decision of who was to be the leader more often than in any other group, 91 per cent of the time *appointing the man*. The study suggests that men are not necessarily more "dominant" in character than women, but women are more reluctant to assume leadership, particularly when the subordinate is male (Megaree, 1969). The leadership strategies chosen by successful women executives in Hennig's research (1970) tend to confirm this kind of laboratory finding. The women tended to minimize the authoritative exercise of power and maximize subordinate autonomy and learning through delegation.

But a leader's style may be ultimately less important for the impact on his or her subordinates than another resource unequally distributed between the sexes: power outside of the immediate work group. Early theory in organizational behavior assumed a direct relation between leader behavior and group satisfaction and morale. However, Donald Pelz discovered in the early 1950s that perceived external power was an intervening variable. He compared high- and low-morale work groups to test the hypothesis that the supervisor in high-morale groups would be better at communicating, more supportive, and more likely to recommend promotion. Yet, when he analyzed the data, the association seemed to be nonexistent or even reversed. In some cases supervisors who frequently recommended people for promotion and offered sincere praise for a job well done had *lower* morale scores. The differentiating variable was whether or not the leader had power outside and upward: influence on his or her own superiors and how decisions were made in the department. The combination of good human relations *and* power was associated with high morale. Human-relations skills and low power (a likely combination for women leaders) sometimes had negative consequences (Pelz, 1952).

The implications for female leadership in organizations are significant. A woman's generally more limited power (partly a function of her rarity and isolation in management), as well as her similarity to a subordinate clerical class rather than the elite, may interfere with her effective exercise of leadership *regardless* of her own style and competence. This hypothesis also helps explain the greater resistance to working for a woman. It also may account for the evidence of the importance of a male sponsor in the success of women executives (Cussler, 1958; Hennig, 1970). A high-status man bringing the woman up behind him may provide the visible sign that the woman does have influence upward. While sponsors serve multiple functions (e.g., coaching and socialization in the informal routines) and are found in the careers of men, the "reflected power" they provide may be even more pivotal for women.

Conclusion: Women and the Infrastructure of Organizations

Women's places in organizations have largely had limited visibility and low status; they have been part of the unexamined infrastructure. When men and women interact in organizations, they often do it across barriers like that of social class; women's mobility has largely been restricted to the infrastructure. In this the women within organizations have a kinship with the "women's auxiliary" outside of it—the network of wives of managers and leaders that perform unpaid tasks, play unofficial but normatively expected roles for the organization, and whose behavior can potentially affect relations in the official organization (Kanter, 1974). Just as managers have a group of women behind them in the office, they do at home, for male managers are largely married to women not employed in the paid labor force.[18]

I have suggested a few of the issues surrounding the sexual structure of organizations and groups that deserve further attention—from the problems of token women to the nature of internal labor markets for managers or secretaries. The sexual division of broad administrative classes was solidified very early in the history of large corporations. But the nature of organizational life for these broad groupings and other occupational subgroups, and how their opportunities and interactions vary in different kinds of organizations (e.g., those with fewer barriers to leader-

18. A total of 93.19 per cent of the male managers earning $15,000 or more in 1969 were married; 72.25 per cent of their wives were not in the paid labor force (Bureau of Census, 1973b).

ship for women), still require investigation. The ideological underpinnings of modern organizations, such as the connection between a "masculine ethic" and a "spirit of managerialism," need further examination. To understand the structural conditions for men and women in organizations and the organizational behavior of men and women is critical for both social inquiry and social change.

References

ARGYRIS, CHRIS.
1957. *Personality and Organization.* New York: Harper & Brothers.
1972. *The Applicability of Organizational Sociology.* New York: Cambridge University Press.
1973. "Some Limits of Rational Man Organization Theory," *Public Administration Review* May–June: 253–67.

BARNARD, CHESTER I.
1938. *The Functions of the Executive.* Cambridge, Mass.: Harvard University Press.

BELL, DANIEL.
1956. "Work and Its Discontents: The Cult of Efficiency in America," *The End of Ideology,* rev. ed. New York: Collier Books, 1961, pp. 227–72.
1957. "The Breakup of Family Capitalism," *The End of Ideology,* rev. ed. New York: Collier Books, 1961.

BENDIX, REINHARD.
1956. *Work and Authority in Industry: Ideologies of Management in the Course of Industrialization.* New York: Harper & Row.
1960. *Max Weber: An Intellectual Portrait.* Garden City, New York: Anchor Books, 1962.

BENET, MARY KATHLEEN.
1973. *The Secretarial Ghetto.* New York: McGraw-Hill.

BLAU, PETER M., and SCOTT, W. RICHARD.
1962. *Formal Organizations.* San Francisco: Chandler.

BOWMAN, G. W.; WORTHY, N. B.; and GREYSER, S. A.
1965. "Are Women Executives People?," *Harvard Business Review* 43 July–August: 14–30.

BUREAU OF THE CENSUS, U.S.
1973a. *Occupational Characteristics.* Washington, D.C.: U.S. Government Printing Office.
1973b. *Occupations of Persons with Higher Earnings.*

BUREAU OF LABOR STATISTICS, U.S.
1971. *Handbook of Labor Statistics.* Washington, D.C.: U.S. Department of Labor.

BURGER, CHESTER.
1964. *Survival in the Executive Jungle.* New York: Macmillan.

BURNHAM, JAMES.
1941. *The Managerial Revolution.* New York: John Day.

CATTELL, RAYMOND B., and LAWSON, EDWIN D.
1962. "Sex Differences in Small Group Performance," *The Journal of Social Psychology* 58:141–45.
COCHRAN, THOMAS C.
1957. *The American Business System: A Historical Perspective, 1900–1955.* Cambridge, Mass.: Harvard University Press.
CONSTANTINI, EDMOND, and CRAIK, KENNETH H.
1972. "Women as Politicians: The Social Background, Personality, and Political Careers of Female Party Leaders," *Journal of Social Issues* 28:217–36.
COUNCIL OF ECONOMIC ADVISERS.
1973. *Annual Report of the Council of Economic Advisers.* Washington, D.C.: U.S. Government Printing Office.
CROZIER, MICHEL.
1965. *The World of the Office Worker,* trans. David Landau. Chicago: University of Chicago Press, 1971.
CUSSLER, MARGARET.
1958. *The Woman Executive.* New York: Harcourt, Brace.
DAVIES, MARGERY.
1974. "Woman's Place Is at the Typewriter: The Feminization of the Clerical Labor Force." Waltham, Mass.: Brandeis University Department of Sociology.
DAVIS, KEITH.
1967. *Human Relations at Work.* New York: McGraw-Hill.
DOERINGER, PETER B., and PIORE, MICHAEL J.
1971. *Internal Labor Markets and Manpower Analysis.* Lexington, Mass.: D.C. Heath.
EPSTEIN, CYNTHIA FUCHS.
1970. *Woman's Place: Options and Limits on Professional Careers.* Berkeley: University of California Press.
ETZIONI, AMITAI.
1964. *Modern Organizations.* Englewood Cliffs, N.J.: Prentice-Hall.
FREUD, SIGMUND.
1930. *Civilization and Its Discontents,* trans. James Strachey. New York: Norton, 1962.
GARSON, BARBARA.
1973. "Women's Work," *Working Papers for a New Society* 1 Fall: 5–14.
GERTH, HANS, and MILLS, C. WRIGHT (eds.).
1958. *From Max Weber: Essays in Sociology.* New York: Oxford University Press.
GOULDNER, ALVIN W.
1959. "Organizational Analysis," *Sociology Today: Problems and Prospects,* ed. R. K. Merton, L. Broom, and L. S. Cottrell, Jr. New York: Basic Books, pp. 400–28.
HALTER, MARILYN; SCHNEIDER, ERIC; and WEINER, LYNN.
1973. "Report from the 'Enormous File': A Case Study of Office Work." Boston: Boston University Department of History.
HENNIG, MARGARET.
1970. "Career Development for Women Executives," unpublished doctoral

dissertation. Cambridge, Mass.: Harvard University Graduate School of Business Administration.

HEYDEBRAND, WOLF (ed.).

1974. *Comparative Organizations.* Englewood Cliffs, N.J.: Prentice-Hall.

HILL, JOSEPH A.

1929. *Women in Gainful Occupations, 1870–1920.* Census Monographs IX. Washington, D.C.: U.S. Government Printing Office. New York: Johnson Reprint Corporation, 1972.

HORNER, MATINA.

1968. "Sex Differences in Achievement Motivation and Performance in Competitive and Non-Competitive Situations," unpublished doctoral dissertation. Ann Arbor, Mich.: University of Michigan.

HURWITZ, JACOB I.; ZANDER, ALVIN F.; and HYMOVICH, BERNARD.

1968. "Some Effects of Power on the Relations Among Group Members," *Group Dynamics,* ed. D. Cartwright and A. Zander. New York: Harper & Row, pp. 291–97.

JAY, ANTHONY.

1967. *Management and Machiavelli: An Inquiry into the Politics of Corporate Life.* New York: Holt, Rinehart & Winston.

1971. *Corporation Man.* New York: Random House. Kanter, Rosabeth Moss.

1974. "The Auxiliary Organization." Waltham, Mass.: Brandeis University Department of Sociology.

1975. "Women in Organizations: Sex Roles, Group Dynamics, and Change Strategies," *Beyond Sex Roles,* ed. A. Sargent. St. Paul, Minn.: West Publishing.

LANGER, ELINOR.

1970. "Inside the New York Telephone Company," *Women at Work,* ed. W. L. O'Neill. Chicago: Quadrangle, 1972, pp. 305–60.

LIEBERSON, STANLEY, and O'CONNOR, JOHN F.

1972. "Leadership and Organizational Performance: A Study of Large Corporations," *American Sociological Review* 37 April: 117–30.

LYNCH, EDITH M.

1973. *The Executive Suite: Feminine Style:* New York: AMACOM.

MANN, R. D.

1959. "A Review of the Relationship between Personality and Performance in Small Groups," *Psychological Bulletin* 56:241–70.

MAYO, ELTON.

1933. *The Human Problems of an Industrial Civilization.* New York: Macmillan.

MEGAREE, EDWIN, I.

1969. "Influence of Sex Roles on the Manifestation of Leadership," *Journal of Applied Psychology* 53:377–82.

MILLER, WILLIAM.

1950. "The Recruitment of the American Business Elite," *Men in Business,* ed. W. Miller. Cambridge, Mass.: Harvard University Press. New York: Harper & Row, 1962.

1952. "The Business Elite in Business Bureaucracies: Careers of Top Executives in the Early Twentieth Century," *Men in Business,* ed. W. Miller. Cambridge, Mass.: Harvard University Press, pp. 286–305; New York: Harper & Row, 1962.

MILLS, C. WRIGHT.
1951. *White Collar: The American Middle Classes.* New York: Oxford University Press.

MORSE, NANCY C.
1953. *Satisfaction in the White Collar Job.* Ann Arbor, Mich.: Survey Research Center, University of Michigan.

PARSONS, H. M.
1974. "What Happened at Hawthorne?," *Science* 183 March: 922–32.

PELZ, DONALD C.
1952. "Influence: A Key to Effective Leadership in the First-line Supervisor," *Personnel* 29:3–11.

Report of a Special Task force to the Secretary of Health, Education, and Welfare.
1972. *Work in America.* Cambridge, Mass.: MIT Press.

ROETHLISBERGER, F. J., and DICKSON, WILLIAM J.
1939. *Management and the Worker.* Cambridge, Mass.: Harvard University Press.

SARASON, SEYMOUR B.
1973. "Jewishness, Blackishness, and the Nature-Nurture Controversy," *American Psychologist* 28 November: 962–71.

SCOTT, W. RICHARD.
1964. "Theory of Organizations," *Handbook of Modern Sociology,* ed. R. E. L. Faris. Chicago: Rand McNally, pp. 485–529.

SEXTON, PATRICIA CAYO.
1974. "Workers (Female) Arise!," *Dissent* Summer: 380–95.

SIKULA, ANDREW F.
1973. "The Uniqueness of Secretaries as Employees," *Journal of Business Education* 48 Fall: 203–5.

STEIN, BARRY A.
1974. *Size, Efficiency, and Community Enterprise,* Cambridge, Mass.: Center for Community Economic Development.

SUTTON, FRANCIS X.; HARRIS, SEYMOUR E.; KAYSEN, CARL; and TOBIN, JAMES.
1956. *The American Business Creed.* Cambridge, Mass.: Harvard University Press.

TAYLOR, FREDERICK W.
1947. *Scientific Management.* New York: Harper & Brothers.

TIGER, LIONEL.
1969. *Men in Groups.* New York: Random House.

TILLETT, ANTHONY; KEMPNER, THOMAS; and WILLS, GORDON. (eds.).
1970. *Management Thinkers.* Baltimore, Md.: Penguin Books.

TRESEMER, DAVID.
1973. "Fear of Success: Popular but Unproven," *Psychology Today* 7 November.

UESUGI, THOMAS K., and VINACKE, W. EDGAR.
1963. "Strategy in a Feminine Game," *Sociometry* 26:35–88.

VINACKE, W. EDGAR.
1959. "Sex Roles in a Three-person Game," *Sociometry* 22 December: 343–60.
WALLACH, MICHAEL A.; KOGAN, NATHAN; and BEM, DARYL J.
1968. "Group Influence on Individual Risk-taking," *Group Dynamics,* ed. D. Cartwright and A. Zander. New York: Harper & Row, pp. 430–43.
WARNER, W. LLOYD, and ABEGGLEN, JAMES C.
1955. *Big Business Leaders in America.* New York: Harper & Brothers.
WINTER, J. ALAN.
1974. "Elective Affinities Between Religious Beliefs and Ideologies of Management in Two Eras," *American Journal of Sociology* 79 March: 1,134–50.
WOLMAN, CAROL, and FRANK, HAROLD.
1975. "The Solo Woman in a Professional Peer Group," *American Journal of Orthopsychiatry* 45: February.
ZEITLIN, MAURICE.
1974. "Corporate Ownership and Control: The Large Corporation and the Capitalist Class," *American Journal of Sociology* 79 March: 1,073–1,119.

Technology
and Organization
in Manufacturing[1]

Peter M. Blau
Cecilia McHugh Falbe
William McKinley
Phelps K. Tracy

Few would question the impact of technology on society. Technological developments have caused the movement of people from farms to cities and from industrial to service occupations. They have stimulated the evolution of the modern economic organization, altered class structures, and affected political institutions. Technological change today occurs primarily in large organizations, both public and private. Yet, research on the structural implications of technology for the organization of work has uncovered few unambiguous patterns.

In one of the pioneering attempts to examine these implications with comparative data from many organizations, Woodward's (1958, 1965) study of 100 firms in England reported systematic differences in structure accompanying various types of production technology. But in another carefully designed research effort involving 46 British organizations a decade later, Hickson, Pugh, and Pheysey (1969) failed to replicate Woodward's findings. Their study found few associations between production technology and the organization of work. Its results indicated that differences in organizational structure depend not so much on technology as on the size of a firm. Since the publication of these two classic studies, several attempts have been made to replicate them in different

SOURCE: *Administrative Science Quarterly* 21, no. 1 (March 1976): 20–40. Reprinted by permission of the authors and the publisher.

1. The research reported here was supported by grant Soc-71-03617-A05 from the National Science Foundation; this support is gratefully acknowledged. The authors also want to thank Andrew Karmen for his assistance at early stages of the research and Hilary Silver for hers at later stages. This is report Number 20 of the Comparative Organization Research Program at Columbia University.

industrial and economic contexts, but so far the debate between the proponents of size and technology as prime determinants of structure remains largely unresolved.

Child and Mansfield (1972) applied the Aston questionnaire (Pugh *et al.,* 1968) to a national sample of 82 British firms, while Hickson and his colleagues (1974) extended their original research to United States and Canadian corporations. In each case, organizational size rather than production technology appeared to exert the more significant influence on the division of labor and organization of work. During this period, Zwerman (1970) followed Woodward's basic approach in his study of 55 Minnesota firms and reported patterns inconsistent with the Aston-type findings. Organizational size was associated with number of levels and the average span of control of the chief executive officer, but, apart from these results, his findings largely supported Woodward's conclusion that technology is most influential.

The inconsistency in these findings suggests the need for further study. Research, however, should not stop with an examination of production technology. Technological innovation in factories used to be confined largely to production, substituting machines for manual labor, but the recent development and spread of computer systems now also substitutes automated operations for white-collar work. Like its blue-collar counterpart a half-century ago, administrative work is becoming increasingly mechanized and automated, leading to structural changes which are also widely debated. Studies of the impact of computers on organizational structure and decision making are following a course similar to that taken by research on production technologies, with impressionistic observations preceding more systematic comparative efforts and yielding inconsistent findings and disagreements.

For example, Whisler (1970a, 1970b) and Argyris (1970) noted strong parallels between technological displacement of labor in blue-collar and white-collar work, with more formal centralized control and less individual skill and autonomy. These conclusions are supported by Mumford and Banks's (1967) study of a British banking firm. A more extensive report by Withington (1969), which drew upon impressionistic evidence in manufacturing, government, and service organizations, came to opposite conclusions. While acknowledging that computers may provide opportunities for greater centralized control, he indicated that this has occurred only in routine areas. Withington's observations agreed with those made earlier by Bavelas (1960) that computers, by and large, do not alter the evolution toward increasingly more specialized and complex managerial structures.

This article clarifies the influence of technology on the structure of white-collar and blue-collar work in factories by analyzing data obtained from interviews with key executives in 110 American manufacturing establishments. To insure comparability with earlier empirical research, the concept of technology employed here refers to the substitution of mechanical equipment for human labor, and therefore does not take direct account of other dimensions of technology—knowledge, strategies, techniques, and skills—discussed by such theorists as Thompson (1967) and Perrow (1967). After a description of research procedures, the influence of the production technology and of automation of support functions on the organization of work is discussed. The last section preceding the conclusions examines and compares the relationships of mechanization and automation to the decentralization of authority in manufacturing plants.

Research Procedures

Data were collected from a random sample of 331 New Jersey manufacturing establishments employing 200 or more persons. New Jersey was selected as the location of the study because its wide variety of manufacturing firms are representative of American industry as a whole. All the two-digit Standard Industrial Classification codes, for instance, are found in this state. One-third of the plants in the original random sample agreed to participate in the study.[2] Reliability checks indicated that the 110 plants participating did not differ significantly from the sample of 331 in terms of size (number of employees), product type (two-digit SIC code), or whether the manufacturing organization was a single-site company or a branch of a larger firm. Although these findings do not preclude the existence of significant differences in other areas, they suggest that the data are fairly representative of larger New Jersey manufacturing concerns, and probably typical of manufacturing establishments in the country.

Information was collected at each of the 110 plants with a structured questionnaire administered to senior managers; these included the chief executive officer (plant manager), the head of production, and the personnel manager. Data were gathered at the site on day-to-day operations, including information on decision making, personnel breakdowns, computer usage, and mechanization of production machinery. All the data obtained refer to attributes of a plant's social structure and objective conditions, such as size, personnel distributions, production technology, and automation. No information was gathered on psychological attitudes.

The unit of analysis was the manufacturing site at a particular location, not the entire corporation that owned the site. If a plant had a parent company—as all but 11 of the 110 establishments did—some information was collected on the larger corporate structure, but it was kept separate from data pertaining to the site, even when the site was located at parent

2. Twenty-two of the 110 participants had fewer than 200 employees, owing to inaccurate source information on the universe and to the general shrinkage of New Jersey's industrial labor force in recent years.

company headquarters. The mean number of employees in the 110 plants was 497 in 1973, but more than half of them had fewer than 360. Personnel totals ranged from less than 100 to more than 4,000, and the standard deviation of plant size was 553, indicating a highly skewed distribution. On the average, plants were smaller than those studied by Hickson, Pugh, and Pheysey (1969), Child and Mansfield (1972), or Zwerman (1970), but larger than Woodward's (1958, 1965). The corporations owning the New Jersey manufacturing establishments employed an average total of 38,480 persons.

A majority of the plants surveyed experienced a decline of 5 percent or more in their labor force from 1967 to 1973. There was some decrease in size for 60 percent of the 110 factories, while only 27 percent were larger in 1973 than in 1967. The average factory in 1973 was composed of 57 percent direct production workers, 18 percent workers in indirect production, and 21 percent nonproduction—white-collar—workers, including supervisors, other exempt staff, and clerks. The average plant was differentiated horizontally into 5 major subunits or divisions with heads reporting directly to the chief executive officer, and vertically into 5 administrative levels. The mean span of control of the plant manager (CEO) was 7—5 division heads and 2 assistants—and the spans of control of first-line supervisors averaged 21 for foremen in direct production, 12 for those in indirect production, and 5 for white-collar supervisors.

The two main independent variables were production technology and the automation of functions through computers. Several measures of production technology refer to the degree of mechanization of manufacturing equipment, which is defined according to Amber and Amber's (1962) automaticity scale. Their scheme measures the extent to which human energy and control over the production process are replaced by machines; it distinguishes five levels of automaticity, ranging from powered machine tools—all work is mechanized but control is dependent on the operator—to computerized equipment—both labor and control functions are taken over by the machine. Estimates of the percentage of total production machinery operating at each of these levels and equivalent figures for the percentage of machines basic to the manufacturing process—the core technology—were obtained. From these data, two principal measures were computed: Mech111, the percentage of total production equipment operating at or above Amber level 3—self-feeding machines which repeat cycles automatically, and Mech111B, the percentage of basic machines at the same stage of mechanization. Another index of the production technology is Woodward's (1958, 1965) 11-point score of the technical complexity of the production process; a 7-point version of the Woodward score, eliminating her two mixed types and combining her first two and last two categories, was used. The three main types of manufacturing Woodward derives from combinations of her score—complex units and small batch, large batch and mass production, and process production—were also used. Straightforward measures were preferred to complex scales or scales based on factor analysis, like Hickson, Pugh, and Pheysey's (1969) technology index, "workflow integration," [3] but since the major component of their index is also based on the Amber and Amber classification, their measure is roughly comparable to the present mechanization score.

The second dimension of technology was the automation of various functions by using a computer. Since some plants have their own data-processing facilities at the site, while others have most of their computer work done elsewhere—at corporate headquarters or by time-sharing services—separate measures of automation were devised. Aut11 is the number of different functions for which a computer at the site is used; AutOut is the number of functions automated by off-site computer systems. [4] A third index, Aut111, refers to total computer use, the number of functions in which a computer is used either on or off the site. In addition, Aut1, a dummy variable, indicates whether a plant has its own data-processing facilities. Parallel measures were provided for the estimated minutes per day a computer is used at the site, off the site, and both combined.

Major dependent variables to be related to mechanization and automation were structural differentiation, personnel components, and spans of control of supervisors at various levels of a plant's administrative hierarchy. Vertical differentiation was measured by the number of managerial levels; horizontal differentiation was indicated by the number of divisions—units whose heads report to the plant manager—or sections—subunits of divisions whose managers were not first-line supervisors. Three measures of the division of labor were the number of job titles, an index of occupational diversity, and the Aston measure of functional specialization. [5] Detailed information furnished by the personnel manager made it possible to calculate the percentages of three main personnel components—direct and indirect production workers and employees performing white-collar jobs—and to divide the last group into three subcomponents: the percentage of full-time supervisors, salaried staff, and clerical workers. Finally, average subordinate-supervisor ratios—spans of control—were obtained for various ranks of supervisors, including the chief executive officer, the division heads who report to that officer, section managers,

3. Child and Mansfield (1972: 384–388) saw that in their national British sample some components of this index of workflow integration are virtually orthogonal and do not have the same correlations with structural variables.
4. The 16 plant functions distinguished in computing these measures are direct production, shipping and receiving, production control, industrial engineering, quality control, inventory control, marketing, purchasing, sales, systems analysis, research and development, accounting, billing and paying, payroll, personnel, and miscellaneous.
5. The index of occupational diversity uses the procedure proposed by Gibbs and Martin (1962), based on ten major occupational categories. The measure of functional specialization indicates how many of the functions listed in fn. 4 have at least one full-time employee.

and first-line supervisors, who oversee workflow operations and represent the lowest administrative level.

To measure decentralization of decision-making authority, information was gathered on the administrative level at which 25 key decisions are made, and intermediate scores were given for decisions made jointly by managers on two different levels. These data were combined into two composite indices, one measuring decentralization of operational decisions, and the other decentralization of authority in personnel matters.[6] Although the decision as to which items to include in the two measures was guided by factor analysis, the actual weighting of components was based on arbitrary loading rather than factor scores. The first index refers primarily to marketing decisions, but includes such other decision-making areas as purchasing, production control, and budget allocations. In these areas, authority is rarely decentralized below the plant manager's level, and most decisions are made at divisional and company headquarters, or even by the corporate board of directors. The second index pertains to personnel decisions—the authority to hire, promote, or fire employees at various hierarchical levels. Decentralization of personnel authority is considerably more pronounced than decentralization of operational authority; middle managers—section or division heads—can often hire or fire employees up to the level immediately below them, although decisions on promotion are usually made in consultation with the plant manager.

Mechanization of Production Operations

In manufacturing, differences in production technology are largely, though not entirely, reflected in the type of equipment used and the degree of its mechanization. The central thesis of the Woodward (1958, 1965) study—that the degree of technical complexity[7] is the critical factor in explaining variation in organization structure—is not supported by the work of Hickson, Pugh, and Pheysey (1969). In contrast to Woodward, they found that the operations technology is not strongly associated with organizational structure. Child and Mansfield (1972), using a national British sample, arrived at the same conclusion: production technology is not a major determinant of organizational structure. These two studies in the Aston tradition challenge Woodward's notion of a technological imperative.

6. Sixteen of the 25 original decision-making variables are included in the two decentralization scores.
7. The Woodward measure has been criticized as reflecting smoothness (Starbuck, 1965:503) or continuity (Hickson, Pugh, and Pheysey, 1969:389), rather than technological complexity. While Woodward (1965:188;1970) acknowledged some problems with the measure, her score is substantially associated with the degree of mechanization of production, as indicated by its correlations with the Aston measure in the original study (.46) and the national sample (.58) (Child and Mansfield, 1972:379, Table 2) and with the present Mech111 index (.37).

The data from the New Jersey sample of manufacturing concerns uphold the general conclusions of Hickson, Pugh, and Pheysey, while contradicting those of Woodward. The degree of mechanization (Mech111) is not related to the six dimensions of structural differentiation (Table 1, column 1, rows 1–6), nor is there a significant zero-order correlation between mechanization and the five indicators of spans of control (Table 1, column 1, rows 17–21). Furthermore, among the personnel components (column 1, rows 7–16), only 2 of the 10 reveal a significant relationship with degree of mechanization. The Woodward scale (Table 1, column 2) exhibits a similar pattern: absence of a significant association with aspects of differentiation and, with a few exceptions, an overall lack of association with either spans of control or personnel components.

The degree of technical sophistication in production does not determine the structure of factories as predicted by Woodward.[8] Specifically, the data do not support Woodward's (1965:51–60) claims that an advanced technology increases the number of levels in the organization (Table 1, row 1), widens the chief executive officer's span of control (row 17), increases the ratio of managers and supervisors (row 8), raises the proportion of clerical and administrative staff (rows 9–10), and enlarges the proportion of college graduates among the staff (row 12). Although the findings generally do not support Woodward, there are some exceptions. Mechanization is associated with a larger proportion of workers in indirect production (Table 1, row 13), specifically, with workers in maintenance (row 14). A positive association between the maintenance component and operations technology was also found by Child and Mansfield (1972:380); Hickson, Pugh, and Pheysey, however, observed a ∩-shaped relationship between the proportion of maintenance workers and production technology. In the Woodward study, an advanced technology narrowed the span of control of middle managers: the present findings support this conclusion fork one level of middle management, division heads (row 18), though not for another, section heads (row 19).

In contrast to mechanization, size exerts a considerable influence on the structure of factories. The size of the labor force (log 10 of the number of employees) exhibits substantial correlations with five of the six measures of differentiation (Table 1, column 3). Thus, the larger an

8. There is no association between size and technology in the present survey; correlations for size are—.03 with Mech111 and .10 with the Woodward score. The relationship is ambiguous in previous studies. Woodward (1965: 46) found no significant relation between size and type of production system. Hickson, Pugh, and Pheysey (1969) reported correlations between size and workflow integration of .08—the entire sample—and .30—manufacturing organizations only—and .47 between size and the Woodward measure—manufacturing organizations only. In the Child and Mansfield data (1972), correlations between size and workflow integration are .24—the national sample—and .17—manufacturing organizations only; and –.08 between size and the Woodward measure—manufacturing organizations only.

TABLE 1. Selected measures of association between size, indices of technology, and dimensions of plant structure

	1 MECH111	2 WOODWARD SCORE	3 SIZE (LOG)	4 SIZE (LOG)• W/CONTROLS	5 WOOD-WARD	6 PRO-DUCTION	7 TYPES	8 AUTIL
	r	r	—	BETA	ETA	ETA CONTROLLING SIZE (LOG)	PATTERN OF RELATION	r
Differentiation								
1. Number of levels	.10	.10	.49••		.04	.08	○	.27••
2. Number of divisions	.03	.01	.41••		.06	.14	∪	−.14
3. Number of sections	.08	.14	.68••		.13	.25	∪	.19••
4. Number of job titles	−.08	−.10	.62••	.43••	.13	.15	∪	.21••
5. Occupational diversity	.02	.09	.06	−.26	.28••	.30	∪	.30••
6. Functional specialization	−.01	.11	.25••	.01	.07	.12	○	.56••
Personnel components (%'s)								
7. Nonproduction	−.08	.01	−.06	−.59••	.21	.20	∪	.33••
8. Supervisors	.04	.14	−.28••	−.88••	.35••	.30	∪	.22••
9. Staff	−.04	−.07	.04	−.40••	.17	.18	∪	.30••
10. Clerks	−.15	.02	−.01	−.34••	.09	.09	○	.27••
11. Professionals	−.04	−.01	.16	−.38••	.17	.20	∪	.19
12. College graduates	.07	.12	−.08	−.56••	.23	.23	∪	.09
13. Indirect production	.24••	.34••	−.01	−.09	.32••	.33	±/	−.24••
14. Maintenance	.24••	.43••	−.04	−.31••	.49••	.50	±/	−.18
15. Direct production	−.09	−.21••	.05	.56••	.33••	.33	∩	−.15
16. Craftsmen	.11	.01	−.03	−.11	.26••	.26	∪	.03
Spans of control								
17. Chief executive officers	.08	.06	.15	−.21••	.20	.24	∪	−.19••
18. Division heads (X)	−.18	−.25••	.01	.35••	.20	.20	−	−.04
19. Section heads (X)	−.12	−.01	.08	.41••	.25	.25	∩	.23••
20. FLS—All (X)	−.06	−.09	.25••	.79••	.24••	.20	∩	−.22••
21. FLS—Direct production (X)	−.13	−.03	.24••	.71••	.36••	.32	∩	−.02

• Controlling levels, divisions, and sections.
•• Significant at .05 level (significance levels are not presented for the eta under controls—column 6—but they can be inferred from the eta in column 5).

organization, the more it is divided into vertical levels, horizontal sub-units, and occupational specialties.. Although the associations of size with personnel components (column 3, rows 7–16) and with spans of control (rows 17–21) are generally weak, these zero-order correlations are misleading, because the effects of size on most personnel components and spans of control are concealed by the opposite influences of structural differentiation on them, as previous research indicated (Blau, 1972). When the three main forms of structural differentiation—number of levels, divisions, and sections—are controlled (Table 1, column 4), size is revealed to exert strong influences on nearly all personnel components and spans of control. The only exceptions are that the proportion of indirect production workers is unrelated to size, but correlated positively with mechanization, and that the proportion of skilled craftsmen is unrelated to either size or mechanization.

Thus, large factories have complex, differentiated structures, and their large work force reduces the proportionate size of most supportive components and widens the spans of control of middle managers and first-line supervisors—whereas their differentiated structures have the opposite effects. These findings parallel those in other types of organizations, including government agencies, department stores, and universities and colleges (Blau, 1972). Furthermore, the findings are similar to those of Hickson and his associates (1969:387), who reported that correlations of structural variables with size are considerably stronger than those with technology. Although some of the Aston measures differed from those of the present study and not all of the results are identical—compare Table 1 in the present study with Table 8 in Hickson, Pugh, and Pheysey (1969: 386)—the overall conclusion in both cases is that the structure of factories, like that of other organizations, depends greatly on their size.

In spite of these findings, it is not plausible that a factory's structure is affected as little by its production technology as the data reveal so far. Hickson and his colleagues (1969:393–395), in attempting to reconcile their conclusions with those of Woodward, suggested two hypotheses to explain the conflicting results. The first was that the technology of an organization affects only production-linked aspects of the administrative structure, such as the maintenance component. In order to test this hypothesis, correlations were computed for both degree of mechanization and Woodward scores with a number of variables within the production sector only of the factories. None of these correlations is appreciably greater than zero or larger than the corresponding correlation for the entire manufacturing plant. For example, within the production sector only, the proportion of supervisors is correlated with Mech111 .09 (and with the Woodward score, .07); that of staff, .02 (.03); that of clerks, −.09 (−.07); the span of control of division heads, −.15 (−.17); of section heads, −.17 (−.17); and of first-line supervisors, −.13 (−.03). These weak associations are quite similar to the corresponding ones for the total plant (Table 1, column 1–2). The hypothesis that structural variables directly linked to production will reveal stronger associations with degree of mechanization is not confirmed by these data.

The second hypothesis advanced by the Hickson study is that the smaller size of the manufacturing concerns in Woodward's sample is responsible for the difference in findings. Specifically, Hickson, Pugh, and Pheysey suggested that the technology will exert more influence on the administrative structure in small manufacturing concerns because administration is less removed from production than in large concerns. To test this hypothesis, separate correlations of Mech111 with the variables in Table 1 were computed for the smallest quartile of the sample—the 28 manufacturing concerns with fewer than 233 employees—and for the remainder of the 110 plants. The results show that only four variables have a correlation coefficient of .20 or more in either size category, and two of these four negate the hypothesis. The proportion of workers in indirect production is correlated with mechanization in large (.23), as well as small (.29), manufacturing concerns. In addition, the proportion of maintenance workers is correlated only in large (.30), and not in small (.06), factories. The two remaining variables with correlations above .20 support the hypothesis: mechanization reduces the number of divisions in small manufacturing concerns (−.23), but not in large ones (.11), and mechanization narrows the span of control of division heads only in small (−.47), and not in large (−.06), factories.

In general, the current data do not support the size hypothesis, for only 10 percent of the comparisons indicate that mechanization exerts a stronger influence in small than in large organizations. Furthermore, Child and Mansfield's (1972:384, Table 6) findings provided only weak support for Hickson, Pugh, and Pheysey's proposition regarding the influence of technology on administrative structure in small organizations. The hypothesis may yet prove tenable in very small organizations, that is, concerns with a work force under 100 employees. The quartile *small* in the present study contains only one plant with fewer than 100 members, and the mean of the group is 172. More important, however, is that the technology is associated with the structure of factories independent of their size, though these effects become apparent only if types of technical systems are distinguished and procedures are employed that reveal curvilinear relationships.

Type of Production Technology

In her study of industrial organizations in South Essex, Woodward (1965: 38) combined the categories in her score to distinguish three types of production technology according to degree of technical advancement. The three types of production are (1) unit and small-batch, the least technologically advanced; (2) large-batch, assembly, and mass production, an intermediate category; and (3) process production, the most technologically advanced. Although these three types of production exhibit linear differences in mechanization,[9] their influence on the factory tends to be curvilinear. These curvilinear effects were observed by Woodward (1965:60–67), as well as by Hickson, Pugh, and Pheysey (1969:392–393) and Child and Mansfield (1972:381–383). For example, all found the span of control of first-line supervisors in direct production to have a curvilinear relation to production technology; but this observation did not alter the main conclusion of the two latter studies that technology does not have important effects on administrative structure. Neither Hickson, Pugh, and Pheysey nor Child and Mansfield realized the pervasiveness of this curvilinear pattern, partly because their principal measures of association—zero-order and partial correlation coefficients—only indicate linear relationships.

Mass-production plants are generally larger—with a mean work force of 631—than small-batch plants—with 421, and process plants tend to be smaller than either—with 326.[10] These differences in size are accompanied by differences in skills and in administrative structure that are independent of plant size. To reveal this pattern, the correlation ratio (eta) of the three production types with the variables in Table 1 is presented (Table 1, column 5); since size has been shown to be strongly related to many of these variables, the eta with size (log) controlled is also shown (column 6).[11] Because the eta, which has no sign, indicates a linear relationship as well as a nonlinear one, only a value of eta substantially greater than the Pearsonian correlation coefficient provides evidence of curvilinearity; the pattern of relationship is illustrated in column 7. Table 2 presents a comparison of means for these variables that discloses their curvilinear relationships with the three types of technology, both without controls (columns 2–4) and controlling log size (columns 5–7).

The data indicate that mass production plants contrast most sharply with process-production plants, with small-batch-production concerns occupying the intermediate position. While not all of the relationships are

9. These linear differences are revealed by the index Mech111 in the present study: in the average small-batch factory, 19 percent of the machines are self-feeding or more highly mechanized; in the average mass-production factory, 32 percent are; and in the average process factory, 53 percent are.
10. Process production, like that in the chemical industry, is characterized by large companies but relatively small plants, as Blauner (1964: 127) noted.
11. The number of plants in each of the three Woodward production categories is 55 in unit and small-batch, 41 in large-batch and mass, and 12 in process. For two, information is missing.

TABLE 2. Means of structural dimensions for 3 Woodward production types

	1 GRAND MEAN	2 UNADJUSTED MEANS	3	4	5 ADJUSTED FOR LOG SIZE	6	7
		Unit and small-batch	*Mass*	*Process*	*Unit and small-batch*	*Mass*	*Process*
Differentiation							
1. Number of levels	5.14	5.11	5.17	5.18	5.14	5.08	5.35
2. Number of divisions	4.95	5.03	4.80	5.09	5.10	4.61	5.44
3. Number of sections	2.88	2.73	2.73	3.19	2.91	2.23	5.12
4. Number of job titles	125.14	135.15	120.74	94.80	139.04	108.83	121.76
5. Occupational diversity	.70	.71	.66	.76	.71	.66	.76
6. Functional specialization	12.38	12.17	12.50	13.12	12.22	12.21	13.78
Personnel components (%'s)							
7. Nonproduction	.25	.26	.22	.30	.26	.22	.30
8. Supervisors	.09	.09	.08	.12	.09	.08	.12
9. Staff	.07	.08	.06	.08	.08	.05	.08
10. Clerks	.09	.09	.08	.10	.09	.08	.10
11. Professionals	.04	.05	.03	.05	.05	.03	.06
12. College graduates	.05	.05	.04	.09	.05	.04	.09
13. Indirect production	.19	.18	.18	.28	.18	.18	.28
14. Maintenance	.08	.07	.07	.19	.07	.07	.19
15. Direct production	.56	.56	.60	.42	.56	.60	.42
16. Craftsmen	.18	.20	.14	.22	.20	.14	.22
Spans of control							
17. Chief executive officers	7.15	7.33	6.60	8.27	7.37	6.48	8.50
18. Division heads (X)	6.14	6.58	5.88	4.94	6.58	5.86	4.97
19. Section heads (X)	5.65	5.26	6.50	4.66	5.25	6.51	4.65
20. FLS—All (X)	14.72	14.55	16.13	10.30	14.71	15.76	10.91
21. FLS—Direct production (X)	21.22	19.63	25.40	13.46	19.82	24.94	14.23

statistically significant, the consistency of the pattern is impressive. For example, as one moves from the least mechanized small-batch to the more mechanized mass-production and on to the most mechanized process plants, there is first an increase and then a sharper decrease in the proportion of workers in direct production (Table 2, row 15) and in the spans of control of first-line supervisors and of middle managers (rows 19–21).

Spans of control, with one exception, exhibit a curvilinear relationship with type of technology, but the relationship gradually changes as one moves from the top of the pyramid to the production floor. For the chief executive officer's span, the relationship is U-shaped (row 17),[12] while the relationship with division head span is linear and negative (row 18).[13] For the spans of section heads and first-line supervisors, the association is ∩ -shaped (rows 19–20), and it is most pronounced for the foremen in direct production (row 21). Production foremen generally have wider spans of control than first-line supervisors in either indirect production or the white-collar sector,[14] since the large volume of routine work in direct production enables foremen to supervise many persons. Work in mass production is more routine than that in small-batch factories, while work in process production is the least routine (Blauner, 1964:132–142). These differences are reflected in the pronounced ∩ -shaped relationship of the spans of control of production foremen with the three types of technology (row 21). Parallel differences are observable for middle managers on lower levels (row 19), but not for higher managers far removed from the production floor (rows 17–18). These findings lend some support to the hypothesis of Hickson, Pugh, and Pheysey that production-linked aspects of structure are most influenced by the technology of the organization, but the hypothesis is substantiated only for curvilinear relationships, not for linear associations.

Thus, the nature of work in mass production and in process production differs in opposite ways from that in the technically least advanced small-batch production, and this is reflected in U-shaped relationships with specialization and nonproduction components. Specialized training and skills of both white-collar and blue-collar workers are less frequent in mass production, but more frequent in process production than in small-batch production (Table 2, rows 11–12 and 16). The proportionate size of the nonproduction component reveals the same U-shaped curve (row 7); the differences are substantial, however, only for the proportion of managers and supervisors (row 8); they are less for the proportion of staff and virtually nil for the proportion of clerks (rows 9–10). The proportions

12. The same relation was observed by Child and Mansfield (1972: 381).
13. This was also observed by Woodward (1965: 53).
14. Mean spans of control of first-line supervisors are 21.2 in direct production, 12.4 in indirect production, and 5.2 in white-collar work.

of indirect production workers and of those in maintenance do not differ in small-batch and mass production, but are substantially higher in process production (rows 13–14), which accounts for the positive correlations of positive slopes curve sharply upward.[15]

These U-shaped differences in specialization and in the nonproduction component give rise to corresponding differences in occupational diversity. The work force is less diverse in mass production and more diverse in process production than in small-batch production (Table 2, columns 2–4, row 5). The Aston measure of functional specialization (row 6) reveals no such differences, however, nor do most of the other measures of differentiation (row 1–4), except for very slight curvilinear tendencies. The dominant influence of size on differentiation in the structure obliterates the influence of technology. But when size is controlled, some curvilinear effects of the technology on differentiation become apparent, as observed in the comparison of means adjusted for log size (Table 2, columns 5–7, rows 1–5).

To summarize, advances in production technology do not have linear, but do have curvilinear, relationships with various aspects of plant structure. As one moves from small-batch to mass production, the nature of manufacturing tasks becomes more uniform, which is reflected in an increase in routine work,[16] a lower skill level of the labor force, and reductions in support components. The data indicate that these trends are reversed in advanced production technologies. Thus, production jobs are least standardized in process plants, since they generally involve maintenance of complex equipment or responsible monitoring functions there. Process plants usually have not only the most highly skilled blue-collar work force, but also the largest proportion of white-collar jobs requiring specialized skills.

Computer Automated Support

The use of automated data processing is prevalent in the 110 plants in the sample: nine-tenths of them employ computers in some of the 16 functions listed in footnote 4. Yet nearly two-thirds (68) of the plants do not have data-processing facilities at their own site. The reason for this

15. Hickson, Pugh, and Pheysey (1969: 393) observed an opposite curve, which implies that process production has the smallest number of maintenance workers. This figure may be due to a mistake in reporting, since the positive slope accompanying this curve (Table 8: 386) implies the reverse.

16. The proportion of routine work—measured by managers' estimates of jobs requiring little skills—conforms to the familiar U-shaped pattern, and measures of skill required reflect the inverse, so that the proportion of routine work is highest for mass production, while white- and blue-collar skill levels are the lowest. This pattern is reversed in process production, which requires the lowest proportion of routine work and the highest skill levels (Table 2, rows 11–12 and 16).

disparity is the extensive use of off-site computers at divisional or corporate headquarters, or time-sharing services. Of the 68 sites which do not maintain a separate computer installation, most have access to off-site systems for at least some of their data-processing work. In addition, many of the plants with their own systems also use off-site computers, because for some functions, such as payroll and accounting, it is more efficient to take advantage of the standardized programs offered by time-sharing contractors than to create one's own software. As would be expected, on- and off-site computer use are inversely correlated (for automation of functions, $-.62$; for minutes per day, $-.44$). Data from this study also show that branch plants are the most likely to utilize off-site computer systems, since they usually have one available at their parent company's headquarters. Total computer use, whether on- or off-site, however, hardly differs for branch plants and independent factories. On the average, eight functions in branch plants and 8.4 in others are automated. This finding indicates that the demand for automated data processing is determined by functional requirements of manufacturing establishments and not by geographical location or structural position within the parent company hierarchy.

Even factories that have an in-house computer rarely use it to automate the production process itself. For example, only five of the plants in the sample had any computer-controlled production equipment (Amber level 5) in 1973, and none of the machinery basic to the manufacturing operation—the core technology—was computerized. These observations are corroborated by the lack of a significant positive relationship between mechanization of production and the indices of computer use. Thus, the correlation between Mech111 and Aut11, the number of functions using on-site computers, is $-.03$, and Mech111's association with Aut11, the number of functions with any computer use, is .07. By the same token, the number of minutes per day of on-site computer time is correlated $-.07$ with Mech111, while total computer use in minutes per day actually has a significant negative relationship ($-.26$) with this mechanization index.[17] From these data, it can be concluded that the automated factory is still a rare exception, and the tentative inference can be drawn that extensive mechanization of production machinery may discourage instituting automated data processing.

Although computers are used very little in direct control of manufacturing equipment, they are employed widely in administrative support of production, as well as in marketing and distribution. The functions which are most frequently automated are accounting, billing and paying, payroll,

17. Since production is only one of the 16 possible functions included in Aut11 and Aut111, the total variance of these measures would not be greatly changed if manufacturing equipment were automated. For this reason, the findings for automation of functional areas are supplemented by using the corresponding measures of on-site and total computer use in minutes per day.

inventory control, and sales. Computers are also often used in immediate support of the manufacturing operation itself, notably in production scheduling. In the current sample, 30 plants applied their on-site computer in production control, and 39 others used an off-site computer for the same purpose. Thus, production control is automated in almost two-thirds of the 110 manufacturing concerns surveyed. Withington (1969) also emphasized the role of computers in production scheduling, citing several detailed case studies that showed how automated data transmission and analysis allow managers to control the flow of supplies on the factory floor and thereby improve the cost-effectiveness of tool and raw material distribution.[18] It might be inferred from Withington's examples and the present data that most production-related computer use involves analysis of ongoing operations, while actual implementation of manufacturing tasks remains essentially in the hands of human operators. Moreover, these data may help explain the negative correlation between Mech111 and total minutes of computer use, inasmuch as production scheduling consumes much computer time and mechanization, which makes the production process less flexible, and reduces the need for detailed scheduling.

In recent years, there has been much conjecture about the effects of automation on the administrative structure of formal organizations. For example, Whisler (1970a: 3–6, 30–45, and 68) basing his claims on other sources as well as on his own research, stated that computer use leads to consolidation of departments and hence fewer departments, a smaller number of levels in the managerial hierarchy, and narrower spans of control on lower supervisory levels. Withington (1969:82–83) noted that the introduction of automated data-processing methods tend to enlarge the administrative component and reduce supervisory spans of control. These propositions, however, are only partially supported by the present study, as the correlations between Aut11 and the various structural indices (Table 1, column 8) demonstrate.[19] The automation of plant functions with on-site computer systems does narrow the span of control of all first-line supervisors (Table 1, row 20), though it has a negligible effect on the span of control of direct production foremen (row 21). This is not surprising, since automation is largely confined to support functions and very rarely involves direct production itself. The data in Table 1 also show that computer use has no influence on the span of control of division heads (row 18), and that it widens the span of control of their subordinates,

18. Withington's case studies are not derived from comparative research, but are based on his experience as a management consultant.
19. Aut11, the measure of in-house automation, is used here because it is the most appropriate measure for testing the effects of automation on internal plant structure. Total computer use (Aut111) is correlated more than .20 with only three of the 21 variables in Table 1—number of levels, .23; number of sections, .27; total number of job titles, .51. The associations with on-site and total use in minutes per day parallel those of Aut11 and Aut111, respectively.

section heads (row 19). The negative association between in-house automation and the chief executive officer's span of control is spurious. Thus, the findings contradict past predictions that computer use will reduce subordinate-supervisor ratios throughout the administrative hierarchy.

Neither is there any evidence that automation of plant functions by on-site computers leads to the consolidation of departments—in the present study's terms, sections or divisions—and a reduction in their number. The correlation between Aut11 and number of divisions (row 2) is negative, but insignificant, while automation has a positive effect on the number of sections. If any shrinkage of the administrative structure occurs, it is on the level just below the chief executive officer, and not in the lower middle-management ranks, as has been claimed. Contrary to Whisler's assumption, moreover, computer use tends to increase rather than decrease the number of administrative levels in the plant hierarchy (Table 1, row 1). The reason probably is that a computer system serves as an impersonal mechanism of control, which makes it less disadvantageous for top management to be separated from the workflow by many hierarchical levels. By establishing guidelines for the computer's design and programming, high-level executives can direct ongoing operations without passing directives down a human chain of command, which often delays the directives' execution.[20] Automation also provides a shortened feedback loop, furnishing immediate information to management about work in progress, thereby reducing dependence on hierarchical channels of communication, reporting and accountability. The tendency of automation to be associated with an increased number of administrative levels has also been observed in government agencies (Blau and Schoenherr, 1971: 74–77). The influence of automation on vertical differentiation in manufacturing concerns persists when size (log) is controlled; the beta weight is .21, which is more than twice its standard error.

Computer use at the site increases the proportion of nonproduction workers (Table 1, row 7) and each of its three subcomponents—supervisors, salaried staff, and clerks (rows 8–10). This finding supports the observation of Withington (1969: 82–83) that automated operations generally require more administrative personnel and a larger white-collar staff. Since automation of plant functions enlarges the white-collar support component, it must necessarily reduce the proportion of workers engaged in direct and indirect production activities (rows 13–15). In-house computer use has mixed effects on the training and skill of employees: it raises the percentage of professionals somewhat (row 11), but it does not increase appreciably the need for college graduates (row 12), nor does it affect the proportion of skilled craftsmen.

20. Automation may enable top executives to set specific guidelines for day-to-day operations, while leaving the responsibility for implementing these guidelines decentralized.

The technical complexity of automation is associated with greater structural complexity in manufacturing plants. Computer use (Aut11) is positively related to most forms of differentiation (Table 1, column 8, rows 1–6), the only major exception being number of divisions. These relationships raise the possibility that correlations observed between Aut11 and other variables in Table 1 are spurious, owing to the influences of differentiation, for the three major forms of differentiation—levels, divisions, and sections—are also associated with many of the variables in rows 7–21. To check this, these three forms of differentiation were controlled through multiple regression techniques; that is, each of the remaining variables in Table 1 was regressed on size (log), number of levels, number of divisions, number of sections, and on-site computer use.[21] Most of the beta weights for Aut11 derived from this analysis closely resemble the corresponding zero-order correlations (column 8), and all the correlations above .20 have matching beta weights that are more than twice their standard error. Only three of the regression coefficients differ as much as .05 from the simple correlation with Aut11. The beta weight for staff is .25 ($r = .30$), for section head span .28 ($r = .23$), and the chief executive officer's span $-.09$, revealing the zero-order correlation of $-.19$ to be spurious. Thus, the influences of automation discussed are observable even when size and differentiation are controlled.

The automation of support functions creates a more differentiated structure in factories, and it exerts additional influences that parallel and reinforce those of structural differentiation.[22] Independently, both automation and differentiation enlarge the proportion of all kinds of administrative personnel, narrow the spans of control of first-line supervisors, and raise the professional skills of the salaried staff. Since automation also increases differentiation, part of its effects on the variables in rows 7–21 is mediated through differentiation. Thus, automation influences the composition of the work force in part directly and in part by engendering differentiation, which affects it further. In particular, both technological and structural complexity expand the administrative apparatus in manufacturing plants, and their effects on it are cumulative.

A process technology in production and the automation of support functions by on-site computers also exert numerous parallel influences on the administrative structure (compare columns 7–8 in Table 1).[23] Both

21. In other words, the regression analyses are the same as those on which the beta weights in column 4 of Table 1 are based, except for the addition of Aut11 as another independent predictor.

22. Since the effects of differentiation are not the focus of this article, they are not discussed in full. But they can be inferred from the data in columns 3 and 4: whenever the beta weight of size, controlling for the three indicators of differentiation, substantially exceeds its simple correlation with a variable, the influence of differentiation on the variable is in the opposite direction from that of size.

23. These effects are independent, since process production, which lies at the upper end of the Woodward scale, is unrelated to automation. The correlation ratio (eta)

process production and automation enlarge a plant's administrative apparatus (rows 7–10), particularly the supervisory and staff components. In addition, both promote the division of labor into diverse, specialized occupations (rows 4–5) and somewhat raise professional skills (row 11). Finally, through their positive influence on white-collar components, computer use and process manufacturing both narrow the average span of control of first-line supervisors (row 20), since the ratio of first-line supervisors to subordinates is higher in specialized white-collar work than in more routine production operations. Most variables that do not exhibit parallel relationships with the two technologies fall into one of two categories. As might be expected, ratios of production personnel (rows 13–16 and 21) are influenced by manufacturing technology, but only weakly by automation of support functions. In addition, spans of control of middle and senior managers (rows 17–19) do not reveal parallel influences.[24]

In sum, process production generates changes in factories that reverse the trends mass production has introduced. Whereas mass production routinizes work and simplifies the administrative structure, process manufacturing leads to the development of specialized skills and a complex administrative apparatus. The automation of support functions produces changes that continue these new trends; it is tempting to infer that automation of the production process itself will accelerate these changes in the future.

Technology and Authority

Whereas the influences of automation on administrative structures at first appeared to far outweigh those of production technology, these initial findings obscured important curvilinear relationships between type of production system and structure. When probing further by comparing structural characteristics in less mechanized mass-production plants with those in plants utilizing advanced process technologies, many similarities with automation appeared. But despite these parallels, there is one important area in which the influences of production technology and of automation are very different, namely, the distribution of authority over important operational and personnel decisions.

Highly mechanized production technologies reduce the autonomy of plant managers and discourage decentralization. The index of decentral-

for Aut11 and the three main Woodward categories is .08 (.07 with log size controlled); and there are no significant differences in the means of Aut11 for any of the three production types. If Aut11 as well as size (log) is controlled, none of the etas of Woodward type with the variables in Table 1 differ by more than .01 from those shown in column 6.

24. Of the three main forms of structural differentiation (rows 1–3), levels are affected only by automation, divisions by neither technology, and sections by both.

ization of marketing and production decisions is negatively correlated with the Woodward scale (−.27). The corresponding eta, which lacks a sign, is similar to the zero-order correlation, whether or not size (log) is controlled (.28 in both cases). This implies that the negative relationship is linear. The average decentralization score for operational decisions, independent of size (log) differences, is .78 for small-batch plants, .57 for mass production, and .41 for process plants. These data suggest that the more highly mechanized production is, the more likely is it that the final authority for making key production and marketing decisions rests above the plant manager's level (scored 0) than at his level (scored 1) or below (scored 2 or more, depending on the level). In the present sample, as one proceeds from small-batch to mass production and then to process plants, the autonomy of the plant manager to make major operational decisions decreases and authority becomes more centralized at corporate headquarters.[25]

For decisions involving the hiring, promotion, and dismissal of plant personnel, however, delegation of authority is little correlated with the Woodward score (−.07). But the corresponding eta is substantially larger (.42) than the zero-order correlation, disclosing a curvilinear relationship between production technology and the decentralization of personnel decisions. Contrary to the stereotypical view of mass production plants as being most regimented, personnel decisions, controlling for size (log), are most decentralized in mass production (2.05), even slightly more than in small-batch production (1.85), and substantially more than in process plants, which have the lowest decentralization score (1.30). Hence, in process plants, which have the most advanced production technologies, both personnel and operational decisions tend to be most centralized. Generalizations from these findings must be made with extreme caution,[26] but some conjectures interpreting the result in terms of the economic character in the plants in the sample may be permissible.

Of the 110 plants in the random sample of New Jersey manufacturing establishments, all but 11 belong to larger corporate units. This accounts for the great discrepancy between the average plant size of 500 employees and the average size for the parent company, which is nearly

25. The index of operational decision making used here reflects essentially the autonomy of the plant management, rather than variations in authority within the plant itself. The index is correlated .95 with a pure measure of plant autonomy in operational decisions, for which the same items were scored 0 for decisions made above the plant level and 1 for those made either by the chief executive or any other manager at the site.
26. The conclusion that a highly mechanized production technology is usually accompanied by a centralized authority should be considered tentative, since the empirical findings in this area vary greatly (Hickson, Pugh, and Pheysey, 1969: 386; Child and Mansfield, 1972: 379; Hickson et al., 1974: 71). The inconsistencies in published results probably derive from the small sample size in most of these studies, which makes correlations of .30 or even higher insignificant and unstable.

40,000. In other words, most plants analyzed here are not fully indepen-dent economic units, but must rely upon resources provided by the parent company. The more corporate resources are invested in expensive, mech-anized plant equipment, which must be depreciated over many years,[27] the more caution one would expect corporate managements to exercise in delegating authority over production and marketing decisions to plant managers. Large capital investments must be protected against unpre-dictable events, and delegating autonomy to plant managers, though it may yield unforeseeable benefits, undoubtedly lessens predictability. Besides, corporations own many plants—the average number owned by the parent companies in this sample was 46—and the coordination of operations in many establishments fosters centralization at corporate headquarters. The most highly mechanized establishments are most likely to be owned by large corporations, since large capital investments are required for their equipment, which may explain why authority is most centralized in them. Another factor may contribute to the delegation of personnel decisions in mass-production plants. Since employees in mass-production factories are least specialized and skilled, personnel decisions assume less import there and are perhaps for this reason more likely to be delegated in these than in other factories.

In contrast to the centralizing influence of an advanced production technology, an in-house computer to automate support functions pro-motes decentralization, though primarily in the form of granting autonomy to the plant manager. The correlation of Aut1, indicating the presence of an on-site computer, with decentralization of operational decisions is strong and positive (.59).[28] Its correlation with decentralization of per-sonnel decisions is weak (.13). The implication is that on-site computers foster decentralization to the level of plant managers, but hardly below this level.

These results at first seem to contradict the argument that large in-vestments in capital equipment foster centralization. But the cost of a computer relative to expenditures for production machinery is apparently small. The measure of capital invested in equipment per employee for the 40 plants where data are available is negatively correlated with Aut1 ($-.21$), which agrees with statements by industry experts that the amount of money invested in computer technologies is small when compared with that invested in production machinery (*Business Week,* 1975). The find-

27. Capital investment in plant, machinery, and other equipment per employee is correlated .52 with the Woodward technology score for the 39 cases on which data for both indices are available.
28. The relationship of Aut1 to the measure of pure site autonomy for operational decisions (fn. 25) is also positive and large (.56). The correlations with Aut11 are similar—with operational decisions, 57; with personnel decisions, .13; with pure autonomy, .57. Since the sheer presence of an on-site computer suffices to influence decentralization, Aut1 is used in this discussion.

ings, based upon data from 110 manufacturing plants in many different industries, are particularly significant in light of the ongoing debate about the implications of computers for the locus of organizational decision making.

In an early article addressing the future consequences of computers for middle-level and senior management, Leavitt and Whisler (1958) predicted that the spread of automation would "extend the thinking range" of top executives by providing them with immediate access to current information about ongoing operations. The authors forecasted loss of autonomy for many middle-management positions and a recentralization of control to more senior levels. A decade later, Whisler (1970b), in a study of 19 insurance agencies, found some support for his arguments that computers reduce clerical and middle-managerial positions, and that their introduction facilitates the recentralization of decision-making authority. Although case studies by Mumford and Banks (1967) and Argyris (1970) arrived at parallel conclusions, there is still disagreement on the broader implications of Whisler's results for firms outside the insurance industry.

Withington's (1969) examination of a broad variety of organizations in both the public and the private sector led him to conclude that automation, while it may result in centralized data processing, tends to promote decentralization of line responsibilities for a variety of reasons. Since few senior managers have sufficient first-hand information to specify data-processing requirements, he pointed out that attempts to recentralize decision making often result in the generation of huge amounts of output which quickly overburden top management and encourage delegation. Automation of record-keeping does permit the development of large, centralized information files, but Withington noted that this readily available information reduces top management's monopoly on company-wide data and enhances the decision-making capability of middle managers. For more routine accounting and budgeting purposes, which are generally some of the first functions to be automated, Withington agreed with Whisler that computers do displace some clerical employees. This does not result in the elimination of hierarchical levels or the recentralization of control, however, because the easy access to extensive information which computers provide to managers on all levels strengthens the authority of junior managers.

The finding in the present study that on-site computer use is associated with decentralization of operational decisions supports Withington's predictions and contradicts those of Whisler and others. But further analysis of those plants that utilize time-sharing facilities linked to off-site computers indicates that the influences of automation may be more complex than either Withington's or Whisler's arguments suggested. Seventy of the 110 plants use off-site computers, and the correlation between outside computer use and the decentralization of operational decisions is strongly negative ($-.55$). While data are not available to determine whether these time-sharing facilities are supplied by corporate headquarters or by an outside contractor, most are probably located at the parent company headquarters. If this is the case, the data imply that the location of computer facilities governs the locus of decision-making authority. If a plant has its own computer, its management is likely to have much autonomy, but if a plant uses an off-site computer, presumably in most cases at corporate headquarters, chances are that authority is centralized there.

Inasmuch as on-site and off-site computer use have opposite implications for decentralization, it is of interest to ascertain the factors associated with a plant's having its own data-processing facilities. The extent to which factories handle their own sales avtivities is an important condition associated with the presence of on-site computers. In plants that do not have their own computer, sales personnel constitute only 1 percent of all employees, while in those plants that do have their own computer system, the sales force is four times as great. The correlation between Aut1 and the percentage of sales personnel is .46. Although these findings are not surprising, since sales is one of the two functions for which on-site computers are most often used—accounting is the other—they have important implications. Plants that must process their own orders and invoices as well as perform their own sales analyses and market research greatly benefit from having a computer on the premises. But the size of the sales force is also strongly correlated with the decentralization of both operational (.62) and personnel decisions (.30), and this raises the possibility that the relationships noted earlier between on-site computer use and decentralization may be spurious.

Regression analysis reveals, however, that this is not the case and that in-house computers as well as extensive selling foster decentralization. Aut1 (beta weight, .41) and percent of personnel in sales (.40) exert independent influences on the decentralization of marketing and production decisions, and they account for nearly one-half (47 percent) of the variance in this decentralization measure. The demands of the market constrain corporations to enlarge the autonomy of managers of plants that are much involved in market transactions and to furnish them with on-site computers to facilitate adjusting to market demands. And the location of a computer at a plant further strengthens the autonomy of its management and lessens centralized corporate authority.

The costs of installing on-site computers include not only the initial capital investment, but additional organizational expenses resulting from structural changes. Plants using on-site systems must hire or retrain specialists to develop the software capabilities necessary for automation. The current study's findings suggest that costs do not end there. For automated factories exhibit higher levels of functional specialization, narrower spans of control, and greater differentiation, all of which increase administrative overhead. Nevertheless, avoiding these costs by centralizing computer facilities at corporate headquarters carries perhaps an even greater long-run cost, namely, that of reduced ability to adjust quickly to changing environmental conditions at the plant. With the recent advent of inexpensive minicomputers, it is likely that many more plants will acquire their own computer facilities in the near future. If the patterns observed here continue to apply, this trend will not lead to recentralization, but foster greater structural complexity and more autonomy at the plant level.

Concluding Conjectures

One important reason for the disagreement over the implications of technology for organizational structure is that the technical developments of the last century have not affected factory structures in any simple, uni-linear fashion. Some plants utilize the mass-production methods first instituted in the early decades of this century, while others continue to use small-batch technologies reminiscent of earlier days, and still others employ process technologies which rose to prominence prior to World War II. Since all these different production techniques are in wide use today, their historical influences, as well as those of more recent computer technologies, can be inferred from the present cross-sectional comparison.

The rise of mass-production technology at the turn of the century relied heavily upon the routinization of work and provided attractive employment for untrained migrants moving to industrial centers. Mass-production plants were much larger than small-batch factories, providing work for many, but few opportunities for upward mobility into the ranks of craftsmen or supervisors. Thus, routinization and its structural consequences in mass-production plants contributed to frustration, thereby stimulating the growth of the industrial labor movement. The development of the technically more advanced process-production methods in the 1930s started a reversal of the trends in factory structure. While corporations grew larger, as did investments in process equipment, which was changing rapidly, the size of plants was reduced and process production fostered the specialization of responsibilities in both blue-collar and white-collar work. The more diverse work force made coordination at the plant level and above more complex and required more supervisors, managers, and staff experts. This in turn provided greater opportunities and discouraged alienation, as Blauner's (1964) study has shown.

Whereas the impact of the computer is quite recent and cuts across industries with very different production technologies, automation appears to reinforce the trends begun by process technologies. Computers are most frequently used for routine data-processing operations in accounting and sales, yet their influence extends far beyond the clerical level. Automation, like process production, promotes specialization and increases ratios of supervisory and staff personnel. In addition to reinforcing changes initiated by the advent of process technologies, automation also has effected changes of its own. Computers in factories encourage the development of multilevel hierarchies and decentralization of authority from corporate headquarters to plant managers.

These changes in factory structure are not simply the result of advances in technology, however. The technology interacts with contemporary social conditions in complex ways. Mass-production methods, for example, were first developed when the majority of the labor force had little education or technical training. It is doubtful that the level of technical knowledge at the turn of the century predetermined the nature of mass-production factories. What seems more likely is that the low level of available skills influenced the manner in which this knowledge was applied to the organization of work. Mass-production techniques simply made it possible to produce complex products with a largely unskilled work force. Efficiencies generated by the development and spread of mass production made it possible to shorten the years people must work and extend their years of schooling, thus raising the education of the labor force.

The better educated labor force, in turn, affected the ways in which advances in technical knowledge were translated into production methods. It permitted designing process-production procedures that require most workers to assume considerable responsibility. As education expands further and growing proportions of the labor force acquire technical and professional competence, the adaptation of computer technologies to production and office work will undoubtedly take these higher skills into account. While it is possible to automate many operations without raising the skills workers use, a highly trained labor force makes this increasingly unnecessary. Hence, one can expect the growing automation of factories to raise the level of skill and responsibility of workers.

References

AMBER, GEORGE S., and PAUL S. AMBER
  1962 Anatomy of Automation. Englewood Cliffs, N.J.: Prentice-Hall.
ARGYRIS, CHRIS
  1970 "Resistance to rational management systems." Innovation, 10: 28–35.
BAVELAS, ALEX
  1960 "Communication and organization." In G. Shultz and T. Whisler (eds.), Management Organization and the Computer: 119–130. Glencoe, Ill.: Free Press.
BLAU, PETER M.
  1972 "Interdependence and hierarchy in organizations." Social Science Research, 1: 1–24.

ORGANIZATIONAL STRUCTURE

BLAU, PETER M., and RICHARD A. SCHOENHERR
1971 The Structure of Organizations. New York: Basic Books.
BLAUNER, ROBERT
1964 Alienation and Freedom. Chicago: University of Chicago Press.
BUSINESS WEEK
1975 "The office of the future." No. 2387, June 30.
CHILD, JOHN, and ROGER MANSFIELD
1972 "Technology, size and organization structure." Sociology, 6: 369–393.
GIBBS, JACK P., and WALTER T. MARTIN
1962 "Urbanization, technology and the division of labor." American Sociological Review, 27: 667–677.
HICKSON, DAVID J., D. S. PUGH, and DIANA C. PHEYSEY
1969 "Operations technology and organization structure: an empirical reappraisal." Administrative Science Quarterly, 14: 378–397.
HICKSON, DAVID J., C. R. HININGS, C. J. MCMILLAN, and J. P. SCHWITTER
1974 "The culture-free context of organization structure: a trinational comparison." Sociology, 8: 59–80.
LEAVITT, HAROLD, and THOMAS WHISLER
1958 "Management in the 1980's." Harvard Business Review, 36: 41–48.
MUMFORD, ENID, and OLIVE BANKS
1967 The Computer and the Clerk. London: Routledge and Kegan Paul.
PERROW, CHARLES
1967 "A framework for the comparative analysis of organizations." American Sociological Review, 32: 194–208.
PUGH, D. S., D. J. HICKSON, C. R. HININGS, and C. TURNER.
1968 "Dimensions of organization structure." Administrative Science Quarterly, 13: 65–105.
STARBUCK, WILLIAM H.
1965 "Organizational growth and development." In J. March (ed.), Handbook of Organizations: 451–533. Chicago: Rand McNally.
THOMPSON, JAMES D.
1967 Organizations in Action. New York: McGraw-Hill.
WHISLER, THOMAS
1970a Information Technology and Organizational Change. Belmont, Calif.: Wadsworth.
1970b The Impact of Computers on Organizations. New York: Praeger.
WITHINGTON, FREDERIC G.
1969 The Real Computer: Its Influence, Uses, and Effects. Reading, Mass.: Addison-Wesley.
WOODWARD, JOAN
1958 Management and Technology. London: Her Majesty's Stationary Office.
1965 Industrial Organization: Theory and Practice. Oxford: Oxford University Press.
ZWERMAN, WILLIAM L.
1970 New Perspectives on Organization Theory. Westport, Conn.: Greenwood Publishing.

PART FIVE

Organizations and Their Environments

One of the major "discoveries" of the 1970s was the importance of the environment for understanding organizational behavior. Of course Weber, Michels, and other pioneer theorists were aware of the impact of the environment on organizations. What is different about current efforts is the explicit attempt to conceptualize environmental effects. Each of the four selections in this part show how particular segments of the environment impinge upon organizational processes and thereby affect their structure and functioning. The range of organizational types considered is substantial and includes book publishing, phonograph records, films, county and city organizations dealing with problem youth, automobile factories, and educational organizations.

The first paper, by Hirsch, argues forcefully for the concept of industry system as a means of understanding how entrepreneurial sectors of the book-publishing, record, and motion picture industries operate. Hirsch's analysis is novel because it focuses not on a single organization but on an entire industry or set of organizations. To comprehend industry practices it is essential to understand the complex web of interdependencies and institutional norms that bind the activities of each unit. All three of the mass cultural industries Hirsch studied strove to limit their dependence on an uncertain environment. Several methods for doing this are described: using contact men, deliberately overproducing, selectively promoting new items, and seeking to coopt key media persons who can affect product sales.

The study by Richard H. Hall and his associates focused explicitly on the problem of coordination, that is, "the extent to which organizations attempt to ensure that their activities take into account those of other organizations." The authors distinguished three bases for interorganizational coordination: voluntary relationships, those mandated by law, and those based on formal agreements. Questionnaires were distributed to staffs of seventy six organizations that dealt with youth 10 to 18 years of age (such as juvenile courts, police, schools, county welfare departments, and YMCAs) located in twelve large urban areas all around the nation. It was assumed that organizations seek to acquire resources both to meet their program needs and to strengthen their particular mode of adaptation to their environment. To do this requires some adjustment to the needs of other organizations with whom they share a domain. The investigators found that exchanges did not automatically take place when the organizations they studied interacted with one another as exchange theory would have predicted (S. Levine and P. E. White, "Exchange as a Conceptual Framework for the Study of Interorganizational Relationships," *Administrative Science Quarterly*, 5 [March 1961], 583–610). Instead, the exchange perspective was supported only when the basis of interaction was voluntary, and not when it was based on formal agreement or legal mandate.

"Work Dedesign in Japan: An Evaluation" is a portion of Robert E. Cole's study, *Work, Mobility, and Participation: A Comparative Study of American and Japanese Industry* (1979). Cole identifies five major features of Japanese work redesign and participatory management efforts. First, as revealed in his analysis of QC (quality control) circles, the company's policies were designed to facilitate worker control over job content. Quality control circles are relatively independent units, usually led by a foreman, consisting of small groups of three to twenty workers, which attempt to solve job-related problems so as to improve production. Simultaneously, QC circles focus on worker self-improvement, including skill development and morale enhancement. One major characteristic of QC circles is the training of foremen in statistical methods that are applicable to shop problems. (Most workers and foremen receive superior training in mathematics in the public schools, at least by our standards.) Cole reports that company officials are firmly convinced of the effectiveness of QC circles and there seems to be no doubt that they enhance worker participation in decision making.

Second, the company emphasizes worker participation in order to encourage attainment of management goals. The focus is not on worker participation for its own sake but instead on what Cole calls "controlled participation," meaning that job redesign is deliberately aimed to maintain existing authority structures. Toyota's job redesign program certainly does not threaten management power and to a certain extent consolidates it. This contrasts sharply with Scandinavian approaches. Even more surprisingly, Cole sees some similarities between Chinese and Japanese management practices.

Third, Toyota Auto Body's job redesign practices emphasize the responsibility of small work units. The QC circles are illustrative.

Fourth, although worker job participation is enhanced, this program has not meant greater participation in industry profits.

Fifth is the emphasis on career development rather than simply job enlargement. Unlike American programs, which stress job enlargement, Toyota Auto Body assumes a long-term employee commitment and, as a result, invests heavily in programs designed to maximize blue-collar workers' chances to develop their skills through a wide variety of training and educational programs.

In summary, two features characterize Toyota job redesign programs: "a lack of sharp jurisdictional definition of job duties" and "a strong internal labor market . . . with employees manifesting a career commitment to the company."

In our last selection, Meyer and Rowan argue that institutionalization, "the processes by which social processes, obligations, or actualities come to take on a rule like status in social thought and action," governs the expansion and increased complexity of formal organization structures. This conception sharply challenges the prevailing Weberian view that sees the expansion and development of organizations as a response to technical requirements and bureaucratic needs for greater coordination and control.

Meyer and Rowan assert that it is the society's characteristics, such as its highly rationalized institutional rules and its degree of modernization, that are primarily responsible for organizational expansion. Bureaucratization is a consequence of the proliferation of myths, such as those concerning the need for new school curricula or new personnel and advertising departments in business firms. Those organizations that incorporate these legitimate, societally approved elements into their formal structures further enhance their legitimacy and are able to obtain additional resources. Successful organizations are those that become isomorphic with their environment by perpetuating institutionalized myths. Two devices for reconciling conflicts between ceremonial rules and efficiency, "decoupling" and the "logic of efficiency," are described.

Processing Fads and Fashions: An Organization-Set Analysis of Cultural Industry Systems[1]

Paul M. Hirsch

Some years ago I had the opportunity to study rather extensively and at first hand the women's fashion industry. I was forcibly impressed by the fact that the setting or determination of fashion takes place actually through an intense process of selection. At a seasonal opening of a major Parisian fashion house there may be presented a hundred or more designs of women's evening wear before an audience of from one to two hundred buyers. The managerial corps of the fashion house is able to indicate a group of about thirty designs of the entire lot, inside of which will fall the small number, usually about six to eight designs, that are chosen by the buyers, but the managerial staff is typically unable to predict this small number on which the choices converge. Now, these choices are made by the buyers—a highly competitive and secretive lot—independently of each other and without knowledge of each other's selections. Why should their choices converge on a few designs as they do? When the buyers were asked why they chose one dress in preference to another—between which my inexperienced eye could see no appreciable difference—the typical,

SOURCE: *American Journal of Sociology* 77, no. 4 (January 1972): 639–59. Copyright © 1972 by The University of Chicago. Reprinted by permission of the author and the publisher.

1. This paper was developed in connection with a study of the popular music industry and its audience conducted at the Survey Research Center, University of Michigan, under the supervision of Dr. Stephen B. Withey and supported by grant numbers 1-RO1-MH17064-01 and 1-FO1-MH48847-01 from the National Institute of Mental Health. I wish to thank Edward O. Laumann, Albert J. Reiss, Jr., Randall Collins, Theodore L. Reed, David R. Segal, and an anonymous reviewer for critical comments on an earlier version of this paper, presented at the sixty-fifth annual meeting of the American Sociological Association, August 1970.

honest, yet largely uninformative answer was that the dress was "stunning." [Blumer 1969, pp. 278–79]

The preselection of goods for potential consumption is a feature common to all industries. In order for new products or ideas to reach consumers, they must first be processed favorably through a system of organizations whose units filter out a large proportion of candidates before they arrive at the consumption stage (Barnett 1953). Much theory and research on complex organizations is concerned with isolated aspects of this process by which innovations flow through organization systems—such as the relation of research and development units to the industrial firm (Burns and Stalker 1961; Wilensky 1968); or problems encountered by public agencies attempting to implement new policy decisions (Selznick 1949; Bailey and Mosher 1968; Moynihan 1969).

Most studies of the "careers" of innovations, however, treat only the invention and the ultimate adoption stages as problematic. The "throughput" sector, comprised of organizations which filter the overflow of information and materials intended for consumers, is generally ignored.[2] Literature on the diffusion of innovations, for example, is concerned solely with the reception accorded a new product by consumers *subsequent* to its release into the marketplace by sponsoring organizations (Rogers 1962). From an organizational perspective, two questions pertaining to any innovation are logically prior to its experience in the marketplace: (1) by what criteria was it selected for sponsorship over available alternatives? and (2) might certain characteristics of its organizational sponsor, such as prestige or the size of an advertising budget, substantially aid in explaining the ultimate success or failure of the new product or idea?

In modern, industrial societies, the production and distribution of both fine art and popular culture entail relationships among a complex network of organizations which both facilitate and regulate the innovation process. Each object must be "discovered," sponsored, and brought to public attention by entrepreneurial organizations or nonprofit agencies before the originating artist or writer can be linked successfully to the intended audience. Decisions taken in organizations whose actions can block or facilitate communication, therefore, may wield great influence over the access of artist and audience to one another. The content of a nation's popular culture is especially subject to economic constraints due to the larger scale of capital investment required in this area to link creators and consumers effectively.[3]

2. A notable exception is Alfred Chandler's classic study of corporate innovation (1962). In the areas of fine art and popular culture, this problem has been noted by Albrecht (1968), Barnett (1959), Baumol and Bowen (1968), and Gans (1966).
3. As Lane (1970*a*, p. 240) puts it, a central sociological question is the extent to which sponsoring organizations "manage and control values and knowledge rather than simply purvey." An organizational approach to the study of American mass

This paper will outline the structure and operation of entrepreneurial organizations engaged in the production and mass distribution of three types of "cultural" items: books, recordings, and motion pictures. Entrepreneurial organizations in cultural industries confront a set of problems especially interesting to students of interorganizational relations, mainly: goal dissensus, boundary-spanning role occupants with nonorganizational norms, legal and value constraints against vertical integration, and, hence, dependence on autonomous agencies (especially mass-media gatekeepers) for linking the organization to its customers. In response to environmental uncertainties, mainly a high-risk element and changing patterns of distribution, they have evolved a rich assortment of adaptive "coping" strategies and, thus, offer a promising arena in which to develop and apply tentative propositions derived from studies of other types of organizations and advanced in the field of organization studies. Our focal organizations (Evan 1963) are the commercial publishing house, the movie studio, and the record company. My description of their operation is based on information and impressions gathered from (1) an extensive sampling of trade papers directed at members of these industries, primarily: *Publishers' Weekly, Billboard,* and *Variety;* (2) 53 open-ended interviews with individuals at all levels of the publishing, recording, and broadcasting industries,[4] and (3) a thorough review of available secondary sources.

Definitions and Conceptual Framework

Cultural products may be defined tentatively as "nonmaterial" goods directed at a public of consumers, for whom they generally serve an esthetic or expressive, rather than a clearly utilitarian function. Insofar as one of its goals is to create and satisfy consumer demand for new fads and fashions, every consumer industry is engaged to some extent in the production of cultural goods, and any consumer good can thus be placed along

---

culture suggests that changes in content can be caused by shrinking markets only partially due to shifts in consumer taste preferences. Industry observers see increased public access since 1955 to "art" films (Houston 1963; Guback 1969) and popular-song lyrics with protest themes (Carey 1969) as reflecting the near-total loss of a once-dependable audience, whose unchanged predispositions now receive confirmation from television fare. The advent of television forced movie exhibitors and radio-station managers to relinquish the majority audience and alter program content to attract minority subcultures *previously neglected for economic reasons.* The production of "rock 'n' roll" records and films by independent producers was stimulated by unprecedented opportunity for radio air play and exhibition (Hirsch 1971). While the altered content represents the best market share now available to many producers and distributors, it is directed at the teenage and intellectual markets, respectively, and not to former patrons.

4. Large firms and record-industry personnel are disproportionately represented.

the implied continuum between cultural and utilitarian products. The two poles, however, should be intuitively distinct. Movies, plays, books, art prints, phonograph records, and pro football games are predominantly cultural products; each is nonmaterial in the sense that it embodies a live, one-of-a-kind performance and/or contains a unique set of ideas. Foods and detergents, on the other hand, serve more obvious utilitarian needs. The term "cultural organization" refers here only to *profit-seeking firms producing cultural products for national distribution.* Noncommercial or strictly local organizations, such as university presses and athletic teams, respectively, are thus excluded from consideration. A fundamental difference between entrepreneurial organizations and nonprofit agencies is summarized by Toffler (1965, pp. 181–82):

> In the non-profit sector the end-product is most frequently a live performance—a concert, a recital, a play. If for purposes of economic analysis we consider a live performance to be a commodity, we are immediately struck by the fact that, unlike most commodities offered for sale in our society, this commodity is not standardized. It is not machine made. It is a handicrafted item. . . . Contrast the output of the non-profit performing arts with that of the record manufacturer. He, too, sells what appears to be a performance. But it is not. It is a replica of a performance, a mass-produced embodiment of a performance. . . . The book publisher, in effect, does the same. The original manuscript of the poem or novel represents the author's work of art, the individual, the prototype. The book in which it is subsequently embodied is a [manufactured] replica of the original. Its form of production is fully in keeping with the level of technology in the surrounding society.

Our frame of reference is the cultural industry system, comprised of all organizations engaged in the process of filtering new products and ideas as they flow from "creative" personnel in the technical subsystem to the managerial, institutional, and societal levels of organization (Parsons 1960). Each industry system is seen as a single, concrete, and stable network of identifiable and interacting components. The concept of organization levels, proposed initially to analyze transactions within the boundaries of a single, large-scale organization, is easily applied to the analysis of interorganizational systems. Artist and mass audience are linked by an ordered sequence of events: before it can elicit any audience response, an art object first must succeed in (*a*) competition against others for selection and promotion by an entrepreneurial organization, and then in (*b*) receiving mass-media coverage in such forms as book reviews, radio-station air play, and film criticism. It must be ordered by retail outlets for display or exhibition to consumers and, ideally, its author or performer will appear on television talk shows [5] and be written up as an interesting news

5. An excellent, first-person account of this experience is provided by Cowan (1970).

story. Drawing on a functionalist model of organizational control and facilitation of innovations proposed by Boskoff (1964), we view the mass media in their gatekeeping role as a primary "institutional regulator of innovation."

A number of concepts and assumptions implicit in this paper are taken from the developing field of interorganizational relations and elaborated on more fully by Thompson (1967).[6] Studies in this emerging tradition typically view all phenomena from the standpoint of the organization under analysis. It seldom inquires into the functions performed by the organization for the social system but asks rather, as a temporary partisan, how the goals of the organization may be constrained by society. The organization is assumed to act under norms of rationality, and the subject of analysis becomes its forms of adaptation of constraints imposed by its technology and "task environment." The term "organization-set" has been proposed by Evan (1963) as analogous to the role-set concept developed by Merton (1957) for analyzing role relationships:

> Instead of taking a particular status as the unit of analysis, as Merton does in his role-set analysis. I take . . . an organization, or a class of organizations, and trace its interactions with the network of organizations in its environment, i.e., with elements of its organization-set. As a partial social system, a focal organization depends on input organizations for various types of resources: personnel, matériel, capital, legality, and legitimacy. . . . The focal organization in turn produces a product or a service for a market, an audience, a client system, etc. [Evan, 1963, pp. 177–79]

After examining transactions between the focal organization and elements of its task environment,[7] we will describe three adaptive strategies developed by cultural organizations to minimize uncertainty. Finally, variations within each industry will be reviewed.

Input and Output Organization-Sets

The publishing house, movie studio, and record company each invests entrepreneurial capital in the creations and services of affiliated organizations and individuals at its input (product selection) and output (marketing) boundaries. Each effects volume sales by linking individual creators and producer organizations with receptive consumers and mass-media

6. For a more far-ranging consideration of the genesis and life cycle of fads and fashions from the standpoint of classic sociological theories, see Meyersohn and Katz (1957), Blumer (1968), and Denzin (1970).
7. A focal organization's task environment consists of other organizations located on its input and output boundaries.

gatekeepers. New material is sought constantly because of the rapid turnover of books, films, and recordings.

Cultural organizations constitute the managerial subsystems of the industry systems in which they must operate. From a universe of innovations proposed by "artists" in the "creative" (technical) subsystem, they select ("discover") a sample of cultural products for organizational sponsorship and promotion. A distinctive feature of cultural industry systems at the present time is the organizational segregation of functional units and subsystems. In the production sector, the technical and managerial levels of organization are linked by boundary-spanning talent scouts—for example, acquisitions editors, record "producers," and film directors—located on the input boundary of the focal organization.

To this point, cultural industries resemble the construction industry and other organization systems characterized by what Stinchcombe (1959) calls "craft administration of production." The location of professionals in the technical subsystem, and administrators in the managerial one, indicates that production may be organized along craft rather than bureaucratic lines (Stinchcombe 1959). In the cultural industry system, lower-level personnel (artists and talent scouts) are accorded professional status and seldom are associated with any one focal organization for long time periods. Although company executives may tamper with the final product of their collaborations, contracted artists and talent scouts are *delegated* the responsibility of producing marketable creations, with little or no interference from the front office beyond the setting of budgetary limits (Peterson and Berger 1971). Due to widespread uncertainty over the precise ingredients of a best-seller formula, administrators are forced to trust the professional judgment of their employees. Close supervision in the production sector is impeded by ignorance of relations between cause and effect.[8] A highly placed spokesman for the recording industry (Brief 1964, pp. 4–5) has stated the problem as follows:

> We have made records that appeared to have all the necessary ingredients —artist, song, arrangements, promotion, etc.—to guarantee they wind up as best sellers. . . . Yet they fell flat on their faces. On the other hand we have produced records for which only a modest success was anticipated that became runaway best sellers. . . . There are a large number of companies in our industry employing a large number of talented performers and creative producers who combine their talents, their ingenuity and their creativity to produce a record that each is sure will captivate the American public. The fact that only a small proportion of the output achieves

8. "Production" here refers to the performances or manuscripts created by artists and talent scouts for later replication in the form of books, film-negative prints, and phonograph records. The physical manufacture of these goods is sufficiently amenable to control as to be nearly irrelevant to our discussion.

hit status is not only true of our industry. . . . There are no formulas for producing a hit record . . . just as there are no pat answers for producing hit plays, or sell-out movies or best-selling books.

Stinchcombe's (1959, 1968) association of craft administration with a minimization of fixed overhead costs is supported in the case of cultural organizations. Here, we find, for example, artists (i.e., authors, singers, actors) contracted on a *royalty* basis and offered no tenure beyond the expiration of the contract. Remuneration (less advance payment on royalties) is contingent on the number of books, records, or theater tickets sold *after* the artist's product is released into the marketplace.[9] In addition, movie-production companies minimize overhead by hiring on a per-picture basis and renting sets and costumes as needed (Stinchcombe 1968), and publishers and record companies frequently subcontract out standardized printing and record-pressing jobs.

The organization of cultural industries' technical subsystems along craft lines is a function of (*a*) demand uncertainty and (*b*) a "cheap" technology. Demand uncertainty is caused by: shifts in consumer taste preferences and patronage (Gans 1964; Meyersohn and Katz 1957); legal and normative constraints on vertical integration (Conant 1960; Brockway 1967); and widespread variability in the criteria employed by mass-media gatekeepers in selecting cultural items to be awarded coverage (Hirsch 1969). A cheap technology enables numerous cultural organizations to compete in producing a surplus of books, records, and low-budget films on relatively small capital investments. The cost of producing and manufacturing a new long-play record or hard-cover book for the general public is usually less than $25,000 (Brief 1964; Frase 1968). Once sales pass the break-even point (about 7,000 copies for books and 12,000 for records, *very roughly*), the new product begins to show a profit.[10] On reaching sales of 20,000 a new book is eligible for best-seller status: "hit records" frequently sell over several hundred thousand copies each. Mass media exposure and volume sales of a single item generally cover earlier losses and yield additional returns. Sponsoring organizations tend to judge the success of each new book or record on the basis of its performance

---

9. Royalty payments in the motion-picture industry are an alternative to costly, long-term contracts with established movie stars and permit producers to partially defer expenditures until the picture is in exhibition. Contracts specifying royalties (in addition to negotiated fees) are limited to well-known actors with proven "track records." Author-publisher contracts are more uniform, specifying royalties of at least 10% to all authors. Record companies seldom provide royalties higher than 3%–5% of sales. Since popular records are frequently purchased in greater quantities than best-selling books, however, musicians' royalties may equal or exceed those of authors.

10. The cost of producing and manufacturing (45 rpm) record "singles" averages only $2,500 (Brief 1964).

in the marketplace during the first six weeks of its release. Movies require a far more substantial investment but follow a similar pattern.[11]

These sources of variance best account for the craft administration of production at the input boundary of the cultural organization. It is interesting to note that in an earlier, more stable environment, that is, less heterogeneous markets and fewer constraints on vertical integration, the production of both films and popular records was administered more bureaucratically: lower-level personnel were delegated less responsibility, overhead costs were less often minimized, and the status of artists resembled more closely the salaried employee's than the free-lance professional's (Coser 1965; Brown 1968; Powdermaker 1950; Rosten 1941; Hughes 1959; Montagu 1964; Peterson and Berger 1971).

At their output boundaries, cultural organizations confront high levels of uncertainty concerning the commercial prospects of goods shipped out to national networks of promoters and distributors. Stratification within each industry is based partly on each firm's ability to control the distribution of marginally differentiated products. Competitive advantage lies with firms best able to link available input to reliable and established distribution channels. In the book industry, distribution "for the great majority of titles is limited, ineffective, and costly. In part this weakness in distribution is a direct consequence of the strength of the industry in issuing materials. . . . If it were harder to get a book published, it would be easier to get it distributed" (Lacy 1963, pp. 53–54).[12]

The mass distribution of cultural items requires more *bureaucratic* organizational arrangements than the administration of production, for example, a higher proportion of salaried clerks to process information, greater continuity of personnel and ease of supervision, less delegation of responsibility, and higher fixed overhead (Stinchcombe 1959). Whereas the building contractor produces custom goods to meet the specifications of a clearly defined client-set, cultural organizations release a wide variety of items which must be publicized and made attractive to thousands of

11. Low-budget feature films range in cost from $100,000 to $2 million each. The break-even point for movies is believed to be $4 in box-office receipts for each dollar invested in the film. A recent film, *Easy Rider,* produced on a low budget of $360,000, is reported to have earned $50 million in box-office receipts and netted its producers approximately $10 million. "Rather than make one expensive film, with all the correct box-office insurance in the way of story and star-casting, and see the whole thing go down the drain," many producers have tried putting "the same kind of money into three or four cheap films by young directors, gambling that at least one of them would prove [to be a smash]" (Houston 1963, p. 101). Houston's description of French filmmaking has since come to characterize its American counterpart.

12. Prior to implementation of a (1948) judgment by the U.S. Supreme Court, independent and foreign film-production companies without powerful distribution arms were blocked most effectively from access to consumers through movie exhibition. The *Paramount Decrees* divested movie-theater-chain ownership from nine major film producers and distributors (Conant 1960).

consumers in order to succeed. Larger organizations generally maintain their own sales forces, which may contract with smaller firms to distribute their output as well as the parent company's.

The more highly bureaucratized distribution sector of cultural industries is characterized by more economic concentration than the craft-administered production sector, where lower costs pose fewer barriers to entry. Although heavy expenditures required for product promotion and marketing may be reduced by contracting with independent sales organizations on a commission basis, this practice is engaged in primarily by smaller, weaker, and poorly capitalized firms. As one publishing company executive explains:

> If a company does not have a big sales force, it's far more difficult for them to have a best seller. But unless a firm does $7,500,000 worth of trade book business a year, they can't afford to maintain an adequate sales force. Many publishing houses, consequently, do not have any sales force at all. They rely on middlemen—jobbers—to get their books into bookstores. But jobbers, of course, don't attend sales conferences. They handle so many books for so many publishers that they can't be expected to "push" certain books from a certain house. [Mann 1967, p. 14]

Contracting with autonomous sales organizations places the entrepreneurial firm in a position of dependence on outsiders, with the attendant risk of having cultural products regarded highly by the sponsoring organization assigned a low priority by its distributor. In the absence of media coverage and/or advertising by the sponsoring organization, retail outlets generally fail to stock new books or records.

A functional equivalent of direct advertising for cultural organizations is provided by the selective coverage afforded new styles and titles in books, recordings, and movies by the mass media. Cultural products provide "copy" and "programming" for newspapers, magazines, radio stations, and television programs; in exchange, they receive "free" publicity. The presence or absence of coverage, rather than its favorable or unfavorable interpretation, is the important variable here. Public awareness of the existence and availability of a new cultural product often is contingent on feature stories in newspapers and national magazines, review columns, and broadcast talk shows, and, for recordings, radio-station air play. While the total number of products to be awarded media coverage may be predicted in the aggregate, the estimation of *which ones* will be selected from the potential universe is problematic.

The organizational segregation of the producers of cultural items from their disseminators places definite restrictions on the forms of power which cultural organizations may exercise over mass-media gatekeepers to effect the selection of particular items for coverage. Widely shared social norms mandate the independence of book-review editors, radio-station personnel, film critics, and other arbiters of coverage from the special needs and commercial interests of cultural organizations.[13] Thus, autonomous gate-keepers present the producer organization with the "control" problem of favorably influencing the probability that a given new release will be selected for exposure to consumers.

For publishing houses and record firms, especially, it would be uneconomical to engage in direct, large-scale advertising campaigns to bring more than a few releases to public attention.[14]

> The fact that each one of the thousands of titles every year must be separately advertised imposes almost insuperable obstacles in the way of effective national advertising. It is as though General Motors for each tenth Chevrolet had to change the name, design, and characteristics of the car and launch a new national advertising campaign to sell the next ten cars. . . . The advertising problem . . . is thus wholly different from that of the advertiser of a single brand that remains on sale indefinitely. [Lacy 1963, pp. 54–55]

> The publisher's advertising problem is greatly aggravated by what we have all agreed is true—too many books are published, most of them doomed in advance to a short and inglorious life. . . . Many a novel is dead the day it is published, many others survive a month or two or three. The sales of such books are always small, and what little advertising they get may be rendered doubly useless by the fact that the bookseller tends to return to the publisher his stock of slow-moving books before they have had time to be exposed to very many potential customers. . . . Well then, what does make a book sell? Charles Darwin gave the right answer to Samuel Butler when he was asked this question: "Getting talked about is what makes a book sell." [Knopf 1964, p. 17]

> Record companies are dependent on radio . . . to introduce new artists as well as to introduce new records of all artists and to get them exposed to the public. . . . [We] cannot expose their performances because it's just on grooves and the public will not know what they sound like. (Q.) "Would it be fair to say that radio accounts for 75, or 90 percent of the promotion of new releases?" (A.) I think your figures are probably accurate, yes. [Davis 1967, p. 5]

For book publishers, record companies, and, to a lesser extent, movie studios, then, the crucial target audience for promotional campaigns consists of autonomous gatekeepers, or "surrogate consumers" such as disk

13. Public reaction to the "payola" scandals in the late 1950s demonstrated a widespread belief that the disseminators of mass culture should be independent of its producers. Disk jockeys, book reviewers, and film critics are expected to remain free from the influence or manipulations of record companies, book publishers, and movie studios, respectively. This feeling is shared generally by members of each industry system as well as embodied in our legal system.
14. New movies, faced with fewer competitors and representing far greater investment per capita, are advertised more heavily directly.

jockeys, film critics, and book reviewers, employed by mass-media organizations to serve as fashion experts and opinion leaders for their respective constituencies.

The mass media constitute the institutional subsystem of the cultural industry system. *The diffusion of particular fads and fashions is either blocked or facilitated at this strategic checkpoint.* Cultural innovations are seen as originating in the technical subsystem. A sample selected for sponsorship by cultural organizations in the managerial subsystem is introduced into the marketplace. This output is filtered by mass-media gatekeepers serving as "institutional regulators of innovation" (Boskoff 1964). Organizations in the managerial subsystem are highly responsive to feedback from institutional regulators: styles afforded coverage are imitated and reproduced on a large scale until the fad has "run its course" (Boskoff 1964; Meyersohn and Katz 1957).[15]

We see the consumer's role in this process as essentially one of rank ordering cultural styles and items "preselected" for consideration by role occupants in the managerial and institutional subsystems. Feedback from consumers, in the form of sales figures and box-office receipts, cues producers and disseminators of cultural innovations as to which experiments may be imitated profitably and which should probably be dropped.[16] This process is analogous to the preselection of electoral candidates by political parties, followed by voter feedback at the ballot box. The orderly sequence of events and the possibility of only two outcomes at each checkpoint resemble a Markov process.

This model assumes a surplus of available "raw material" at the outset (e.g., writers, singers, politicians) and pinpoints a number of strategic checkpoints at which the oversupply is filtered out. It is "value added" in the sense that no product can enter the societal subsystem (e.g., retail outlets) until it has been processed favorably through each of the preceding levels of organization, respectively.[17]

Organizational Response to Task-Environment Uncertainties

Our analysis suggests that organizations at the managerial level of cultural industry systems are confronted by (1) constraints on output dis-

15. Boskoff (1964, p. 224) sees the sources of innovations within any social system as the "technical and/or managerial levels of organization, or external sources. . . . By its very nature, the institutional level is uncongenial to innovative roles for itself." Changes occur at an increasing rate when "the institutional level is ineffective in controlling the cumulation of variations. . . . This may be called change by institutional default." Changes in pop-culture content consistently follow this pattern.
16. Two interesting formal models of aspects of this process are presented by McPhee (1963).
17. For a more detailed discussion of the *role-set* engaged in the processing of fads and fashions, with particular application to "hit" records, see Hirsch (1969).

tribution imposed by mass-media gatekeepers, and (2) contingencies in recruiting creative "raw materials" for organizational sponsorship. To minimize dependence on these elements of their task environments, publishing houses, record companies, and movie studios have developed three proactive strategies: (1) the allocation of numerous personnel to boundary-spanning roles; (2) overproduction and differential promotion of new items; and (3) cooptation of mass-media gatekeepers.

Proliferation of Contact Men

Entrepreneurial organizations in cultural industries require competent intelligence agents and representatives to actively monitor developments at their input and output boundaries. Inability to locate and successfully market new cultural items leads to organizational failure: new manuscripts must be located, new singers recorded, and new movies produced. Boundary-spanning units have therefore been established, and a large proportion of personnel allocated to serve as "contact men" (Wilensky 1956), with titles such as talent scout, promoter, press coordinator, and vice-president in charge of public relations. The centrality of information on boundary developments to managers and executives in cultural organizations is suggested in these industries' trade papers: coverage of artist relations and selections by mass-media gatekeepers far exceeds that of matters managed more easily in a standardized manner, such as inflation in warehousing, shipping, and physical production costs.

Contact men linking the cultural organization to the artist community contract for creative raw material on behalf of the organization and supervise its production. Much of their work is performed in the field. In publishing, for example:

"You have to get out to lunch to find out what's going on out there—and what's going on out there is where an editor's books come from," says James Silberman, editor-in-chief of Random House. "Over the years, I've watched people in the book business stop having lunch, and they stop getting books."

There are, in general, three kinds of publishing lunches. The first, and most common, takes place between editor and agent: its purpose is to generate book ideas for the agent's clients; also, it provides an opportunity for the agent to grow to like the editor enough to send him completed manuscripts. The second kind is set up by publicists with whomever they want to push their books: television people, critics, book-review editors. . . .

The third kind takes place between authors and editors, and it falls into three phases: the precontract phase, where the editor woos the author with good food and book ideas; the postcontract phase, where the author is given assistance on his manuscript and the impetus to go on; and the postpublication phase, where the editor explains to the author why the publishing house took so few advertisements for his book. [Ephron 1969, p. 8]

Professional agents on the input boundary must be allowed a great deal of discretion in their activities on behalf of the cultural organization. Successful editors, record "producers," and film directors and producers thus pose control problems for the focal organization. In fields characterized by uncertainty over cause/effect relations, their talent has been "validated" by the successful marketplace performance of "their discoveries"—providing high visibility and opportunities for mobility outside a single firm. Their value to the cultural organization as recruiters and intelligence agents is indicated by high salaries, commissions, and prestige within the industry system.

Cultural organizations deploy additional contact men at their output boundaries, linking the organization to (1) retail outlets and (2) surrogate consumers in mass-media organizations. The tasks of promoting and distributing new cultural items are analytically distinct, although boundary units combining both functions may be established. Transactions between retailers and boundary personnel at the wholesale level are easily programmed and supervised. In terms of Thompson's (1962) typology of output transactions, the retailer's "degree of nonmember discretion" is limited to a small number of fixed options concerning such matters as discount schedules and return privileges.[18] In contrast, where organizations are dependent on "surrogate consumers" for coverage of new products, the latter enjoy a high degree of discretion: tactics employed by contact men at this boundary entail more "personal influence"; close supervision by the organization is more difficult and may be politically inexpedient. Further development of Thompson's typology would facilitate tracing the flow of innovations through organization systems by extending the analysis of transactions "at the end of the line"—that is, between salesmen and consumers or bureaucrats and clients—to encompass boundary transactions at all levels of organization through which new products are processed.

A high ratio of promotional personnel to surrogate consumers appears to be a structural feature of any industry system in which: (*a*) goods are marginally differentiated; (*b*) producers' access to consumer markets is regulated by independent gatekeepers; and (*c*) large-scale, *direct* advertising campaigns are uneconomical or prohibited by law. Cultural products

---

18. Sponsoring organizations without access to established channels of distribution, however, experience great difficulty in obtaining orders for their products from retail outlets and consumers. Thompson's (1962) typology of interaction between organization members and nonmembers consists of two dimensions: Degree of nonmember discretion, and specificity of organizational control over members in output roles. Output roles are defined as those which arrange for the distribution of an organization's ultimate product (or service) to other agents in society.

are advertised *indirectly* to independent gatekeepers within the industry system in order to reduce demand uncertainty over which products will be selected for exposure to consumers. Where independent gatekeepers neither filter information nor mediate between producer and consumer, the importance of contact men at the organization's output boundary is correspondingly diminished. In industry systems where products are advertised more directly to consumers, the contact man is superseded by full-page advertisements and sponsored commercials, purchased outright by the producer organization and directed at the lay consumer.

Overproduction and Differential Promotion of Cultural Items

Differential promotion of new items, in conjunction with overproduction, is a second proactive strategy employed by cultural organizations to overcome dependence on mass-media gatekeepers. Overproduction is a rational organizational response in an environment of low capital investments and demand uncertainty. "Fortunately, from a cultural point of view if not from the publisher's, the market is full of uncertainties. . . . A wise publisher will hedge his bets" (Bailey 1970, pp. 144, 170).

Under these conditions it apparently is more efficient to produce many "failures" for each success than to sponsor fewer items and pretest each on a massive scale to increase media coverage and consumer sales. The number of books, records, and low-budget films released annually far exceeds coverage capacity and consumer demand for these products.[19] The publisher's "books cannibalize one another. And even if he hasn't deliberately lowered his editorial standards (and he almost certainly has) he is still publishing more books than he can possibly do justice to" (Knopf 1964, p. 18). While over 15,000 new titles are issued annually, the probability of any one appearing in a given bookstore is only 10% (Lacy 1963). Similarly, fewer than 20% of over 6,000 (45 rpm) "singles" appear in retail record outlets (Shemel and Krasilovsky 1964). Movie theaters exhibit a larger proportion of approximately 400 feature films released annually, fewer than half of which, however, are believed to recoup the initial investment. The production of a surplus is facilitated further by contracts negotiated with artists on a royalty basis and other cost-minimizing features of the craft administration of production.

Cultural organizations ideally maximize profits by mobilizing promotional resources in support of volume sales for a small number of items. These resources are not divided equally among each firm's new releases.

---

19. This is not to say that "uneconomical" selections may not appeal to a fair number of consumers. Each industry defines consumer demand according to its own costs and convenience. Thus, a network television program with only 14 million viewers fails for inadequate consumer demand.

Only a small proportion of all new books and records "sponsored" by cultural organizations is selected by company policy makers for large-scale promotion within the industry system. In the record industry:

> The strategy of massive promotion is employed by policymakers is an attempt to influence the coverage of their product by media over which they exert little control. They must rely on independently owned trade papers to bring new records to the attention of radio programmers and disk jockeys, and upon radio airplay and journalists to reach the consumer market. For this reason, selected artists are sent to visit key radio stations, and parties are arranged in cities throughout the country to bring together the artist and this advanced audience. It seems likely that if . . . policymakers could better predict exposure for particular releases, then fewer would be recorded. . . . Records are released (1) with no advance publicity, (2) with minimal fanfare, or (3) only after a large-scale advance promotional campaign. The extent of a record's promotion informs the policymakers' immediate audience of regional promoters and Top 40 programmers of their expectations for, and evaluation of their product. In this way the company rank orders its own material. The differential promotion of records serves to sensitize Top 40 programmers to the names of certain songs and artists. Heavily promoted records are publicized long before their release through full-page advertisements in the trade press, special mailings, and personal appearances by the recording's artists. The program director is made familiar with the record long before he receives it. It is "expected" to be a hit. In this way, though radio stations receive records gratis, anticipation and "demand" for selected releases are created. . . . The best indicator of a record's potential for becoming a hit at this stage is the amount of promotion it is allocated. [Hirsch 1969, pp. 34, 36]

Similarly, in the publishing industry:

> Publishers' advertising has several subsidiary functions to perform besides that of selling books, or even making readers. Among them are:
>
> 1. Influencing the "trade"—that is impressing book jobbers and retail booksellers with the fact that the publisher is actively backing a certain title and that it would be good business for them to stock and push it.
> 2. Influencing authors and their agents. Many an author has left one publisher for another because he felt that the first publisher was not giving his book enough advertising support.
> 3. Influencing reviewers. The implication here is not that any reputable reviewer can be "bought" by the use of his paper's advertising columns, but reviewers are apt to watch publishers' announcements (particularly those that appear in the trade papers) for information which will aid them in selecting books for review, and in deciding which ones to feature or to review at length.
> 4. Influencing the sale of book club, reprint, and other subsidiary rights. Publishers sometimes advertise solely to keep a book on the best-seller list while a projected movie sale is in prospect. Occasionally this works

469

the other way round: movie producers have been known to contribute generously to the ad budget of the initial hardcover edition so as to reap the benefit of the best-seller publicity for their film when it finally appears. [Spier 1967, pp. 155–56]

Most cultural items are allocated minimal amounts for promotion and are "expected" to fail (recall the description of postpublication author-editor luncheons cited earlier). Such long shots constitute a pool of "understudies," from which substitutes may be drawn in the event that either mass-media gatekeepers or consumers reject more heavily plugged items.[20] We see the strategy of differential promotion as an attempt by cultural organizations to "buffer" their technical core from demand uncertainties by smoothing out output transactions (Thompson 1967).

Cooptation of "Institutional Regulators"

Mass-media gatekeepers report a wide variety of mechanisms developed by cultural organizations to influence and manipulate their coverage decisions. These range from "indications" by the sponsoring organization of high expectations for particular new "discoveries" (e.g., full-page advertisements in the trade press, parties arranged to introduce the artist to recognized opinion leaders) to personal requests and continuous barrages of indirect advertising, encouraging and cajoling the gatekeeper to "cover," endorse, and otherwise contribute toward the fulfillment of the organization's prophesy of great success for its new product.

The goals of cultural and mass-media organizations come into conflict over two issues. First, public opinion, professional ethics, and, to a lesser extent, job security, all require that institutional gatekeepers maintain independent standards of judgment and quality rather than endorse only those items which cultural organizations elect to promote. Second, the primary goal of commercial mass-media organizations is to maximize revenue by "delivering" audiences for sponsored messages rather than to serve as promotional vehicles for particular cultural items. His records, for example, are featured by commercial radio stations primarily to sell advertising:

Q. Do you play this music because it is the most popular?
A. Exactly for that reason. . . . We use the entertainment part of our programming, which is music, essentially, to attract the largest possible audience, so that what else we have to say . . . in terms of advertising message . . . [is] exposed to the largest number of people possible— and the way to get the largest number to tune in is to play the kind of music they like . . . so that you have a mass audience at the other end.

20. Two recent successful long shots are the best-selling reissue of turn-of-the-century Sears Roebuck catalogs and the film *Endless Summer*. For a discussion of criteria employed to choose pop records for differential promotion, see Hirsch 1969.

Q. If, let's say that by some freak of nature, a year from now the most popular music was chamber music, would you be playing that?

A. Absolutely . . . , and the year after that, if it's Chinese madrigals, we'll be playing them. [Strauss 1966, p. 3] [21]

Goal conflict and value dissensus are reflected in frequent disputes among cultural organizations, mass-media gatekeepers, and public representatives concerning the legitimacy (or legality) of promoters' attempts to acquire power over the decision autonomy of surrogate consumers.

Cultural organizations strive to control gatekeepers decision autonomy to the extent that coverage for new items is (*a*) crucial for building consumer demand, and (*b*) problematic. Promotional campaigns aimed at coopting institutional gatekeepers are most likely to require proportionately large budgets and illegitimate tactics when consumers' awareness of the product hinges almost exclusively on coverage by these personnel. As noted earlier, cultural organizations are less likely to deploy boundary agents or sanction high-pressure tactics for items whose sale is less contingent on gatekeepers' actions.

Variability within Cultural Industries

Up to this point, we have tended to minimize variability among cultural organizations, cultural products, and the markets at which they are directed. Our generalizations apply mainly to the most *speculative* and entrepreneurial segments of the publishing, recording, and motion picture industries, that is, adult trade books, popular records, and low-budget movies. [22] Within each of these categories, organizations subscribe, in varying degrees, to normative as well as to the more economic goals we have assumed thus far. Certain publishing houses, record companies, and movie producers command high prestige within each industry system for financing cultural products of high quality but of doubtful commercial value. To the extent they do *not* conform to economic norms of rationality, these organizations should be considered separately from the more dominant pattern of operations described above. [23]

21. Similarly, the recent demise of the *Saturday Evening Post* was precipitated by an inability to attract sufficient advertising revenue: too many of its 6 million subscribers lived in rural areas and fell into low-income categories (Friedrich 1970).
22. Adult trade books account for less than 10% of all sales in the book-publishing industry, excluding book-club sales (Bowker 1969). Recordings of popular music (subsuming folk and country and western categories) provide the majority of sales in the record industry (Brief 1964). Figures on the contribution of low-budget films to movie industry sales were not obtained. Low-budget films are more speculative than high-budget "blockbusters" on a *per picture* basis only, where their probability of box-office success as well as their costs appear to be lower.
23. Lane (1970*b*) presents a valuable portrait of one such publishing house; Miller (1949) provides an excellent study of cross-pressures within the book industry.

Whether our generalizations might also characterize less-uncertain industry segments, such as educational textbook and children's-book publishing divisions, or classical record production is also subject to question. In each of these instances, cost factors and/or degree of demand uncertainty may be quite different, which, in turn, would affect the structure and operation of the producer organizations. Textbook publishers, for example, face a more predictable market than do publishers (or divisions) specializing in trade books: more capital investment is required, and larger sales forces must be utilized for school-to-school canvassing (Brammer 1967). In the case of children's books, some differences might be expected in that libraries rather than retail stores account for 80% of sales (Lacy 1968).

Within the adult-trade-book category, coverage in book-review columns is more crucial to the success of literary novels than to detective stories or science-fiction books (Blum 1959). Review coverage is also problematic: "Even *The New York Times,* which reviews many more books than any other journal addressed to the general public, covers only about 20 percent of the annual output. Many books of major importance in specialized fields go entirely unnoticed in such general media, and it is by no means unknown for even National Book Award winners to go unreviewed in the major national journals" (Lacy 1963, p. 55). We would therefore expect publishers' agents to push novels selected for national promotion more heavily than either detective stories or science-fiction works. Serious novels should be promoted more differentially than others.

Similarly, coverage in the form of radio-station air play is far more crucial in building consumer demand for recordings of popular music than for classical selections. Control over the selection of new "pop" releases by radio-station programmers and disk jockeys is highly problematic. Record companies are dependent on radio air play as the *only* effective vehicle of exposure for new pop records. In this setting—where access to consumers hinges almost exclusively on coverage decisions by autonomous gatekeepers—institutionalized side payments ("payola") emerged as a central tactic in the overall strategy of cooptation employed by producer organizations to assure desired coverage.

Radio air play for classical records is less crucial for building consumer demand; the probability of obtaining coverage for classical releases is also easier to estimate. Whereas producers and consumers of pop records are often unsure about a song's likely sales appeal or musical worth, criteria of both musical merit and consumer demand are comparatively clear in the classical field. Record companies, therefore, allocate proportionately fewer promotional resources to assure coverage of classical releases by mass-media gatekeepers, and record-company agents promoting classical releases employ more legitimate tactics to influence coverage decisions than promoters of pop records employ to coopt the decision autonomy of institutional regulators.

Thompson (1967, p. 36) has proposed that "when support capacity is concentrated but demand dispersed, the weaker organization will attempt to handle its dependence through coopting." In our analysis, cultural organizations represent a class of weaker organizations, dependent on support capacity concentrated in mass-media organizations; demand is dispersed among retail outlets and consumers. While all cultural organizations attempt to coopt autonomous consumer surrogates, the intensity of the tactics employed tends to vary with degree of dependence. Thus, cultural organizations most dependent on mass-media gatekeepers (i.e., companies producing pop records) resorted to the most costly and illegitimate tactics; the institution of payola may be seen as an indication of their weaker power position.

Conclusion

This paper has outlined the structure of entrepreneurial organizations engaged in the production and distribution of cultural items and has examined three adaptive strategies employed to minimize dependence on elements of their task environments: the deployment of contact men to organizational boundaries, overproduction and differential promotion of new items, and the cooptation of mass-media gatekeepers. It is suggested that in order for new products or ideas to reach a public of consumers, they first must be processed favorably through a system of organizations whose units filter out large numbers of candidates before they arrive at the consumption stage. The concept of an industry system is proposed as a useful frame of reference in which to (1) trace the flow of new products and ideas as they are filtered at each level or organization, and (2) examine relations among organizations.

References

ALBRECHT, MILTON C. 1968. "Art as an Institution." *American Sociological Review* 33 (June): 383–96.

BAILEY, HERBERT S. 1970. *The Art and Science of Book Publishing.* New York: Harper & Row.

BAILEY, STEPHEN K., and EDITH K. MOSHER. 1968. *ESEA: The Office of Education Administers a Law.* Syracuse, N.Y.: Syracuse University Press.

BARNETT, H. G. 1958. *Innovation: The Basis of Cultural Change.* New York: McGraw-Hill.

BARNETT, JAMES H. 1959. "The Sociology of Art." In *Sociology Today,* edited by Robert K. Merton, Leonard Broom, and Leonard S. Cottrell, Jr. New York: Basic.

BAUMOL, WILLIAM J., and WILLIAM G. BOWEN. 1968. *Performing Arts: The Economic Dilemma.* Cambridge, Mass.: M.I.T. Press.

BLUM, ELEANOR. 1959. "Paperback Book Publishing: A Survey of Content." *Journalism Quarterly* 36 (Fall): 447–54.

BLUMER, HERBERT. 1968. "Fashion." In *International Encyclopedia of the Social Sciences.* 2d ed. New York: Macmillan.

———. 1969. "Fashion: From Class Differentiation to Collective Selection." *Sociological Quarterly* 10 (Summer): 275–91.

BOSKOFF, ALVIN. 1964. "Functional Analysis as a Source of a Theoretical Repertory and Research Tasks in the Study of Social Change." In *Explorations in Social Change,* edited by George K. Zollschan and Walter Hirsch. Boston: Houghton Mifflin.

BOWKER, R. R., Co. 1969. *The Bowker Annual of Library and Book Trade Information.* New York: R. R. Bowker Co.

BRAMMER, MAUCK. 1967. "Textbook Publishing." In *What Happens in Book Publishing,* edited by Chandler B. Grannis. 2d ed. New York: Columbia University Press.

BRIEF, HENRY. 1964. *Radio and Records: A Presentation by the Record Industry Association of America at the 1964 Regional Meetings of the National Association of Broadcasters.* New York: Record Industry Association of America.

BROCKWAY, GEORGE P. 1967. "Business Management and Accounting." In *What Happens in Book Publishing,* edited by Chandler B. Grannis. 2d ed. New York: Columbia University Press.

BROWN, ROGER L. 1968. "The Creative Process in the Popular Arts." *International Social Science Journal* 20 (4): 613–24.

BURNS, TOM, and G. M. STALKER. 1961. *The Management of Innovation.* London: Tavistock.

CAREY, JAMES T. 1969. "Changing Courtship Patterns in the Popular Song." *American Journal of Sociology* 74 (May): 720–31.

CHANDLER, ALFRED D., JR. 1962. *Strategy and Structure: Chapters in the History of the American Industrial Enterprise.* Cambridge, Mass.: M.I.T. Press.

CONANT, MICHAEL. 1960. *Antitrust in the Motion Picture Industry.* Berkeley: University of California Press.

COSER, LEWIS A. 1965. *Men of Ideas.* New York: Free Press.

COWAN, PAUL. 1970. "Electronic Vaudeville Tour: Miking of an Un-American." *Village Voice,* April 16, 1970, p. 5.

DAVIS, CLIVE. 1967. "The Truth About Radio: A WNEW Inquiry." Transcript of interview with general manager CBS Records. Mimeographed. New York: WNEW.

DENZIN, NORMAN K. 1970. "Problems in Analyzing Elements of Mass Culture: Notes on the Popular Song and Other Artistic Productions." *American Journal of Sociology* 75 (May): 1035–38.

EPHRON, NORA. 1969. "Where Bookmen Meet to Eat." *New York Times Book Review,* June 22, 1969, 8–12.

EVAN, WILLIAM M. 1963. "Toward a Theory of Inter-Organizational Relations." *Management Science* 11:B217–30. Reprinted in *Approaches to Organizational Design*, edited by James D. Thompson. Pittsburgh: University of Pittsburgh Press, 1966.

FRASE, ROBERT W. 1968. "The Economics of Publishing." In *Trends in American Publishing*, edited by Kathryn L. Henderson. Champaign: Graduate School of Library Science, University of Illinois.

FRIEDRICH, OTTO. 1970. *Decline and Fall*. New York: Harper & Row.

GANS, HERBERT J. 1964. "The Rise of the Problem Film." *Social Problems* 11 (Spring): 327–36.

———. 1966. "Popular Culture in America: Social Problem in a Mass Society or Social Asset in a Pluralist Society?" In *Social Problems: A Modern Approach*, edited by Howard S. Becker. New York: Wiley.

GUBACK, THOMAS H. 1969. *The International Film Industry: Western Europe and America Since 1945*. Bloomington: Indiana University Press.

HIRSCH, PAUL M. 1969. *The Structure of the Popular Music Industry*. Ann Arbor: Survey Research Center, University of Michigan.

———. 1971. "Sociological Approaches to the Pop Music Phenomenon." *American Behavioral Scientist* 14 (January): 371–88.

HOUSTON, PENELOPE. 1963. *The Contemporary Cinema: 1945–1963*. Baltimore: Penguin.

HUGHES, RICHARD, ed. 1950. *Film: The Audience and the Filmmaker*. Vol. 1. New York: Grove.

KNOPF, ALFRED A. 1964. "Publishing Then and Now, 1912–1964." Twenty-first of the R. R. Bowker Memorial Lectures. New York: New York Public Library.

LACY, DAN. 1963. "The Economics of Publishing, or Adam Smith and Literature." In "The American Reading Public," edited by Stephen R. Graubard. *Daedalus* (Winter), pp. 42–62.

———. 1968. "Major Trends in American Book Publishing." In *Trends in American Book Publishing*, edited by Kathryn L. Henderson. Champaign: Graduate School of Library Science, University of Illinois.

LANE, MICHAEL. 1970a. "Books and Their Publishers." In *Media Sociology*, edited by Jeremy Tunstall. Urbana: University of Illinois Press.

———. 1970b. "Publishing Managers, Publishing House Organization and Role Conflict." *Sociology* 4:367–83.

McPHEE, WILLIAM. 1963. "Survival Theory in Culture," and "Natural Exposure and the Theory of Popularity." In *Formal Theories of Mass Behavior*. Glencoe, Ill.: Free Press.

MANN, PEGGY. 1967. "A Dual Portrait and Market Report: Harper and Row." *Writer's Yearbook* 37:10–17.

MERTON, ROBERT K. 1957. *Social Theory and Social Structure*. Rev. ed. Glencoe, Ill.: Free Press.

MEYERSOHN, ROLF, and ELIHU KATZ. 1957. "Notes on a Natural History of Fads." *American Journal of Sociology* 62 (May): 594–601.

MILLER, WILLIAM. 1949. *The Book Industry: A Report of the Public Library Inquiry of the Social Science Research Council*. New York: Columbia University Press.

475

MONTAGU, IVOR. 1964. *Film World*. Baltimore: Penguin.

MOYNIHAN, DANIEL P. 1969. *Maximum Feasible Misunderstanding*. New York: Free Press.

PARSONS, TALCOTT. 1960. *Structure and Process in Modern Societies*. Glencoe, Ill.: Free Press.

PETERSON, RICHARD, and DAVID BERGER. 1971. "Entrepreneurship in Organizations: Evidence from the Popular Music Industry." *Administrative Science Quarterly* 16 (March): 97–107.

POWDERMAKER, HORTENSE. 1950. *Hollywood: The Dream Factory*. New York: Grosset & Dunlap.

ROGERS, EVERETT. 1962. *Diffusion of Innovations*. Glencoe, Ill.: Free Press.

ROSTEN, LEO. 1941. *Hollywood*. New York: Harcourt Brace.

SELZNICK, PHILLIP. 1949. *TVA and the Grass Roots*. Berkeley: University of California Press.

SHEMEL, SIDNEY, and M. WILLIAM KRASILOVSKY. 1964. *This Business of Music*. New York: Billboard.

SPIER, FRANKLIN. 1967. "Book Advertising." In *What Happens in Book Publishing*, edited by Chandler B. Grannis. 2d ed. New York: Columbia University Press.

STINCHCOMBE, ARTHUR L. 1959. "Bureaucratic and Craft Administration of Production: A Comparative Study." *Administrative Science Quarterly* 4 (September): 168–87.

———. 1968. *Constructing Social Theories*. New York: Harcourt, Brace & World.

STRAUSS, R. PETER. 1966. "The Truth About Radio: A WNEW Inquiry." Transcript of interview. Mimeographed. New York: WNEW.

THOMPSON, JAMES D. 1962. "Organizations and Output Transactions." *American Journal of Sociology* 68 (November): 309–24.

———. 1967. *Organizations in Action*. New York: McGraw-Hill.

TOFFLER, ALVIN. 1965. *The Culture Consumers*. Baltimore: Penguin.

WILENSKY, HAROLD. 1956. *Intellectuals in Labor Unions*. Glencoe, Ill.: Free Press.

———. 1968. "Organizational Intelligence." In *International Encyclopedia of the Social Sciences*. 2d ed. New York: Macmillan.

Patterns of Interorganizational Relationships

Richard H. Hall
John P. Clark
Peggy C. Giordano
Paul V. Johnson
Martha Van Roekel

The systematic analysis of interorganizational relationships has increased markedly in recent years. As the analysis of organizations has moved toward an open systems approach, it has become immediately apparent that other organizations are a critical part of the environment of any organization. Analysts of social power at the local, national, and international levels have begun to realize that it is interlocking organizations, rather than individuals, that are at the center of power systems. Consumers or clients of organizations are usually served, processed, changed, or harassed not by a single organization, but by a number of related organizations. Organizational members themselves are influenced when there are mergers, acquisitions, and vertical integration among organizations.

The present study focuses on dyadic relationships among organizations that deal with problem youth. The analysis demonstrates that the political-economic or exchange model of interorganizational relationships is useful, that this model loses its explanatory power under some conditions, and that different forms of interorganizational relationships are found in the same relationships.*

SOURCE: *Administrative Science Quarterly* 22, no. 3 (September 1977): 457–71. Reprinted by permission of the authors and the publisher.

* This research was supported by NIMH grant #RO 1 MH17508-03MHS. We are grateful to Steven McLaughlin and Michael Carter for assistance on part of the data analysis and Jean Kelley and Barbara Wilson for computer assistance. The comments of anonymous ASQ reviewers on an earlier version of the present paper also were helpful.

Background

The primary focus of this investigation was the degree of coordination among the organizations studied. As Yep (1974) has suggested, coordination has been an explicit or implicit concern of most interorganizational analyses (Miller, 1958; Reid, 1964). According to Yep, coordination occurs as organizations try to adapt to their environment or to maximize their own goal attainment. Coordination is also the implicit or explicit goal of most social policy makers (Kahn, 1969), even though there have been some suggestions that competitive relations among social agencies might serve clients better (Warren, 1970).

Exchange As a Basis for Interaction

The dominant theoretical perspective on interorganizational relationships is exchange theory. The formulation of Levine and White (1961) stressed goal attainment as the basis for exchange relationships. For example, when a patient is referred from one hospital to another for treatment, nonreciprocal exchange occurs as each hospital maximizes its goal attainment. Levine and White stressed that exchanges did not necessarily involve elements of economic value; they could involve services, clients, and economic units. Part of the exchange process was the development of domain consensus, which, once developed, led to other exchanges.

Benson (1975) extended the basic exchange framework. He argued, on the basis of Yuchtman and Seashore's (1967) model of acquisition of resources, that organizations seek an adequate supply of money and authority to fulfill program requirements, maintain their domain, ensure their flow resources, and extend and defend the organization's paradigm or way of doing things. Resources are acquired from the political economy, and it is through exchanges with this macrostructure as well as other organizations that the organization is able to maximize its supply of money and authority. Benson also suggested that when relationships among organizations were in balance or equilibrium, there would be domain consensus, ideological consensus, positive evaluations of other organizations, and work coordination among them. The balance could be upset, however, by inadequacies among the organizations or by external forces.

Other Bases of Interaction

The emphasis in these exchange approaches is on voluntary interorganizational relationships. A second major basis of interorganizational relationships that has received much less theoretical attention is mandated relationships among organizations. Aldrich (1976) found that mandated interactions tended to be more intense, imbalanced in favor of one of the organizations studied, and associated with lower perceived cooperation. Turk (1970, 1973) also examined how such mandated interactions were affected by characteristics of urban areas. Mandated interactions involve laws or regulations specifying areas of domain, information and client flows, and financial obligations. Examples include juvenile-justice programs, model city programs, many poverty programs, and increasingly, health-service programs. Often, the domain is subdivided so that the interorganizational network becomes a situation of "sequential interdependence" (Thompson, 1974: 9) in which there is "a value-added system of specialists, each performing his portion of the larger task and passing the job onto the next one." Other interorganizational relationships appear to be mandated interactions. Relationships between the public and private sectors are most typically governed by laws and regulations. Relationships among governmental agencies (aside from budget-decision periods) operate on the basis of sequential interdependence and mandated domain. The most obvious form of mandate is the externally imposed law or regulation by the legal or political system.

A third basis for interaction is voluntary, but standardized through some form of formal agreement. Exchanges occur in the development of the formal agreement, but interactions subsequent to the agreement are guided by it. Private business organizations engage in exchange when agreeing upon a contract, but once the contract is signed, the relationship is formalized. Exchanges may continue through interlocking boards of directors or other personnel shifts (Pfeffer, 1972; Pfeffer and Leblebici, 1973), but the ongoing activities of the organizations are primarily governed by the formal agreement. Other types of formal agreements include contracts to share facilities or personnel and agreements to share information about a particular set of clients.

Few interorganizational relationships would be exclusively voluntary, standardized-voluntary, or mandated. In a mandated situation, for example, voluntary exchanges would still take place. Also, many relationships that are voluntary in the beginning could later become standardized when the organizations decided it was time to regularize the relationships. Nonetheless, these distinctions appear to be crucial for the analysis of interactions among organizations, and so for the study of coordination, a major form of interaction.

Coordination

For the purposes of the present analysis, coordination is defined as the extent to which organizations attempt to ensure that their activities take into account those of other organizations. This definition makes it possible to examine interorganizational conflict as a phenomenon distinct from coordination. Guetzkow (1966) argued that conflict and coordination vary among organizations engaged in specialized and differentiated activities and Assael (1969) argued that "partial conflict" contributes to coordination.

Coordination occurs as organizations attempt to attain their goals or carry out their programs and probably at the same time that they are trying to cope with their environment. As Warren (1967) noted, relationships could be minimal, only occurring when a particular focal organization had to take another organization into account. Or, at the other extreme, organizations could merge as programs and cost conditions make the maintenance of separate entities difficult. Coordination can be formalized, as in computerized transmittal of routine information, or informal, as when a member of one organization telephones to check some information with a friend in another organization. Coordination may cover only a few facets of the potential interactions among organizations, or the organizations can participate in joint meetings in which all phases of their operations are discussed and plans for continued coordination developed. Coordination can also involve the resolution of conflict among organizations.

In the present research, coordination is studied as it occurs under different bases of interaction. Except for Aldrich (1976), not enough attention has been paid to the consequences of different bases of interaction as they affect the quality of interactions among organizations. Our observations in the set of organizations studied and consideration of the literature led us to develop a set of hypotheses about bases of interaction and coordination.

Hypotheses and Assumptions

In voluntary nonmandated situations, it is hypothesized that the domain consensus and positive evaluation (Benson, 1975) are preconditions for coordination, and the organizations attempt to exert power as the exchange with other organizations occurs. On the other hand, when coordination is mandated by law, domain consensus is not an issue, so that it is hypothesized that positive evaluations are important to the parties involved under conditions of a legal mandate, since few legal mandates would prescribe that total scope of coordination. Inasmuch as the legal mandate already defined the roles of the interacting organizations, power would be less important in the ongoing relationships, since it could not be readily manipulated. In standardized-voluntary cases, where relationships are standardized by formal agreement, domain consensus has already been achieved and is no longer a major issue. In such situations, it is hypothesized that it is important for the interacting organizations to see each other as performing well, since mutual recognition of good performance undoubtedly entered into the decision to reach a formal agreement in the first place. With a formal agreement, it is also hypothesized that power relationships have been resolved, so that the exercise of power in such situations is not an important variable.

Two important assumptions were made in this study. First, interorganizational (and interpersonal) relationships were not of one kind. At any particular time, organizations could be interacting with other organizations on multiple bases—on one issue on a voluntary basis, on another on the basis of a formal agreement, and on a third on the basis of a legal mandate. Obviously, some interorganizational interactions occur on just one basis. The second assumption was that at any particular time, interorganizational relationships serve as a major basis for subsequent relationships. The evolution of a formal agreement is preceded by voluntary interactions; voluntary interactions are preceded by earlier voluntary interactions. As organizations interact, their members gather impressions about the personnel in other organizations as well as about the organization as a whole. Since the present study is not longitudinal, it is not possible to specify the flow of interorganizational interactions in the manner just described. It is possible, however, to examine the patterns of relationships as they exist under different bases, which is important in understanding the consequences of such relationships.

Research Setting

The organizations studied were all concerned with problem youth. They comprised what Aldrich (1977) calls an "action set." The frame of reference was the interactions among the organizations. This approach must be distinguished from approaches that concentrate on characteristics of particular focal organizations (Evan, 1966) or on a complete network of interorganizational relationships (Warren, Bergunder, and Rose, 1974). The organizations were both "people-processing" and "people-changing" (Hasenfeld, 1972). Although Hasenfeld suggested that people-changing organizations had their technology located primarily within the organizations it was assumed here that such organizations also had important interorganizational linkages. This is particularly the case in organizations such as probation departments, which are located in the community, rather than isolated from it. Mental hospitals or prisons are people-changing organizations which would have a much greater intraorganizational locus, given their isolation from the community.

The organizations were specifically charged with dealing with youth 10–18 years of age. The youths came to the organizations on their own initiative (the organization's definitions of the youth's actions) or by referral from another individual or organization. The research began in a midwestern city, where a year-long period of intensive observation was conducted. In the course of the observations a core set of agencies was identified. At the end of the observational phase, the professional staff of each agency completed a questionnaire, which asked for the identification of other agencies in the city with which they had contacts about problem youth. From the organizations listed, sociograms or "orgiograms" were constructed. Eight core organizations were identified: (1) the county juvenile court, (2) the county juvenile probation, (3) the county juvenile detention, (4) the city police (juvenile division), (5) city schools (social work division), (6) county welfare (child and adolescent and family services divisions), (7) county mental health (child and adolescent division), and (8) YMCA (detached worker program).

Although most of these organizations were units of larger organizations, they were treated as separate organizations in the present analysis. With the exception of the YMCA, they were public organizations. The schools' and police jurisdictions were part of the central city, while the other organizations were county-wide. Each organization had interactions with other sets of organizations in addition to those which formed this core set of organizations. The focus on problem youth led to the inclusion of organizations outside the strict framework of juvenile justice, since many such youth do not have contact with the juvenile justice system itself; many welfare clients are adjudicated through the courts, but without contact with the balance of the juvenile justice system.

The observational phase of the research revealed many forms of interaction among these agencies. Some were essentially voluntary, as when a police officer would telephone the probation department for information about a particular youth or when the schools would refer a youth to the mental health center. In other cases there was a formal agreement between organizations. For example, the schools and the juvenile police developed a school liaison officer program in which a juvenile officer was housed in a specific school to work with youths and the school staff. This apparently very effective program was periodically reviewed by both parties to the agreement. The court and the mental health agency also had a formal agreement, in which the mental health agency agreed to do all of the psychological diagnostic work for the court. Legal mandates for interaction occurred in cases such as the welfare-court interactions for the placement of youths in foster homes. The welfare department was required to go through the court for such placements. Similarly, the police were required to take youths to the detention center after their formal arrest. The basis for the interactions appeared to be unrelated to the qualities of the relationship, since distrust and trust were found in relationships regardless of the basis of interaction.

When this phase of the project was completed, the research was expanded to 11 cities of comparable size to the original city: Atlanta, Baltimore, Boston, Buffalo, Dallas, Denver, Indianapolis, Minneapolis, Oakland, St. Paul, San Diego, and Seattle.

At least one of the authors visited each of these cities to conduct the research. The first step was the identification of the core agencies in each city. There were identical agencies in each city, except for the absence of a detention program in one city, detached worker programs in all but one city, and the presence of a youth diversion program in one city. Since 8 organizations declined to participate, a total of 76 organizations in 12 cities constitute the data base for the present analysis.

A total of 3,853 questionnaires were distributed in the 76 organizations, and 2,311 were returned (60 percent). The organizations ranged in size from 3 to 209 members. The proportions of refusals were similar for different hierarchical levels in the organizations, and sampling bias across organizations appeared to be negligible. The response rates from the different organizations varied, but the returns appeared representative of the organizations. Pennings (1973: 691), in a discussion of the use of questionnaires to measure organizational characteristics, pointed out that, "Because the subject matter of the scales deals with the perception of structural properties of organizations rather than with attitudes, opinions or feelings, low response rates probably affect possible distortions to a much smaller extent than do refusal rates in research on attitudes and opinions, where systematic biases may be strongly associated with the very attitudes that are measured." The same point would appear to be revelant for our analysis of interorganizational relationships.

Measurement of Variables

The measurement of social relationships has always been a nagging and unresolved problem for social scientists. Interorganizational relationships are no exception. The observational phase of the research indicated that the personnel of the organizations could verbalize the contents and meanings of the contacts of their organization with other organizations. This phase of the research also indicated that organizational records of such interactions were either inadequate or missing. It was also found that the use of key informants would not be a meaningful approach, since it was frequently observed that the personnel in the top positions of the organizations were unaware of the extent and quality of interactions of their subordinates with other organizations. These observations led to the decision to obtain information from the entire professional staffs of the organization.

The use of the professional staffs as respondents and the types of questions asked meant that the perceptions of the respondents were the basis for the data on interorganizational relationships. The use of such perceptual data has been the subject of a growing but inconclusive debate (Pennings, 1973; Seidler, 1974). In the present research we proceeded on the belief that the professional staffs who were in contact with each other would interact on the basis of their individual and collective definitions of the situation. This approach assumed that the perceptions of the situation became the operative data for the personnel in interaction.

In the present research an attempt was made to ask each respondent in each organization to describe the qualities of the relationships with each of the other organizations serving problem youth in their city. Thus, each member of the juvenile court was asked about the relationships with each of the other organizations in that network. If there were eight organizations in a city, each respondent was asked about relationships between his or her organization and the seven other organizations.

The extensiveness of the coverage created a methodological problem. If each variable were to be ideally measured, multiple items or indicators should be used. In the present case we were interested in 14 basic interorganizational variables. If we had used five items or indicators for each variable and had asked respondents from a focal organization about interactions with seven other organizations in a city, it would have required 490 items for each questionnaire on interorganizational relationships alone. This would have been impossible in itself, but when coupled with the additional variable of the total research project, an alternative strategy had to be developed.

The strategy selected was to ask a single question about each variable. Most of the questions were answered on the basis of a five-point scale; others required a choice among discrete categories. This is not the optimal approach to measurement, but since the focus of the study was a broad conceptualization of interorganizational relationships, it appeared to be the best strategy available.

Single-item measures administered on a single occasion do not lend themselves to tests of reliability, so that the findings of the study will have to be interpreted with this in mind. However, from the observational and record-gathering phase of the study, the evidence suggests that we obtained valid information, even with the single-item measures.

The observational and record-gathering phase of the study indicated that there was a high level of conflict between the probation and welfare departments. The results from the questionnaire are validated by these observations. The welfare-probation relationships had the highest level of conflict (and the lowest level of coordination) among all the sets of relationships. The school system and the juvenile police, as previously noted, had established a school-police liaison officer program. In addition to efforts to keep order in the schools, the officers worked with the youths and school personnel, such as the principals, school social workers, and assistant principals. The observations indicated that both the schools and police liked the program and believed that it was effective. The results from the questionnaire again were that this relationship exhibited the highest level of coordination and least conflict in this particular relationship than in any of the other cities. Similar validating evidence for the other variables was also obtained.

An additional methodological problem in the present research was one that may be characteristic of such relational analyses. The problem was in determining a score for the relationships. A mean score on each variable was computed for each relationship with each other organization. An array of scores was thus obtained on the interorganizational relationships of the mental health unit, for example, with each of its interacting organizations. The members of the other organizations had similarly indicated the quality of the relationships of their organization with the mental health unit. The problem arose when an attempt was made to specify the level of coordination (or any other variable) between a pair of agencies, such as mental health and probation. At first glance it appeared that the mental health and probation scores on coordination could be simply combined to yield a coordination score, but a closer examination of the issue suggested that such a combination was neither feasible nor desirable.

This conclusion was based on the researchers' knowledge of the organizations and their interactions in the city in which the intensive observations and record collection were conducted. For example, the juvenile court might believe that it had a high quality of communication with the mental health unit, because that unit was always cooperative, even deferential, to members of the court. The members of the mental health unit, on the other hand, might feel that the court, because of its power and the fact that its members expected deferential treatment did not really communicate well with them and hence rated the quality of communication as low. A combination of the scores from these two organizations would yield a composite score of "average." However, the same score would be obtained by combining the communications scores from two organizations, both of which rated the communications as "average" in the first place. Consequently, such a combination would distort important elements of the relationships.

An additional source of problems in combining scores lies in the scope of the operations of the organizations studied. Welfare departments are involved in many more activities than just those that deal with problem youths, while probation departments are solely concerned with such youths. The probation departments are thus more heavily involved with the set of organizations being studied than are the welfare departments. On issues such as the frequency of interaction, the probation department might indicate that its interactions with welfare were very frequent, while welfare would indicate that its interactions with probation were relatively low, when compared with all of their other interactions.

The resolution of these problems was based on the notion that the members of each organization would act on their individual and collective definitions of the situation; that is, if they perceived high coordination or low quality of communications, their actions would be based on such definitions. The relational score for each organization with respect to its relationships with each other organization was used as the basis for the analysis of interorganizational relationships. The data to be analyzed in the next section thus represent the total number of dyadic interorganizational relationships reported. The maximum possible number of such relationships was N organizations $(N-1)$, from each city. Because some organizations in some cities did not participate in the research, the data analysis was based upon 470 cases of the reported one-way interorganizational relationships.[1]

Results and Discussion

The results are presented in two steps: first, a brief examination of the zero-order correlations among the variables; and, second, a multiple regression analysis with coordination as the dependent variable, in which there are controls for the basis of interaction—legal mandate, formal agreement, and voluntary.

The use of the question about the bases of interaction requires some explanation. The percentage of respondents indicating interaction based on specific cases, common practice, formal agreement, and legal mandate was used as a score for that particular variable. The same procedure was followed for the questions about the mode of interaction, such as by telephone or letter, and the reason for interaction, such as requesting information or giving information. For the critical variable of the basis of interaction, then, an organization could have a score for each interactional basis, if these were in fact indicated. These are perceptual measures on which unanimity is seldom achieved. As will be seen agreement was achieved in some cases in which there was no legal mandate or formal agreement. In other cases, some respondents in the organizations listed one

1. There was in fact a high level of agreement between organizations on these types of interactions. If a welfare department reported that its basis of interaction with the court was a legal mandate, the court responded in the same manner. In only three cases was there significant disagreement. It should also be noted that the responses to questions about interaction patterns, such as coordination or conflict, were broadly distributed. There appeared to be no tendency to rate all interactions at the same end of the continua presented. A few exceptions to this occurred among some welfare and school social work departments, but the extent of this was so low that the correlations among the variables appear not to be inflated.

basis as the most important, while others listed another. For those organizations in which there were mixed reponses, there was a percentage of responses indicating the basis for interaction. This percentage was used as the basis for determining correlation coefficients.[2] In the rest of the analyses, the percentage response was used as a control. For some organizations it was thus possible that a percentage was indicated for each of the possible responses on that particular question.

Most of the relationships among these organizations had a voluntary basis. Some 74 percent of the relationships were reported to be primarily based on a specific need or common practice, with 15 percent primarily based on a legal mandate and 11 percent primarily based on a formal agreement. Most of the relationships between any two organizations had mixed bases. For example, interactions occurred on the basis of specific need and a legal mandate.

One of the most interesting findings in the zero-order correlations was the fact that frequency of interaction was related to both coordination ($r = .60$) and conflict ($r = .30$). Although the data were insufficient for a causal analysis of this point, it appeared that conflict and coordination could both be a consequence of frequent interorganizational interactions. A second finding was that person-to-person interaction was strongly related ($r = .51$) to coordination, while other modes of interacting were not. The question about reasons for interacting did not yield very strong relationships with the other interorganizational variables. A voluntary basis for interaction was much less strongly related to coordination than interactions mandated by law. Interestingly, when there was a formal agreement, there was little relationship to coordination ($r = .06$) or any other interorganizational variable.

Other patterns of relationships were largely as expected. Good assessments of organizations in terms of personnel competence, performance, quality of communications, and compatibility of philosophy were positively related to coordination among the organizations and negatively related to conflict. The power of the focal organization was also related to higher levels of coordination.

The major concern of the present analysis was to identify differences in patterns of interorganizational relationships that were related to different bases of interaction. To examine the influence of different bases of relationships, a series of stepwise multiple regressions was performed with coordination as the dependent variable. The regressions were run in the following order: (1) no controls, (2) controlling for no formal agreement and no mandate by law, (3) controlling for no formal agreement, (4) controlling for no mandate by law, (5) controlling for high degree of formal agreement, and (6) controlling for high degree of mandate by law.

2. The table of correlation coefficients is available from the authors on request.

Since most of the relationships among these organizations had mixed bases, the controls in the analysis had to be developed accordingly. Control for no formal agreement and no legal mandate meant that none of the respondents indicated that there were formal agreements or legal mandates. The same was true for the controls for no formal agreement or no legal mandate. The controls for high formal agreement and high requirement by law were based on those interactions in which at least 25 percent of the respondents from the organization noted a formal agreement or legal mandate. Even when agreements or mandates were present, a great deal of voluntary interaction did take place. The controls for high formal agreement and high legal mandate were thus high in a relative sense.

The regression analyses thus offer a strong test of the importance of the basis of the relationships, since instances in which voluntary and low legal mandate or formal agreement were combined were excluded from the analysis since these were assumed to be representative of the paucity of such programs. Another possibility was that the organizational members were not aware of the interactional bases, although our observations suggested that they were in fact quite aware of the reasons for their interactions. Also, the conflict-resolution variable was not included in the regressions. The wording of the conflict resolution question was regrettably close to that of the coordination question, and it was felt that multicollinearity here was too certain.

The results of the regression analyses are shown in Tables 1–4. It should be noted that two "sheaf coefficients" (Heise, 1972) were used in the tables. The sheaf coefficient is "a single measure of multiple effects" (Heise, 1972: 157). Because of the problem of collinearity among the power variables and among the variables indicating a generally positive assessment of the other organization, sheaf coefficients were calculated for these variables in combination.[3]

The most striking aspect of these findings was that coordination was achieved through different means, depending upon the basis for the interaction. Under each condition there were strong relationships with coordination. The strongest prediction was found when there was a formal agreement, suggesting that reaching a formal agreement was itself a step toward coordination. The high prediction of coordination with a legal mandate was contrary to Aldrich's (1976) suggestion that mandated relationships would result in less cooperation. This does not suggest that the legal mandate is the answer to coordination problems, but rather that organizations are able to work within the framework of legal mandates and achieve coordination.

For the total sample (Table 1), a rather large number of variables

3. In Table 4, the positive-assessment sheaf is composed of only the perception of performance and competence of personnel variables. The other variable, compatibility of philosophy, was negatively and nonlinearly related in this case.

TABLE 1. Multiple regression coefficients with coordination as dependent variable for total sample *

Positive-assessment sheaf	.407
Power sheaf	.219
Frequency of contact	.185
Conflict	−.258
Quality of communications	.124
Person-to-person contact	.003
Contact based on formal agreement	.003
Contact based on common practice	.002

Multiple $r = .870$ $N = 462$
* All variables enter the equation at the .05 level of significance or better.

was significantly related to coordination, including the positive-assessment sheaf and the power sheafs. The presence of a positive-assessment sheaf here and in most of the other conditions is partial confirmation of Benson's (1975) argument that domain consensus, positive evaluation, and work coordination vary together, and that the exchange process was operating. Our variables were quite similar to those that he suggested. The presence of the power sheaf was also suggestive of exchange relationships. It would appear that both parties in the dyadic relationships struggled to maximize their position and benefit from the exchange. The other variables included for the total sample were not surprising. Frequency of contact, the negative relationship with conflict, and quality of communications would be expected to be related to coordination. The other variables, while statistically significant, had weaker predictive values.

In those situations in which there was neither a legal mandate nor a formal agreement, and in which there was no formal agreement, the patterns found were nearly identical (Table 2). The positive-assessment sheaf

TABLE 2. Multiple regression coefficients with coordination as dependent variable *

	WITHOUT FORMAL AGREEMENT †	WITHOUT FORMAL AGREEMENT OR LEGAL MANDATE ‡
Positive-assessment sheaf	.546	.490
Frequency of contact	.207	.238
Person-to-person contact	.004	.007

* All variables enter the equation at the .05 level of significance or better.
† Multiple $r = .862$ $N = 154$
‡ Multiple $r = .845$ $N = 95$

TABLE 3. Multiple regression coefficients with coordination as dependent variable *

	WITH FORMAL AGREEMENT †	WITHOUT LEGAL MANDATE ‡
Positive-assessment sheaf	—	.371
Power sheaf	.359	.212
Frequency of contact	.231	.212
Importance of contact	.295	—
Conflict	−.828	−.267
Person-to-person contact	—	.005
Contact based on formal agreement	—	.007
Contact based on specific need	—	.004
Quality of communications	—	.132
Contacts to plan programs	—	−.002
Contact based on common practice	—	.003

* All variables enter the equation at the .05 level of significance or better.
† Multiple $r = .919$ $N = 49$
‡ Multiple $r = .852$ $N = 213$

was the major predictor, with frequency of contact also strongly related and person-to-person contact also in the equation. The smaller number of cases here probably had the effect of limiting the number of variables that would enter the equation.

The pattern found when there was no mandate by law (Table 3) was very similar to that for the entire sample. Since this set of data involves almost half of the total number of cases, this was not unexpected. The pattern shifted dramatically when there was a formal agreement. For the first time, the positive-assessment sheaf was not in the equation. Perhaps the issues of competence, performance, and compatibility of philosophies were resolved before the formal agreement was reached and were no longer important. The presence of the power sheaf here suggested that negotiations were still carried out, even after the formal agreement had been reached. These findings were contrary to our expectations. The fact that the interactions were viewed as important was not unexpected, since there was little likelihood that formal agreements would be developed over trivial procedures.

The pattern shifted again when there was a legal mandate (Table 4). The positive-assessment sheaf, minus compatibility of philosophy, was a strong predictor. The strong negative relationships with conflict suggested that when there was a legal mandate, conflicts which arose were very disruptive. The same was also true when there was a formal agreement. The absence of the power sheaf here would appear to mean that the organizations did not engage in power struggles when issues were already decided

TABLE 4. Multiple regression coefficients with coordination as dependent variable, with high degree of legal mandate *

Positive-assessment sheaf	.532
Frequency of contact	.167
Conflict	−.343
Quality of communications	.074

Multiple $r = .873$ $N = 89$
* All variables enter the equation at the .05 level of significance or better.

by the external legal mandate. Also, the fact that compatibility of philosophy had to be removed from the positive-assessment sheaf suggested that compatibility was in itself not very relevant when interactions were mandated.

The cross-sectional character of these data must be taken into consideration in these interpretations. The discussion of some types of linkages among the variables is speculative. Nonetheless, the distinctly different patterns found among the different bases of relationships indicate that the basis of relationships was crucial in understanding different patterns of interorganizational relationships. Since the organizations may have multiple bases of interactions, some caution should be used in interpreting these results. When the dominant bases are voluntary, but there are legal mandates for a small proportion of the interactions, it is likely that these cases would be included in the condition of no formal agreement in Table 2. In the present analysis there is no way in which the influence of the proportionately small legal mandate for the overall interaction pattern would emerge from the way in which the controls were employed. It is thus possible that the legally mandated part of the interaction could have a greater influence on the staffs' shared perceptions than the part that was voluntary, although the strikingly different patterns found under the different control conditions would appear to reduce this possibility.

Summary and Conclusions

The purpose of this analysis has been to explore patterns of interorganizational relationships as they occur under different conditions. We began by noting that the dominant theoretical perspective has been exchange theory, which stresses goal attainment as the basis for interorganizational interactions. Organizations interact with the macrostructure and other organizations to obtain clients, services, and economic support. Similarly, exchanges take place as organizations try to maintain their domain and extend or defend their paradigm. The findings of the present study support the exchange perspective, when the basis of interaction is voluntary. When the basis of interaction is a formal agreement or a legal mandate, exchange theory is not as useful. With a formal agreement, many of the issues involved in exchange situations are apparently resolved, since the issues of competence of personnel, performance, and compatibility of operating philosophy no longer appear to be relevant, although power is still operative in these situations. When the basis of interaction is a legal mandate, the power issue is apparently resolved to the extent that it does not become part of the pattern. This is not to say that there are not power differences but that these have apparently been accepted by the parties involved and are no longer an issue. Conflict is disruptive in legally mandated situations and a positive assessment of the organizations involved is important for coordination.

Inasmuch as many interorganizational relationships are legally mandated or based upon formal agreements, these findings suggest that one cannot rely exclusively on exchange theory as the explanation of patterns of interorganizational relationships. As legal mandates or formal agreements are being developed, exchanges between organizations and with the political economy of the macrostructure would be interesting to observe. Once mandates have been issued or agreements reached, it is probably most appropriate to focus upon approaches other than exchanges. What appears to be operating is a more Durkheimian division of labor in which interdependencies are maintained. These interdependencies, as mandated by law or formal agreement are based upon the sequence of tasks performed.

Investigators concerned with interorganizational relationships must be particularly careful in their determination of the bases of the relationships, so that critical elements of the relationships are neither assumed nor missed. The findings of this study also demonstrate that if interorganizational coordination is desired, different mechanisms must be utilized, depending on the basis of the relationship itself.

References

ALDRICH, HOWARD
1976 "Resource dependence and interorganizational relations: local employment service offices and social services sector organizations." Administration and Society, 7: 419–454.
1977 "Organization-sets, action-sets and networks: making the most of simplicity." In Paul Nystrom and William Starbuck (eds.), Handbook of Organizational Design. Amsterdam: Elsevier (forthcoming).
ASSAEL, HENRY
1969 "Constructive role of interorganizational conflict." Administrative Science Quarterly, 14: 573–582.

BENSON, J. KENNETH
1975 "The interorganizational network as a political economy." Administrative Science Quarterly, 20: 229–249.

EVAN, WILLIAM
1966 "The organization set." In James Thompson (ed.), Approaches to Organizational Design: 173–191. Pittsburgh: University of Pi.tsburgh Press.

GUETZKOW, HAROLD
1966 "Relations among organizations." In Raymond V. Bowers (ed.), Studies on Behavior in Organizations: 13–44. Athens, GA: University of Georgia Press.

HASENFELD, YEHESKEL
1972 "People processing organizations: an exchange approach." American Sociological Review, 37: 256–263.

HEISE, DAVID R.
1972 "Employing nominal variables, induced variables, and block variables in path analyses." Sociological Methods and Research, 1: 147–173.

KAHN, ALFRED J.
1969 Studies in Social Policy and Planning. New York: Russell Sage Foundation.

LEVINE, SOL, and PAUL E. WHITE
1961 "Exchange as a conceptual framework for the study of interorganizational relations." Administrative Science Quarterly, 5: 583–601.

MILLER, WALTER B.
1958 "Inter-institutional conflict as a major impediment to delinquency prevention." Human Organization, 17: 20–23.

PENNINGS, JOHANNES
1973 "Measures of organizational structure: a methodological note." American Journal of Sociology, 79: 686–704.

PFEFFER, JEFFREY
1972 "Size and composition of corporate boards of directors." Administrative Science Quarterly, 17: 218–228.

PFEFFER, JEFFREY, and HUSEYIM LEBLEBICI
1973 "Executive recruitment and the development of interfirm organizations." Administrative Science Quarterly, 18: 449–461.

REID, WILLIAM
1964 "Interagency coordination in delinquency prevention and control." Social Service Review, 38: 418–428.

SEIDLER, JOHN
1974 "On using information: a technique for collecting quantitative data and controlling measurement error in organization analysis." American Sociological Review, 39: 816–831.

TANNENBAUM, ARNOLD
1968 Control in Organizations. New York: McGraw-Hill.

THOMPSON, JAMES D.
1974 "Technology, polity, and societal development." Administrative Science Quarterly, 19: 6–21.

TURK, HERMAN

1970 "Interorganizational networks in urban society: initial perspectives and comparative research." American Sociological Review, 35: 1–19.

1973 Interorganizational Activation in Urban Communities: Deductions from the Concept of System. Washington, D.C.: The Arnold and Caroline Rose Monograph Series, American Sociological Association.

WARREN, ROLAND

1967 "The interorganizational field as a focus of investigation." Administrative Science Quarterly, 12: 396–419.

1970 "Alternative strategies of interagency planning." In Paul E. White and George J. Vlasak (eds.), Interorganizational Research in Health Conference Proceedings: 114–128. Washington, D.C.: National Center for Health Services Research and Development, (HEW).

WARREN, ROLAND, ANN BERGUNDER, and STEPHEN ROSE

1974 The Structure of Urban Reform. Lexington, MA: D.C. Heath & Co.

YEP, BENJAMIN

1974 An Elaboration of the Concept of Coordination in Interorganizational Research. Ames, IA: Iowa State University (mimeo).

YUCHTMAN, EPHRAIM, and STANLEY SEASHORE

1967 "A system resource approach to organizational effectiveness." American Sociological Review, 32: 891–902.

Work Redesign in Japan: An Evaluation

Robert E. Cole

In summarizing characteristics of the rather minimal experience with participatory management in the United States, the HEW task force report *Work in America* (1972, pp. 103–10) delineated the range of decisions in which workers participate. They may determine:

1. Their own production methods.
2. The internal distribution of tasks.
3. Questions regarding internal leadership.
4. What additional tasks to take on.
5. When they will work.

With regard to job content the emphasis in the American literature on job redesign and job enlargement has been on expanding the scope of individual jobs and job rotation in particular. The HEW report also places strong emphasis on the need for profit sharing to be associated with these innovations.

At first glance these foci seem not inconsistent with the [situation of the Japanese automobile industry]. To leave the matter here, however, ignores some subtle though, in the last analysis, fundamental differences in the style, content and direction of participatory management in the two nations.

The Basic Differences

The reorganization of work at Toyota Auto Body is more radical than most U.S. activities in this area. The head of the personnel section summarizes their approach as follows:

SOURCE: *Work, Mobility, and Participation: A Comparative Study of American and Japanese Industry*, pp. 196–223. Copyright © 1979 by The Regents of the University of California. Reprinted by permission of the author and the University of California Press.

495

We believe that an individual job and the way it is performed must be
activities into which are woven the original ideas of workers, not to be
thought of as simply a fixed job which superiors order one to perform.
The individual jobs must be carefully thought out with this aim in mind.

We may ask ourselves what obstacles would have to be removed in the
United States before we could imagine successful institutionalization of
these seemingly utopian assumptions. First, it may be noted, machine design is by and large not a function of each specific company. Rather, it is
a highly centralized operation that came into being in the middle of the
nineteenth century in the United States. The machine-tool industry developed as a response to the common processes and problems in the production of a wide range of disparate products in a variety of different industries. This technology involved the spread of specialized machines, each
designed to insure speedy performance of limited tasks. This presumed a
sequential productive process involving large numbers of special-purpose
machines, with each one advancing the product one small step further toward its completed form. It was the growing nineteenth-century success in
development of machine technology which culminated in the assembly-line
system in the early twentieth century. The tendency towards "pre-set tools"
which culminated in the revolutionary numerical-control machine technology of the post-World War II period reduced the skills required by the
machine operator (Rosenberg 1972, pp. 98–110).

Yet this perspective is based on a conceptualization of technological
change exclusively in terms of large-scale innovations. Nathan Rosenberg
(1972, p. 164) notes that much less attention is paid to small-scale, often
anonymous, improvements in design and minor adjustments and modifications of practices. Stinchcombe (1974, pp. 8, 17–18, 30) makes the same
point in resisting "the easy theoretical distinction between innovation and
routine administration." Only by innovation can the routine problems of
production be solved. The cumulative impact of frequent small-scale
changes can be enormous, and without their consideration approaches to
technological change are incomplete. These small-scale changes, often introduced by workers and foremen, are far more critical to raising industrial
efficiency than is commonly realized. It is here at the "margins," in short,
that workers may have their most significant opportunity of determining
production methods. The extent to which the opportunity is exploited may
be treated as variable. In this connection, American organizational sociologists generally assume that because a task is routinized, job occupants
do not have the potential for non-routinized decision making. They interpret this situation as one in which job designers are simply responding to a
universal organizational logic in situations of high clarity of task objectives, high predictability of expected problems and high capability in developing regular procedures for handling these problems (e.g., Dornbusch

and Scott 1975, pp. 82–83). Our analysis suggests to the contrary that the potential organizational benefits of greater employee discretion may be higher in routinized tasks than is commonly recognized. In this sense American organizational sociologists confuse organizational logic with the political power of engineers to make a particular set of decisions.

Historically in Japan and the United States, as with all successful industrializers, industrialization has been associated with the breaking down of traditional skills. Concomitant with this development has been the separation of work associated with conception (intellectual work) from that associated with execution (manual work). As Frederick Taylor himself wrote:

> Establishing a planning department merely concentrates the planning and much other brainwork in a few men especially fitted for their task and trained in their especial lines, instead of having it done, as heretofore in most cases, by high priced mechanics, well fitted to work at their trades, but poorly trained for work more or less clerical in nature. (Taylor 1947, pp. 65–66, cited in Braverman 1974).

Historically this involved a process of management systematically gathering up knowledge of the work process and then distributing it to individual workers in the form of detailed instructions. Such arrangements do not begin to tap the potential for training and knowledge that workers have. Indeed it is a strategy systematically to denude workers of this potential (Braverman 1974, p. 84).

Within the Japanese automobile industry the process of breaking down traditional craft skills and substituting semiskilled jobs and assembly-line operations took place in the 1950s and 1960s. Toyota Auto Body did not establish its first fully mass production operation until 1957; at the time the No. 1 Kariya assembly plant was the industry's most modern facility. Now Toyota Auto Body managers are seeking to reverse these historical processes.

In the United States, as a "natural" corollary of having engineers design the basic machinery, the engineers, along with line managers, have assumed responsibility for job design as well (Glueck 1974, p. 111). Industrial engineers generally adopt the norm that a machine design which breaks the operation down to (cheaper) less skilled operations is a superior one. These are the labor "requirements" which shape their design (Braverman 1974, pp. 199–200). In the American auto industry it is not uncommon to hear industrial engineers talk about the need to design equipment that is "idiot proof." They mean, of course, that it must be designed to minimize any possible interference by those blue-collar workers who must operate it on a daily basis. Toyota Auto Body managers are increasingly questioning these assumptions, and they are doing so in two ways. First they are bringing the industrial engineers into working relationships with the workers and line managers through such activities as QC circles and improvement groups, and secondly they are trying to upgrade the level of worker competence through education; this permits workers to participate more fully in the design of the production process.

The following discussion should give us further insight into the implications of these different strategies. When a persistent quality problem develops the tendency of American auto companies is to turn not only to the inspectors, as noted earlier, but to the engineers, to see if the problem can be designed away. Thus, for example, the American auto producers are increasingly moving away from nut-and-bolt assemblies to rivets. The reason is that nuts must be tightened with just the right torque to insure that they will not loosen when subject to vibration. This has been a significant problem for U.S. auto companies, as reflected in consumer complaints. Unwilling to wrestle with the task of upgrading worker quality, they are turning to rivets, which require considerably less worker skill and discretion. As an alternate solution an auto parts firm began in 1977 to market a newly developed "microencapsulated epoxy" that automatically creates a permanent seal when nuts are fastened to bolts. In both developments we see the tendency of the U.S. auto industry to look for technological solutions to their quality problem. A similar response may be seen in the change of types of welding operations for putting panels together. The U.S. auto industry joins exterior body panels by flanging the panels and welding the flanges. The Japanese carmakers often use lap joints with exposed welds where the panels overlap. The flanged joint offers two "advantages":

1. Dimensional control does not require dependence on worker care and skill.
2. Appearance does not require as precise positioning of the weld gun.

The contrast with the Japanese auto industry in these respects is instructive. In terms of design one might call Toyota "backward," since they still rely heavily on nut-and-bolt assemblies and lap joint welding operations. Yet they have consistently produced a superior product as measured by independent quality ratings; it is a more labor intensive operation relying on higher quality labor. They have been able to do so by working to upgrade labor quality rather than seeking to simplify skill requirements whenever quality problems arise. But to present the matter in this fashion conceals the nature of the ongoing process. Because labor quality is high they have fewer incentives to seek out technological solutions which lower skill requirements. This particular example should not be overdone. There has been an enormous amount of technological innovation in the Japanese auto industry over the last decade, often involving the simplification of tasks and including, for example, welding operations. But the primary incentives for these innovations have been the labor shortage, and a desire to reduce physically exhausting and tedious tasks and increase international competitive ability (see Koshiro 1977).

Our discussion thus far suggests that a major obstacle to institutionalizing the participation of workers in job design is the conflict with the jurisdiction of industrial engineers. Our conclusion, however, is that the jurisdictional boundaries are not as fixed as at first appears. A second obstacle to increasing worker involvement in job design lies in the attitudes and vested interests of workers, managers and unions in existing job structures. Grinker and associates (1970, p. 9) summarize the American situation as follows:

> Even if an industry wanted to alter significantly certain job structures quickly, these patterns have been enforced by unionism and entrenchment of existing workers to the extent that they are almost immutable without cataclysmic consequences, or so most employers and union leaders believe.

Although U.S. manufacturers have a relatively free hand to reorganize jobs below the level of skilled worker, there can hardly be meaningful job enrichment if semiskilled workers are systematically excluded from the job tasks requiring the greatest discretion and responsibility. Monopolization of these tasks by skilled workers is a serious barrier to job redesign. The contrast with the approach adopted by Toyota Auto Body managers is stark. In the context of diffuse job definitions the Japanese manager seeks to organize job duties around qualified individuals. From an employer point of view the costs resulting from ambiguity in job definitions are compensated for by great flexibility in adaptive capacity. The union adopts a hands-off policy. From an employee point of view there is the benefit of having a higher probability of being assigned to jobs that suit one's interest and/or serve company goals. On the cost side there is less protection for the worker in terms of insuring that individual interests will not be sacrificed to company interests. In America, the employer benefits from having clearly defined jobs so that job occupants can be more easily treated as replaceable parts. This provides an important kind of flexibility for employers, though it is, so to speak, a flexibility "between" occupants, while the Japanese emphasize a flexibility in using the occupant himself. These differences may reflect the different supply-and-demand functions for labor in the respective nations. Historically labor surplus and weak unions in Japan have allowed employers to take the initiative in constructing job structures. These different strategies may also rest on different conceptions of human nature. In assessing the distinctive job-related worker evaluation strategies practiced by India, Malaysia, Singapore, Pakistan, Canada, and the U.S.A., as compared to ability-based evaluations in Japan and Thailand, Shiba (1973, p. 65) concludes:

Those countries relying on job-related evaluation presuppose inequality of human ability and believe that these differences must be recognized and assessed and jobs allocated accordingly. The basic assumption in countries like Japan and Thailand, however, seems to be that human ability is basically constant; that any employee satisfying minimum requirements will, given experience, be able to do any job.

He attributes these differences in perception to the degree of cultural homogeneity in a given society, with the belief in equality of human ability stemming from a more homogeneous cultural base.

It is interesting that the American and Japanese educational systems have been contrasted in exactly the same terms. Cummings (1976) notes the strong egalitarian character of Japanese elementary schools relative to U.S. schools. In contrast to the American schools, which assume that individuals have different abilities, Japanese teachers are less ready to concede the point and act accordingly. Instead they assume that differences in performance result from lack of effort and other factors than can be overcome.

In summary, the HEW report's list of decisions in which workers participate gives us a sense of tinkering, while managers at Toyota Auto Body are acting to enable workers to control the content of the job itself. In the analysis of most Western scholars and engineers, technology is usually designated as the critical causal agent. In line with the heritage of scientific management, work is assigned and jobs designed on the basis of the perceived imperatives flowing from the mechanical processes to be carried out by relating the machine and the man, in a way which maximizes efficiency. This conception limits our capacity to examine all available options, though its dominance, no doubt, reflects the social, political, economic, and cultural conditions prevailing in America. This is not to say conditions are so different in Japan that managers at Toyota Auto Body have entirely succeeded in their efforts to weave worker ideas into the very concept of the job itself. They themselves see this as a policy to be seriously pursued, though hardly at all costs.

The Japanese efforts do have many parallels to the new approaches being explored in Western Europe. In particular, the methods developed at the Tavistock Institute in London and applied in Norway and Sweden through the work of Einar Thorsrud appear quite similar (Emery and Trist 1969; Thorsrud 1969). The emphasis in their approaches is on the development of the organization as an "open socio-technical system" which focuses on the interaction of social and technical factors. The aim is to develop small work groups which maintain a high level of independence and autonomy. As a consequence it is expected that jobs will be enriched, individual responsibility increased, and learning possibilities enhanced. These same statements could be applied to the Japanese efforts.

500

Controlled Participation

A second characteristic of job redesign at Toyota Auto Body is that the emphasis is not on participation per se, but rather on achieving the consent of workers for policies which management wants to pursue, as well as on guiding workers in the direction in which management would like to see them move. This is apparent in the rhetoric the company uses; the term *sanka* (participation) is not used, rather the focus is on *nattokusei* (consent) and *kobetsu shidō* (individual guidance). We have here a carefully controlled participation in which management often takes the lead informally or formally in initiating policies that workers are then guided to accept and pursue. The operation of the QC circles clearly corresponds to this description, as do the programs for career guidance and life planning. In a similar vein, when asked if the job redesign program at the company was aimed more at the increase of responsibility of each individual employee rather than at employee participation in management, a company official stated:

> Yes, this is correct. We believe that the heavier duties (more important jobs) will enhance employees' motivation to see their jobs as a challenge. We believe that taking jobs with heavier duties is related to employees' participation. . . . The QC circles in our company necessarily result in participatory management because they heighten job quality.

Job redesign occurs in a context of unquestioned management authority at Toyota Auto Body, though the maintenance of this authority is something that the managers self-consciously work very hard to uphold. The belief that they can build increasing responsibility into employees' jobs suggests the considerable trust and confidence that Japanese managers have in their employees. Above all, they do not appear to be concerned that given worker groups will acquire the power to keep their area of work under their own control free from outside interference. Crozier (1964, pp. 153–59) describes such an outcome in a French firm; it is a situation where the power of (maintenance) workers is insured by their exclusive knowledge and the resultant unpredictability of their behavior. There are a number of possible explanations for Japanese management's self-confidence in this regard. The increased responsibility given to workers occurs in a context in which management controls the training, the amount of job rotation, and the content of career patterns. This gives management enormous leverage in preventing the hardening of worker privilege. Furthermore, foremen maintain responsibility for QC circles in their workshop; thus the existing structure of line authority is not threatened. Moreover management cultivates the ideology of shared organizational goals to legitimize still further its attempt to limit "selfish" efforts devoted to the exclusive enhancement of worker rights and privileges. It is, of course, possible that management may be misreading the situation. There is a line of reasoning about organizational change and worker participation, in particular, which emphasizes its incremental character (Jenkins 1973, pp. 291–93). Small changes work their way through the system gradually modifying structural arrangements, so that in the long run profound changes, often unnoticed in the beginning, end up transforming organizational practices and power relationships. Whether this will be the case with job redesign in Japan is not something we can predict with confidence. As yet management maintains firm control of the innovative process.

Another approach to examining the degree of control management retains over the work process is to directly examine decision making concerning the determination of the speed of production, number of items to be produced, and the size of the workgroup. These are crucial decisions for both the firm and employees. We would expect that if job redesign were being implemented in the fashion envisioned by the report *Work in America,* workers would have significant inputs into the decision-making process. Instead we find that at Toyota Auto Body the speed of production, number of units to be produced, and size of the workgroup are decided through consultation at three levels, by the department chief, the section chief, and the supervisor and foreman. These production decisions are made for the section level, not for individual jobs. It is the responsibility of the section chief and lower-level supervisors to set the workpace for the workgroup or individuals where appropriate. Workers and unions have no direct input into the determination of workpace, amount of production, and size of workgroup. To be sure they can make their views known indirectly through complaints to the foreman if they feel that staffing is inadequate or the workpace too rapid. What about QC-circle activity? Is this not a realm in which they have a direct impact? Apparently this is not the case. Company representatives set the production goals for each workgroup; QC circles act to implement these goals whenever there is a gap between the goal and actual performance. In short, QC circles act in the framework of decisions determined by management.

This leads many Japanese scholars to see QC circles as a device to break worker collective resistance and rebuild group solidarity on the basis of management goals. Our understanding of decision making in organizations must rely heavily on a grasp of the distribution of power in the organization and how power is used. This ought to be a commonplace observation. Yet, while social scientists have treated the subject of power in organizations (e.g., Thompson 1967; Zald 1970), the subject has only recently been receiving more systematic attention (Salancik and Pfeffer 1974, pp. 135–51). The failure to recognize the role of power in organizational decision making is even more apparent in the work of American social scientists studying Japan, many of whom still treat Japan as a consensual society with "bottom-up" participation (Vogel 1975). What our analysis reveals is that the heavy expressive and instrumental reliance on consensus in a Japanese organization is in no way incompatible with the strong exercise of management power and authority.

It is here that Japanese efforts may be clearly distinguished from Scandinavian ones. In the Swedish and Norwegian developments, the aim is to achieve a fundamental change in the basic structure of the organization, with rather open-ended possibilities for worker influence. There is a high level of public discussion, with the dialogue punctuated by concern for democracy and social justice. This has heightened worker expectations. The forward movement has been sustained by labor governments and strong union support. These conditions are not present in Japan and consequently management has been able to proceed without making radical commitments, conceding only those areas in which it is convinced its interests are being fully served. The Japanese effort focused on blue-collar employees in the private sector while as noted the Scandinavian efforts developed more as a national social and political movement. Consequently, the Scandinavian approach included public sector as well as white-collar employees. In the case of the Japanese public sector, strong conflict between the government and public sector unions discouraged any such effort. On the other hand, there is a strong class consciousness and a certain mistrust which interacts with a pragmatic cooperation between management and labor in the Scandinavian private sector that has no counterpart in Japan. This class consciousness focuses attention on relative and absolute wage levels. No discussion of new forms of work organization takes place in Scandinavia without raising important issues of wage equity and giving rise to union and worker suspicion of management motives. These are not significant issues in Japan.

One should not exaggerate these differences. Although the Swedish and Norwegian unions and the social democratic politicians have strongly shaped the public debate and thereby constrained management behavior, they have not been so active at the individual firm level. The central labor union federations fear (especially in Norway) that the existing centralized decision-making process of wage determination would be threatened by the new increase in shopfloor decision-making. Consequently, although the unions support the movement in principle, they have adopted a much more passive and defensive role at the firm level than is commonly recognized. This has allowed management to play the dominant role in the articulation of shopfloor participation. Still, there is no doubt that Scandinavian management has been constrained by anticipated reactions from the unions, the social democratic parties and the workers to an extent that has no counterpart in Japan.[1]

1. I am indebted to Professor Sigvard Rubenowitz for the opportunity to meet with his research staff at the Department of Applied Psychology of the University of

It was not until the late 1970s that some Japanese Socialist party and union theoreticians began seriously to consider *jishu kanri* (workers' self-management) as a new route to increased democratization and socialism (see Hori 1977, pp. 10–15). They see this decentralized approach as an alternative to the centralized Soviet model, advocated by many extreme leftist members of the Socialist party, and as a means to rejuvenate a shattered Socialist party. The popular socialist leader Asukata Ichio, chairman of the Socialist Party, is particularly attracted to the Yugoslav model.

The Chinese and Yugoslav Cases: Some Comparisons

In fact, the nature of Japanese controlled participation has a number of similarities with the socialist model. The most widely studied socialist case is that of Yugoslavia, with the practice of "self-managing socialism" (e.g., Hunnius 1973). This system calls for the gradual introduction of direct management of both politics and the economy by the workers, a radical solution which, of course, has little in common with what Japanese managers have in mind. But the central building blocks thus far set in place in Yugoslavia are the "basic organizations of associated labor," which contain from six to several hundred workers each. Within a carefully defined framework of rules each unit is supposed to hold its own meetings, decide what work is to be carried out and how, as well as decide the distribution of rewards. Members of the League of Communists carefully guide the proceedings at all levels to insure the achievement of designated goals. As in Japan, despite the controls from above, workers do participate in decisions affecting their workshop, and control by peers is more likely in Yugoslavia than in Western nations such as Italy and the United States (Tannenbaum et al. 1974, p. 210). The range of decisions made by workers, however, is much wider in Yugoslavia than in Japan. Yet although the range of decisions is wider, the results achieved are not necessarily superior. Notwithstanding the extensive controls built into the Yugoslav innovation, enormous losses of productivity are said to occur just as a result of endless meetings. Poorly motivated workers continue to plague the operation of the economy (Browne 1975). To be sure a labor force characterized by low levels of education and limited industrial experience further limits the effectiveness of workers' self-management. Whatever the reason, the structure of control exercised by Japanese management appears far more effective than the controls built into the Yugoslav experi-

Göteborg. We had numerous discussions in the summer of 1978 concerning similarities and differences between Swedish and Japanese modes of worker participation.

ment. The ability to reconcile the power and control of superiors with voluntaristic participation by subordinates is, after all, at best a most delicate matter—and Japanese managers seem very good at it. Perhaps a cultural inheritance of collective organization explains Japanese success here.

There is another difference between the Japanese system and the socialist model as represented by Yugoslavia, which may explain the seemingly different results. The Japanese manager, despite some occasional claims to the contrary, is constitutionally unable to take the broader interests of consumers and society at large into consideration unless pressured by the government. Such pressure has occurred quite rarely in postwar Japan, where until recently it seemed to many that the interests of the society were enhanced by letting management pursue its corporate goals. Practically speaking, it is difficult to take into account the interests of society at large and consumers because the participants in the whole range of worker-participation and labor-management consultation activities are company employees (Shirai 1975, pp. 70–77). In contrast, Yugoslav enterprises are public institutions. The League of Communists, the trade unions, the local commune, the banks and the territorially-based industrial associations all operate to exercise powerful social controls on the enterprise. These social controls, though somewhat curbed in recent years, insure that society's interests—as perceived and interpreted by the party— are taken into consideration (Hunnius 1973, pp. 286–91; Jenkins 1973, p. 98). This system of social control means that workers see less direct payoff for advancing their own short-run interests through positive cooperation with self-managing socialism. There is indeed evidence that persistent attitudes of "excessive self-interest" at the expense of wider community interests are quite prevalent (Hunnius 1973, p. 309). This being so it would in all likelihood be reflected in lesser rates of productivity increases than would otherwise be the case where worker motivation is a factor.

We might also note that it is in this area of taking the wider interests of society into consideration that the Japanese model diverges most sharply from the Maoist organizational model. The highly publicized charter of the Anshan Iron and Steel Company, promulgated in the early 1960s, lays down the fundamental principles for running Chinese socialist enterprises as follows:

> keep politics firmly in command; strengthen Party leadership, launch vigorous mass movements; institute the system of cadre participation in productive labour and worker participation in management, reform irrational and outdated rules and regulations, and close cooperation among workers, cadres and technicians; and go full steam ahead with technical innovations and the technical revolution. (Peking Review 1976, p. 9)

Yet, apart from keeping politics in command, it is also clear from this statement that there are a number of interesting similarities between the Maoist organizational style and the Japanese approaches outlined above. For more explicit comparisons, we reproduce Whyte's (1973, p. 157) comparison of Western and Maoist ideal organizational types (see Table 1). Our previous discussions suggest that the Japanese score closer to the Maoists than to the Western type on many of these conceptions. The major discrepancies appear in the emphasis on organizational autonomy (number 2) promoted by the Japanese in contrast to the Chinese, and the Japanese firm's emphasis on job security and career orientations (number 10), which the Chinese disdain (at least in theory).

What explains the surprising similarities in organizational style between Japan, a highly industrialized nation, and China, still in the early stages of industrialization? Several possible explanations come to mind. The first is that one of the two nations is studying the other's experiences and learning from them. An examination of the Japanese managerial literature suggests that it is not the Japanese who are studying the Chinese, nor does it appear that the Chinese have been paying particular attention to Japanese personnel methods. One possible variant of this diffusion thesis is that during World War II the Chinese were exposed to Japanese managerial methods in China and absorbed them. It is suggestive that many of the key management models spread from the Northeast (Manchuria) to other parts of China in the 1950s. It is in Manchuria, especially in large firms, that most plants were exposed to Japanese influence (e.g., Anshan Iron and Steel Company). Most large plants there were controlled and run by Japanese managers and engineers. Moreover the Japanese stayed on in key roles until as late as 1953 in some cases (Office of the Prime Minister 1956, pp. 245, 262, 298–99). Yet whatever the impact of the Japanese it should be kept in mind that they would have been inculcating prewar Japanese patterns; such patterns were a good deal more authoritarian and less oriented towards participation than the postwar patterns. The possibility that this channel of influence was important represents a provocative hypothesis, but unfortunately no current research results are available which allow for a disposition of the thesis.[2]

A second explanation is that the two nations, as late developers, share the common need of late developers to mobilize their population on behalf of political goals. This explanation does seem to have some potential in explaining twentieth-century revolutionary movements, such as that of China, which base their legitimacy on mass support. The explanation, however, hardly fits the pre-World War II Japanese experience. The late-developer hypothesis cannot be stretched to cover two such diverse historical experiences as those of Japan and China, in this regard at least.

2. This analysis draws heavily on the observations of Thomas Rawski.

TABLE 1. Contrasting organizational styles in China and the West [a]

WESTERN CONCEPTIONS	MAOIST CONCEPTIONS
	CONTRASTS

WESTERN CONCEPTIONS	MAOIST CONCEPTIONS
1. Use criteria of technical competence in personnel allocation	1. Use both political purity and technical competence
2. Promote organizational autonomy	2. Politics takes command, and openness to outside political demands
3. Legal-rational authority	
4. Informal social groups unavoidably occur	3. Mass line participative-charismatic authority
5. Differentiated reward to office and performance encouraged	4. Informal groups can and should be fully co-opted
6. Varied compliance strategies needed, depending on the organization	5. Differentiated reward to office and performance deemphasized
7. Formalistic impersonality	6. Normative and social compliance should play the main role everywhere
8. Unemotionality	7. Comradeship
9. Partial inclusion and limited contractual obligations of officeholders	8. Political zeal encouraged
10. Job security encouraged	9. Near total inclusion and theoretically unlimited obligations
	10. Job security not valued, and career orientations not encouraged
11. Calculability through rules and established procedures	11. Flexibility and rapid change valued, rules and procedures looked on with suspicion
12. Unity of command and strict hierarchy of communications	12. Collective leadership and flexible consultation

SIMILARITIES	
1. Organizations have specific goals	1. Same
2. Organizations utilize a hierarchy of specialized offices	2. Same
3. Authority and rewards greater at the top of an organization	3. Same, although efforts to deemphasize
4. Universalistic hiring and promotion criteria	4. Same, although criteria differ
5. Files, rules, and written communications regulate organizational life	5. Same, although not always viewed positively
6. Offices separated from officeholders	6. Same

[a] Reproduced from Martin Whyte, "Bureaucracy and modernization in China: The Maoist critique," *American Sociological Review* 38: 149–63.

A third explanation sees common organizational outcomes as a result of common cultural heritages (see Brugger 1976). The rapid spread of QC circles to South Korea and Taiwan is suggestive in this regard. Ronald Dore (1973, pp. 401–2) makes the following rather pertinent observation:

> The modified Confucian world-view which prevailed in late nineteenth-century Japan assumed original virtue rather than original sin. Confucianists in positions of authority—whether in Tokugawa samurai bureaucracies, in Japanese nineteenth-century railway workshops, or in modern Peking party offices—have been rather less predisposed than their Western counterparts to see their subordinates as donkeys responsive to sticks and carrots, and more disposed to see them as human beings responsive to moral agents.

Perhaps the clearest indication of this disposition in Japanese firms is the reliance on a succession of publicly announced goals, policies, annual objectives, programs, and slogans designed to mobilize worker activity on behalf of the company. For example, in the evolution of personnel management at Toyota Auto Body each new program (e.g., workshop university, QC circles) is inaugurated with great fanfare and a series of slogans. In the case of QC-circle activities, each of the four periods into which the company divides QC-circle development had its own slogan: "Please everybody gather," "Let's try together," "Let's study harder," and "To be a powerful QC circle." In every new activity undertaken by the company the slogan writers are busy at work. The president of the company commonly plays the key ritual role of announcing goals, slogans, and policies. The successive attempts to revitalize worker participation are also characteristic of the Chinese efforts. As Whyte (1974, p. 213) notes, campaigns recur "precisely because their efforts tend to wear off in time" (see also Andors 1971 and Skinner and Winckler 1969).

Finally, we ought not to overdo the extent of these similarities. In this post-Mao era the new Chinese leaders are charging that in preceding years production goals were continually sacrificed to political ends. This simply has not been the case in Japan. Moreover, although many Western observers see a renewed Chinese interest in raising production in the future, all signs now point to a downplaying of the participatory approach under the new leadership.

Organizational Control and Coordination

A third feature of the job-redesign policies present at Toyota Auto Body involves the extensive emphasis on the responsibility of small work units. This theme appears in the Western job-redesign literature as well, though it does not appear to be as central to U.S. efforts as in the case of

Japan and Scandinavia. The emphasis on responsibility of small work units is hardly novel to Japanese job-redesign efforts but is rather a continuing feature of Japanese work organization. It includes a strong implicit, if not explicit, focus on the stimulation of competition among small-group units. The operation of the QC circles discussed previously amply demonstrates the existence of these practices. Historically the stimulation of small-group competition in order to coerce workers to perform according to management desires has had an important place in the arsenal of management techniques. Tekiji Kobayashi's classic proletarian novelette *Kani Kosen* (The Cannery Boat), written in 1927, is one of the most graphic literary descriptions of exploitative aspects of this technique (Motofuji 1973, p. 34). Present-day practices are a far cry from the openly coercive prodding of competition that was all too common in the pre-World War II period. Since the current management ideology and practice calls for obtaining worker consent for management policies, the emphasis is on a voluntaristic competition. No doubt this is more effective than the coercive methods of the past, at least when a high level of worker skill is required. Yet it is clear that a coercive element remains even in the contemporary approach, as seen in the fact that QC circles are often established on orders from top management and with the requirement that all employees participate. Moreover, socialist and labor union militants emphasize that Japanese management uses worker self-management primarily to rationalize the firm and raise production (Hori 1977, p. 14).

Whatever success the Japanese have had with QC circles, zero defect and the like is not explained simply by their ability to apply statistical methods to production. These various practices are built on the submerged portion of the iceberg reflecting traditional Japanese human relations. The ability to integrate hierarchy with the traditional small-group collective organization separates the Japanese experience with job redesign from the more technological character of the movement in the United States. Emphasizing small-groupism, to the extent that it is accepted by workers, brings the weight of informal ties to the commitment-building process, thereby adding affective and normative pressures to the instrumental company ties (see Rohlen 1975, p. 188).

This leads us to a consideration of hierarchy. Job redesign and participatory management require decentralization; this is true by definition and certainly characterizes the Japanese experience. Yet decentralization at Toyota Auto Body has been accompanied, if anything, by an increase in the authority and role of the foreman. There certainly has been no diminution of foreman authority.

Yet the Western literature on the subject is full of suggestions of the "withering away of the role of the foreman" as workers come to take up the full range of decision making affecting their work lives. This must be understood in the broader context of the attack on bureaucracy and the particular evil identified as hierarchy in the United States. Indeed the very same people who believe that job mobility must increase in the modern organization of the future are also those who would maintain that hierarchy in organizations is doomed (e.g., Bennis and Slater 1968). They reason that hierarchy in bureaucracy is inconsistent with the "turbulent environment" that characterizes advanced societies and the increased importance attached to democratic principles. The decline of hierarchy is also a major theme of those who see the Chinese model as the wave of the future—even as the Chinese leaders now move to modify their approach. Students of Japan also argue that as Japanese organizations move toward a more participatory mode of decision making, hierarchy will decline and worker morale will improve (Azumi and McMillan 1976, pp. 225–26).

It is one thing to argue that there is variation in the power and privilege associated with hierarchy across organizations and societies, but it is quite another to demonstrate that hierarchy is doomed or rapidly declining (Tannenbaum et al. 1974). The prophets of industrial democratization are on extremely shaky empirical and theoretical grounds, as Charles Perrow (1972) among others has demonstrated. An examination of the literature on complex organizations suggests in fact that hierarchy and decentralization may be joined together to meet certain organizational contingencies. One organizational response to increased internal and external complexity is to choose "tall hierarchies" and decentralized decision making (see Chandler 1962; Blau 1968; Blau and Schoenherr 1971; Child 1972). The need to reduce operating overhead by eliminating supervisory levels provides one such incentive. This is the response of some U.S. auto companies to having to scale down their cars and accept the lowered profit margins associated with the downsizing. Job redesign constitutes a mode of decentralization whereby workers assume greater responsibility for their work behavior, thereby reducing some supervisory overhead costs. This does not mean that hierarchy or the supervisory authority that persists will be diminished; indeed it may be strengthened. Hierarchical control implies a source of authority located at the top of the organization, but is not inconsistent with decentralization (Child 1972, p. 174). In short there is no strong basis for predicting that were job-redesign efforts successful in the United States, they would involve substantial reduction of foreman authority. Of course, we can build such a reduction of foreman authority into our definition of job redesign, but then we are dealing with tautology.

Japan's experience here is enlightening, and Toyota Auto Body's practices are not particularly unique in this respect. If it can be demonstrated that foreman authority is not diminished as job-redesign efforts are institutionalized in an advanced industrial society such as Japan, it becomes difficult to take seriously the argument that hierarchy is inevitably slated to disappear.

Japanese managers see nothing inconsistent in the continuation of hierarchical principles of organization as they develop participation. The situation at Toyota Auto Body is rather clear-cut in this regard. Hierarchy is not diminished by the various developments we have described. It has been shown how the QC-circle activity is very carefully orchestrated, and operates within the boundaries designated by management; it fits into the existing structure of line authority. The chief of the personnel section makes it clear that he is in charge of the job-redesign plan, though it is done in consultation with the heads of other departments. The role and authority of the foreman in this area involve:

1. The enforcement of job rotation within teams.
2. The operationalization of job-redesign plans received from his superiors into workable plans at the respective workshop levels.
3. The fair evaluation of worker performance under these plans in terms of what the workers can do and what they have actually done.
4. The provision of education and training for subordinates.

Workers do not select their foremen in any formal sense. Moreover the foreman role has probably been strengthened. Management has sought to upgrade foreman leadership abilities; this was central to its whole re-organization plan. Management's idea was that by strengthening the role of the foreman through shifting many functions previously carried out in the personnel department to the shop level, they would be able to increase worker participation. This is because the foreman can more effectively absorb the ideas of subordinates than can distant functionaries. In short, there appears to be no conflict between increasing worker participation and the strengthening of the foreman role. The Japanese brand of worker participation clearly relies on principles of hierarchical control.

Interestingly, when the Toyota Auto Body managers were asked what work-related and personnel policy-related problems are caused by decentralization, they did not mention either growing worker power or threats to hierarchical control through a diminution of foreman authority. Their concern was with hierarchical control, but at the level of departments—exactly what we might expect, based on the classic studies of business organizations (see Chandler 1962). The head of the management planning office explained:

> If the chief of each department had complete freedom to make policy then management of the whole organization would collapse. If, for example, as sometimes happens, department heads emphasize a different aspect of individual guidance, it creates a big problem for the organization as a whole. To combat this we have adopted several measures:
>
> 1. The personnel department collects data by department and feeds the information back to each department so that each knows what the others are doing.

2. Every month meetings are held between the personnel department and department heads and section heads. In these meetings the personnel section representatives raise issues and try to smooth out differences.
3. Four times a year campaigns are initiated company-wide to deal with issues of concern to all. Thus in one recent campaign the goal was to have a company-wide assessment of educational training. The results of these campaigns are then fed back to each department so that they can work to bring themselves into line if necessary.

In summary, the company tries to deal with the classic problems of organizational control and coordination stemming from ongoing decentralization. These problems are sources of continued difficulty, but they are problems with at least partial solutions—solutions which involve development of new modes for coordination and hierarchical control. This is not to say that decentralization cannot lead to a reduction of hierarchy. In Sweden and especially Norway, the early movement for job redesign stressed the absorption of the foreman role by autonomous groups. More recently, the trend is to recognize the necessity of the foreman and emphasize the transformation of the foreman role to that of long-range planner and coordinator. Similar developments seem to be taking place in Japan.

The "Profit Motive"

The fourth characteristic of participatory management at Toyota Auto Body is its disdain for engaging in direct worker participation in profits. Central to the ideology of the job-enlargement movement in the U.S. is the view that direct worker participation in profits is necessary if workers are going to avoid believing that "participatory management is merely a refined Tayloristic technique for improving productivity at their expense" (HEW Task Force 1972, p. 105). Profit sharing is the solution proposed by the HEW report in order to avoid having workers believe they have been manipulated into raising productivity for the employer's benefit. Moreover it is emphasized that profit sharing must be tied to the productivity of the individual worker or to that of his or her small group as opposed to the profitability of the entire firm. The rationale here is that workers must be able to relate their efforts to raise productivity to specific rewards. The HEW report also urges that the return on increased worker productivity must be immediate. Annual profit-sharing plans are inadequate, because the reward may be too far in the future to affect worker or group performance. Finally, the profit-sharing arrangements must be contractual to avoid workers seeing them as paternalistic or capable of being arbitrarily rescinded by management.

Although Toyota Auto Body officials pay great attention to measuring productivity increases at the individual and small-group levels, we have seen from our examination of the wage system that it is only loosely tied to productivity increases (the semiannual bonuses constitute a partial exception).[3] Nor is this approach unusual for large Japanese firms. If we accept that Japanese managers have had as much or more success in motivating the work force as their American counterparts, how are we to explain this discrepancy? Workers believe that their activities in raising productivity through participation in QC circles and the like do lead to company growth, and that this should be reflected in increased wages. There is no attempt, however, to measure these relationships. This relaxed approach makes sense in the context of the delayed-reward system built into arrangements for career advancement. Where probability of job changing is low, delayed gratification becomes much more acceptable policy from the viewpoint of both employers and employees.

The HEW recommendation on profit sharing reads like a stereotyped Skinnerian model of resurrected economic man. Inherent in the presentation is the view that instant reward is necessary to reinforce desirable behavior, lest it be extinguished. Perhaps in the context of a higher rate of job changing and little management commitment to career planning for blue-collar workers, this model does make sense. Yet it seems to be based on a perception of workers as narrowly self-interested automatons to be used by management as it sees fit. The Japanese approach highlights an alternative which permits the elaboration of some very different kinds of behavioral models. The alternative model assumes a conception of the worker as having socio-psychological needs which, if nurtured, will yield economic returns to the firm.

Career Enlargement

The most distinguishing feature of the Toyota Auto Body approach to job redesign lies in the company's emphasis on career enlargement rather than job enlargement. Their achievements are particularly impressive in that they occur in an industry notorious for its early occupational ceiling and preponderance of routine semiskilled work. Would not the potential to pursue such policies be much higher in industries that already have a good deal of variety built into the technological constraints?

3. Sixty-five percent of all Japanese companies listed on the national stock exchanges report some sort of employee stock-ownership program in 1974. However this accounted for only 0.59 to the total volume of stock issued by the listed companies, and only 1.8 percent of the total amount of stock held by Japanese private investors. In short, employee stock-ownership programs do not constitute a significant portion of private investors, nor does employee stock-ownership appear to be a major employer strategy for mobilizing worker identification with the goals of the firm (Zenkoku Shōken Torihikijo 1975, p. 17).

The American approach, as summarized in documents such as the HEW report, is focused on the narrow concept of job enlargement and job enrichment. Toyota Auto Body, however, operates from the assumption of long-term employee commitment (even if not in fact always true). They seek to operationalize policies based on career enlargement. This involves attention to individual blue-collar aspirations, job progressions carefully coordinated with heavy investment in educational and training inputs, and policies designed to maximize the utilization of worker knowledge and talents in designing jobs and raising productivity. The company has increasingly drawn back from the policy of relying on university-trained technical engineers to implement proposals for changes in work and production organization. Again Toyota Auto Body practices appear not as unique innovations of recent vintage but rather as characteristic Japanese practices. Rohlen (1975, p. 207) observes, for example, that Japanese work groups tend to be granted a great deal of autonomy within the company and that experts are not expected to solve ongoing operational problems. This would be viewed as outside interference, leading to an undermining of group morale and leadership.

The reliance on segregated units to initiate and execute innovations is the commonplace American organizational solution, and it fails to efficiently utilize the talents and training of ordinary workers. Victor Thompson (1965, pp. 1–20) refers to this situation as the "overspecification of resources whereby jobs end up requiring only a small part of the worker's training and knowledge."

Toyota Auto Body managers have instituted practices designed to maximize the blue-collar workers' opportunities for skill development and for contribution to productivity increase. One is reminded of the oft-mentioned observation of Japanese managers: "American managers are much better at performing managerial functions than the Japanese but Japanese production workers perform much better than U.S. workers." Generally speaking it may be said that fairly extensive educational opportunities are open to the roughly 16 percent of the U.S. blue-collar autoworkers who may be characterized as skilled tradesmen. The remaining 84 percent of blue-collar autoworkers who are overwhelmingly operatives benefit, however, from only the most rudimentary on-the-job training (Grinker et al. 1970). They are expected to look out for their own interests or trust in union regulations, especially seniority, which guarantee job rights and insure some degree of wage progression with increased length of service (see Northrup et al. 1975, p. 23).

A different way to examine these arrangements is to describe the forms and scope of training programs for acquiring higher-level skills open to American blue-collar workers. In the case of General Motors two forms of training are open for hourly-rated production employees to acquire skills. They are the formal apprenticeship program and the employee-in-training (EIT) program. EIT primarily involves on-the-job training and the taking of specified courses outside the company, which the company pays for at the straight hourly rate the employee is currently receiving. This program is particularly suitable for older married employees. In addition the company runs a formal apprenticeship program (in conjunction with the UAW) which involves considerably more schooling and is particularly suited for younger workers. Of the 400,000 hourly-rated employees there are roughly 12,000 enrolled in EIT and 5,500 in the apprenticeship program, a total of 4.4 percent of all hourly-rated employees. Moreover General Motors undoubtedly invests more in this training function than do its American competitors. It is to the bulk of unskilled operatives, left for the most part untouched by the formal training efforts of U.S. auto employers, that Toyota Auto Body managers have sought to expand educational opportunities. We have shown in the preceding chapter that Toyota Auto Body policies on career enlargement represent fairly standard policies in large Japanese firms.

The impact of the rapid economic growth of the automobile industry on the development of career enlargement policies deserves some elaboration. It is quite clear that in Japan the automobile industry has been a growth industry for the past twenty years. The producers exploited an almost virgin domestic market and rapidly expanded exports. This provided ample organizational opportunities and resources for worker upgrading; talented workers knew that they would be required to spend only a few years on the assembly lines. The normal blue-collar worker could expect promotion to subforeman before the age of thirty, and even promotion to foreman was a realistic expectation for normally qualified workers (see Osako 1973, pp. 150–51, 154). Heavy educational investment by the company could be recaptured because the vacancies being created required increased skills. In the United States, however, the automobile industry has been a cyclical industry over the last twenty years. Employment in the industry has risen and fallen with fluctuations in consumer demand. If we examine the postwar period, employment in the U.S. auto industry (motor vehicles and equipment) in 1971 stood at 842,100, just slightly above the total of 833,300 in 1951 (with about 80 percent classified as blue-collar workers). In the twenty years from 1951 to 1971, total annual employment in the industry increased twelve times over the previous year and declined eight times (U.S. Department of Labor 1973, p. 268). By contrast, employment in the Japanese automobile and parts-manufacturing industry rose almost steadily from 101,000 in 1951 to 617,062 in 1972 (Ueno and Muto 1974; Office of the Prime Minister 1973, pp. 8–9). The aggregate data, of course, do not necessarily mean that all firms are growing; indeed many firms either merged or went out of business. Yet for the many Japanese firms in which the aggregate data do reflect the company experience it is clear that planning for manpower development must have been greatly facilitated by these growth rates. In contrast, the U.S. situation has been one in which the opportunities for worker upgrading and career planning have been sharply constrained by the lack of growth in organizational employment. Employers have not been able to anticipate vacancies to insure that educational investment will be recaptured.

This analysis has important implications for industrial sociology and, more generally, for the sociology of complex organizations. In recent years Western sociologists have devoted an enormous amount of scholarly attention to the character of technology in their interpretation of work behavior (e.g., Blauner 1964; Woodward 1965; Perrow 1970). In some versions the degree of uncertainty in an organizational task imposed by technology is viewed as critical (Crozier 1964; Thompson 1967). Rates of growth of an industry or firm have not been given their due consideration. A major reason for this bias is that analysis of work organizations, like most sociological research, relies primarily on cross-sectional data. Institutional variables, such as technology and the organization's relation to the environment (e.g., location, public policy, and product market), can easily be measured at one point in time (see Northrup et al. 1974). The research of William Form (1976) demonstrates some of the problems with this approach; using just four national cases surveyed at one point in time to construct a measure of the technological complexity of automobile production, he proceeds to make broad generalizations concerning the impact of the industrialization process on work and non-work behavior. By contrast, inclusion of rates of growth as an independent variable requires more dynamic models of work behavior than have heretofore been developed.[4]

In this light it would be interesting to compare rapidly growing industries in Japan and the United States, such as the basic computer industry, to see whether the options for career development are exercised equally by managements in both industries. A cursory examination of IBM personnel policies indicates that great importance is attached to avoiding layoffs whenever possible, high investment in employee education, early exploration and development of job-enrichment programs, emphasis on respecting individual dignity, and utilization of behavioral science approaches (Foy 1975). Although it remains to be seen just how similar these programs are to Japanese arrangements, the initial similarities are striking. One logical implication of the above line of reasoning is that the

4. To be sure those who have emphasized the impact of different kinds of technologies have often pointed out the incompleteness of their analysis. Blauner (1964, p. 9) writes, for example, "Whereas technology sets limits on the organization of work, it does not fully determine it, since a number of different organizations of the work process may be possible in the same technological system." Yet these caveats came to be ignored in subsequent scholarhip. One scholar who has explicitly focused on the causal implications of rate of organizational growth is Arthur Stinchcombe (1974, pp. 123–50).

slowdown in the rate of growth of Japanese industry may make it exceedingly difficult for Japanese industry to maintain career-development policies. Most importantly, the reduction in the rate of creation of new vacancies and an aging labor force will put severe pressures on existing management policies. With respect to the Japanese automobile industry, a government advisory organ to the Ministry of International Trade and Industry estimated in 1976 that the average annual production increase will be only 2.8 percent in the period 1974–85. This compares to the spectacular average annual growth rate of 17.4 percent recorded in the period 1965–73. The upshot of these projections is that the European and American pattern of sales rising when the economy is strong and falling when it fares poorly is expected to take root in Japan within the next ten years. The implications of this shift for employment and personnel administration policies should be profound.

Additional Participatory Practices

The aforementioned arrangements do not exhaust the forms of participatory management currently operative at Toyota Auto Body. There is also a production conference, held once a month, at which management and union officials discuss in advance how to achieve the company's monthly production plans. Workshop consultation meetings (*shokuba kondankai*) are then held at which management and union representatives in each workshop discuss how to achieve those parts of the goals agreed on in the production conference that apply to them.

These arrangements are part of the broad labor-management consultation systems (*rōshi kyōgisei*) that have evolved in postwar Japan. They derived originally from an amalgam of practices including the prewar factory committees, the Whitley Committee in Great Britain, and the *Betriebsrat* in Germany. They also drew strength from post-World War II conditions in which management took the initiative in responding to the aggressive character of the labor movement by seeking to prevent stress and increase productivity. A third phase developed between 1955 and 1965, in which management began to make extensive use of human relations techniques stressing the importance of communication. This was an attempt to harmonize workers' desires with the goals of the firm. From 1965 to the present there has been an intensification of use of more sophisticated types of management techniques grounded in the social sciences; these provide a basis for further elaborating the joint consultation systems (see Keiya 1972, 247–48; Yasui 1975, pp. 2–16).[5] Unions also took the initiative in many cases in establishing joint councils. A 1972

5. In addition to these named sources the following section draws upon Okamoto (1974) and the Japan Institute of Labour (1973).

Ministry of Labor "Survey on Labor-Management Communications" found that over 60 percent of all firms surveyed had some system of joint consultation in which employers and employees discussed management policies and plans—the larger the firm, the greater the likelihood of its having such a system. Some 90 percent of those firms employing 1,000 or more employees have joint consultation systems. In these firms the consultation generally takes place at the plant level, though both firm- and plant-level consultation may exist in the same firm. Industry-level consultation exists in such industries as shipbuilding and textiles, but generally it remains weakly developed. The subjects of joint consultation meetings, as reported in the 1972 survey, included "dealing with the running of the workshop" (92 percent of the establishments), "dealing with the workshop environment" (85 percent), and "involving management policy, programs and workshop organizations" (58 percent).

The distinction between collective bargaining and joint consultation is not sharply drawn. It is not unusual for issues that cannot be resolved through joint consultation to be taken up in the collective bargaining process (Shirai 1975, p. 275). Joint consultation does, however, provide a framework for negotiations on working conditions to be conducted on a continuous basis. The system is not seen by participants as providing the primary basis for increased worker participation in management. In the aforementioned 1972 survey only 6 percent of the unions involved reported that the objective was increased participation in running the operation (see Okamoto 1974, p. 7). Rather the focus was on improvement of communications between management and labor (29 percent), improvement of working conditions (28 percent) and stabilizing labor relations (18 percent). Subsequent surveys by the Japan Productivity Center come to the same conclusion.

Interestingly enough when Japanese managers and, to a lesser extent, unionists are pressed as to why the joint-consultation system is being advanced in Japan instead of formal labor participation in management, the answer is commonly that the joint-consultation system already in operation is quite sufficient.[6] Yet in many of the Western European nations the major emphasis is not on job enlargement as described earlier nor on the kinds of labor-management consultation just mentioned. Rather it is on having worker or union representatives sit directly on corporate boards of directors. Labor participation in management is aleady legally required in some form in such countries as West Germany, Sweden, Norway and the Netherlands (Levinson 1974, p. 95). In these countries it is required by law that every corporation above a minimum size have its workers represented on its board of executives, or auditors, or equivalent machinery. Al-

6. For a sample of union comment see the remarks of Mr. Asano representing the Japan Automobile Workers Union (International Metalworkers Federation—Japan Council 1974, p. 23).

though some Japanese unionists and academics have proposed having a union representative participate as an auditor, these suggestions have not had much currency in Japan. Unions in the Domei Federation, representing the majority of workers in the private sector, until recently were interested in having representatives on boards of directors; the Textile Workers Union (Zensen Domei) has pursued this goal. However, none of these unions have strongly advocated legislative enactment, a common pattern in Western Europe. Unions in the more militant Sohyo Federation, which dominates the public sector, have tended to be opposed to worker participation on boards of directors. The Chemical Workers Union (Gōkarōren) maintains that such proposals would lead to a co-optation of labor and a sapping of union vitality. There are indications, however, that the grass roots support among Sōhyō union leaders for worker representation on boards of directors is quite strong, notwithstanding the official Sōhyō position (Hanami, Koshiro and Inagami 1977).

Japanese management is strongly opposed to legislating worker representation on boards of directors, with the Federation of Employers' Associations urging members to do everything possible to forestall such moves. In 1976 the Japan Committee for Economic Development (Keizai Doyukai) also announced its opposition to worker participation in management. These organizations agree only to the need for expanding the "quite effective" labor-management consultation system currently in operation. They also cite the success of small-group participatory activities such as QC-circle activities at the workshop level. With respect to the former, management concedes labor only the commitment to consult. It still retains the initiative in introducing subjects, so that questions of company productivity plans and equipment investment policies dominate much of the discussions. Yasui (1975, p. 16) notes that matters relating to the operation of the firm, production, and personnel are most often settled by company notification or explanation. It is generally only matters relating to health, safety and working conditions that are settled by binding consultation (*kyōgi kettei*).

In short, management retains its prerogative to act unilaterally but, where possible, uses the joint consultation system to elicit worker and union opinion. With regard to small-group participatory activities, we have seen that management carefully controls and guides the activities into channels which flow toward the achievement of basic management goals. No surprise then that management would seek to forestall more direct threats to its prerogatives through legislation.

The United States and Japan have almost entirely avoided the form of representative participation on boards of directors.[7] This reflects the

---

7. In 1975 Hitachi Shipbuilding and Engineering became the first major Japanese firm to conclude a union contract providing for union participation in management.

absence of the powerful political role of labor as manifest in the labor parties of Western Europe. Instead management is much more firmly in control of labor-management practices, though this is modified in the case of the United States by the powerful influence of collective bargaining on workshop operations. In the case of the United States the movement for increased worker participation takes the form of calls for job redesign and job enlargement. This has the characteristics of the typical American search for solutions when confronted with social problems—that is, to look for the solution in technical virtuosity, whether it be physical hardware or organizational software. This contrasts with an approach that recognizes differing interests and makes adjustments in power relations. At the same time there is an almost utopian quality to the proposals for job redesign in the United States. The call for worker control of all shopfloor decisions relating to them has relatively little backing from organized labor. Government interest, as shown in the now defunct National Center for Productivity and the Quality of Working Life, reflected a primary concern with creating an environment for improved productivity, rather than participation per se. The major advocates of worker participation appear to be a small but vocal minority among intellectuals, selected union leaders, and occasional foundation officials. Although not to be dismissed, they hardly provide the organizational force to bring about the innovation in question. The enormous academic literature on organizations is seldom applied to worker participation and job design. In those few firms and industries in the United States in which labor has cooperated with management in trying to institute new approaches to job redesign, the efforts have been voluntary. They are designed to solve specific productivity problems rather than being programmatic responses to well-articulated demands for worker participation (Weinberg 1976, pp. 13–22). They arise from the traditional concerns with job security and company or industry survival.

In the case of Japan, despite enhanced participation at the lower levels, it may well be that management has not given up any of its prerogatives; the net result, in fact, may be a strengthening of management and the bureaucratic structures of the firm (see Yasui 1975). This is potentially the greatest paradox of worker participation in Japan. In the mid-1970s the tone of Japanese labor's pronouncements on participation in management began to shift from a concentration on democratization of the workshop to joint determination of economic policies on a national level by management and labor (Inagami 1975). The Federation of Iron and Steel Workers (Tekkorōren) has taken the lead in this area. At their 1977 convention, they called for the establishment of a "social contract" involving the creation of a consultative organ among government, labor and management to discuss economic management and wage determination. The slowdown in economic growth, the gradual weakening of the Liberal Democratic party and the likelihood that they would be forced into a coalition government with at least one of the opposition parties no doubt served as background for these developments.

Conclusions

The research at Toyota Auto Body provides a unique opportunity to "test" some of the conclusions drawn from analysis of the Detroit-Yokohama comparative study.

One observation on the analytical strategy adopted here is in order. The conventional practice is to state that case-study research is designed to develop hypotheses that can later be tested systematically through careful sampling methods, commonly in a survey research format. Those who collect case study data are usually quite defensive on this matter, rushing to point out the limitations of their research as if to defuse their critics in this age of quantification in the social sciences. The strategy adopted here is quite contrary to this convention. We are saying instead that the use of systematic sampling and survey techniques has permitted us to generate a set of propositions and their corollaries. We would like to examine the validity of these propositions and corollaries in a specific case. If our propositions fit the empirical realities of this case we will claim support for them (though of course we cannot empirically demonstrate the correctness of these propositions through the use of only one case). Similarly, if the propositions do not hold, we may conclude either that they are wrong or that the case selected is somehow unique.

We can summarize the conclusions as they apply to a typical Japanese factory job system with the following two propositions and their corollaries.

I. The social organization of a Japanese firm is characterized by a lack of sharp jurisdictional definition of job duties.
   a. Low concern with promotion to particular jobs but existence of rough categorizations designed to locate employee progress in company.
   b. Job performance not a major determinant of wages.
   c. Extensive job rotation.
   d. Task performance perceived as a goal of work group (group production norms) rather than individual—strong work-group ties.
   e. Low commitment of employees to particular jobs.
II. The social organization of a Japanese firm is characterized by a strong internal labor market (relative to the importance of the external labor market) with employees manifesting a career commitment to the company.
   a. Low quit rate.

    b. Strong company training programs designed to sustain and adapt worker skills throughout employment with company.

    c. Minimal concern of employees with job security.

    d. Selective recruitment of new employees.

    e. Job assignments primarily a management prerogative with low union involvement.

Parenthetically, these propositions and their corollaries represent ideal conditions for the introduction of extensive job-redesign programs. Indeed, were such characteristics as extensive job rotation already present, we would be right to conclude that many of the goals of the job-redesign movement as articulated in the United States have already been achieved in Japanese firms.

    We turn now to our first proposition, that the social organization of the Japanese firm is characterized by a lack of sharp jurisdictional definition of job duties. It is apparent that over the last ten years Toyota Auto Body has moved strongly into the area of job-evaluation systems and shifted the wage system to give greater weight to job rankings. This transition became quite common in major Japanese firms as the slogan "ability first" took hold. Clearly this sharpened the jurisdictional boundaries between jobs. Yet on balance one cannot help but be impressed that, by American standards, job boundaries are grouped in extremely broad categories for purposes of wage remuneration. Although the job wage accounts for 40 percent of the total wage (excluding bonuses), we have seen that the bulk of production employees are grouped in only two job grades. Although we report no data on the degree of employee concern for promotion, we can document the existence of an extremely rough categorization of employees by job and ability grades. These grades are designed to locate employee progress in the company (corollary a). In short, the payoffs are not for the detailed job classifications but for extremely broad categories. Job performance is a significant determinant of wages, contrary to corollary b, but not in the sense of providing detailed internal differentiation of jobs and job holders. We do find associated with this outcome the existence of extensive job rotation, as predicted in corollary c. Task performance does appear to be perceived as a goal of the work group rather than the individual (corollary d); the most clear-cut manifestation of this lies in QC-circle activity and the overall ability of the company to foster small-group activity and establish the small group as the locus of responsibility. We do not have direct evidence concerning the degree of employee commitment to particular jobs and therefore cannot arrive at a definitive judgment on the applicability of corollary d. Overall, Proposition I and the associated corollaries find substantial support in our examination of Toyota Auto Body. They do, however, underestimate the role of job performance as a determinant of wages.

Proposition II predicts that the social organization of the factory will be characterized by a strong internal labor market with career commitment by employees to the company. Our evidence supports this proposition with the important exception that turnover is relatively high; the company reports a loss of 50 percent of the annual cohort of new recruits after five years. This requires modification of corollary a. Turnover is generally high in the Japanese automobile industry relative to other manufacturing industries, but it is still remarkably low by American automobile industry standards. On the other hand, high turnover of new recruits may be seen as a continuation of the selection process. Since the selection process for initial entry to the labor market is never perfect, a further sorting out before the internal labor market takes over seems like a rational qualification of the dominance of internal labor markets in Japan. Viewed from a comparative perspective, this initial sorting-out process appears quite similar to Western market economies. The Japanese Ministry of Labor (1973, p. 69) reports that in France 50 percent of non-university school graduates change jobs within three years of entering the labor force, while in the United States 30 percent of high school graduates change jobs within two years. The ministry estimates that in Japan some 30 to 40 percent of high school and middle school graduates change jobs within two years and 50 percent within three years. In short, the volume of turnover seems roughly equivalent. If the internal labor market does operate differently in Japan, and we think it does, it is only after this initial period.

In the case of Toyota Auto Body, as reported above, the annual retention rate has been high and has been rising in recent years. The company has systematically pursued a policy of career enlargement. Although we are unable to report any subjective measure of career commitment by employees, the objective structure of career enlargement does appear to have been institutionalized to an unusually high degree. Closely associated with the structure of career enlargement is an intensive development and systemization of educational opportunities within the firm, reaching down to blue-collar workers. This training is not reserved for an elaborately screened elite who qualify for skilled tradesman jobs; rather it is available to all regular blue-collar workers. The amount of company investment in employee training is impressive, though it comes primarily in the form of on-the-job training and is not directly obvious (corollary b). We can report no direct subjective data on the concern workers express for job security (corollary c). However, the strong worker involvement in individual and group suggestion systems, as institutionalized through QC-circle activity, suggests that for many employees working themselves out of a job is not a major preoccupation. The rapid growth of the auto industry over the last ten years has meant that workers who demonstrated their ability did so in a relatively open opportunity structure, which allowed them to be rewarded in the firm through upgrading. The persistence of the selective recruitment which we would expect to be associated with strong internal labor markets is a bit more difficult to evaluate (corollary d). It would seem that selective recruitment has on balance been weakened. The higher proportion of new recruits with prior work experience suggests that the company, under pressure from the labor shortage, has had to lower its standards considerably. These new recruits enter the firm with work habits not necessarily suited to the personnel policies enforced by management. By contrast, new school graduates, being without work experience, are more amenable to shaping by the company. The second element in an evaluation of selective recruitment involves the shift from recruiting primarily middle school to high school graduates. This shift has been enforced by the rapid increase in the proportion of middle school graduates going on to complete high school. The companies have not eagerly sought to recruit high school graduates. They were increasingly forced to do so as a consequence of the disappearance of middle school graduates who were prepared to enter the labor force.[8] For routine blue-collar jobs one might argue that the shift to high school-educated recruits reflects on balance a lowering of recruitment standards from the perspective of existing organizational practices in large Japanese firms. This is because large Japanese firms have been accustomed to recruiting young middle school graduates whom they could train and mold to the form desired by the company.

Finally, it is clear that management determines job assignments and unions do not (corollary e). The unions do exercise some indirect influence over job assignments through their participation in the monthly production conference and the workshop consultation meetings, but this is a secondary rather than primary function of these meetings. Moreover the union has no established power base for gaining acceptance of its view in this area.

In summary, there is considerable evidence in our study for support of Proposition II and its corollaries, although again with some qualifications. The notable exception is the high rate of turnover for each annual cohort of new recruits.

● ● ●

8. General Motors executives claim that the situation has been quite similar for them. The proportion of those General Motors employees in assembly plants classified as modal production workers with a high school education or more rose from 30 percent in 1950 to 67 percent in 1972. Moreover of that 67 percent 7 percent were college graduates, 10 percent had more than a high school education, and 50 percent were high school graduates. General Motors executives assert that this was not part of a general strategy, but that they simply drew from the existing labor force. The federal affirmative action guidelines have, if anything, forced the company to reconsider its selection procedures and encouraged more aggressive recruitment of non-high school graduates.

524

To further summarize our discussion it is appropriate to suggest a third proposition and associated corollaries that seem to underlie many of our findings concerning management strategies and policies.

III. Management operates with a model of human nature which stresses the perfectibility of human nature.
   a. Development of QC circles.
   b. Provision of extensive training and encourage skill acquisition.
   c. Career development programs evolve.
   d. Research findings of the social sciences acted on.

Whether it be based on Confucianist values, cultural homogeneity, rapid economic growth, or some combination thereof, the Japanese manager views his employees as having socio-psychological needs, which, if nurtured, will yield economic returns to the firm. Japanese management sees all regular male employees as resources with substantial potentialities for human growth. Because they apply these views to all regular male workers they are prepared to accept a quite egalitarian distribution of rewards and status. As a consequence, moreover, they are prepared to invest in the various strategies listed above as corollaries of the initial proposition.

It must be noted that these benevolent views of human nature were hardly characteristic of much of pre-World War II industry, nor are they necessarily dominant in small-scale industry today. A set of facilitating conditions has, however, come into being since World War II, which has allowed these evolving managerial attitudes to become dominant in large-scale firms. The most notable enabling conditions have undoubtedly been the growth of an educated managerial class, the spread of democratic ideology, the rapid growth of the economy and associated development of strong internal labor markets, and the crushing of the militant left-wing unions of the early postwar period, though not until they had brought about the diffusion of many white-collar privileges to blue-collar workers. To be sure, enlightened views on the perfectibility of man do not necessarily spring from the noblest of antecedents. Nor do they necessarily apply to female employees.

We have throughout been concerned with the analysis of boundaries: boundaries between organizations and job boundaries within organizations. It is the strength and permeability of these boundaries that constitute the major variables of our study. Moreover, the permeability of one boundary is inextricably linked with the permeability of the other. Our major finding is that the restricted job movement between organizations in Japan is closely associated with a strong internal labor market characterized by relaxed jurisdictional boundaries for jobs within the organization. Indeed, these boundaries are so permeable that the very concept "job" takes on a different meaning in Japan than in the United States.

This permeability lends itself, in particular, to the institutionalization of many social arrangements we characterize in America as job redesign.

References

ANDORS, STEPHEN.
  1971. Revolution and modernization: Man and machine in industrializing societies, the Chinese case. In Edward Friedman and Mark Selden (eds.), *America's Asia.* New York: Vintage.
AZUMI, KOYA, and McMILLAN, CHARLES.
  1976. Worker sentiment in the Japanese factory: Its organizational determinants. In *Japan: The paradox of progress,* ed. Lewis Austin. New Haven: Yale University Press.
BENNIS, WARREN, and SLATER, PHILIP.
  1968. *The temporary society.* New York: Harper and Row.
BLAU, PETER.
  1968. The hierarchy of authority in organizations. *American Journal of Sociology* 73:453–67.
  1967. *The American occupational structure.* New York: John Wiley and Sons.
BLAU, PETER, and SCHOENHERR, RICHARD.
  1971. *The structure of organizations.* New York: Basic Books, Inc.
BLAUNER, ROBERT.
  1964. *Alienation and freedom.* Chicago: University of Chicago Press.
BRAVERMAN, HARRY.
  1974. *Labor and monopoly capital.* New York: Monthly Review Press.
BROWNE, MALCOLM.
  1975. Yugoslav output off, cracking down on loafers. *New York Times,* 11 September, p. 10.
BRUGGER, WILLIAM.
  1976. *Democracy and organization in the Chinese industrial enterprise, 1948–1953.* London: Cambridge University Press.
CHANDLER, ALFRED, JR.
  1962. *Strategy and structure: Chapters in the history of the American industrial enterprise.* Cambridge, Mass.: MIT Press.
CHILD, JOHN.
  1972. Organization structure and strategies of control: A replication of the Aston study. *Administrative Science Quarterly* 17:163–77.
CROZIER, MICHEL.
  1964. *The bureaucratic phenomenon.* Chicago: University of Chicago Press.
CUMMINGS, WILLIAM.
  1976. Egalitarian education. Unpublished paper, University of Chicago.
DORE, RONALD.
  1973. *British factory–Japanese factory.* Berkeley and Los Angeles: University of California Press.
DORNBUSCH, SANFORD, and SCOTT, W. RICHARD.
  1975. *Evaluation and the exercise of authority.* San Francisco: Jossey-Bass.

EMERY, F. E., and TRIST, E. L.
1969. Socio-technical systems. In *Systems thinking,* ed. F. E. Emery. London: Penguin Books.

FORM, WILLIAM.
1976. *Blue-collar stratification.* Princeton, N.J.: Princeton University Press.

FOY, NANCY.
1975. *The sun never sets on IBM.* New York: William Morrow.

GLUECK, WILLIAM.
1974. *Personnel: A diagnostic approach.* Dallas: Business Publications.

GRINKER, WILLIAM; COOKE, DONALD; and KIRSCH, ARTHUR.
1970. *Climbing the job ladder.* New York: E. F. Shelley and Co. Reprinted ERIC Reports, National Institute of Education, U.S. Department of Health, Education and Welfare.

HANAMI, TADASHI; KOSHIRO, KAZUTOSHI; and INAGAMI, TAKESHI.
1977. Worker participation in management today. *Japan Labor Bulletin* 16, no. 8, pp. 5–8.

HORI, MASAO.
1977. Atarashii shakaishugi e no michi (Road to a new socialism). *Ekonomisuto* 55 (No. 36, August 30): 10–15.

HUNNIUS, GERRY; GARSON, G.; and CASE, JOHN, eds.
1973. *Workers' control.* New York: Random House.

INAGAMI, TAKESHI.
1975. Keiei sanka to rōdō ishiki (Worker participation and worker consciousness). *Nihon Rōdō Kyōkai Zasshi* 17 (September):2–14.

JAPAN INSTITUTE OF LABOUR.
1973. Labor management communications and worker participation. *Japan Labor Bulletin* 12 (October):6–8.

JENKINS, DAVID.
1973. *Job power.* New York: Doubleday.

KEIYA, YOSHIO.
1972. Some aspects of workers' participation in industry in Japan. In *Proceedings of the 1971 Asian Regional Conference on Industrial Relations.* Tokyo: Japan Institute of Labour.

KOSHIRO, KAZUTOSHI.
1975. Bijon no iki o dekinai Nihonteki keiei sanka ron (Theory of Japanese-style management participation is no better than an ideal vision). *Gekkan Ekonomisuto* 18 (August):80–86.
1977. Humane organization of work in the plants: Production techniques and the organization of work in Japanese factories. Paper presented at the Sixth Japanese-German Economic and Social Conference, Düsseldorf, October 3–9.

LEVINSON, CHARLES.
1974. *Industry's democratic revolution.* London: George Allen and Unwin Ltd.

MOTOFUJI, FRANK.
1973. *"The factory ship" and "the absentee landlord."* Tokyo: University of Tokyo Press.

527

NORTHRUP, HERBERT, ET AL.
  1975. *In-plant upgrading and mobility patterns.* Final Report: Office of Research and Development Manpower Administration. U.S. Department of Labor. Miscellaneous Series No. 21. Philadelphia. Industrial Relations Unit, Wharton School, University of Pennsylvania.
OFFICE OF THE PRIME MINISTER, JAPAN.
  1956. *Chūkyō tekkōgyō chōsa hōkokusho (Survey report on the steel industry of Communist China).* Vol. 1. Tokyo: Office of the Prime Minister.
  1973. *Jigyōsho tōkei chōsa hōkoku (1972 establishment census of Japan).* Vol. 1. Tokyo: Bureau of Statistics.
OKAMOTO, HIDEAKI.
  1974. The union management relationship at the enterprise level. *Japan Labor Bulletin* 13, no. 7, pp. 5–8.
OSAKO, MASAKO.
  1973. Auto assembly technology and social integration in a Japanese factory: A case study. Ph.D. dissertation. Northwestern University.
Peking Review.
  1976. Always act as a locomotive in grasping revolution, promoting production. November 12. Pp. 9–10.
PERROW, CHARLES.
  1972. *Complex organizations: A critical essay.* Glenview, Ill.: Scott, Foresman and Co.
ROHLEN, THOMAS.
  1974. *For harmony and strength.* Berkeley and Los Angeles: University of California Press.
  1975. The company work group. In *Modern Japanese organization and decision-making,* ed. Ezra Vogel. Berkeley and Los Angeles: University of California Press.
ROSENBERG, NATHAN.
  1972. *Technology and American economic growth.* New York: Harper and Row.
SALANCIK, GERALD, and PFEFFER, JEFFREY.
  1974. The bases and use of power in organizational decision making: The case of a university. *Administrative Science Quarterly* 19:135–51.
SHIBA, SHOJI.
  1973. *A cross-national comparison of labor management with reference to technology transfer.* Institute of Developing Economies Occasional Papers Series No. 11. Tokyo: Institute of Developing Economies.
  1973a. *Rōdō no kokusai hikaku (An international comparison of labor).* Tokyo: Tōyō Keizai Shinpōsha.
SHIRAI, TAISHIRO.
  1975. Nihon teki keiei sanka no mondaiten (Key questions concerning Japanese-style management participation). *Tōyō Keizai,* special issue, no. 31 (January), pp. 70–77.
SKINNER, WILLIAM, and WINCKLER, EDWIN.
  1969. Compliance succession in rural Communist China: A cyclical theory. In *A sociological reader on complex organizations,* ed. Amitai Etzioni. 2nd ed. New York: Holt, Rinehart and Winston.

STINCHCOMBE, ARTHUR.
1959. Bureaucratic and craft administration of production: A comparative study. *Administrative Science Quarterly* 4:168–87.
1974. *Creating efficient industrial administrations.* New York: Academic Press.

TANNENBAUM, ARNOLD, ET AL.
1974. *Hierarchy in organizations.* San Francisco: Jossey-Bass.

TAYLOR, FREDERICK.
1911. *Shop management.* New York: Harper and Brothers.
1947. Scientific management. In *Compiled writings.* New York: Harper.

THOMPSON, JAMES.
1967. *Organization in action.* New York: McGraw-Hill.

THOMPSON, VICTOR.
1965. Bureaucracy and innovation. *Administrative Science Quarterly* 10:1–20.

THORSRUD, EINAR.
1969. *Mot en ny bedriftsorganisasjon (Toward a new performance organization).* Oslo: Tanum.

UENO, HIROYA, and MUTO, HIROMICHI.
1974. The automobile industry of Japan. *Japanese Economic Studies* 3 (Fall): 3–90.

U.S. DEPARTMENT OF HEALTH, EDUCATION and WELFARE SPECIAL TASK FORCE.
1972. *Work in America.* Cambridge, Mass.: MIT Press.

U.S. DEPARTMENT OF LABOR
1973. *Employment and earnings: United States, 1909–1972.* Bulletin 1312.9. Washington, D.C.: Bureau of Labor Statistics.

VOGEL, EZRA, ED.
1975. *Modern Japanese organization and decision-making.* Berkeley and Los Angeles: University of California Press.

WEINBERG, EDGAR.
1976. Labor-management cooperation: A report on recent initiatives. *Monthly Labor Review* 99, no. 4, pp. 13–22.

WHYTE, MARTIN.
1973. Bureaucracy and modernization in China: The Maoist critique. *American Sociological Review* 38:149–63.
1974. *Small groups and political rituals in China.* Berkeley and Los Angeles: University of California Press.

WOODWARD, JOAN.
1965. *Industrial organization: Theory and practice.* London: Oxford University Press.

YASUI, JIRO.
1975. Rōdō no ningenka to sanka kakumei (The humanization of work and the participation revolution: A personal view of Japanese efforts). *Nihon Rōdō Kyōkai Zasshi* 17 (May):2–16.

ZALD, MAYER.
1970. *Power in organizations.* Nashville, Tenn.: Vanderbilt University Press.

ZENKOKU SHŌKEN TORIHIKYO.
1975. *Kabushiki bumpu jōkyō chōsa, Showa 49 nendo (Survey of stock distribution, fiscal year 1974).* Tokyo: National Stock Exchange.

Institutionalized Organizations: Formal Structure as Myth and Ceremony[1]

John W. Meyer
Brian Rowan

Formal organizations are generally understood to be systems of co-ordinated and controlled activities that arise when work is embedded in complex networks of technical relations and boundary-spanning exchanges. But in modern societies formal organizational structures arise in highly institutionalized contexts. Professions, policies, and programs are created along with the products and services that they are understood to produce rationally. This permits many new organizations to spring up and forces existing ones to incorporate new practices and procedures. That is, organizations are driven to incorporate the practices and procedures defined by prevailing rationalized concepts of organizational work and institutionalized in society. Organizations that do so increase their legitimacy and their survival prospects, independent of the immediate efficacy of the acquired practices and procedures.

Institutionalized products, services, techniques, policies, and programs function as powerful myths, and many organizations adopt them ceremonially. But conformity to institutionalized rules often conflicts sharply with efficiency criteria and, conversely, to coordinate and control activity in order to promote efficiency undermines an organization's ceremonial conformity and sacrifices its support and legitimacy. To maintain cere-

SOURCE: *American Journal of Sociology* 83, no. 2 (September 1977): 340–63. Copyright © 1977 by The University of Chicago. Reprinted by permission of the authors and the publisher.

1. Work on this paper was conducted at the Stanford Center for Research and Development in Teaching (SCRDT) and was supported by the National Institute of Education (contract no. NE-C-00-3-0062). The views expressed here do not, of course, reflect NIE positions. Many colleagues in the SCRDT, the Stanford Organizations Training Program, the American Sociological Association's work group on Organizations and Environments, and the NIE gave help and encouragement. In particular, H. Acland, A. Bergesen, J. Boli-Bennett, T. Deal, J. Freeman, P. Hirsch, J. G. March, W. R. Scott, and W. Starbuck made helpful suggestions.

monial conformity, organizations that reflect institutional rules tend to buffer their formal structures from the uncertainties of technical activities by becoming loosely coupled, building gaps between their formal structures and actual work activities.

This paper argues that the formal structures of many organizations in postindustrial society (Bell 1973) dramatically reflect the myths of their institutional environments instead of the demands of their work activities. The first part describes prevailing theories of the origins of formal structures and the main problem the theories confront. The second part discusses an alternative source of formal structures: myths embedded in the institutional environment. The third part develops the argument that organizations reflecting institutionalized environments maintain gaps between their formal structures and their ongoing work activities. The final part summarizes by discussing some research implications.

Throughout the paper, institutionalized rules are distinguished sharply from prevailing social behaviors. Institutionalized rules are classifications built into society as reciprocated typifications or interpretations (Berger and Luckmann 1967, p. 54). Such rules may be simply taken for granted or may be supported by public opinion or the force of law (Starbuck 1976). Institutions inevitably involve normative obligations but often enter into social life primarily as facts which must be taken into account by actors. Institutionalization involves the processes by which social processes, obligations, or actualities come to take on a rulelike status in social thought and action. So, for example, the social status of doctor is a highly institutionalized rule (both normative and cognitive) for managing illness as well as a social role made up of particular behaviors, relations, and expectations. Research and development is an institutionalized category of organizational activity which has meaning and value in many sectors of society, as well as a collection of actual research and development activities. In a smaller way, a No Smoking sign is an institution with legal status and implications, as well as an attempt to regulate smoking behavior. It is fundamental to the argument of this paper that institutional rules may have effects on organizational structures and their implementation in actual technical work which are very different from the effects generated by the networks of social behavior and relationships which compose and surround a given organization.

Prevailing Theories of Formal Structure

A sharp distinction should be made between the formal structure of an organization and its actual day-to-day work activities. Formal structure is a blueprint for activities which includes, first of all, the table of organization: a listing of offices, departments, positions, and programs. These elements are linked by explicit goals and policies that make up a rational theory of how, and to what end, activities are to be fitted together. The essence of a modern bureaucratic organization lies in the rationalized and impersonal character of these structural elements and of the goals that link them.

One of the central problems in organization theory is to describe the conditions that give rise to rationalized formal structure. In conventional theories, rational formal structure is assumed to be the most effective way to coordinate and control the complex relational networks involved in modern technical or work activities (see Scott 1975 for a review). This assumption derives from Weber's (1930, 1946, 1947) discussions of the historical emergence of bureaucracies as consequences of economic markets and centralized states. Economic markets place a premium on rationality and coordination. As markets expand, the relational networks in a given domain become more complex and differentiated, and organizations in that domain must manage more internal and boundary-spanning interdependencies. Such factors as size (Blau 1970) and technology (Woodward 1965) increase the complexity of internal relations, and the division of labor among organizations increases boundary-spanning problems (Aiken and Hage 1968; Freeman 1973; Thompson 1967). Because the need for coordination increases under these conditions, and because formally coordinated work has competitive advantages, organizations with rationalized formal structures tend to develop.

The formation of centralized states and the penetration of societies by political centers also contribute to the rise and spread of formal organization. When the relational networks involved in economic exchange and political management become extremely complex, bureaucratic structures are thought to be the most effective and rational means to standardize and control subunits. Bureaucratic control is especially useful for expanding political centers, and standardization is often demanded by both centers and peripheral units (Bendix 1964, 1968). Political centers organize layers of offices that manage to extend conformity and to displace traditional activities throughout societies.

The problem. *Prevailing theories assume that the coordination and control of activity are the critical dimensions on which formal organizations have succeeded in the modern world.* This assumption is based on the view that organizations function according to their formal blueprints: coordination is routine, rules and procedures are followed, and actual activities conform to the prescriptions of formal structure. But much of the empirical research on organizations casts doubt on this assumption. An earlier generation of researchers concluded that there was a great gap between the formal and the informal organization (e.g., Dalton 1959; Downs 1967; Homans 1950). A related observation is that formal organizations are often loosely coupled (March and Olsen 1976; Weick 1976):

structural elements are only loosely linked to each other and to activities, rules are often violated, decisions are often unimplemented, or if implemented have uncertain consequences, technologies are of problematic efficiency, and evaluation and inspection systems are subverted or rendered so vague as to provide little coordination.

Formal organizations are endemic in modern societies. There is need for an explanation of their rise that is partially free from the assumption that, in practice, formal structures actually coordinate and control work. Such an explanation should account for the elaboration of purposes, positions, policies, and procedural rules that characterizes formal organizations, but must do so without supposing that these structural features are implemented in routine work activity.

Institutional Sources of Formal Structure

By focusing on the management of complex relational networks and the exercise of coordination and control, prevailing theories have neglected an alternative Weberian source of formal structure: the legitimacy of rationalized formal structures. In prevailing theories, legitimacy is a given: assertions about bureaucratization rest on the assumption of norms of rationality (Thompson 1967). When norms do play causal roles in theories of bureaucratization, it is because they are thought to be built into modern societies and personalities as very general values, which are thought to facilitate formal organization. But norms of rationality are not simply general values. They exist in much more specific and powerful ways in the rules, understandings, and meanings attached to institutionalized social structures. The causal importance of such institutions in the process of bureaucratization has been neglected.

Formal structures are not only creatures of their relational networks in the social organization. In modern societies, the elements of rationalized formal structure are deeply ingrained in, and reflect, widespread understandings of social reality. Many of the positions, policies, programs, and procedures of modern organizations are enforced by public opinion, by the views of important constituents, by knowledge legitimated through the educational system, by social prestige, by the laws, and by the definitions of negligence and prudence used by the courts. Such elements of formal structure are manifestations of powerful institutional rules which function as highly rationalized myths that are binding on particular organizations.

In modern societies, the myths generating formal organizational structure have two key properties. First, they are rationalized and impersonal prescriptions that identify various social purposes as technical ones and specify in a rulelike way the appropriate means to pursue these technical purposes rationally (Ellul 1964). Second, they are highly insti-

533

tutionalized and thus in some measure beyond the discretion of any individual participant or organization. They must, therefore, be taken for granted as legitimate, apart from evaluations of their impact on work outcomes.

Many elements of formal structure are highly institutionalized and function as myths. Examples include professions, programs, and technologies:

> Large numbers of rationalized professions emerge (Wilensky 1965; Bell 1973). These are occupations controlled, not only by direct inspection of work outcomes but also by social rules of licensing, certifying, and schooling. The occupations are rationalized, being understood to control impersonal techniques rather than moral mysteries. Further, they are highly institutionalized: the delegation of activities to the appropriate occupations is socially expected and often legally obligatory over and above any calculations of its efficiency.

> Many formalized organizational programs are also institutionalized in society. Ideologies define the functions appropriate to a business— such as sales, production, advertising, or accounting; to a university— such as instruction and research in history, engineering, and literature; and to a hospital—such as surgery, internal medicine, and obstetrics. Such classifications of organizational functions, and the specifications for conducting each function, are prefabricated formulae available for use by any given organization.

> Similarly, technologies are institutionalized and become myths binding on organizations. Technical procedures of production, accounting, personnel selection, or data processing become taken-for-granted means to accomplish organizational ends. Quite apart from their possible efficiency, such institutionalized techniques establish an organization as appropriate, rational, and modern. Their use displays responsibility and avoids claims of negligence.

The impact of such rationalized institutional elements on organizations and organizing situations is enormous. These rules define new organizing situations, redefine existing ones, and specify the means for coping rationally with each. They enable, and often require, participants to organize along prescribed lines. And they spread very rapidly in modern society as part of the rise of postindustrial society (Bell 1973). New and extant domains of activity are codified in institutionalized programs, professions, or techniques, and organizations incorporate the packaged codes. For example:

> The discipline of psychology creates a rationalized theory of personnel selection and certifies personnel professionals. Personnel departments and functionaries appear in all sorts of extant organizations, and new specialized personnel agencies also appear.

> As programs of research and development are created and profes-

sionals with expertise in these fields are trained and defined, organizations come under increasing pressure to incorporate R & D units.

As the prerational profession of prostitution is rationalized along medical lines, bureaucratized organizations—sex-therapy clinics, massage parlors, and the like—spring up more easily.

As the issues of safety and environmental pollution arise, and as relevant professions and programs become institutionalized in laws, union ideologies, and public opinion, organizations incorporate these programs and professions.

The growth of rationalized institutional structures in society makes formal organizations more common and more elaborate. Such institutions are myths which make formal organizations both easier to create and more necessary. After all, the building blocks for organizations come to be littered around the societal landscape; it takes only a little entrepreneurial energy to assemble them into a structure. And because these building blocks are considered proper, adequate, rational, and necessary, organizations must incorporate them to avoid illegitimacy. Thus, the myths built into rationalized institutional elements create the necessity, the opportunity, and the impulse to organize rationally, over and above pressures in this direction created by the need to manage proximate relational networks:

Proposition 1. *As rationalized institutional rules arise in given domains of work activity, formal organizations form and expand by incorporating these rules as structural elements.*

Two distinct ideas are implied here: (1A) As institutionalized myths define new domains of rationalized activity, formal organizations emerge in these domains. (1B) As rationalizing institutional myths arise in existing domains of activity, extant organizations expand their formal structures so as to become isomorphic with these new myths.

To understand the larger historical process it is useful to note that:

Proposition 2. *The more modernized the society, the more extended the rationalized institutional structure in given domains and the greater the number of domains containing rationalized institutions.*

Modern institutions, then, are thoroughly rationalized, and these rationalized elements act as myths giving rise to more formal organization. When propositions 1 and 2 are combined, two more specific ideas follow: (2A) Formal organizations are more likely to emerge in more modernized societies, even with the complexity of immediate relational networks held constant. (2B) Formal organizations in a given domain of activity are likely to have more elaborated structures in more modernized societies, even with the complexity of immediate relational networks held constant.

Combining the ideas above with prevailing organization theory, it becomes clear that modern societies are filled with rationalized bureaucracies for two reasons. First, as the prevailing theories have asserted,

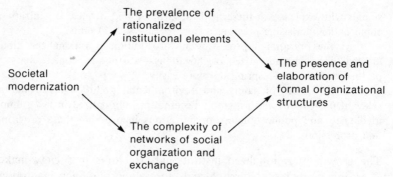

FIGURE 1. The origins and elaboration of formal organizational structures.

relational networks become increasingly complex as societies modernize. Second, modern societies are filled with institutional rules which function as myths depicting various formal structures as rational means to the attainment of desirable ends. Figure 1 summarizes these two lines of theory. Both lines suggest that the postindustrial society—the society dominated by rational organization even more than by the forces of production— arises both out of the complexity of the modern social organizational network and, more directly, as an ideological matter. Once institutionalized, rationality becomes a myth with explosive organizing potential, as both Ellul (1964) and Bell (1973)—though with rather different reactions— observe.

The Relation of Organizations to Their Institutional Environments

The observation is not new that organizations are structured by phenomena in their environments and tend to become isomorphic with them. One explanation of such isomorphism is that formal organizations become matched with their environments by technical and exchange interdependencies. This line of reasoning can be seen in the works of Aiken and Hage (1968), Hawley (1968), and Thompson (1967). This explanation asserts that structural elements diffuse because environments create boundary-spanning exigencies for organizations, and that organizations which incorporate structural elements isomorphic with the environment are able to manage such interdependencies.

A second explanation for the parallelism between organizations and their environments—and the one emphasized here—is that organizations structurally reflect socially constructed reality (Berger and Luckmann 1967). This view is suggested in the work of Parsons (1956) and Udy (1970), who see organizations as greatly conditioned by their general institutional environments and therefore as institutions themselves in part. Emery and Trist (1965) also see organizations as responding directly to environmental structures and distinguish such effects sharply from those that occur through boundary-spanning exchanges. According to the institutional conception as developed here, organizations tend to disappear as distinct and bounded units. Quite beyond the environmental interrelations suggested in open-systems theories, institutional theories in their extreme forms define organizations as dramatic enactments of the rationalized myths pervading modern societies, rather than as units involved in exchange—no matter how complex—with their environments.

The two explanations of environmental isomorphism are not entirely inconsistent. Organizations both deal with their environments at their boundaries and imitate environmental elements in their structures. However, the two lines of explanation have very different implications for internal organizational processes, as will be argued below.

The Origins of Rational Institutional Myths

Bureaucratization is caused in part by the proliferation of rationalized myths in society, and this in turn involves the evolution of the whole modern institutional system. Although the latter topic is beyond the scope of this paper, three specific processes that generate rationalized myths of organizational structure can be noted.

The elaboration of complex relational networks. As the relational networks in societies become dense and interconnected, increasing numbers of rationalized myths arise. Some of them are highly generalized: for example, the principles of universalism (Parsons 1971), contracts (Spencer 1897), restitution (Durkheim 1933), and expertise (Weber 1947) are generalized to diverse occupations, organizational programs, and organizational practices. Other myths describe specific structural elements. These myths may originate from narrow contexts and be applied in different ones. For example, in modern societies the relational contexts of business organizations in a single industry are roughly similar from place to place. Under these conditions a particularly effective practice, occupational specialty, or principle of coordination can be codified into mythlike form. The laws, the educational and credentialing systems, and public opinion then make it necessary or advantageous for organizations to incorporate the new structures.

The degree of collective organization of the environment. The myths generated by particular organizational practices and diffused through relational networks have legitimacy based on the supposition that they are rationally effective. But many myths also have official legitimacy based on legal mandates. Societies that, through nation building and state formation, have developed rational-legal orders are especially prone to give collective (legal) authority to institutions which legitimate particular organizational structures. The rise of centralized states and integrated nations means that organized agents of society assume jurisdiction over large numbers of activity domains (Swanson 1971). Legislative and judicial authorities create and interpret legal mandates; administrative agencies—such as state and federal governments, port authorities, and school districts—establish rules of practice; and licenses and credentials become necessary in order to practice occupations. The stronger the rational-legal order, the greater the extent to which rationalized rules and procedures and personnel become institutional requirements. New formal organizations emerge and extant organizations acquire new structural elements.

Leadership efforts of local organizations. The rise of the state and the expansion of collective jurisdiction are often thought to result in domesticated organizations (Carlson 1962) subject to high levels of goal displacement (Clark 1956; Selznick 1949; and Zald and Denton 1963). This view is misleading: organizations do often adapt to their institutional contexts, but they often play active roles in shaping those contexts (Dowling and Pfeffer 1975; Parsons 1956; Perrow 1970; Thompson 1967). Many organizations actively seek charters from collective authorities and manage to institutionalize their goals and structures in the rules of such authorities.

Efforts to mold institutional environments proceed along two dimensions. First, powerful organizations force their immediate relational networks to adapt to their structures and relations. For instance, automobile producers help create demands for particular kinds of roads, transportation systems, and fuels that make automobiles virtual necessities; competitive forms of transportation have to adapt to the existing relational context. But second, powerful organizations attempt to build their goals and procedures directly into society as institutional rules. Automobile producers, for instance, attempt to create the standards in public opinion defining desirable cars, to influence legal standards defining satisfactory cars, to affect judicial rules defining cars adequate enough to avoid manufacturer liability, and to force agents of the collectivity to purchase only their cars. Rivals must then compete both in social networks or markets and in contexts of institutional rules which are defined by extant organizations. In this fashion, given organizational forms perpetuate themselves by becoming institutionalized rules. For example:

> School administrators who create new curricula or training programs attempt to validate them as legitimate innovations in educational theory and governmental requirements. If they are successful, the new procedures can be perpetuated as authoritatively required or at least satisfactory.
>
> New departments within business enterprises, such as personnel, advertising, or research and development departments, attempt to profes-

sionalize by creating rules of practice and personnel certification that are
enforced by the schools, prestige systems, and the laws.

Organizations under attack in competitive environments—small
farms, passenger railways, or Rolls Royce—attempt to establish themselves as central to the cultural traditions of their societies in order to receive official protection.

The Impact of Institutional Environments on Organizations

Isomorphism with environmental institutions has some crucial consequences for organizations: (a) they incorporate elements which are legitimated externally, rather than in terms of efficiency; (b) they employ
external or ceremonial assessment criteria to define the value of structural
elements; and (c) dependence on externally fixed institutions reduces
turbulence and maintains stability. As a result, it is argued here, institut-
tional isomorphism promotes the success and survival of organizations.
Incorporating externally legitimated formal structures increases the commitment of internal participants and external constituents. And the use
of external assessment criteria—that is, moving toward the status in society
of a subunit rather than an independent system—can enable an organization to remain successful by social definition, buffering it from failure.

Changing formal structures. By designing a formal structure that
adheres to the prescriptions of myths in the institutional environment, an
organization demonstrates that it is acting on collectively valued purposes
in a proper and adequate manner (Dowling and Pfeffer 1975; Meyer and
Rowan 1975). The incorporation of institutionalized elements provides
an account (Scott and Stanford 1968) of its activities that protects the
organization from having its conduct questioned. The organization becomes, in a word, legitimate, and it uses its legitimacy to strengthen its
support and secure its survival.

From an institutional perspective, then, a most important aspect of
isomorphism with environmental institutions is the evolution of organizational language. The labels of the organization chart as well as the vocabulary used to delineate organizational goals, procedures, and policies are
analogous to the vocabularies of motive used to account for the activities
of individuals (Blum and McHugh 1971; Mills 1940). Just as jealousy,
anger, altruism, and love are myths that interpret and explain the actions
of individuals, the myths of doctors, of accountants, or of the assembly
line explain organizational activities. Thus, some can say that the engineers
will solve a specific problem or that the secretaries will perform certain
tasks, without knowing who these engineers or secretaries will be or exactly
what they will do. Both the speaker and the listeners understand such
statements to describe how certain responsibilities will be carried out.

Vocabularies of structure which are isomorphic with institutional rules provide prudent, rational, and legitimate accounts. Organizations described in legitimated vocabularies are assumed to be oriented to collectively defined, and often collectively mandated, ends. The myths of personnel services, for example, not only account for the rationality of employment practices but also indicate that personnel services are valuable to an organization. Employees, applicants, managers, trustees, and governmental agencies are predisposed to trust the hiring practices of organizations that follow legitimated procedures—such as equal opportunity programs, or personality testing—and they are more willing to participate in or to fund such organizations. On the other hand, organizations that omit environmentally legitimated elements of structure or create unique structures lack acceptable legitimated accounts of their activities. Such organizations are more vulnerable to claims that they are negligent, irrational, or unnecessary. Claims of this kind, whether made by internal participants, external constituents, or the government, can cause organizations to incur real costs. For example:

> With the rise of modern medical institutions, large organizations that do not arrange medical-care facilities for their workers come to be seen as negligent—by the workers, by management factions, by insurers, by courts which legally define negligence, and often by laws. The costs of illegitimacy in insurance premiums and legal liabilities are very real.
>
> Similarly, environmental safety institutions make it important for organizations to create formal safety rules, safety departments, and safety programs. No Smoking rules and signs, regardless of their enforcement, are necessary to avoid charges of negligence to avoid the extreme of illegitimation: the closing of buildings by the state.
>
> The rise of professionalized economics makes it useful for organizations to incorporate groups of economists and econometric analyses. Though no one may read, understand, or believe them, econometric analyses help legitimate the organization's plans in the eyes of investors, customers (as with Defense Department contractors), and internal participants. Such analyses can also provide rational accountings after failures occur: managers whose plans have failed can demonstrate to investors, stockholders, and superiors that procedures were prudent and that decisions were made by rational means.

Thus, rationalized institutions create myths of formal structure which shape organizations. Failure to incorporate the proper elements of structure is negligent and irrational; the continued flow of support is threatened and internal dissidents are strengthened. At the same time, these myths present organizations with great opportunities for expansion. Affixing the right labels to activities can change them into valuable services and mobilize the commitments of internal participants and external constituents.

Adopting external assessment criteria. In institutionally elaborated environments organizations also become sensitive to, and employ, external criteria of worth. Such criteria include, for instance, such ceremonial awards as the Nobel Prize, endorsements by important people, the standard prices of professionals and consultants, or the prestige of programs or personnel in external social circles. For example, the conventions of modern accounting attempt to assign value to particular components of organizations on the basis of their contribution—through the organization's production function—to the goods and services the organization produces. But for many units—service departments, administrative sectors, and others—it is utterly unclear what is being produced that has clear or definable value in terms of its contribution to the organizational product. In these situations, accountants employ shadow prices: they assume that given organizational units are necessary and calculate their value from their prices in the world outside the organization. Thus modern accounting creates ceremonial production functions and maps them onto economic production functions: organizations assign externally defined worth to advertising departments, safety departments, managers, econometricians, and occasionally even sociologists, whether or not these units contribute measurably to the production of outputs. Monetary prices, in postindustrial society, reflect hosts of ceremonial influences, as do economic measures of efficiency, profitability, or net worth (Hirsch 1975).

Ceremonial criteria of worth and ceremonially derived production functions are useful to organizations: they legitimate organizations with internal participants, stockholders, the public, and the state, as with the IRS or the SEC. They demonstrate socially the fitness of an organization. The incorporation of structures with high ceremonial value, such as those reflecting the latest expert thinking or those with the most prestige, makes the credit position of an organization more favorable. Loans, donations, or investments are more easily obtained. Finally, units within the organization use ceremonial assessments as accounts of their productive service to the organization. Their internal power rises with their performance on ceremonial measures (Salancik and Pfeffer 1974).

Stabilization. The rise of an elaborate institutional environment stabilizes both external and internal organizational relationships. Centralized states, trade associations, unions, professional associations, and coalitions among organizations standardize and stabilize (see the review by Starbuck 1976).

Market conditions, the characteristics of inputs and outputs, and technological procedures are brought under the jurisdiction of institutional meanings and controls. Stabilization also results as a given organization becomes part of the wider collective system. Support is guaranteed by agreements instead of depending entirely on performance. For example, apart from whether schools educate students, or hospitals cure patients, people and governmental agencies remain committed to these organizations, funding and using them almost automatically year after year.

Institutionally controlled environments buffer organizations from turbulence (Emery and Trist 1965; Terreberry 1968). Adaptations occur less rapidly as increased numbers of agreements are enacted. Collectively granted monopolies guarantee clienteles for organizations like schools, hospitals, or professional associations. The taken-for-granted (and legally regulated) quality of institutional rules makes dramatic instabilities in products, techniques, or policies unlikely. And legitimacy as accepted subunits of society protects organizations from immediate sanctions for variations in technical performance:

> Thus, American school districts (like other governmental units) have near monopolies and are very stable. They must conform to wider rules about proper classifications and credentials of teachers and students, and of topics of study. But they are protected by rules which make education as defined by these classifications compulsory. Alternative or private schools are possible, but must conform so closely to the required structures and classifications as to be able to generate little advantage.
>
> Some business organizations obtain very high levels of institutional stabilization. A large defense contractor may be paid for following agreed-on procedures, even if the product is ineffective. In the extreme, such organizations may be so successful as to survive bankruptcy intact—as Lockheed and Penn Central have done—by becoming partially components of the state. More commonly, such firms are guaranteed survival by state-regulated rates which secure profits regardless of costs, as with American public utility firms.
>
> Large automobile firms are a little less stabilized. They exist in an environment that contains enough structures to make automobiles, as conventionally defined, virtual necessities. But still, customers and governments can inspect each automobile and can evaluate and even legally discredit it. Legal action cannot as easily discredit a high school graduate.

Organizational success and survival. Thus, organizational success depends on factors other than efficient coordination and control of productive activities. Independent of their productive efficiency, organizations which exist in highly elaborated institutional environments and succeed in becoming isomorphic with these environments gain the legitimacy and resources needed to survive. In part, this depends on environmental processes and on the capacity of given organizational leadership to mold these processes (Hirsch 1975). In part, it depends on the ability of given organizations to conform to, and become legitimated by, environmental institutions. In institutionally elaborated environments, sagacious conformity is required: leadership (in a university, a hospital, or a business) requires an understanding of changing fashions and governmental programs. But this kind of conformity—and the almost guaranteed survival which may accompany it—is possible only in an environment with a highly institutionalized structure. In such a context an organization can be locked into isomorphism, ceremonially reflecting the institutional environment in its structure, functionaries, and procedures. Thus, in addition to the conventionally defined sources of organizational success and survival, the following general assertion can be proposed:

Proposition 3. *Organizations that incorporate societally legitimated rationalized elements in their formal structures maximize their legitimacy and increase their resources and survival capabilities.*

This proposition asserts that the long-run survival prospects of organizations increase as state structures elaborate and as organizations respond to institutionalized rules. In the United States, for instance, schools, hospitals, and welfare organizations show considerable ability to survive, precisely because they are matched with—and almost absorbed by—their institutional environments. In the same way, organizations fail when they deviate from the prescriptions of institutionalizing myths: quite apart from technical efficiency, organizations which innovate in important structural ways bear considerable costs in legitimacy.

Figure 2 summarizes the general argument of this section, alongside the established view that organizations succeed through efficiency.

Institutionalized Structures and Organizational Activities

Rationalized formal structures arise in two contexts. First, the demands of local relational networks encourage the development of structures that coordinate and control activities. Such structures contribute to the efficiency of organizations and give them competitive advantages over less efficient competitors. Second, the interconnectedness of societal relations, the collective organization of society, and the leadership of organizational elites create a highly institutionalized context. In this context rationalized structures present an acceptble account of organizational activities, and organizations gain legitimacy, stability, and resources.

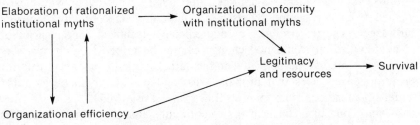

FIGURE 2.   Organizational survival.

All organizations to one degree or another, are embedded in both relational and institutionalized contexts and are therefore concerned both with coordinating and controlling their activities and with prudently accounting for them. Organizations in highly institutionalized environments face internal and boundary-spanning contingencies. Schools, for example, must transport students to and from school under some circumstances and must assign teachers, students, and topics to classrooms. On the other hand, organizations producing in markets that place great emphasis on efficiency build in units whose relation to production is obscure and whose efficiency is determined, not by a true production function, but by ceremonial definition.

Nevertheless, the survival of some organizations depends more on managing the demands of internal and boundary-spanning relations, while the survival of others depends more on the ceremonial demands of highly institutionalized environments. The discussion to follow shows that whether an organization's survival depends primarily on relational or on institutional demands determines the tightness of alignments between structures and activities.

Types of Organizations

Institutionalized myths differ in the completeness with which they describe cause and effect relationships, and in the clarity with which they describe standards that should be used to evaluate outputs (Thompson 1967). Some organizations use routine, clearly defined technologies to produce outputs. When output can be easily evaluated a market often develops, and consumers gain considerable rights of inspection and control. In this context, efficiency often determines success. Organizations must face exigencies of close coordination with their relational networks, and they cope with these exigencies by organizing around immediate technical problems.

But the rise of collectively organized society and the increasing interconnectedness of social relations have eroded many market contexts. Increasingly, such organizations as schools, R & D units, and governmental bureaucracies use variable, ambiguous technologies to produce outputs that are difficult to appraise, and other organizations with clearly defined technologies find themselves unable to adapt to environmental turbulence. The uncertainties of unpredictable technical contingencies or of adapting to environmental change cannot be resolved on the basis of efficiency. Internal participants and external constituents alike call for institutionalized rules that promote trust and confidence in outputs and buffer organizations from failure (Emery and Trist 1965).

Thus, one can conceive of a continuum along which organizations can be ordered. At one end are production organizations under strong output controls (Ouchi and Maguire 1975) whose success depends on the management of relational networks. At the other end are institutionalized organizations whose success depends on the confidence and stability achieved by isomorphism with institutional rules. For two reasons it is important not to assume that an organization's location on this continuum is based on the inherent technical properties of its output and therefore permanent. First, the technical properties of outputs are socially defined and do not exist in some concrete sense that allows them to be empirically discovered. Second, environments and organizations often redefine the nature of products, services, and technologies. Redefinition sometimes clarifies techniques or evaluative standards. But often organizations and environments redefine the nature of techniques and output so that ambiguity is introduced and rights of inspection and control are lowered. For example, American schools have evolved from producing rather specific training that was evaluated according to strict criteria of efficiency to producing ambiguously defined services that are evaluated according to criteria of certification (Callahan 1962; Tyack 1974; Meyer and Rowan 1975).

Structural Inconsistencies in Institutionalized Organizations

Two very general problems face an organization if its success depends primarily on isomorphism with institutionalized rules. First, technical activities and demands for efficiency create conflicts and inconsistencies in an institutionalized organization's efforts to conform to the ceremonial rules of production. Second, because these ceremonial rules are transmitted by myths that may arise from different parts of the environment, the rules may conflict with one another. These inconsistencies make a concern for efficiency and tight coordination and control problematic.

Formal structures that celebrate institutionalized myths differ from structures that act efficiently. Ceremonial activity is significant in relation to categorical rules, not in its concrete effects (Merton 1940; March and Simon 1958). A sick worker must be treated by a doctor using accepted medical procedures; whether the worker is treated effectively is less important. A bus company must service required routes whether or not there are many passengers. A university must maintain appropriate departments independently of the department's enrollments. Activity, that is, has ritual significance: it maintains appearances and validates an organization.

Categorical rules conflict with the logic of efficiency. Organizations often face the dilemma that activities celebrating institutionalized rules, although they count as virtuous ceremonial expenditures, are pure costs from the point of view of efficiency. For example, hiring a Nobel Prize winner brings great ceremonial benefits to a university. The celebrated name can lead to research grants, brighter students, or reputational gains. But from the point of view of immediate outcomes, the expenditure lowers the instructional return per dollar expended and lowers the university's ability to solve immediate logistical problems. Also, expensive technologies, which bring prestige to hospitals and business firms, may be simply excessive costs from the point of view of immediate production. Similarly, highly professionalized consultants who bring external blessings on an organization are often difficult to justify in terms of improved productivity, yet may be very important in maintaining internal and external legitimacy.

Other conflicts between categorical rules and efficiency arise because institutional rules are couched at high levels of generalization (Durkheim 1933) whereas technical activities vary with specific, unstandardized, and possibly unique conditions. Because standardized ceremonial categories must confront technical variations and anomalies, the generalized rules of the institutional environment are often inappropriate to specific situations. A governmentally mandated curriculum may be inappropriate for the students at hand, a conventional medical treatment may make little sense given the characteristics of a patient, and federal safety inspectors may intolerably delay boundary-spanning exchanges.

Yet another source of conflict between categorical rules and efficiency is the inconsistency among institutionalized elements. Institutional environments are often pluralistic (Udy 1970), and societies promulgate sharply inconsistent myths. As a result, organizations in search of external support and stability incorporate all sorts of incompatible structural elements. Professions are incorporated although they make overlapping jurisdictional claims. Programs are adopted which contend with each other for authority over a given domain. For instance, if one inquires who decides what curricula will be taught in schools, any number of parties from the various governments down to individual teachers may say that they decide.

In institutionalized organizations, then, concern with the efficiency of day-to-day activities creates enormous uncertainties. Specific contexts highlight the inadequacies of the prescriptions of generalized myths, and inconsistent structural elements conflict over jurisdictional rights. Thus the organization must struggle to link the requirements of ceremonial elements to technical activities and to link inconsistent ceremonial elements to each other.

Resolving Inconsistencies

There are four partial solutions to these inconsistencies. First, an organization can resist ceremonial requirements. But an organization that neglects ceremonial requirements and portrays itself as efficient may be unsuccessful in documenting its efficiency. Also, rejecting ceremonial requirements neglects an important source of resources and stability. Second, an organization can maintain rigid conformity to institutionalized prescriptions by cutting off external relations. Although such isolation upholds ceremonial requirements, internal participants and external constituents may soon become disillusioned with their inability to manage boundary-spanning exchanges. Institutionalized organizations must not only conform to myths but must also maintain the appearance that the myths actually work. Third, an organization can cynically acknowledge that its structure is inconsistent with work requirements. But this strategy denies the validity of institutionalized myths and sabotages the legitimacy of the organization. Fourth, an organization can promise reform. People may picture the present as unworkable but the future as filled with promising reforms of both structure and activity. But by defining the organization's valid structure as lying in the future, this strategy makes the organization's current structure illegitimate.

Instead of relying on a partial solution, an organization can resolve conflicts between ceremonial rules and efficiency by employing two interrelated devices: decoupling and the logic of confidence.

Decoupling. Ideally, organizations built around efficiency attempt to maintain close alignments between structures and activities. Conformity is enforced through inspection, output quality is continually monitored, the efficiency of various units is evaluated, and the various goals are unified and coordinated. But a policy of close alignment in institutionalized organizations merely makes public a record of inefficiency and inconsistency.

Institutionalized organizations protect their formal structures from evaluation on the basis of technical performance: inspection, evaluation, and control of activities are minimized, and coordination, interdependence, and mutual adjustments among structural units are handled informally.

Proposition 4. *Because attempts to control and coordinate activities in institutionalized organizations lead to conflicts and loss of legitimacy, elements of structure are decoupled from activities and from each other.*

Some well-known properties of organizations illustrate the decoupling process:

Activities are performed beyond the purview of managers. In particular, organizations actively encourage professionalism, and activities are delegated to professionals.

Goals are made ambiguous or vacuous, and categorical ends are substituted for technical ends. Hospitals treat, not cure, patients. Schools produce students, not learning. In fact, data on technical performance are eliminated or rendered invisible. Hospitals try to ignore information on cure rates, public services avoid data about effectiveness, and schools de-emphasize measures of achievement.

Integration is avoided, program implementation is neglected, and inspection and evaluation are ceremonialized.

Human relations are made very important. The organization cannot formally coordinate activities because its formal rules, if applied, would generate inconsistencies. Therefore individuals are left to work out technical interdependencies informally. The ability to coordinate things in violation of the rules—that is, to get along with other people—is highly valued.

The advantages of decoupling are clear. The assumption that formal structures are really working is buffered from the inconsistencies and anomalies involved in technical activities. Also, because integration is avoided disputes and conflicts are minimized, and an organization can mobilize support from a broader range of external constituents.

Thus, decoupling enables organizations to maintain standardized, legitimating, formal structures while their activities vary in response to practical considerations. The organizations in an industry tend to be similar in formal structure—reflecting their common institutional origins—but may show much diversity in actual practice.

The logic of confidence and good faith. Despite the lack of coordination and control, decoupled organizations are not anarchies. Day-to-day activities proceed in an orderly fashion. What legitimates institutionalized organizations, enabling them to appear useful in spite of the lack of technical validation, is the confidence and good faith of their internal participants and their external constituents.

Considerations of face characterize ceremonial management (Goffman 1967). Confidence in structural elements is maintained through three practices—avoidance, discretion, and overlooking (Goffman 1967, pp. 12–18). Avoidance and discretion are encouraged by decoupling autonomous subunits; overlooking anomalies is also quite common. Both internal participants and external constituents cooperate in these practices. Assuring that individual participants maintain face sustains confidence in the organization, and ultimately reinforces confidence in the myths that rationalize the organization's existence.

Delegation, professionalization, goal, ambiguity, the elimination of output data, and maintenance of face are all mechanisms for absorbing uncertainty while preserving the formal structure of the organization (March and Simon 1958). They contribute to a general aura of confidence within and outside the organization. Although the literature on informal organization often treats these practices as mechanisms for the achievement of deviant and subgroup purposes (Downs 1967), such treatment ignores a critical feature of organization life: effectively absorbing uncertainty and maintaining confidence requires people to assume that everyone is acting in good faith. The assumption that things are as they seem, that employees and managers are performing their roles properly, allows an organization to perform its daily routines with a decoupled structure.

Decoupling and maintenance of face, in other words, are mechanisms that maintain the assumption that people are acting in good faith. Professionalization is not merely a way of avoiding inspection—it binds both supervisors and subordinates to act in good faith. So in a smaller way does strategic leniency (Blau 1956). And so do the public displays of morale and satisfaction which are characteristic of many organizations. Organizations employ a host of mechanisms to dramatize the ritual commitments which their participants make to basic structural elements. These mechanisms are especially common in organizations which strongly reflect their institutionalized environments.

Proposition 5. *The more an organization's structure is derived from institutionalized myths, the more it maintains elaborate displays of confidence, satisfaction, and good faith, internally and externally.*

The commitments built up by displays of morale and satisfaction are not simply vacuous affirmations of institutionalized myths. Participants not only commit themselves to supporting an organization's ceremonial facade but also commit themselves to making things work out backstage. The committed participants engage in informal coordination that, although often formally inappropriate, keeps technical activities running smoothly and avoids public embarrassments. In this sense the confidence and good faith generated by ceremonial action is in no way fraudulent. It may even be the most reasonable way to get participants to make their best efforts in situations that are made problematic by institutionalized myths that are at odds with immediate technical demands.

Ceremonial inspection and evaluation. All organizations, even those maintaining high levels of confidence and good faith, are in environments that have institutionalized the rationalized rituals of inspection and evaluation. And inspection and evaluation can uncover events and deviations that undermine legitimacy. So institutionalized organizations minimize and ceremonialize inspection and evaluation.

In institutionalized organizations, in fact, evaluation accompanies and produces illegitimacy. The interest in evaluation research by the American federal government, for instance, is partly intended to undercut the state, local, and private authorities which have managed social services in the United States. The federal authorities, of course, have usually not evaluated those programs which are completely under federal jurisdiction; they have only evaluated those over which federal controls are incomplete. Similarly, state governments have often insisted on evaluating the special fundings they create in welfare and education but ordinarily do not evaluate the programs which they fund in a routine way.

Evaluation and inspection are public assertions of societal control which violate the assumption that everyone is acting with competence and in good faith. Violating this assumption lowers morale and confidence.

Thus, evaluation and inspection undermine the ceremonial aspects of organizations.

Proposition 6. *Institutionalized organizations seek to minimize inspection and evaluation by both internal managers and external constituents.*

Decoupling and the avoidance of inspection and evaluation are not merely devices used by the organization. External constituents, too, avoid inspecting and controlling institutionalized organizations (Meyer and Rowan 1975). Accrediting agencies, boards of trustees, government agencies, and individuals accept ceremonially at face value the credentials, ambiguous goals, and categorical evaluations that are characteristic of ceremonial organizations. In elaborate institutional environments these external constituents are themselves likely to be corporately organized agents of society. Maintaining categorical relationships with their organizational subunits is more stable and more certain than is relying on inspection and control.

Figure 3 summarizes the main arguments of this section of our discussion.

Summary and Research Implications

Organizational structures are created and made more elaborate with the rise of institutionalized myths, and, in highly institutionalized contexts, organizational action must support these myths. But an organization must also attend to practical activity. The two requirements are at odds. A stable solution is to maintain the organization in a loosely coupled state.

No position is taken here on the overall social effectiveness of isomorphic and loosely coupled organizations. To some extent such structures buffer activity from efficiency criteria and produce ineffectiveness. On the other hand, by binding participants to act in good faith, and to adhere to the larger rationalities of the wider structure, they may maximize long-run effectiveness. It should not be assumed that the creation of microscopic rationalities in the daily activity of workers effects social ends more efficiently than commitment to larger institutional claims and purposes.

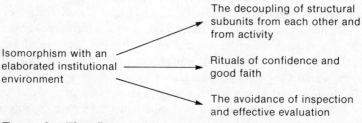

FIGURE 3.   The effects of institutional isomorphism on organizations.

Research Implications

The argument presented here generates several major theses that have clear research implications.

1. Environments and environmental domains which have institutionalized a greater number of rational myths generate more formal organization. This thesis leads to the research hypothesis that formal organizations rise and become more complex as a result of the rise of the elaborated state and other institutions for collective action. This hypothesis should hold true even when economic and technical development are held constant. Studies could trace the diffusion to formal organizations of specific institutions: professions, clearly labeled programs, and the like. For instance, the effects of the rise of theories and professions of personnel selection on the creation of personnel departments in organizations could be studied. Other studies could follow the diffusion of sales departments or research and development departments. Organizations should be found to adapt to such environmental changes, even if no evidence of their effectiveness exists.

Experimentally, one could study the impact on the decisions of organizational managers, in planning or altering organizational structures, of hypothetical variations in environmental institutionalization. Do managers plan differently if they are informed about the existence of established occupations or programmatic institutions in their environments? Do they plan differently if they are designing organizations for more or less institutionally elaborated environments?

2. Organizations which incorporate institutionalized myths are more legitimate, successful, and likely to survive. Here, research should compare similar organizations in different contexts. For instance, the presence of personnel departments or research and development units should predict success in environments in which they are widely institutionalized. Organizations which have structural elements not institutionalized in their environments should be more likely to fail, as such unauthorized complexity must be justified by claims of efficiency and effectiveness.

More generally, organizations whose claims to support are based on evaluations should be less likely to survive than those which are more highly institutionalized. An implication of this argument is that organizations existing in a highly institutionalized environment are generally more likely to survive.

Experimentally, one could study the size of the loans banks would be willing to provide organizations which vary only in (1) the degree of environmental institutionalization, and (2) the degree to which the organization structurally incorporates environmental institutions. Are banks willing to lend more money to firms whose plans are accompanied by

551

econometric projections? And is this tendency greater in societies in which such projections are more widely institutionalized?

3. Organizational control efforts, especially in highly institutionalized contexts, are devoted to ritual conformity, both internally and externally. Such organizations, that is, decouple structure from activity and structures from each other. The idea here is that the more highly institutionalized the environment, the more time and energy organizational elites devote to managing their organization's public image and status and the less they devote to coordination and to managing particular boundary-spanning relationships. Further, the argument is that in such contexts managers devote more time to articulating internal structures and relationships at an abstract or ritual level, in contrast to managing particular relationships among activities and interdependencies.

Experimentally, the time and energy allocations proposed by managers presented with differently described environments could be studied. Do managers, presented with the description of an elaborately institutionalized environment, propose to spend more energy maintaining ritual isomorphism and less on monitoring internal conformity? Do they tend to become inattentive to evaluation? Do they elaborate doctrines of professionalism and good faith?

The arguments here, in other words, suggest both comparative and experimental studies examining the effects on organizational structure and coordination of variations in the institutional structure of the wider environment. Variations in organizational structure among societies, and within any society across time, are central to this conception of the problem.

References

AIKEN, MICHAEL, and JERALD HAGE. 1968. "Organizational Interdependence and Intra-organizational Structure." *American Sociological Review* 33 (December): 912–30.

BELL, DANIEL. 1973. *The Coming of Post-industrial Society.* New York: Basic.

BENDIX, REINHARD. 1964. *Nation-Building and Citizenship.* New York: Wiley.

———. 1968. "Bureaucracy." Pp. 206–19 in *International Encyclopedia of the Social Sciences,* edited by David L. Sills. New York: Macmillan.

BERGER, PETER L., and THOMAS LUCKMANN. 1967. *The Social Construction of Reality.* New York: Doubleday.

BLAU, PETER M. 1956. *Bureaucracy in Modern Society.* New York: Random House.

———. 1970. "A Formal Theory of Differentiation in Organizations." *American Sociological Review* 35 (April): 201–18.

BLUM, ALAN F., and PETER McHUGH. 1971. "The Social Ascription of Motives." *American Sociological Review* 36 (December): 98–109.

CALLAHAN, RAYMOND E. 1962. *Education and the Cult of Efficiency*. Chicago: University of Chicago Press.

CARLSON, RICHARD O. 1962. *Executive Succession and Organizational Change*. Chicago: Midwest Administration Center, University of Chicago.

CLARK, BURTON R. 1956. *Adult Education in Transition*. Berkeley: University of California Press.

DALTON, MELVILLE. 1959. *Men Who Manage*. New York: Wiley.

DOWLING, JOHN, and JEFFREY PFEFFER. 1975. "Organizational Legitimacy." *Pacific Sociological Review* 18 (January): 122–36.

DOWNS, ANTHONY. 1967. *Inside Bureaucracy*. Boston: Little, Brown.

DURKHEIM, ÉMILE. 1933. *The Division of Labor in Society*. New York: Macmillan.

ELLUL, JACQUES. 1964. *The Technological Society*. New York: Knopf.

EMERY, FRED L., and ERIC L. TRIST. 1965. "The Causal Texture of Organizational Environments." *Human Relations* 18 (February): 21–32.

FREEMAN, JOHN HENRY. 1973. "Environment, Technology and Administrative Intensity of Manufacturing Organizations." *American Sociological Review* 38 (December): 750–63.

GOFFMAN, ERVING. 1967. *Interaction Ritual*. Garden City, N.Y.: Anchor.

HAWLEY, AMOS H. 1968. "Human Ecology." Pp. 328–37 in *International Encyclopedia of the Social Sciences*, edited by David L. Sills. New York: Macmillan.

HIRSCH, PAUL M. 1975. "Organizational Effectiveness and the Institutional Environment." *Administrative Science Quarterly* 20 (September): 327–44.

HOMANS, GEORGE C. 1950. *The Human Group*. New York: Harcourt, Brace.

MARCH, JAMES G., and JOHAN P. OLSEN. 1976. *Ambiguity and Choice in Organizations*. Bergen: Universitetsforlaget.

MARCH, JAMES G., and HERBERT A. SIMON. 1958. *Organizations*. New York: Wiley.

MERTON, ROBERT K. 1940. "Bureaucratic Structure and Personality." *Social Forces* 18 (May): 560–68.

MEYER, JOHN W., and BRIAN ROWAN. 1975. "Notes on the Structure of Educational Organizations." Paper presented at annual meeting of the American Sociological Association, San Francisco.

MILLS, C. WRIGHT. 1940. "Situated Actions and Vocabularies of Motive." *American Sociological Review* 5 (February): 904–13.

OUCHI, WILLIAM, and MARY ANN MAGUIRE. 1975. "Organizational Control: Two Functions." *Administrative Science Quarterly* 20 (December): 559–69.

PARSONS, TALCOTT. 1956. "Suggestions for a Sociological Approach to the Theory of Organizations I." *Administrative Science Quarterly* 1 (June): 63–85.

———. 1971. *The System of Modern Societies*. Englewood Cliffs, N.J.: Prentice Hall.

PERROW, CHARLES. 1970. *Organizational Analysis: A Sociological View*. Belmont, Calif.: Wadsworth.

SALANCIK, GERALD R., and JEFFREY PFEFFER. 1974. "The Bases and Use of

Power in Organizational Decision Making." *Administrative Science Quarterly* 19 (December): 453–73.

SCOTT, MARVIN B., and STANFORD, M. LYMAN. 1968. "Accounts." *American Sociological Review* 33 (February): 46–62.

SCOTT, W. RICHARD. 1975. "Organizational Structure." Pp. 1–20 in *Annual Review of Sociology*. Vol. 1, edited by Alex Inkeles. Palo Alto, Calif.: Annual Reviews.

SELZNICK, PHILIP. 1949. *TVA and the Grass Roots*. Berkeley: University of California Press.

SPENCER, HERBERT. 1897. *Principles of Sociology*. New York: Appleton.

STARBUCK, WILLIAM H. 1976. "Organizations and their Environments." Pp. 1069–1123 in *Handbook of Industrial and Organizational Psychology*, edited by Marvin D. Dunnette. New York: Rand McNally.

SWANSON, GUY E. 1971. "An Organizational Analysis of Collectivities." *American Sociological Review* 36 (August): 607–24.

TERREBERRY, SHIRLEY. 1968. "The Evolution of Organizational Environments." *Administrative Science Quarterly* 12 (March): 590–613.

THOMPSON, JAMES D. 1967. *Organizations in Action*. New York: McGraw-Hill.

TYACK, DAVID B. 1974. *The One Best System*. Cambridge, Mass.: Harvard University Press.

UDY, STANLEY H., JR. 1970. *Work in Traditional and Modern Society*. Englewood Cliffs, N.J.: Prentice-Hall.

WEBER, MAX. 1930. *The Protestant's Ethic and the Spirit of Capitalism*. New York: Scribner's.

———. 1946. *Essays in Sociology*. New York: Oxford University Press.

———. 1947. *The Theory of Social and Economic Organization*. New York: Oxford University Press.

WEICK, KARL E. 1976. "Educational Organizations as Loosely Coupled Systems." *Administrative Science Quarterly* 21 (March): 1–19.

WILENSKY, HAROLD L. 1965. "The Professionalization of Everyone?" *American Journal of Sociology* 70 (September): 137–58.

WOODWARD, JOAN. 1965. *Industrial Organization, Theory and Practice*. London: Oxford University Press.

ZALD, MAYER N., and PATRICIA DENTON. 1963. "From Evangelism to General Service: The Transformation of the YMCA." *Administrative Science Quarterly* 8 (September): 214–34.

Index

Index

Blau, Peter M., 4–5, 110–128, 129, 130, 142, 151–175, 184, 185, 202n, 208, 213, 348–349, 411, 425–450, 510, 532, 549
Blauner, Robert, 437, 448, 516
Blum, Alan F., 539
Blum, Eleanor, 472
Blum, J. M., 268
Blumer, Herbert, 456, 459n
Bogoslovsky, Boris B., 325n
Bolton, J. E., 194
Bonus plan, 57
Boskoff, Alvin, 459, 465
Boulding, Kenneth, 185, 230
Bowen, William G., 465n
Bowman, G. W., 397, 407, 417
Bracketing, enactment as, 270–271
Brammer, Mauck, 472
Braverman, Harry, 497
Braybrooke, D., 266
Bribery, 330n
Brief, Henry, 460, 461, 471n
Brockway, George P., 461
Bronowski, J., 324n
Browne, Malcolm, 504
Brugger, William, 508
Bryson, L., 324n
Bucher, Rue, 208, 210, 221
Buddhism, 32
Bukharin, Nikolai, 362–363
Bureaucracy
  concentration of means of administration, 21–24
  leveling of social differences, 24–26
  permanent character of, 26–27
  position of officials, 10–15
  qualitative changes of administrative tasks, 17–19
  quantitative development of administrative tasks, 15–17
  succession and, 296–299
  technical advantages, 19–21
  Weber on, 1–2, 7–36, 122–127
Burger, Chester, 410n
Burke, Kenneth, 325n
Burnham, James, 402, 403
Burns, Tom, 112n, 178, 456
Burtt, E. A., 325n
Butler, D. E., 359n

"Caesarism," 13
Calder, Bobby J., 229
Caldwell, 319n
Callahan, Raymond E., 545
Cantine, 310n, 319n
Capital, 101

Capitalist market economy, 20
Caplow, Theodore, 185
Career enlargement, 513–517
Career stability, 123, 125
Carey, Alex, 3, 220
Carlson, Richard O., 538
Case studies on organizations, 111, 120–121, 128
Caste system, 34
Cattell, Raymond B., 412
Centralization versus decentralization issue, 347–348, 370–394
Certainty, 135
Chaffee, S. H., 275
Chandler, Alfred D., Jr., 208, 456n, 510
Charades, enactment in, 269
Charismatic authority, 1, 7–8, 28–36
Cherbuliez, Antoine Elisée, 46n
Child, John, 228, 426, 428, 429n, 430, 431, 437n, 444n, 510
China, organizational style in, 505–508
Churchill, Betty C., 194
Clark, Burton R., 538
Clark, John P., 451–452, 477–494
Classical theoretical perspectives, 1–128
  Barnard, 4, 84–97
  Blau, 4–5, 110–128
  Michels, 2, 37–54
  Parsons, 4, 98–109
  Roethlisberger and Dickson, 3, 67–83
  Taylor, 2–3, 55–66
  Weber, 1–2, 7–36
Clemmer, Donald, 306
Coalition model of organizations, 231, 236
Cochran, Thomas C., 404
Cohen, Michael D., 132, 255, 260, 261
Cole, Arthur H., 325n
Cole, Robert E., 452–453, 495–529
Coleman, James S., 2, 260, 347, 351–369
Colvin, Fred H., 328n
Commons, John R., 148, 149, 298n
Communication, 19, 89–90, 93–96
Communists, 362–364
Community Action Agencies, 386, 389–390
Comparative study of organizations, 4–5, 110–128
Competence multiplier, 272
Competition theory, 186–187, 193
Complexity, 123, 124, 126
Comprehensive Employment and Training Act (CETA) of 1973, 371, 374, 377, 384, 386–390, 392, 393
Computer automation, 142, 428–429, 438–443, 445–449
Conant, Michael, 461

Index

Index

Index